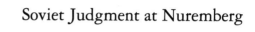

Soviet Judgment at Nuremberg

FRANCINE HIRSCH

Soviet Judgment at Nuremberg

A New History of

the International Military

Tribunal after World War II

OXFORD
UNIVERSITY PRESS

OXFORD
UNIVERSITY PRESS

Oxford University Press is a department of the University of Oxford. It furthers
the University's objective of excellence in research, scholarship, and education
by publishing worldwide. Oxford is a registered trade mark of Oxford University
Press in the UK and certain other countries.

Published in the United States of America by Oxford University Press
198 Madison Avenue, New York, NY 10016, United States of America.

CIP data is on file at the Library of Congress.
ISBN 978–0–19–937793–0

9 8 7 6 5 4 3 2 1

Printed by LSC Communications, United States of America

To Mark

CONTENTS

ILLUSTRATIONS

MAPS

ABBREVIATIONS

International Institutions

IADL   International Association of Democratic Lawyers
IMT   International Military Tribunal
UNWCC   United Nations War Crimes Commission

American Institutions

JAG   Judge Advocate General's Department of the U.S. Armed Forces
OSS   Office of Strategic Services

German Institutions

Gestapo   Geheime Staatspolizei; Secret State Police
RSHA   Reichssicherheitshauptamt; Reich Central Security Office
SS   Schutzstaffel; Protection Squadron
SA   Sturmabteilung; Storm Battalion, Storm Troopers
SD   Sicherheitsdienst; Security Service
SiPo   Sicherheitspolizei; Security Police

Soviet Institutions, Places, Territorial Designations

NKVD   Narodnyi komissariat vnutrennikh del; People's Commissariat for
        Internal Affairs (until March 1946); Ministry of Internal Affairs
NKGB   Narodnyi komissariat gosudarstvennoi bezopasnosti; People's
        Commissariat for State Security (until March 1946); Ministry of
        State Security

RSFSR	Rossiiskaia Sovetskaia Federativnaia Sotsialisticheskaia Respublika; Russian Soviet Federative Socialist Republic
SMERSH	Smert Shpionam!; Death to Spies!, Chief Counterintelligence Directorate
SSR	Sovetskaia Sotsialisticheskaia Respublika; Soviet Socialist Republic
SVAG	Sovetskaia voennaia administratsiia v Germanii; Soviet Military Administration in Germany
Sovinformburo	Sovetskoe informatsionnoe biuro; Soviet Information Bureau
TASS	Telegrafnoe agentstvo SSSR; Telegraph Agency of the Soviet Union

A Note About Soviet Institutions and Name Changes

In March 1946 all people's commissariats were renamed ministries. I use the names Ministry of Internal Affairs, Ministry of State Security, and Ministry of Foreign Affairs throughout the book (even for the period before March 1946 when the institutions were officially called commissariats).

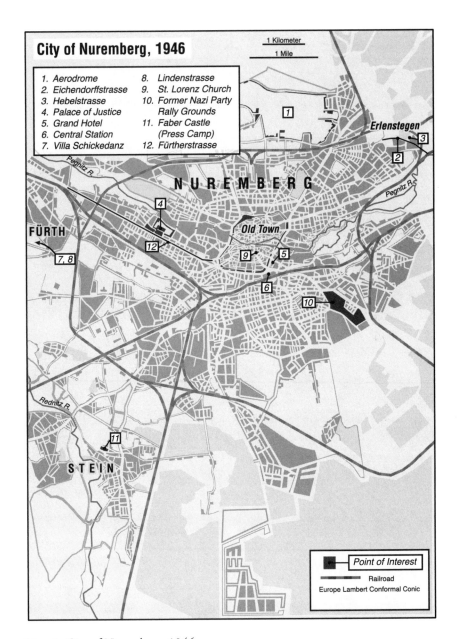

City of Nuremberg, 1946

1 Kilometer
1 Mile

1. Aerodrome
2. Eichendorffstrasse
3. Hebelstrasse
4. Palace of Justice
5. Grand Hotel
6. Central Station
7. Villa Schickedanz
8. Lindenstrasse
9. St. Lorenz Church
10. Former Nazi Party Rally Grounds
11. Faber Castle (Press Camp)
12. Fürtherstrasse

Erlenstegen

NUREMBERG

Pegnitz R.

FÜRTH

Old Town

STEIN

Rednitz R.

Point of Interest
Railroad
Europe Lambert Conformal Conic

Map 1 City of Nuremberg, 1946.

Introduction: The Untold Story

IN NOVEMBER 1945, roughly six months after the end of the Second World War in Europe, the International Military Tribunal (IMT) convened in the Palace of Justice in the city of Nuremberg, in the American zone of what had been Nazi Germany. The flags of the United States, Great Britain, the Soviet Union, and France flew over the entrance to the imposing sandstone building, and honor guards from all four countries stood at attention outside—visible reminders that this trial of the former Nazi leaders was being held by the four military powers occupying Germany.

Nuremberg was rich with symbolic significance. The city had been the cradle of the Nazi movement, the site of choreographed mass rallies—recorded for posterity in Leni Riefenstahl's *Triumph of the Will*—at which Adolf Hitler had announced the Third Reich's race laws and roused millions of followers with the promise of a resurgent Germany. It had also been one of the last holdouts of German forces, the setting of one of the final battles of the war in Europe. This was a fitting place for a postwar reckoning.

Among those who came to observe the trial was the Soviet filmmaker Roman Karmen, a special correspondent for the Soviet press who was tasked with documenting the proceedings. Making his way through the city in a car on the day of his arrival, Karmen was struck by the devastation. "You do not see one intact structure in Nuremberg," he observed. "It is sheer ruins." Karmen had spent the last few years as a cameraman embedded with the Red Army, shooting footage in Leningrad, on the Don, and on the Belorussian front. He had seen what war could do. Even so, he was taken aback by what he now encountered. Nuremberg had been nearly leveled by repeated Allied bombing campaigns and street-to-street fighting. The medieval town center as well as the more modern parts of the city had been reduced to piles of rubble and debris. Before leaving Moscow, Karmen had watched German newsreels and documentary films showing the city in its glory days under the Nazis. He recalled scenes of extraordinary splendor, the Nazi Party Rally Grounds, and the endless parades of SS units, Hitler Youth, and soldiers. It seemed impossible to believe that this was the same city.[1]

After dropping off his luggage at the Press Camp, located southwest of the city, Karmen headed directly to the courthouse. He was in a hurry. His arrival in Nuremberg had been delayed because of bad weather. It was already November 22; he had missed the first two days of the trial and did not want to waste any more time. His car turned onto the Fürtherstrasse, one of the few streets that had escaped significant damage. There, behind cast-iron gates, stood the Palace of Justice. Four stories high and built early in the century, it appeared relatively unscathed by the war. Thousands of German prisoners of war had been put to work by American occupation forces to fill in bullet holes and otherwise repair the building. Noticing the Soviet soldiers in the honor guard, Karmen felt a surge of pride, recalling the Red Army's "valorous path from Stalingrad to the Volga to Moscow to Berlin."[2]

Inside the Palace of Justice, Karmen marveled at the mixture of grandeur and functionality. The courtroom itself had been demolished and expanded to include space for the eight judges, the four teams of prosecutors, the defendants and their attorneys, and the hundreds of representatives of the press who now crowded the back of the room. A special booth had been built for the interpreters behind the witness box; an upstairs gallery had been added for spectators. The air smelled of fresh wood and paint. A bronze bas-relief of Adam and Eve and the serpent, original to the building, hung on one of the walls. American military police in white helmets stood guard. Directly across from the judges' bench was the dock; Karmen immediately recognized both Hermann Goering and Rudolf Hess among the defendants. Later, in the thick of the trials, Karmen would recall the great satisfaction he had felt at this precise moment—knowing that this was the place where "the peoples of the world would judge the band of fascist hangmen."[3] This was where he would spend the next ten months filming the trials for posterity.

Karmen brought a profound sense of responsibility with him to Nuremberg. His mission throughout the war had been to bring Nazi atrocities to light. His footage of razed villages, bombed-out cities, and slaughtered civilians had been used in dozens of newsreels and documentaries at home and abroad. In the summer of 1944, he had filmed the Soviet liberation of the Majdanek

FIGURE I.1 The Palace of Justice in Nuremberg, the site of the International Military Tribunal, ca. 1945–1946.

Credit: United States Holocaust Memorial Museum, courtesy of Harry S. Truman Library. Photographer: Charles Alexander.

death camp in Poland. He described the workings of the gas chambers and the crematorium in an article that ran in both the *Daily Worker* and the *Los Angeles Times,* noting that the entire enterprise of wiping out over a half million people "was organized with diabolical efficiency." "Save for 1,000 living corpses the Red Army found when it entered, no inmate escaped from here alive."[4] From Poland, Karmen had accompanied the Red Army west, where he documented the taking of Berlin and the Nazi surrender.

At Nuremberg, Karmen was the head of a small team of Soviet cameramen who would produce newsreels as well as a feature-length film about the trial. They were committed to crafting a visual narrative that showed the world the immense sacrifices the Soviet Union had made in order to defeat the Nazis. "If it were not for the Soviet Army, not for the heroic Soviet people who played a decisive role in the victory over Germany, there would have been no Nuremberg," Karmen reflected while working on the film.[5]

Karmen was a gifted filmmaker and a seasoned Soviet propagandist who could exert a great deal of control over the ideas and images he presented on the screen. For the Soviet delegation to Nuremberg as a whole, however—the judge and his alternate, the prosecution team, the translators and interpreters, and a bevy of assistants—exerting control over the trials would prove to be far more of a challenge.

It was not as if the Soviets were caught by surprise by the convening of the IMT; they had been key actors in its creation. During the darkest days of the war—when it was unclear whether the Soviet Union would even survive—Joseph Stalin and his foreign minister, Vyacheslav Molotov, had called for a "special international tribunal" to try Nazi leaders, partly as a means of establishing a legal claim for reparations, which they already understood would be necessary for rebuilding their country's shattered cities and industries. The Soviets took it as a given that the Nazi leaders were guilty and deserved to be hanged. They envisioned the Nuremberg Trials as they had the Moscow Trials of 1936 to 1938: as a grand political spectacle whose outcome was certain. Nuremberg would expose the depths of Nazi depravity and hand out death sentences to the defendants.

That was how things were supposed to go. However, even before Karmen set up his Eyemo movie camera in the Palace of Justice and began to film, the proceedings had begun to veer away from Moscow's expectations. The countries of the prosecution were not just facing off against the defendants in the Nuremberg courtroom—they were also competing against each other.

The four Allies had all had vastly different experiences of the war. They came to Nuremberg with varying degrees of vengefulness and very different sets of concerns. The French had to reckon with their legacy of wartime collaboration; the war had exposed and exacerbated social and political fissures, and the new French government was uncertain how to move on. The British, who had stood alone against Germany for a year, had been bankrupted by the war and worried about losing influence and empire. The United States, whose late entrance into the war had ended a long period of isolationism, was poised to take a more involved role in world affairs, likely even a dominant one. Compared with the civilian losses among the European combatants, those of the United States were minuscule; unlike the other Allied powers, the United States had emerged from the war an economic powerhouse, brimming with confidence. Meanwhile, the Soviets had been savaged by the Nazi assault and occupation: the number of casualties beggared the imagination. Celebrating their ultimate triumph over the enemy while coming to terms with these staggering losses, the Soviets were determined to take their rightful place at the table of the victors.

All of the Allies were intent on using the trials to put forward their own history of the war and to shape the postwar future. They also came to Nuremberg with conflicting ideas about the very meaning of justice and how it should be served. The prosecutors and the judges, coming from these four countries with their different political systems and legal traditions, had competing ideas about even such basic matters as evidence, witnesses, and the rights of the defendants.

And what about the defendants? Reich Marshal Hermann Goering, German foreign minister Joachim von Ribbentrop, Reich minister Alfred Rosenberg, and the other Nazi leaders were largely unrepentant; to them, Nuremberg was a travesty of justice. To the surprise and consternation of the prosecuting countries, the former Nazi leaders and their attorneys vehemently challenged the legitimacy of the proceedings and exploited the tensions among the countries of the prosecution—tensions that were embarrassingly evident from the beginning. If the defendants were going to the gallows, they would fight every step of the way.

All of this was apparent to the participants, and certainly to a keen observer like Roman Karmen. Like the other Soviet correspondents in Nuremberg, he felt the strain of the trials from the very moment he arrived. Listening to testimony about the most horrific crimes conceivable over the many months that followed, he was forced to relive the war. He was appalled by the defense's claims that Germany had launched a "preventive invasion" to defend against an imminent Soviet attack. He recoiled from the defense's efforts to challenge the right of the victors to judge the vanquished. He found it almost excruciating to focus his camera day after day on the faces of the "loathsome creatures" and "most vile beasts" sitting in the dock. But he kept his camera trained on them nonetheless, determined to capture their true nature and thus to reveal the meaning of evil.[6]

Karmen's film, *Judgment of the Peoples* (*Sud narodov*), was released in the Soviet Union a month after the judges issued their verdicts in October 1946. The fifty-five-minute documentary set out the Soviet account of the Second

World War in no uncertain terms. It cut back and forth between scenes of the courtroom and footage of Nazi atrocities that Karmen and other Soviet cameramen had shot in territories freshly liberated from German occupation. It juxtaposed close-ups of the defendants in the dock with haunting images of leveled cities and stacks of corpses in concentration camps. The film, released in the United States as *The Nuremberg Trials,* opened in New York in the spring of 1947. The *New York Times* called it a "grim and impressive recount of the horror of Nazi war crimes and of the guilt of the top-level leaders."[7] The *New York Herald Tribune* on the other hand dismissed the film as "an elongated newsreel" and characterized its assertion "that the Nazi menace was about to engulf the world until halted by the Red armies" as the kind of propaganda that was unlikely to win the Soviet Union any friends. The truth was that Karmen's film was too raw and intense, at least for American audiences who were done with the war and ready to move forward. Its message about the Soviet Union's role in saving Europe from Hitler clashed with America's vision of itself as Europe's liberator and protector. The film would soon be forgotten in the United States—as would the role the Soviets had played in all aspects of the Nuremberg Trials.[8]

The IMT remains a landmark event of the twentieth century, a starting point for conversations about transitional justice, international law, genocide, and human rights. Yet, even with all the popular and scholarly attention the IMT has received over the decades, its story remains incompletely told. This book presents a new history of the Nuremberg Trials by restoring a central and missing piece: the role of the Soviet Union. In so doing it offers a new way of understanding the origins and development of the postwar movement for human rights.

Why were the Soviets essential to Nuremberg? And why has their part in the IMT been largely forgotten? The reasons for the latter should come as no great surprise. The IMT was not just the last hurrah of wartime cooperation for the Allied powers. It was also an early front of the Cold War, taking place at a juncture when the postwar relationship between the United States and the Soviet Union was still largely unformed, before either state had become a superpower. Even before the trials were over, the politics of the Cold War gave rise to the myth of "the Nuremberg Moment"—a myth which erased the Soviet role in bringing the trials to fruition. For decades, when Soviet participation in Nuremberg was discussed at all in the United States, it was described as regrettable but unavoidable—a sort of Faustian bargain that American and British leaders had made in order to bring closure to the war and bring the Nazis to justice.[9]

In the myth of the Nuremberg Moment, the Americans led the way, putting the desire for vengeance aside to give the Nazis a fair trial before the law and ushering in a new era of international human rights. The 1961 Stanley Kramer film *Judgment at Nuremberg* and the 2000 docudrama *Nuremberg* both adhere to this storyline. In *Nuremberg*, the square-jawed U.S. chief prosecutor Robert H. Jackson (played by Alec Baldwin) emerges as the hero, insisting on a fair hearing for even the most monstrous Nazi leaders. The British and the French play gallant but supporting roles. As for the Soviets, they make cameo appearances in which they come off as coarse, brutish, and vengeful—obstacles to the high-minded pursuit of justice rather than equal partners. In some scenes, the Germans are portrayed more sympathetically than the Soviets.[10]

The docudrama was adapted from Joseph E. Persico's *Nuremberg: Infamy on Trial*, which he based in large part on the accounts of American and British participants.[11] Western judges and prosecutors, who produced the earliest and most enduring accounts of the IMT, saw the fact of Soviet participation as a threat to the legitimacy of Nuremberg and to its legacy. They had good reason for this. Germany and the Soviet Union had jointly invaded Poland in September 1939; it was widely suspected that the Soviets, and not the Nazis, were responsible for the murder of thousands of Polish officers in the Katyn Forest outside Smolensk in Russia; Red Army troops had committed atrocities during their march to Berlin in the final months of the war; and the Soviets were carrying out deportations in Poland and Hungary even as the IMT was hearing evidence against the Nazis.[12] To many members of the Western delegations and the international press corps the Soviets were little better than the Nazi defendants.

The idea of the Nuremberg Moment as a triumph of Western leadership and liberal idealism has remained surprisingly resilient even as new histories have shifted the focus to look in greater depth at the role of international-law experts in shaping the trials. Philippe Sands's haunting book *East West Street* (2016) illuminates the contributions of the Polish-American lawyer Raphael Lemkin and the Polish-British lawyer Hersch Lauterpacht in developing some of the key concepts used at Nuremberg, such as "genocide" and "crimes against humanity," but gives scant mention to the Soviet lawyer Aron Trainin, whose contribution was arguably even more significant. All three men hailed from Jewish families in the former Russian Empire—but Lemkin and Lauterpacht emigrated to the West, while Trainin remained in Russia and served the Soviet government.[13] Lemkin and Lauterpacht are exemplars of a liberal legal tradition. They fit the storyline. Trainin—who made his way in Stalin's Soviet Union and whose earlier writings helped justify the Soviet show trials—clearly does not.[14]

The narrative of the Nuremberg Moment allows no room for ambiguity. But to tell the history of the IMT without a full accounting of the role of the Soviets is to capture the moment but miss the story. Stalin's Soviet Union fundamentally shaped the IMT and was key to its success, setting in motion what has become widely regarded as a revolution in international law that criminalized wars of conquest and sought to protect individuals from repressive states.[15] That a country known for show trials and for a demonstrated callousness toward human life should have played this role is surprising, perhaps even disconcerting. The full story of Nuremberg confronts us with two awkward truths: illiberal authoritarian states have at times positively shaped international law, and international justice is an inherently political process.[16]

Of all the Allies, the Soviets had pushed the hardest to try the Nazis not just for crimes committed during the course of the war, but also for the crime of launching what they called a "war of aggression" to begin with. The experience of total war, a war not just of armies but of civilizations, inspired Soviet lawyers to make their mark on international law in a way that changed it forever. It was Aron Trainin who first articulated the concept of a "crime against peace"—describing the planning and waging of an unprovoked war of conquest as a punishable criminal act. This would become the most important charge in the Indictment, the document which provided the legal framework for the entire trial.[17] Trainin also brought Soviet ideas about criminal responsibility and complicity into the international discussion about war crimes well in advance of the Allied victory. At a time when British leaders and some American politicians (including Treasury Secretary Henry Morgenthau Jr.) favored the summary execution of Nazi leaders as a simpler and more straightforward approach, the Soviets insisted on the convening of an international tribunal. The Nuremberg Trials might not have happened at all had the Soviet view not prevailed.

The tribunal the Soviets thought they were calling for, however, was not the tribunal they wound up with. They had no idea what they were getting into at Nuremberg. The crimes of the Nazis were so abhorrent, the evidence of mass atrocities so extensive, that Stalin and Molotov had assumed that the scripting of the trials would be straightforward. Soviet leaders had been so confident of guilty verdicts that they did not hesitate to add one of their own war crimes—the Katyn massacre of Polish officers—to the Indictment. They did not expect that the defendants would be allowed to challenge official war crimes reports, call military leaders and SS men as witnesses, or take the stand to lob counter-accusations at the prosecution. Nor did the Soviets anticipate that the other Allies would have significantly differing opinions on how the trials should proceed—or how effective the Americans would be in setting and carrying out their own agenda.

Stalin and Molotov had also thought that controlling the Soviet prosecutors and judges, and thus steering the trials from afar, would be easy. They were imagining Nuremberg as a grand exercise in education and enlightenment, a sort of show trial writ large.[18] Stalin appointed Andrei Vyshinsky, who had prosecuted the spectacularly staged Moscow Trials, to head a secret Moscow-based commission that would direct the Soviet work on the Nuremberg Trials.[19] When selecting Soviet judges and prosecutors for the IMT, Stalin similarly looked to people with show trial experience. Soviet judge Iona Nikitchenko had made his career as a judge in the Moscow Trials; Soviet chief prosecutor Roman Rudenko had served as the prosecutor for show trials in the 1930s in Ukraine, and more recently as the prosecutor for a show trial of Polish leaders held in Moscow. The Soviet assistant prosecutors had similar credentials.

Stalin and the rest of the Soviet leadership were nevertheless unable to exert anywhere near this degree of control. They realized the extent of their miscalculation only once the trials were under way. Ironically, the Soviet Union's highly centralized command structure proved to be its biggest obstacle at Nuremberg, preventing the Soviet legal team from achieving some of the outcomes Moscow wanted most. Stalin held Vyshinsky responsible for all aspects of the Soviet case, including the screening and selection of evidence and witnesses. Vyshinsky, in turn, required the Soviet prosecutors and judges to consult with him about each decision regarding the IMT, no matter how small. This entailed frequent secret long-distance check-ins, often via back channels and usually with tight deadlines. Making the situation still more complicated was the fact that even Vyshinsky lacked the authority to give directives about most matters on his own. Many decisions required a round robin of consultations with Soviet leaders—up to and including Stalin himself. All of this deprived the Soviet delegation of an ability to quickly react to the unexpected.

And much of what happened was indeed unexpected—at least from the Soviet perspective. Rivalries among the Allies dictated what transpired in the Nuremberg courtroom as much as the demands of justice did. None of the countries of the prosecution wanted to have their own foreign policies and wartime actions scrutinized on the international stage, and so the Nuremberg Charter was written to circumscribe the Tribunal's jurisdiction to trying the European Axis powers. However, in response to noisy allegations of "victors' justice" from the defense, and in reaction to Nikitchenko's repeated statements about the unquestioned guilt of the defendants, the Western judges redoubled their efforts to make sure that the accused were seen as receiving a fair trial.

The wartime alliance fractured; Cold War tensions flared. The Western judges gave the Nazi defendants ever greater leeway as the trial proceeded, allowing them nearly free rein to denounce Soviet breaches of international law in open court. Soviet wartime atrocities and crimes against peace—including the secret protocols to the German-Soviet Non-Aggression Pact of August 1939, in which Soviet and Nazi leaders had plotted out the conquest and division of much of Eastern Europe—became first an open secret and then not a secret at all. The Soviets had intended to use an international tribunal to elaborate a narrative about Soviet heroism and German treachery, about Soviet suffering and German guilt. The story quickly got away from them. They ultimately found themselves cast as co-conspirators of the Nazi regime—denied both the respect of victory and the self-righteousness of victimhood.

To tell the full story of the Nuremberg Trials requires a broad focus, one that illuminates the relationships among the four countries of the prosecution on the ground in the American zone of Germany. It also means showing what went on behind the scenes. Nuremberg saw the crystallization of high-minded ideals about justice and human rights—but at the same time it was "a boiling, seething *internationale*" (in Karmen's words), a polyglot community rife with late-night boozing, dealmaking, and intrigue.[20] Telegrams, intelligence reports, and secret meeting transcripts from the former Soviet archives, as well as private letters and unpublished diaries from the United States, Great Britain, and Russia, make clear that what went on in the back rooms and barrooms and at private parties was almost as consequential as what happened in the courtroom. Here the prosecutors traded secrets with one another, forged alliances and blocs, and leaked highly sensitive information to the press. Here the journalists from all over the world shared gossip about the defendants and even organized a betting pool to place wagers on the verdicts.

While this book tells a story about international law and politics, it is also a human drama. Rebecca West, the British journalist who covered the trials for the *New Yorker*, described the emotional burden of the experience: "What irked was the isolation in a small area, cut off from normal life by the barbed wire of army regulations; the perpetual confrontation with the dreary details of an ugly chapter in history . . . the continued enslavement by the war machine."[21] The hundreds of foreign correspondents and the members of the American, British, French, and Soviet delegations, a long way from home, felt marooned at Nuremberg. Forced to confront evidence of the most unthinkable atrocities in the courtroom of the Palace of Justice, they chased down whatever pleasure and human connection they could after hours.[22] The raucous dinner parties, the cheap whiskey at the Press Camp bar, and the (sometimes bawdy) entertainment at the city's Grand Hotel made it possible to keep going. For the Soviet correspondents and lawyers, warned by Moscow not to fraternize with Westerners and under surveillance by their own security agents, Nuremberg's nightlife offered unique opportunities and dangers. Lubricated by alcohol, the Soviets would sometimes forget themselves.

The Soviet press corps in Nuremberg included some forty-five correspondents—many hand-picked by Stalin to cover the trials for Soviet audiences as well as for the foreign press.[23] Karmen kept company with the writer Ilya Ehrenburg, the photographer Evgeny Khaldei (whose pictures of Soviet soldiers are among the most iconic of the war), the journalist Boris Polevoi, the playwright Vsevolod Vishnevsky, Stalin's favorite political cartoonist Boris Efimov, and other accomplished propagandists. Many of them knew each other well from the front lines. A number of them, including Karmen, were Jewish; a couple, including Ehrenburg, had worked during the war for the Jewish Anti-Fascist Committee, an official Soviet agency that had publicized evidence of Nazi atrocities and raised money abroad for the Red Army. All of the correspondents defined themselves first and foremost as loyal Soviet citizens. They had all established their careers in the political cauldron of the Stalinist 1930s, spent the war years at the front or otherwise defending their homeland, and then found themselves thrown together at Nuremberg.

Some were better prepared than others to be part of a new and improvised foreign-relations apparatus. Many of the Soviet correspondents embraced the opportunity to mingle with foreign journalists and share stories about the war. "They slapped us on the shoulders, became acquainted with us, shook our hands, invited us to drink whisky at the bar," Karmen remembered.[24] Others experienced a deep sense of alienation at Nuremberg, certain that the British and especially the Americans could never truly understand what the Soviet people had endured under German occupation. "Much here is ridiculous, a lot of boorishness, a lot of absurdity," noted Vishnevsky in one letter home, taken aback by the business-as-usual attitude of the Americans toward the trials and by "the revelry" of Nuremberg's nightlife.[25]

The members of the Soviet legal team often seemed inscrutable to their Western counterparts. The American, British, and French prosecutors and judges could relate to Aron Trainin, who had studied abroad and whose ideas about war crimes had been circulating in the West. Nikitchenko and

FIGURE I.2 Roman Karmen (second from right), Vsevolod Vishnevsky (second from left), and other Soviet correspondents explore the demolished city of Nuremberg during their free time, ca. 1945–1946.

Credit: Russian State Archive of Literature and Art f. 2989, op. 1, d. 870, l. 2.

Rudenko, Communist Party members and career bureaucrats who had received only rudimentary educations and who grasped neither the niceties nor the subtleties of international relations, frequently confounded them. Trainin was the Soviet Union's face to the West where questions of postwar justice were concerned; Rudenko and Nikitchenko represented the Soviet Union's show trial tradition and came off as Party hacks. All three took orders from Vyshinsky, the éminence grise of the Soviet contingent. Vyshinsky had no official role in the trials—but he was the linchpin of the Soviet effort to shape the trials and their verdicts. As the middleman between the Kremlin and the Soviet delegation, he was the gatekeeper, doling out sensitive information about the Soviet past (including details about Soviet-German collaboration) to Nikitchenko and Rudenko on a strictly need-to-know basis. He strove assiduously to keep evidence of the Soviet Union's own war crimes out of the courtroom.

Rounding out the Soviet delegation in Nuremberg were the translators, interpreters, stenographers, typists, and drivers—and, inevitably, the secret police agents, who answered to Kremlin figures such as Lavrenty Beria, the chief of the Ministry of Internal Affairs (NKVD), and Viktor Abakumov, the chief of SMERSH (the military counterintelligence agency whose acronym derives from the phrase "Death to Spies").[26] The agents spent much of their time monitoring and reporting on the other members of the Soviet delegation. In practice, the line between the secret police agents and the rest of the Soviet delegation was often blurry. Members of the Soviet press corps—and even some of the Soviet assistant prosecutors—also reported regularly to Moscow about the latest developments in the trials and about the comings and goings of Soviet personnel. This practice of reporting was a regular part of Stalinist culture. The paper trail it produced is a boon for the historian.

In the end, Nuremberg was simultaneously about justice and politics. It involved a mixture of principle, self-interest, and compromise. The full story is far messier than the myth—but it is no less heroic. All of the prosecutors and judges, journalists and interpreters, lawyers and diplomats—American, French, British, and Soviet—worked long hours, shuttling between their overcrowded rooms and the wood-paneled courtroom with its "ghastly greenish" light, day after day, week after week, month after month for nearly a year.[27] Representing four different governments with four very different legal systems, they persisted in their effort to expose Nazi crimes that, in the words of the U.S. chief prosecutor Robert H. Jackson, were "so calculated, so malignant, and so devastating, that civilization cannot tolerate their being ignored, because it cannot survive their being repeated."[28] It was emotionally grueling work. Hearing eyewitnesses describe the smoke and stench of the death camps, studying photographs of mass graves and dismembered bodies, reading countless atrocity reports into the court record—all of this made the members of all four delegations long desperately for home even as it reminded them of what was as stake.[29]

These men and women worked hard to find common ground in Nuremberg, and in important ways they succeeded. They created a comprehensive record of the crimes of the Third Reich, shared moments of catharsis, and pushed forward the work of denazification. They set the precedent that launching an aggressive war was a crime, and they laid a foundation for the development of new international laws and institutions devoted to the protection of human rights in wartime and in peacetime.

This was a collective effort—but not all the partners were equal. The Americans, who had jurisdiction over the Nazi defendants and witnesses in the prison attached to the Palace of Justice, did what they could to shut the Soviets out. Jackson did not trust the Soviets and had little patience with the French, and he set out from the start to seize control over the bulk of the case. The Americans and the British got along well enough but also competed for the limelight.

What the myth of the Nuremberg Moment got right was its depiction of American initiative and energy. Once the trials were under way, the American prosecutors and judges did their utmost to drive the agenda. The Soviets, who had done so much to set the trials in motion, found themselves perpetually a step behind. They also found themselves increasingly isolated—especially when it came to refuting countercharges from the defense. Over the course of the trials, the Nuremberg courtroom became a forum not just for indicting former Nazis but for censuring the Soviet Union. The Western powers sent a clear message to Moscow that the international courtroom would not be free from the politics of postwar competition. The Soviets in turn saw the Western judges' refusal to shut down the defense's attacks on the Soviet Union as a calculated political tactic against which they had only limited recourse. The Soviets, with their shaky understanding of the free press, saw the publication of evidence of their own war crimes in American and British newspapers as proof that the Western journalists (no matter how friendly they might be after a few drinks in the Press Camp bar) were conspiring with their governments to pursue an anti-Soviet agenda.

The Soviet Union had won the war; at Nuremberg it lost the victory. As the fate of the defendants hung in the balance, the postwar order did as well. Ideas and arguments about justice, war crimes, and human rights that were articulated in the Palace of Justice would soon kindle discussions at the United Nations and elsewhere about the inclusion of "the Nuremberg principles" (including "crimes against peace" and "crimes against humanity") in a new international criminal code. The Soviets had shaped these principles—but had also come to understand how the institutions and language of international law could be harnessed and used against them. As a result of Nuremberg, the ideals of human rights would be intertwined with the politics of the Cold War for decades to come.

PART I | The Road
to Nuremberg

CHAPTER 1 | When War Became a Crime

T HE IDEA OF bringing Nazi leaders before an international tribunal was forged in the Soviet Union, during the bleakest days of the German occupation. The Red Army had halted the German advance on Moscow in January 1942. "Under the powerful blows of the Red Army the German troops are reeling back to the West sustaining huge losses in men and equipment," Stalin declared in a speech the next month.[1] Hope had been sparked, but the reality was grim. From the start of the German invasion in June 1941, German forces (the Wehrmacht) had advanced 600 miles into the Soviet Union, laying waste to some of its most industrialized and fertile regions. Moscow had not been captured, but the Germans had taken Kiev and most of Crimea and had laid siege to Leningrad. Moscow itself bore the scars of German aerial bombing raids. While German troops had suffered significant casualties, Soviet losses were far, far greater. Over two and a half million Soviet soldiers had been killed in combat during the first eight months of the war, and another three million had been captured. For every dead German soldier, twenty Soviet soldiers had perished.[2]

As the Red Army pushed south through Russia and Ukraine over the next few months of 1942 in a series of offenses and counter-offenses, the soldiers saw up close the damage the Nazis had inflicted. Most Soviet soldiers and war correspondents had some sense of what they would find—Foreign Minister Molotov had been publicly chronicling German atrocities since November 1941—but even the most hardened among them had not imagined the extent of the devastation. Entire city blocks were reduced to dust and ashes;

corpses were stacked on corpses. In some towns soldiers found scaffolds with bodies still hanging from them. One soldier wrote home in February 1942 that no matter what "they write in the newspapers" about the German occupation, the reality was "much worse." Refugees and what survivors there were shared stories of torture, rape, mutilation, and mass murder.[3]

Molotov continued to publicize these crimes at home and abroad, emphasizing their premeditated nature and the invaders' complete disregard for international law. His "Third Note on German Atrocities" of April 1942 cited evidence captured from the headquarters of defeated German army units that proved that these acts—including the razing of villages and the massacre of civilians—were part of a deliberate plan drawn up by the Nazi government. Molotov vowed that the German leaders and their accomplices would not escape punishment.[4] He set out to centralize the work of documenting each and every act of destruction wrought on the lands and peoples of the Soviet Union. The Nazis would be held accountable.[5]

With victory—or even survival—far from assured in the spring of 1942, the Soviets took up questions of war crimes, reparations, and international law that would have vital importance for the postwar future. At the center of this effort stood Andrei Vyshinsky, who had prosecuted the Moscow Trials of 1936–1938 and was now Molotov's deputy foreign minister.[6] Vyshinsky had until recently served as the director of the Institute of Law within the Soviet Academy of Sciences. In the spring of 1942, Molotov appointed him to a special commission charged with determining the "international-law perspective" on compensation for war damages. Vyshinsky turned to the Institute of Law, asking its international-law experts to investigate how the question of reparations had been dealt with in past peace treaties, especially after the First World War at Versailles.[7] The Institute of Law got down to work. Aron Trainin, whose career was already entwined with Vyshinsky's, took the lead.

Vyshinsky and Trainin would together craft the Soviet Union's approach to postwar justice. By 1942 the two knew each other well. Born four months apart in 1883, both men had been inspired by the revolutionary currents of their time. Both came from national minorities that had been persecuted under the Tsarist regime. Both had embraced the Bolshevik Revolution and their new Soviet identities. Both had made their marks in the field of law— but via very different paths. These paths had converged in the 1930s.

Vyshinsky's career had been shaped by luck and by his almost preternatural ability to ride the winds of change. Born to a Polish Catholic family in Odessa, he moved with his parents to the port city of Baku. As a young man, he participated in underground Marxist circles and became known for assassinating police agents. In 1908, after being arrested for organizing a workers' militia, he spent four months in an overcrowded prison cell in Baku, where he debated revolutionary theory with another young prisoner, Joseph Stalin. After his release he resumed his studies, earning a law degree at Kiev University in 1913. Vyshinsky and Stalin met again after the October Revolution of 1917; three years later, at Stalin's urging, Vyshinsky joined the Bolsheviks. He rose through the Party ranks, occupying various posts and distinguishing himself as a state prosecutor. Beginning in 1921 he also taught law at Moscow University. In 1925 he was named rector of the university and led the campaign to rid the institution of "politically unreliable" faculty and students.[8]

Stalin admired Vyshinsky's ruthlessness and recruited him in 1928 to serve as the judge in the first major Soviet show trial. Fifty-three engineers from the town of Shakhty in the North Caucasus had been charged with membership in a criminal organization that had purportedly conspired with foreigners to sabotage the Soviet mining industry. For six weeks Vyshinsky

FIGURE 1.1 Andrei Vyshinsky, 1934.
Credit: ITAR-TASS News Agency/Alamy Stock Photo.

presided over the proceedings in Moscow's House of Trade Unions, impressing the foreign journalists and dignitaries in the audience with his cool logic. All but four of the defendants were convicted; five were executed.[9] Two years later, Vyshinsky served as presiding judge in the Industrial Party Trial, in which eight eminent economists and scientists were accused of plotting with France and England to overthrow the Soviet government; all were convicted. Soon after, Stalin appointed him deputy procurator general of the USSR and deputy people's commissar of justice of the Russian Soviet Federative Socialist Republic.[10]

Vyshinsky's showmanship and ability to use the law to serve any desired end had earned him Stalin's respect. That, along with Hitler's rise to power in 1933, catapulted Vyshinsky to prominence. The mid-1930s saw the birth of a new kind of internationalism in the USSR as Soviet leaders looked for allies against the emerging Nazi threat. These years brought the fall of Marxist legal theorists such as Evgeny Pashukanis (the first director of the Institute of Law) who rejected international law as a cover for the imperialist aims of capitalist states.[11] Vyshinsky took a more pragmatic approach—viewing international law as a set of norms regulating the relations among states which the Soviet state could use to reinforce and project its authority.[12]

Trainin had been born to a Jewish merchant family in the provincial city of Vitebsk and educated in Western European legal traditions at Moscow University. As a student he, too, had thrown his lot in with the revolutionary movement; like Vyshinsky, his political activities had landed him briefly in prison. Trainin graduated from Moscow University's Faculty of Law in 1908 and became a criminologist and justice of the peace in the years before the First World War, criticizing the Imperial government from within and calling for reform. He spent extensive time abroad, primarily in Berlin, where he studied comparative law.[13] After 1917, he became a law professor at his alma mater, where he soon met Vyshinsky. He also served the new Bolshevik government, developing a criminal code.[14] By the early 1930s he had earned a reputation as a sharp legal mind and occupied a post at the Institute of Law.

Vyshinsky had an eye for talent, and he took Trainin under his wing. After the Soviet Union joined the League of Nations in 1934, Trainin worked with Vyshinsky to define a Soviet approach to international law. He began by studying international legal projects pursued after the First World War. Trainin's 1935 work *Criminal Intervention* was his first take on the subject. He argued that the movement to unify international law in the 1920s and early 1930s had failed because the League of Nations had been so preoccupied with halting the spread of communism that it had ignored what Trainin characterized as the real problem: how to prevent "aggressive war." Trainin called out several jurists for their myopia, including the Warsaw-based lawyer Raphael Lemkin and the Romanian lawyer Vespasian Pella. Describing "military aggression" as "an enormous evil, threatening death and destruction" to millions of innocent people, Trainin proclaimed that the Soviet Union was ready to play an energetic role in the "struggle for peace."[15]

Trainin took his critique of international law further in *The Defense of Peace and Criminal Law*, published in 1937 (at the height of Stalin's Great Terror). Again he derided the League of Nations for taking the legality of war as a given. He conceded that the Kellogg-Briand Pact of 1928, an ambitious multilateral peacekeeping agreement that the Soviet Union and sixty-one other countries had signed on to, had been an important step forward. But it had not gone far enough. The signatories had renounced war "as an instrument of national policy"—but had fallen short of making the waging of war a punishable offense. Trainin observed that in current international law "unlawfully hunting rabbits is punished more severely than organizing the military destruction of people." He called for the creation of an international criminal court to try "persons violating peace."[16]

Vyshinsky attached his name to this work as its editor and wrote an introduction in which he suggested that all acts "infringing on peace" be the subject of a new international criminal law convention.[17] This bold proposal was prompted by the looming threat of Germany and Japan, who had just signed an Anti-Comintern Pact that was clearly directed against the Soviet Union.

Hitler's Germany had made the publication of Trainin's works timely, but Vyshinsky's influence had made it possible. In 1935, Vyshinsky had become procurator general of the USSR and was serving as Stalin's right-hand man in his campaign against purported "enemies of the people." As prosecutor in the three Moscow Trials (staged in August 1936, January 1937, and March 1938), Vyshinsky drafted the indictments before the trumped-up investigations were even completed. In these show trials, he appropriated the language of international law, elaborated in part through the work of Trainin, to demand the execution of the defendants as "terrorists" who were serving hostile foreign governments. Using the concept of "complicity" to spin a web of guilt, Vyshinsky charged the defendants with participation in a "conspiratorial group" that was plotting to undermine the Soviet regime. Here was Stalin's paranoia given a legal vocabulary.

In January 1937, Vyshinsky became the director of the Institute of Law—replacing Pashukanis, who had been arrested and shot (like hundreds of thousands of others) on charges of "Trotskyism."[18] From this post, Vyshinsky continued to rewrite Soviet law to fit Stalin's schemes, with Trainin's assistance. In 1940 Stalin named Vyshinsky deputy foreign minister. The next year, Trainin published *On the Doctrine of Complicity*, wrapping the concept Vyshinsky had used during the Moscow Trials in a cloak of legal legitimacy.[19]

It is thus not surprising that when faced in the spring of 1942 with urgent questions about war crimes, international law, and reparations, Vyshinsky looked to Trainin. For his part, Trainin, who had been evacuated with the Institute of Law to Tashkent and wanted to do what he could to stand against the Nazi invaders, was eager to serve. He and other international-law experts were already working as consultants to the Soviet government, addressing critical questions such as the legal status of partisans—who were playing a vital part in the Soviet struggle against the Nazis in the occupied territories.[20] The ruthlessness of the Nazis toward civilians seemed to require a complete reimagining of the law. On receiving Vyshinsky's request, Trainin turned his attention to the problem of criminal responsibility, ultimately asking questions that went well beyond reparations: What state actions during wartime could be considered punishable offenses under international law? What did international law have to say about atrocities committed during a war of aggression? What kinds of sanctions could be taken against the leaders of a "bandit" state that invaded other countries and made "a mockery of the principles and the norms recognized by civilized humanity" in pursuit of "predatory goals"?[21] Trainin's answers, which evolved in dialogue with Vyshinsky and in response to reports about the horrors of the Nazi occupation, would ultimately shape the Allied approach to war crimes.

The British and the Americans were also confronting the issue of what to do about German atrocities in the spring of 1942. The deportation and murder of civilians in Nazi-occupied Europe was on a scale no one could quite believe—but the evidence kept coming in, thanks to the tireless efforts of the European governments-in-exile. Back in January, representatives from Poland, Czechoslovakia, Yugoslavia, Greece, Belgium, the Netherlands, Norway, Luxembourg, and the Free French Committee of National Liberation (the French government-in-exile) had met in London and declared their determination to use the channels of international justice to punish the Nazis and those in league with them. They had asked the other Allied powers to pledge themselves to collective action. The British and the Americans, however, would not commit themselves to bringing war criminals before an international court.[22] They recalled all too well the failure of such efforts after the First World War. They also could not imagine what such a court might look like. How could mass murder at this level be adjudicated?

FIGURE 1.2 Aron Trainin, 1945.

Credit: United States Holocaust Memorial Museum, courtesy of Joseph Eaton.

In June 1942—nine days after the Nazis obliterated the Czechoslovak village of Lidice in retaliation for the assassination of SS leader Reinhard Heydrich—Prime Minister Winston Churchill and President Franklin D. Roosevelt met in Washington and discussed the creation of a commission to track Axis crimes. Both were reluctant to invest such a body with real authority. Harry Hopkins, a former New Deal administrator who had become Roosevelt's closest advisor (living full-time in the White House since May 1940), instead sketched a proposal for an investigative body that would operate independently from the Allied governments and would engage primarily in propaganda. It was not geared toward punishing war crimes but toward publicizing them in order to rally support for the war effort. Hopkins wanted to staff this commission with dignitaries known for their integrity, mentioning the Soviet writer Alexei Tolstoy and the eighty-year-old former chief justice of the Supreme Court Charles Evans Hughes as examples of such men. The commission would disseminate information about German atrocities and report to the Allied governments.[23]

The British Foreign Office, for its part, began outlining plans for a war crimes commission that was more closely tied to the Allied governments but that would similarly serve as a fact-finding body with no power to punish offenders. The British foreign secretary, Anthony Eden, suggested that each Allied government might separately try rank-and-file Germans who had committed crimes against its citizens. Eden contended, however, that the crimes of Hitler, Hermann Goering, and other Nazi leaders were far too great for any trial and should be dealt with by an executive action of the Allied governments. The British government ultimately put together a proposal that reflected Eden's perspective.[24]

As the governments-in-exile circulated more and more evidence about what was happening in occupied Europe and urged retaliatory air raids of German towns, the American and British governments felt increasingly compelled to act. Dissemination of propaganda was clearly not going to be enough. In August 1942, Eden invited representatives from the governments-in-exile to a private meeting in London, where he shared the British proposal for a war crimes commission. Roosevelt, who was evaluating this proposal in Washington, remained noncommittal. On August 21, Roosevelt publicly acknowledged his receipt of new evidence that "acts of oppression and terror" were on the rise in occupied Europe and had the potential to lead to the "extermination of certain populations." He promised that the United States would make use of this evidence, and that the perpetrators would be brought before courts in the countries they were oppressing to "answer for their acts."[25]

Churchill, who did not like being upstaged, proclaimed on September 8 that the British government looked forward to seeing the perpetrators stand before "tribunals in every land." By late September, frustrated that Roosevelt was still sitting on their proposal, the British resolved to move forward with or without the Americans. On October 3, the British Foreign Office sent a memorandum to all the Allied nations stating that the British government would soon announce the creation of a commission to investigate German atrocities and inviting them to sign on. The U.S. government, now faced with a deadline, got on board. On October 7 President Roosevelt and British Lord Chancellor John Simon publicly pledged to establish an Allied commission to bring Nazi war criminals to justice.[26]

This declaration brought the British and the Americans closer together—but it alienated the Soviets. The Soviet Ministry of Foreign Affairs was still in evacuation in Kuibyshev (present-day Samara) after fleeing the Nazi advance on Moscow the previous year, and had not even received the British Foreign Office's memorandum until October 6. Stalin and Molotov were furious that the British had not waited for their reply. Their anger deepened on learning that the British and American governments had been discussing the details of some kind of commission behind their backs.[27] All this was fed by Stalin's mistrust of his allies. He was already frustrated with Churchill and FDR for failing to follow through on their promise to open a second front in the West. He also worried that Churchill intended to sign a separate peace with the Nazis. The British government's refusal to initiate criminal proceedings against Hitler's deputy Rudolf Hess fueled this suspicion; Hess had been taken into British custody seventeen months earlier, after flying solo from Germany to Great Britain and proclaiming his goal of negotiating peace between the two states.[28]

Determined now to seize the initiative, Soviet leaders shifted the terms of the discussion by publicly insisting that plans be made at once for an international trial of major war criminals—exactly what the British and the Americans had been hoping to avoid. The Soviets framed this demand as a direct response to the January appeal from the governments-in-exile, choosing to ignore the British memorandum altogether. On October 14, 1942, Deputy Foreign Minister Solomon Lozovsky summoned the Czechoslovak ambassador and a representative from the Free French Committee of National Liberation to a midnight meeting in Kuibyshev and handed them a statement from Molotov about the criminal responsibility of the Nazi perpetrators ("the Hitlerites") for atrocities in occupied Europe. The statement stipulated that Hitler, Goering, Hess, Joachim von Ribbentrop, and other Nazi leaders should be brought before a "special international tribunal" and punished with "all of the severity of criminal law." It called for the cooperation of all interested governments in capturing, trying, and sentencing Nazi leaders and insisted that those already in Allied hands (i.e., Hess) be brought to justice without further delay.[29] The Soviet government broadcast this statement the following day.[30] On October 19, the lead article in *Pravda* attacked the British government for shielding Hess from punishment and described England as "a sanctuary for gangsters."[31]

Moscow also swiftly proceeded with the establishment of its own war crimes commission—which had been in the works ever since Molotov had called for the centralization of the work of exposing German atrocities back in April. While Vyshinsky and Trainin were working on the international-law side of the reparations question, Soviet leaders had been squabbling over the commission's form and function. The British-American announcement focused Soviet efforts. Between October 17 and 20, Molotov, Vyshinsky, and Lozovsky worked out the final details of the Extraordinary State Commission for Ascertaining and Investigating German-Fascist Crimes in the USSR. Stalin approved their proposal in late October; on November 2, the Soviet government passed a decree bringing the commission into being.[32]

The Extraordinary State Commission was something entirely new. It was made up of government officials as well as cultural figures, the latter chosen mainly for their potential to communicate what was happening in terms that the world might understand. Its members included the writers Alexei Tolstoy and Ilya Ehrenburg, the physician Nikolai Burdenko, the trade union leader Nikolai Shvernik, and Metropolitan Nikolai of Kiev and Galicia (a bishop of the Russian Orthodox Church). The commission oversaw dozens of subcommissions throughout the Soviet Union that would soon undertake the harrowing work of amassing evidence and building a case. The commission had close ties to the Ministry of Foreign Affairs and to the state security apparatus. While Shvernik was its nominal head, Vyshinsky would in fact run the show, at times working with the secret police to shape or even (in at least a few cases) fabricate affidavits and reports.[33] With the establishment of the Extraordinary State Commission, the Soviets set out on their own road toward bringing the Nazis to justice.

In the meantime, there was more diplomatic posturing and hemming and hawing. Back in London, Eden used the floor of the House of Commons on October 21 to complain that the British government was still awaiting the Soviet reply to its proposal for an Allied war crimes commission.[34] The British would wait for two more weeks: Molotov sent an irate note to British ambassador Sir Archibald Clark Kerr on November 3, the day after the creation of the Extraordinary State Commission. The timing was intentional. Lambasting the British government for failing to consult in advance with the Soviets, Molotov called the British proposal too timid to satisfy those peoples who were suffering so catastrophically under German occupation. Any such Allied commission, Molotov emphasized, must be empowered to punish the Nazi leaders. The Extraordinary State Commission was prepared to share evidence of the monstrosity of their crimes.[35]

Two days later, on November 5, Stalin and Molotov received Kerr in the Kremlin. Stalin accused the British government of being hypocritical in calling for the investigation of war crimes while harboring Hess. He inquired, only half-facetiously, whether Goebbels, the Nazi propaganda minister, might expect similar treatment in British hands. Kerr assured Stalin that no one had any intention of coddling anyone—but he questioned the wisdom of bringing Hess and Hitler before an international tribunal, arguing that their crimes were far too great to be dealt with by judicial procedure. Kerr then expressed his personal hope for an executive decree in which Stalin, Roosevelt, and Churchill proclaimed that Hitler should hang. Stalin balked at this suggestion, arguing that without a trial the public could conclude that the Allied leaders had engaged in victors' justice.[36] The hanging could just as easily happen after the trial.

The Soviets had no problem with victors' justice per se: Stalin had meted it out to his opponents for many years. He was, however, keenly attuned to the propaganda value of an international tribunal versus punishment by executive decree. In the Moscow Trials, Vyshinsky had prosecuted Lev Kamenev, Nikolai Bukharin, and other Bolshevik leaders on the trumped-up charge that they were Nazi collaborators who had been plotting with Hitler "to establish a fascist dictatorship in Russia."[37] A trial of actual Nazi leaders would rally the war-weary Soviet people and provide collective catharsis, while laying the groundwork for reparations.

Stalin and Kerr were imagining dramatically different things. The Soviets took Nazi guilt as a given; they could not conceive of a trial in which the defendants did anything other than confess their crimes, preferably from a prepared script, and then get hustled off for execution. The British, on the other hand, envisioned a trial with all of the usual pomp and procedure in which the defendants were presumed innocent and had bewigged counsel at their ready. They could not see the point of such a trial—especially when an executive decree would make it possible to impose punishment far more efficiently.[38]

While Soviet leaders still had their sights set on bringing Hitler, Hess, and others before an international tribunal, Molotov's response, sent on November 12, struck a conciliatory note: he agreed that the Allied governments would collectively decide on the punishment of the Nazi leaders, by a means to be determined later. At another meeting at the end of November, Molotov expressed understanding when Kerr related that the British and American governments wanted to wait until after the war to punish captured Nazi leaders (such as Hess) for fear of German reprisals. Then a fresh disagreement flared over whether rank-and-file war criminals would face national trials or be brought before an international tribunal.[39]

While the Soviets and the British wrangled over the details of trying war criminals, Nazi forces were brutalizing Europe. On December 17, 1942, Britain, the United States, the Soviet Union, and the European governments-in-exile issued a joint statement citing reports of the slaughter of "many hundreds of thousands" of innocent Jewish men, women, and children whom the Nazis had deported to Eastern Europe. (At this point, the actual number of Jewish victims was already in the millions.) The signatories proclaimed that those responsible would not escape punishment.[40] The next day, the Soviet Union put out its own report, "On the Implementation of the Nazi Plan to Exterminate the Jewish Population of Europe." Printed in the major Soviet newspapers and distributed in English abroad, it voiced solidarity with the European governments-in-exile and documented the "bloody orgy of extermination" being carried out against the Jews in Ukraine, Belorussia, Lithuania, Latvia, Estonia, and other regions of the Soviet Union.[41] The Ministry of Foreign Affairs, with help from the Extraordinary State Commission and the

NKVD, had amassed overwhelming evidence of Nazi efforts to annihilate the Jews. This was a decisive step toward making it public knowledge.[42]

As Soviet troops encircled the Wehrmacht in a bombed-out Stalingrad in January 1943, the Soviets adjusted their position about rank-and-file war criminals, now agreeing to the British suggestion that each of the Allied powers should deal with them in national trials. With the Red Army's capture of thousands of German officers and soldiers, such an approach was suddenly in Moscow's interests. Soviet leaders also expressed a new willingness to participate in an Allied war crimes commission, but with a caveat: this commission should include only representatives of those countries that were actively fighting the Axis powers and had "borne the brunt" of the war and occupation. This was not a simple request, for the British already had invited the United States, the USSR, China, the European governments-in-exile, India, and the British Dominions of Australia, Canada, New Zealand, and South Africa to participate in the commission.[43] Stalin, keenly attuned to the balance of power, believed that the inclusion of the Dominions would allow the British to shape the commission's agenda.

Over the course of the next few months, the Red Army marched across the steppe and into Ukraine, liberating key areas from German forces. In February 1943 the Red Army retook Kursk, Rostov, and Kharkov. It found shattered and depopulated cities, blown-out apartment buildings, women and children with swollen bellies wandering about in rags. In Kharkov the people spoke of deportations, mass executions, and public hangings; melting snow revealed mass graves. The Extraordinary State Commission sent photographers to document the ruins. The Red Army held on to Kharkov for only a month before being driven back in mid-March, leaving the inhabitants to the revenge of the returning German forces.[44]

The question of Soviet participation in an Allied war crimes commission meanwhile remained unresolved. The British government moved forward with its plans to organize the commission, proposing London as the headquarters and branches in Chungking, Washington, and Moscow.[45] A Moscow branch was meant to appeal to the Soviets, but Stalin was uninterested; he did not want the British and the Americans meddling in the Soviet investigation of war crimes.

Stalin had reason to be wary of Western interference, for evidence had surfaced of a Soviet atrocity. In April 1943, Radio Berlin announced that German authorities had discovered the bodies of 10,000 Polish officers buried in pits in the Katyn Forest outside Smolensk. The Nazis blamed the Bolsheviks for the crime. The Soviets dismissed this accusation as a lie and contended that the

"German-Fascist scoundrels" had themselves murdered the Poles along with Soviet civilians in the summer of 1941, after Soviet troops had withdrawn from the region. The Polish government-in-exile asked the International Red Cross to investigate the gravesite. The Soviets opposed this request and severed diplomatic relations with the Polish government-in-exile, accusing it of treachery.[46] Soon thereafter, a German-sponsored International Katyn Commission, with forensic scientists mostly from the Axis powers, excavated the area and reaffirmed Soviet responsibility for the crime.[47]

For American and British leaders, Katyn presented a political predicament. Roosevelt and Churchill had reports from Western diplomats and intelligence agents pointing to Soviet culpability for the massacre—but chose to ignore them, worried that a split with Stalin would undermine the alliance against Germany. Churchill went so far as to assure Stalin that he would "oppose vigorously" a Red Cross investigation.[48] The Soviets, of course, did have something to hide. In the spring of 1940, the NKVD, acting on Party orders, had executed some 22,000 Polish officers and intellectuals at several sites, including Katyn.[49] Now, Soviet leaders began to engineer a cover-up—including the fabrication of evidence to be planted at the crime scene.[50]

In an effort to draw international attention away from Katyn and back to Axis crimes, the Soviets held their first public trial of Nazi collaborators—using evidence that had been collected by the Extraordinary State Commission. In July 1943, eleven men, all Russians or Ukrainians, were brought before a military tribunal in Krasnodar, in the North Caucasus, and charged with committing treason during the German occupation of the region. Almost all of the defendants had served in a special detachment of the mobile killing unit Einsatzgruppe D, which had murdered more than 7,000 Soviet citizens, mostly Jews. Experts and eyewitnesses provided general testimony about Nazi atrocities in the region. The judge and prosecutor pressed the defendants to confess the details of their crimes before hundreds of spectators, including correspondents from the world press. All of the defendants were found guilty. Three received prison sentences, and eight were hanged before a crowd of 30,000 observers. Cameramen filmed the spectacle, and the footage was shown in movie theaters throughout the Soviet Union. Stalin deemed the trial a triumph.[51]

In staging the Krasnodar Trial, Soviet leaders honed their narrative about the war and the German occupation. The victims were described during the trial and in the press coverage as "peaceful Soviet citizens," emphasizing the shared suffering of the entire Soviet people. This did not mean that Soviet leaders were attempting to suppress the substantial evidence that the Extraordinary State Commission had gathered about the targeted murder of Jews. The commission member Tolstoy published an article in the Soviet newspaper *Krasnaya zvezda* (*Red Star*) after the trial describing Nazi efforts to wipe out the Jewish communities of the North Caucasus: he told how Jews were forced to wear yellow Stars of David, prohibited from public places, and ultimately herded onto trains and taken to killing sites where they were gassed in vans or shot. For Soviet leaders, who wanted to use the trial to foster the unity of the Soviet people, the fate of the Jews was not the central narrative. But it was there for the reading in the Soviet press.[52]

After the Krasnodar Trial, the Soviets again considered the possibility of participating in the Allied war crimes commission, which, though stalled, was still in the works. In late July 1943, Soviet leaders agreed to London as the home base, provided that Britain, the United States, the USSR, and China assumed equal leadership positions. They signed off on the creation of Washington and Chungking branches but insisted that a Moscow branch was unnecessary, given that the Extraordinary State Commission was already investigating Nazi atrocities in the Soviet Union and was ready to share its findings. The ultimate dealbreaker on Soviet participation, though, remained the commission's composition. Soviet leaders cannily agreed to the inclusion of the British Dominions and India—on the condition that Ukraine, Belorussia, Moldavia, Lithuania, Latvia, Estonia, and Karelia-Finland were also brought onto the commission.[53] The British rejected this Soviet proposition on the grounds that it would raise "insurmountable difficulties."[54] The Red Army had invaded Latvia, Lithuania, and Estonia after the signing of the German-Soviet Non-Aggression Pact; the British and U.S. governments refused to recognize the USSR's annexation of these countries. The British also argued that the international legal status of the Dominions and India bore no relation to that of even the recognized Soviet republics, which were dependent on Moscow "for all of their dealings with the outside world."[55] The Soviets continued on their separate path.

The United Nations War Crimes Commission (UNWCC) thus convened in London on October 26, 1943, without Soviet participation. As the only Allied power not at the table, the Soviets were conspicuous in their absence. The chair of the commission, Sir Cecil Hurst, a British judge with ties to the Foreign Office, tried to limit the UNWCC's role from the start. He pushed to define the term "war crime" narrowly as a "criminal action violating the laws and customs of war" as set out in the Geneva and Hague Conventions before the First World War.[56] But the delegates from occupied Europe had come with far more ambitious agendas. The Czechoslovak jurist Bohuslav Ečer, whose country was being ravaged by the Nazis, argued that "the methods of total war," which targeted civilians as a matter of course, had made older ideas about war crimes obsolete: any definition must include acts such as mass deportations and the razing of villages. The Belgian delegate, Marcel de Baer (the president of his country's military court), agreed with Ečer and insisted that the UNWCC pursue the punishment of crimes that might slip through the cracks of existing international law, including the persecution of Germany's Jews. The jurists similarly split on the relationship between war crimes and what some of them were calling "the crime of war." Ečer and de Baer argued that "the preparation and waging of an aggressive war" was the essential crime to be punished, while Hurst insisted that this view lacked any legal basis.[57]

Discussions about definitions dragged on for weeks and prevented the UNWCC from getting down to the work of investigating atrocities. By December, at their wits' end, the commission's members agreed to accept Hurst's narrow understanding of war crimes as a starting point. Even then, the jurists remained uncertain about the task before them. Hurst argued that the commission's sole purpose was to gather information. Ečer thought it should promote the creation of inter-Allied tribunals to prosecute international crimes, which he defined as crimes "committed on the territory of several Allied nations" as well as those aimed "against the very foundations of the International Community."[58]

In Russia, Soviet jurists were considering some of the same questions as the UNWCC—but without the hand-wringing. Trainin, who had recently returned to Moscow with the Institute of Law, was at the center of this effort. He had completed his report for Vyshinsky over the summer, and after vetting by his colleagues it was passed on to the Ministry of Foreign Affairs.[59] By the early fall, some of Trainin's key arguments had been publicized abroad. Addressing the question of reparations, Trainin maintained that there was no question that Germany must be held "materially responsible" for all of its war crimes—including the planning and waging of the current war. He also argued that this wasn't enough: those persons who had committed or conspired to commit criminal acts in the name of the state must be tried and punished.[60]

For the British and the Americans, the failure of Versailles a generation earlier haunted their thinking. It was reason enough to steer clear of an international tribunal. Trainin disagreed: it was an object lesson in why a tribunal was necessary. The Treaty of Versailles had called for the punishment of Kaiser Wilhelm II and his associates for systematically violating the laws and customs of war. The failure to follow through, Trainin suggested, had emboldened Hitler. While the UNWCC stumbled over the definition of "war crimes," Trainin argued for the criminal responsibility of "Hitlerites" at all levels. He rejected the plea of "acting on superior orders," which was still a standard defense in international law, arguing that rank-and-file soldiers who "plunder and kill on the orders of their superiors" were just as guilty as those who "plunder and kill of their own accord." The greatest degree of criminal responsibility, however, belonged to Germany's leaders. Here Trainin called particular attention to Hitler and his ministers, the leadership of the Nazi Party, Nazi authorities in the occupied territories, the Wehrmacht's High Command, and German financial and industrial magnates, noting their "grievous violations of the principles of international intercourse and human ethics."[61]

All eyes turned to Moscow in October 1943 as Molotov received Eden and the U.S. secretary of state, Cordell Hull, to discuss the course of the war and to plan for its aftermath. One outcome was the Moscow Declaration, in which the United States, the USSR, Britain, and China pledged to pursue the unconditional surrender of the Axis powers and called for the creation of an international organization committed to peace and security. The declaration included a Statement of Atrocities, in which Roosevelt, Churchill, and Stalin decried German "atrocities, massacres, and cold-blooded mass executions" in the occupied territories and promised the punishment of all who were responsible. One of the atrocities this statement listed was the massacre of Polish officers, implying Nazi responsibility for Katyn.[62] Stalin had gambled correctly that Roosevelt and Churchill would not object.

The Statement of Atrocities stipulated that German officers, soldiers, and others who had planned or participated in criminal acts would be sent back to the scenes of their crimes for judgment in national courts. War criminals whose offenses spanned more than one geographical area would be punished by a joint decision of the Allied governments. Whether this decision would be reached by means of a trial or by other means was left open.[63]

The Tehran Conference of late November and early December did not bring clarity to this question. Roosevelt, Churchill, and Stalin, together for their first face-to-face meeting, coordinated their military strategies and pledged postwar cooperation. The British and the Americans again promised to open a second front, and Stalin agreed to declare war on Japan after the Nazi defeat. In discussions about postwar Europe, Stalin won concessions on his demand to revise Poland's borders (to the so-called Curzon Line) and shared his ideas for a punitive program to permanently weaken Germany.[64] During a conference dinner at the Soviet embassy, Stalin warned that unless such a program were implemented, Germany would "rise again within 15 or 20 years to plunge the world into another war." One measure he recommended was the execution of 50,000 to 100,000 German military officers. American and British attendees were uncertain whether he was joking.[65] But this was no joke: Stalin's purge of his own military leadership had taken place quietly behind the scenes during the Great Terror. Some 35,000 officers had been removed from their positions; around 10,000 of them were arrested, and many of those were shot.[66]

In the wake of Tehran, Soviet leaders set out to show the world that they were committed to the expeditious trial and punishment of war criminals. On December 3, two days after the conference ended, the Soviet Union held its first public hanging of a German soldier for war crimes near the town of Kremenchug in Ukraine, following a field court-martial. Two weeks later, the Soviets convened a military tribunal in Kharkov, which the Red Army had again retaken, and tried three Gestapo officials and a Ukrainian collaborator for their roles in the slaughter of civilians. The Kharkov Trial was the first public war crimes trial of German nationals held by any Allied power. It took place over four days before a large rotating audience that included foreign correspondents. The Extraordinary State Commission provided much of the evidence. The victims, numbering more than 14,000 and overwhelmingly Jewish, were referred to as "peaceful Soviet citizens" (as in the Krasnodar Trial), even as an article by Ehrenburg in *Krasnaya zvezda* called attention to the massacre of the city's Jews.[67]

A key purpose of the Kharkov Trial was to establish the invalidity of the defense of "following superior orders," which Trainin was continuing to denounce in his articles as a "saving bunker" for war criminals "during the stern hour of vengeance."[68] When the accused attempted to enter this plea, the tribunal rejected it as inadmissible. All four defendants were found guilty and hanged in public: a clear example of Soviet justice. The trial and the hangings were widely covered in the international press just as Stalin had hoped. *Life* included a two-page photo essay with grisly images of the convicted men swinging from the scaffolds.[69] Soviet filmmakers produced a full-length documentary of the trial, *Sud idet!* (*The Trial Begins!*), released in English as *The Kharkov Trials*, which shocked audiences in New York and London with its vivid account of Nazi atrocities—including the murder of women and children in gas vans. In an editorial, the *Times* of London called the film "grim and unrelenting," musing that "the story it unfolds" of the German occupation "is so appalling that nerves can hardly react to it."[70]

Even as the Soviets were influencing the Allied approach to German war crimes, they were continuing to engage in a massive cover-up of Katyn. Between October 1943 (when the Red Army recaptured the Katyn area) and

January 1944, Soviet secret police agents with the NKVD and the Ministry of State Security (NKGB) were opening burial pits in the Katyn Forest and planting evidence among the corpses, to be discovered during future exhumations; they were also using intimidation and force to collect false witness testimony. On January 10, the NKVD and NKGB produced a joint report concluding that the massacre had been carried out in the fall of 1941 by an unknown German military unit that had been stationed in the region.[71]

That same month, Soviet leaders convened a special commission under Extraordinary State Commission member Nikolai Burdenko to "investigate" the Katyn massacre. Known as the Burdenko Commission, this body included Alexei Tolstoy and Metropolitan Nikolai of Kiev and Galicia, as well as forensic scientists and other notables. It worked closely with Vyshinsky, who had been entrusted with the cover-up. The NKVD deputy chief Sergei Kruglov—who had co-authored the NKVD-NKGB report—attended the commission's meetings. Kruglov was far from a disinterested party. He had been part of the "troika" responsible for implementing the NKVD's plan to carry out the massacre in 1940. The commission's findings, announced on January 24, unsurprisingly upheld the Soviet claim of German responsibility for the atrocity.[72]

Three days later, on January 27, the Red Army lifted the siege of Leningrad, which had lasted nearly 900 days. The Extraordinary State Commission immediately set to work interviewing survivors. With Katyn presumably taken care of and evidence about Nazi war crimes continuing to pile up, Soviet leaders again considered participation in the UNWCC, going so far as to amend the USSR's constitution to give the republics the right to establish foreign relations with other states—putting them on an equal footing with the British Dominions. When the British continued to reject the participation of the republics in the commission, negotiations again ground to a halt.[73]

The UNWCC meanwhile had become a forum for heated discussions about justice. When Cecil Hurst proposed that the UNWCC focus exclusively on crimes against the citizens of the Allied governments, Bohuslav Ečer vehemently objected—exclaiming that it would "shock the public conscience" if the Allies decided that the murder of German Jews fell outside their reach. The U.S. delegate Herbert Pell, who was deeply troubled by the news coming out of Europe (and whose vision for the UNWCC was far more ambitious than the State Department's), agreed with Ečer; he introduced a motion to treat crimes against stateless persons, as well as crimes committed because of the religion or race of the victims, as war crimes. Pell argued that the fight against Nazism demanded the punishment of "crimes against humanity"—intentionally using a term that had made its public debut in a 1915 declaration by the French, Russians, and British condemning the Ottoman slaughter of Armenians. Ečer then suggested that the UNWCC extend the concept of war crimes to include attacks on "fundamental human rights." When the question arose of whether membership in the SS and Gestapo might be considered a crime, the French representative René Cassin (the legal advisor to the Free French Committee of National Liberation) noted that the concept of a criminal organization was well known in French and Belgian criminal law.[74] The Soviets were still not involved in the UNWCC—but Trainin's ideas about the criminal responsibility of the Nazi leaders and their organizations were about to enter its discussions.

By the late spring of 1944, the Soviet Union had reclaimed much of southern Russia and Ukraine, and the Wehrmacht was in full retreat. That summer, the Red Army launched its most ambitious offensive of the war, recapturing Belorussia and marching into Poland. Fresh from these victories, the Soviets sharpened and publicized their arguments for bringing the Nazi leaders before an international tribunal. Trainin and Vyshinsky were, not surprisingly, central to this effort. Moscow published Trainin's report as a book, *The Criminal Responsibility of the Hitlerites,* in July 1944; Vyshinsky once again signed on as editor and wrote the introduction.

Trainin argued that the scope of the war was so overwhelming, "the methods used by the Hitlerites" so unprecedented, that it would be unthinkable not to hold the perpetrators to account. Evidence compiled by the Extraordinary State Commission and presented at the Krasnodar and Kharkov trials had revealed what he termed "a stunning picture" of the organized mass murder of civilians. While the German state should face political and economic sanctions for these crimes, criminal responsibility, he argued, must be borne by individuals.

Trainin insisted that Nazi leaders should be tried not only for crimes committed in the course of the war but also for launching the war—committing a "crime against peace"—in the first place. The idea of treating aggressive war as a punishable criminal act (which Trainin had long been arguing for) was at that moment being debated by the UNWCC. But Trainin now coined the term "crimes against peace" and gave it its definitive formulation: acts of aggression; propaganda of aggression; the conclusion of international agreements with aggressive aims; the violation of peace treaties; provocations designed to stir up trouble between countries; terrorism; and the support of fifth columns. Trainin called for the creation of an international tribunal to try the Hitlerites and proposed that "crimes against peace" be included in a new international-law convention.[75]

In this book Trainin also elaborated his earlier argument that Nazi leaders and their organizations should be tried for participating in a criminal conspiracy. He devoted a chapter to the concept of "complicity" (building on his 1940 book on the topic), defining it as the joint participation of people in committing a crime whereby each accomplice is linked with the criminal outcome. Complicity often entails participation in a conspiracy or criminal organization, he argued, and even if the members of a group do not know one another they each can still "be responsible for all the crimes" the group commits. Trainin noted matter-of-factly that he was borrowing from the definition of complicity that Vyshinsky had set out in the Moscow Trials. He maintained that the concept of complicity, which was firmly established in Soviet domestic law, was even more important for international law—because in international crime the perpetrator seldom acts alone. Trainin also added to his earlier critique of the defense of "superior orders"—explaining that "an order to commit a crime is not a military order" but "an instigation to evil-doing, for which both the instigator and the agents can and must bear full responsibility."[76]

Trainin's concepts of criminal responsibility, complicity, and crimes against peace soon spread across the European continent, to London, and then to Washington. In September and early October 1944, while British and American forces were advancing across France and toward Germany, articles by Trainin appeared in *Soviet War News, New Masses*, and other leftist publications in the United States and Great Britain.[77] The real breakthrough came in October, when Trainin's ideas were discussed at the UNWCC in London. Ečer, who knew Russian, served as a middleman.

On October 6, Ečer again implored his colleagues to consider the preparation and waging of the present war a crime, one for which the Axis leaders must be punished. He quoted the French lawyer Cassin, who had referred to the current war as a "total war" that had manifested itself in "total criminality." He then put forth Trainin's argument (excerpted from *Soviet War News*) that those bearing the greatest guilt included Hitler and other German leaders. They had not waged war: they had prepared, organized, and perpetrated a crime. Soviet arguments about Nazi criminality were beginning to take hold.[78] On October 10, UNWCC chairman Hurst reported the receipt of three copies of Trainin's book, which a former commission member from Luxembourg had sent for the commission's review. One copy was given to Ečer, who was asked to read it and report back to the commission with his analysis.[79]

Throughout October, leading members of the UNWCC continued to oppose the idea of holding political leaders responsible for launching a war. They felt there was simply no legal basis for it: the Kellogg-Briand Pact of 1928, while denouncing war, had been vague on the question of individual responsibility. The Yugoslav delegate Radomir Živković criticized his colleagues for being overly cautious. There was nothing in international law preventing the Allied governments from declaring that aggressive war was a punishable crime, he argued. The delegates needed to decide whether it was politically desirable to do so. Ečer agreed that if there were, as he put it, "gaps" in international law, the commission should "fill them." He again referenced the Soviet Union, whose international-law and criminal-law experts "strongly support the opinion that the preparation and launching of this war are crimes for which the authors must bear penal responsibility." Now using Trainin's terminology, Ečer proclaimed that the "preparation and launching of the present war must be punished as a crime against peace."[80]

Trainin's term "crimes against peace"—which would have a profound effect on postwar justice and on the very perception of the war—thus entered the international legal lexicon. On October 31, Ečer presented the UNWCC with a detailed report on Trainin's book. This report was circulated to the delegates, many of whom brought it back to their governments.[81] On November 11 Ečer's analysis was forwarded to the U.S. State Department.[82] A short time later, the State Department assessed Trainin's book (now translated into English) and sent it, along with Ečer's analysis, on to the White House.[83]

On January 4, 1945, two lawyers from the War Department's Special Projects Branch, Lieutenant Colonel Murray Bernays (a Russian Jewish émigré who happened to be married to the niece of Sigmund Freud) and his colleague D. W. Brown, wrote a secret report for FDR addressing the question of whether starting the Second World War was a crime for which the Axis leaders could be tried and punished. They concluded that it was. This opinion completely broke from U.S. policy, they acknowledged, but the events in Europe demanded that international law evolve "with the growth and development of the public conscience." According to Bernays and Brown, regardless of earlier opinions, it could "not be disputed that the launching of a war of aggression today is condemned by the vast majority of mankind as a crime."[84]

Bernays had been a reluctant advocate for trials of Nazi war criminals, concerned about reprisals against American prisoners of war. He, and the rest of the War Department, had been pushed into considering this question largely in response to an August 1944 proposal by U.S. Treasury Secretary

Henry Morgenthau Jr. for dismantling Nazi Germany after the war (known as the Morgenthau Plan). Morgenthau had suggested using German prisoners of war to rebuild Europe and advocated shooting the major Nazi leaders upon capture, without trial.[85]

Over two weeks in early September, Bernays wrote a memorandum arguing that shooting Nazi leaders in the manner Morgenthau advised would make a mockery of those ideals for which the Allied powers had gone to war. Instead, he proposed what the Soviets had been calling for all along: an international trial of Nazi leaders grounded in the concept of "criminal conspiracy." Bernays recommended that a tribunal be convened to try the Nazi leaders and their organizations (including the Gestapo and the SS) for conspiring to terrorize and murder civilians in violation of the laws of war. This approach became known by the War Department and the State Department as the Bernays Plan. Bernays did not mention Trainin or Ečer in his September memorandum.[86] But by November or December he had made a thorough study of their arguments—and he cited Trainin's work at length in his and Brown's January 1945 report to FDR on the criminality of the present war.[87]

Bernays and Brown had done extensive research for this report. They cited previous international treaties, including the Kellogg-Briand Pact. They also noted that Polish-British law professor Hersch Lauterpacht and U.S. Secretary of War Henry L. Stimson had both referred to the idea of a criminal or illegal war. Finally, they referenced the "Soviet view," which held, as they put it, "that the launching of an aggressive war is today a crime in international law." Bernays and Brown gave special attention to Trainin's concept of crimes against peace. Given these precedents, they concluded that a formal declaration by the Allied governments calling out the criminality of aggressive war would "rest on solid grounds" and would itself take on the power of "valid international law."[88]

As his concepts were getting attention and shaping the discussion in the West, Trainin was publicly criticizing the UNWCC's pursuit of what he dismissed as "justice with the brakes on."[89] He wasn't the only Soviet lawyer who thought that the UNWCC didn't understand what was at stake. In January, two lawyers with the Ministry of Foreign Affairs (Sergei Golunsky and Semyon Bazarov) observed in a report to Molotov that the UNWCC's attention had been completely diverted to questions of legal theory.[90] Meanwhile, the Ministry of Foreign Affairs, anticipating the end of the war, made plans for the translation and dissemination abroad of Extraordinary State Commission reports cataloguing Nazi atrocities in the Soviet Union. On January 5, Deputy Foreign Minister Lozovsky recommended to Molotov the publication of ten to fifteen volumes of these reports, with photographs. Lozovsky emphasized the urgency of publicizing these materials before Germany capitulated, for they would enable the Soviet government to press hard its demands for reparations.[91]

By mid-January of 1945, the U.S. government was leaning toward a more active and engaged approach to postwar justice. On January 22, in anticipation of the Yalta Conference, Secretary of War Stimson, new Secretary of State Edward Stettinius Jr., and Attorney General Francis Biddle gave FDR their recommendations for dealing with Axis war criminals. They pointed to the criminality of Nazi leaders, who had carried out "a systematic and planned reign of terror" inside Germany and throughout Europe. They also called out the guilt of Nazi organizations such as the SS and the Gestapo. After criticizing the UNWCC as ineffectual, they conceded the challenges in front of them. Nazi crimes had been so enormous and so widespread that identifying and trying the perpetrators presented a situation unique in the history of international criminal law. Moreover, atrocities committed within Germany before the start of the war were not war crimes in the traditional sense. Yet the Allied governments had pledged to punish these crimes, and "the interest of postwar security and a necessary rehabilitation of the German people, as well as the demands of justice, require that this be done."[92]

Stimson, Stettinius, and Biddle opposed the idea of punishing the Nazi leaders by executive decree. They argued that ordering the execution of Hitler and other high-ranking Nazis would be efficient but would violate "the most fundamental principles of justice" and would encourage the German people to turn them into martyrs. A trial, by contrast, would receive popular support as well as "the respect of history." They suggested charging the German leaders and their organizations with committing heinous war crimes and with jointly participating in a criminal conspiracy. The latter charge would cover atrocities committed before the war, including crimes against the Jews, as well as the crime of planning and waging "an illegal war of aggression." They further recommended a two-stage judicial process. Initially, the Allied powers would convene an international tribunal to try some of the top German leaders who also represented those organizations that had been charged with complicity in the criminal conspiracy. Later, the Allied powers would identify other participants in the conspiracy; they would either be sent back to the scenes of their crimes for trial or brought before occupation courts.[93]

The Stimson-Stettinius-Biddle proposal drew extensively from the Bernays Plan—but also reflected Trainin's ideas about criminal responsibility and French ideas about criminal organizations. It rested heavily on the idea that Trainin, Ečer, and others had put forward that a war of conquest and exploitation—what was increasingly being called a "war of aggression"—was an international crime. The authors explained that the Soviets seemed ready to cooperate and already favored the creation of an international tribunal. The British, they noted, continued to oppose a trial of the top Nazi leaders—and it was not clear whether they could be won over.[94]

When Stalin, Molotov, and Vyshinsky welcomed Churchill and Roosevelt at the resort town of Yalta on February 4, 1945, questions of shaping the postwar future were paramount. This was a long way from the early months of the siege of Leningrad, when the notion of punishing the Nazis was purely theoretical. The Red Army was rapidly approaching Berlin—and the Soviets were now in a position of strength. The leaders gathered at a large round table in the ballroom of the opulent Livadia Palace, flanked by interpreters and advisors. Stalin, playing the role of gracious host, insisted that Roosevelt chair the meeting. The Soviet leader then sat back and, speaking with what others in the room would later remember as "simple unquestionable finality," began to usher through his agenda.[95]

Stalin called for the joint occupation of a defeated Germany, and insisted on territorial concessions and reparations. The three leaders agreed to divide Germany into four occupation zones: one for each of their countries, and one for France. They also affirmed that reparations in kind would be extracted from Germany, in part, as their joint proclamation expressed it, "through the use of German labor." Roosevelt and Churchill also acquiesced to Stalin's demand for Soviet influence over Poland (which was already under Red Army occupation) in exchange for his promise to allow free elections. Stalin, in turn, again pledged that the Soviets would join the war against Japan. Looking ahead, the leaders agreed that representatives of the Allied governments should meet in San Francisco that spring with the aim of establishing an international organization to maintain the future peace.[96]

At the close of the Yalta conference on February 11, Stalin, Churchill, and Roosevelt pledged to bring all war criminals to just punishment and to prosecute the leaders of the Axis powers after the Allies achieved victory in Europe. The specifics were not discussed; it was agreed that the three foreign ministers would work out the details at a later date.[97] Stalin left Yalta satisfied that he and the Western leaders had seen eye to eye, that Churchill and Roosevelt had agreed to Soviet influence in Eastern Europe and had accepted Soviet ideas about reparations that anticipated the use of German forced labor to rebuild the Soviet Union. For Stalin, of course, the latter point was key.[98] What Stalin could not have anticipated was Roosevelt's death in mid-April—and how it would completely unhinge his relationship with the United States.

Back in London, the members of the UNWCC wondered when (and whether) the Allied governments would agree on the specifics of a plan for postwar justice. In late March, the delegates sent a progress report to their governments urging cooperation between the UNWCC and the Extraordinary State Commission and posing the key question: did the Allied governments intend to punish Nazi leaders (the major war criminals) by executive decree or by an international criminal court?[99]

This question continued to divide the British and the Americans. In early April, shortly before FDR's death, the British Foreign Office invited representatives of the U.S. government to London to privately discuss the problem of war crimes. Roosevelt sent one of his most trusted advisors, U.S. judge Samuel I. Rosenman (the speechwriter who had coined the term "New Deal"), to meet with Lord Chancellor Simon and Sir William Malkin, the legal advisor to the Foreign Office.[100] Rosenman and Simon readily affirmed their governments' commitment to the Moscow Declaration's pledge to return rank-and-file war criminals to the scenes of their crimes. At issue was how to deal with the main Nazi leaders and organizations, whose crimes were international in scope.[101]

Neither the British nor the Americans favored the type of inter-Allied court envisioned by some members of the UNWCC, but they acknowledged that some kind of "appropriate substitute" must be put forward. Malkin noted the British preference for military courts, which could consider any evidence that was deemed to have probative value.[102] Simon then put forward a British proposal for dealing with Hitler and other "arch-criminals" that, he suggested, would avoid the extremes of summary executions on the one hand and a prolonged trial with a parade of defense witnesses on the other. The Allied governments could draw up an indictment and appoint an inter-Allied tribunal with specific powers. This tribunal would allow Hitler and the other defendants to be heard and to produce witnesses behind closed doors. It would then notify the Allies if any of the charges had been disproved. Afterward, the Allied governments would determine the punishments. Simon emphasized that this would not be a war crimes trial as currently known in international law: there would be no consideration as to whether the charges were already on the books as criminal offenses. The charges could thus include crimes against Germany's Jews, Simon explained, since Hitler would not be able to argue in his defense "that international law does not forbid a ruler to maltreat his own subjects." Rosenman sent Simon's plan on to Washington for assessment.[103]

In short, by the end of the war in Europe, the British government, American leaders, and the Soviets were all still imagining different models for postwar justice. Nonetheless, something had changed. Soviet ideas about the criminal responsibility of the Hitlerites had filtered through. The latest British proposal—Simon's plan—shared a key element with the Soviet idea of a special international tribunal: both would use the courtroom to demonstrate Nazi guilt without getting bogged down by legal debate. In other ways, however, the British and the Soviets remained far apart. The British envisioned a closed hearing, followed by punishment by executive decree; the Soviets, by contrast, wanted a public spectacle, and had the Moscow Trials and the more recent Kharkov Trial in mind as models. Stimson and his colleagues, for their part, shared the Soviet preference for a public trial of Nazi leaders—but wanted to use such a forum to showcase American leadership and the rule of law.

With Roosevelt's death on April 12, it fell to President Harry S. Truman to determine the American approach to postwar justice. Truman didn't think much of the British proposal for a closed hearing, which seemed undemocratic. He approved the Stimson-Stettinius-Biddle plan for a public international tribunal of the German leaders and their organizations.[104] On April 13, at Truman's request, James F. Byrnes, a close advisor of FDR who had been at Yalta, reached out to Soviet ambassador Nikolai Novikov to sell Moscow on the specifics of the American approach. Byrnes reminded Novikov that the Moscow Declaration had not fixed a policy for punishing the major war criminals or the members of the main Nazi organizations like the SS and the Gestapo. Now, in light of the rapid advance of the Allied armies on Germany, the time had come to do so. The Allied governments could probably agree to execute the "most notorious" Nazi war criminals without a trial, Byrnes noted. But the U.S. government believed that it would be preferable to come up with "a suitable judicial process."[105]

Byrnes highlighted the key similarities between the American approach and the Soviet idea of a special international tribunal. He cited a "distinguished Soviet author" who had recently argued that Nazi crimes were part of a premeditated plan of "aggressive actions" aimed at initiating "a reign of terror" in Germany and throughout all of Europe. This author had further argued that the Nazi leaders and everyone in the main Nazi organizations shared criminal responsibility for this program. Byrnes identified this author as Aron Trainin. Having established common ground, Byrnes presented for Soviet consideration a brief outline of principles for trying Nazi leaders and their organizations before an inter-Allied military court. Such a court would not interfere with the punishment of rank-and-file "Hitlerites" at the scenes of their crimes, Byrnes assured Novikov (using Soviet terminology). But it would, he said, "ensure the punishment" of Nazi leaders and the members of the principal Nazi organizations. Byrnes suggested that representatives of the United States, the Soviet Union, Great Britain, and France meet to discuss this proposal.[106]

By early April 1945, the Soviet Union and the United States, in spite of their vastly different political systems, experiences of the war, and ideas about the law, had come to share basic concepts for the trial of the major Nazi war criminals by an international tribunal. They would soon diverge over the details of this tribunal, over the question of reparations, and over plans for the future of Germany and postwar Europe. They would soon want to forget the fact that they had ever been Allies at all. But for now, with the war against the European Axis powers almost but not quite won, the wartime alliance remained strong. On April 16, the Red Army began a major offensive against Berlin. As Soviet soldiers descended on the city, and as British and American forces approached from the west, the need for all of the major Allied powers to agree on a plan to deal with captured Nazi leaders became more pressing than ever.

CHAPTER 2 | But What Is Justice?

A S THE RED Army closed in on Berlin on April 24, 1945, Foreign Minister Vyacheslav Molotov was in San Francisco. Hundreds of delegates from all over the world had flocked to the American city to finalize plans for the United Nations, a new organization dedicated to preventing future wars. Lavish welcoming receptions offered the delegates free food, free movies, and even free blimp rides. The word coming out of Europe was that the Nazis were near defeat. The world seemed poised for resurrection and change.[1]

Before arriving in San Francisco, where he was put up in the St. Francis Hotel and chased down for autographs as if he were a movie star, Molotov had stopped in Washington to call on the new president, Harry S. Truman. Molotov, who was used to dealing with FDR, had been expecting a congenial visit. Instead, Truman had berated him for Stalin's failure to allow free elections in Poland.[2] Truman's scolding tone had put him on the defensive and had given him second thoughts about American intentions. Now, taking in the dazzling sights of the City by the Bay and adjusting to the rhythms of a country seemingly unscathed by war, Molotov was still quietly stewing. He pointedly reminded Secretary of State Edward Stettinius Jr. in a private meeting that evening that the USSR was "in the first rank of the powers and would not be pushed back into the second rank."[3] If U.S. leaders did not treat the Soviet Union as an equal partner, Molotov warned, they would come to regret it.

On May 2, the Red Army took the Reich Chancellery, the last holdout of the Nazi leadership. The defenders of Berlin surrendered. Soviet soldiers

FIGURE 2.1 Vyacheslav Molotov (center) in San Francisco, spring of 1945.
Credit: Russian State Documentary Film and Photo Archive A-6831.

scoured the streets for SS men and German generals—making the question of how to deal with war criminals not just urgent but immediate.[4] Truman seized the moment. That very afternoon, without consulting the Soviets or the British, he announced to the press the establishment of an international military tribunal. Supreme Court Justice Robert H. Jackson would represent the U.S. government in the preparation and prosecution of the case against the former Nazi leaders.[5]

Truman's public announcement, coming hard on the heels of the Soviet victory in Berlin and while all the Allied foreign ministers were still on

American soil, put plans for what would become the Nuremberg Trials into motion. The speed with which Truman acted allowed Washington to set the agenda, forcing the Soviets—who had initially taken the lead in calling for an international tribunal—into a subsidiary role. Molotov was determined that this would not remain the case.

The road from Truman's announcement on May 2 to the conclusion that August of a four-power agreement to try the major Nazi war criminals would expose just how far apart the Allied powers were about the very meaning of "justice" and how it should be served. While the United States, the Soviet Union, Great Britain, and France ultimately reached a mutual accord to convene an international tribunal, the distance would remain—reflecting gaps in understanding that greatly affected the trials themselves.

Molotov remained guarded as discussions with the Americans and the British about the proposed international tribunal got off to a brisk start on May 3, the day after Truman's announcement. The U.S. judge Samuel Rosenman presented Molotov, Stettinius, and the British foreign secretary, Anthony Eden, with the U.S. plan—which Stettinius had coauthored with Henry Stimson and Francis Biddle before Roosevelt's death. Just three weeks earlier, James Byrnes had provided Soviet ambassador Nikolai Novikov with an outline of this plan and had suggested that U.S., Soviet, British, and French representatives meet to discuss its details. The Soviets had not yet responded when Truman pushed the issue forward.

Rosenman had of course been involved in the earlier discussions about postwar justice and was well aware that Molotov had been calling for a public trial of Nazi leaders, with reparations as a primary goal. Now, Rosenman walked the foreign ministers through the essentials of the U.S. plan, explaining that it proposed trying Nazi leaders and their organizations (such as the Gestapo and the SS) for "engaging in a criminal conspiracy." Once the organizations were convicted, their members "would ipso facto be guilty" of war crimes. The United States was not necessarily looking for death sentences, he added. However, it did intend to sentence the guilty to hard labor—"to rehabilitate the countries which the Germans had despoiled." This last bit, as Rosenman surely knew, was music to Molotov's ears, signaling American acceptance of the Soviet demand for labor reparations. Rosenman suggested that the United States, Great Britain, the USSR, and France each appoint one representative to serve on the tribunal and another to serve on the Committee of Inquiry, which would prepare and prosecute the cases.[6]

Molotov's and Eden's reactions were candid and quick. Eden explained that British opposition to convening an international tribunal had softened after Hitler's suicide on April 30. The British War Cabinet still had reservations about trying the "most notorious Nazis"—but if the Soviets and the Americans were intent on doing so, his government would likely go along. Molotov declared that the U.S. plan concerned "a matter of great importance" but scoffed at the suggestion that any meaningful agreement could be reached before the foreign ministers left San Francisco. Eden, Molotov, and Stettinius agreed to bring the French foreign minister, Georges Bidault, into the discussion; he was furnished with a copy of the draft agreement the next day.[7]

At Molotov's direction, two Soviet experts from the Ministry of Foreign Affairs who had accompanied him to San Francisco—the lawyer Sergei Golunsky and the diplomat Amazasp Arutunian—studied all twenty-six articles of the U.S. plan. The main charges, they reported to Molotov, were enumerated in Article 6, and included violating the rules and customs of warfare, invading another country, launching a war of aggression, and using war as an instrument of foreign policy. Article 8, they explained, established that organizations could be charged with criminal acts or with complicity in criminal acts, and that a finding of guilt would set in motion subsequent trials of that organization's members.[8] Golunsky also discussed these charges with British and French international lawyers, who raised concerns about ex post facto, or retroactive, law. William Malkin, the legal advisor to the British Foreign Office, hoped that the court would declare that the illegality of aggressive war had been "existing doctrine" when the Nazis began their march across Europe, lest charges of unfairness turn the defendants into martyrs.[9]

By May 6, the French, British, Soviet, and American representatives in San Francisco had expressed their general support for the idea of an international military tribunal—but beyond that, the discussion stalled. Eden needed to report to the British government and Molotov needed to confer with Stalin before signing off on any plan.[10] Stalin at this point was focused on the details of the German capitulation. On May 7, General Alfred Jodl signed an unconditional surrender of German forces at Allied headquarters in Reims, France. Early in the morning on May 9, at Soviet insistence, Field Marshal Wilhelm Keitel signed a second document of surrender before Marshal Georgy Zhukov at Soviet headquarters in Berlin.[11] On the afternoon of May 10, Molotov left the startling beauty of San Francisco behind him and boarded a plane to Moscow with the U.S. plan in hand.[12]

In Washington, Jackson had spent the last days of April getting up to speed on the U.S. plan, which he found to be both "too impassioned" and "too detailed." He cautioned Rosenman and Truman against giving the impression of "setting up a court organized to convict." He also urged greater flexibility in the document to deal with the novelty of the task at hand, warning that "it is surprising how much litigation can be hung on a single word of limitation."[13]

Jackson, age fifty-three, was largely self-taught as a lawyer. A former trial lawyer and longtime political ally of FDR, he had briefly served as attorney general before being appointed in 1941 to the Supreme Court. As one of only a few Democrats in a strongly Republican upstate New York, he had become known for his fierce independence. His intelligent eyes often showed a glint of mischief. During his time on the Court, he had authored a number of influential dissents—including one in which he had denounced the U.S. government's internment of Japanese Americans.[14] Jackson was a man of action who did not like to waste time. He was already gathering evidence about Nazi war crimes from the Office of Strategic Services (OSS), a wartime intelligence agency of the U.S. government, and from the War Crimes Section of the Judge Advocate General's Department (JAG) of the U.S. Army—evidence that, he noted in his diary, "confirmed all the gruesome things" the press had reported about atrocities and then some.[15]

While Jackson was deeply disturbed by the news coming out of Europe, he was also uneasy about what he was hearing of the United States' plans for postwar Germany. On Friday, May 4, the War Department lawyer Murray Bernays told him about a secret document from the Allied Reparations Commission that matter-of-factly referred to an agreement made at Yalta about extracting labor reparations from Germany. No one seemed to know whether there was a signed agreement or whether terms for labor reparations had been set. Either way, Jackson considered the news "a bombshell"— contrary to everything the United States had fought for in the war. Did the U.S. government really intend to sanction the use of forced labor? Bernays confided to Jackson that the War Department was similarly taken aback by the document, which was said to have originated with Treasury Secretary Morgenthau. Jackson speculated in his diary that evening that the whole business was a Russian demand, since the Soviet Union was the only Allied country that could use "slave labor in large numbers."[16]

That evening, Jackson spoke by phone with Rosenman, who had been with FDR at Yalta and who assured him that everything had been left "very vague" regarding reparations.[17] (This was of course at odds with the impression he had given Molotov a day earlier.) But another secret document, which Bernays passed along to Jackson on May 6, reignited Jackson's concerns. Issued by the U.S. government's Informal Policy Committee on Germany (which coordinated planning among the State, War, and Treasury

FIGURE 2.2 Robert H. Jackson, 1945.

Credit: United States Holocaust Memorial Museum, courtesy of
John W. Mosenthal.

Departments for the U.S. zone of occupation), it specified that "reparations
in kind" would be extracted partly as German labor, which would be used for
postwar reconstruction. The document further noted that such labor would
be compelled "only from convicted war criminals" or from those who were
judged by an "appropriate process" to have belonged to the Gestapo (Secret
State Police), the SS (Protection Squadron), or the SA (Storm Battalion).[18]
Jackson thought this just raised more questions. What was an appropriate
process? Would the suspected members of these organizations stand trial or
face a closed hearing? If the Gestapo, SS, and SA were already assumed to be
guilty, why bother trying them at all?

Jackson was learning firsthand that FDR's death had left U.S. policymakers
in a quandary. No one seemed to be able to say what exactly FDR had promised Stalin at Yalta. On Saturday, May 12, Jackson attended a lunch with oil
magnate Edwin Pauley (the Truman-appointed U.S. representative on the
Allied Reparations Commission) and Averell Harriman, the U.S. ambassador

to the Soviet Union, both of whom had been at Yalta. Jackson questioned them about FDR's intentions. Harriman insisted that Roosevelt had agreed only to the phrase "use of German labor," which could be interpreted as paid labor. He also told Jackson that the Soviets were not alone in wanting German labor: the Soviets were seeking five million German workers, but France had requested two million, and England had said it would take "a small number for a short time." Jackson, outraged, declared that he would not proceed with "pretended trials."[19]

After the lunch, Jackson fired off a memorandum to Pauley objecting to the idea that Germans could be conscripted into labor brigades simply because they had been members of Nazi organizations. He cautioned that even a well-monitored program of labor reparations would "destroy the moral position of the United States." Stories about the mistreatment of forced laborers would "come drifting out of Russia" in a couple of years, he predicted, which would likely be "all too well-founded."[20] Jackson shared his objections with Truman on May 15 and received a sympathetic if noncommittal response. He then spoke with OSS chief William J. ("Wild Bill") Donovan, who agreed with him that the whole reparations plan would give the impression that trials were all about providing forced labor to the victors. Jackson, recognizing Donovan (a former New York political rival) as a valuable ally, brought him onto his staff as an advisor.[21]

He and Donovan also discussed the Soviet attitude toward postwar justice. They noted that Soviet newspapers, which never printed anything without Stalin's approval, had recently attacked the United States for not shooting Goering immediately after his surrender to the Seventh Army. Jackson speculated that the Soviets were getting cold feet about the "aggressive war" charge. He told Donovan that he had recently heard that there was "a good deal of evidence" indicating that Russia had been preparing extensively for war before 1941. He asked him to find out from Goering and other Nazi leaders in U.S. custody what they thought had prompted Germany to declare war on Russia.[22]

Jackson did not know that much of the impetus to prosecute Nazi leaders for waging "aggressive war" had initially come from the Soviets. Donovan began to educate Jackson on this topic by giving him a report that the OSS had just prepared: "Soviet Intentions to Punish War Criminals." This sixty-one-page document explained that the Soviets differentiated between more traditional war crimes and acts that disturbed the peaceful relations between states. It noted that the Soviets had proposed defining "aggressive war" as an international crime and had announced their intention to prosecute Germany's leaders, including members of the military High Command, for this act. The study described the work of the Extraordinary State Commission as well as the Kharkov Trial, noting that the USSR had been the first Allied power to publicly try war criminals. Much of the study was devoted to an explication of Aron Trainin's book *The Criminal Responsibility of the Hitlerites*. The study observed that Trainin's views warranted close attention, for his book bore Andrei Vyshinsky's name as editor. Trainin's division of war crimes into "ordinary crimes" and "war guilt" (for waging a war of aggression), as well as his critique of the defense of following orders, the study concluded, seemed to guide other Soviet pronouncements about these issues.[23]

After his initial briefing by Donovan, Jackson set out to learn more about the Soviet approach to justice. On May 17, he and the members of his staff, which now also included Bernays, Army intelligence officer John Harlan Amen, Washington attorney Sidney S. Alderman, and others, viewed the Soviet film on the Kharkov Trial. Jackson found it an eye-opening lesson in the Soviet method "of proving a case by the defendants themselves."[24] He also obtained a copy of Trainin's book. Jackson remained highly suspicious of the Soviets, as he would throughout the trials, but he absorbed Trainin's ideas; his own reports soon included some of Trainin's phraseology.

The issue of labor reparations, meanwhile, continued to fester. For Jackson it was a dealbreaker. On May 18, he attended a meeting at Morgenthau's office with Pauley. Morgenthau angrily declared that the Allied Reparations Commission had been sitting for four or five days and this was the first he had heard that either FDR or Truman had not been on board with the plan "to furnish reparations labor irrespective of conviction." He dismissed the idea of trials as foolish and impractical. Trying Nazi organizations would take far too much time, he argued, and could not possibly produce the large amount of labor that would be needed in Europe in the next few months for planting, harvesting, and coal mining. When Jackson protested that the American people would not abide a program of slave labor, Pauley agreed to consider some form of "voluntary recruitment," presumably for paid labor supplied by Germany in lieu of reparations payments.[25]

News of the Morgenthau meeting leaked to the press, and on May 23 the *Washington Post* columnist Drew Pearson ran with the story. A possible plan to use "German prison labor to rebuild Russia and France" had been thrown into question "by a secret opinion" made by Justice Jackson, who would be leading the U.S. prosecution of German war criminals, he reported. The issue was now "up in the air."[26] The same day, TASS (the main Soviet news agency) pointedly reminded the German people that they could only redeem themselves from Nazism by doing what it called "honest work" to repair the material damage they had wrought in other countries.[27] By now, the Soviets had already organized labor brigades in their zone of Germany and were sending them to Russia to repair buildings, factories, and railroads that had been destroyed during the war.[28]

Jackson and the Soviets were working at cross purposes—but the Soviets, who were unaware of the hullabaloo over reparations in Washington, did not yet realize this. For them, labor reparations were the epitome of justice. The Soviet Union had been devastated by the Nazi occupation. German troops had carried out systematic destruction that was not militarily necessary, Trainin had pointed out in numerous articles, and those who had participated in such campaigns "must repair what they have destroyed." Putting SS men to work in this way was common sense.[29] Jackson, by contrast, had come to embrace an international tribunal as a means to demonstrate American moral leadership—and saw all forced labor as deplorable.

Plans for an international tribunal moved forward even as the ground was being laid for future disagreements. On May 24, the U.S. government sent notes to the Soviet, British, and French governments, requesting that they each send a representative to Washington to complete the negotiations.[30] Jackson and Donovan had flown to Europe a couple of days earlier to meet privately with European leaders—including Bidault, who provided assurances that the French government was on board with the U.S. plan. Jackson and Donovan spent a few days in Paris and in Frankfurt being briefed by OSS officers about Nazi war crimes and the political situation in postwar Germany.[31] The OSS, Jackson quickly learned, was the one U.S. government agency that had been seriously investigating and compiling evidence of Nazi war crimes.[32]

Jackson and Donovan flew into London on May 28. The war had left its mark on the city. "Whole blocks gone—roofs blown off," Jackson wrote in his diary. As bad as this was, Jackson acknowledged that it was "mild—hardly noticeable in comparison with the total destruction visible upon the German cities." That afternoon, Jackson and Donovan met with British Attorney General Sir David Maxwell Fyfe, Foreign Office legal advisor Patrick Dean, and Treasury Solicitor Sir Thomas Barnes in the small ballroom at Claridge's, the city's oldest and most luxurious hotel.[33] A popular meeting place for diplomats, statesmen, and nobility, Claridge's had survived the war intact.

The talks went remarkably well given the British government's continuing skepticism about trying the Nazi leaders. The men amicably discussed several proposed revisions to the U.S. plan, only one of which Jackson considered significant. The British had consolidated the charges in Article 6 into two parts: violating the rules and customs of warfare as defined in the Hague and

Geneva Conventions, and pursuing a policy aimed at "dominating Europe by a war of aggression." This echoed Trainin's division of war crimes into two categories: "ordinary crimes" and the far more serious crime of waging aggressive war.[34]

Churchill announced the following day that Maxwell Fyfe would represent the British government in the prosecution of the case before the international tribunal; Barnes and Dean would serve as his assistants. That afternoon, Jackson and Donovan sat down with Maxwell Fyfe to discuss possible defendants. Maxwell Fyfe suggested Goering, Alfred Rosenberg, Joachim von Ribbentrop, and German Labor Front leader Robert Ley. Donovan added Rudolf Hess and the former German chancellor Franz von Papen. When the conversation turned to the framework for the tribunal, Jackson and Maxwell Fyfe discovered that they had been working under differing assumptions: Jackson was anticipating a single, highly public trial, whereas Maxwell Fyfe had foreseen multiple trials. He acceded to Jackson's vision. Jackson and Maxwell Fyfe agreed that it would be more convenient to hold further negotiations in London, instead of in Washington as initially planned. They both understood that the Soviets would bristle at having been left out of these initial talks—and decided that each would reach out to the Soviet Union separately. They also resolved that if the Soviets did not come to the next meeting they would proceed without them, agreeing that they could not "take the time to go to Moscow."[35]

Jackson was by this point highly ambivalent about collaborating with the Soviets at all. While traveling around Europe that week, he had heard all kinds of disturbing stories about Soviet behavior. The commander of the American forces in Frankfurt had complained that the Russians were "stripping the territory they occupy" and shooting intellectuals and anyone else who might rally opposition to them. U.S. brigadier general Edward C. Betts of the European Theater of Operations had told Jackson that the Soviets had set up concentration camps in Poland and were "filling them with Poles" who objected to the Soviet-sponsored Polish government.[36] The British seemed less troubled about the Soviets and did not understand Jackson's indignation about their demand for labor reparations. Prisoners of war were already laboring in Britain and France, Barnes told Jackson, and a labor reparations program "would not differ in principle."[37] Just a couple of days earlier, the British government had informed the U.S. Informal Policy Committee on Germany that it had no objections to labor reparations.[38]

On May 30, there was progress. The British Cabinet formally accepted the U.S. plan for an international tribunal as a starting point for negotiations. The same day, Jackson called on the Soviet ambassador in London, Fedor

Gusev, and expressed the hope that the Soviet government would quickly come on board.[39] Soon after, Jackson asked the State Department to send telegrams urging the French and the Soviet governments to appoint representatives to meet with him and Maxwell Fyfe "at the earliest date possible in London."[40] He had resolved with the British that the talks would start no later than June 25.

When Jackson updated Truman on June 7 about the status of the negotiations for an international tribunal, his exposure to ideas from Trainin was apparent, whether or not he openly acknowledged this or even was aware of it himself. He described the Nazis as a "band of brigands" who had seized the German government and embarked on a policy of religious, political, and racial persecution that was "preparatory to the launching of an international course of aggression." He then detailed the three main charges as now set out in Article 6: the committing of war crimes recognized by international conventions; the domestic persecution, maltreatment, or murder of racial or religious groups, which was not recognized in such conventions but violated "the laws of humanity"; and the preparation and launching of an aggressive war. Jackson insisted that the illegality of aggressive war was an established doctrine. He cited the distinction that the seventeenth-century jurist Hugo Grotius made between a war of defense and a war of aggression and argued that it was only during the nineteenth century that lawyers had accepted war-making as a part of foreign policy. According to Jackson, the "shock to civilization" of the First World War had reestablished the "principle of unjustifiable war," which was then codified in the Kellogg-Briand Pact of 1928. By the time Hitler came to power it had been "thoroughly established that launching an aggressive war or the institution of war by treachery was illegal," Jackson concluded. It was high time for "the forces of the law to be mobilized on the side of peace."[41] This last part was pure Trainin.

On the afternoon of June 7, the same day Jackson was briefing Truman, Molotov sent Stalin a report from the Ministry of Foreign Affairs evaluating the U.S. plan (unaware that it had just been accepted by the British). The report spoke favorably of the plan while strongly objecting to one of its main premises: the trial of Nazi organizations like the SS and the Gestapo. The Yalta Agreement, Molotov pointed out, had already empowered the Allied Control Commission (the temporary occupation government) to dissolve and ban these organizations, and inter-Allied or national tribunals could already try their individual members. Molotov's report also recommended a number of revisions aimed at bolstering Soviet influence and furthering Soviet interests. It argued that the international tribunal's meetings should be chaired by rotation and that the Committee of Inquiry should automatically accept evidence from national war crimes commissions such as the Soviets' own Extraordinary State Commission. Molotov also called for the insertion of a clause about extradition, obligating the signatories to hand indictable persons (such as Hess) over to the tribunal.[42]

Stalin approved Molotov's report, and on June 9 the Ministry of Foreign Affairs penned a memorandum accepting the U.S. plan as a basis for discussion—pending the acceptance of the revisions Molotov had specified (which were detailed in the document).[43] Soviet ambassador Novikov passed this memorandum on to Jackson in Washington on June 14. Novikov expressed shock and bewilderment on hearing from Jackson that talks were being moved to London. He told Jackson that Soviet leaders had delegated him to complete the negotiations in Washington.[44]

Jackson perused the Soviet memorandum and brushed off many of the proposed revisions as "matters of detail." A couple of issues seemed more substantive, but even these looked to him to be the result of misunderstandings. In particular, he noted several paragraphs questioning the proposed trial of Nazi organizations on the grounds that they had been dissolved at Yalta. Not fully understanding the Soviets' concerns, Jackson concluded—naïvely—that this objection could be answered with the assurance that these organizations no longer legally existed. He was, however, wary of the Soviet demand for the extradition of war criminals.[45] He knew that extradition was a controversial issue and that a number of countries were insisting on their sovereign right to grant asylum.[46] Other proposed revisions were just as substantive but did not draw his immediate attention. The Soviets had expanded Article 14 to prohibit the accused from using the trials to engage in propaganda. Perhaps most significantly, they had supplemented Article 21 to open the door to the automatic acceptance of evidence provided by national war crimes commissions like the Extraordinary State Commission—ensuring the admissibility of Soviet evidence now being prepared by Vyshinsky.[47]

Jackson told Novikov that the Americans had done more work on the plan since San Francisco, believing that as an important document for "future International Law . . . it could be better arranged and more accurately expressed." He promised to share the updated version.[48] On June 16 the State Department sent copies to the Soviet, British, and French embassies in London. That same day, Jackson told Truman about Novikov's apparent surprise over the change in venue and wondered what this meant. What if Moscow didn't send someone to London? They agreed that if the Soviets didn't show up for the start of the meeting on June 25, Jackson would announce a one-week postponement to allow them more time. If they didn't arrive by the end of that week, he would move forward without them.[49]

Jackson would have liked nothing more than to move forward without the Soviets, whom he was already regarding as the Achilles' heel of the entire plan for a four-power tribunal. He was learning more by the day, from the OSS and other sources, about Soviet actions during the war. At a June 11 meeting with American religious leaders, he had shared his anxiety about potential problems arising during the trial as a result of the Soviet Union's 1939 invasions of Poland and Finland.[50] The Soviet Union could not exactly be uninvited or excluded from participating in the prosecution of the former Nazi leaders. Molotov had been first to propose an international tribunal, and Trainin had provided key arguments about Nazi criminality and the illegality of aggressive war. But Jackson worried that the Soviets would undermine the tribunal's legitimacy just by participating, and he was beginning to ponder ways of minimizing their impact. It would be so much easier if they simply didn't show up.

The Soviets had no intention of not showing up. In June 1945, Soviet leaders were still gaining a full realization of what their country had endured during the war. The Soviet Union's losses were almost beyond belief. Some twenty-seven million Soviet citizens had perished: one out of every seven people. Two-thirds of the dead were civilians. (By comparison, American war casualties came to around 407,000 soldiers and included hardly any civilians.) The Nazi invasion and the Soviet defense, both employing a scorched-earth policy, had destroyed 1,700 towns, 70,000 villages, and 30,000 factories.[51] The world did not seem to grasp the sheer magnitude of Soviet losses. An international tribunal would provide the Soviets with a public forum for a reckoning. It would expose Nazi crimes and, Soviet leaders believed, would facilitate Moscow's claims for material compensation and German labor.

The stakes for the Soviet Union were thus extremely high. Stalin and Vyshinsky, who now grasped that the Americans and the British were planning a four-power conference in London, knew the right men to send: Iona Nikitchenko and Trainin.[52] Nikitchenko, the fifty-year-old deputy chairman of the Supreme Court of the USSR, would be the main Soviet representative; Trainin would serve as his assistant. Alike as they were in their unwavering devotion to the Soviet cause, these two men had very different backgrounds and represented different parts of the Soviet legal system. Trainin was a highly educated and well-traveled academic. Nikitchenko, of peasant origins, had never received a formal legal education. He had proven his loyalty as the head of a military tribunal in the Russian Civil War and was known abroad only as a judge in the infamous Moscow Trials—as a faithful executor of Stalin's will.[53] The appointment of Trainin was at least partly intended to reassure Western leaders and lawyers, who admired his book on Nazi war crimes.[54]

On June 23, Vyshinsky notified the British Foreign Office that Nikitchenko and Trainin would fly into London on June 25 and that negotiations could begin the next day.[55] They would be late, but they would be there, and the four powers were now in general agreement about how to proceed. It was the end of the beginning.

Jackson had flown back to London the previous week and was using the time to get to know his British and French colleagues. With the British there was ease. He and Maxwell Fyfe spent a "delightful evening" at Claridge's, where the Americans were staying, "exchanging stories like country lawyers," as Jackson wrote in his diary. Jackson was pleasantly surprised by Maxwell Fyfe's conviviality, noting that he went around the restaurant "with napkin in hand" to "find his favorite waiter to bring us wine." The British took Jackson and his assistants to see the dog races and to visit Hyde Park—and the men found time in between these outings to chat about the details of the case. Jackson also had a chance to dine with the French jurist Robert Falco, whom Charles de Gaulle's government had recently appointed as its representative for negotiations about the international tribunal. He was pleased to discover that Falco spoke "fairly good English."[56] Falco had been a judge on the Paris Court of Appeal before being fired in 1940 by the Vichy government because he was Jewish.[57]

Jackson also took advantage of the delay to investigate possible locations for the tribunal. On June 22, he told American occupation authorities in Germany that the proceedings would require secure facilities for some 150 prisoners and witnesses, as well as rooms for conducting the trial and for the press. He wanted to stay in U.S.-controlled territory and out of the Soviet zone, where everyone would be at Moscow's mercy for communications and supplies. He asked U.S. authorities whether Munich might work. If not, maybe Heidelberg or Nuremberg would do. Jackson soon heard back that Nuremberg, located in the American zone, was the most desirable choice from both a "historical and accommodations point of view." The Palace of Justice had a large courtroom that could hold some 200 people, plus an adjoining prison that could accommodate 150 prisoners. The Faber Castle on the outskirts of town—the family estate of the famed pencil manufacturing dynasty—could provide accommodations; so could the suburb of Fürth.[58]

Truman had given Jackson a great deal of autonomy to make arrangements for the international tribunal, far more than any other figure involved. Truman trusted Jackson implicitly and was convinced that his integrity, along with

Germany under Four-Power Occupation, 1945

- City
* Allied Control Council

100 Kilometers
100 Miles

NORTH
SEA

Berlin

French

British   Soviet

American

5 miles

Baltic Sea

NETHERLANDS

Hamburg
Bremen

SOVIET

POLAND

BRITISH

Hannover

Berlin
Potsdam

Essen

Leipzig
Dresden

Düsseldorf

Frankfurt
Mainz

CZECHOSLOVAKIA

FRENCH

Heidelberg
AMERICAN

Nuremberg

Stuttgart
Tübingen

Munich

FRANCE

AUSTRIA

SWITZERLAND

Europe Lambert Conformal Conic

MAP 2 Germany under Four-Power Occupation, 1945.

his reputation and experience, would lend credibility to the proceedings.[59] In very sharp contrast, Soviet leaders were aiming to keep Nikitchenko and Trainin on as short a leash as possible. Before they boarded the plane for London, Vyshinsky issued them strict directives. The Americans had revised their plan after San Francisco; Nikitchenko and Trainin were to review the new document from every possible angle and send Moscow their assessment.

They were also to insist on the inclusion of the Soviet revisions Novikov had given to Jackson on June 14 as well as the incorporation of new edits provided by the Ministry of Foreign Affairs. They were to push hard for the provision requiring the extradition of war criminals and to make sure that Extraordinary State Commission reports carried the same weight as other evidence. The representatives of the four powers would put together a list of defendants, discuss the rules for summoning witnesses, and define the role of the defense attorneys. Vyshinsky instructed Nikitchenko and Trainin to make no decisions without his explicit approval. If any of the delegations introduced new proposals, they were to send him a full report and await directions.[60] In short, while Jackson was calling his own shots, Nikitchenko and Trainin had marching orders.

Arriving in London on the evening of June 25, Nikitchenko and Trainin were already behind. They had their first look at the revised U.S. plan that night; the Soviet embassy in London had not forwarded it to Moscow.[61] The next morning they set out for Church House, a squat structure located next to Westminster Abbey that had housed the British Parliament after the Blitz. On their arrival, Trainin, Nikitchenko, and their interpreter, Oleg Troyanovsky, exchanged introductions with Jackson, Falco, Maxwell Fyfe, and their assistants—all of whom had already gotten to know one another. It was not a promising beginning. Jackson found Nikitchenko to be "an inscrutable person" with "eyes that look past you." He thought Trainin was a "more versatile man" but noted that he "scarcely seemed to be acting friendly."[62] Maxwell Fyfe took note of Nikitchenko's "strong face" and his "powerful and pugnacious jaw."[63] At least Troyanovsky, a recent Swarthmore graduate and the son of a former Soviet ambassador, impressed the Americans with his fluent English, which he spoke with an American accent.[64]

The representatives found their places at a large square table in a dimly lit conference room. The first day's meeting was slow going. The Soviets were out of their element. While Trainin had at least lived and studied in Europe, Nikitchenko had no real experience abroad. Neither had any experience with the work of international diplomacy. Nikitchenko politely praised the U.S. plan—and immediately began demanding specific changes. Jackson suggested in response that he circulate a memorandum outlining the Soviet position. Nikitchenko agreed but said that it would take a couple of days to put together.[65]

When Jackson walked the group through the revised U.S. plan during the afternoon session, Nikitchenko and Trainin peppered him with requests for clarification. What was the point of prosecuting the Nazi organizations

Figure 2.3 Iona Nikitchenko, Aron Trainin, and Oleg Troyanovsky (center, sitting left to right) during deliberations at the London Conference, 1945.

Credit: United States Holocaust Memorial Museum, courtesy of Harry S. Truman Library. Photographer: Charles Alexander.

when Stalin, Churchill, and Roosevelt had already declared them to be illegal at Yalta? Jackson replied that this was the best way to cast a wide net of guilt. What was the American understanding of an indictment? When Jackson explained that the indictment made an accusation but did not include the evidence, Nikitchenko and Trainin voiced surprise. In Soviet law, the indictment included all of the evidence supporting the charges and could run thousands of pages long.[66]

Jackson's explanation gave rise to a discussion of the key difference between the common law system of the British and the Americans and the civil law system of the French and the Soviets: the relationship between the prosecutor and the judge. The common law system was adversarial, whereas the civil law system was inquisitorial. In England and the United States, the prosecutor was expected to demonstrate first that there was a case against the accused and then to prove this case to the judge in open court. In France and the Soviet Union, the prosecution and the judges worked more closely together. An examining magistrate (*juge d'instruction*) conducted pretrial investigations and forwarded a dossier of evidence to the prosecutor, who filed it with the criminal trial court; the judges of this court then examined the accused on the basis of this evidence.[67] It was generally understood (but not openly acknowledged at this meeting) that political trials in Stalin's Soviet Union had certain "nuances" of their own. Evidence was frequently attained through coercion or wholly fabricated, and the defendants were primed to be compliant by the secret police.[68] What is clear from this first meeting of the main architects of the International Military Tribunal (IMT) is that none of them fully grasped how their familiarity with one legal system versus another had profoundly shaped their expectations for postwar justice.

On the night of June 28, Nikitchenko and Trainin sent along their memorandum of position.[69] When the group convened the next day, Nikitchenko boldly proclaimed that the major war criminals had "already been convicted" in the Moscow and Yalta declarations and the purpose of the tribunal was, therefore, to demonstrate to the world their guilt and then punish them. It would be ridiculous to think of the judge presiding over any such trial as a disinterested party without previous knowledge of the case, he continued, for this would create unnecessary delays. Sensing the discomfort in the room, Nikitchenko quickly added that the rules of a "fair trial must, of course, apply." Still, he insisted, once the evidence was gathered, reviewed by the prosecution, and presented to the judges, the trials themselves should not take more than several weeks.[70]

The others were appalled at this legal scenario. Maxwell Fyfe later posited that Nikitchenko had been envisioning the Committee of Inquiry as a committee of examining magistrates, who would begin with the assumption that the accused "had been already condemned by Churchill, Roosevelt, and Stalin."[71] Jackson heard Nikitchenko as calling for a kangaroo court.[72] Neither was entirely wrong. Jackson immediately countered Nikitchenko's understanding of the Moscow and Yalta declarations: they were accusations, not convictions. A conviction required "a judicial finding."[73]

Nikitchenko insisted during this same session that the trial of Nazi organizations—the Gestapo, SS, and so on—be removed from the plan. He could not envision a situation in which any of them were not found to be criminal. Jackson, growing more exasperated, explained that his government was aiming to use the case against the organizations to expose "the whole Nazi drive to dominate the world" and kick off the denazification of Germany.[74]

Jackson resolved to stand strong against Soviet objections to the U.S. plan.[75] The next morning, he delivered a redraft to the other delegations. He had accepted a suggestion from Trainin to divide the draft into two documents: an agreement establishing the tribunal and a statute outlining its rules and procedures. But the plan's substance remained unchanged. It called for a full trial of the Nazi leaders and their organizations based largely on the American model, in which the prosecutor presented all of the evidence and proved his case in open court. Jackson struck a conciliatory note in an accompanying memo, stating that he did not propose adopting American court procedure wholesale and was extremely interested in Russian, French, and British suggestions. He added that the Americans shared Trainin's view that "aggressive war" was a crime. Jackson then reminded the others that the American people had not witnessed Nazi atrocities firsthand. Evidence mattered. It was necessary to document Nazi crimes in a trial that the American people could trust.[76]

Reconvening at Church House on Monday, July 2, the group focused again on the question of trying Nazi organizations. Jackson explained that he wanted to make use of the idea of "conspiracy," by now familiar to everyone in the room, whereby the Nazi participants in a "common plan" were held liable for one another's crimes. Falco's assistant André Gros, a professor of international law in Paris, chimed in that both French and Soviet law recognized collective guilt. Nikitchenko concurred but added that under Soviet law perpetrators still had to be tried as individuals. He conceded that from the Soviet perspective a tribunal could try groups of individuals (such as a collection of individual SS members) and that many persons could stand trial at the same time. Through this approach, he noted, the court could establish the criminal responsibility of the organization.[77]

Jackson was keen to get this matter settled. The Americans sought to reach each organization through proof of what its individuals did, "just as you suggest," he agreed. Once the guilt of the organization was established, the tribunal could attribute the criminality embodied in it to its other members. Of course, each member of a guilty organization would have to be given the opportunity to prove that he had been forced to join or had been mistakenly identified as a member, Jackson added. But he could not question the organization's guilt. Jackson left the meeting believing that he and Nikitchenko had seen eye to eye.[78]

The location of the tribunal, unsurprisingly, also sparked debate. Nikitchenko and Trainin had strict orders from Moscow to insist on Berlin, which had been the site of the Nazi capitulation in the East and was now in the Soviet zone of Germany. Jackson argued for Nuremberg, on the grounds that it was most convenient and was "the birthplace," as he put it, of the Nazi movement. Both sides stood firm on the issue. When this discussion grew contentious on July 4, Nikitchenko suggested a way around the impasse. There could be several main trials, he offered: the international tribunal might try Karl Hermann Frank (the Nazi governor of the Czech protectorate) in Czechoslovakia, and other Nazi leaders in Poland, for example. Given Goering's responsibility for the Blitz, the British government might want his trial to be held in England. Nikitchenko's proposal came as a surprise. Barnes interjected that his government had come to believe that all the major war criminals should stand trial in Germany.[79] As the lunch hour approached, Jackson asked to be excused in order to observe America's "day of hostility with the British." For the first time in days, according to Jackson's diary, Nikitchenko cracked a smile.[80]

The long and fraught discussions about legal and organizational questions wore on all of the participants. Occasional after-hours gatherings helped the Soviets and the Western representatives unwind. On the evening of July 6, Jackson hosted the Soviets for a dinner at Claridge's. The Americans wore black tie; Nikitchenko, Trainin, and Troyanovsky showed up in gray suits, while Ambassador Gusev donned a dark suit jacket and striped trousers. After the meal, Jackson proposed a toast to Generalissimo Stalin, and Gusev proposed one to President Truman. The Americans made speeches, and Jackson praised Trainin's book. The Americans invited Nikitchenko to make a speech, and he did so, Jackson observed, "with evident pleasure," speaking a few sentences and then waiting for the translation. Jackson found the speech to be "dignified, friendly and when he spoke of the sufferings of Russia rather eloquent." Trainin also gave "a very commendable short address." Writing in his diary that evening, Jackson judged the dinner to have been "very successful from the point of view of cultivating better relations," even as he noted that the Soviets "drank very little and were somewhat scornful of the yellow liquid claimed to be vodka which was served."[81]

While the Allied representatives were trying to work out their differences in London, the heads of their governments were planning a face-to-face meeting in Germany. On July 3, James F. Byrnes, whom Truman had just appointed secretary of state, had informed Jackson by telegram that the matter of war criminals would likely be discussed at the Big Three Meeting in Potsdam (a suburb of Berlin) slated to start on July 17. This would be the first face-to-face meeting of British, American, and Soviet leaders since FDR's death. Writing back on July 4, Jackson—who knew Byrnes from a brief stint together on the Supreme Court—related that the negotiations in London were going slowly, largely because the Soviets and the Americans were finding it difficult to understand each other's legal systems. Although some problems had abated, there were "deep differences in legal philosophy and attitude," he wrote, and "even after words are agreed upon we find them understood to mean different things." Jackson explained that he was doing his best to adopt enough of the Soviet suggestions to achieve a four-power agreement while keeping the substance of the U.S. plan.[82]

In London, the deliberations were entering a new and critical phase. Beginning on July 5 and continuing through the next week, a drafting subcommittee, which included Alderman, Trainin, Falco, Barnes, and Dean, compared the U.S. plan against each side's proposed amendments and tried to work toward an agreement. Extradition turned out to be a thorny issue. Alderman and Barnes insisted that they did not have the authority to commit their governments to negotiate with other states for the turnover of war criminals, especially those who had been granted asylum or immunity from prosecution. Trainin suggested that this was a possible dealbreaker—and the discussion was shelved for the time being.[83]

The group did reach a consensus on some key questions. The presidency of the tribunal would rotate for subsequent trials, and a government could replace a judge for reasons of ill health. On most questions, the judges would take a majority vote, with the president's vote breaking any ties. Convictions and sentences, however, would require affirmative votes of three out of the four judges. The group agreed that the plea of superior orders could not exempt a defendant from responsibility, but left open the possibility of the judges considering it as a mitigating factor for sentencing. They also agreed that the document they had been calling a "statute" would henceforth be called a "charter."[84] The bigger issues still loomed—location, for example— but some of the smaller ones were falling into place.

Jackson and Donovan flew to Germany on the morning of July 7 to gather more evidence. Jackson was still getting a sense of the immensity of Nazi atrocities. They spent their first evening at an OSS headquarters in Wiesbaden, a working champagne factory whose product "was wonderful and good," as Jackson wrote in his diary. John Harlan Amen joined the group from Paris and brought a collection of documents, including the minutes of the November 5, 1937 meeting between Hitler and his generals in the Reich Chancellery at which Hitler had first revealed his plans for Germany's acquisition of Lebensraum ("living space") through war. (The meeting later became known as the Hossbach Conference.) Allen Dulles, the OSS station chief in Bern, came in from Switzerland, bringing with him four possible German witnesses, including a former employee of the German Foreign Office.[85]

The next morning Jackson and Donovan drove to Frankfurt to discuss the location of the trial with Lieutenant General Lucius D. Clay, the deputy military governor of the American zone of occupied Germany. Clay, who had just returned from Berlin, told them that the city would work as a site for the international tribunal. As it was under four-power occupation, the U.S. delegation would remain under American control. If Jackson had the ability to choose, though, Clay strongly recommended Nuremberg. In Frankfurt, Jackson and Donovan also called on the U.S. diplomat Robert D. Murphy, who told them grim stories about what was happening in Berlin. The Soviets had already deported thousands of men from their sector of Berlin to the Soviet Union as forced laborers. From Frankfurt, Jackson made a quick stop in Nuremberg and toured the courthouse and the prison. Satisfied with what he saw, he made plans to return with his British, French, and Soviet colleagues later in the month.[86]

Back in London, Jackson quickly understood that there was still a long way to go toward an agreement. Meeting with Nikitchenko, Trainin, Gros, and Maxwell Fyfe on July 13, he tried to get them to commit to a timeline for the trials. Maxwell Fyfe suggested that the indictment could be ready in a month and that the trial might begin some three weeks later. Nikitchenko and Gros balked at setting a date. The Soviets had no sense of "the state of the evidence," Nikitchenko protested (not unreasonably). He added that he didn't know whether he and Trainin would serve as the Soviet representatives on the Committee of Inquiry: that remained for Moscow to decide.[87]

The men turned next to some of the more tendentious aspects of the plan—including the trial of the Nazi organizations. The most recent redraft stated, somewhat matter-of-factly, that while trying each former Nazi leader the tribunal might declare that an organization to which he belonged was "criminal." Jackson warned that no American judge would accept this formula, which made no provision for the organization to defend itself. The tribunal would need to announce in advance that the Gestapo and the SS (for example) were being charged with criminality so that their former members could come forward in the organizations' defense. Nikitchenko was perplexed. What would happen if hundreds of SS men asked to defend the SS before the international tribunal? Jackson dismissed this as far-fetched. Maxwell Fyfe agreed that no one would knowingly "put his head into the noose."[88]

To Trainin and Nikitchenko, what Jackson was proposing seemed absurd. It was one thing to allow an individual to claim that he had joined the SS or the Gestapo under duress or that it had been a case of mistaken identity. It was something else entirely to allow unrepentant Gestapo or SS members to publicly defend these organizations. Besides, Trainin asserted, everyone knew what the Gestapo had done. Jackson disagreed and emphasized that they should not rely on American judges "to know all about the Gestapo." He reminded them that the American people had been far removed from the theater of war. He noted that the evidence he had seen since coming to Europe, which he had been getting from the OSS and other sources, had "utterly astonished" him, and as a highly placed public official he had been relatively in the know. Jackson again assured Nikitchenko and Trainin that what he wanted above all was a surefire way to proceed against as many Nazi war criminals as possible.[89]

The Soviets were apparently moved by Jackson's assurances. A couple of days later Nikitchenko and Trainin, along with the British and the French, tentatively accepted the American amendment: the tribunal would give notice about the indictment of the organizations, and members wishing to testify would be given a chance to be heard in a manner the judges deemed just.[90] The Soviets had accepted the explanation that this was a formality, aimed at American sensibilities, and that no former Gestapo or SS members would dare come forward and risk arrest.

Everyone tried over the next week to reach compromises on other issues. The Americans and the British agreed that the prosecution would attach the most important evidence to the indictment and turn it over to the tribunal before the case was heard. The French and the Soviets agreed, in turn, that this evidence would be produced in open court—and that the prosecution could introduce additional evidence at that time. Jackson and Nikitchenko continued to disagree, however, about how to prevent the defendants from using the court to launch countercharges against the Allied powers. Nikitchenko insisted that this would be best handled by explicitly banning Nazi propaganda. Jackson urged a more subtle approach. He predicted that the defense would attempt to use the court to accuse the Allied governments of taking actions that had compelled them "to make war defensively." This could be avoided, he argued, by including a definition of "aggressive war" in Article 6. Jackson was acting on the advice of the War Crimes Section of JAG, which had warned him that the defense would try to litigate the causes of the war.[91] Maxwell Fyfe supported Jackson's suggestion. Nikitchenko and Gros viewed the inclusion of a definition as unnecessary.

Tensions over whether or not to define "aggressive war" exposed fissures. Nikitchenko and Gros argued at a July 19 meeting that German actions had already been described as "aggressive" in Allied documents and that the tribunal thus did not need to further address this issue. Jackson retorted that the prosecution needed to define the term now in order to avoid any controversy over its meaning during the trials. Nikitchenko dismissed Jackson's concerns—confident that the prosecutors could parry any defense arguments and that the judges could be counted on to keep the trials on track. Besides, he reiterated, the criminality of the Nazi leaders was already established;

the tribunal was being convened to determine each defendant's "measure of guilt."[92] He was still working off of the model of a Soviet show trial.

Maxwell Fyfe, like Jackson, was anticipating a robust defense from the former Nazi leaders, who were already on record justifying their actions during the war. He reminded the others of Ribbentrop's claims that there had been "no policy of aggression." He further related the British intelligence service's prediction that the defendants would claim that they had attacked Norway in order to avert a British act of aggression. "I think we are rather opening the door for trouble," he warned, if "aggression" is not defined. Jackson agreed, postulating that the defendants would accuse Britain, France, and the Soviet Union of pursuing foreign policies that had "forced them to war." Documents seized by Allied forces from the German Foreign Office showed that this had long been their position, he noted, and it was not clear how the judges—who would be selected by the four powers, one for each country of the prosecution—would respond to this line of argument. Gros summed up the choice at hand: either define "aggression" in Article 6 or leave things to the judges. He favored the latter option, arguing that for the sake of world opinion it was important not to give the impression of preemptively "shutting out a defense."[93]

This core matter was still simmering when the Soviets hosted their Western colleagues for lunch at the Savoy Hotel on Friday, July 20. Nikitchenko was supposed to fly to Nuremberg the following day with Jackson, Falco, Maxwell Fyfe, and their assistants in order to assess Jackson's selection of the site for the tribunal. At the lunch, however, Nikitchenko announced (with "visible embarrassment" according to the Americans) that he and Trainin would be unable to make the trip. Jackson offered to reschedule— but Nikitchenko said that he and Trainin would still be unable to go. The Americans assumed that Nikitchenko was acting on Moscow's orders. They were right.[94] Soviet leaders understood that the visit more or less committed everyone to Nuremberg if conditions there were found to be acceptable.

Jackson and the others went to Nuremberg on July 21, without the Soviets. The state of the city made a strong impression on Maxwell Fyfe, who was making his first postwar visit to Germany. "The old walled town was a heap of ruins," he later wrote, recalling how piles of rubble were littered with decomposing corpses.[95] The group agreed that for practical and symbolic reasons Nuremberg's courthouse "was the place for the trial," as Jackson noted.[96] The same day, the Soviet Military Administration in Germany sent Moscow a secret report about the further deterioration of conditions in Berlin, noting an increase in crimes against locals perpetrated by men in "Red Army uniform."[97] The report was intentionally vague. In fact, Red

FIGURE 2.4 Robert Jackson (fourth from right), David Maxwell Fyfe (third from right), and others on their way to inspect Nuremberg as a possible site for the International Military Tribunal, July 1945.

Credit: Office of the U.S. Chief of Counsel, Charles Alexander, courtesy of Harry S. Truman Library & Museum.

Army soldiers, who had rampaged through the city after its surrender, were continuing to rape and plunder even as Soviet occupation authorities half-heartedly attempted to introduce law and order.[98] While the Soviets continued to argue that the tribunal should convene in Berlin, the prospect of actually playing host looked increasingly daunting.

Reconvening in London, the representatives continued to wrangle over the language of Article 6. Nikitchenko shared a Soviet redraft on July 23 that called out the criminality of violating the rules and customs of warfare, of committing atrocities against civilians—and of planning or waging "aggressive war" specifically on behalf of the European Axis powers. Nikitchenko reiterated his opposition to defining "aggression," noting that it had not even been defined in the Charter of the new United Nations. "Apparently, when people speak about 'aggression,' they know what that means," Nikitchenko noted, "but when they come to define it, they come up against difficulties which it has not been possible to overcome up to the present time."[99]

FIGURE 2.5 Nuremberg in ruins, July 1945.

Credit: Office of the U.S. Chief of Counsel, Charles Alexander, courtesy of Harry S. Truman Library & Museum. Photograph donated by Robert Jackson.

Jackson wouldn't accept the presumption that a war of conquest was only criminal when waged by certain states. This ran counter to his deeply held ideas about justice. A crime was a crime regardless of who committed it, he argued. Trainin tried to convince Jackson that his concerns were misplaced. While a permanent international court might be created in the future, this tribunal was being established specifically to try former Nazi leaders. Jackson came back the following day with a counter-suggestion. The preamble to Article 6 could state that the tribunal would have jurisdiction only over those who had carried out criminal acts on behalf of the European Axis powers. This would introduce the kind of qualification the Soviets sought without writing it into a definition.[100] Nikitchenko was noncommittal.

Jackson also objected to a French redraft of the charge of "crimes against civilians" (also part of Article 6), though for less high-minded reasons. It was a long-standing tenet of U.S. foreign policy to stay out of the internal affairs of other countries, he explained—noting "regrettable circumstances at times in our own country in which minorities are unfairly treated." Germany's oppression of minorities and extermination of the Jews had risen to "international concern" and had become subject to international law, he explained, only because these actions had been an integral part of its plan to wage aggressive war. He wanted the charter to make this connection explicit. Gros took issue with Jackson's call for restrictive language, pointing out that there had been many humanitarian interventions in the last century to defend national minorities from persecution. It would be a travesty, he argued, to suggest that such interventions were only justified when a government waged "aggressive war." Here, Nikitchenko and Maxwell Fyfe threw their support behind Jackson.[101]

Jackson submitted a redraft of Article 6 on July 25—this one characterizing atrocities or "crimes against civilians" as violations of international law when carried out in connection with "aggressive war." Gros protested that he and the others had not been charged with codifying international law. He then made a larger point, one that went to the very heart of the matter. The Americans seemed intent on winning the trial on the grounds that the war "was illegal," while the Europeans wanted to expose the horrors of the Nazi occupation. Jackson insisted that it was possible to do both—but for the trial to have a lasting impact, the countries of the prosecution must insist on the criminality of "aggressive war." The Soviets had been arguing this same point from early on, of course—but now they had their worries. Would Jackson's redraft of the preamble really protect the Allied powers from scrutiny?[102]

Nikitchenko suggested adjourning for a few days so that everyone could review the proposals at hand.[103] The others understood that this would allow him to consult with the Soviet leadership. The lines of communication were shorter than usual: Stalin, Molotov, and Vyshinsky were all in Potsdam.

In a long telegram to Vyshinsky that same afternoon, Nikitchenko reported that the negotiations in London were moving along. Two points of significant contention remained: the place of the tribunal and the crimes under its jurisdiction. The first was straightforward. The British and the Americans wanted Nuremberg, while he and Trainin were following Moscow's directives and continuing to argue for Berlin. The second was more complicated. He and Trainin objected to the wording of Article 6, which they believed might make it possible to characterize "defensive acts" by the Soviet Union and the other Allied nations as "international crimes."[104]

Vyshinsky passed this on to Molotov, who in turn gave a full report to Stalin. There was general agreement, Molotov reported, that the international tribunal should investigate the cases of the major German war criminals in violating the rules and customs of warfare, committing atrocities, and waging aggressive war. The plan had undergone numerous revisions, and many of the Soviet edits had been accepted. Molotov then related the news about the continuing disagreements over the location of the tribunal and the wording of the "aggressive war" charge. The Ministry of Foreign Affairs considered it imperative that Article 6 be reworded to make clear "that we are talking about fascist aggression," he emphasized, adding that Nikitchenko and Trainin had thus far been unable to win over the Western representatives to this point of view.[105]

While Nikitchenko's report made the rounds of Soviet leaders, Jackson flew to Germany for a private meeting with Byrnes. The two men talked frankly with each other. Jackson despaired over his negotiations with the Soviets. Byrnes shared his view that it would be "a very good thing" to reach an agreement, but not at the cost of a fair trial. He was in complete agreement with Jackson that any definition of war crimes "could not be limited" to the European Axis powers. That was not how international law was supposed to work. Byrnes related that he was having a similarly exasperating time in his discussions with Soviet ambassador Ivan Maisky about reparations. Maisky wanted the United States to deliver all reparations from the countries it was occupying directly to the Soviet Union rather than to the smaller countries of Eastern Europe. Meanwhile, the Soviets had grabbed "everything moveable" from their zone of Germany, including telephone switchboards, toilets, and horses. Byrnes related his opinion that it would be "foolish" to stand with the Soviets "in trying anybody for looting" given what they were doing in Germany.[106]

Before returning to London, Jackson visited Berlin. He had been there in 1935 and wanted to see it again for himself. The city, he wrote in his diary, was "a mass of rubble and ruin under which thousands of bodies still lie buried and unidentified." There were laborers everywhere, "mostly women, and none of them young men." Jackson toured destroyed palaces and opera houses and explored the Reich Chancellery. He discovered that Hitler's desk was overturned in his room and that letters addressed to Goering were strewn about. "If the Russians had done no better job than this in collecting evidence we will not get much from that source."[107]

The Potsdam Conference briefly recessed on July 25, when Churchill flew to London to await the results of the British general election. When the conference resumed on July 28, the new British prime minister, Clement Attlee, and his foreign secretary, Ernest Bevin, replaced Churchill (who had been voted out of office) and Eden. Before the break, the foreign ministers had been edging toward an agreement on how to deal with Nazi war criminals. Molotov, Byrnes, and Bevin—all having been briefed on the status of the London negotiations—were eager to bring this question to a successful conclusion. On July 30, Molotov suggested that the international tribunal should begin with the cases against major war criminals, such as Goering, Ribbentrop, Hess, Rosenberg, Keitel, and Krupp. He also declared, in a marked shift of position, that the Soviet Union was amenable "to any choice of venue." Molotov did insist, however, that the governments take a clear stand on extradition by pledging to use all means available to transfer war criminals, including those being harbored in neutral countries, to the court.[108]

By now, the Potsdam Conference had brought a partial resolution to the reparations question—removing a major obstacle in the way of the IMT. The Allied leaders had given up on trying to establish a unified approach, agreeing instead that each of the four powers occupying Germany would extract reparations in its own way from its own occupation zone—which the Soviets were already doing. Stalin also secured a promise of German machinery and other capital equipment from the British and American zones in exchange for deliveries of food, coal, and other raw materials from the Soviet zone. The so-called Potsdam Agreement did not explicitly mention labor reparations, thus removing one of Jackson's worries. But Soviet leaders interpreted it as sanctioning their approach.[109]

The Soviets now no longer needed an international tribunal to press their case for reparations from Germany. But Stalin still saw great value in Soviet participation. The tribunal would give the Soviets the opportunity to take their place among the postwar powers and to make clear what they had sacrificed to win the war. When the Potsdam Conference ended on August 2, Stalin, along with Truman and Attlee, reaffirmed his intention to bring the major war criminals "to swift and sure justice" and expressed the hope that the London negotiations would result in an agreement toward this end. At Stalin's insistence, the leaders pledged that the list of principal Nazi defendants would be published before September 1.[110]

At Potsdam Stalin had given a clear signal of support for the IMT—and when the negotiations in London resumed, Nikitchenko and Trainin were much more cooperative. Attlee's Labor government designated Lord Chancellor William Jowitt to complete the negotiations on behalf of the British, replacing Maxwell Fyfe (a Churchill appointee). Jowitt skillfully mediated between Nikitchenko and Jackson, and the group reached consensus on the main outstanding issues, including the wording of Article 6. The Americans and the British were delighted by this turn of events, gloating that the Soviets had "swallowed our program 'hook, line, and sinker,'" as Jackson noted in his diary.[111]

The truth was more complicated, for the Soviets had also gotten much of what they wanted. Nikitchenko had agreed that the "first trials" of the international tribunal would be held in Nuremberg, but Berlin would serve as the tribunal's permanent seat. The Soviets would have the prestige of hosting the tribunal without the burden of providing logistical support for the trials. Nikitchenko had stopped insisting on a revision that would have deemed "aggressive war" to be criminal only when waged by the European Axis powers—but only because Moscow had agreed that explicitly limiting the IMT's jurisdiction to trying European Axis war criminals was an acceptable approach.[112] This, Soviet leaders believed, should prevent the trials from becoming a free-for-all. As an act of goodwill toward the Soviets (at Jowitt's suggestion), the phrase "the crime of war," which Jackson had put forward as a substitute for "aggression," was replaced in Article 6 with Trainin's term "crimes against peace."[113] Regarding extradition, the other thorny issue of the past two months, the signatories had agreed to take the needed steps to make major war criminals within their borders available to the IMT, and to make an effort to extradite those major war criminals who had taken shelter in other countries.[114]

In the end, all four delegations had made compromises. Jackson had dropped his insistence on defining "aggression" and had at least temporarily put aside his aspiration to use the Nuremberg Charter to shape international law. Gros had settled for a somewhat watered-down charge of "crimes against civilians." It was relabeled "crimes against humanity" on Jackson's suggestion (using the term that the American lawyer Herbert Pell had introduced into the discussions of the UNWCC and that the influential Polish-British lawyer Hersch Lauterpacht favored) but was limited to crimes committed "in execution of or in connection with" another crime "within the jurisdiction of the Tribunal." This meant, in practice, that it was restricted specifically to crimes committed on behalf of the aggressor state in connection with the planning or waging of an aggressive war.[115] Finally, the British had abandoned their vision of justice by executive decree.[116]

The London Conference came to a close on August 8 at Church House. At 11 a.m., before a small crowd of journalists and photographers, the representatives signed the London Agreement and the Nuremberg Charter in a public ceremony. It was announced at the gathering that Nikitchenko would serve as the Soviet chief prosecutor and Gros would serve as deputy to whomever the French appointed.[117] This would turn out to be François de Menthon, the former minister of justice and current attorney general of the new French government, who had just overseen the trials of key members of the Vichy regime. Jackson's appointment as U.S. chief prosecutor had long been public knowledge. The British representatives were still unknown, but it was soon revealed that Sir Hartley Shawcross would serve as chief prosecutor and Maxwell Fyfe would assist him.

On August 13, Vyshinsky informed Molotov that the Committee of Chief Prosecutors (formerly the Committee of Inquiry) would begin its work on the indictment in a week in London and asked him to select four assistant prosecutors, two typists, a stenographer, and two translators with English and German to assist Nikitchenko.[118] Soviet leaders also began to seriously consider their contribution to the list of defendants to be tried at Nuremberg. The Soviets did not have anyone as high up as a Goering or a Ribbentrop in their prisons; most of the senior Nazis had surrendered to the Americans. Vyshinsky and Molotov discussed the major German war criminals who were in Soviet custody and agreed on a list of five names: Field Marshal Ferdinand Schörner; Vice Admiral Hans-Erich Voss; General Lieutenant Reiner Stahel; the former German ambassador to Bulgaria, Adolf Beckerle; and Deputy Minister of Propaganda Hans Fritzsche (who had been with Hitler in the bunker during his last days). Vyshinsky forwarded this list to NKVD chief Lavrenty Beria on August 20. Beria did not respond for more than a week. Turning prisoners over to the IMT would mean a loss of NKVD control.[119]

In London, the Committee of Chief Prosecutors began finalizing the list of defendants. At their August 23 meeting, the prosecutors agreed that the list should be released to the press on August 28 so that it could be published by September 1 (the deadline Stalin had insisted on at Potsdam).[120] Nikitchenko still had not heard from Moscow. On August 27 Beria finally informed Molotov that the five Nazi prisoners could be given to the international tribunal. He also provided a list of an additional nine military leaders who were in Soviet custody and who in the NKVD's opinion could be included among the defendants; among them were General Lieutenant Willi Moser, Grand Admiral Erich Raeder, and SS Obergruppenführer Friedrich Jeckeln (who had overseen the mass killing of Jews in Ukraine and other

FIGURE 2.6 The signing of the London Agreement and the Nuremberg Charter on August 8, 1945. Seated at the table from left to right: Aron Trainin, Iona Nikitchenko, William Jowitt, Robert Jackson, and Robert Falco.

Credit: United States Holocaust Memorial Museum, courtesy of Joseph Eaton.

parts of the Soviet Union). Then Beria set out a condition for the inclusion of any Soviet prisoners as defendants: NKVD oversight. If Soviet leaders were going to send these men to be tried outside Soviet borders, the state security apparatus must be directly involved. Beria suggested the creation of a special commission under Vyshinsky, with representatives from the NKVD, the Ministry of Defense, SMERSH, the Office of the Military Procurator, and other security agencies—bringing to bear the full weight of the Soviet security apparatus.[121]

Stalin approved Beria's proposal for an oversight commission and sent word to Nikitchenko to secure the inclusion of the additional Nazi leaders on the list of defendants.[122] Nikitchenko received his instructions from Moscow after the Committee of Chief Prosecutors had finalized its list. Given the timing, he did well: Raeder and Fritzsche were added to the list, which was published on August 30. The Western prosecutors assured Nikitchenko that additional defendants in Soviet custody would be brought before the international tribunal in a second trial, whose details would be worked out at a later date.[123]

In all, the twenty-four defendants were a diverse cast of characters. They included some of the most notorious Nazi leaders, such as Goering, Hess, Ribbentrop, and Keitel, as well as key representatives of major industries and institutions that had supported the Nazi Party, such as Gustav Krupp (whose family ran the Krupp AG Heavy Industry Conglomerate) and the former Reichsbank president Hjalmar Schacht. The *Times* of London noted approvingly that this "first list, bringing in men from the economic and financial arms of the German war machine, and bringing leading officers of the General Staff, proves how widely and thoroughly the net has been cast." It also predicted that the trials would not take long.[124]

Soviet preparations now moved forward quickly. On the evening of August 31 Nikitchenko left Nuremberg—flying first to Berlin and then to Moscow. He gave Vyshinsky a full report about the negotiations at Church House and reported on the expected timeline.[125] On September 3, Molotov, having been briefed by Vyshinsky, informed Stalin that the four countries of the prosecution should finish preparing the indictment by mid-September and that the trials would begin at the end of October. Stalin, meanwhile, was quietly making key decisions about the IMT and would soon surprise everyone with the announcement that Roman Rudenko (the procurator of the Ukrainian SSR), and not Nikitchenko, would serve as the Soviet chief prosecutor.[126]

Soviet newspapers featured positive reports on the outcome of the London negotiations. Trainin wrote an article for *Izvestiia* proclaiming that the will to strike "a swift and accurate blow" at the Nazi war criminals had brought the four delegations together to establish an international tribunal. Justice was at hand.[127] On the face of things he was right: Soviet, American, French, and British jurists had navigated daunting legal and political differences to come up with the London Agreement and the Nuremberg Charter. They had found common ground and a common language—although, as Jackson, who remained highly skeptical of the Soviets, observed, the different delegations sometimes understood the agreed-on words to mean entirely different things. These gaps, especially about the meaning of justice and what constituted a fair trial, would create tensions among the wartime allies in the weeks and months ahead. At the same time, significant gaps in experience—between those countries that had endured Nazi occupation and those that had not, between those countries that had collaborated with the Nazis and those that had not—would exacerbate those tensions and affect all aspects of the trials, starting with the writing of the IMT's foundational document: the Indictment.

CHAPTER 3 | Countdown to Indictment

O N SEPTEMBER 14, 1945, Roman Rudenko, the procurator general of the Ukrainian SSR, set out from Moscow for London. Nine days earlier, Stalin had hand-picked Rudenko, just thirty-eight years old, to serve as the Soviet chief prosecutor for the IMT in Nuremberg. It was the assignment of a lifetime.[1]

Rudenko seemed a logical choice for this position. A devoted Party member from the age of nineteen, he had proven his political mettle in the 1930s, prosecuting a series of Soviet show trials in the Donbas region of Ukraine and sending dozens of guiltless defendants to their deaths or to labor camps.[1] More recently, he had impressed Stalin with his performance as chief prosecutor in a show trial of sixteen leaders of the Polish underground state, a network of anti-Nazi resistance organizations that had been loyal to the Polish government-in-exile in London. Staged in Moscow in June 1945 before a large audience that included Western diplomats and journalists, this trial had turned reality upside down. The defendants—after being kidnapped and tortured by the NKVD—had confessed to collaborating with Nazi Germany. The trial had helped solidify the Soviet Union's hold on Poland and from Stalin's perspective had gone off brilliantly.[2]

Rudenko was a talented orator and an expert in Soviet-style justice but had only a rudimentary education. He had left school after the seventh grade to work in a sugar factory and had gotten involved with his local Party organization. Later, after his performance in the Donbas trials, the Party had sent him to take a two-year law course to get credentialed. During the war,

Nikita Khrushchev (then the head of the Communist Party of the Ukrainian SSR) had promoted Rudenko up through the ranks in Ukraine to his current post as procurator general.[3] But how prepared was Rudenko to serve as the Soviet chief prosecutor in a high-stakes international tribunal? Like most Soviet functionaries, he had no experience abroad. He had limited knowledge of international politics. What's more, he had no idea what he did not know—and he did not know a lot, even about his own country's recent history. This would put the Soviet Union at a disadvantage even before the Nuremberg Trials began, as negotiations got under way in London about the Indictment—the document that would establish the framework of the entire case.

Rudenko's appointment as Soviet chief prosecutor took the Western powers by surprise. After all, the Kremlin had already confirmed that Iona Nikitchenko would fill this post. In the days after Nikitchenko's departure from Nuremberg on August 31, the London-based Soviet diplomat Nikolai Ivanov had repeatedly assured everyone that he would soon return with a staff and evidence.[4] It was not until the eve of Rudenko's arrival that the Americans learned about the switch.[5] Robert Jackson expressed disappointment upon hearing that the Soviets had replaced Nikitchenko "with God knows whom and God knows why." He had gotten used to Nikitchenko and now would have to start from scratch with someone new.[6]

If Nikitchenko's dismissal as Soviet chief prosecutor was surprising for Jackson, his new position—as the Soviet judge—came as a complete shock. Nikitchenko had been irrepressibly vocal about the guilt of the defendants. How could his new role not evoke cries of "victors' justice"? For Soviet leaders this was of no concern; they refused to consider the idea that a judge should be a disinterested party without prior knowledge of the case, as Nikitchenko had made clear at the London Conference that summer. From their perspective, Nikitchenko, who had served as the presiding judge in the Moscow Trials and who understood Stalin's expectations for the international tribunal (quick decision, quick punishment), was the man for the job.

Stalin had kept the Western powers in the dark about Soviet personnel changes until Rudenko was on his way to London. He had appointed both Rudenko and Nikitchenko to their new positions on September 5—the same day he had tapped Andrei Vyshinsky to head a secret Indictment Commission (officially called the Commission for Directing the Preparation of the Indictment Materials and the Work of the Soviet Representatives in the International Tribunal and in the Committee of Prosecutors).[7] Back in the spring, U.S. judge Samuel Rosenman had speculated to Jackson that the

FIGURE 3.1 Roman Rudenko, Soviet chief prosecutor at the International Military Tribunal, ca. 1945–1946.

Credit: State Archive of the Russian Federation f. 10140, op. 2, d. 153, l. 2. Photographer: Viktor Temin.

Soviets would choose Vyshinsky as their chief prosecutor, given his well-known success in prosecuting "the famous Soviet trials."[8] While Vyshinsky would have no official role in the IMT, his behind-the-scenes influence would shape Soviet participation in ways both large and small.

Stalin had created the Indictment Commission in response to NKVD chief Beria's insistence on secret police oversight of the defendants and witnesses the Soviet Union sent to Germany. Vyshinsky immediately began to expand this commission's role. The commission would help build the case against the former Nazi leaders: it would screen evidence, conduct its own investigations, and interrogate witnesses. It would also monitor Soviet personnel abroad. Above all, it would do everything possible to protect Soviet interests and guard Soviet secrets.

In keeping with Beria's wishes, the Indictment Commission included a sort of who's who of high-ranking state security personnel: Bogdan Kobulov, deputy chief of the NKGB; Viktor Abakumov, chief of SMERSH; and Sergei Kruglov, deputy chief of the NKVD. The other members were chosen by Vyshinsky because of their international-law expertise or their familiarity with the evidence of Nazi crimes: Procurator General Konstantin Gorshenin, Aron Trainin, Extraordinary State Commission members Dmitry Kudryavtsev and Pavel Bogyavlensky, and Ivan Goliakov, head of the Soviet Union's Supreme Court. The commission reported directly to Beria, Molotov, Georgy Malenkov, and Anastas Mikoyan—the "Politburo Four." (The Politburo, the supreme decision-making body of the Party, had a dozen or so members; these four were part of Stalin's inner circle.) Stalin, naturally, had the final word on all decisions.[9] While the other Allied powers had committees and commissions that dealt with various aspects of the Nuremberg Trials, and the OSS was heavily involved in gathering evidence for the American case, this degree of centralization and control was unique to the Soviet Union.

Telford Taylor, one of the U.S. assistant prosecutors, later remembered Rudenko making his appearance on Monday, September 17, in a brown Foreign Service uniform with epaulets showing the high rank of lieutenant general. Short, pale, stocky, and looking ill at ease, Rudenko did not make a commanding first impression.[10] Deputy chief prosecutor Yuri Pokrovsky accompanied him, along with Ivanov and their interpreter from the Ministry of Foreign Affairs, Elena Dmitrieva. The forty-three-year-old Pokrovsky, who had fought with the Imperial Russian Army before going over to the Bolsheviks during the civil war and serving as a Red Army procurator, impressed David Maxwell Fyfe with his "Old World" charm and warmth.[11] Rudenko, by contrast, came off as stern and charmless.

The Western prosecutors had been waiting impatiently for the Soviets. They were ready to begin their formal discussion of the Indictment. Back in August, after the signing of the London Agreement and the Nuremberg Charter, Jackson, Nikitchenko, Maxwell Fyfe, and Robert Falco had divided up the work of preparing the Indictment. They had agreed that the British would chair a committee that would write up the charge of "crimes against peace" (envisioned as Count One). The Soviets and the French would oversee the work on the "war crimes" and "crimes against humanity" sections (envisioned as Counts Two and Three), bringing in evidence from the Eastern Front and the Western Front, respectively. The Americans would outline the case against the Nazi organizations and would draft general language for the Indictment on the overarching Nazi conspiracy. At the time, Bill Whitney, an OSS operative and one of Jackson's assistants in London, had reported to Washington that the Russian attitude about all this was "remarkably cooperative."[12] Since that initial discussion, the Americans and the British had combined their efforts and jointly drafted the "crimes against peace" section—expanding it to include a detailed accounting of the Nazi conspiracy to wage aggressive war against Europe.[13]

Now, with the Soviet chief prosecutor finally at the table, the Committee of Chief Prosecutors reviewed this Anglo-American draft. Rudenko had a lot to catch up on. Taylor later wrote that this first meeting "did not go well": both Rudenko and the French chief prosecutor, François de Menthon, were unfamiliar with the long discussions that had shaped the London Agreement and the Nuremberg Charter, and de Menthon voiced reservations about the charge of aggressive war. Rudenko brought a pile of Extraordinary State Commission reports with him to the meeting, all in Russian, only to learn that his delegation would be responsible for translating all of its evidence into German in order for it to be included in the Indictment. He understood immediately that this would be impossible. He left this meeting deeply shaken: the Soviet delegation was perilously short-staffed, especially when it came to translators. That evening, he sent a telegram to Vyshinsky requesting additional evidence as well as the rapid dispatch of assistants, translators, stenographers, and typists.[14]

The following day, September 18, negotiations moved much more briskly. That evening, Rudenko reported to Vyshinsky that the British, American, and French prosecutors had read through the Anglo-American draft of Count One and had spoken "approvingly" about accepting it as a starting point for work toward a final text. He added that he had not objected, because it more or less corresponded to the Soviet outline.[15] He was displaying startling political naïveté. He had not read the document, as it had not yet been translated from English—a language he did not know. Unaccustomed to having any kind of real authority, he had gotten carried away by the momentum of the meeting, reasoning that changes could always be made later.

Rudenko sent Vyshinsky the English-language document (several dozen pages), explaining that translating it into Russian had not been possible for what he called "technical reasons." He again requested more evidence, including data on the extermination of Soviet civilians. He also alerted Vyshinsky that the tribunal's standards for evidence would be more exacting than Soviet leaders in Moscow had been anticipating. He needed original war crimes reports; summaries of reports, or newspaper articles with data about atrocities, would not do. The matter of evidence was urgent, Rudenko added, for a subgroup of the prosecutors would soon be selecting evidence about German atrocities committed on the territory of the Soviet Union.[16]

In Moscow, Vyshinsky and his Indictment Commission now had a brief window to review the materials Rudenko had sent from London. The

Committee of Chief Prosecutors would not reconvene for at least a week, because the Americans were flying to Nuremberg and the French to Paris.[17] Taylor later recalled that at this point the Americans were impatient to decamp for Nuremberg, where Jackson was already setting up the Document Room to house and organize the evidence for the trials. Jackson had in fact left for Nuremberg on the same day Rudenko arrived in London; the two men had not yet met. Sidney Alderman, the U.S. deputy chief prosecutor, also left for Nuremberg with most of the American staff on September 20. Only Taylor and his assistants remained behind. Maxwell Fyfe and de Menthon soon headed to Nuremberg as well. Rudenko, who had of course only just arrived, told his Western colleagues that he would stay put for at least two weeks.[18] He and Pokrovsky had not received permission from Moscow to go to Germany and would await further directives while sifting through whatever evidence remained in London.

Rudenko and Pokrovsky were in a tight spot—through no fault of their own. Moscow had been amply forewarned that work would soon commence in Nuremberg. A week before Rudenko's arrival in London, Ivanov had alerted Soviet leaders that sending personnel to both England and Germany could no longer be delayed. Preparations were beginning in earnest, he had reported, and it was necessary for the Soviet representatives to get down to work on the Indictment in London and also to study the evidence the Americans were amassing in Nuremberg. The Americans were surging ahead. They had already installed a staff in Nuremberg to translate the most important documents from German into English—and had told Ivanov that if the Soviet prosecution wanted Russian translations, Moscow would need to dispatch to Nuremberg at least "ten people who know German and English" posthaste.[19]

The translation issue had taken everyone by surprise. The Nuremberg Charter had stipulated that all official documents for the IMT would be produced "in English, French, and Russian, and in the language of the Defendant." This had made perfect sense—until it didn't. Jackson had a dozen or so people translating documents for him at this point, and even so he was having a terrible time trying to keep pace with all of the evidence pouring in. He noted in his diary that a "considerable accumulation" of untranslated material had "piled up."[20] This was an understatement. There were millions of pages of documents to contend with.

The assignment of responsibility for the translation work had not been clarified during the earlier negotiations in London. Nobody had expected this much evidence. The U.S. War Department had only recently informed Jackson that the State Department had been unable to recruit a sufficient number of qualified translators for Russian, French, and German, and that the other Allied countries would need to send more personnel to make up the shortfall.[21] The Soviets were now coming to understand that they would be fully responsible for translating their own documents into German, English, and French and all of the other countries' documents into Russian. The Party had initially approved just two interpreters to travel abroad, assuming that they could also translate documents.[22]

Vyshinsky did not grasp the gravity of the situation until September 18—when Rudenko revealed that he had been unable to have the first part of the Indictment translated into Russian. He immediately informed Party leaders that at least eight translators with knowledge of English, French, and German were needed immediately in London and that no fewer than six translators would be required in Nuremberg for the duration of the trials.[23] It was no small task to find qualified foreign-language experts in the Soviet Union, especially after the wartime anti-German campaign—when just being overheard speaking German could get you arrested and shot. It was even harder to get the NKVD to clear people who knew foreign languages for travel abroad. Their ability to communicate with the outside world—the very thing that was needed to operate on the international stage—also made them highly suspect in the eyes of the Soviet security apparatus.

On September 21, Vyshinsky sent Rudenko a small batch of captured German documents in Russian translation, including key memoranda from Alfred Rosenberg (former Reich minister for the Occupied Eastern Territories) about colonizing the Caucasus as well as a report from the Nazi Security Police (SiPo) detailing the extermination of the Soviet Union's Jews in the territories of Belorussia, Latvia, Lithuania, Estonia, and the Leningrad region in the period between October 1941 and January 1942.[24] These documents—laying bare the Nazi plan for Lebensraum and describing the mass slaughter of civilians—had been seized by the Red Army. Vyshinsky promised that more evidence would be coming once it was rendered into Russian. In the meantime, these documents would provide an irrefutable picture of Nazi criminality. In turn, Rudenko passed along to Vyshinsky a draft of the Indictment's sections on war crimes and crimes against humanity: twenty-three pages, only partially translated into Russian.[25]

The politics of the Indictment were the politics of history. The four wartime Allies understood that in putting together the case against the Nazi elite and their organizations, the prosecutors were also setting out a version of events for posterity. The Soviets had extensive experience using trials to shape the historical record—but this time they weren't running the show. It was only after reviewing the Anglo-American text of the "crimes against peace" section sent by Rudenko that Soviet leaders even understood that the international agreements of the late 1930s might be included in the Indictment as part of the narrative about the rise of the Nazis and the start of the war. This was precisely the kind of thing Stalin and Molotov wanted to avoid. What would happen at Nuremberg if the German-Soviet Non-Aggression Pact of 1939—the Molotov-Ribbentrop Pact—became a topic of scrutiny and discussion? Everyone knew that Stalin's promise of neutrality had freed Hitler to invade Poland.

The Soviets weren't the only ones who had negotiated an agreement with Hitler, of course. In September 1938, France and Britain had signed the Munich Pact, in which they turned their backs on Czechoslovakia and surrendered the Sudetenland to the Nazis in an effort to avoid war. But there were key differences. Unlike the Soviet Union, Britain and France had new leaders who were not implicated in the policies of their predecessors: Clement Attlee and Charles de Gaulle had been staunch opponents of appeasement. There was also a great deal more to the Molotov-Ribbentrop Pact than met the eye. The pact had included secret protocols in which Stalin and Hitler agreed to divide up Eastern Europe between them. During 1939 and 1940, the Soviets had seized the eastern half of Poland, the Baltic states of Latvia, Lithuania, and Estonia, part of Finland, and Bessarabia. The secret protocols would show that they had done so with Hitler's blessing.

Given these concerns, Moscow's first critique of the "crimes against peace" section, coming from the Legal Department of the Ministry of Foreign Affairs, was remarkably mild. The Legal Department notified Rudenko on September 20 that the text contained some "factual errors," such as its positive characterization of the Munich Pact as an agreement aimed at preventing war and its assumption that international agreements signed by Tsarist Russia were binding on the Soviet Union. The Legal Department also criticized the assertion that the Nazi leadership's exercise of "total control" over the German economy was proof of a nefarious plot to establish a system of total rule in Germany.[26] This could be read as a veiled critique of the Soviet Union, which also had a state-controlled economy.

Three days later, Vyshinsky and his commission, having completed their own review, sent Rudenko a much harsher assessment calling for extensive changes. Vyshinsky forwarded no fewer than fifteen corrections for the "crimes against peace" section, focused primarily on matters of historical interpretation. The commission demanded the deletion of all lines suggesting that Hitler and his clique had "forced" Germany to secretly rearm and plot against other countries, since this gave the impression that the German

Poland Divided between Germany and the USSR, 1939

- City
- − − 08/23/39 Planned Nazi-Soviet Demarcation Line
- ▬ ▬ 09/28/39 Nazi-Soviet Demarcation Line Post-Invasion
- ▦ Annexed by Germany on October 8, 1939
- ▨ Incorporated into Lithuanian borders on October 10, 1939

Latvia, Lithuania, and Estonia were all annexed by the USSR in 1940.

ESTONIA

LATVIA

Baltic Sea

LITHUANIA

EAST PRUSSIA

Danzig (Gdansk)

Vilna (Wilno, Vilnius)

Minsk

USSR

Narew

Bialystok

Vistula

Bug

Poznan

Warsaw

Lodz

P O L A N D

Vistula

Lublin

Bug

GERMANY

Vistula

San

Cracow

Lvov (Lwow)

100 Kilometers
100 Miles

SLOVAKIA

HUNGARY

ROMANIA

Europe Lambert Conformal Conic

MAP 3   Poland Divided between Germany and the USSR, 1939.

government bore no responsibility for Nazi crimes. It objected even more strongly to the description of the Nazi conspiracy to wage aggressive war, which described the German-Soviet Non-Aggression Pact as an indirect cause of the Nazi invasion of Poland. Vyshinsky ordered Rudenko to insist that these lines be rewritten so that the pact could under no circumstances be interpreted as the "springboard," as he put it, for Nazi actions. He also commanded Rudenko to "send us the final editing" of this section for approval before signing off on it.[27]

Substantial as these revisions were, they were almost minor in comparison to the sweeping changes Vyshinsky demanded for the sections on war crimes and crimes against humanity on the Eastern Front, which the Soviet delegation had drafted with some input from Taylor. The commission had found "this entire part" of the document unsatisfactory and would be sending on the next plane to London a new Russian text to translate into English as a substitute. This new text drew extensively from Extraordinary State Commission reports; it enumerated a long list of Nazi atrocities committed against civilians and prisoners of war during the German occupation of the Soviet Union. The list included the deportation of Soviet citizens to Germany to work as slave laborers—as well as the "German" murder of 925 Polish officers in the Katyn Forest near Smolensk.[28]

Adding Katyn to the Indictment was a bold and potentially reckless move for the Soviets. Ever since the discovery of the mass graves in April 1943 the Soviets and the Germans had been publicly blaming each other for the massacre. In January 1944, Soviet leaders had organized a trip for eighteen Western correspondents and Kathleen Harriman (the twenty-five-year-old daughter of the U.S. ambassador) to the Katyn Forest with the aim of publicizing the findings of the Burdenko Commission.[29] After traveling to the region in a luxurious train car well stocked with food, wine, vodka, and cigarettes, the correspondents had visited the mass graves and examined items said to have been excavated from the gravesite. They had met with Nikolai Burdenko, Alexei Tolstoy, and Metropolitan Nikolai as well as with Soviet forensic experts and several supposed witnesses. The reportage had been as favorable as Moscow had hoped it would be. Stalin and Vyshinsky were considering holding a Katyn trial in the Soviet-controlled Polish People's Republic as a next step.[30] Instead, they seized on the IMT as an opportunity to tar the Nazis with the crime on the most public stage in the world. Though the Germans and the Soviets had bruited about the figure of 10,000 corpses for over two years, the Indictment Commission had chosen to go with the more conservative figure of 925—which corresponded to the number of exhumed bodies noted in the Burdenko Report.[31]

Accustomed as he was to Soviet show trials, Vyshinsky did not grasp the dangers of the game he was playing. He was operating under the assumptions that the Allied judges in Nuremberg would keep the proceedings focused exclusively on the crimes of the European Axis powers and that evidence from the Extraordinary State Commission and other official war crimes commissions would be considered incontrovertible and thus go unchallenged. Vyshinsky directed Rudenko to inform him immediately of the other chief prosecutors' responses to the proposed revisions.[32]

Jackson, too, had been dissatisfied with the Indictment. While Rudenko was grounded in London, Jackson, Maxwell Fyfe, and de Menthon were meeting in Nuremberg. On September 22, just before Maxwell Fyfe returned to London for a few days, Jackson handed him a rewrite that differed dramatically from the version they had been discussing.

Unbeknownst to the other prosecutors, Jackson had been spending his free moments rewriting the first half of the Anglo-American draft. In a fit of inspiration, he had separated out the charge of conspiracy, designated it as Count One, and made it into the linchpin of the entire case. The new Count One would charge the defendants with participating in the formulation or execution of a common plan or conspiracy "to commit crimes against peace, war crimes, and crimes against humanity, as defined in the Nuremberg Charter." It held them "individually responsible for their own acts and for all acts committed by any persons in the execution of such plan or conspiracy." As reconceived by Jackson, Nazi crimes against peace, war crimes, and crimes against humanity (now Counts Two, Three, and Four) all had their roots in a larger conspiracy. Whoever presented on Count One—a role Jackson was intent on claiming for himself—would also have the opportunity to address all of the other counts.[33]

Jackson had made this change, as he privately admitted to U.S. assistant prosecutor Robert Storey, with the explicit aim of "keeping control of the bulk of the case in American hands." Jackson was hoping to engineer a scenario in which the British, the French, and the Soviets documented the evidence of Nazi breaches of treaties, atrocities, and other specific crimes, while the U.S. prosecution developed the overarching framework for the case.[34] He continued to believe that the IMT could play a foundational role in the future development of international law. While he recognized the symbolic importance of a four-power trial, he was unwilling to entrust the vital arguments of the case to others.

Maxwell Fyfe was nonplussed by Jackson's move, which had bumped the "crimes against peace" charge to Count Two and limited its scope. Patrick Dean, the legal advisor to the British Foreign Office, went to Nuremberg to meet with Jackson—who insisted that a separate conspiracy count was essential in order to fully demonstrate the breadth and depth of Nazi criminality. The British again caved in to American demands. Maxwell Fyfe, on his return to Nuremberg on September 27, agreed to the new division of the case.[35]

All of this happened while Soviet leaders in Moscow were reviewing and commenting on the sections of the Indictment that Rudenko had sent them on September 18 and 21. Rudenko would not learn about the new Count One until days later.

Soviet leaders had done remarkably little to prepare Rudenko and Pokrovsky for their time abroad, assuming that the Indictment Commission would be able to direct their every move from Moscow. This was not working out as expected. Ivanov, who had been posted as a diplomat at the Soviet embassy in Berlin in 1938 and 1939 and knew substantially more than Rudenko about the history of Soviet-German relations, had been at first surprised and then alarmed at Rudenko's ignorance.[36] Ivanov now used the downtime in London to fire off a warning to Moscow: Rudenko's lack of knowledge about the Soviet-German relationship could dangerously weaken the Soviet position at the trials. How could he defend against what he didn't know? Ivanov urged Soviet leaders to brief Rudenko about the diplomatic intrigues of the 1930s and to enlighten him as to the causes of the war. Ivanov suggested that they supply Rudenko with "specific materials from German sources (the speeches of Hitler, Goebbels, Ribbentrop and others) revealing the main reasons and goals of the attack on the USSR in 1941." They should also tell him "what position to take and how to respond to questions relating to the conclusion of the non-aggression pact and so on between Germany and the USSR in 1939." The "and so on" was a veiled reference to the secret protocols. If Soviet leaders did not take such steps, Ivanov warned, Rudenko and his assistant would be "defenseless" should the accused, or even the British or the Americans, "attempt to falsify any of the historical facts."[37]

The exposure of the truth about the Molotov-Ribbentrop Pact posed an especially grave danger to the Soviets. Neither Rudenko nor Pokrovsky knew about the existence of the pact's secret protocols. This left them at a great disadvantage, given that one of the defendants, former German foreign minister Ribbentrop, had been intimately involved in writing them. Ivanov advised Soviet leaders to send experts on German history and international relations in order to ensure that Rudenko had the facts necessary to interrogate the defendants and to evaluate the evidence. He also recommended that Soviet leaders assign an experienced diplomat to accompany Rudenko to Nuremberg as an advisor.[38]

Ivanov's concerns did not stop there. The Soviet delegation was at a further disadvantage, he reported, because its members had no real experience with international organizations. Rudenko and Pokrovsky had trouble setting meeting agendas and posing questions for discussion and did not seem to understand the basic tactics, let alone the subtleties, of negotiation—all of which impeded their ability to advance Soviet goals.[39] The Soviet shortage of interpreters and translators was exacerbating these problems. The negotiations in London were taking place in English, which meant that Rudenko was dependent on his support staff for assistance. Elena Dmitrieva had poor command of English and German and was unable to translate even a fraction of the material that the Western governments had turned over to the prosecution. If this were not addressed, the Soviet prosecution would be in the dark during the trials, unable to anticipate and object to the introduction of evidence that might send things "in an unfavorable direction," Ivanov cautioned. Dmitrieva's incompetence was already making the Soviets look bad, he added, for she frequently mistranslated Rudenko's words.[40]

Ivanov was not exaggerating. The Americans were having a hard time understanding Dmitrieva and found her efforts as an interpreter "often comical." Taylor later noted that Dmitrieva, "though personally rather winsome," was "wholly unequal" to the task of translating legal concepts. Alderman compared trying to talk with Rudenko to having a "conversation through a double mattress."[41] Ivanov implored Vyshinsky to immediately dispatch qualified translators with English, French, and German to London and Nuremberg. Time was running out. While Rudenko and Pokrovsky were bumbling along in London, the Americans had sent most of their evidence to Nuremberg, and the British and the French had sent their delegations to join the Americans there.[42]

The Soviet delegation's shortcomings—the lack of translators, Rudenko's ignorance, and the difficulty addressing both of these issues—arose from the very nature of the Stalinist system. In part, they were direct consequences of the suspicion and fear that had been sown during the years of the Great Terror. Between 1937 and 1939, the NKVD had ruthlessly purged the Ministry of Foreign Affairs; about a third of its officials had been arrested and shot, and many posts had been left vacant.[43] It had been dangerous to study foreign languages, especially German, lest one be accused of working for the enemy. Very few Soviet citizens had been allowed to travel outside Soviet borders before the war took the Red Army westward. Expertise and experience abroad, in other words, were in short supply.

Stalin's paranoia and the conspiratorial nature of the Soviet regime had also given rise to the politics of secrecy. Rudenko's and Pokrovsky's ignorance about Soviet-German relations was a direct consequence of the Stalinist policy of sharing information only on a need-to-know basis. Ivanov, a diplomat who had been stationed in Germany, had a higher security clearance than Rudenko and Pokrovsky—but he could not share what he knew without explicit permission. Perhaps it hadn't occurred to Stalin and Vyshinsky to brief Rudenko about the details of Soviet-German collaboration. After all, Soviet leaders were used to using trials to build whatever narrative they wanted; they had not been expecting the Indictment to deal with the events of the 1930s. Or perhaps they had chosen to keep Rudenko uninformed.

Ivanov's warnings elicited an immediate response. Vyshinsky promptly enlisted Trainin and another international-law expert, Boris Mankovsky, as well as the diplomat Vladimir Semenov (who had been posted in Germany in 1940 and 1941), to assist the Soviet prosecution in Nuremberg. Semenov and Mankovsky were already in Berlin working for the Soviet Military Administration in Germany (SVAG). It proved impossible, however, to recruit translators and interpreters quickly. The NKVD refused to expedite the process of vetting personnel for political reliability—a prerequisite for travel abroad. In reaction, Vyshinsky and Gorshenin looked for foreign-language experts who had already passed muster with the NKVD. They sent an appeal for interpreters to SVAG. They also asked Abakumov, chief of SMERSH, for German-speaking personnel who had assisted with the Kharkov Trial two years earlier.[44]

Back in Nuremberg, the translation problem was moving from urgent to dire. On Saturday, September 29, Jackson sent Rudenko a message alerting him that the shortage of translators was liable to "result in serious embarrassment" for all of the countries of the prosecution. According to Jackson, more than 600 German-language documents that had been identified as vital for the prosecution's case had been translated into English but not into Russian or French, and another 2,000 such documents had not been translated at all. While the American and British delegations were attempting to translate these materials into English, they would not be able to also render them into Russian or French. Jackson invoked the Nuremberg Charter's requirement that all evidence be made available in English, Russian, French, and German. If the Soviet and French delegations did not pick up the slack, he warned, much of the case that had been built up thus far would have to be dropped.[45]

Rudenko passed this information along to Vyshinsky the following day, alerting him that the Soviets would need to provide not six but a dozen translators in Nuremberg. He also asked Vyshinsky to dispatch Nikitchenko immediately to London and from there to Berlin, where the tribunal would hold its first public session. Noting that the U.S. judge, Francis Biddle, had already left for Berlin, he emphasized that time was of the essence. The Americans and the British wanted the chief prosecutors and the judges to gather in Berlin no later than October 8 or 10. Rudenko assured Vyshinsky that he was faithfully carrying out his orders: he had sent the

Soviet revisions to the Western prosecutors, and they would be discussed along with suggestions from the other delegations over the next several days, once Jackson returned to London for the next scheduled meeting of the Committee of Chief Prosecutors.[46]

At this point Rudenko was still unaware that Jackson had completely redrafted the first part of the Indictment. He also did not know that Jackson had decided to remain in Nuremberg and send Alderman to London in his place. Rudenko learned about the discussions that had taken place in Nuremberg only when Dean brought the new Counts One and Two to London on the afternoon of September 30.[47]

Rudenko was blindsided by the news that so much had happened without him. Dean told him that the British and American delegations were intending to put forward the redraft at the upcoming Committee of Chief Prosecutors meeting, and that he was passing it along so the Soviet prosecutors would have time to translate and evaluate it. Alderman arrived the next day, bringing with him the newly drafted description of the charges against the Nazi organizations.[48]

Stalin had appointed Rudenko as chief prosecutor because of his way with words, not because of his ability to navigate the subtleties of foreign relations. The shaping of the Indictment had become a struggle for control of the case against the Nazis—but the subtleties of the situation were lost on Rudenko. He did not realize that Jackson was angling to use the conspiracy charge to seize control over the entire case. He did not even bother to forward the new Counts One and Two to Moscow. Rudenko still did not have translators in London who could render the English-language materials Dean had just given him (several dozen more pages) into Russian. In all likelihood, he only skimmed them, with Dmitrieva's assistance.

Rudenko was thus at a disadvantage when the prosecutors convened in London on Tuesday, October 2, to finalize the Indictment. Over several days, Alderman, Rudenko, British chief prosecutor Sir Hartley Shawcross, and French deputy chief prosecutor Charles Dubost reviewed all four counts. Deliberations were mostly congenial, despite disagreements over some of the proposed American and Soviet revisions. The list of organizations to be indicted at this point included the Reich Cabinet, the Leadership Corps of the Nazi Party, the SA, the SS, the Gestapo, and the SD (Security Service). The SD (which had functioned as the intelligence agency of the SS and the Nazi Party) and the Gestapo were indicted as a single organization. The U.S. prosecution was intent on expanding this list to include the Wehrmacht's General Staff and High Command, and also wanted to add more individual defendants—primarily several industrialists and generals who were in U.S. custody. Alderman carried the day on the first issue (the General Staff and High Command was added to the list of organizations) but lost the vote on the second: the list of individual defendants would not be lengthened. The other delegations had their own wish lists of additional defendants and were unwilling to support the U.S. request without similar consideration.[49]

It was also during these meetings that the prosecutors agreed to use the term "genocide" in the war crimes section of the Indictment to refer to the systematic extermination of "national, racial, or religious groups."[50] Raphael Lemkin, a lawyer with the U.S. War Department and a Polish-Jewish refugee, had coined the term in his 1944 book *Axis Rule in Occupied Europe* and had been lobbying Jackson to use it to describe the crimes of the Nazis. Lemkin had created the word by combining the ancient Greek word *genos* (race, tribe) with the Latin *cide* (to kill). Genocide, Lemkin had argued, was different from murder because it was aimed at the destruction of a group "as an entity."[51] A decade earlier, Trainin had criticized Lemkin, Vespasian Pella, and other international-law experts for refusing to address the problem of "military aggression." This problem was no longer theoretical. Lemkin had lost forty-nine family members at the hands of the Nazis. In the wake of the war, creating new laws to protect humankind had become his obsession. For now, the Soviets gave the adoption of Lemkin's new term no real notice. Only in the aftermath of the Nuremberg Trials, when talk turned to human rights and the creation of a permanent international criminal court, would Moscow come to see this concept as a political weapon that might also be wielded against the Soviet Union.[52]

Many of the Soviet changes to the Indictment were approved without much ado. The language about the Nazis forcing Germany to act was eliminated, and more details were added about Nazi crimes against Soviet civilians, including a paragraph about deportations and enslavement. However, the Western prosecutors balked at two of the Soviet revisions. The first concerned the insertion of a paragraph referring in passing to Latvia, Estonia, and Lithuania as part of the Soviet Union. The American and British prosecutors rejected this outright: their governments refused to recognize the Soviet annexation of these states. Rudenko declared that he could not alter the language without flying back to Moscow and consulting with Stalin, and that this would require a two-week delay. "The thought of delay drove our British brethren frantic," Jackson noted in his diary. Jackson consulted the State Department, which assured him that signing the Indictment did not constitute "recognition of Russia's absorption of these territories."[53]

The second controversial revision was the addition of the Katyn massacre to the list of Nazi war crimes. Jackson, Maxwell Fyfe, and de Menthon (along with the rest of the world) had been watching the Soviets and the Germans accuse each other of this massacre for several years now. They appealed to Rudenko to leave Katyn out of the case on legal and pragmatic grounds. Jackson argued that there weren't any witnesses who "would meet the high standards of credibility required in a criminal trial."[54] The Western prosecutors all expressed concern that, whatever the actual truth might be, the inclusion of Katyn in the Indictment would make it possible for the German defense to try to shift the blame back to the Soviets—accusing one of the countries of the prosecution of a war crime.[55] Rudenko refused to budge. He had orders from Moscow; his hands were tied.

On October 5, the Kremlin finally sent a small team of investigators to Nuremberg. At its helm was Georgy N. Alexandrov, who was an expert, after a career in the procurator general's office in Moscow, in the Stalinist techniques of putting together a case. Jackson, who had been complaining for weeks that the other chief prosecutors had not yet established their staffs in Nuremberg, noted in his diary that the Russians upon their arrival "were astonished to find the accumulation of evidence." Alexandrov and his team had been expecting to go through all of the relevant documents that evening before interrogating the defendants in the Nuremberg prison the following morning. A roomful of evidence piled high in teetering stacks—along with American regulations restricting access to the prisoners—stopped them in their tracks.[56]

Over the next few days, Alexandrov and his team began the task of sorting through documents while petitioning for permission to begin their work in the Nuremberg prison.[57] They soon contacted Moscow, again stressing the urgent need for personnel who knew German, and complaining that Jackson's team would not allow them to interrogate defendants or witnesses on their own but had instead instructed them to present their questions through one of the American investigators and wait for a written response.[58]

In response to Alexandrov's plea, Vyshinsky once again appealed to SVAG, asking it to assist the Soviet investigators in Nuremberg and to lend them an interpreter. He also tried to put reliable communication lines in place, instructing SVAG to negotiate with the Americans to allow the unimpeded travel of Soviet couriers between Berlin and Nuremberg (through the American zone) and inquiring whether it would be possible to establish a direct phone line from Nuremberg to Moscow. Vyshinsky also asked SVAG to look into the problem of accommodations. A residential building the Americans had given the Soviets on the outskirts of the city (on the

FIGURE 3.2 The Document Room at Nuremberg with its teetering stacks of evidence, November 1945.

Credit: United States Holocaust Memorial Museum, courtesy of National Archives and Records Administration, College Park. Photographer: Charles Alexander.

Eichendorffstrasse) could house most of their legal team of approximately twelve. But as Soviet leaders in Moscow began to better understand just how process-heavy this trial would be—and how different it would be from the trials they were used to, where quick guilty verdicts were a foregone conclusion—they added more legal and support personnel. They now sought housing for around a hundred people.[59]

Though Stalin had agreed to the Americans' choice of Nuremberg as the setting for the IMT, Berlin remained a potent symbol of victory in the Soviet imagination, synonymous with the last battle of the war and the German surrender to Marshal Georgy Zhukov. It was the former capital of the Third Reich. Now under four-power occupation but physically inside the Soviet zone, it was the headquarters of the Allied Control Council (the occupation government of Germany that had been established in August) and of SVAG.

FIGURE 3.3 Aerial view of the Palace of Justice (center), showing the Nuremberg prison compound with its four wings (immediately behind), November 1945. The defendants were housed in the far right wing, the witnesses in the left wing, and other prisoners in the two center wings.

Credit: United States Holocaust Memorial Museum, courtesy of National Archives and Records Administration, College Park.

The IMT would hold its first public session in Berlin, where the Indictment would be filed with the judges. As a preliminary to this session, the prosecutors had agreed to meet on October 6 at the former People's Palace of Justice in Berlin to sign this critical document. This date had been set before Jackson had surprised everyone with his rewrite. While a week of intense discussion in London had yielded a sixty-five-page document that the prosecutors could more or less agree on, Rudenko still had not been able to carefully evaluate the new Count One, or the complete text as a whole. He had not yet sent the current draft to Moscow; his team had not finished translating it into Russian.

The details of Rudenko's time in Berlin are murky—largely because he later tried to conceal his missteps from Moscow. He showed up for the scheduled meeting on October 6 but promptly announced that the printed copy of the Indictment contained a number of errors that would have to be corrected before it could be filed with the Tribunal. When pressed, he refused to elaborate.[60] This was a ploy to hold up the proceedings. He had good reason to want a delay. He was not supposed to sign anything without explicit permission from Moscow—and this version of the Indictment was significantly different from the one Soviet leaders had reviewed weeks earlier. The Indictment Commission was not even aware of the existence of the new Count One.

The Western prosecutors pressured Rudenko to sign the English-language copy of the Indictment, using what Maxwell Fyfe described in his memoir as "friendship and sweet reasonableness."[61] They assured him that corrections could be made later and that his signature could be annulled if the English-language and Russian-language texts significantly diverged. They also warned him that the Soviet Union would publicly take the heat for delaying the start of the Nuremberg Trials if he did not comply.[62]

Rudenko knew that his options were limited. There was not enough time to explain the situation to Moscow and wait for instructions. Plus, what would Vyshinsky say about his carelessness in not sending along the redraft earlier? Stalin had ordered people shot for less. That afternoon, Rudenko, throwing his fate to the winds, joined his Western colleagues and signed the English-language document with the understanding that it "would be held open for the correction of minor errors" and for "reconciliation" with the still unfinished French and Russian translations.[63] The prosecutors made plans to deliver the Indictment to the Tribunal and to publish it in the press the following week.

Rudenko had acted without Moscow's permission—and he promptly panicked. That evening, he fled Berlin for London, without appointing anyone to serve as his deputy. Taylor later recounted that this unannounced departure took everyone by surprise and "contributed greatly to the delays and confusions of the next ten days."[64] Later that night, Rudenko sent Vyshinsky a telegram from London stating that he would send him a Russian-language copy of the revised Indictment on Monday, October 8, and that the signing would take place in Berlin. Rudenko gave no indication that he had already signed the document.[65] He then fell silent and did not write Moscow again until October 10. One wonders how he was spending his time in London. Was he walking the streets of the city pondering his options? Was he trying to find a way to get the full Indictment translated into Russian? Or was he holed up in his hotel room, paralyzed with fear?

While Rudenko was incommunicado, the British and American prosecutors tried to move things along, calling for a meeting with the judges in Berlin to obtain instructions about lodging the Indictment with the

Tribunal. On October 7, British officials informed the Soviet government that the British and American judges had flown to Berlin earlier that day; they asked that the Soviet judges arrive by October 9. They also expressed the hope that the Soviets would deliver the defendants Erich Raeder and Hans Fritzsche, who were being held in a prison in Berlin, to Nuremberg by the same date.[66]

This was a much quicker timetable than Soviet leaders had been anticipating. Before receiving Rudenko's note, they had been planning to send Nikitchenko to Berlin around October 19. But the Soviets had little leverage. Indeed, it was right around this time that Vyshinsky learned that Rudenko had signed the Indictment in Berlin. Soviet leaders promptly dispatched Nikitchenko, alternate judge Alexander Volchkov, and Trainin to Berlin to assess the situation. Volchkov had served in the Legal Department of the Red Army during the war; he also had a decent command of English, having been stationed as a Soviet diplomat in London earlier in his career.[67]

At this point, both Jackson and Vyshinsky were asking the same question: Where was Rudenko? Jackson noted in his diary on October 9 that he had spent the afternoon "attempting to learn what had become of the Russian delegation."[68] Vyshinsky later wrote in a report that for several days "no communication whatsoever from Comrade Rudenko came through."[69] On October 10, Rudenko finally sent a telegram from London to Moscow informing the Ministry of Foreign Affairs that the Indictment had been signed in Berlin on October 6 and would be published in the international press on Friday, October 12. He added that it would be lodged with the Tribunal on Friday, October 19 (though he surely knew that the Americans and British were intent on doing so earlier).[70]

Also on October 10, the judges convened in closed session in Berlin. Questioned about Rudenko's whereabouts, Nikitchenko told his colleagues that he was not sure when the Soviet chief prosecutor would turn up.[71] Meanwhile, the Western prosecutors were pushing hard to call the first public session of the Tribunal. Nikitchenko protested that such a meeting could not be held in Rudenko's absence.[72] That evening, Nikitchenko and Trainin warned Vyshinsky that things would probably move forward in Berlin with or without Soviet participation. The British and the Americans, with backing from the French, kept raising the issue of submitting the Indictment to the Tribunal. In spite of Soviet objections, a meeting had been scheduled for the next day for the prosecutors to sign the Russian and French versions and a second English-language copy of the document.[73] The Russian-language translation was still not ready.[74]

Nikitchenko and Trainin also informed Vyshinsky that they had just spoken by telephone with Rudenko, who was in London, and that they had implored him to come to Berlin as quickly as possible. Rudenko had assured them that he would arrive shortly and had promised to send the Russian translation of the Indictment from London to Moscow by airplane that evening. Nikitchenko and Trainin apparently had their doubts: they told Vyshinsky that they, too, would send him the English-language original as well as a Russian translation. Warning that their translation might not be "fully satisfactory," since they had had no time to make more than a quick pass through it, they closed their letter with another appeal for Moscow to send translators to Germany.[75]

By now, it seemed like everyone in Berlin was waiting for Rudenko. Taylor dubbed Thursday, October 11 "Waiting for Rudenko Day." Having received news from London that Rudenko would show up around midday, Maxwell Fyfe and one of Jackson's assistants set out to the airport to meet him and to get him to agree to an immediate meeting of the Committee of Chief Prosecutors. Rudenko finally appeared at 3:30 in the afternoon. The prosecutors' meeting was held that evening. After heartily agreeing with the others that they should move quickly to present the Indictment to the Tribunal, Rudenko announced that checking the Russian translation and comparing it to the English text would take two more days.[76]

What exactly Nikitchenko and Trainin had told Rudenko during their telephone conversation is not known. Nonetheless, it is clear that they had formulated a plan; from this point forward, Rudenko's actions were being choreographed by the entire Soviet delegation. After much grumbling, the other Allied prosecutors agreed to Monday, October 15, as the absolute deadline for filing the Indictment.[77]

On the evening of October 11, the Soviet diplomat Semenov notified Vyshinsky that Rudenko had gotten the other prosecutors to agree to a postponement, and that nothing further would happen without Moscow's approval.[78] However, a telegram from Rudenko to Vyshinsky the next morning suggested that things were continuing to move along. The prosecutors had resolved to deliver the Indictment to the Tribunal on the morning of October 15 and to publish it that evening.[79]

Vyshinsky finally received the copy of the Indictment that Nikitchenko and Trainin had sent from Berlin on the afternoon of October 12. The one Rudenko had promised never arrived.[80] Later that day, Vyshinsky sent Rudenko a message, informing him that the Indictment Commission would be sending him a number of major corrections. He would try to send all of the corrections by Sunday, October 14, but he warned that they might be late. Rudenko was not to sign off on the final document—under any circumstances—until he received word from Moscow.[81]

Life in Berlin had not stood still while everyone was waiting for Rudenko to show up; the judges were making a series of decisions that would affect the staging of the trials. On October 10, for example, they broached the question of wardrobe. The French judge Henri Donnedieu de Vabres, a sixty-five-year-old professor of criminal law at the Sorbonne, insisted on black robes as befitting the Tribunal's dignity. Nikitchenko dismissed such gowns as "medieval." In the spirit of compromise, it was agreed that each judge could wear whatever he considered appropriate—leaving the Soviet judges free to wear their military uniforms.[82]

Discussions on other topics were more contentious. On October 11, the three Western judges decided, over Nikitchenko's objections, that the presidency of the Tribunal would not rotate during the trials at Nuremberg. A couple of days later, the judges selected the British judge, Sir Geoffrey Lawrence, as the Tribunal's president. Lawrence, a High Court judge, was known for his even temper and blunt manner. Biddle, who back in January 1945 had coauthored the original U.S. plan to convene an international tribunal, had coveted this post. Jackson had convinced Biddle to support Lawrence lest the Americans, who were playing host and supplying the majority of the defendants, be seen as completely running the show. Jackson explained his thinking in a letter to President Truman: if an American judge were to head the Tribunal and anything went wrong, "all of the animosities and blame would be centered upon the United States."[83] Nikitchenko also went along with the choice of Lawrence, largely because he, in turn, was selected to preside over the Tribunal during its public meetings in Berlin.[84]

Back in Moscow, Vyshinsky focused his attention on the Indictment, well aware that the October 15 deadline was looming. On Saturday morning, October 13, he sent Russian-language copies (based on the roughly translated version that Nikitchenko and Trainin had sent him) to Gorshenin, Kobulov, and the other members of the Indictment Commission. Explaining that the translation had just been completed from the text received the day before, Vyshinsky asked his colleagues to send their comments that afternoon.[85]

Complicating matters further for the Soviets, Stalin had left Moscow on October 9 for his villa in Sochi, near the Black Sea in the Caucasus. It was Stalin's first vacation in nine years. He was visibly exhausted, and speculation abounded that he was seriously ill. The *Chicago Tribune, Newsweek*, and other publications were reporting (based on no hard evidence) that he had suffered two heart attacks during the Potsdam Conference a couple of months earlier.[86] Molotov and Beria kept Stalin abreast of international developments and received instructions from him, but the lines of communication among the Soviet leadership were stretched further than usual.[87]

Comments on the Indictment came in on the afternoon of October 13. Many were petty—there wasn't enough time for a thorough critique. Bogyavlensky and Kudryavtsev (from the Extraordinary State Commission) wrote that since it was "now pointless to introduce structural changes" they were sending "minor comments." Most of these were focused on matters of historical interpretation. For example, they wanted to make clear that the Jewish ghetto in Lvov (a part of Poland that had experienced both Soviet and German occupation) had been "created by the Germans." One change, however, was anything but minor. Bogyavlensky and Kudryavtsev had rewritten the line about Katyn to state that the Germans had shot 11,000 Polish officers.[88] This was much closer to the figure that everyone else had been citing.

Many of Gorshenin's comments were geared toward setting the story straight about the origins and course of the war. He wanted the Indictment to state explicitly that Austria had been forcibly united with Germany—countering German claims that the Anschluss had been an act of national self-determination. He also wanted it to clarify that the Jews had been wiped out from "a significant part" of Europe rather than the entire continent, since the Soviet Union was "a part of Europe" and the Jewish population of territories that had not fallen under German occupation had survived. Reiterating key points that the Ministry of Foreign Affairs and the Indictment Commission had made earlier, Gorshenin argued that it was imperative to describe how the meeting between British prime minister Neville Chamberlain, French prime minister Edouard Daladier, and Hitler at Munich in 1938 had changed the fate of Czechoslovakia. He also asserted that the characterization of the German-Soviet Non-Aggression Pact did not sufficiently emphasize German treachery. He wanted a revision stating that German leaders had concluded this pact with the express intention of using it as cover while planning a surprise attack.[89]

Gorshenin suggested other edits that were aimed at squaring the document with Soviet values. For example, he questioned a paragraph in the American-authored conspiracy section that condemned the Nazis for attempting to end the influence of the church on the German people. The Soviet Union was itself an atheistic state—and only during wartime had Stalin reached a detente with the Russian Orthodox Church in an effort to rally the Soviet people to the defense of the motherland. Gorshenin rewrote this paragraph to emphasize that Nazi leaders had destroyed churches with the explicit aim of replacing them with fascist institutions and fascist doctrine.[90]

One of Gorshenin's biggest criticisms of the Indictment was that it belittled the Soviet Union's role in the war and underestimated its losses. This, he knew, could directly affect the pursuit of reparations as well as the historical record. Why was there only a partial accounting of the material damage the Nazis had inflicted on the lands, industries, and institutions of the USSR? Why was there only an abbreviated list of the places where the German invaders had carried out mass atrocities? Gorshenin wanted the document to make clear that the Nazis had targeted for mass extinction not only the Soviet Union's "Jews, Poles, and Gypsies" but "also the Russians." Gorshenin also urged Vyshinsky to verify all figures—especially relating to Katyn.[91]

Vyshinsky reviewed the recommended revisions that evening and approved them all, with one small change. Regarding the peoples the Nazis had targeted for extermination, he crossed out Russians and substituted "Slavs"—which could also cover the Ukrainians and the Belorussians. He also approved the change regarding Katyn. He then forwarded the Indictment, along with the revisions, to the Politburo Four.[92]

Molotov and Malenkov replied with several additional changes, which Vyshinsky added the next day—October 14—with the deadline now only a day away. Two of these were particularly notable. First, both leaders had disagreed with Gorshenin's characterization of the German-Soviet Non-Aggression Pact. They wanted the Indictment to state that "in spite of" the conclusion of the pact in August 1939, Nazi leaders had begun making preparations in late 1940 to invade the Soviet Union. This softened the charge of German treachery—no longer suggesting that Nazi leaders had signed the pact with the intention of launching a surprise attack. It also made Stalin and Molotov look less like fools vis-à-vis Hitler. Second, Molotov and Malenkov advised cutting the word "totalitarian," which the Americans had used throughout Count One as an adjective describing Nazi policies. By now, American and British politicians were using this term in the international press to warn of the dangers of communism and socialism.[93] Vyshinsky made the changes and sent the document back to Molotov for approval.[94]

Nikitchenko and Rudenko awaited final directives from the Kremlin. When it seemed like word was not coming, they initiated more stalling tactics. On the afternoon of October 14, Nikitchenko informed his fellow judges that he had just received word that the Indictment was not ready for presentation and that the first public meeting of the Tribunal in Berlin might have to be postponed.[95] Later in the day, Rudenko, who already knew (likely from Gorshenin) about some of Moscow's edits, told the other prosecutors that he had discovered numerous errors in the English-language versions of the "war crimes" and "crimes against humanity" sections when he had compared them against the Russian text. He insisted on another postponement.[96]

Jackson, who was back in Nuremberg, learned that afternoon from one of his assistants in Berlin, Francis Shea, that Rudenko was arguing that the prosecutors could not file the Indictment until another round of changes were made and that the Russian text would not be finished before Thursday. This was the last straw. Out of patience, he told Shea to "force the issue" and see if the British and French prosecutors would agree to make the Indictment public without the Soviets. Jackson dismissed as "trivial" the changes Rudenko was raising, noting that they mostly concerned matters of translation or adjustments to the number of people killed in different locations.[97] But as Taylor later remembered, the edit involving "the already controversial Katyn Forest Massacre" was hardly trivial.[98]

That evening, the judges summoned the prosecutors to a private meeting. Rudenko told the group that to his "great regret" the Russian-language text of the Indictment was "in a very bad form" and it was necessary to postpone the opening of the Tribunal. He added that his assistants had discovered some serious mistakes in the English-language original. Pressed for an example, he spoke of Katyn: the "whole world" knew that 11,000 people, not 925, had been murdered there. He said that it would take "two or three days" to check several other figures with his colleagues in London and in Moscow—and that this would also allow enough time to finalize the Russian text and check it against the English-language original. After fielding numerous questions from the Western judges and sensing their reluctance to grant the postponement, he pointedly reminded everyone that he could have his signature annulled on the English-language text if he chose. He assured them that he was not inclined to do so. But his options were limited. If the Tribunal convened as scheduled, he would have to publicly refuse to present the Russian copy of the Indictment. "I would have no other way out."[99]

After some discussion, the judges asked the prosecutors to leave the room but ordered them to stay in the building—probably to make sure that Rudenko didn't disappear again. Lawrence proposed that the first public session of the Tribunal be held the next day as planned and that Rudenko be permitted to insert corrected figures into the English-language text and submit the Russian version later. Biddle agreed, warning that any delay would come as "a profound shock to those who were expecting a prompt trial" and would result in negative press coverage. At this point, Nikitchenko made an emotional appeal. Moving ahead without a completed Russian-language text "would harm the interests" of the Soviet Union, the country that had "suffered the most in the war with Germany." But not only that: publicity about Soviet objections to the Indictment would discredit the entire Tribunal.[100] This was unmistakably a threat—and it succeeded. The Western judges asked Nikitchenko and Volchkov to leave the room, and after conferring in private ultimately agreed to a three-day postponement, moving the first public session of the Tribunal to Thursday, October 18. The prosecutors learned around midnight that the postponement had been granted.[101]

Everyone knew that Rudenko and Nikitchenko were acting under direct orders from Moscow. Taylor later speculated that the main issue was the Kremlin's "reluctance," as he put it, to have the Tribunal's first public session take place without a completed Russian text to submit along with the French and English ones.[102] For Moscow, though, it wasn't just a matter of the translation. The Indictment Commission was still finalizing its list of changes to the document.

Soviet leaders were also trying to determine what had happened earlier that month in Berlin. On October 16, Rudenko sent Molotov a telegram with his version of events. He admitted that he had signed the Indictment on October 6—but explained that he had done so only after having been assured by the British that he would be permitted to make changes later or annul his signature if necessary. He said nothing about his reasons for fleeing Berlin or what he had been attempting to accomplish in London.[103]

Whether or not Soviet leaders believed Rudenko's explanation, they had gotten their postponement. Still, it was unlikely that the Western prosecutors would agree to substantial revisions this late in the game. On October 15, Vyshinsky, Molotov, and Malenkov sketched out a strategy for Rudenko to use when negotiating with the other chief prosecutors and forwarded it to Beria and Mikoyan for review. The plan was as follows: Rudenko would propose the real Soviet revisions alongside several bogus revisions, which he could use as bargaining chips. The bogus revisions had no bearing on the Soviet case; for example, one of them was a call for the inclusion of more evidence about German attacks on British civilians.[104]

The Soviet leaders elaborated three real revisions in their memorandum, two of which reflected their concerns about the Munich Pact and the German-Soviet Non-Aggression Pact. According to the memorandum, the Indictment skirted the issue of French and British appeasement by suggesting that Germany had coerced Czechoslovakia into handing over "its fate and the fate of its people" to "the Führer and the Reich Chancellor," without attempting to resolve their "dispute" by peaceful means. Rudenko was to insist on a more accurate historical account, making it clear that Germany had seized first the Sudetenland and then all of Czechoslovakia by force without cause or provocation.[105]

The Indictment's characterization of the German-Soviet Non-Aggression Pact, the memorandum continued, was riddled with errors. Soviet leaders sent along a total rewrite of this section, which took the focus away from the signing of the pact in 1939 and placed it instead on the Nazis' violation of the pact and invasion of the Soviet Union less than two years later. The redraft emphasized the premeditated nature of the Nazis' invasion and subjugation of the Soviet people, noting "the annihilation of adults, women, old people, and children, especially Russians, Belorussians, and Ukrainians, and the extermination of the Jews." It stated that German troops had perpetrated these crimes on the direct orders of the Nazi government and the military's High Command. The memorandum stressed that this correction had "the greatest significance" for the USSR—and that Rudenko should refuse to sign the Indictment if the other prosecutors rejected it.[106]

The third real Soviet revision concerned the internal politics of Germany—at least on its face. It focused on a section in the new Count One that described the creation of a one-party state as a crime. Here again, the accusation hit too close to home: the Soviet Union was also a one-party state. The memorandum called for the omission of this section or for a reformulation that placed the emphasis on the criminal rather than the political nature of the Nazi Party. Finally, the memorandum enumerated a list of minor corrections to the Russian-language version of the document. Most of these were matters of word choice and translation—such as the replacement of the word *vozhd* with the word *furer* [Führer] throughout the document when referring to Hitler. *Vozhd*, the Russian word for "leader," was a common designation for Stalin.[107]

At midday on October 16, the Politburo Four finally sent Stalin the full text of the Indictment along with the draft of their memorandum for Rudenko. Stalin reviewed these materials in Sochi that afternoon. He resolved to focus Soviet efforts on securing the most important revision: the redraft of the paragraph about the German-Soviet Non-Aggression Pact. Stalin left the bogus revisions in place but took his pen to the rest of the memorandum. He crossed out the revision dealing with the one-party state and edited the instructions to Rudenko regarding the revision about the Munich Pact. Rudenko was now directed to back down if he encountered "serious opposition" to the Soviet edits. In the end, only the redraft about the German-Soviet Non-Aggression Pact remained nonnegotiable. Here, too, Stalin toned down the instructions to Rudenko. Under no circumstances was Rudenko to refuse to sign the document. If the other prosecutors objected to the Soviet revision, Rudenko was to stall for more time and consult immediately with Moscow.[108] Stalin had two main goals. He wanted the pact he had signed with Hitler to be put in the proper perspective. And he wanted the Nuremberg Trials to go forward with the participation of the Soviet Union.

With Stalin's approval, the Politburo Four forwarded the directives to Rudenko that night—instructing him to present the Soviet revisions to the Western prosecutors the following day, October 17. They also sent him a secret telegram spelling out what should have been obvious: the only "real" revision was the one about the German-Soviet Non-Aggression Pact.[109] After all that had transpired over the past few weeks, Soviet leaders did not want to risk any possible misunderstanding. They certainly didn't trust Rudenko to read between the lines.

Rudenko followed through the next morning and proposed the Soviet changes. Taylor later remembered how Rudenko uncharacteristically had "stepped out of his own area of primary concern" to suggest that the British expand their accusations to include additional German war crimes such as the bombing of England. This change was not made. Gazing out the windows at the cratered streets and leveled buildings of Berlin, the British prosecutors understood that the illegality of aerial bombings would be a difficult charge for them to make.[110] Soviet leaders had no problem with the rejection of this and other bargaining-chip revisions. Their plan worked beautifully. Rudenko successfully ushered through the revision about the German-Soviet Non-Aggression Pact. The Soviet-authored paragraph was adopted almost verbatim. (In the published version there was one small but notable difference from what Stalin had provided: the paragraph noted "the annihilation of Belorussians and Ukrainians, and the extermination of Jews," but omitted special mention of the Russians.)[111]

On the other hand, the Soviet rewrite of the section about the Munich Pact was rejected. A compromise was reached instead: the final version of the document made a link between the conclusion of the Munich Pact and the Nazi seizure of Czechoslovakia but let the Western powers off the hook by emphasizing that the Nazis had acted contrary to the pact's provisions.[112] In the end, the prosecutors chose to tread with care around the issue of appeasement.

The Soviets would have preferred more sweeping changes, but they were not negotiating from a position of strength. The Anglo-American alliance (which was stronger than ever under Truman), Rudenko's various missteps, and the shortage of translators had all put the Soviet Union at a disadvantage. The Americans had set the timeline, pressured the rest of the prosecution to keep pace, and shaped the Indictment in ways that had taken everyone—and especially the Soviets—by surprise. Many of the Americans' flourishes remained in the final document, including the charge that Nazi leaders had striven for and achieved "totalitarian control" over Germany. Most notably, the new Count One provided a means for Jackson and his team to exercise significant influence over the entire case. Nazi crimes against peace, war crimes, and crimes against humanity, Jackson would insist, could all be traced back to the Nazi conspiracy.[113]

Considering all he had been up against, Rudenko's mission had been a relative success. The Soviets had gotten the changes they had wanted the most, even over and above the ones concerning the German-Soviet Non-Aggression Pact. Critical Soviet line edits had made it into the final version of the Indictment—including the reference to the Latvian, Lithuanian, and Estonian republics and the accusation that the Germans had slaughtered 11,000 Poles in Katyn.[114] The Western prosecutors were now complicit in this Soviet lie—even if they did not yet know it.

On the morning of October 18, the IMT at long last convened its first public session in the large, ornate hall of the former People's Palace of Justice in Berlin. Nikitchenko presided as representatives of the four countries of the prosecution made brief statements and presented their copies of the Indictment to the Tribunal.[115] The entire ceremony took less than an hour. Later that day the Soviets served the Indictment on the two defendants they were guarding in Berlin, Raeder and Fritzsche. Afterward Nikitchenko and the other judges flew to Nuremberg, joined by many of the prosecutors. On October 19, the judges held an informal meeting in Nuremberg, and British major Airey Neave served the Indictment on the twenty defendants who were already in the Nuremberg prison. It was a fitting role for Neave, who had achieved world fame with his daring escape from Colditz Castle, a prisoner-of-war camp in Saxony.[116]

After brief discussions, the judges set the opening date of the Nuremberg Trials for November 20. They then dispersed, agreeing to reconvene in Nuremberg on October 29 in order to review defense petitions and the rules for the Tribunal.[117] In Moscow, Soviet leaders took stock of all that had happened over the past few months and contemplated their next moves. The October countdown had been a sign of what was to come for the Soviets. The next four weeks would be a frenetic race to the starting line.

CHAPTER 4 | Ready or Not

WITH THE NUREMBERG Trials set to start on November 20, Iona Nikitchenko now fully realized that the Soviets were in over their heads. There was far more work to do in the next four weeks than the Soviet delegation could handle. But that wasn't the only challenge the Soviets faced. Nikitchenko had also come to understand that the Western judges were envisioning a very different kind of trial from the ones he was used to. In the Soviet judicial system, guilty verdicts could be assured; it was not uncommon for prosecutors, judges, investigators, and defense attorneys to all work together toward a common goal that everyone had agreed on ahead of time. At Nuremberg, none of this would be the case.

Nikitchenko's visit to Nuremberg with the Western judges on October 18 and 19 had only heightened his unease. On October 22, shortly after returning to Berlin, he sent a telegram to Vyshinsky to share his concerns. The Americans were planning to maintain sole control over all the defendants in the Nuremberg prison, he reported. This meant that the two defendants the Soviets were delivering to Nuremberg, Erich Raeder and Hans Fritzsche, would be under American authority. At the same time, the Americans were expecting all the countries of the prosecution to provide their own interpreters and translators. This would not be easy for the Soviets, who had shot many of their German speakers as suspected spies. While the Party had recently sent some interpreters to Nuremberg, few could accurately translate from spoken English, French, or German into

Russian, or vice versa. Unless Moscow remedied this problem—and fast—
the Soviet case would be in serious trouble. Nikitchenko's telegram was
pushed up the chain of command to Stalin.[1]

Soviet leaders, already informed of the need for translators by Vyshinsky,
were in the process of finalizing their selection of all kinds of personnel
for Nuremberg. On October 20, Stalin personally approved twenty-four
correspondents to cover the trials. This list included writers and artists whose
wartime reporting had roused the Soviet population, such as the novelist and
journalist Ilya Ehrenburg, the playwright Vsevolod Vishnevsky, and the political cartoonist Boris Efimov. It also included special correspondents from
the Soviet news agency TASS, such as the photographer Evgeny Khaldei,
who had followed the Red Army to Germany and documented the Battle

FIGURE 4.1 The four judges and their alternates met briefly in Nuremberg on
October 19, 1945. From left: British alternate judge Norman Birkett, British
judge (and Tribunal president) Geoffrey Lawrence, Soviet alternate judge Alexander
Volchkov, Soviet judge Iona Nikitchenko, American alternate judge John Parker,
American judge Francis Biddle, French alternate judge Robert Falco, French judge
Henri Donnedieu de Vabres. Both Nikitchenko and Falco had participated in the
deliberations at the London Conference before being moved by their governments
to the judges' bench.

Credit: State Archive of the Russian Federation f. 10140, op. 2, d. 152, l. 1.
Photographer: Viktor Temin.

of Berlin.[2] These were more than just writers and artists; they were the conscience of the Soviet Union.

Even with Stalin directly involved, rivalries within the Soviet government shaped the process of filling out the Soviet delegation. The press corps was no exception. TASS was not the only major Soviet news organization; Deputy Foreign Minister Solomon Lozovsky had been hoping that the Soviet Information Bureau (Sovinformburo), which he oversaw and which had conducted the Soviet Union's international press campaign during the war, would also have a role in covering the IMT. He asked Party leaders on October 22 to approve the dispatch of at least five Sovinformburo correspondents to Nuremberg to write articles and place Soviet materials in the foreign press. When only two were approved (the writer Mikhail Dolgopolov and the photographer Viktor Kinelovsky), Lozovsky turned to Molotov with an appeal to Soviet pride.[3] According to the British trade paper *World's Press News,* American authorities had given the Soviet Union far fewer spots for its press corps in Nuremberg than they had allowed for the other countries of the prosecution: the United States would have around 100 correspondents, Britain fifty, France around forty-five, and the USSR between twenty-five and thirty. These numbers were insulting, Lozovsky argued. He further observed that almost all of the Soviet correspondents selected thus far were from the major newspapers in Moscow and Leningrad, when by rights there should be correspondents from all of the republics that had endured the German occupation. He urged Molotov to talk to the Americans about increasing the number of Soviet spots to fifty. In fact, Stalin himself did not want to send a large contingent of correspondents into the American zone, outside the Party's direct control; the Soviets had requested only twenty-five to thirty spots. Molotov dismissed Lozovsky's appeal for the time being.[4]

While Lozovsky's focus was on Soviet prestige, Stalin's greater concern at the moment was control. Only the most loyal personnel would be sent to Nuremberg, and even they would be shadowed by Soviet security agents. Soviet leaders expected to oversee all activity from afar. The Soviet prosecutors and judges in particular were supposed to check in with Moscow on a regular basis and receive sign-off on all decisions, large and small. Rudenko's antics around the signing of the Indictment had made such an approach seem especially necessary. In theory, this degree of surveillance and supervision would give the Soviets the ability to shape the trials. In actual practice, it ended up depriving the Soviet delegation of flexibility and reducing Soviet influence. In the run-up to the start of the trials, the other Allies would make decisions that would determine the course of Nuremberg while the Soviet representatives were sending reports to Moscow and waiting for responses.

The serious business of finalizing preparations for the IMT sometimes played out as a farce.

Even as Soviet leaders carefully vetted personnel for Nuremberg, some of their plans for the IMT were already unraveling for reasons outside anyone's control. On October 24, Jackson sent Rudenko a telegram informing him that the industrialist Gustav Krupp had been paralyzed by a stroke and the case against him would likely be dismissed. Krupp and his firm had financed Hitler and had later made a huge profit exploiting slave labor from the concentration camps. Soviet leaders had been intending to use the Krupp case to demonstrate the role of capital in German crimes and to establish the guilt of German industrialists as a group, setting a precedent for future trials. These plans were now thrown into question. Stalin and Molotov learned about this development from the Soviet ambassador in London, Fedor Gusev, who had intercepted the telegram before forwarding it to Rudenko in Germany.[5]

A few hours later, Rudenko, who had just arrived in Nuremberg, sent Vyshinsky the same news—but with additional information. Jackson had floated the idea of bringing Krupp's son, Alfried, to trial in his father's place, along with two or three other industrialists. Alfried Krupp had taken over the family business before the war and had fostered ties with Hitler. Rudenko suggested to Vyshinsky that it would be prudent to seek medical confirmation of Gustav Krupp's illness. He added that the prosecutors had raised the possibility of requesting medical evaluations of several of the defendants, partly to counter rumors that Hess, who was claiming amnesia, was unfit to stand trial. Noting that the chief prosecutors would soon be discussing these questions, he asked for instructions. Vyshinsky directed Rudenko to oppose any supposition that the case against Gustav was in peril; if the defendant was too ill to be moved to Nuremberg, he could be tried separately.[6]

Soviet leaders had settled on telephoned telegrams as the best approach for transmitting information from Nuremberg to Berlin to Moscow and back again. Encrypted messages could be sent quickly over the phone lines in pieces. Those phone lines were about to see a lot of activity. After the October 26 meeting of the Committee of Chief Prosecutors in Nuremberg, Rudenko informed Vyshinsky that the prosecutors had agreed to seek a four-power medical evaluation of Gustav Krupp and asked him to send an eminent Soviet physician to Nuremberg. He also conveyed Jackson's proposal to add Alfried Krupp and other industrialists to the Indictment. Nikitchenko (who was reading Rudenko's messages in Berlin before sending them on) tacked on his opinion that adding more defendants would delay the start of the trials by almost two weeks. Rudenko also reported that the prosecutors were contemplating the creation of a four-power psychiatric commission to examine Hess, Goering, Robert Ley, and any other defendants who showed signs of mental illness.[7] (In fact, Ley had committed suicide the night before, hanging himself with a towel in his prison cell.)[8]

Vyshinsky instructed Rudenko not to question the mental health of any of the defendants. If the other prosecutors pushed for a psychiatric commission, Rudenko should plan for the participation of a Soviet psychiatrist, to be named later. Most critically, Rudenko was to oppose the addition of Alfried Krupp or other industrialists to the case, since this would result in a postponement of the trial, which, as Vyshinsky put it, would be "undesirable."[9]

The translation problem meanwhile continued to vex the Soviets. The diplomat Vladimir Semenov sent a separate message to Vyshinsky from Berlin that evening, imploring Soviet leaders to swiftly send someone from the Ministry of Foreign Affairs who spoke top-notch German to assist Rudenko. The Americans had given the Soviet prosecution access to evidence from the archive of the German Foreign Office and the archive of the former Reich minister for the Occupied Eastern Territories, Alfred Rosenberg—evidence that, he stressed, the Ministry of Foreign Affairs had not yet seen.[10] What Semenov did not report but had prompted his note was that Jackson had angrily threatened to cut off Soviet and French access to these materials until the two delegations fixed their translation problems. Jackson had further warned that if the Soviets were unable to translate their Russian-language documents into German, the entire Soviet part of the case would be thrown out of court.[11]

David Maxwell Fyfe thought that Jackson was behaving unfairly. When the Committee of Chief Prosecutors reconvened on October 27 it became apparent that he had gone behind Jackson's back to offer assistance to the Soviets and the French. Rudenko and Charles Dubost made a show of expressing their gratitude to Maxwell Fyfe and announced that "thanks to the British" their German translations would soon be ready.[12] Jackson's attempt to play hardball had backfired.

In a show of camaraderie, Rudenko, Dubost, and Maxwell Fyfe stood together at the October 27 meeting to vote down Jackson's proposal to add Alfried Krupp to the case, on the grounds that it would delay the start of the trial. From there the alliances shifted. Dubost proposed the organization of a second trial that would focus on the German industrialists who had aided Hitler. Rudenko supported Dubost—but Maxwell Fyfe and Jackson, unwilling to commit their governments to anything beyond Nuremberg, argued against him. The four prosecutors did agree to request a psychiatric

FIGURE 4.2 The creation of windows in the courtroom for the use of radio commentators, photographers, and cameramen, September 1945. The courtroom was under construction for much of the fall.

Credit: United States Holocaust Memorial Museum, courtesy of National Archives and Records Administration, College Park.

examination of Hess, prompting the Soviet government to prepare three experts for travel: a psychiatrist, a neurologist, and an internist.[13]

Nikitchenko arrived in Nuremberg on October 28. The first informal meeting of the Tribunal, held the next morning in a small room in the Palace of Justice, was an understated affair. The four judges and their alternates sat around a table covered by a U.S. Army blanket and tried to ignore the din of hammering and sawing coming from the courtroom down the hall, now under heavy construction, while discussing the selection of defense attorneys. Airey Neave, who had delivered the Indictment to most of the defendants and was now responsible for helping them secure counsel, appealed to the judges for guidance. A number of defendants, including Goering, were requesting former Nazi Party members as attorneys, and Neave was uncertain how to respond.[14]

The judges offered their opinions—and Nikitchenko and the Soviet alternate judge Alexander Volchkov found themselves in sharp disagreement

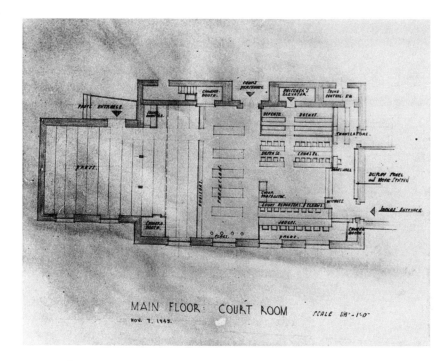

MAIN FLOOR: COURT ROOM   *SCALE 1/8"-1'-0"*
NOV. 7. 1945.

FIGURE 4.3 An American sketch of the main floor of the Nuremberg courtroom, November 7, 1945. The sketch shows the press box—but not the visitors' gallery, which was above it on the second floor.

Credit: United States Holocaust Memorial Museum, courtesy of Randy Cole.

with their Western colleagues. Francis Biddle argued that the Nuremberg Charter "stated unequivocally" that defendants were entitled to "the counsel of their choice." Tribunal president Geoffrey Lawrence agreed that this included anyone credentialed to practice law in the German courts. The Soviet judges expressed astonishment that former Nazis would be allowed to serve as defense attorneys. Nikitchenko protested that such men should themselves be sitting "in the dock" and not playing official roles in the trial. Neave later recalled that this argument continued well into the night by the dim light of an army lamp. In the end the Soviet judges were overruled. Nearly half of the defendants would select former Nazis as their attorneys.[15]

The judges met in closed session several more times that week. After approving the prosecutors' request to appoint a joint medical commission to examine Gustav Krupp and dealing with logistical questions such as the salaries for defense counsel, they turned to the Tribunal's rules of procedure. Here again the Soviet judges were flabbergasted by just how much latitude was being given to the defendants. Nikitchenko was especially upset about

Rule Four, which allowed the defendants to request any witnesses who might help their cases. He argued unsuccessfully to give each of the prosecutors veto power.[16]

The judges also discussed using a system of simultaneous interpretation based on a translation system that had been developed by IBM and installed at the League of Nations in 1931. At the League of Nations, interpretation had been consecutive: speeches had been translated ahead of time and then read simultaneously in multiple languages. With this new system—which would make its debut in Nuremberg—interpreters for the four languages of the Tribunal (English, Russian, French, and German), using microphones and headsets, would directly translate the speaker's words over separate channels while he or she was speaking. The judges viewed this innovative technology with a mixture of enthusiasm and skepticism. Would it actually work? (No one talked about the fact that IBM, like the Krupps, had done a lucrative business with Hitler.)[17] On the evening of October 31, Nikitchenko informed Vyshinsky that the Tribunal was planning to test the IBM system in a couple of weeks, which would require a group of skilled Soviet interpreters to be in Nuremberg and at their stations.[18]

Jackson's determination to maintain American control over as much of the case as possible only increased. He was peeved that Maxwell Fyfe had gone out of his way to help the French and the Soviets, whom he continued to regard with irritation and sometimes outright disdain. Events unfolding in Europe had convinced him that neither the French nor the Soviets shared American sensibilities about what constituted a fair trial. Writing to President Truman, he complained that the French trial of Pierre Laval (the prime minister of the collaborationist Vichy regime) had been "a scandal throughout Europe" and that the Soviet-run trials taking place in Hungary and the Balkans were "nothing that we would recognize as trials." Jackson was also incensed that the Soviet Union and France were doing "some of the very things we are prosecuting Germans for." The Soviet Union "asserts sovereignty over the Baltic States based on no title except conquest"; French violations of the Geneva Convention were so egregious that the American command was "taking back prisoners sent to them."[19]

As the judges debated the Tribunal's regulations, Jackson lamented having to cooperate with the Soviets at all. He was most worried about Katyn and how it might undermine the Allied case. He had good reason for concern. On October 20, Bill Donovan (who had arrived in Nuremberg in early October, after President Truman's shutdown of the OSS) had passed him a top-secret report he had just received alleging Soviet guilt for the massacre.[20]

As detailed in the report, Fabian von Schlabrendorff, a former German soldier who had attempted to assassinate Hitler in 1943, had told the OSS that the Indictment contained a glaring inaccuracy: Katyn was not a Nazi crime. Schlabrendorff stated that he had been an eyewitness to the discovery of the gravesite and was certain that the Soviets had carried out the massacre. He further reported that this "undeniable fact" was also known by countless German soldiers and officers, as well as non-German doctors, Polish priests, and British officers. Schlabrendorff advised switching out this line in the Indictment with an actual German crime, such as the shooting of captured Soviet commissars.[21]

This information had come too late: the Indictment had been lodged with the Tribunal two days before and had already been made public. There was little Jackson could do short of convincing Rudenko to not offer evidence supporting the Katyn charge and thus to let the matter drop.[22] Jackson knew this was unlikely. Since receiving Donovan's report, he had been seething about having given in to the Soviets about Katyn and potentially contaminating the case. Around November 1, he confided to Maxwell Fyfe his fear that "there will be trouble about Katyn."[23]

More recently, Jackson had been briefed about the details of Soviet-German collaboration on the eve of the war. He had reviewed a secret report provided by U.S. Army Military Intelligence on the interrogation of former German ambassador Gustav Hilger, who had been the interpreter at Ribbentrop's August 1939 meeting with Molotov and Stalin in Moscow. Hilger had told his American interrogators precisely how the German and Soviet leaders had plotted to divide up Eastern Europe. Ribbentrop had made a "sweeping gesture on a map," affirming German indifference to Latvia, Estonia, and Finland. He and Stalin had agreed initially that Lithuania would remain in what they called Germany's "zone of influence," that the Soviets could have Bessarabia, and that Poland would be divided along the Vistula River. After the German and Soviet invasion of Poland, Hilger had attested, the final borders were adjusted in a second agreement.[24] A member of Jackson's investigative team had alerted him on October 5 that Hilger was willing to serve as a witness for the prosecution but had cautioned that this might cause "complications."[25] Those complications, it was now clear, concerned the Soviets.

By early November, Jackson had seen more, and more detailed, information than he had probably wanted concerning Soviet war crimes and crimes against peace—and from witnesses whom U.S. intelligence considered absolutely reliable. What he did not suspect was that he now knew more about all of this than Rudenko or Yuri Pokrovsky.

While Jackson stewed about the Soviets, Soviet leaders could not understand why Rudenko and Nikitchenko had been ceding so much ground to the other countries of the prosecution. They had managed to get key Soviet edits—including the one about Katyn—into the Indictment but after that had been outvoted or outmaneuvered on many other issues. The Tribunal's recent rulings to allow the defendants to select Nazi attorneys and to call witnesses of their choice heightened Moscow's worries.

Molotov was also troubled by the trial plan, which Vyshinsky had just sent to him for review. The U.S. prosecution would open with a presentation on the Nazi conspiracy; the British would speak next on crimes against peace; the French and then the Soviets would follow up with presentations on war crimes and crimes against humanity (with the French focusing on Western Europe and the Soviets covering Eastern Europe and the Soviet Union). In his memorandum to Molotov, Vyshinsky had played up the significance of the "war crimes" section.[26] Molotov was not impressed. He continued to see the "crimes against peace" charge as the heart of the case—and he wanted the Soviet chief prosecutor to give this presentation.

On the evening of November 1, Vyshinsky sent Rudenko urgent instructions to reopen discussions with the other prosecutors about the division of the case. Rudenko was to prevail on the British, who had proven more sympathetic than the Americans, to cede to him the presentation on crimes against peace. He was to withhold his agreement to the trial plan until he received the go-ahead from Moscow.[27] The problem was that Rudenko had already agreed to the trial plan. Furthermore, the Western prosecutors seemed to think that Nikitchenko had signed off on this division of the case back in August, when he was a member of the Committee of Chief Prosecutors. (Nikitchenko, for his part, believed that he had only agreed to the division of work for the writing of the Indictment.) Making success even less likely was the fact that the British were already fighting off American encroachment into this part of the case. There was significant overlap between Counts One and Two (conspiring to wage aggressive war was by definition a crime against peace)—and Maxwell Fyfe and Jackson both wanted to present the most sensational documents.[28]

Vyshinsky summoned Rudenko and Nikitchenko back to Moscow on November 5 to appear before the Indictment Commission. It was the worst possible time for them to leave Nuremberg. At a November 7 meeting, in Rudenko's absence, Jackson and Maxwell Fyfe worked out an agreement about dividing up the evidence for Counts One and Two. The U.S. prosecution would present on the Nazi "conspiracy to wage aggressive war" up through the invasion of Poland in September 1939. The British prosecution would finish the presentation on Poland and cover the Nazi takeover of southern and northern Europe. Next, the U.S. prosecution would come back in to prove the predatory nature of the attack on the Soviet Union. Jackson and Maxwell Fyfe were now in accord, but Rudenko had been shut out. The setbacks for the Soviets continued that afternoon when the four-power medical commission submitted to the Tribunal its opinion that Gustav Krupp was unfit to stand trial.[29]

November 7 had been a difficult day for the Soviets in Nuremberg; nonetheless, they prepared for a celebration. That evening, in honor of the twenty-eighth anniversary of the October Revolution, Soviet investigator Georgy Alexandrov hosted a party for all of the prosecutors and their staffs at the Soviet compound on the Eichendorffstrasse. Maxwell Fyfe, Dubost, Donovan, and Pokrovsky toasted the Red Army and the Russian people with large glasses of cognac. Bowls of caviar and other hors d'oeuvres were served, and a member of the Soviet delegation played piano in the background. Jackson refused to join this celebration—even after Alexandrov drove twenty miles to Jackson's lodgings on the Lindenstrasse to get him. Writing home about this incident, Maxwell Fyfe noted the "horror which Jackson's conduct caused" among the other Allies and criticized his lack of "good manners." Jackson was "a funny man if you think that sort of thing is funny," he wrote, "even funny-peculiar."[30]

Rudenko and Nikitchenko missed all of this. They were back in Moscow, being skewered for their mistakes. Vyshinsky opened a November 9 meeting of the Indictment Commission by reminding Rudenko of his "irresponsible actions" and "breaches of duty" in London and Berlin, including his many failures to fulfill Moscow's directives. Because of Rudenko's recklessness, he complained, the Soviets had lost valuable opportunities to negotiate. He next rebuked Nikitchenko for keeping "aloof" from the work of the Soviet prosecution in London and Germany and for consenting in October to the appointment of Lawrence as Tribunal president. "Really, we did not give such directives!"[31] Rudenko's and Nikitchenko's protestations and deflections of blame fell on deaf ears. Both were ordered to submit full explanations of their actions in writing and to follow Party discipline going forward.[32]

With Rudenko and Nikitchenko duly chastised and still in the room, the Indictment Commission reviewed a preliminary draft of the Soviet prosecution's opening speech and discussed the Tribunal's pending decisions about Krupp and Hess.[33] The night before, Volchkov, who was sitting in for Nikitchenko in Nuremberg, had informed Vyshinsky that the Tribunal was establishing a psychiatric commission to examine Hess and that it would announce its decision concerning Gustav Krupp at its November 13 meeting.[34] Acknowledging that the case against Krupp was likely a lost cause, the commission directed Rudenko and Nikitchenko to focus their efforts on insisting that Hess was sane. The commission also approved the oath for witnesses that Volchkov had recently sent from Nuremberg, but only after changing "absolute truth" to "truth."[35]

The Indictment Commission also addressed outstanding personnel issues. Vyshinsky announced that the USSR would be sending roughly twice as many correspondents to Nuremberg as previously anticipated. The correspondents on the expanded list included the filmmaker Roman Karmen and journalists from a number of the Soviet republics. The Party had taken Lozovsky's advice after all. More concerning to Vyshinsky was the continuing shortage of interpreters. The Ministry of Foreign Affairs had just dispatched several more interpreters to Nuremberg, including the Swarthmore-educated Oleg Troyanovsky (who had interpreted for Nikitchenko and Trainin in London); the All-Union Society for Cultural Ties Abroad had agreed to send six interpreters who had already been cleared with the NKVD. Viktor Abakumov, chief of SMERSH, suggested that the German interpreter he had sent to Nuremberg with Raeder could also be used for the trials.[36]

Finally, Vyshinsky addressed the question of witnesses. The Indictment Commission had tentatively approved eighteen possible witnesses for the Soviet prosecution—and Vyshinsky suggested that it select another seventy to hold in reserve. For this task, the Indictment Commission created a subcommission that included Extraordinary State Commission members Pavel Bogyavlensky and Dmitry Kudryavtsev.[37] Vyshinsky directed them to find specific types of witnesses—particularly civilians who had witnessed the murder of children, as well as Red Army soldiers who had liberated German-occupied cities, villages, and death camps. He told Rudenko and Nikitchenko to find out if the Western prosecutors definitely intended to call witnesses and, if so, how many and when.[38]

Immediately after the meeting, Vyshinsky asked the Party to prepare multi-entry visas for Rudenko and Nikitchenko, noting that they would be summoned repeatedly to Moscow for further instructions.[39] For now Nikitchenko and Rudenko would remain in Moscow a little longer to work on the Soviet case. Vyshinsky told Volchkov to expect Nikitchenko in Nuremberg around November 15, with interpreters in tow. He instructed Volchkov to have the Tribunal reschedule the testing of the IBM interpretation equipment to accommodate this time frame.[40]

Back in Nuremberg, Jackson was trying to keep things on course. Members of his staff who were interrogating defendants in the Nuremberg prison had been warning him about a German defense plan to use the courtroom to expose Soviet, French, and British crimes against peace. Then on November 6 (the day before Alexandrov's party) Donovan had shared with him intelligence indicating that the defense would seek to call witnesses to testify about Soviet guilt for Katyn.[41]

On November 9—the same day Rudenko and Nikitchenko were being disciplined in Moscow—Jackson alerted Maxwell Fyfe, Dubost, and Pokrovsky that trouble lay ahead. At a meeting of the Committee of Chief Prosecutors, he warned that the defense was planning to launch "political attacks" on the countries of the prosecution during the trials. He shared the information he had received indicating that the accused and their attorneys would likely focus on the actions of England, Russia, and France in connection with the "aggressive war" charge. This of course was an area where the Soviets were particularly vulnerable, given the secret protocols and the subsequent Soviet invasions of Latvia, Lithuania, Estonia, Finland, and Poland. Jackson suggested that the United States, "being late to the war and remote from the scene," was immune to these kinds of attacks and therefore in the best position to shut them down. He proposed that each of the prosecutors draw up a confidential memorandum enumerating those wartime practices and policies of his own government that could be fodder for the defense's allegations.[42] In effect, Jackson had just asked his colleagues to come clean about their countries' war crimes.

The Soviets had little reason to trust Jackson and his motives. The Soviet Union and the United States were simultaneously allies and rivals: they shared the goal of bringing the former Nazi leaders to justice, but it was clear by the fall of 1945 that they had competing visions for the future of Europe. American and British leaders had been watching Soviet actions in Eastern Europe with growing unease. By this point the Soviets had installed a puppet government in Poland and were carrying out mass arrests and deportations of political opponents (as well as Nazi collaborators) throughout Eastern Europe. At the same time, Soviet leaders worried about the postwar Anglo-American alignment.[43]

Cooperation and mistrust coexisted on many levels. The United States and the Soviet Union were cooperating in the prosecution of Nazi leaders and organizations. But U.S. officials in the American zone of Germany were refusing to repatriate Soviet citizens (including groups of Ukrainians) whom Soviet leaders accused of having actively collaborated with the Nazis.[44] Then of course there was Jackson himself, who was frequently impatient with the

Soviet delegation and dismissive of Soviet concerns. He had snubbed the Soviets on more than one occasion and had threatened and rebuked them over their lack of preparation. He routinely insisted on deadlines that were difficult for the Soviets to meet and then expressed impatience when they could not keep up.

Those deadlines kept coming, and the Soviets continued to lag behind. On November 12, Volchkov informed Nikitchenko (who was still in Moscow, along with Rudenko) that the Tribunal would be testing the IBM simultaneous interpretation system the next day as planned—without waiting for the Soviet interpreters. Volchkov also reported that Jackson was still pushing hard for the addition of Alfried Krupp to the Indictment, in spite of the other prosecutors' objections. The judges had decided, Volchkov added, that the full Tribunal—the four judges and their alternates—should consider this matter. Volchkov also updated Nikitchenko on issues raised by the defense, including a request from defendant Julius Streicher's attorney, Hanns Marx, to delay the start of the trial for two to three weeks. Marx, another former Nazi Party member, had signed on to the case late and was asking for more time to prepare his defense. Vyshinsky jumped into the exchange and responded to Volchkov at once: "You should not object to delaying the trial and exchanging G. Krupp with A. Krupp."[45]

This marked a complete reversal of Vyshinsky's earlier instructions. He had come to understand just how unprepared the Soviet prosecution was for the start of the trials, now little more than a week away. Earlier that day, the Party's Department of Agitation and Propaganda had sent Vyshinsky a scathing critique of the proposed Soviet opening speech, deriding it as "carelessly put together" and calling out its many "hackneyed phrases" and "factual errors." Some of those errors were egregious. The speech stated that the German army had taken aggressive action against France and England in September 1939, when the invasion of France had actually taken place in May 1940. It praised the Red Army for having "disrupted" Nazi plans but did not describe its heroic role in defeating Hitler's forces and liberating the peoples of Europe.[46] The speech would have to be revised.

Vyshinsky's instructions to Volchkov to support a postponement had come from Stalin's inner circle. Using the Krupp case to delay the opening of the trials now seemed like the last best hope to regroup and catch up. Early in the morning on Wednesday, November 14, Rudenko phoned Jackson and Dubost from Moscow and offered support for the motion to add Alfried Krupp to the Indictment.[47]

So began another round of Soviet delaying tactics. On November 14, the Tribunal held its first public hearing in Nuremberg—again without Nikitchenko. The judges and prosecutors gathered in the remodeled courtroom. There was no fanfare, no crush of reporters: most of the correspondents had not yet arrived. All the Western judges and their alternates were present, but Volchkov alone represented the Soviets.

The main item of discussion was the Krupps. The Krupps' attorney, Theodor Klefisch, a criminal defense lawyer from Cologne, presented a motion to sever Gustav from the case on the grounds that he was too ill to stand trial. Klefisch also argued against the proposal to try Alfried, citing the injustice of indicting a man in place of his father. When it was time for the prosecutors to speak, Pokrovsky made a show of deferring to Dubost and Jackson—who agreed that Gustav could not be tried but insisted that Alfried be added to the case. The French government, Dubost stated, was intent on bringing the industrialists to justice. British chief prosecutor Hartley Shawcross (who had recently arrived in Nuremberg) opposed them, calling instead for the trial of Gustav in absentia. "This is a court of justice, not a game in which you can play a substitute if one member of the team falls sick," he argued.[48]

The Tribunal met in closed session that afternoon and voted unanimously to drop Gustav from the case. Volchkov found himself alone among the judges, however, in supporting the plan to try Alfried in his place.[49]

After midnight, Rudenko sent Volchkov and Pokrovsky news from Moscow that Nikitchenko would be flying to Germany in the morning. Rudenko predicted optimistically that the question of delaying the trial would be settled "favorably and exactly according to the plan we put forward." (Volchkov had not yet told him about the judges' closed session.) When morning came, Rudenko sent Pokrovsky another message, emphasizing that Moscow did not want the proposal for a delay to come from the Soviet delegation.[50]

The Tribunal convened its second public hearing in Nuremberg on November 15, with Volchkov again sitting in for Nikitchenko. After announcing their decision about Gustav Krupp, the judges fielded questions from the defense attorneys. The Tribunal had been planning to rule on Marx's request to postpone the trial, but he withdrew his petition after Lawrence assured defense counsel that they could continue working on their clients' cases after the trials opened. Marx did, however, raise doubts about Streicher's sanity. He urged the Tribunal to pursue a psychiatric evaluation of his client—but refused to file a formal motion, because Streicher insisted he was "mentally completely normal." When Lawrence explained that such a motion had to be made, Pokrovsky, seeing another chance for a delay, offered to file one, noting that he too had questions about Streicher's mental state.[51]

Nikitchenko arrived in Berlin on the evening of November 15, and Volchkov briefed him by phone about the day's events. After midnight, Nikitchenko broke the news to Vyshinsky that the Western judges had opposed adding Alfried Krupp to the list of defendants, and shared Volchkov's rundown of the judges' deliberations. The British judges were completely against trying Alfried. The French judges wanted to try him but had argued that this would require a separate Indictment, since adding another name to the original document would mean serving it anew to all of the accused and would thus delay the trial by a month. The American judges had pointed out that the prosecutors had the right to append a separate Indictment to the main one and that two weeks should be enough time for Krupp's attorney to prepare—but they had noted that this time frame would violate the rules of procedure, which stipulated that the Indictment had to be delivered to the accused thirty days before the start of the trial (which was still set for November 20).[52]

Nikitchenko then assured Vyshinsky that Volchkov had hatched a plan. During an informal exchange of opinions among the judges, Volchkov had shrewdly posited that the prosecutors originally had proposed a thirty-day window because the full Indictment was "a bulky document" and that less time should be needed to review the charges against one person. The American and French judges, Nikitchenko relayed, had "liked this idea." Volchkov and Pokrovsky had then agreed that Pokrovsky would bring a proposal to the Committee of Chief Prosecutors to amend the rules of procedure to allow for a two-week window between serving the Indictment and starting the trial— and to move the trial's opening date to December 2. Pokrovsky could then work with Jackson's team to draw up an Indictment against Alfried Krupp.[53]

With the clock ticking, Vyshinsky convened another meeting of the Indictment Commission on November 16 in Moscow and shared his skepticism about the Soviets being ready even by December 2. Rudenko still did not have a plan for conducting the trial, and the Soviet prosecution desperately needed a few more weeks to study the evidence and prepare its presentations, Vyshinsky reported. He also passed on the recent news from Nikitchenko about the Krupps—and noted that the outcome remained uncertain. Bogdan Kobulov, deputy chief of the NKGB, then took the floor and shared disturbing intelligence he had received from Nuremberg: Goering, Wilhelm Keitel, Alfred Jodl, and other defendants were using the pretrial interrogations to make allegations against the Soviet Union. Raeder had even told British investigators on film that he had confessed to the Russians under duress. Vyshinsky agreed that this was an outrage. A delay, he noted hopefully, would enable the Indictment Commission to install one of its members in Nuremberg as an observer.[54]

While hoping for a postponement, Vyshinsky continued to make preparations for the imminent start of the trials. That afternoon, he directed the General Staff of the Red Army to dispatch more cipher clerks and portable radio transmitters to Nuremberg. He also asked the Extraordinary State Commission to send one or two experts to Nuremberg to assist the Soviet prosecution with evidentiary materials.[55] Around 8 p.m., Vyshinsky received word from Semenov that Pokrovsky had succeeded: the Committee of Chief Prosecutors had voted three to one, with Shawcross dissenting, to submit a motion to the Tribunal to try Alfried Krupp and to change the rules of procedure along the lines Pokrovsky had recommended. The judges were now considering this motion in closed session. Semenov also noted that the American, British, and French honor guards had all arrived and asked if the Soviet Military Administration in Germany (SVAG) might send twenty-five or so of its guards from Berlin to join them. (The Soviets apparently had not planned for this ahead of time.) This must be done before November 19, he stressed, lest there be speculation that the Soviets were "striving to delay the start of the trial."[56]

Two hours later, the postponement strategy collapsed. Pokrovsky sent Rudenko the bad news: the Western judges had rejected the prosecutors' motion to amend the Indictment to add Alfried Krupp. They had instead agreed to leave Gustav Krupp's name on the document, in the event that he recovered after the trials started. The IMT would therefore open on November 20 as planned. Pokrovsky added that there was still a glimmer of hope for a delay. The judges had ordered a psychiatric evaluation of Streicher—and Jackson had confided to him that the American specialist would not arrive until November 19. The Tribunal would also consider the matter of trying Martin Bormann, Hitler's private secretary, in absentia, which might provide another possible avenue for a postponement.[57] (Bormann had in fact died in Berlin on May 2, though this would not be confirmed for another twenty-seven years.)

Noting that Nikitchenko had finally appeared in Nuremberg that evening, Pokrovsky asked Rudenko about his travel plans. Pokrovsky then added, matter-of-factly, that in response to similar questions from the Western prosecutors he had started a rumor that Rudenko had fallen ill and was showing symptoms of malaria. He asked Rudenko to communicate whether his health would allow him to be in Nuremberg on November 20 or if "the doctors" would require him to convalesce in Moscow for several more days.[58]

Pokrovsky was clever to choose malaria as Rudenko's putative illness. Wartime conditions had led to an increase in the disease in Ukraine and other parts of the Soviet Union. Malaria could take months to develop and could attack in cycles of severity and relative remission; it was unpredictable enough to give the Soviets some cover.[59] Pokrovsky's gambit provided the inspiration for a final Soviet campaign to delay the opening of the IMT. Just before midnight on November 16, Vyshinsky told Pokrovsky to give the Tribunal a written statement explaining that the Soviet chief prosecutor was ill and would need two weeks to recover. If there was talk of moving ahead before Rudenko returned, Pokrovsky was to claim that he was not familiar enough with the case to stand in for him and that Rudenko was strongly opposed to the proceedings starting without him. Pokrovsky was to carry out these orders at once and report the results to Moscow.[60] Rudenko's "malaria" was beginning to take on substance.

On the morning of November 17, Pokrovsky informed the Western prosecutors that his supposition about Rudenko's health had been correct. He assured them that Rudenko's condition was not so serious as to raise the question of replacing him with another member of the Soviet prosecution. Reminding his colleagues that according to the Nuremberg Charter the chief prosecutor alone could carry out certain duties, he asked them to join him in informing the judges that "unforeseen circumstances" would prevent the trials from opening on November 20. He emphasized that the Soviet government had not approved a substitute for Rudenko; none of his assistants had the authority to represent the Soviet prosecution at the trials.[61]

Rudenko's malaria became a topic of gossip even as things were proceeding in Nuremberg. The Tribunal held its third public hearing that morning, now before a small crowd of correspondents, and Maxwell Fyfe and Pokrovsky both spoke out in favor of trying Bormann in absentia. The judges agreed.[62] When the Tribunal went into closed session that afternoon, Nikitchenko tried, unsuccessfully, to reopen the matter of Alfried Krupp. He laid out a number of reasons for delaying the start of the trials: the four countries of the prosecution had not yet coordinated their opening speeches; the psychiatric commission had not submitted its report about Hess; Bormann's attorney, who had yet to be named, would need time to prepare; and Rudenko needed time to convalesce. A postponement, he added almost as an afterthought, would also give Alfried Krupp's attorney enough time to prepare his case. The Western judges were unmoved. The trials would still open in three days.[63]

Nikitchenko sent Vyshinsky an update before midnight on November 17, noting that the Tribunal would formally consider Pokrovsky's request for a postponement in the morning. Anticipating a rejection, Nikitchenko posited that it might be necessary for him to declare that in Rudenko's absence the Soviets would not be able to participate in the opening of the trials on November 20. Vyshinsky's response was immediate: Nikitchenko was to give no such statement. Instead, he should quickly relay the Tribunal's decision to Moscow and await word as to his next steps.[64]

As Nikitchenko tried to maneuver for a delay, Moscow received more bad news about the situation in Nuremberg from TASS's Secret Department—a division of the news agency that provided intelligence to the Party. Soviet leaders had dispatched the lawyer Arkady Poltorak, the photographer Khaldei, and several other TASS correspondents to Nuremberg on November 12 to check on the arrangements for the Soviet delegation. The correspondents prepared a report afterward that TASS's Secret Department forwarded to Stalin, the Politburo Four, Vyshinsky, and other leaders.[65]

The report gave Soviet leaders their first real picture of what was happening on the ground in Nuremberg. The TASS correspondents reported that American authorities in Nuremberg had received them "courteously, but with reserve," providing them with food and lodging but discouraging them from exploring the city on their own. From what they had seen, the preparations for the IMT were almost complete. The Palace of Justice had been repaired, and the Americans already had a staff of 450 people working there. The Press Camp had been set up in the outskirts of the city at the Faber Castle; a small building on the grounds would house the Soviet correspondents. The American authorities had been bewildered at Moscow's lack of interest in the organizational and logistical work of getting ready for the trials. The Soviet Union was the lone country of the prosecution that had not helped to equip the Press Camp—and as a result there were no Russian newspapers or magazines to be found in its reading room. Books on Soviet law were similarly absent from the library that had been set up at the Palace of Justice.[66]

Insofar as the TASS correspondents had been able to become acquainted with the evidence, they were impressed and alarmed in equal measure. The Americans had captured three German archives (those of the German Foreign Office, the military High Command, and the Reich minister for the Occupied Eastern Territories), and their contents had been organized to correspond to the counts of the Indictment. Among these materials were documents detailing Germany's secret preparations to invade the Soviet Union and memoranda proving that Germany, Finland, and Romania had conspired in planning the attack. There were also documents proving that Nazi leaders had given explicit directives to murder Soviet civilians and that German soldiers had used the pretense of "the Russian partisan war" to shoot anyone they wanted. These and other documents would make a huge impression on world opinion during the trials. Yet the Soviet prosecution's poor mastery of this evidence, much of which was in German, was cause for concern.[67]

The TASS correspondents also provided disquieting information about the interrogation of defendants and witnesses in the Nuremberg prison—illustrating just how much of an advantage the Americans had gained from the decision to hold the trials in the American zone. Before the Soviet prosecution team arrived in Nuremberg, the British and French had agreed that American investigators would conduct all of the interrogations and that the other delegations would submit written questions through the U.S. prosecution. After much negotiation, the Soviet investigators were permitted to conduct their own interrogations, but an American observer always remained in the room along with his stenographer.

The Americans themselves meanwhile had questioned all of the defendants and about 200 witnesses, including several field marshals and generals. The correspondents noted that these interrogations lacked rigor; most of the defendants had denied their guilt completely or insisted that they had been compelled to fulfill Hitler's orders. The interrogators had not challenged the defendants on these claims. Some defendants and witnesses had even used these interrogations to assert that the war against the Soviet Union had been "preventive," the TASS correspondents reported (echoing Kobulov). The witnesses General Walter Warlimont and Field Marshal Walther von Brauchitsch, two of the highest-ranking military leaders in custody, had taken this line, claiming that they had seen evidence of Soviet plans to invade Germany. Judging from the interrogation transcripts, the American as well as the British investigators "freely tolerate verbose speeches" on this topic, the correspondents added.[68]

The week in Nuremberg had convinced the TASS correspondents that the defense would try to use the courtroom to launch an anti-Soviet propaganda campaign. They also predicted that the accused and their attorneys would attempt to justify German atrocities against Soviet prisoners of war and civilians by alleging that German prisoners of war had received similar treatment in Soviet hands. It was unclear how the Americans and the British would respond to such efforts. The correspondents were especially wary of the British, and speculated that their economic stake in large German industries was making them reluctant to bring industrialists like Alfried Krupp to justice.[69] In short, the TASS report confirmed Moscow's fears about the Soviet delegation's state of unreadiness—and about the double threat posed by the defense and the Anglo-American alliance. It provided even more reason for delaying the start of the trials.

As the TASS report was making the rounds in Moscow, the Western prosecutors were consulting with their governments about the Soviet chief prosecutor's illness. The Western prosecutors were fairly certain that Pokrovsky was lying or that (as one British official put it) Rudenko's malaria was "of the diplomatic variety."[70] But they still had to respond.

Outside the Palace of Justice on November 18, the British, French, and American honor guards were practicing in full dress uniform. Journalists and photographers from all over the world had arrived on the scene and were speculating about whether or not the trials would begin on time.[71] Things were bustling inside as well. A group of French, British, and Soviet psychiatrists went ahead without their American colleague and examined Streicher. They found him to be sane (in spite of what they called his "neurotic obsession" with Jews), and the Tribunal accepted their report. The Tribunal also directed Neave to obtain an attorney for Bormann.[72]

Pokrovsky informed Rudenko that morning that he had received replies to his request for a postponement from the French and British prosecutors, though not from the Americans. Dubost had suggested that he wanted to support the Soviet position but would not put this support in writing. The British had refused to hear of a postponement and had assured Pokrovsky that Rudenko would not be needed in Nuremberg for almost a month: the opening speeches of Jackson, Shawcross, and François de Menthon would together take three to four weeks. Pokrovsky asked Rudenko whether he should announce that the Soviet delegation could not participate in the opening of the Nuremberg Trials if it was not delayed. He requested a swift reply, noting that he planned to call a meeting of the Committee of Chief Prosecutors for the following morning.[73]

Vyshinsky again stepped in. Pokrovsky was to refrain from making "any kind of declarations" and wait for the judges' final decision. Vyshinsky also instructed him to verify how long the chief prosecutors were planning to take for their opening speeches. The news that the American, British, and French opening speeches would take three to four weeks made no sense. An earlier communication had stated that each would be a couple of hours. Had there been some kind of misunderstanding? Would each opening speech really go on for days?[74]

Pokrovsky sent Vyshinsky more information that night. Yes, the Committee of Chief Prosecutors had initially agreed that each chief prosecutor would take up to two hours for his opening presentation. But around four days ago the prosecutors had determined that much more time would be needed. Pokrovsky claimed to have notified Rudenko about the updated timetable, which would run as follows: Jackson would begin with a presentation on "the common plan or conspiracy," which would likely take two to three days. His assistants would then present the documents he had referenced. Next, Shawcross would present his speech on "crimes against peace," which would take a full day; then the British would present their documents. The French would give the third presentation. Rudenko would go last, in three to four weeks' time.[75]

The opening speeches would rest on a foundation of documentary evidence, Pokrovsky added, explaining that Jackson planned to take statements of a paragraph or two from the Indictment and support them with "incontrovertible documents." He suggested that Rudenko's opening speech should be similarly detailed, and recommended that it include historical information such as facts about Germany's breaches of international agreements. Pokrovsky added that the Western prosecutors thought it wise to assemble a small number of witnesses somewhere not too far from Nuremberg, perhaps in Berlin or Paris, who could be brought in quickly should the defense try to dispute the veracity of any of the evidence.[76]

Finally, Pokrovsky tried to assuage Moscow's worries that the defendants would turn Nuremberg into a forum for Nazi propaganda. All of the prosecutors wished to deprive the defendants of opportunities to draw the court into discussions about the Allied governments, he noted. It was toward this end, he explained, that the prosecutors had deemed it desirable to share with each other "lists of questions that should not be discussed in court." Pokrovsky then gave Vyshinsky what he saw as proof of the prosecution's commitment to keep the case focused on the defendants: the Committee of Chief Prosecutors had opposed a request by Rosenberg to call witnesses to testify that the Soviets had carried out deportations in Latvia, Lithuania, and Estonia, on the grounds that the IMT was being convened only to judge the European Axis powers.[77] Pokrovsky did not consider the possibility that the judges might see things differently.

This new information did little to reassure Vyshinsky about Soviet preparedness. It now looked like there was even more work to be done on Rudenko's opening speech. What's more, the Indictment Commission had yet to decide how to respond to Jackson's request for a list of taboo topics. Less than thirty minutes after receiving Pokrovsky's report, Vyshinsky fired off a reply instructing Pokrovsky to continue to press for a delay. If the majority of the prosecutors voted down the Soviet petition for a postponement, then Pokrovsky was to declare that he had not been authorized to participate in the trial without Rudenko and that he was duty-bound to tell Moscow that his proposal had been rejected. Vyshinsky then spelled things out to be sure that Pokrovsky grasped the subtleties: the statement would carry a threat of refusing to participate in the opening of the trials but was not an actual refusal. Vyshinsky added that Nikitchenko should follow this same directive.[78]

On the morning of November 19, with the start of the trials just twenty-four hours away, the Committee of Chief Prosecutors met at the request of Pokrovsky and Dubost. U.S. assistant prosecutor Telford Taylor later recalled that this was an especially "tense and rancorous" meeting. Dubost was refusing to let the Krupp case drop. He presented a separate Indictment for Alfried Krupp and asked the other prosecutors to join him in submitting it to the Tribunal. He also proposed submitting a motion to consolidate this case against Alfried with the case against the other defendants, in order to try them at the same time. Pokrovsky raised the matter of the Soviet chief prosecutor's illness and pointed out that adding Alfried to the case would cause no delay beyond what Rudenko's recovery would already require. Shawcross opposed any delay; to appease the French, though, he offered to announce publicly that the British planned to indict Alfried and other industrialists with the intention of bringing them before a second international tribunal.[79] Jackson rejected both Dubost's proposal and Pokrovsky's appeal to wait for Rudenko, declaring that the American people would respond "extremely negatively" to a last-minute postponement and would blame the prosecutors and the judges for being unable to properly manage things.[80]

That afternoon, the Tribunal summoned the prosecutors to a closed meeting. When the room was cleared of everyone but the judges, prosecutors, and interpreters, Lawrence brought forward the matter of Rudenko's illness. Nikitchenko said a few words in support of a postponement, and then the prosecutors took the floor. Dubost (still hoping to bide enough time to add Alfried to the case) maintained that it would be unfair to proceed without Rudenko. If the Russians could not be at the opening of the trials, then the French, too, would not participate. Shawcross declared that his government remained set against postponing the trial, but he agreed not to oppose the Soviet request if it was made publicly and if the Soviet government took full responsibility for the delay.[81]

Pokrovsky, who had been conspicuously absent at the start of this meeting, burst into the room in the middle of this exchange. He announced that he had just been on the phone with Moscow and had learned that a delay of

five days should now suffice. Thanks to a "marvelous new medical application," Rudenko was on the mend. He would only need three more days
of bed rest and could be in Nuremberg in five days. (Jackson wrote in his
diary that Pokrovsky delivered this news "without a smile.")[82] Pokrovsky
reiterated that Rudenko had not designated anyone to stand in for him and
asked that everyone wait for his return. Jackson remained unsympathetic. He
vowed to publicly oppose the Soviet appeal for a delay, noting that he could
not take it upon himself "to represent or protect Russian interests" in this
situation. The three Western judges—Lawrence, Biddle, and French judge
Henri Donnedieu de Vabres—signaled their opposition to the Soviet request.
Lawrence asked Pokrovsky with exasperation why his government could not
simply delegate him to stand in for Rudenko. Pokrovsky promised to again
call Moscow.[83]

Taylor later speculated in his memoir that either Rudenko was actually ill
and wanted to be at the opening of the trials or the Soviets were "collaborating
with Dubost to cause a delay as a device" to push for including the case
against Alfried Krupp. He thought it improbable that the need for additional time played any real part in the Soviet effort to postpone the trial.[84]
Taylor was wrong. The need for time was fundamental: the Soviets were further behind than anyone could have imagined. The amount of work to be
done on the Soviet prosecution's opening presentation alone was daunting.
The French also had a good deal of work to do but were not hampered by
a Soviet-style bureaucracy. The Americans and the British, in comparison,
were ready to go.

Shortly after emerging from the Tribunal's closed meeting, Pokrovsky
and Nikitchenko updated Vyshinsky about the day's events. Pokrovsky related the ins and outs of the prosecutors' deliberations and advised that it
was not in the Soviet Union's interest to sign a hastily prepared document
indicting Krupp. Nikitchenko agreed; filling Vyshinsky in on the Tribunal's
private deliberations, he broke the news that postponing the trials was a lost
cause.[85]

By late afternoon on November 19, it was clear that the Nuremberg
Trials were going to begin on time, with or without the Soviet Union. Soviet
leaders called a halt to their delaying tactics. Late that afternoon, Pokrovsky
informed the Tribunal that he had received the authority to represent the
Soviet prosecution until Rudenko's arrival. He was thus no longer opposed
to the November 20 opening date, as long as certain conditions were met.
Most critically, no defendant would be questioned in court or allowed to offer
a defense until Rudenko showed up. The judges agreed.[86]

On the evening of November 19, Semenov reported to Vyshinsky that the Soviet Union's agreement to begin the trial the following day had been received by everyone "with great satisfaction."[87] Vyshinsky passed this news up the chain of command, and plans were made for the dispatch of Rudenko and other Soviet personnel from Moscow to Germany. Vyshinsky meanwhile had a great deal to consider besides the Soviet delegation's lack of readiness. Given Jackson's request for a list of taboo topics, Vyshinsky had to wonder exactly what the Western prosecutors and judges knew about Soviet-German collaboration. He and the rest of the Indictment Commission also had to decide what to share not just with Jackson but also with Rudenko and with the rest of the Soviet delegation. These were not simple questions.

With the Nuremberg Trials about to begin, the Soviets were on edge. The Soviet Union had emerged from the war as a major power, but its key personnel had little experience on the international stage, and it showed. Their efforts first in London and then in Berlin and Nuremberg had at times played out like a comedy of errors—replete with amateurish interpreters, a disappearing act, and a feigned illness. The Western delegations had taken full note of the Soviet delegation's difficulties. Would the defense do so as well? Could the judges be counted on to keep the trials focused on the crimes of the European Axis powers? All of the prosecutors—Soviet, American, British, and French—braced themselves for what lay ahead.

PART II | The Prosecution's Case

CHAPTER 5 | The Trial Begins

THE SOVIET FILMMAKER Roman Karmen had a terrible time getting to Nuremberg. He showed up at the Central Moscow Aerodrome on the morning of November 20 and boarded a small plane that was soon packed with more than twenty writers, journalists, artists, and cameramen. The plane took off in clear skies and set a course west to Soviet-occupied Berlin, where officers from the Soviet Military Administration in Germany greeted the passengers and shuttled them to Karlshorst for the night.[1]

Karmen and his travel companions took in Berlin during the drive to their lodgings. It was dreary—far drearier than Moscow, where the joy of victory eased the work of rebuilding. Pedestrians shuffled down the avenues, looking broken-down and bone-tired.[2]

Early the next morning, Karmen and the others boarded a plane for Nuremberg. This time the weather was foggy, and the passengers endured a wrenching flight. Some of the correspondents tried to soothe their nerves by paging through the German-language daily *Tägliche Rundschau,* which included an article recapping the first day of the trial. Karmen had hoped to arrive at the Palace of Justice in time for most of the day's proceedings. Instead, the plane circled over a fog-covered Nuremberg several times before turning back for Berlin.[3]

The nonlanding in Nuremberg seemed of a piece with the events of the past couple of months for the Soviets. The international tribunal was supposed to be the Soviet Union's triumph and redemption—the vindication of its people's suffering and sacrifice. But instead the Soviets were living a logistical nightmare. While striving to delay the start of the trials, Soviet leaders had held off on sending critical personnel to Nuremberg. The lousy weather had further delayed Soviet arrivals and contributed to the already entrenched sense of being behind.

Karmen was far more than a chronicler of events—he was an active and fully engaged participant, revered for his artistic genius as well as his daring. His newsreels and documentaries of the Spanish Civil War, including the 1937 *Madrid in Flames*, had brought him international fame.[4] He had spent the last few years embedded with the Red Army, capturing on film the profound devastation the Nazi occupiers had wrought on the Soviet Union. Karmen had been everywhere. In February 1943 he had filmed the surrender and interrogation of German Field Marshal Friedrich von Paulus in Stalingrad. After filming the Soviet liberation of the Majdanek death camp in Lublin, Poland, in July 1944, he had accompanied the Red Army farther west. In April 1945 he had documented the taking of Berlin and the Nazi surrender. He was now headed to Nuremberg on Stalin's orders to capture for posterity the world's final reckoning with the Nazi regime.[5]

Karmen was joined by some of the Soviet Union's most eminent writers and artists, whose job would be to cover the Nuremberg Trials for audiences at home and abroad. These were seasoned men and talented propagandists. They had seen the death pits of Babi Yar and the concentration camps up close; they had walked through the remains of bombed-out cities that stank of decaying corpses. They brought to their work a visceral power. Vsevolod Vishnevsky had gotten his start as a playwright in the wake of the Bolshevik Revolution, staging mock trials such as *The Trial of the Kronstadt Mutineers*. He had remained in his native Leningrad during the Nazi blockade, writing for *Pravda* and broadcasting near-daily radio announcements to the city's desperate inhabitants. In the spring of 1945 he, too, had marched with the Red Army to Berlin.[6] Another passenger was Boris Efimov, who had spent the war years on the front working as an artist-correspondent for the Red Army newspaper *Krasnaya zvezda* (*Red Star*) and illustrating leaflets for Soviet fighter planes to airdrop into German-occupied territories.[7]

When the fog lifted the next day, Karmen and his companions were finally transported (some by plane and some by car) from Berlin to Nuremberg. Karmen chose to fly, and this time all went well. An American colonel registered the new arrivals with the U.S. military government and drove them to the Faber Castle.

The castle, which was located in Stein, a city about five miles from Nuremberg, was an immense Gothic-style building with grand arches and

FIGURE 5.1 Roman Karmen in Berlin, where he filmed the German capitulation, May 10, 1945.

Credit: SPUTNIK/Alamy Stock Photo.

corner turrets. Once the home of the aristocratic Bavarian family that made pencils, it had been transformed into the Press Camp. Karmen took note of its elaborate marble staircases and enormous library. It had been outfitted with offices, sitting rooms, typing rooms, and other amenities to serve the more than 300 correspondents who were covering the trials. The colonel pointed out the bar and the cafeteria to the Soviets, explained how to sign in for breakfast and supper, and then ushered them to their living quarters—a house on the castle grounds that, he casually mentioned, had formerly served as the headquarters of the local committee of the Nazi Party. The Americans

Figure 5.2 The Faber Castle, the home of the Press Camp, southwest of Nuremberg in Stein, 1946.

Credit: Office of the U.S. Chief of Counsel, Charles Alexander, courtesy of Harry S. Truman Library & Museum.

had dubbed the house "the Russian palace" in anticipation of its Soviet lodgers. Everything had been cleaned and painted, but the quarters were cramped; the correspondents would be living three or four people to a room. The weary travelers dropped off their belongings and set off immediately for the Palace of Justice, a twenty-minute drive away through neighborhoods that had largely been reduced to rubble.[8]

The IMT was well under way by this point, having opened on November 20, the day the Soviet press delegation had left Moscow. Tribunal president Geoffrey Lawrence had inaugurated the proceedings with a short statement delivered in English and translated simultaneously into German, French, and Russian. The trial that was about to begin was "unique in the history of the jurisprudence of the world," he had proclaimed, calling on all involved "to discharge their duties without fear or favor, in accordance with the sacred principles of law and justice."[9] These noble sentiments were well received.

The rest of that first day in court had been devoted to reading out the Indictment. David Maxwell Fyfe, U.S. deputy chief prosecutor Sidney Alderman, and several junior members of the French and Soviet delegations had walked through the four major counts—conspiracy, crimes against peace, war crimes, and crimes against humanity—and made brief reference to the evidence.[10]

The defendants, who had already seen the Indictment in written form, had watched all of this from their seats in the dock. Even without key members of the regime's top leadership (Hitler, Goebbels, and Heinrich Himmler had all committed suicide in the final days of the war) it was a collection of men who had brought the world to ruin. Here they were now, sitting according to the rank they had once held in the Nazi hierarchy, looking small, old, and ordinary without their uniforms and insignia. In the first row were Hermann Goering, Rudolf Hess, Joachim von Ribbentrop, Wilhelm Keitel, Ernst von Kaltenbrunner, Alfred Rosenberg, Hans Frank, Wilhelm Frick, Julius Streicher, Walther Funk, and Hjalmar Schacht. Behind them were Karl Doenitz, Erich Raeder, Baldur von Schirach, Fritz Sauckel, Alfred Jodl, Franz von Papen, Arthur Seyss-Inquart, Albert Speer, Konstantin von Neurath, and Hans Fritzsche. Martin Bormann, whose whereabouts remained unknown, would be tried in absentia. Some of the defendants seemed impassive; others showed signs of strain; still others looked far more at ease than they had any right to be.[11]

As a result of the failed stalling tactics, key members of the Soviet prosecution had been absent on that first day of the proceedings. Roman Rudenko was still in Moscow, recovering from his bout with "malaria." Yuri Pokrovsky had stood in for him in the courtroom, accompanied by Georgy Alexandrov. That first evening Pokrovsky sent Andrei Vyshinsky a telegram whose brevity conveyed a degree of relief: "The first day of the trial is over. The Indictment was read. There were no incidents."[12]

In fact, there had been an incident, just not in open court. Goering's attorney, Otto Stahmer, a seventy-year-old judge and a known Nazi sympathizer, had submitted a four-page petition to the Tribunal complaining that the judges, as representatives of the victors, could not be impartial. The petition also challenged the legal grounds of the case—contending that neither the Kellogg-Briand Pact of 1928 nor any international treaty of the prewar years had established the criminality of waging "an unjust war," and accusing the prosecution of creating ex post facto law.[13] Pokrovsky sent Moscow a short note about Stahmer's petition the following day, explaining that it asked for experts in international law to be summoned to evaluate the

FIGURE 5.3 The defendants, seated in the dock according to the importance of their positions in the Nazi leadership, ca. 1945–1946. Front row, from left: Hermann Goering, Rudolf Hess, Joachim von Ribbentrop, Wilhelm Keitel, Ernst von Kaltenburnner, Alfred Rosenberg, Hans Frank, Wilhelm Frick, Julius Streicher, Walther Funk, and Hjalmar Schacht. Second row: Karl Doenitz, Erich Raeder, Baldur von Schirach, Fritz Sauckel, Alfred Jodl, Franz von Papen, Arthur Seyss-Inquart, Albert Speer, Konstantin von Neurath, and Hans Fritzsche. Martin Bormann was tried in absentia.

Credit: United States Holocaust Memorial Museum, courtesy of Gerald (Gerd) Schwab. Photographer: Charles Alexander.

Tribunal's competency to try these cases.[14] This was just the beginning of the defense's challenges to the IMT.

The second day of the trial had begun with the defendants responding individually to the charges brought against them. All had pled "not guilty," and some had tried to use the occasion to grandstand, joining Stahmer in questioning the very premise of the proceedings. Goering, known by all as "Nazi no. 2," attempted to deliver a prepared speech rejecting the jurisdiction of the Tribunal, but Judge Lawrence cut him short. (His speech would, however, find its way to the press.) Jodl, a career soldier who had helped plan and conduct most of Germany's military campaigns during the war, attested that "for what I have done or had to do I have a pure conscience before God, before history and my people." Hess, Hitler's former deputy, whose eyes bulged wildly in his gaunt face, simply bellowed "Nein!" When Lawrence noted that this would be recorded as a plea of "not guilty," a wave of laughter swept through the courtroom. Lawrence sternly warned those assembled—correspondents, dignitaries, diplomats, soldiers, and a small number of Germans—to observe the proper decorum.[15]

After the pleas were entered, Robert Jackson rose and strode to the rostrum with the ease and determination of an experienced trial lawyer. This was the moment he had been waiting for and he was ready. After bowing to the judges and surveying the courtroom, he delivered the opening statement for the prosecution. This would be the "first trial in history for crimes against the peace of the world" and as such imposed a "grave responsibility," he began. That the Allied nations had chosen to "stay the hand of vengeance and voluntarily submit their captive enemies to the judgment of the law" was, he said, "one of the most significant tributes that Power has ever paid to Reason." Speaking directly to the charges of victors' justice, Jackson declared that the tremendous scope of Nazi aggression had "left but few real neutrals." The victors would judge the vanquished but would seek "a just and measured retribution," knowing that they, too, would face the judgment of history.[16]

Jackson spent much of his speech outlining the conspiracy charge (Count One) and describing its connection to the three other counts. The prosecution's case, he promised, would show that the defendants had joined together to carry out a common plan that could be accomplished only by waging a war of conquest. All of their actions, from the "seizure of the German state" to the physical annihilation of dissidents and enemies to the mistreatment of prisoners of war and conquered populations, he argued, were part of this conspiracy.[17]

Jackson read for the court passages from captured German documents—including the reports of the SS Einsatzgruppen, the mobile death squads that had massacred millions of Jews, Gypsies, and other Soviet citizens. In one report from October 1941, Einsatzgruppe A had boasted about its success in encouraging "native anti-Semitic forces" to start pogroms against the Jews in Latvia, Lithuania, and Estonia before sending in its own execution squads. More than 105,000 Jews had been murdered in Latvia and Lithuania over just a few weeks. Another report spoke of men, women, and children being "locked into barns and burned alive." These and other atrocities were not just inhuman but were part of a Nazi plan for the extermination of the Jews, a plan for which each of the defendants—whatever his place in the conspiracy—bore personal responsibility, Jackson charged. He had not found a single instance in which any of the defendants had "opposed the policy it-self or sought to revoke or even modify it."[18] While the defendants remained largely impassive, as Jackson continued to speak they began to look less at ease.

Jackson devoted the last part of his speech to an explanation of the prosecution's rationale for treating "aggressive war" as a punishable criminal act. This part of the case had the least precedent—and he knew this. The riskiest charge, it was to his mind also the most important. "Civilization," he told the court, "does not expect that you can make war impossible. It does ex-pect that your juridical action will put the forces of international law . . . on the side of peace."[19]

That afternoon, Pokrovsky sent another message to Moscow, summing up the day's events and praising Jackson's "oratorical mastery." He had been genuinely impressed by Jackson's argument about the importance of a fair trial and quoted directly from the speech: "If we bring a cup with poison to the lips of the accused, then we bring it to our own lips." Pokrovsky suggested that the speech be circulated widely in the Soviet press.[20] *Pravda* and *Izvestiia* both printed long excerpts.[21]

On the same afternoon as Jackson's speech, Vladimir Semenov wrote to Vyshinsky about the logistical problems continuing to plague the Soviet delegation in Nuremberg. Housing was in short supply, he noted, but the American authorities claimed to be "working on it." (The problem of accommodations affected all of the delegations: hundreds of typists, stenographers, translators, and correspondents from all over the world were jammed into close quarters, sometimes as many as ten to a room, and some of the buildings housing them lacked baths or showers.) Semenov also complained about the bland meals the Americans had been organizing. He urged Vyshinsky to send Soviet foodstuffs on the next flight to Nuremberg. The cafeteria in the Press Camp served American officer rations, but the Soviets were finding it difficult to get used to watery oatmeal and dry white toast. Complaints about American food would become a recurrent theme and were a matter of taste as well as national pride.[22]

The unreliability of the communication lines between Nuremberg and Moscow, which had already been delaying correspondence in both directions, was a more serious issue. Unless fixed, Semenov warned Vyshinsky, this problem could leave the Soviet delegation dangerously isolated. Finally, there was the urgent need for more cipher clerks to encode and decode messages. Semenov stressed that this was particularly pressing in connection with Vyshinsky's imminent arrival in Nuremberg along with the rest of the "com-mission under your leadership" for "directing the Soviet part of the IMT."[23]

The fact was that the Soviets were still finalizing their preparations for the trials. They had not finished assembling their delegation to Nuremberg or vetting cipher clerks for travel abroad. Stalin had given his final approval only that morning to the commission whose arrival Semenov was anticipating: the Commission for Directing the Work of the Soviet Representatives in the International Tribunal and the Committee of Chief Prosecutors in Nuremberg, headed by Vyshinsky (hereafter referred to as the Vyshinsky Commission).[24]

This commission was charged with secretly directing all aspects of Soviet participation in the IMT. Its members were accomplished figures in the fields of law, state security, or propaganda. Aron Trainin and Boris Mankovsky would advise the Soviet delegation on international-law questions, while the assistant director of the Party's propaganda department, Lev Kuzmin, would watch over the Soviet press corps. Bogdan Kobulov, deputy chief of the NKGB, would handle security matters, and Procurator General Konstantin Gorshenin would deal with personnel issues. (Kobulov, Gorshenin, and Trainin had all been members of the Indictment Commission.)[25]

The Vyshinsky Commission was a combination of watchdog and support staff. The other delegations had nothing similar. It would discreetly provide assistance to the Soviet delegation, while also keeping Soviet leaders closely informed about the course of the trial and forwarding all proposals (regarding procedure, documentary evidence, witnesses, and so on) to them for review.[26]

One secret commission for the Nuremberg Trials was not enough for Stalin, who prized centralized control above all else. He simultaneously set up a second commission—a shadow commission within the Politburo: the Politburo Commission for the Nuremberg Trials. This was the true successor to the Indictment Commission. Like its predecessor, it included Vyshinsky, Gorshenin, and Kobulov in its ranks; its other members were the highest-ranking officials from the world of Soviet state security and law. It took over from the Indictment Commission the work of selecting and screening witnesses for the Soviet prosecution. At least two of its members, NKVD deputy chief Sergei Kruglov and SMERSH chief Viktor Abakumov, would verify that potential witnesses were completely loyal to the Soviet Union and could keep their testimonies straight under pressure.[27]

The Politburo Commission reported directly to Molotov, who conferred with Beria, Malenkov, and Mikoyan (the rest of the Politburo Four)—and ultimately of course with Stalin.[28] The logistics were complicated, since for the first two months of the trials Stalin was still recuperating in Sochi near the Black Sea. He kept to a regular work routine, sleeping late and then working into the night. He maintained contact with the Politburo Four, communicating with them over a high-frequency telegraph line or via mail couriers and, less frequently, by phone.[29]

The particularities of the Stalinist system—top-down management taken to extremes—would continue to shape Soviet participation in the IMT. While the American, British, and French delegations were also in regular communication with their governments, they had far more autonomy than Soviet personnel in Nuremberg. The Soviet regime's insistence on highly centralized decision-making and dependence on secret channels of communication were of an entirely different order of magnitude from Jackson's routine updates to Truman and check-ins with the OSS.

By November 22, the third day of the trial, Rudenko's malaria had outlasted its usefulness. He set out from Moscow to Nuremberg with Gorshenin, Trainin, and several other members of Vyshinsky's inner circle, including Mark Raginsky, who had just been added to the Soviet prosecution team.[30] Raginsky, like Rudenko and Nikitchenko and nearly everyone else on the Soviet side with any real responsibility, had proven his mettle to Vyshinsky in the 1930s show trials, where his lack of scruples as an investigator had helped seal the fate of Stalin's enemies.[31]

The pedigrees of the Soviet prosecutors and judges presented Jackson and the others with a problem. They all knew what a travesty of justice the Moscow Trials of 1936-1938 had been. The Americans in particular were sensitive to the defense's accusations of victors' justice. While Rudenko and his colleagues were en route to Nuremberg, the U.S. assistant prosecutors were using their presentations to make it absolutely clear that this would not be a show trial in any way, shape, or form. The IMT would strictly follow due process and would adhere to the rule of law as understood in the American context, considering the defendants innocent until proven guilty.[32] The proceedings had barely started, and Soviet and American intentions were already on a collision course.

November 22 was also the day Karmen arrived in Nuremberg with his Eyemo movie camera. It was an overcast day, and dark clouds hung low over the Palace of Justice.[33] Arriving at the bustling courthouse, he spent a few moments taking things in. He was surprised to find an "endless number" of rooms in the building, including document rooms, telegraph rooms, and even movie montage rooms. Security was tight. On each hallway and at each door Karmen noticed an American soldier who "indifferently yells the word 'pass' and will not let you through until you show your pass."[34] Karmen got his pass and went straight into the courtroom, looking for the best places from which to film. He saw that several windows had been cut out of the courtroom walls and that photographers and cameramen were positioned to look in through them from neighboring rooms. He also saw that the press box (which seated around 250 people) and the visitors' gallery (which could hold another 130) were both overflowing. Other Soviet correspondents had a harder time gaining access to the courtroom. Ilya Ehrenburg eventually became so frustrated by his inability to obtain a pass that he borrowed one from a colleague and bluffed his way past the guards.[35]

The U.S. prosecution continued to present its case as the Soviet correspondents got their bearings. By the time that the journalist Boris Polevoi showed up on Monday, November 26, most of the other correspondents had established familiar routines. Polevoi, who had just come from covering Bulgaria's postwar elections, soon realized his disadvantage. The other Soviet journalists had already gotten chummy and had started to become acclimated

FIGURE 5.4 The courtroom, November 1945. The defendants sit in the dock (front, right) with the defense lawyers seated in front of them. Facing them on the left are the judges, against the wall, with the court reporters and stenographers seated in front of them. Beyond the defendants and judges (center) are the tables of the prosecution. Beyond these tables (rear) is the press box, with the visitor's gallery above it; both were especially packed at the beginning of the trial and on high-interest days.

Credit: dpa Picture-Alliance/Alamy Stock Photo.

to the trials, which Polevoi found to be "unusual and complex." The Soviet correspondents had by this point divided themselves into "two tribes": the "Big Wigs" and the "Khaldeians." The first group was made up of around a dozen of the Soviet Union's most famous artists and writers, including Karmen, Vishnevsky, and Ehrenburg. The second group, which included war reporters from across the USSR, had been given the sobriquet of its most celebrated member, the photographer Evgeny Khaldei.[36] While the two groups got along, it was clear that the Big Wigs felt their nickname was well deserved.

The Soviets found the living conditions in Nuremberg much more rugged than expected. By the time of Polevoi's arrival, the Big Wigs had fled the Press Camp and had joined some members of the Soviet legal team downtown in the once-magnificent Grand Hotel, which American engineers had rushed to refurbish. It included 270 rooms, a nightclub, a ballroom, and two banquet halls for dining, but there were large holes in the roof, and parts of the floors were still missing. The Khaldeians had resigned themselves to

FIGURE 5.5 The photographer Evgeny Khaldei (left), one of the best-known Soviet war correspondents, in the Nuremberg courtroom, 1946. He shot some of the most iconic images of the war and of the trials. In this image Hermann Goering is on the right, covering his face with his hand; behind Goering is Karl Doenitz.
Credit: dpa Picture-Alliance /Alamy Stock Photo.

making the Press Camp's "Russian palace" their home and invited Polevoi to join them there. The building had a malfunctioning furnace whose fumes gave everyone headaches. Residents had to leave the windows wide open at night to ventilate their rooms. Karmen, Ehrenburg, Efimov, and the others who had decamped for the Grand Hotel now at least had functioning heat and hot water.[37] Their new quarters were more comfortable, with just two to a room, but were hardly luxurious. Ehrenburg later recalled how it had been necessary to clamber to his second-floor room "partly by ladder, partly over loose boards," because the staircase was still under repair.[38]

Karmen spent his first few days in Nuremberg establishing what soon became a daily ritual. Setting up his camera in the Palace of Justice each morning, he would watch the courtroom come to life. The American guards would bring in the defendants and then open the heavy green drapes to let in some daylight. The defendants freely chatted with each other in the dock and rose to greet their attorneys as they arrived. Gradually, the courtroom filled. Before the judges made their entrance at 10 a.m., the drapes were closed and the electric lights switched on. The feeling, the playwright Vishnevsky wrote in his diary, was of "animation, as before a premiere."[39]

All of the Soviet correspondents were acclimating to the rhythms of the trial. By day, they listened to the U.S. prosecution lay out the details of the Nazi conspiracy. On November 23, for example, the U.S. assistant prosecutor Thomas Dodd introduced evidence documenting the roles of Goering, former Reichsbank president Schacht, and other defendants in rearming Germany and developing its war economy. Other members of Jackson's team detailed the means by which the Nazi conspirators acquired what the Americans continued to call "totalitarian control of Germany," focusing on the reshaping of education and the organization of the Hitler Youth.[40] The correspondents busily took notes and filed stories with their newspapers back home through the Associated Press (AP), United Press International (UPI), and other Western telegraph agencies or via the Soviet military wire. At lunchtime, always 1 p.m., everyone headed over to the cafeteria attached to the court. Ehrenburg later recalled how they all took trays and "filed past ten American soldiers who, like expert jugglers, ladled out soup, poured coffee, and slung potatoes and slices of bread on to the plates."[41] Vishnevsky was reminded of a Charlie Chaplin film.[42]

The afternoon's court session ended promptly at 5 p.m. (earlier on Saturdays), leaving most of the participants with abundant free time. At night Nuremberg became a town of postwar decadence—at least from the Soviet point of view. The Grand Hotel's nightclub was packed with lawyers, journalists, and military personnel intent on escaping the depressing business

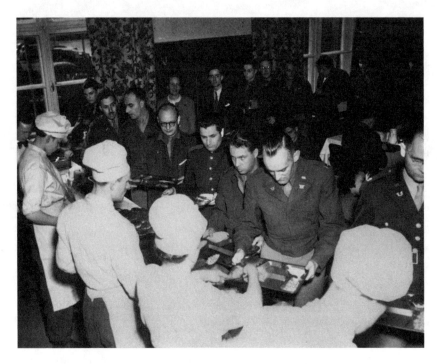

FIGURE 5.6 The cafeteria in the Palace of Justice reminded the Soviet correspondent Vsevolod Vishnevsky of a Charlie Chaplin film, 1945.

Credit: Office of the U.S. Chief of Counsel, Charles Alexander, courtesy of Harry S. Truman Library & Museum.

of the trials. Ehrenburg later recalled how people would gather there and order cocktails while "a lady in a very low-cut dress sang American songs (with a German accent)."[43] Vishnevsky wrote in his diary about German vaudeville shows complete with acrobats.[44]

The Khaldeians found their own watering hole close to the Press Camp. Polevoi later recalled how reporters from all over the world made themselves at home in a bar run "by a jovial American with dazzling white teeth" who "poured out drinks and mixed cocktails so expertly that our bottles, wine glasses and tumblers seemed to dance in his agile hands." Polevoi was fascinated by the names of the drinks: " 'Black Cat,' 'Manhattan,' 'Bloody Mary,' and so on." The Soviet correspondents preferred vodka and drank it straight. They observed with curiosity and amusement that the Western journalists treated their gin and whiskey with caution, "topped with water and loaded with ice."[45]

The Soviet correspondents were taken aback by the informality of life in the American zone. They believed that the American officers in the Palace of Justice behaved far too casually for the occasion and that the defendants were allowed too many indulgences. Vishnevsky noted with disapproval that Keitel sat "gobbling chocolate" in the dock; he also took offense at all of the "whistling and gum chewing" that went on while discussing "the blood of the Russian people."[46] Such things would be unimaginable in a Soviet court-room. The Soviet correspondents were also upset to discover that many of the drivers employed for the journalists were Germans.[47]

"It's a very alien world here," Vishnevsky wrote *Pravda* chief Peter Pospelov after his first week in Nuremberg. People "stare wide-eyed when I tell them about Leningrad and Stalingrad. . . . On their faces and in their souls, there are almost no traces of Russia's struggle." In Vishnevsky's opinion, the trials should have happened right after the German surrender. The Americans now were preoccupied with their own affairs, he noted, and were more concerned about "unemployment, China, Eisenhower, and who arrived back home" than about the fate of the Nazi war criminals. The British, for their part, were thinking about the latest soccer matches. Even the locals were indif-ferent: "if they hang them, shoot them, or send them to penal servitude—it is no longer interesting."[48]

While some Nurembergers were uninterested in the trials, others were openly hostile. Daily life was a struggle for much of the population. The American writer John Dos Passos, speaking with Germans living in impro-vised shelters and cooking food on makeshift stoves on the street, had come to understand that to many residents what was going on at the Palace of Justice was just another display of Allied power.[49] Vishnevsky thought that the locals were particularly antagonistic to the Soviets and complained in his letter to Pospelov that the local newspapers were running all kinds of articles disparaging the USSR.[50] He was aghast at the American authorities' laissez-faire attitude about this situation, noting in his diary that Jackson had brushed off his complaint about the press with the explanation that the newspapers had to spin these sorts of stories in order to make money.[51]

Another constant for the Soviet delegation was surveillance and informing. The Soviets had established not just one but several networks of informants in Nuremberg who were already busy writing up reports for Moscow— about the course of the trials, life in the American zone, the foreigners they met, and, inevitably, one another. The informants were a diverse group representing various Soviet institutions and agencies. Investigators from the NKVD reported directly to Beria in Moscow. Informants who worked for the Secret Department of TASS had a direct line to Stalin and Molotov; they culled articles from Western newspapers about the Soviet Union and about the trials, reported on local conditions, and studied the behavior of fellow

Soviet personnel. Other members of the Soviet press corps reported to their editors and to Sovinformburo chief (and deputy foreign minister) Solomon Lozovsky. Finally, certain members of the Vyshinsky Commission, the Soviet press corps, and the Soviet delegation sent regular reports to Malenkov, Molotov, or Vyshinsky.

The Soviets were as busy covering each other as they were covering the trials. This level of monitoring was typical for Stalin's Soviet Union, where the NKVD maintained a vast network of informants and schoolchildren were encouraged to report on their parents.[52] But it created an unusual situation in the small community of Nuremberg, where the members of the Soviet delegation shared extremely close quarters, mixed with foreigners every day, and encountered innumerable opportunities to get into trouble. Buying clothing and toiletries on Nuremberg's black market, dancing the jitterbug in the Grand Hotel ballroom, flirting with Westerners—any of this could prompt a report to Moscow.

Intrigue abounded. Soviet personnel knew that they were being followed—but were rarely certain as to who was spying on whom. Some became convinced that British and American spies were trailing them, and they may have been right: U.S. Counterintelligence Corps agents were keeping an eye on the Soviet delegation. Then again, so was the NKVD.[53]

On Sunday, November 25, Vyshinsky arrived in Nuremberg for a weeklong stay. His presence created a state of heightened alert among the members of the Soviet delegation. As Stalin's envoy and as the head of one of the two secret commissions overseeing Soviet participation in the trials, Vyshinsky was feared and respected. The Soviet prosecutors, judges, and support staff all knew that they were in Nuremberg to do his bidding and that their fates rested in his hands. Even the Western prosecutors were stirred up by Vyshinsky's arrival. According to Telford Taylor, the U.S. delegation had regarded Vyshinsky as "an ominous figure" because of his role in the Moscow Trials.[54] Everyone eyed him with curiosity: What exactly was his business? How would he behave?

Vyshinsky had come to Nuremberg primarily to ensure that Rudenko successfully repelled a push for the IMT to consider highly sensitive evidence about the German-Soviet Non-Aggression Pact—which, of course, had been a matter of concern all along. The instigator of this particular request was Alfred Seidl, the defense attorney for Hans Frank and a former member of the Nazi Party, who claimed to have "dug up" some documents about the pact's secret protocols and wanted to introduce them in court. There were rumors that members of the U.S. delegation, including Jackson, were prepared to support Seidl's request.[55]

This was just the kind of situation Beria had been anticipating when he insisted on NKVD oversight of the trials. The secret protocols, in which Hitler and Stalin had plotted out the conquest and division of Poland, Finland, Latvia, Lithuania, Estonia, and Bessarabia, implicated the Soviets in crimes against peace. Vyshinsky was there to make sure that this information stayed out of the courtroom. He got down to business quickly and quietly, becoming acquainted with the day-to-day work of the judges, investigators, and prosecutors and meeting with key members of the Soviet delegation.[56]

For Western observers, Vyshinsky's role in the IMT was never clear—exactly as Stalin had intended. He was not officially part of the Soviet delegation; when he appeared at the Palace of Justice, it was as a distinguished guest. While the Party had designated Nuremberg as the Vyshinsky Commission's place of residence, it had stipulated that Vyshinsky himself would be present only when necessary.[57] Vyshinsky's trip to Nuremberg had pulled him away from other critical assignments for Stalin and Molotov. When the trials began he was deeply involved in Soviet efforts to establish a communist government in Romania.[58] He was also overseeing the organization of military tribunals throughout the Soviet Union to try German soldiers who had committed atrocities during the Nazi occupation.[59] The secret protocols took precedence, however; Vyshinsky's other responsibilities would wait.

On Monday, November 26, the day after Vyshinsky's arrival, the U.S. prosecution presented evidence on the conspiracy to wage aggressive war. Alderman read from captured Nazi documents such as the Hossbach Memorandum—the minutes of the November 5, 1937 meeting in the Reich Chancellery at which Hitler had told his generals of his intention to take over Europe. Alderman also quoted passages from the Barbarossa File, showing that Nazi leaders had drawn up detailed plans to attack the Soviet Union months before the actual invasion, using the nonaggression pact to shield their intentions.[60]

That evening Pokrovsky sent an update to Moscow noting that Alderman had presented documents "of great interest" regarding the "unleashing of war" against Poland in September 1939.[61] Polevoi and the rest of the Soviet correspondents were similarly impressed. They observed that while the documents Alderman produced about Hitler's plans for the invasion of the Soviet Union were not surprising, the details were revelatory. Polevoi considered this the first time that Soviet journalists "were taken right into the Nazi devil's kitchen and shown *how* the plans were devised at the secret meetings between Hitler and his accomplices to Germanize the Soviet Union, and *how monstrous* these plans were."[62]

While the Americans presented their evidence, the German attorneys were formulating their defense. Pokrovsky warned Moscow that Ribbentrop's attorney, Fritz Sauter, had requested a number of witnesses who could give "clear and intelligible answers" to questions about German foreign policy under Hitler—including Andor Hencke, the former under state secretary of the German Foreign Office, and Friedrich Gaus, the former head of its Legal Department.[63] This was cause for real concern for the Soviets. Both of these witnesses could testify about the meetings between Ribbentrop and Molotov in 1939 and 1940. They needed to be kept out of the witness box.

After the trials recessed for the day, Vyshinsky convened his commission for its first on-the-ground meeting in Nuremberg. The commission's members (Trainin, Gorshenin, Mankovsky, Kobulov, and Kuzmin) were in attendance; also present were Nikitchenko and Volchkov, Rudenko and Pokrovsky, and a battery of assistant prosecutors, including Alexandrov, Raginsky, and Lev Sheinin. Sheinin, who headed the Evidence Department of the procurator general's office, had worked with Vyshinsky as a special investigator in the Moscow Trials and, like the others, knew how he operated.[64] But this of course was not the Moscow Trials. As partners in an international undertaking, the Soviet prosecutors and judges were frequently at a loss, unable to assert control over developing situations.

Vyshinsky for one was tired of Rudenko's and Nikitchenko's excuses. It was time to stand up to the Americans and the British. Discussing the defendants, Vyshinsky instructed Rudenko and Nikitchenko to ensure that Hess remained on the docket. Soviet leaders saw Hess as exceptionally treacherous; they also continued to fear that the British were trying to shield him, possibly to protect themselves from scrutiny. A group of physicians and psychiatrists had examined Hess earlier in the month and had been unable to agree on whether or not he was feigning amnesia. Vyshinsky directed Rudenko to come to an agreement with the Western prosecutors that Hess was of sound mind and could stand trial. If there were differences of opinion, he and Nikitchenko were to demand that the Tribunal bring in additional medical experts.[65]

Vyshinsky also addressed the question of Rudenko's opening speech, which was taking on increasing urgency. Moscow remained intent on using Nuremberg to cement the Soviet Union's position as a major European and international power. Vyshinsky saw that the Americans, vying for leadership of the postwar world, were not keen to share the limelight. He had learned barely a week earlier that the other chief prosecutors would be delivering lengthy opening speeches. Rudenko's opening speech as written was barely two hours long, while the speech Jackson had delivered and the ones the British and French were preparing ranged from four to eight hours. This obviously would not do. Vyshinsky now deemed it imperative to significantly lengthen Rudenko's speech and to "saturate it," as he put it, with documentary evidence. He divided those assembled into four groups. Each would prepare a section of the speech on an assigned theme: war crimes and crimes against humanity; fascist ideology; aggression against Czechoslovakia, Poland, and Yugoslavia; and aggression against the USSR.[66]

Vyshinsky feared that by the time Rudenko delivered his opening speech there would be nothing left to say. Earlier that fall, Rudenko had stood by while Jackson made the conspiracy charge the linchpin of the case. Since then, Jackson had been pressing Rudenko for the originals of all kinds of Soviet documents, insisting that they were needed to prove the Nazi conspiracy.[67] Already during that first week in court, the U.S. prosecution had read out a steady stream of evidence about crimes against the Soviet people. Vyshinsky ordered Rudenko to confront Jackson and demand that the U.S. prosecution leave all documents "touching upon the USSR" for the Soviet prosecution.[68] Vyshinsky was not about to let their thunder be stolen.

Vyshinsky waited until the end of the commission's inaugural meeting to raise the most sensitive issue of all: Jackson's November 9 request that the British, French, and Soviet chief prosecutors write up secret memoranda essentially detailing their countries' war crimes, in anticipation of potential allegations from the defense.[69] Back in Moscow, Soviet leaders had put their own spin on Jackson's request. Without admitting to any wrongdoing, they had compiled a list of "taboo topics" they wanted kept out of the courtroom. Vyshinsky now presented it to those assembled for discussion.

Not surprisingly, this highly secret list—which had been typed out in Moscow on a single sheet of paper—included a number of items about Soviet-German relations: "the relationship of the USSR to the Versailles peace"; "the German-Soviet Non-Aggression Pact of 1939 and all questions relating to it"; "Molotov's visit to Berlin and Ribbentrop's visit to Moscow"; and "the Soviet-German agreement about the exchange of the German population of Lithuania, Latvia, and Estonia with Germany." It also included more general topics concerning Soviet foreign policy, including "questions about the [Dardanelles] Straits and about the alleged territorial pretensions of the USSR"; "the Balkan question"; and "Soviet-Polish relations" (in particular regarding "Western Ukraine and Western Belorussia"). Off limits as well were any and all questions "connected with the socio-political structure of the USSR" and "the Soviet Baltic republics."[70]

After some discussion about the dangers posed by the German defense, the members of the Vyshinsky Commission reviewed the list. Vyshinsky ordered Rudenko to reach a verbal agreement with the other prosecutors that they would "not touch on the questions that the USSR, USA, England, France, and other United Nations do not want to become subjects of criticism from the side of the accused." To be safe, he also instructed Rudenko and Nikitchenko to make arrangements to review ahead of time the hundreds of documents the other countries of the prosecution were planning to present to the Tribunal, in order to identify any that broached the topics on Moscow's list or were otherwise harmful to Soviet interests.[71] Vyshinsky stopped short of fully complying with Jackson's request: he did not give Rudenko permission to share a physical copy of the list with any of the Western prosecutors. He had not received clearance from Stalin and Molotov to do so. He also understood that once a copy was in circulation the Soviets would lose the shield of plausible deniability.

Vyshinsky's visit was an occasion even to those who were unaware of his direct involvement with the trials and knew him only as a Soviet dignitary. Jackson gave a dinner at the Grand Hotel in his honor. Telford Taylor later remembered that all the "senior people" attended—except for the British, who had other commitments. This dinner took place almost immediately after the Vyshinsky Commission's meeting; Vyshinsky and Gorshenin arrived fresh from their discussions with the Soviet delegation about Jackson and his motivations. At one point in the evening, Vyshinsky rose and proposed a toast to the defendants. "May their paths lead straight from the courthouse to the grave!" Everyone had drained their glasses before the translation was finished, and the American judges were appalled to hear that they had drunk to the deaths of the accused.[72] This was perhaps the only time the Soviets did not mind the sluggish pace of interpretation from Russian into English. Vyshinsky visibly enjoyed the moment.[73]

The rest of the week was a blur of evidence by day and private parties by night. In the courtroom, Alderman documented the Nazi conspiracy to conquer Austria, Poland, and Czechoslovakia. Vyshinsky sat with Gorshenin, balefully eyeing the accused. Vishnevsky noted in his diary that Goering, Ribbentrop, and others "tensely" eyed Vyshinsky back.[74] In the evenings, the festivities continued. In spite of postwar shortages, booze was somehow plentiful in Nuremberg. French brandies and liqueurs were especially abundant, but scotch, whiskey, or vodka might also appear, depending on who was hosting.[75] The British held a dinner featuring the traditional Scottish dish of haggis in honor of the Russian guests and introduced them to the sounds of the bagpipe, played by a piper from the Scots Guards. Vyshinsky, Gorshenin,

Rudenko, Alexandrov, and Pokrovsky all attended and seemed to enjoy the music as well as the food.[76] (Haggis, made from sheep's innards, was apparently a welcome change from American officer rations.) On another evening Rudenko played host. Taylor later remembered that there were "no fewer than twenty-five vodka toasts."[77] British alternate judge Norman Birkett was impressed by the quantity of vodka, champagne, and cognac provided by the Soviets and by the "cartloads of food."[78]

These parties were an important part of the informal diplomatic relations of Nuremberg—the behind-the-scenes interactions that profoundly shaped the developing course of the trials. In this case, the revelry seemed to foster friendly relations among the prosecutors. Rudenko reached a verbal agreement with Maxwell Fyfe, Charles Dubost, and Jackson that they would work together to steer clear of topics that might be damaging to any of the countries of the prosecution. In addition, the prosecutors agreed to allow one another to review their speeches and evidence in advance. Vyshinsky informed Molotov of this victory.[79]

FIGURE 5.7 Andrei Vyshinsky (leaning forward) and Konstantin Gorshenin (on his left), in the seats reserved for honored guests in the Nuremberg courtroom, ca. November–December 1945.

Credit: Russian State Documentary Film and Photo Archive B-3208.
Photographer: Evgeny Khaldei.

The last few days of Vyshinsky's visit were filled with courtroom drama. On the evening of November 29, the U.S. prosecution showed a film about Nazi concentration camps in the zones that had been liberated by Western forces. The footage had been shot by American and British cameramen at Dachau, Buchenwald, and Bergen-Belsen.[80] This was the first film of the trials, and it made an "incredibly strong impression" on all who were there, Karmen later wrote. The experience was made even more powerful by the fact that all those in attendance were able to monitor the expressions of the defendants, who were watching the film from the dock. Before the screening began, the courtroom lights were dimmed, and small spotlights were aimed at the accused. Karmen recalled that expert psychiatrists, some Soviet, sat in the courtroom and took notes: recording "when Goering shut his eyes," "when Keitel took off his headphones and turned away," and when Rosenberg began to shake uncontrollably from nerves.[81] The Soviet assistant prosecutor Dmitry Karev (a professor of criminal law at Moscow State University who was in charge of organizing the Soviet documentary evidence) was also struck by the reaction in the dock, and reported to Moscow that Hjalmar Schacht would "not look at the screen."[82] Karmen believed that the defendants, seeing "with their own eyes what they were accused of," finally understood that the trials were "not a farce."[83]

The drama continued the following morning when the U.S. prosecution unexpectedly called its first witness: Major General Erwin Lahousen, a former German military intelligence officer and one of the survivors of a small group of plotters who had tried to assassinate Hitler in July 1944. Lahousen's appearance caused a commotion, with the defense protesting vociferously that it had not been informed about this witness in advance. The defense had reason to panic. Lahousen had been a true Third Reich insider and could directly implicate Ribbentrop, Keitel, and other former Nazi leaders in war crimes and in the "conspiracy to wage aggressive war." He proceeded to do exactly that. He spoke at length about Nazi plans and procedures and described efforts to exterminate entire categories of people—including prisoners of war who "could be identified as thoroughly bolshevized or as active representatives of the Bolshevik ideology."[84]

That evening, Karev reported to Moscow that Lahousen had given powerful testimony about the particularly brutal treatment of Russian prisoners of war. He also noted that Lahousen, on being questioned by Rudenko, had revealed that the Nazi intelligence service had recruited Ukrainian emigrants from Galicia to carry out "acts of sabotage" in Poland and other countries.[85] This fed right into Soviet anxieties about Ukrainian fifth columnists.

The afternoon of Friday, November 30 brought still more excitement when the Tribunal held a closed hearing to consider Rudolf Hess's fitness to stand trial. Hess, who typically sat in the dock reading paperback novels and ignoring the activity around him, had asserted repeatedly that he did not remember any aspect of his Nazi past. Now the Tribunal would consider the reports that the medical experts had filed several weeks earlier about his purported amnesia. Rudenko showed up in court primed for a fight, but also confident of the support of the British, French, and American chief prosecutors. They had met privately the day before and had all agreed that Hess should be tried.[86]

The correspondents arrived in the courtroom ready for a show but were told that the afternoon session would be held "in camera." Before leaving, Polevoi noticed that Hess seemed more attentive than usual and sat "with his detective story unopened." Once the courtroom had been cleared, Hess's attorney, Gunter von Rohrscheidt, stated that while his client saw himself as "fit to plead," he was in fact mentally ill and could not stand trial. The prosecutors launched into their counterarguments—but their presentation came to an unexpected halt when Hess himself insisted on addressing the Tribunal and immediately confessed to faking his amnesia.[87]

The Tribunal called the correspondents back in, and Lawrence announced that Hess would make a statement. Hess then astonished the press corps by declaring that his memory would, as he put it, "again respond to the outside world" and that his reasons for pretending to have amnesia were purely of "a tactical nature." No one really knew what had sparked this unexpected confession, but the Soviets promptly gave credit to one of their own experts, the psychiatrist Evgeny Krasnushkin, for having "caught Hess out." According to Soviet journalists, on Krasnushkin's instructions Hess had been shown old Nazi films and had smiled repeatedly at the scenes of himself with Hitler, not realizing that he was being observed.[88] The next morning the Tribunal announced its opinion that Hess was capable of standing trial. Whatever had motivated him to retract his claims of amnesia, the Soviets were quite pleased with this turn of events.[89]

On December 1, in the wake of the ruckus over the Hess case, Vyshinsky called another meeting of his commission. All of its members were present except for Kobulov, who had flown back to Moscow to brief Soviet leaders about the trial's progress. Also at the table were Nikitchenko, Volchkov, Rudenko, Pokrovsky, and the assistant prosecutors who had been at the first meeting. Most of the discussion focused on the preparation of documentary evidence for the Soviet part of the case. The Soviet prosecution had been reviewing evidence, and Pokrovsky informed the commission that some sixty documents, including Nazi directives, letters from the defendants' personal archives, and Extraordinary State Commission reports, had been selected and translated and could be registered with the Tribunal.[90]

In spite of the recent goodwill among the chief prosecutors, Vyshinsky remained concerned about the other delegations grabbing up key Soviet evidence and shutting the Soviets out of the case. He reiterated that Rudenko and Nikitchenko should promptly "secure the receipt" from the other chief prosecutors of all documents focused on the Soviet Union, Yugoslavia, Czechoslovakia, and Poland, in order to ensure that the Soviets could present them in court. If the other delegations insisted on presenting these documents themselves, Rudenko was to lay claim to those sections that, as Vyshinsky put it, "were of direct interest to the USSR."[91]

Vyshinsky also deemed it critical for the Soviets to make a strong impression by adding more original evidence to their case. He ordered Rudenko and his team to review another large batch of documents from the Extraordinary State Commission and to choose the most significant ones to present to the Tribunal, seeing to it that they were translated into German. The commission also discussed making use of different kinds of evidence. Impressed by the American documentary film shown two days prior, the commission resolved to determine the status of the Soviet footage of German atrocities that had been shot by Karmen and others. Finally, prompted by the testimony of Lahousen the day before, the commission discussed the merits of calling witnesses for the Soviet prosecution.[92]

Soviet leaders had harbored serious doubts about the wisdom of calling witnesses and had been considering building the Soviet case on documentary evidence alone. While Stalin and Vyshinsky certainly appreciated the potential power of live testimony, they also understood the dangers. Witnesses would be subject to cross-examination by defense attorneys and would not be able to rely on a prepared script. Leaving so much to chance seemed extremely risky. Even so, the Soviets had been actively evaluating witnesses for some time. Over the first half of November, the Indictment Commission had sorted through lists of hundreds of potential witnesses from every region of the Soviet Union—and had come up with a draft list of eighty persons who could conceivably be called on to testify. Gorshenin and Kobulov had then directed local state security personnel to interview these witnesses and determine their fitness to appear before the IMT.[93] The responses had already started coming in to Moscow and had shown just how challenging it might be to find witnesses who were both politically reliable and able to speak persuasively about Nazi atrocities.

In some cases, local state security personnel had discovered what they considered "compromising" information disqualifying potential witnesses. Officials from the Moscow region had reported to Gorshenin that several eyewitnesses had questionable pasts and that a couple of them were serving prison sentences. According to local investigators, one witness, Ivan Frolov, had been taken prisoner by German forces in 1941 and interned in a POW camp, where he had been forced to dig graves and bury corpses for his captors. After being freed, he had lived in a Soviet processing camp before being arrested in August 1943 as a traitor to the Soviet Union for having abetted the Nazis.[94] Frolov's situation was not unique, given Stalin's conviction that any Soviet soldier who had done anything to help the enemy—even under duress—was a traitor to the motherland.

In other cases, listed witnesses had been found to be too ill or damaged by their wartime experiences to testify. While interned in a Nazi labor camp in Ukraine, for example, a certain Ismail Khuazhev had witnessed the mass extermination of prisoners by means of "infecting them with tuber-culosis, typhus, and dysentery." But according to North Caucasus officials, Khuazhev himself was seriously ill. During his interview, he had given a "muddled" statement full of jumbled facts and had spoken "unconvincingly and uncertainly."[95]

Those witnesses who had made it through the NKVD's screening process were, by contrast, well spoken, able to provide detailed information about German atrocities, and completely loyal to the Soviet regime. Ivan Egorov, for example, was a career soldier who had enlisted in the Red Army in 1927 and served during the war as head medic of the Second Latvian Partisan Brigade. He had been captured by the Germans in June 1941 and interned at the Stalag 347 prisoner-of-war camp in Latvia until 1943. He had witnessed what he described as "the torment, torture, and murder" of Soviet servicemen who were ill or wounded and had provided NKVD investigators with a com-prehensive report on the "inhumane conditions" in the camp, as well as a list of specific Nazi crimes.[96]

Metropolitan Nikolai (now the head of the Moscow Eparchy of the Russian Orthodox Church) had also been deemed an exemplary witness. As a member of the Extraordinary State Commission, he had participated in dozens of trips to investigate and document some of the most brutal crimes committed by the Nazis in cities and villages throughout the USSR. In January 1944, he had been part of the Soviet commission that investigated the Katyn grave-site. A few months later he had participated in the work of a special commis-sion to investigate German atrocities in the Leningrad region. Soviet leaders had judged that testimony from Metropolitan Nikolai, a man of religion, would play especially well in the West. Their assessment noted that he was highly educated, knew foreign languages, and would be invaluable "also in public relations" as a witness at Nuremberg.[97]

At the time of its initial meeting on November 26, the Vyshinsky Commission had been on the fence about summoning witnesses. Vyshinsky had nonetheless suggested that Moscow dispatch fifteen to twenty witnesses to Nuremberg "in case of necessity."[98] The Politburo Commission for the Nuremberg Trials, meeting on November 28 in the Kremlin, had followed up by approving a tentative list of twenty-five witnesses, summoning five of them to Moscow to prepare their testimony. They were the director of the Hermitage, Joseph Orbeli; the poets Jacob Kolas and Pavel Tychkin; the priest Nikolai Lomakin; and Metropolitan Nikolai. Kobulov and several NKVD agents were to deliver the rest of the witnesses to Moscow in two weeks' time and determine who should be sent along to Nuremberg.[99]

Reports from Nuremberg about Lahousen's testimony had quickly convinced the Politburo Commission that it was imperative for the Soviet prosecution to call its own witnesses in open court, lest Jackson and his team completely steal the show. By the time the Vyshinsky Commission held its second meeting, on December 1, the issue had been decided: the Soviet case would not rely on written evidence alone. Vyshinsky passed along this information, and also declared that Soviet prosecutors should examine all witnesses in court regardless of which delegation had called them. Finally, Vyshinsky directed Rudenko to reach an agreement with the other chief prosecutors to not call any more witnesses until after all four countries' prosecutors had presented their documentary evidence in court. If this failed, Rudenko was to insist that witnesses be called sooner only in "exceptional circumstances."[100] Vyshinsky was tired of the Soviets being upstaged.

Over the next few weeks, NKVD special investigators in Moscow prepared the Soviet witnesses and streamlined their testimonies. Meanwhile, local procurators and state security personnel continued to send Gorshenin and Kobulov information about possible additional witnesses, as well as the transcripts of their depositions. The Politburo Commission, in addition to overseeing all of this, carefully studied a list of former Nazi leaders in Soviet custody. The commission set out to prepare a couple of surprises of its own for the Tribunal—not to be unveiled until the Soviet prosecution presented its case.[101]

Vyshinsky departed Nuremberg on December 2 to prepare for the upcoming meeting of American, British, and Soviet foreign ministers in Moscow and to confer with Molotov and Stalin about joint Allied efforts toward the denazification of Germany. During his brief stay in Nuremberg, Vyshinsky had worked hard to get the Soviet case on the right course. Before leaving town, he deputized Gorshenin to oversee the work of the Vyshinsky Commission and tapped Raginsky to serve as his eyes and ears within the Soviet delegation. Vyshinsky instructed the members of the commission to meet regularly with Nikitchenko and Rudenko and to report all developments to Moscow. He also ordered Nikitchenko to keep Rudenko informed about the details of the judges' private deliberations—flouting one of the Tribunal's most basic rules.[102]

There was only so much Vyshinsky could control. After Lahousen's testimony, the accused and their attorneys began bombarding the judges with petitions to produce former Nazi leaders as defense witnesses. On December 3, the day after Vyshinsky's departure, the Vyshinsky Commission discussed a developing fiasco. Apparently, the Soviet prosecution had naïvely agreed in early November to the calling of forty-nine defense witnesses, including two top German generals, Field Marshal Walther von Brauchitsch and Field Marshal Gerd von Rundstedt, and an officer with Army Group Center, Lieutenant Reinhard von Eichborn, who had been stationed near Katyn.[103] Was this true? If so, what could be done?

Raginsky looked for scapegoats. He reported to Vyshinsky on December 4 that Rudenko and Pokrovsky were to blame. They had not opposed these witnesses when they had the chance, and some had already been summoned. Raginsky theorized that the defense was intent on "exhausting" the prosecution; he noted that Sauckel already had ten witnesses lined up and had submitted a petition to call another thirty-six. Raginsky anticipated that defense witness testimony would drag out the trials and might even create the misconception that some sort of "historical justification" existed for Nazi crimes.[104]

Raginsky reported on other worrisome developments as well. He noted, for example, that the Tribunal had accepted a defense petition to use a transcript of Anthony Eden's October 1942 speech in the House of Commons about Hess's flight to Great Britain and that this threatened the entire prosecution with "serious unpleasantness." (Eden had proclaimed that Hess had flown to Scotland in May 1941 on a peace mission.) Raginsky also criticized Rudenko's continuing failure to obtain evidence needed for the Soviet case from Jackson and complained that this was hampering work on the Soviet opening speech.[105]

Finally, Raginsky forwarded to Moscow a copy of a memorandum Maxwell Fyfe had circulated among the chief prosecutors in response to Jackson's request for information about each country's areas of vulnerability vis-à-vis the defense. In it, Maxwell Fyfe had noted Britain's wartime policy toward Norway as well as the history of British imperialism—and had affirmed the British prosecution's commitment to forcefully object if the defendants attempted, either while testifying or through their attorneys, to make counter-accusations against any of the countries of the prosecution.[106]

Maxwell Fyfe's memorandum did not put the Soviets at ease. At a December 5 meeting of the Vyshinsky Commission (the second since Vyshinsky's departure), Gorshenin and Raginsky denounced what they saw as Anglo-American plotting. Earlier that day, Maxwell Fyfe had announced that Alderman would present British as well as American documents on the Nazi war of aggression against the Soviet Union. Still furious about the Anglo-American refusal to share the "crimes against peace" charge with the Soviets, the commission instructed Rudenko to again insist that the other delegations immediately hand over to him all "documents about aggression relating to the USSR" as well as lists of all the documents that the Americans and the British were planning to present to the court. He was also to censure his American and British colleagues for violating what the commission called the "principle of collegiality."[107]

Back in Moscow, Raginsky's report had put Vyshinsky on edge. On December 6 he demanded an immediate update from Gorshenin about Jackson's response to Rudenko's most recent request for documents about the Nazi invasion of the Soviet Union. Gorshenin was to do everything possible to drive this to a successful outcome. "Act quickly and immediately," Vyshinsky instructed. Sensing a loss of resolve since his departure, he also directed Gorshenin and Raginsky to quickly develop a plan for the balance of the trials: to establish precisely when Rudenko would make his opening speech, when the Soviet prosecution needed to submit its petitions to call witnesses, and when Soviet prosecutors would have the opportunity to cross-examine witnesses called by the other countries of the prosecution or by the defense. The calling of any further witnesses, he reiterated, must be delayed until after the Soviet prosecution had presented its case.[108]

Finally—and most important—Vyshinsky addressed the issue of Jackson's continuing warnings about possible efforts by the defense to bring up Soviet crimes against peace.[109] Soviet leaders were not about to share a physical copy of their list of taboo topics with the Western powers. Instead they added another insider, Nikolai Zorya, to the Soviet prosecution team, entrusting him with keeping Soviet state secrets out of the courtroom.[110] Zorya, who was the head of the Department of the Supervision of the Military in the procurator general's office, knew the breadth of Soviet machinations and the depth of Soviet vulnerability—and understood just how much was on the line.

The NKVD, meanwhile, had taken Vyshinsky's demand for vigilance as a green light to denounce individual members of the Soviet delegation for failing to protect Soviet interests. The Soviet politics of denunciation, a hugely destructive feature of Stalinism, had been transplanted to Nuremberg. State security personnel now accused assistant prosecutor Georgy Alexandrov of working against Soviet interests. They reported to Moscow that he had allowed Nazi defendants to insult the Soviet Union while he was interrogating them in the Nuremberg prison back in October. Desperate to correct the record, Alexandrov told Gorshenin that no such insults had been made and that Pokrovsky (who had been present at all of these interrogations) could back this up. For Alexandrov, everything was at stake in clearing his name. Contending that lies and rumors created "an unhealthy environment," he requested that Soviet leaders conduct a special investigation to establish who was "guilty" of spreading misinformation and to call the perpetrators to account.[111] Soviet leaders instead let the matter fester.

Karmen had come to Nuremberg to record the trials for posterity and to highlight the leading role of the Soviet people in the victory over Germany.[112] But the start of the Nuremberg Trials was turning out to be an American show, with Jackson as the star of the moment and Alderman playing the key supporting role. Day in and day out, Polevoi, Vishnevsky, and the other Soviet journalists and writers reported on the details of the American case, while Khaldei took photographs and Karmen captured the courtroom drama on film.

Equally dramatic, though, were the behind-the-scenes politics of the IMT—the "offstage" interactions among the prosecutors as well as the secret meetings of the Vyshinsky Commission, all of which fundamentally shaped what happened in the Nuremberg courtroom. The first few weeks of the trials had brought rising temperatures among the countries of the prosecution and within the Soviet delegation. Vyshinsky's visit to Nuremberg had been a catalyst to both action and further dysfunction for the Soviets. The American case was continuing to expand and take on topics the Soviets thought they owned, while the German defense team was continuing to line up witnesses who could attest to Soviet-German collaboration. The representatives at the London Conference had agreed that the IMT would focus exclusively on European Axis crimes—but Stalin had little reason to believe that the Western powers would keep their word. In this novel forum of postwar justice it was still not completely clear who would be judging whom.

CHAPTER 6 | Stuck on the Sidelines

L IFE IN NUREMBERG maintained a familiar rhythm, a kind of punctu-
ated tedium, during the first weeks of December 1945 as the Tribunal
continued to hear evidence against the former Nazi leaders. The Soviet
correspondents sat in the press box of the Palace of Justice, absorbing details
about the Nazi conspiracy and filing their stories at the end of the day over
the Soviet military wire. Boris Efimov spent those weeks with a pencil in his
hand, listening to the wind howl through the gaps in the courtroom windows, staring at the defendants, and quietly sketching.[1]

Efimov had perfected the art of political caricature in the 1930s, while
covering the Moscow Trials for *Izvestiia*. He had delighted Stalin with his gro-
tesque portraits of Nikolai Bukharin, Leon Trotsky, and other old Bolsheviks,
depicting them as Gestapo agents, spies, and slobbering pigs eating from a
trough labeled "Fatherland." Following the German-Soviet Non-Aggression
Pact of 1939 Efimov had turned his talent to lampooning FDR and Churchill.
And then, with the German invasion of the Soviet Union in June 1941, his
attention had shifted to Hitler. His drawings of the Nazi elite, rendered com-
ically as the "Berlin gang of bandits," had inspired Soviet soldiers and had
brought him international recognition. Goebbels was said to have pledged
that Efimov "would be among the first to hang after the Germans captured
Moscow."[2]

At the end of the war, Efimov, a Jew who had grown up in Bialystok in
the Pale of Settlement, had accompanied Red Army troops to the Majdanek
and Treblinka concentration camps just after they had been liberated. At

FIGURE 6.1 Boris Efimov, reputed to have been Stalin's favorite cartoonist, pictured during the Second World War, ca. early 1940s.

Credit: Russian State Documentary Film and Photo Archive No. 4-34559. Photographer: M. S. Nappelbaum.

Majdanek he had examined the barracks, the cells, and the office of the camp commandant (noting a sign over the toilet that read "Only for SS!"). He had walked along a much-trodden path that "step by step," he knew, had brought hundreds of thousands of new arrivals at the camp to their deaths: it led to the so-called bathhouse. Standing on the gray-tiled floor of the showers, looking at the heavy iron doors, thinking about the last breaths of frightened human beings, he had shaken with sadness and rage. "What kind of human imagination is capable of visualizing what happened here in these minutes?" he later reflected while recalling this experience.[3]

Now Efimov drew the former leaders of the Third Reich as strange and hideous beasts in a "fascist zoo": reptiles, rodents, wolves, and apes with mixed-up features and physiognomies, formerly savage creatures now rendered pathetic. Ribbentrop was a rat-like hyena, Kaltenbrunner an ape-like vulture, Goering an enormous slug.[4] These sketches appeared in *Izvestiia* as part of the Soviet coverage of the trials, under the heading "Fascist Beasts." Efimov reflected in his memoir that the term "beasts" fit the defendants perfectly. "Is not each of them repulsive, a cruel creature, now harmless, who only recently had carried the magnificent title of Reich Marshal, Reich Minister, Reich Leader, or Grand Admiral?"[5]

These "fascist beasts" had been driven to the dock instead of straight to the gallows. The Soviets had anticipated a quick hearing with a clear accounting of Nazi guilt, followed by hangings. But the Western powers, sensitive to charges of victors' justice, were intent on showing the world that the defendants were receiving a fair trial. The defendants, petitioning for witnesses and preparing their own testimonies, still had a lot of fight in them—and were determined to put forward their own version of events. Efimov's images of diminished beasts, like all propaganda, reflected a large degree of wishful thinking.

Efimov sketched the former Nazi leaders while Hartley Shawcross delivered the British opening speech on Tuesday, December 4, addressing the charge of "crimes against peace" (Count Two of the Indictment). Soviet leaders had always seen this charge as the crux of the case—and had wanted Rudenko to give this presentation. To the Soviets, Shawcross seemed to channel Aron Trainin as he argued that launching a "war of aggression" had long been considered a criminal act and described the Kellogg-Briand Pact as part of a body of "positive international law" on which the charge of "crimes against peace" was based. The Tribunal would be applying "not the law of the victor," Shawcross told the court, but long-accepted principles that would "safeguard the future peace and security" of humankind.[6]

Shawcross went on to describe how the duplicitous making and breaking of treaties in pursuit of the conquest of Europe lay at the heart of Nazi criminality. The defendants were those men who had enabled Hitler "to tear up existing treaties, to enter into new ones and to flout them, to reduce international negotiations and diplomacy to a hollow mockery." While the story of Nazi diplomacy was perhaps "less gruesome" than the story of Nazi atrocities,

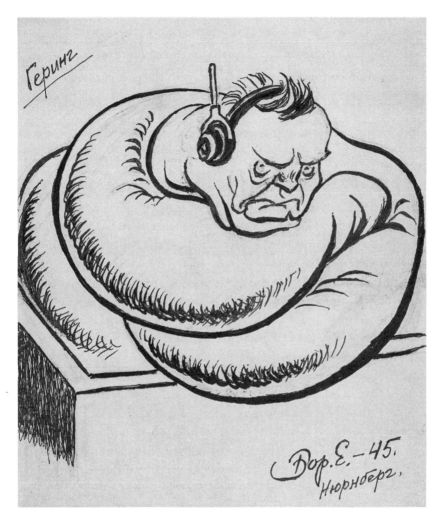

FIGURE 6.2 Boris Efimov's caricature of Hermann Goering, *Izvestiia,* December 5, 1945, part of Efimov's series "Fascist Beasts (from the Hall of Justice)." Efimov's political cartoons appeared in the Soviet press alongside articles about the course of the trials.

Credit: Reproduced courtesy of Boris Efimov and the Ne Boltai! Collection.

it was no less evil. The kind of treachery the German leadership had engaged in would just as surely "lead to the end of civilized society."[7]

Shawcross, an experienced barrister and politician, had two thorny issues to deal with in his presentation on crimes against peace. First, there was the problem of Norway. The defense was expected to argue that Germany had attacked Norway in April 1940 in order to preempt a British plan to invade and occupy the country. Shawcross confronted this straight on: "even if the allegations were true—and they were patently false—they would afford no conceivable justification for the action of invading without warning, without declaration of war, without any attempt at mediation or conciliation." Second, there was the problem of the German-Soviet Non-Aggression Pact, which had precipitated the German and Soviet invasions of Poland in 1939. Rudenko, who had read an earlier draft of Shawcross's speech (in keeping with the informal agreement the chief prosecutors had reached in November), had asked Shawcross to omit several mentions of Soviet-German cooperation. Shawcross had obliged. The line that remained highlighted Nazi deceit, noting that Germany had concluded the nonaggression pact even as it harbored an intention "to attack Russia at some convenient opportunity."[8]

After Shawcross's speech, the Americans and the British took turns further documenting Nazi crimes against peace. This was a delicate arrangement. Shawcross had interrupted the American presentation of evidence on the "conspiracy to wage aggressive war" in order to give his speech. The British, like the Soviets, were wary of U.S. ambitions, especially given the overlap between Counts One and Two. Maxwell Fyfe had insisted that the British begin laying out their case in the middle of the American presentation in order to avoid being shut out. He complained in a letter home that he'd "had to fight" to get the Americans to put aside enough of their case to make sure Shawcross had "sufficient material" to present and the British prosecution as a whole had "enough to do."[9] The Soviets of course had had no such luck. And so Rudenko and his team now watched as their Western colleagues began to tell the story of Hitler's unprovoked attacks on Eastern Europe and the Soviet Union. Over the next couple of days, Alderman presented evidence of the Nazi takeover of Czechoslovakia, and the British assistant prosecutor Mervyn Griffith-Jones took the court through the Nazi leadership's planning and waging of war against Poland.[10]

The Soviets remained on the sidelines at the end of the week as the U.S. prosecution kicked off its presentation on the German assault on the USSR. Alderman began by declaring that the "spirit of opportunism" had motivated Hitler to sign a nonaggression pact with the Soviet Union and that it was thus "not very surprising" that he had abandoned it when it no longer suited him. Even in 1939, while Germany was at war with France and England and while the Soviets were supplying the Nazis with food and other resources, Hitler was considering the possibility of attacking the Soviet Union, Alderman maintained. Nazi ideology had long made clear that "Germany's key to political and economic domination lay in the elimination of the USSR as a political factor and in the acquisition of Lebensraum at her expense." He introduced key pieces of evidence from the Barbarossa File, including the war diary of Franz Halder, the chief of staff of the military High Command. An entry from December 1940 indicated that Halder and Hitler had discussed the role of the Luftwaffe (the German air force) in taking out key Soviet industrial centers.[11]

As the court recessed for the weekend the Soviets faced the fact that they had been scooped: deprived of the opportunity to tell their story of Nazi treachery in their own words. That evening, the Vyshinsky Commission convened (minus Vyshinsky) and acknowledged this bitter reality. Rudenko and Nikitchenko now admitted to Gorshenin and the others that the Americans had been within their rights in presenting evidence about the Nazi assault on the USSR. The Committee of Chief Prosecutors had agreed during its deliberations about the Indictment that the Americans and the British would cover the planning and waging of aggressive war, they conceded, and this had made meeting Molotov's demand that the Soviets present this evidence next to impossible all along.[12]

Meanwhile, earlier that day, Jackson had made a small gesture of collegiality. He had sent the Soviet prosecution a list of documents in the Americans'

FIGURE 6.3 Roman Rudenko (on the right, with his head resting on his hand), Yuri Pokrovsky (on the left, taking notes), and other members of the Soviet prosecution are stuck on the sidelines while the Americans and the British present their parts of the case, 1945.

Credit: Russian State Documentary Film and Photo Archive No. A-9222.

possession about German war crimes and crimes against humanity committed against Soviet soldiers and civilians. The Vyshinsky Commission now directed its international-law experts (Trainin and Boris Mankovsky) to work with the Soviet prosecution to review this list and to obtain critical evidence from Jackson. Frustrated by recent developments, the commission also set out to learn why Georgy Alexandrov, who had led the Soviet investigation team back in October, had not known about these documents earlier. This boded poorly for Alexandrov, who was already in trouble for his supposed lack of vigilance while interrogating the defendants in the Nuremberg prison.[13]

The Vyshinsky Commission next discussed the defense's continuing effort to line up witnesses who were likely to speak on the topic of Soviet-German collaboration. Gorshenin instructed Nikitchenko to use his role on the Tribunal to defer the review of defense petitions for witnesses until after all four countries of the prosecution had concluded their opening speeches. Finally, the commission set to work with the Soviet prosecutors and judges on a general strategy against the defense, aiming to be better prepared for the later stages of the trials. The commission's members read through evidence and drafted questionnaires to guide the Soviet prosecutors in their cross-examinations of the defendants.[14] These were crib sheets consisting of leading questions and anticipated answers, intended to entrap the accused and elicit statements of guilt. If the defendants could not be given prepared scripts to recite in court—a common characteristic of Soviet show trials—then at least the Soviet prosecutors could be armed with them.

The Soviets had been concerned for months about shutting down Nazi propaganda inside the Nuremberg courtroom. They had not even considered the possibility that they would also have to deal with its dissemination in the Western press. As the third week of the trials came to a close, Soviet leaders were fuming about a series of so-called interviews with the defendants that American newspapers were running—picked up from the Associated Press (AP) newswire, which was giving the former Nazi leaders a mouthpiece.

Several AP correspondents had been putting together their own questionnaires for the former Nazi leaders—and had found eager intermediaries in the defense counsel, who had passed the questions along and provided their clients' responses. The first of these interviews, with Goering, had appeared in American newspapers on December 1 and 2 under headlines such as "Goering Affirms Belief in Nazism" (*New York Times*) and "Goering Declares He's Still Nazi and Would Support Fuehrer Again" (*Los Angeles Times*).[15] The interview with Keitel, appearing a few days later under headlines such as "Keitel Terms Invasion of Russia Defensive" (*Los Angeles*

Times) and "Nazis Beat Reds to Punch, Keitel Says, Justifying Attack" (*Zanesville {OH} Signal*), was what had really incensed the Soviets. The former chief of Germany's military High Command had used the Western press to launch counter-accusations against the USSR.[16]

The TASS Secret Department had sent long sections from the Keitel interview to Stalin, the Politburo Four, and Vyshinsky immediately after its appearance in the American press. In one excerpt, Keitel denied responsibility for the deaths of hundreds of thousands of Red Army soldiers who had been taken prisoner by the Germans, contending that when German forces captured these soldiers in the summer of 1941 they were already half-starved and dying. Even more galling was Keitel's insistence that Germany's invasion of the Soviet Union had been preventive. Keitel confessed in the interview to signing "the so-called Barbarossa Plan" seven months before the German invasion of the Soviet Union—but claimed that this plan had been drawn up only in response to numerous reports that the Red Army was mobilizing for war. According to Keitel, Hitler had ordered the June 22, 1941 attack on the Soviet Union as a defensive action.[17]

The Goering and Keitel interviews were among a parade of feature stories about the former Nazi leaders that the AP and its affiliates published during the first weeks of the Nuremberg Trials. Sensational stories like these sold newspapers (as Jackson had explained to Vsevolod Vishnevsky) and fed the public's fascination with the former titans of Nazi power. They were also part of a more general trend. The lawyer Arkady Poltorak, the Soviet appointee to the Tribunal's Secretariat (which received all correspondence addressed to the Tribunal and maintained its records), later recalled how American and British publishers "flooded Nuremberg" that fall and, "seeing a quick dollar or pound in the publication of memoirs," eagerly sought to speak with the defense attorneys.[18] Soviet leaders were outraged about the defendants' use of American newspapers to spread their point of view. Not fully grasping the concept of an independent press, they took the Keitel interview as further proof of the U.S. government's anti-Soviet sentiments—certain that Washington had known about and possibly even facilitated its publication.

Even more disturbing to the Soviets was the publication of the AP interviews in the German-language newspaper *Die Neue Zeitung,* which was run by the U.S. military government in Germany. On December 7, *Die Neue Zeitung* carried the interview with Goering. A few days later, it ran an interview with Hess in which he told the world about his "peace mission" to England—and there was talk, the TASS Secret Department reported, that the newspaper was planning to run the Keitel interview as well as interviews with Ribbentrop and Raeder.[19] *Die Neue Zeitung* had been founded with the explicit goal of reeducating the German public. The U.S. military government in Germany insisted that the newspaper was modeling a free press by presenting a multitude of viewpoints.[20] But the Soviets had a legitimate complaint: *Die Neue Zeitung* was actively disseminating the views of the former Nazi leaders within Germany, thereby furthering their interests.

The Soviet correspondents in Nuremberg were struck more generally by the American approach to journalism, replete as it was with wild speculation and drama. As soon as an American correspondent "snatched up something," such as word that "Goering's attorney demands this or that from the Tribunal," he filled out a telegram form and sent it off via courier to his editor, Roman Karmen observed. In the course of a single session of the court, an American correspondent might send off dozens of such telegrams—out of which his editor then constructed an article. Soviet correspondents for *Pravda, Izvestiia*, and other newspapers, by contrast, crafted their articles after leaving the courtroom. At the end of each session, TASS provided them with a detailed, almost stenographic, record of what had transpired in court—and only then did the writers set to work. The final stories were sent over the military wire to Moscow, or first to Berlin. They were often heavily censored before appearing in the Soviet press.[21] This method was cumbersome and time-consuming, but it facilitated the centralized control that Soviet leaders demanded.

It wasn't just the American press that had alarmed the Soviets with blatantly anti-Soviet headlines. The TASS Secret Department advised Stalin and the Politburo Four that the British press, too, was taking an anti-Soviet stance. British journalists in Nuremberg had found out about the late-stage editing of Shawcross's opening speech and had run with the story. London's *Daily Express* had reported that the Soviet prosecution had "in the friendliest manner" asked for the removal of several paragraphs from the British opening speech, as well as the addition of the phrase "it was a lie" following a quote from Hitler describing Soviet economic assistance to Germany during the early months of the war. The newspaper had then compared the original text with the speech Shawcross had delivered, helpfully highlighting the omitted paragraphs for readers.[22] The TASS Secret Department drew the conclusions that the British press and the British prosecution were in cahoots and that the former was helping the latter to achieve the goal it had apparently established of "calling special attention to German-Soviet relations."[23] Vishnevsky presented a similar description of events in a letter home to Moscow a week later, hypothesizing that Shawcross himself had given the removed paragraphs to the British journalists, who had eagerly printed them.[24]

In truth, Shawcross was a conundrum to the Soviet delegation. Rudenko and Yuri Pokrovsky had developed a friendly relationship with Maxwell Fyfe over the preceding months. However, Shawcross had spent relatively little time in Nuremberg; he was attorney general for Clement Attlee's Labor government, which was vocally anticommunist. The TASS Secret Department insinuated that Shawcross's intention was to implicate the Soviet Union in Nazi crimes. Even after the agreed-on edits to his opening speech, the TASS report noted, Shawcross had made a number of "tendentious claims" about the causes of the war and the rise of Hitler—claims the British press was now having a field day airing. The British were trying to "whitewash the Munich politics of the English and French governments" and present themselves as the heroes and the martyrs of the war, the TASS Secret Department complained. Particularly outrageous were Shawcross's assertions that England alone had always stood up to Germany and that Hitler had always looked on England as his main enemy and had sought Soviet assistance in order to destroy it. Even worse, Shawcross had read aloud sections of documents that gave the court the impression that the Soviets had helped Germany to wage war against England. All of this of course ran entirely counter to the Soviet narrative of the war, which presented the Soviets as heroes and martyrs, omitted any mention of Soviet-German cooperation (including economic agreements), and contended that Hitler's chief aim all along had been the conquest of the USSR.[25]

Some of Shawcross's assistants had also made anti-Soviet slurs in their presentations, the TASS Secret Department informed Stalin. Griffith-Jones had twice repeated Hitler's claims that the Soviet Union had willingly handed vast material resources over to Germany for the purpose of waging war against England. He had also read an excerpt from the American interrogation of Goering in which Goering had asserted that the signing of the German-Soviet Non-Aggression Pact had enabled Germany's invasion of Poland. The British press had publicized these claims as well. The TASS Secret Department denounced the transcript of the Goering interrogation as a particularly "dubious document" and concluded that the British had introduced it in court with the explicit goal of maligning the USSR.[26]

Reviewing these and other reports about the Western press in Sochi, Stalin focused his ire on Molotov. He had become increasingly convinced that Molotov and the Ministry of Foreign Affairs were being too conciliatory toward the British and the Americans and not taking a hard enough line in pursuit of Soviet interests abroad. Stalin was toying with the idea of forcing Molotov's resignation—and had secretly directed Beria, Mikoyan, and Malenkov to take Molotov to task for his missteps in international relations. Other articles in the American and British press had also ignited Stalin's rage. The *New York Times* and London's *Daily Herald* had speculated on Stalin's poor health and predicted Molotov's likely ascension to power. Stalin was furious about these "cock-and-bull stories" and about Molotov's relaxation of censorship on foreign correspondents in Moscow. He called for a return to a strict "policy of firmness" in foreign relations: he would not tolerate further smears against himself or the Soviet Union.[27]

Molotov got the message, loud and clear. The Ministry of Foreign Affairs increased its monitoring of foreign journalists in Moscow and of Soviet correspondents abroad; there would be more vigilance going forward. At the same time, Vyshinsky directed Rudenko to appeal to the Committee of Chief Prosecutors and to the Tribunal to try to rein in the defense attorneys as well as the press. The Vyshinsky Commission also began compiling evidence to use if needed against the British, including the notes of a conversation between Hitler and Lord Halifax, the former British foreign secretary, about improving relations between Germany and England. Should the British go public with claims of Soviet treachery, the Soviets could make the counterclaim that Neville Chamberlain and Hitler had contemplated forging an anti-Soviet alliance in the late 1930s.[28] Covering their bases, Molotov and Vyshinsky also reviewed secret documents from Goering's office files about German-American economic relations in the 1930s, looking for evidence of American financial support of Hitler or details of business ties between the United States and Nazi Germany.[29] The Vyshinsky Commission meanwhile reminded the Soviet press corps in Nuremberg to report only on the evidence that had been made public in court—and to refrain from prognosticating in print about the verdicts or succumbing to any other kind of sensationalism.[30]

During the dark evenings of early December, correspondents from all over the world frequented the American bar near the Press Camp, drinking late into the night, playing chess, and occasionally talking politics. The drinks were quite cheap, just 10 to 20 cents each, but the Soviet correspondents were constantly short of pocket money. The foreign journalists often bought a couple of rounds, and conversations ensued in a mishmash of languages.[31] The Soviet journalist Boris Polevoi recalled the after-hours banter among the correspondents as "sometimes fierce, but, more often than not, good-humored." He thought that the foreigners seemed genuinely interested in getting to know the Soviet journalists and gauging their opinions about the war, international politics, and even the role of the press.[32] The American reporter Harold Burson remembered the Soviet correspondents as wickedly funny, frequently edgy, and "very evangelical, as far as Communism was concerned." He also thought that some of them were much more "independent of mind" than they let on.[33]

Efimov, Karmen, Vishnevsky, and the rest of the "Big Wigs" sometimes joined the other correspondents at the American bar near the Press Camp or went out about the city, but mostly they gathered in one another's rooms at the Grand Hotel with a bottle of vodka or whiskey. On a good evening, someone would pull out a parcel with salted herring, caviar, or some other delicacy from home. The men—for they were all men—discussed the most recent gossip from Russia and joked around, trying to forget the war, which they were reliving every day in the courtroom. A favorite leisure activity was to make drunken declamations ("We spit on your atom bomb!") and shout insults in Russian and heavily accented English at the table lamps, which were presumed to be bugged.[34] During the early weeks of the trials Efimov and Karmen roomed together. Efimov found Karmen and his circle to be too rowdy and switched roommates, desperate for a reprieve from the drinking, smoking, and loud company.[35]

On Saturday night, December 8, amid the comings and goings outside the Grand Hotel, a Soviet chauffeur was murdered. According to Soviet reports, Corporal Ivan Buben was sitting in his car around 11 p.m. when a pistol shot was fired through the window. Another Soviet driver was startled and, looking for the source of the noise, saw two American soldiers and two German police officers carrying Buben to the hotel entrance. Buben managed to tell the other driver "an American shot me!"—confirming this twice in the presence of the soldiers before losing consciousness. He was brought to an American hospital; the doctors found a bullet wound, with an entrance hole above his heart and an exit hole below his lungs. He died a couple of hours later.[36]

Buben had been a trusted member of the Soviet delegation. He regularly drove Soviet special investigator Mikhail Likhachev and had been assigned to Vyshinsky during his November visit to Nuremberg. The TASS Secret Department reported to Stalin that a drunk American soldier was likely responsible for the murder and described Buben as an upright character who (unlike some of his compatriots) had stayed away from American bars.[37] The day after the shooting, Rudenko sent Jackson a note suggesting that it was highly suspicious that the murderer had not been apprehended, given that the crime had taken place "at the illuminated entrance of a hotel carefully guarded by the American police." This lack of a swift American response made Soviet personnel fear for their lives, he added.[38] Jackson assured Rudenko that the U.S. military authorities would bring the perpetrator to justice.[39] But in fact no one was arrested. Moreover, rumors had begun to

FIGURE 6.4 Roman Karmen (fourth from left), Vsevolod Vishnevsky (second from left), and other correspondents pose with an American guard in front of the Grand Hotel, ca. 1945-1946.

Credit: Russian State Archive of Literature and Art f. 2989, op. 1, d. 870, l. 2.

spread among the Americans and the British that the real culprit was a disgruntled Russian who had been attempting to assassinate Likhachev (the head of the Soviet security police in Nuremberg) and had mistakenly killed Buben instead. When he was shot, Buben had been resting in the passenger seat of Likhachev's limousine, a conspicuous black-and-white luxury car with red leather upholstery that was purported to be from Hitler's own car pool.[40]

The murder of Buben would remain an unsolved mystery. It is possible that a drunken American soldier fired the shot. The GIs patronized a couple of bars near the courthouse and regularly "borrowed" cars for joy rides, according to the Soviet correspondents. After-hours road accidents had become so frequent that the local authorities had set a smashed jeep on a pedestal in the center of a busy city square as a warning, as Polevoi remembered.[41] The TASS Secret Department chose to play up the inebriated-American scenario in its report to Moscow about the murder, describing other incidents with out-of-control GIs—and implying that an American soldier might have only meant to threaten Buben when he accidentally fired his weapon. According to the report, another Soviet chauffeur had been held at gunpoint by a drunk American soldier near the entrance of the Grand Hotel a week earlier; the soldier had forced the chauffeur to drive him around town. Still another Soviet chauffeur had been similarly threatened by an American soldier but had managed to leap out of his car and find protection in the Grand Hotel.[42]

Soviet leaders called for greater security after reading these reports. But in the case of Buben, the American rumors could well have been true. Someone from the Soviet delegation might have been trying to settle a score with Likhachev, who had been the source of damning reports to Moscow about Alexandrov and other members of the Soviet delegation. During his short time in Nuremberg, Likhachev had earned a reputation as an exceptionally unsavory character. (Rumors spread that he had gotten a member of the Soviet delegation pregnant and had forced her to have an abortion.) Rudenko had personally asked Gorshenin to deal with Likhachev, and Gorshenin in turn had appealed to the Party and SMERSH to replace him. In the wake of Buben's murder, Soviet leaders recalled Likhachev and sent a different investigator (Vsevolod Siuganov) to Nuremberg in his place.[43]

Unease over the Buben murder hung in the air the following week as the U.S. prosecution continued its case against the Nazi leaders. On Monday, December 10, Alderman resumed his account of the German conspiracy to wage aggressive war against the Soviet Union, detailing what he described as the "cold-blooded calculation" that had gone into German military preparations and highlighting the leading roles of Goering, Keitel, and other defendants in preparing the assault. The Nazi conspirators had wanted unfettered use of Soviet foodstuffs, raw materials, and supplies to maintain the German military, Alderman charged. He presented numerous documents from Rosenberg's files outlining Nazi policies in Eastern Europe. These included "General Instructions for all Reich Commissars in the Occupied Eastern Territories," from May 1941, in which Rosenberg anticipated the division of the Soviet Union into different political-economic regions (Reich commissions) on the basis of race. The territories of southern Russia and the northern Caucasus were to have been used to produce food for the German people.[44]

Staring at the dock from his seat in the courtroom, Efimov remembered Rosenberg as Hitler's "steward for oppressing, robbing, and exterminating the inhabitants of the Russian, Ukrainian, and Belorussian lands seized by the Germans." Now Efimov observed that the former Reich minister had the gloomiest appearance of all the defendants and drew him as a rodent with hooves and a long tail. Sketching Alfred Rosenberg's face and trying to imagine his internal state, Efimov recalled lines from "A Terrible Revenge," a nineteenth-century Gothic horror story by the Russian writer Nikolai Gogol about a wicked sorcerer. "Not a single person in the world could tell what was in the soul of the sorcerer."[45]

Karmen thought that Alderman did a masterful job of showing the roles of the defendants in the conspiracy to wage aggressive war, presenting "completely irrefutable" evidence that made them "turn pale." He observed the way Alderman supported every accusation with a top-secret document—a telegram, report, or telegraph conversation signed by Goering or another defendant—that the Nazis had never dreamed would be made public.[46] Polevoi was equally impressed with Alderman's use of evidence, recalling the way he read from transcripts of secret meetings at which Hitler, Goering, Rosenberg, and Keitel had spoken "candidly, in a free and easy manner," about their plans to conquer and exploit the Soviet Union.[47]

The Soviet correspondents also found American visual evidence of the Nazi conspiracy compelling but observed that it did not have the desired effect on the defendants. On December 12, the American prosecution showed *The Nazi Plan*, a documentary film chronicling the rise and fall of National Socialism—which was made in large part from captured German films and excerpts from Leni Riefenstahl's *Triumph of the Will*.[48] The screenwriter Budd Schulberg and the Hollywood director John Ford had worked with OSS officers to piece together the four-hour production.[49] *The Nazi Plan* displayed the close relationship between Hitler and the defendants up close and on-screen. Watching the film from the dock, many of the defendants appeared to relish the trip down memory lane. Telford Taylor later admitted that the reaction of the defendants surprised the Americans. "Far from viewing the film as another nail in their coffin, they enjoyed it hugely."[50]

Efimov drew the defendants watching themselves on the big screen, calling it "Last Performance in Nuremberg." The writer Vsevolod Ivanov (another member of the Soviet press corps) wrote an article that ran alongside Efimov's political cartoon in *Izvestiia* describing the pleasure the defendants took from a scene of their former selves "zealously laughing it up" with Hitler in April 1939 after he had assured FDR and other world leaders that he did not have aggressive aims in Europe. This was of course just after the Nazi invasion of Czechoslovakia. The Soviets became anxious to screen their own footage of the Nazi conspiracy—footage which they were certain the defendants would find much less delightful.[51]

The ineffectiveness of the American documentary provided an opening for the Soviets, a chance to showcase one of their areas of strength: film. On the same day that the Americans screened *The Nazi Plan*, Gorshenin received from Moscow a list of short films and film clips that the Soviet prosecution could draw on as evidence in its case against the former Nazi leaders. The Central Studio of Documentary Films in Moscow—Karmen's studio—had put together these films, which included Russian-language documentaries about Auschwitz and Majdanek as well as English-language documentaries about the devastation of Minsk, Smolensk, and Stalingrad, the destruction of Soviet cultural treasures, and the crimes of the Nazi "doctors."[52]

Back in September, while the Committee of Chief Prosecutors was meeting in London, Rudenko had informed Vyshinsky that there would be opportunities for screening film footage in Nuremberg and had inquired about preparing Soviet documentary films for use as material evidence in the trials.[53] In late October, Vyshinsky and one of his assistants in the Ministry of Foreign Affairs, Mikhail Kharlamov, had viewed footage about the destruction of Soviet cities, churches, industries, and cultural treasures that Karmen's studio had proposed sending to Nuremberg—and had given pointed criticism. They had cautioned that the footage brought too much attention to the German bombardment of Soviet military factories and advised the omission of several scenes. They had also noted that the English-language subtitles were too clumsily propagandistic and that the filmmakers should allow the evidence to "speak for itself." Vyshinsky and Kharlamov had recommended reorganizing the footage into several individual films by theme. One of these films, they suggested, should include the factory in Danzig, Poland where "the Germans made soap from human corpses."[54]

Spurred by the lack of atrocity footage in *The Nazi Plan*, the Party's propaganda department now directed the studio to select the most compelling footage shot by Karmen and other Soviet cameramen during the war and combine it with captured German film footage to create three documentaries to introduce as evidence: *Atrocities Committed by the German Fascist Invaders in the USSR; The German Fascist Destruction of Soviet Cities;* and *The German Fascist Destruction of the Cultural Treasures of the Peoples of the USSR*. Karmen's studio set to work on these films, with completion planned for early January 1946.[55] The Soviets had gotten off to a slow start but were gaining momentum quickly. Karmen was soon bragging to the other correspondents that his studio was preparing a "bomb" whose effects "would be remembered by everyone."[56]

As the Party discussed Soviet film footage and considered the problem of the Western press, Rudenko and his team watched the Americans continue to expand their case. For the rest of the week (December 12–15) a group of U.S. assistant prosecutors detailed the connections between the Nazi conspiracy and Nazi crimes against humanity. Thomas Dodd (a Connecticut lawyer who had served as the assistant to five attorneys general, including Jackson and Biddle) presented evidence on the exploitation of forced labor in the German-occupied Soviet Union; William F. Walsh detailed the persecution of Jews throughout Eastern Europe; and Samuel Harris presented evidence on plunder and mass starvation in Nazi-occupied Russia and Ukraine.[57]

All three elaborated on evidence that Jackson and Alderman had alluded to during the first days of the trials. Dodd quoted at length from communications between Fritz Sauckel (Hitler's head of labor deployment) and Rosenberg. In October 1942, Sauckel had informed Rosenberg that some two million foreign laborers would need to be drafted immediately from Ukraine and other parts of the occupied East to work in the German armament industry. Dodd described what this had meant in practice: the Russians and Ukrainians who were recruited for forced labor in Germany were mercilessly starved and mistreated. Those villages that resisted the call for labor recruitment were burned to the ground. Survivors were beaten, imprisoned, and sent to labor camps. Walsh read from correspondence among German leaders about the extermination of the Jews. One secret report to Rosenberg, dated June 1943, groused that thousands of Jews killed by the SS could have been better used as forced labor. Another report complained about gas leaks in the mobile killing vans being used by the Einsatzgruppen throughout the occupied East; it recommended that when the vans were in operation German soldiers stay as far away as they could in order to preserve their health.[58]

The Americans painted a haunting picture of the German occupation of the Soviet Union. The Soviets were simultaneously moved and troubled. Jackson and his team had continued to hoard evidence of Nazi crimes against Soviet citizens—and were now encroaching still further on the Soviet case. Dodd had introduced and read documents about forced labor, deportations, and concentration camps that were all supposed to have been allocated to the Soviets and the French, who would be presenting on "crimes against humanity." Rudenko and French deputy chief prosecutor Edgar Faure had both asked the Americans to back off—but Jackson had again insisted that all of these documents related to the conspiracy charge.[59]

The Vyshinsky Commission held five meetings that week, and its members privately aired their fury with the Americans. Gorshenin related that he, too, had approached Jackson about the American incursion into the Soviet case, to no avail. He ordered Rudenko to continue his efforts to obtain whatever materials the U.S. prosecution agreed to hand over.[60] Vyshinsky, who was following developments in Nuremberg from afar, had become convinced that Jackson was trying to force the Soviet prosecution into a secondary role in the trials. He was right, of course. Jackson had told several members of his staff as well as President Truman that he did not have faith in the Soviets or in the French and wanted the American prosecution to present as much of the case as possible.[61] But there was also another issue in play. Due in part to concerns about state sovereignty, the "crimes against humanity" charge had been circumscribed in the Nuremberg Charter to cover only crimes committed "in execution of or in connection with" another crime within the Tribunal's jurisdiction. Jackson had come to believe that this charge had a better chance of sticking—and of covering crimes committed before the start of the war—if it was firmly tied to Count One, the Nazi conspiracy.[62]

The Vyshinsky Commission's members moved forward with the Soviet case even as they struggled to keep the Americans at bay. They continued to revise the speeches of the Soviet prosecutors and to approve the selection of documents. They vigorously discussed how to handle the expansion of the American case—which, in addition to being infuriating, carried practical implications for their selection of evidence. Should the Soviet prosecution forge ahead and present documents the Americans and the British had already introduced? They decided to cede no ground. While the Soviet prosecution would make maximum use of evidence that had not yet been presented to the Tribunal, it would use any and all documents that were important for the Soviet case—regardless of whether the Americans or the British had already introduced them in open court. The Vyshinsky Commission did, however, emphasize the desirability of adding fresh evidence to Rudenko's opening speech. Toward this end Vyshinsky asked Soviet leaders to expedite the authentication of newly obtained documents relating to Nazi aggression.[63]

The question of defense witnesses also continued to vex the Soviets. In October, the Tribunal had rejected Nikitchenko's proposal to give each chief prosecutor veto power over defense witnesses.[64] Now the defense was asking to summon more and more German generals and diplomats as witnesses to challenge Soviet evidence and arguments about the war. The Tribunal's regulations were loose. Each defense attorney could petition the Secretariat for the production of any witnesses he pleased, providing no justification other than those facts that the witnesses would provide and why such facts were relevant to his client's defense. The defense had rushed to take advantage of this rule, creating a flood of petitions; the American authorities had established a subcommission in the Secretariat to review them.[65] The Vyshinsky Commission now deemed it imperative for Trainin to participate in this subcommission and told Nikitchenko to make this happen. The commission also gave the Soviet prosecution orders to oppose specific defense requests—such as Otto Stahmer's petition to submit written questions for Lord Halifax. Stahmer wanted Halifax to attest that Goering had tried to keep Germany out of war.[66]

The prosecution's indictment of six fascist organizations—the Reich Cabinet, the Leadership Corps of the Nazi Party, the SA, the SS, the General Staff and High Command of the Wehrmacht, and the Gestapo and SD (indicted as a single organization)—further complicated the matter of witnesses. The Soviets had initially opposed the U.S. proposal to try organizations but had compromised on this issue at the London Conference. Now, much to the surprise of everyone—including Jackson and Maxwell Fyfe—the defense was asking to call dozens of representative members of each organization before the court. The Vyshinsky Commission ordered Rudenko and Nikitchenko to oppose this request by arguing that representatives of these organizations were already among the defendants and that hearing additional witnesses would take up far too much time.[67] The Soviets were concerned about time, but mostly they wanted to stifle the defense. They didn't see what could possibly be gained by having dozens of SS men and German generals testify in court.

Soviet correspondents thought that the defense was scheming to derail the trials. Vishnevsky reported to *Pravda* chief Peter Pospelov on December 15 that the accused and their attorneys were "trying any way they can to drag the trials out and to discredit the accusations as well as the Tribunal itself." Vishnevsky observed that Goering in particular was watching the growing tensions between the Soviets and the Anglo-Americans with special interest, waiting for any flare-up that might help the defendants' cause. He suggested that the defendants were resorting to all kinds of "tricks," engaging in political ploys and focusing in on procedural technicalities. "We have to strike at these methods *mercilessly*," he urged, and pursue "a speedy judgment."[68]

The Vyshinsky Commission was attempting to do just that. Acting on its instructions, Rudenko and Nikitchenko challenged a Tribunal decision requiring the prosecution to read aloud in court all sections of documents on which it intended to base its case.[69] (The Tribunal had recently introduced this rule after the defense had protested that some American evidence had not been made available to it in German; reading the documents into the court record would ensure their simultaneous translation into the four official languages of the IMT.)[70] The Soviets worried that this could precipitate further defense challenges to all kinds of evidence in open court.

The Vyshinsky Commission was also attempting to squelch Stahmer's petition to the Tribunal for copies of all documents relating to his client Goering. Rudenko (duly acting on the commission's instructions) informed the Tribunal that some of these documents, because of their classified character, should not be in private hands and definitely should not be in the hands of former Nazis like Stahmer. He agreed to provide the relevant documents for Stahmer to read—but only under supervision within the Palace of Justice.[71] In an attempt to get rid of Stahmer, the commission also drafted a petition for Rudenko to submit to the Tribunal calling for the dismissal of all defense attorneys who had belonged to the Nazi Party. Gorshenin directed Nikitchenko to feel out the other judges on this question. He also impressed upon Nikitchenko and Volchkov the importance of keeping Moscow in the loop about all of the Tribunal's private deliberations. The Soviet judges dutifully promised to provide "timely and high-quality information."[72]

Goering and "his Nazi attorney" (as the Soviets called Stahmer) were continuing to draw the attention of the entire Soviet delegation. Goering had arrived at the Nuremberg prison in a drug-addled state, addicted to morphine. Now clean, he used his charm and cunning to dominate his codefendants. Karmen noted that even in the dock Goering stood out in his "single-breasted jacket with gold buttons, and trousers tucked in his boots."[73] Vishnevsky deemed Goering the most charismatic of the defendants and observed the way he commanded the others as well as their attorneys.[74] Efimov saw that "Goering carried himself cheekily and brazenly, in every way possible indicating that if in Hitler's hierarchy he was second, then here, in the dock, he is number one." He described how Goering intently followed all aspects of the case, sometimes "shaking his head affirmatively and other times sarcastically twisting his mouth."[75]

In Moscow, Soviet leaders were still up in arms about the efforts Goering had been making, with Stahmer's assistance, to advance his agenda in Western newspapers. Rudenko had lodged a complaint with the Committee of Chief Prosecutors on December 11 about the Goering interview with the AP—but nothing had come of it. Deciding that enough was enough, the Politburo Commission for the Nuremberg Trials drafted a letter of protest in Rudenko's name about the Nazi defense's misuse of the press. Soviet leaders forwarded the letter to Nuremberg with orders for Rudenko to get the other chief prosecutors' signatures and submit the letter to the Tribunal.[76]

On the morning of December 15, Rudenko sent Jackson, Maxwell Fyfe, and Dubost copies of this letter—which lambasted the Western press for allowing the former Nazi leaders to continue their criminal activities by rallying the German people "behind the Tribunal's back." The letter called on the judges to put a stop to what it called an "abnormal and intolerable" situation by prohibiting the publication of interviews with the defendants and other propaganda. Noting Stahmer's role in spreading Goering's "fascist pronouncements," the letter asked the judges to warn the defense lawyers that they would lose the right to defend their clients if they continued to pass information from the defendants to the press. It also asked the judges to warn the press corps that correspondents who spread Nazi ideas would be barred from the courtroom.[77] Maxwell Fyfe and Dubost expressed support for Rudenko's appeal; Dubost even noted that in France a lawyer would be punished if he acted as a middleman between an imprisoned client and a third party. Both stopped short of signing the strongly worded letter.[78]

Rudenko formally submitted this letter to the Tribunal later that day. The Vyshinsky Commission made sure that Nikitchenko understood that it had been lodged on Moscow's orders.[79] On Monday morning, December 17, Judge Lawrence, as the president of the Tribunal, admonished defense counsel to keep to "the highest professional standards" and to stop serving as intermediaries between their clients and the press corps. The Tribunal refused to go further in its warning or to censor the press. Instead, Lawrence gently asked the press to avoid actions "which might conflict with the impartial administration of justice."[80]

Soviet newspapers made Lawrence's statement sound far more authoritative, assuring the Soviet people that the Tribunal was taking "energetic measures" to rein in the Nazi defense.[81] But it was clear to the Soviet correspondents that Lawrence's warning lacked teeth. Writing to Pospelov again on the evening of December 19, Vishnevsky reported that there was a photo of Goering on the third page of that day's local paper, bringing even more publicity to the former Nazi leader. This was par for the course, he lamented. "The capitalist press covers the trial lopsidedly" and was continuing to broadcast the views of the defense. Vishnevsky did assure Pospelov that the prosecution's case, along with news of the recent execution of war criminals in Bergen-Belsen and Dachau, was starting to unnerve some of the defendants. "We have to squeeze them, squeeze some more and hang this entire gang!" he wrote.[82]

Soviet newspapers did not cover the drama the Soviet prosecution was experiencing behind the scenes, of course. While *Pravda* and *Izvestiia* reported on the Tribunal's December 17 warning to the defense, they did not share the other announcements Lawrence had made that morning. To the Soviet prosecution's great disappointment, the Tribunal had approved a number of defense petitions for witnesses and had affirmed that the defense was also entitled to call witnesses on behalf of each of the indicted organizations. On a brighter note for the Soviets, the Tribunal had announced that it would accept as evidence not just those parts of documents that were read aloud in court but also documents that were only cited in court, as long as they had been translated into German and made available to defense counsel. This left the Soviet prosecution free to refer to official war crimes commission reports—such as Extraordinary State Commission reports and the Burdenko Report—without having to read them before the Tribunal.[83]

The U.S. prosecution meanwhile was continuing to preempt the Soviets, presenting powerful evidence of German crimes against humanity in the occupied Soviet Union on the grounds that this evidence, too, supported the conspiracy charge. On December 17, Harris described how the defendants had sought to convert the Crimea, the Volga region, and Baku into German colonies and had planned to ship all foodstuffs from the southern Soviet Union to Germany—starving "millions of Russians" in the process.[84] This presentation, revealing how the Nazis used famine as an instrument of extermination, made a strong impression on the Soviet correspondents.[85] Rudenko and his team had been planning to present some of this very same evidence; they now had to figure out whether and how to rework part of their case.

The Soviet prosecutors remained stuck on the sidelines as the U.S. prosecution shifted focus and began to sum up some of its evidence against the indicted organizations. The assistant prosecutors Robert Storey and Warren F. Farr spoke of the crimes of the Leadership Corps of the Nazi Party, the SA, the SS, the Reich Cabinet, and the Gestapo.[86] The evidence against the SS held the biggest surprise for the Soviet correspondents. Polevoi learned that SS men were not just killers but also engineers, inventors of all kinds of equipment and machinery for mechanized mass slaughter. "Civil and mechanical engineers dressed in black SS uniforms designed gas chambers, furnaces, and machinery for crushing bones," he later wrote in his memoir. One of the most horrifying pieces of machinery of all, he noted, was the gas van.[87]

On Thursday, December 20, the Tribunal voted itself into recess for the Christmas break. While the Soviets publicly complained about this inter-mission as an unnecessary disruption of the trials, they were grateful for the time to work on their case. That afternoon, the Vyshinsky Commission held its final meeting before the holiday and came up with a work plan for the next two weeks. Gorshenin and Raginsky would return to Moscow to meet with Soviet leaders. In their absence, Mankovsky and Alexandrov (no longer under investigation following Likhachev's removal) would oversee the Soviet delegation in Nuremberg. They would secure the urgent translation of documents for the Soviet case and work with other commission members to continue generating the questionnaires the Soviet prosecution would use to cross-examine the defendants. The commission instructed them to avoid posing questions that might elicit "a programmed speech"—and further ad-vised them to omit the anticipated answers.[88]

Finally, the Vyshinsky Commission censured Nikitchenko for failing to convince the other judges to disqualify former Nazis (such as Stahmer and Seidl) from serving as defense attorneys and for failing to bring Trainin into the Secretariat's work of reviewing defense petitions. Neither Nikitchenko nor Volchkov, Gorshenin added, had informed him of any difficulties that might have arisen in fulfilling the commission's orders. Now Nikitchenko and Rudenko were to work with the commission to prepare petitions for the Tribunal with the goal of eliminating undesirable witnesses.[89]

As the holiday approached, an enormous Christmas tree smelling of fresh fir needles appeared in the Faber Castle, carted back from the Bavarian Alps by American troops. Glass balls, trinkets, dried fruits and nuts, and small bottles of gin, whisky, and other liqueurs dangled from the tree's branches. A large Santa Claus that had been flown in from the United States stood guard in front of the tree.[90] The coming of Christmas pro-vided the inspiration for one of Efimov's most memorable drawings of the defendants: Goering, Ribbentrop, Keitel, Jodl, Rosenberg, and Frank stare dolefully out of their cell windows at a scrawny tree "trimmed" with the Barbarossa File, Plan Green, and other evidence of their plans for waging aggressive war.

Nuremberg emptied out for the Christmas break. A number of the Soviet correspondents, including Polevoi, set out on trips around Europe for the Soviet press. Others, such as Mikhail Kuprianov, Porfiry Krylov, and Nikolai Sokolov, flew back to Moscow on orders from *Pravda* to report in person

FIGURE 6.5 Boris Efimov's political cartoon "Design for Putting Up a Christmas Tree," *Izvestiia,* December 27, 1945, part of Efimov's series "Fascist Beasts (from the Hall of Justice)." The tree is decorated with evidence of Nazi crimes. The defendants are Goering, Ribbentrop, Keitel, Jodl, Rosenberg, and Frank (left to right).

Credit: Reproduced courtesy of Boris Efimov and the Ne Boltai! Collection.

on Germany, the course of the trials, and everyday life in Nuremberg.[91] Gorshenin, on his return to Moscow, conferred with Vyshinsky and other members of the Politburo Commission about the Soviet case. Meanwhile, at Vyshinsky's request, the Ministry of Foreign Affairs compiled for the Soviet prosecution packets of materials on designated themes. The packet on "the racial ideology of German fascism" included the Nuremberg race laws as well as quotes culled from Nazi speeches and from Rosenberg's book *The Myth of the Twentieth Century.* The Soviets were preparing to address the topic of German anti-Semitism in court.[92]

The recess was a chance for the Soviets to take stock of their successes and failures at Nuremberg. Soviet informants contributed to this process in their reports for Moscow. Mikhail Dolgopolov, a Sovinformburo correspondent and *Izvestiia* editor, sent Solomon Lozovsky a seven-page missive on December 30 that hit Moscow where it hurt most—comparing Soviet inadequacies to American prowess. The report received immediate attention in Moscow. Copies were forwarded up the Soviet hierarchy; Molotov (still smarting from Stalin's criticism of his failure to protect Soviet interests abroad) called for quick and decisive action to address the issues it raised.[93]

Most of Dolgopolov's observations were old news in Moscow. The communication lines between Moscow and Nuremberg were terrible; Soviet correspondents did not receive Moscow newspapers for weeks on end and did not have a single radio receiver in their residence. The other delegations, by contrast, had recent newspapers and magazines from London, Paris, and New York and set them out in the Press Camp for everyone to read. The Americans found it inconceivable that Soviet correspondents could work under such conditions—and Dolgopolov emphasized that their skepticism was well placed. Soviet personnel were in a state of "complete disinformation," as he put it, and could not respond to questions from the Western correspondents about articles concerning the Soviet Union that appeared in the foreign press. The Soviet delegation, he made clear, was missing precious opportunities to advance Moscow's views to the West.[94]

Dolgopolov also addressed the persistent shortage of skilled Soviet interpreters, a problem that had become more dangerous than ever. The "overwhelming majority" of Soviet interpreters, he reported, were struggling to extemporaneously translate the speeches of the prosecutors and judges and the statements of the lawyers into Russian.[95] Simultaneous translation was presenting unique challenges for all of the delegations. Even the most talented interpreters sometimes faltered when a sudden statement was made, when an attorney or judge asked a question in court, or when the testimony was especially shocking.[96] The Soviets, however, were having a difficult time with even some of the more rudimentary courtroom interpretation. Everyone, Dolgopolov stressed, was "talking about this."[97]

The Soviets were failing on numerous fronts to present their country to the world in the best possible light, according to Dolgopolov. Whereas the American occupation authorities had set up a movie theater to serve the international press corps, the Soviets had no similar venue and were missing the chance to share their great films. Especially embarrassing was the failure of Soviet support personnel to make a good impression, as a result of their shabby appearance. "The clothing of our female personnel is so bad and looks so poor that the Americans and English make fun of them," Dolgopolov reported. If the Soviet Union was going to send its citizens to major international events like the Nuremberg Trials, it was essential to pay some attention to appearances.[98]

Turning to broader questions of politics and propaganda, Dolgopolov shared rumors that had been circulating in the American zone about arrests and deportations in the Soviet Union. He and some Soviet colleagues had visited Munich one weekend and had heard stories about the punishment of Soviet citizens who had returned home after being liberated from German camps and prisons. Dolgopolov recounted his encounter with a Soviet Azerbaijani, a former prisoner of war who was now working for the Americans as a hospital orderly. This man had confided that he and the "many other" Soviet citizens in the American zone wanted to return home but were afraid of punitive measures.[99] Repatriation was a diplomatic quagmire. Stalin was furious about the American refusal to forcibly repatriate all Soviet citizens— and the NKVD was in fact arresting large numbers of returnees on charges of collaboration.[100] Dolgopolov would have known that this information about Soviet citizens in Munich would get Stalin's full attention.

Dolgopolov ended his report with a call for a greater mobilization of the Soviet press corps in the coming months. Based on chatter in the Press Camp, it seemed like the foreign correspondents planned to scale back their coverage of the trials during the Soviet part of the case. Dolgopolov proposed that the Soviets "fill this gap" by sending more of their own journalists, photographers, and writers to Nuremberg and by increasing their coverage of the trials both for the Soviet Union and for foreign newspapers.[101] (Sovinformburo was already translating Soviet articles and attempting to place them in newspapers abroad.)

Dolgopolov's letter was a clear-eyed assessment of the Soviet Union's struggles on the international stage. Molotov responded by expressing surprise to Gorshenin that it had not been possible thus far to set things right. Gorshenin assured Molotov that measures had been taken to improve the communications lines and to recruit more personnel.[102] But both men must have also understood that seriously addressing the difficulties the Soviets were facing would require far-reaching changes in the USSR's foreign relations apparatus that Stalin was unwilling to make.

The Soviets had gone to Nuremberg to take on the Nazis—but had ended up engaged in a struggle on multiple fronts to shape the narrative of the war. American ambitions and American know-how in the realm of diplomatic relations and international organizations presented one set of challenges. The Soviets bristled at the U.S. prosecution's continuing efforts to relegate the Soviet Union to a secondary role in the trials. At the same time, the defendants were taking advantage of the Tribunal's rules and the relatively loose conditions in Nuremberg to launch a vigorous defense—both in the courtroom and beyond its walls via the press. In the pages of Western newspapers, in their petitions to the Tribunal, and in their dismissive attitude toward the proceedings, Goering, Keitel, Ribbentrop, and the other former leaders of Nazi Germany were still fierce and were focusing much of their wrath against the Soviet Union.

Stalin and Vyshinsky had sent talented individuals to Nuremberg. Many of them understood that the entire Soviet delegation needed greater flexibility, and more information and expertise, to function effectively in the American zone of Germany. But Moscow's answer to everything from personnel problems to public relations issues to the preparation of the Soviet case was greater centralization and surveillance. The problem was that the Soviets did have secrets to hide—more so than the other countries of the prosecution—and this would continue to shape the course of the trials. The Soviets were heroes and victims. They were also perpetrators.

CHAPTER 7 | Course Corrections

A S THE NEW YEAR began, the Soviet press corps prepared for the Americans to resume their case against the Nazi organizations. Boris Polevoi steeled himself for his return to the Palace of Justice with its sickly green lighting, where every day the reporters were bombarded with evidence that, as he put it, "gave one the creeps."[1]

Over the holidays Polevoi had briefly escaped Nuremberg for a trip around Western Europe with a group of Yugoslav correspondents—a moment of respite that soon seemed "like a vague dream." The oversized Christmas tree was still standing in the Faber Castle on his return, though he noticed immediately that it had been stripped of its most festive decorations.[2] Vsevolod Vishnevsky had remained in Nuremberg over the break, deeming it "hardly sensible to fly to Moscow, get tired, and fly back" when he could spend the time absorbing himself in the materials of the trial.[3] He devoted himself to researching the defendants' pasts for the Soviet prosecution and writing short biographical sketches for the Soviet press. Several of his pieces appeared in *Pravda* during the winter recess, reminding the Soviet people that Konstantin von Neurath bore responsibility for the massacre of the Czech village of Lidice and that Hans Frank had been planning to empty Poland of all Poles by 1950.[4]

Vishnevsky, an ardent communist, was famous in the Soviet Union and well known in leftist circles in Europe. Stalin had sent him to France and Spain a decade earlier as a cultural representative of the antifascist Popular Front. In Paris, he had rubbed elbows with James Joyce and Pablo Picasso and attended the premiere of the Soviet film *We Are from Kronstadt*, for which he had written the screenplay. (It was based on his play about the 1919 defense of Petrograd.) In Madrid, he wrote the text for *Spain*, a documentary of the Spanish Civil War made from Karmen's newsreel footage.[5] Ilya Ehrenburg, who had been with Vishnevsky in Madrid, described him as "an extremely passionate man" who "reminded one of a good Spanish anarchist. When he began to speak he never knew where it would take him or how it would end."[6] During the Second World War, the timbre and intonation of Vishnevsky's voice became familiar to Leningraders as he gave stirring speeches over the radio, urging the blockaded population to stand strong.[7] Vishnevsky had staged many mock trials in his time as a playwright. Now he studied the defendants in the Nuremberg courtroom and imagined their final act—death by hanging. He was determined to do his part to make this happen.

When the Tribunal reconvened on Wednesday, January 2, Vishnevsky, Polevoi, and the rest of the Soviet correspondents were thrust back into the horrors of the war in the occupied Soviet Union. The U.S. prosecution began by presenting more evidence against the Gestapo and the SS, detailing the murder of Jews and communists in Russia and Ukraine. The U.S. assistant prosecutor Robert Storey read a chilling affidavit by Hermann Friedrich

FIGURE 7.1 Boris Polevoi, Vsevolod Vishnevsky, and the photographer Viktor Temin, 1946.

Credit: Russian State Documentary Film and Photo Archive No. 0-358881.

Graebe, the wartime manager of a German construction firm in Ukraine, describing how SS units and Ukrainian militiamen had jointly stormed the Jewish ghetto of Rovno in July 1942—dragging people from their beds in the middle of the night and herding them to a waiting freight train. "Car after car was filled, and the screaming of women and children and the cracking of whips and rifle shots resounded unceasingly," Storey read. "Women carried their dead children in their arms, children pulled and dragged their dead parents by their arms and legs down the road toward the train." That afternoon, the U.S. assistant prosecutor Whitney R. Harris began to sum up the evidence against Ernst von Kaltenbrunner, the only SS man in the dock.[8]

The next morning, the Americans surprised the Soviets by announcing in court that they would begin calling witnesses to testify about the crimes of the SS. Robert Jackson had ignored the repeated Soviet entreaties to defer additional witness testimony until later in the trials. He had former SS men lined up to testify about the extermination of Europe's Jews—and he understood that their firsthand accounts would carry far more weight than any written evidence.

Assistant prosecutor John Harlan Amen called to the witness box former SS general Otto Ohlendorf, a small, hunched man in a wrinkled grey suit. Ohlendorf had once commanded Einsatzgruppe D, a mobile execution squad that had committed countless atrocities in Ukraine and Crimea. He now dispassionately recounted how his unit had marched into the Soviet Union alongside the Wehrmacht in June 1941, killing 90,000 men, women, and children with gas and machine guns during the first year of the war.[9]

Ohlendorf incriminated a number of organizations, including the SS, the military High Command, and the SD. He testified that the four Einsatzgruppen (A, B, C, and D) and their subunits, the Einsatzkommandos, had operated with the complete support of military leaders and had frequently been under direct military command. The murder of Jews and commissars, Ohlendorf attested, had been premeditated. The Einsatzgruppen had received instructions a month before Operation Barbarossa that these groups "were to be liquidated." Amen interrupted him: "And when you say 'liquidated' do you mean 'killed'?" Ohlendorf answered in the affirmative. On the eve of the invasion, he continued, Himmler assembled the men and repeated the order, adding that those who took part in the campaign would bear "no personal responsibility."[10]

The Soviet prosecutors had not been expecting to examine witnesses at this stage of the trials—let alone an SS man who had overseen Nazi atrocities in the Soviet Union. Yuri Pokrovsky did the best he could on the fly, asking Ohlendorf what had prompted Himmler's decision to use mobile gas vans in the East. Ohlendorf startled everyone by declaring that Himmler had been motivated by compassion—wanting to free the men of the Einsatzkommandos from the emotional burden of shooting women and children. In practice, Ohlendorf added, the men did not like using the gas vans, as they found the removal of the dead to be distressing. Asked by Pokrovsky to elaborate, Ohlendorf alluded to the fact that certain bodily functions had taken place spontaneously, "leaving the corpses lying in filth." Nikitchenko followed up from the bench: "For what reason were the children massacred?" Ohlendorf answered without missing a beat. "The order was that the Jewish population should be totally exterminated." When asked by the attorney for the SS, Ludwig Babel, if he really had had "no scruples" about carrying out such an order, Ohlendorf seemed surprised. It was "inconceivable," he explained, "that a subordinate leader should not carry out orders given by the leaders of the state."[11]

The Americans got more than they had bargained for in Ohlendorf. He provided all the horrific descriptions of SS atrocities they had expected—but, in attesting that the perpetrators had been following their superiors' orders, he was also setting up the defense that Aron Trainin had denounced in his wartime writings. The Soviet effort at the London Conference to ban this defense had resulted in a compromise: the "superior orders" plea would not free a defendant from criminal responsibility, but the judges could choose to consider it as a mitigating factor for sentencing. Ohlendorf was throwing the defense a lifeline.

The next witness for the prosecution, SS officer Dieter Wisliceny, similarly invoked the defense of "just following orders." He had worked for Adolf Eichmann, whose name would soon be synonymous with the Nazi program to wipe out Europe's Jews. Wisliceny testified that Eichmann had shown him a letter from Himmler referring to Hitler's order for "the final solution to the Jewish question" and had explained that this referred to the "biological annihilation of the Jewish race." Wisliceny told the court that when he expressed reservations, Eichmann rebuked him: "It was an order of the Führer's and would have to be carried out."[12] Wisliceny estimated that between four and five million Jews had been murdered in keeping with this order.

The following morning, the Americans called still more witnesses to testify about the crimes of the SS. Walter Schellenberg, an SS intelligence chief, expounded on the Einsatzgruppen's operations in the Soviet Union, corroborating Ohlendorf's testimony. Alois Hollriegel, a former guard at the Mauthausen concentration camp in Austria, described the murder of internees by shooting, gassing, and other means—recounting how guards had made a sport of throwing prisoners off a steep precipice near the camp's quarry, calling the victims "paratroopers." He also added to the evidence against Kaltenbrunner and the Hitler Youth leader Baldur von Schirach by testifying that both men had visited Mauthausen and knew about its operations.[13] Jackson had correctly judged the effect this testimony would have in the courtroom. It left no question as to why the former Nazi leaders and their organizations were on trial.

The week in court ended with Telford Taylor presenting evidence against the last indicted organization, the General Staff and High Command of the Wehrmacht. Taylor emphasized that the German military brass were being charged with criminality not just for committing war crimes and crimes against humanity but also for having conspired with Hitler to wage war with the aim of enlarging Germany. The Soviet prosecutors watched as he read from a great pile of captured German documents—including a roster of officers who had attended a conference Hitler had called in June 1941 to walk through the details of Operation Barbarossa. Taylor also presented affidavits from German generals directly admitting to their complicity in the attack on the Soviet Union. The evidence showed, he emphasized, that the High Command had embarked on the war against the Soviet Union "with ruthless determination backed by careful planning."[14]

The Americans were doing an excellent job presenting evidence of Nazi crimes against the Soviet Union—but Stalin was fed up. He had envisioned the Nuremberg Trials as a means for the Soviet Union to publicly claim its role as an international power. The events playing out in the Palace of Justice were instead making the Soviets look like a secondary player, subordinate to the Americans. Yes, the world was learning more each day about the Nazi assault on the Soviet people. But the Soviets wanted to bear witness to their own suffering and confront the defendants themselves, on their own terms.

The Soviets had repeatedly been caught off guard by the way the Americans had reconfigured the case against the major German war criminals. Jackson and his team had used the conspiracy charge he had insisted upon in London and the organizations case as a rationale to present voluminous evidence on all four counts of the Indictment. Stalin was unwilling to accept a lesser role for the Soviet Union. It was time to correct course.

Stalin, who had recently returned to Moscow from Sochi, now began to show a keen interest in all aspects of the Soviet case. Rudenko, Trainin, Gorshenin, Raginsky, and Sheinin had marked the New Year in Moscow, and remained there after the holiday to work on the Soviet presentations in close consultation with Stalin and other Soviet leaders.[15] Vyshinsky was not in Russia for much of this period; he spent early January on foreign policy business in Romania and flew from there to London for the first meeting of the new United Nations.[16] In Vyshinsky's absence, Gorshenin conferred with others at the Ministry of Foreign Affairs who knew the details of Soviet-German collaboration, including Andrei Smirnov—a career diplomat who had worked at the Soviet embassy in Germany from 1940 to June 1941.[17]

On Friday, January 4, Gorshenin sent Party leaders a draft of Rudenko's opening speech, thoroughly revised from the original November version.[18] Two nights later, Stalin received Rudenko and Gorshenin at his Kremlin office on Red Square for an hour-long meeting. Molotov, Malenkov, Mikoyan, and Beria were all present, as was Andrei Zhdanov (another member of Stalin's inner circle).[19] Rudenko had been summoned to Stalin's Kremlin office only once before, in June 1945, when he was preparing to prosecute the former leaders of the Polish underground.[20] Given the high stakes of the Nuremberg Trials and all that had gone wrong so far, Rudenko must have been terrified.

There is no transcript of their meeting, but it is clear that Stalin expressed his dissatisfaction with the overall course of the trials and with the draft of the Soviet opening speech—and that he gave Rudenko and Gorshenin orders on both fronts. The speech would have to be rewritten. Stalin had announced earlier that day at a meeting of the Politburo that it was imperative to bring in fresh evidence to strengthen the Soviet case and to counter the defense's claims that Hitler had launched a preventive war against the Soviet Union. The Politburo had directed NKGB chief Vsevolod Merkulov, the new NKVD chief Sergei Kruglov, and SMERSH chief Viktor Abakumov (the heads of the three main branches of the Soviet security apparatus) to secure this evidence.[21] They were to procure statements from Romanian and Hungarian leaders in Soviet custody attesting that their nations had been conspiring with Germany to attack the USSR long before Operation Barbarossa was set in motion. The Politburo had also ordered the verification of General Erich Buschenhagen's statement to the NKVD about a German-Finnish agreement to attack the Soviet Union. Buschenhagen, the former chief of staff of the German forces in Norway, was a Soviet prisoner.[22]

Gorshenin had undoubtedly known that Stalin wanted the speech reworked before he and Rudenko walked into Stalin's office in the Kremlin. For two days prior to the meeting, Abakumov had been feeding him strictly secret documents—including sworn testimony from the former Romanian prime minister Ion Antonescu (another Soviet prisoner) about an agreement with Hitler to attack the Soviet Union. Abakumov had also offered Gorshenin access to captured German and Romanian archives that were in the hands of SMERSH and the NKVD.[23]

The morning after their meeting with Stalin, Rudenko and Gorshenin received a memorandum from the Ministry of Foreign Affairs echoing Stalin's concerns about the Soviet opening speech. The Ministry called it "unfortunate" that the current draft relied "almost exclusively" on documents the Americans had already presented, such as the Barbarossa Plan and Plan Green, or documents that had already appeared in print, such as Extraordinary State Commission reports. Again the captured German and Romanian archives were identified as a solution. The speech would have a much greater impact if it included this new evidence.[24] Gorshenin and Rudenko, thoroughly tired of the Soviets being sidelined, could not have agreed more.

Gorshenin and Rudenko had also left Stalin's office with instructions to expand the Soviet case to cover all four of the Indictment's counts. The Americans had made major incursions into the Soviet part of the case; the Soviet prosecution could not be expected to limit itself to presenting on war crimes and crimes against humanity on the Eastern Front. It would have its time in court in equal measure. To assist with the additional work, Stalin added another assistant prosecutor to the Soviet team: Lev Smirnov, who had just finished prosecuting ten members of the SS and the Wehrmacht in a war crimes trial in Smolensk. All ten had been convicted and sentenced to hard labor or death by hanging.[25]

On January 7, less than twenty-four hours after his face-to-face meeting with Stalin, Gorshenin sent Molotov a brief outline of a greatly expanded Soviet trial plan. It covered all four counts. Rudenko would give the Soviet opening speech as planned, but with fresh evidence. Then Pokrovsky and Nikolai Zorya would deliver presentations (to be prepared) on the Nazi conspiracy and crimes against peace. Pokrovsky would focus on the planning and waging of war against Czechoslovakia, Poland, and Yugoslavia; Zorya would address Germany's invasion of the Soviet Union, arguing that preparations had begun as early as 1939. A group of assistant prosecutors would follow up with evidence of German war crimes throughout the occupied Soviet Union and Eastern Europe. Smirnov would conclude with a presentation on crimes against humanity.[26]

The Politburo Commission for the Nuremberg Trials immediately signed off on the new Soviet trial plan, which aligned with Stalin's vision for the Soviet case. Trainin, Raginsky, and Sheinin prepared to fly back to Nuremberg with instructions for the Soviet prosecution.[27] Rudenko and Gorshenin would remain in Moscow until later in the month to work on the Soviet presentations, select new evidence, and interview potential witnesses.[28]

Soviet leaders used the next ten days—until mid-January—to continue Rudenko's better-late-than-never political education, briefing him in greater detail about the history of Soviet-German relations. Abakumov, Kruglov, and Merkulov meanwhile supplied Gorshenin with new evidence from the German Foreign Office and the NKVD for the Soviet presentations on the conspiracy and crimes against peace (Counts One and Two). These materials included a statement from Gheorghe Alexianu, the former Romanian governor of Transnistria, about German-Romanian collaboration against the Soviet Union. Abakumov suggested that the Soviet prosecution use this statement along with affidavits from the other high-ranking Romanians in Soviet custody: former prime minister Ion Antonescu, former foreign minister Mihai Antonescu, and former minister of war Constantin Pantazi.[29] Armed with this new evidence, the Soviet prosecution could confidently say that the Americans had illuminated only part of the Nazi conspiracy. Moscow could marshal some of this same information, after it had received a public hearing, to justify the need for Soviet involvement in postwar Romanian politics.

In Nuremberg the week of January 7 had begun with excitement both outside and inside the Palace of Justice. Early Monday morning a Soviet soldier discovered an unwrapped packet of Russian-language documents near the compound on the Eichendorffstrasse where members of the Soviet prosecution were housed. The packet was found next to an iron stove that the American soldiers who guarded the compound used to keep warm. Closer inspection revealed that the papers were Extraordinary State Commission reports about war crimes in Stalingrad—and that half of the packet was missing. The papers had apparently been taken from the Soviet delegation's Studebaker truck, parked in the compound's courtyard. The Soviet soldier reported this finding to his commanding officer, who saw that the truck was half empty and concluded that reams of Soviet evidence had been burned.[30]

Over the next few days, an American investigation determined that the matter of the destroyed Soviet evidence had been overblown. The truck had originally been only half full of documents; just half of a ream was missing. Pokrovsky verified these details and told the American authorities that the consequences were not serious for the Soviet prosecution. It remained a mystery, however, as to who had removed the documents from the truck. The American guard claimed that he had found the open packet of documents lying on the ground nearby and, assuming it to be waste paper, had used the wrapping paper, the cord, and some of the documents to start a fire. The guard who had been on duty immediately before him had tried to shift the blame to the Soviets, asserting that it was not his job to protect the truck's cargo from the residents of the Soviet compound. The American investigation report was forwarded to Moscow and contributed to growing Soviet frustration with life under the American authorities.[31]

Amid the tumult about the Soviet documents, the U.S. prosecution called witnesses to testify about the crimes of the General Staff and High Command. On the afternoon of January 7, Erich von dem Bach-Zelewski, the former SS leader for central Russia, stepped into the witness box and described the Wehrmacht's role in the antipartisan campaign in the Soviet Union. Under questioning by Taylor, Bach-Zelewski explained that most antipartisan actions had been carried out not by the SS but by regular army troops under Wehrmacht command. He also told the court that reprisals were frequently taken against civilians on the pretext of fighting the partisans, and that the High Command had been fully aware of such actions and the atrocities that resulted. He further maintained that the instructions about these antipartisan operations were intentionally vague, resulting, as expected, in what he now called "a wild state of anarchy."[32]

Pokrovsky followed up with a slew of questions for Bach-Zelewski about the antipartisan campaign. Did he correctly understand that commanders could declare anyone to be a partisan? Was it true that this was used as a pretext to massacre the Slavic and Jewish populations of the occupied East? Bach-Zelewski answered in the affirmative and acknowledged that the military command knew about the aims of the antipartisan campaign. He recounted a speech on the eve of the Russian campaign in which Himmler had declared outright that a goal of the campaign in the Soviet Union and Eastern Europe was to reduce the Slavic population by some "30 million."[33]

The defense attorneys lined up to cross-examine Bach-Zelewski. Rosenberg's lawyer, Alfred Thoma, asked whether the call for the extermination of 30 million people had been an expression of Himmler's personal ambition or was in keeping with Nazi ideology. Bach-Zelewski declared it to be the latter. "If for years, for decades, a doctrine is preached to the effect that the Slav race is an inferior race, that the Jews are not even human beings, then an explosion of this sort is inevitable." When Bach-Zelewski left the stand, Goering erupted in rage. He denounced Bach-Zelewski as "the bloodiest murderer" of all and called him a "swine-dog and a traitor." One Soviet participant later recalled that the interpreters did not translate Goering's words but that "everybody in the courtroom heard and understood" them.[34]

Pokrovsky had done an able job examining Bach-Zelewski and was standing up well in Rudenko's absence. Then Jackson and Maxwell Fyfe announced to the court on January 8 that the Americans and the British would begin the process of summing up the criminal responsibility of the individual defendants for conspiracy and crimes against peace (Counts One and

Two). The objective, they explained, was to bring together for the Tribunal the evidence presented thus far in court. This did not mean that the case against the former Nazi leaders was close to wrapping up, Maxwell Fyfe declared. The French and Soviet prosecutors would soon present evidence about war crimes and crimes against humanity (Counts Three and Four), which they could also relate to the individual defendants.[35]

What was going on here? Jackson was more determined than ever to bring American ideas about justice to postwar Europe. He had devised this strategy in order to solidify American control over what he saw as the most important parts of the case. He considered the Soviets and the French too ethically compromised by their wartime collaborations with Hitler to give, as he told Taylor, "plausible, let alone forceful, support" to the "conspiracy" and "crimes against peace" charges. He had thus convinced Maxwell Fyfe that it would be best to conclude this part of the case before the Soviets and the French even stepped up to the lectern.[36]

Four-power cooperation, tenuous even at the best of times, was giving over to bitterness and suspicion—both at Nuremberg and in the wider world. Truman and Jackson had similarly jaundiced views of the Soviets. A few days earlier Truman had sent a sharply worded letter to Secretary of State James Byrnes denouncing the creation of a Communist-controlled government in Romania (which was at least partially Vyshinsky's doing) as well as the continuing presence of Soviet troops in Iran. At the Potsdam Conference that summer, the United States had been "faced with an accomplished fact" of a Soviet-dominated Poland, Truman grumbled, and the Soviets "have been a headache to us ever since." Further compromises, he made clear, were not in the offing. He was done with "babying the Soviets."[37]

Jackson began implementing his plan to wrap up Counts One and Two even as Rudenko and Gorshenin were still in Moscow executing Stalin's orders to redraft the Soviet trial plan to cover all four counts. The rest of the Soviet prosecution spent the week in Nuremberg watching the Americans and the British take turns summing up their evidence against the defendants in the first row of the dock (temporarily skipping Hess, whose attorney, Gunter von Rohrscheidt, had broken his foot).[38] Maxwell Fyfe presented key evidence of Ribbentrop's treachery against the Soviet Union. He introduced into evidence the German-Soviet Non-Aggression Pact—which Ribbentrop, of course, had ushered to conclusion—and then presented evidence of Ribbentrop's plans to breach this treaty, including his communications with Rosenberg in the spring of 1941 about difficulties that might arise following the German occupation of Russia and Ukraine. Maxwell Fyfe also addressed Ribbentrop's role in the planning of war crimes and crimes against humanity, adding hastily that the defendant's role in executing these crimes would of course "be dealt with by my friends and Soviet colleagues."[39]

The American and British monologues were disrupted on Friday afternoon, January 11, when the U.S. prosecution called a witness who had recently arrived in Nuremberg. Dr. Franz Blaha, a Czech surgeon who had been interned at Dachau, was the first former concentration camp inmate to speak before the Tribunal, and his testimony about Nazi "medical experiments" shook the courtroom. The crowd listened with horror as Blaha described how prisoners were "cooled and warmed, reduced to a coma and then returned to life" before ultimately being killed. Pokrovsky questioned Blaha in an effort to clarify his testimony. Would it be correct to say that Dachau was an extermination camp and that there were various methods of extermination? Blaha answered yes. Everything that happened at the camp was related to the "plan for extermination," he testified, and "it was the Russian prisoners who were always treated the worst of all." Polevoi later recounted how he and the other Soviet correspondents spent the late afternoon in the Press Room of the Palace of Justice, talking over Blaha's testimony and becoming more and more furious. "Vampires—that's what they are," the writer Leonid Leonov proclaimed of the defendants. "Civilized savages, we'll drive a stake into your grave," Vishnevsky put in. "We'll drive it right through."[40]

Rudenko and Gorshenin were continuing to craft the Soviet presentations in conjunction with Soviet leaders in Moscow. On January 12, Gorshenin sent a revised draft of Rudenko's speech to Stalin, the Politburo Four, Zhdanov, and Vyshinsky. That same day, he sent Molotov two other key documents for review. The first enumerated a series of questions the Vyshinsky Commission had written up for the Soviet prosecution to use when cross-examining the defendants. Gorshenin acknowledged that these questions "may change in the course of interrogation." The second was a twenty-one-page inventory of the evidence Gorshenin and Rudenko had selected for the Soviet prosecution, categorized according to the four counts of the Indictment.[41]

This inventory included evidence that the Americans and British had already introduced but also plenty of new materials from captured archives. The "conspiracy" and "crimes against peace" sections included familiar documents, like the Barbarossa Plan, in addition to new evidence provided by the NKVD and SMERSH—including sworn statements from the generals Buschenhagen and Paulus concerning plans to invade the Soviet Union.[42]

The "war crimes" and "crimes against humanity" sections included directives from the military High Command on the treatment of Soviet prisoners of war that the Americans had already introduced, as well as dozens of Extraordinary State Commission reports about Nazi atrocities. To supplement these materials, Gorshenin and Rudenko had added memoranda from Rosenberg's archive and reports from Polish and Yugoslav war crimes commissions. Gorshenin and Rudenko also suggested that the Soviet prosecution introduce photographic and film evidence, as well as material evidence such as soap rendered from the corpses of concentration camp victims.[43]

By now, Karmen's studio had completed the three documentaries planned for Nuremberg—and on January 13 the Party's propaganda department signed off on them. The films had been prepared from footage shot by Soviet cameramen, with frames spliced in from German newsreels. A thirty-minute film about the German destruction of Soviet culture highlighted the shelling of palaces and museums in blockaded Leningrad and the razing of churches throughout Russia and Ukraine. A forty-minute film about the destruction of Soviet cities featured shots of burned-out blocks of buildings in Minsk, Smolensk, Novgorod, Kursk, and other urban areas. The final film, running forty-five minutes, focused on German atrocities against civilians and prisoners of war and included footage that Soviet cameramen had shot in Majdanek and Auschwitz during the Red Army's liberation of the concentration camps.[44] These films would all be shown as part of the Soviet case.

Late at night on January 13, Stalin received Gorshenin and Rudenko in the Kremlin for a follow-up meeting about the Soviet presentations. Minister of Justice Nikolai Rychkov (a recent addition to the Vyshinsky Commission) accompanied them.[45] The meeting lasted just ten minutes—enough time for Stalin to voice his continuing displeasure with the Soviet opening speech.

In the meeting's wake, Rudenko and Gorshenin rewrote parts of the speech to explicitly counter the defense's claims about preventive war. They added a new section reminding the court that "far in advance" of attacking the USSR Hitler and his clique had developed an invasion plan, pinpointed the territories they wanted to seize, and worked out the methods for plundering them and exterminating their populations. The speech now emphasized that the "original documents of Hitler's government" fully exposed the "falsity and ridiculousness" of all arguments about the "preventive" character of the assault.[46]

Rudenko and Gorshenin also revised the "crimes against humanity" section to place greater emphasis on German crimes against religion in Russia and Ukraine, including the desecration of churches, synagogues, and chapels. Stalin knew that this would play well on the international stage. They added vivid details, describing how German soldiers had stabled their horses and dogs among the pews, paraded around in religious vestments, and made bunks out of icons.[47] This approach carried some risks, given that the

Bolsheviks themselves had ransacked and repurposed churches, synagogues, and mosques during their antireligious campaign of the 1920s. But the 1920s seemed far in the past.

As the Soviets finished preparing their case in Moscow, the Americans and the British began to sum up the evidence on Counts One and Two against the defendants in the second row of the dock—and further expanded their reach as they did so. On January 14 and 15, the British summarized the cases thus far against the admirals Karl Doenitz and Erich Raeder. The British assistant prosecutor Frederick Elwyn Jones walked through the evidence of Raeder's role in the attacks on Norway and the Soviet Union. He read from a memorandum dated June 15, 1941 (six days before the invasion of the USSR) in which Raeder called for the immediate destruction of Russian submarines in the Baltic Sea. From there, Elwyn Jones turned to Raeder's war crimes on the high seas—trespassing onto Count Three.[48] The Soviets had carefully prepared their case against Raeder (one of the two Nazi leaders they had brought to Nuremberg) after interrogating him at length in Moscow. Once again they had been scooped.

Nearly two months had passed since the start of the Nuremberg Trials. Aside from Soviet and French cameos to cross-examine witnesses, it had been an entirely Anglo-American affair. This was not what the Soviets had been expecting. None of the members of the Soviet delegation or the Vyshinsky Commission (least of all Vyshinsky himself) had anticipated that the Americans and the British would spend so much time addressing the court or that Jackson would take over so much of the case. The Soviets had made good use of the additional time to develop their presentations—but for months they had been acting largely in reaction to the agenda set by the Americans. Now it was finally time for the French to begin their presentations on war crimes and crimes against humanity. The Soviets would continue to wait in the wings while the French took their turn, but with less unease. They knew they had less to worry about than with the Americans and the British.

On Thursday morning, January 17, François de Menthon, the French chief prosecutor, stepped up to the lectern to give his opening speech, focusing on Nazi war crimes and crimes against humanity in Western Europe. De Menthon, a former French Resistance leader and a close friend of Charles de Gaulle, was well known as a devout antifascist. He had headed the Commission d'Épuration (Purge Commission) to root out collaborators in liberated France and had personally overseen the trials of Philippe Pétain and other leaders of the Vichy regime, which had cooperated with the Nazis in the deportation and murder of Jews during the occupation of France.[49]

De Menthon spoke for four and a half hours, describing the devastation wrought by the Nazis on France and the rest of Europe and calling for justice—carefully steering clear of the sensitive topic of French collaboration. For society to move forward, he argued, the leaders of Nazi Germany must be found guilty and punished for causing "the death of millions of men and the ruin of a great number of nations." It was essential for the Tribunal to condemn both the Nazi "war of aggression" and the immoral acts that Germany had committed in the course of the war. He urged the Tribunal "to make its judgment a decisive act in the history of international law."[50]

De Menthon's presentation stood out from the other opening speeches in that he lingered on the question of collective guilt, which both Jackson and Shawcross had avoided. He declared that the Tribunal's judgment was essential for the reeducation of the German people, who had been "intoxicated by Nazism" and its racial mythology for many years. "The initial condemnation of Nazi Germany by your High Tribunal will be a first lesson for these people and will constitute the best starting point for the work of the revision of values."[51] De Menthon understood from his own experiences in France that the work of denazification would be a long, arduous process, requiring an unblinking confrontation with the past. This speech served as his farewell to Nuremberg; he left for France the next day to take on a more active role in domestic politics as a deputy in the French National Assembly. The jurist Auguste Champetier de Ribes (another former member of the French Resistance) replaced him as head of the French prosecution.

As de Menthon called for the reeducation of the entire German people, at least one member of the U.S. prosecution was growing uneasy about the idea of collective guilt and what it might mean for the future of Europe. Assistant prosecutor Robert Kempner (the head of the U.S. prosecution's rebuttal team and himself a German refugee) advised Jackson on January 23 that the trial of Nazi organizations such as the SS, the Gestapo, and the SA had become a hot political issue in Europe—and especially in Germany. He noted that every household in Germany was likely to include "at least one SA or SS member"; should the breadwinner be arrested as a war criminal, the entire family would be crippled. In the United States, too, there was opposition to the trial of the fascist organizations, Kempner added. Anti-Soviet newspapers had condemned this approach as "a totalitarian technique" and had warned that declarations of organizational guilt would result in mass deportations of people to the Soviet Union as forced laborers.[52]

Of course, it was the Americans, not the Soviets, who had pushed for—and even insisted on—addressing widespread Nazi criminality by putting organizations on trial in Nuremberg. Jackson, Samuel Rosenman, Murray Bernays, and others had seen the organizations case as the best way to cast a wide net of guilt without automatically condemning the entire German people. What's more, the Soviets were neither dependent on nor waiting for the Nuremberg verdicts to recruit forced labor. Stalin, Truman, and Attlee had decided months ago at the Potsdam Conference that each country would extract reparations from its own occupation zone in Germany. The Soviets had been deporting German war criminals from their occupation zone to the Soviet Union as forced laborers even before Potsdam and were poised to continue doing so regardless of the outcome of the organizations case. Jackson knew all this, of course—but he also understood that these newspapers reflected popular sentiment both about the Soviets and about the IMT as a whole.

Jackson had long been worried that Soviet participation in the IMT could endanger perceptions of its legitimacy. He had known for months that the Soviets were very likely responsible for war crimes and crimes against peace—and he had been fretting about this information becoming public. As the trials entered their third month this was looking more likely. On January 21, Lucius Clay, the deputy head of the U.S. military government in Germany, wrote Jackson about rumors coming out of Poland that the Soviets had perpetrated the Katyn massacre. Clay indicated that the Poles were reluctant to pursue the matter lest it create more problems for them with the Soviet Union, which had their country under military occupation.[53] Jackson sensed that it was just a matter of time before Katyn exploded into the open one way or another.

Kempner added to Jackson's worries a few days later with the news that the defense was planning to use evidence about Soviet plans to invade Poland to weaken the prosecution's case. Kempner passed along a memorandum that an "anti-Soviet German politician," Arnold Rechberg, had offered to *Die Neue Zeitung* containing details from Fritz Sauter (whom Ribbentrop had just fired as his attorney) about the secret protocols of the German-Soviet Non-Aggression Pact. Rechberg had claimed in this memorandum that Hitler had not wanted to start a war but "the Red Chiefs" had persuaded him to do so with their offer of a divided Poland. Kempner advised Jackson that Ribbentrop's defense was likely to stress the secret protocols, according to which a "sphere of influence in the European east was divided between Germany and Russia."[54] Kempner's news did not exactly surprise Jackson, who was already anticipating the defense's "political attacks" on France, Britain, and the USSR in connection with the "aggressive war" charge. He had difficult questions to ponder nonetheless. How should he respond when the defense tried to call attention to Soviet crimes in open court? Was it really in the interests of the United States to protect Soviet secrets?

By now, Rudenko had been thoroughly briefed on the secret history of Soviet-German collaboration. At the moment, however, he was more directly focused on what Stalin had identified as the greatest threat from the defense: the claim that Operation Barbarossa had been a preventive action. Rudenko had returned to Nuremberg in time for de Menthon's speech, bringing with him fresh evidence for the Soviet case and orders to directly confront any defense arguments about preventive war. He set the Soviet translators to work rendering the new evidence into German for submission to the Tribunal and enlisted members of the state security apparatus and the Extraordinary State Commission to assist them.[55] The translators needed the extra help, as the NKVD and SMERSH continued to send along witness statements and newly discovered documents relating to all four counts.[56]

As Jackson contemplated the problem of Soviet war crimes and as Rudenko prepared for his day in court, the French continued to argue their case. The French presentations, including a speech on the compulsory recruitment of French labor given by the assistant prosecutor Jacques Herzog on January 18 and 19, made a powerful impression on the Americans and the British. Taylor later noted that "the statistics alone" that Herzog cited were "mindshattering." Herzog had produced evidence showing that more than three million French, Belgian, and Dutch citizens had been forced to serve the Nazi war effort.[57] Maxwell Fyfe was pleasantly surprised by the competence of the French prosecution after the earlier crisis over translating documents. "The French are doing their case much better than anyone expected," he wrote in a letter home after Herzog's presentation. "If we could only get on to the Defense we should feel that the end was within purview if not within sight."[58] There was, of course, much, much more to go—including the entire Soviet case, which was now estimated to start sometime in February.

The French assistant prosecutors Charles Gerthoffer and Henry Delpech began the week of January 21 by describing the organized looting of German-occupied Western Europe. Gerthoffer stared down the defendants while charging that Nazi policies of plunder had caused the deaths of hundreds of thousands of French citizens and had "damaged the health of the nation for generations to come."[59] The Soviet prosecutors took only a perfunctory interest in these presentations. Unlike the Americans and the British, the French did not present evidence relating to the Soviet Union or Eastern Europe. This was a welcome reprieve.

Midweek, however, the French stepped aside to make way for the Americans and the British, who had not yet finished summing up their evidence against the individual defendants under Counts One and Two. They turned their attention now to the last three men in the dock: Franz von Papen, Konstantin von Neurath, and Hans Fritzsche. The U.S. assistant prosecutor Drexel Sprecher condemned Fritzsche, who had headed the Radio Division of Goebbels's propaganda ministry, as a conspirator who had made Nazi crimes palatable to the German people. Fritzsche had justified the invasion of the Soviet Union as a preventive operation to avert an impending Soviet attack. He had also drummed up hatred by repeatedly describing the Soviets as "subhuman creatures" who aimed to obliterate the German people. Such incitements, Sprecher argued, had set the stage for the Nazi policy of extermination in the East.[60] Fritzsche was the most senior German bureaucrat the Soviets had captured, and the Soviet prosecution had been planning to document his role in inciting atrocities in the Soviet Union and Eastern Europe.[61] They watched Sprecher do so instead.

The French case resumed on January 24, with deputy chief prosecutor Charles Dubost presenting on German atrocities in occupied Western Europe. Dubost was a serious and soft-spoken man. The Americans greatly disliked him; Taylor dismissed him as "intense and humorless," and Jackson thought he was a communist.[62] Maxwell Fyfe, on the other hand, regarded him as an unassuming hero and noted how "his valour in the Resistance was the subject of stories which would leave the shocker-writer pale with envy."[63] The Soviets held him in similar esteem.

Until now, the French prosecution had seemed detached.[64] This was about to change. Dubost fully understood the power of eyewitness testimony. The following afternoon, he called Maurice Lampe, the first of seven French witnesses who would testify about the deportations and the concentration camps. Lampe, a survivor of Mauthausen, described what he called "a long cycle of torture and suffering," pausing to dwell on those scenes in the camp that had remained most fixed in his mind. He recalled in detail the brutal murder of prisoners by means of exposure when the barracks became overcrowded: the guards had stripped prisoners naked, drenched them in water, and sent them out into the extreme cold. Those still alive in the morning were "finished off with blows from an axe." Lampe also related the stories he had heard from other prisoners and from SS men about the first Soviet prisoners of war in Mauthausen. Some 4,000 Soviet soldiers, he recounted, had been massacred during the construction of the camp's infirmary. The carnage had "made such a deep impression," he noted, that the infirmary became known as the "Russen Lager" (Russian Camp), and even the SS men referred to it by this name.[65]

When Dubost finished questioning Lampe, Rudenko approached the witness and asked him for more details about the murdered Soviet soldiers. Lampe speculated that the soldiers had been killed because they were too weak and malnourished to perform the relentlessly backbreaking work demanded of them. Some were killed on the spot; the SS herded others to a wire fence on the edge of the camp, where they were mowed down by guards in the watchtowers. Lampe explained that "as a general rule" all Soviet officers, commissars, and communists at Mauthausen were executed. If some of them survived the camp it was only because the SS did not know their backgrounds.[66] Lampe's testimony deeply affected the Soviet delegation. Writing about the trials decades later, the lawyer Arkady Poltorak was still haunted by Lampe's "sad eyes and emaciated face" and by his grisly account of how prisoners of war were beaten, stoned, and worked to death in the Mauthausen quarry.[67] A French survivor like Lampe, unlike the Americans, could bear full witness to Soviet suffering because he had suffered comparably himself. He was, in a sense, one of them.

Dubost called four more witnesses on Monday, January 28. The first was Marie-Claude Vaillant-Couturier, a member of the Resistance and the French Communist Party who had spent three years at Auschwitz. The Soviets were transfixed by Vaillant-Couturier. She approached the witness box in a blue tailored suit with her head held high and shoulders back, radiating quiet dignity. She told the court that she had been quartered in the sewing block at Auschwitz, near the train station, and had watched as soldiers unsealed the train cars and thousands of people spilled out onto the platform. An orchestra made up of prisoners, "all young and pretty girls dressed in little white blouses and navy blue skirts," she recalled, greeted the trains with "gay tunes such as *The Merry Widow.*" The guards routinely told the new arrivals that they were at a work camp, using an elaborate ruse to maintain order while ushering the elderly, young children, and mothers to the bathhouse—to their deaths.[68] In an article for *Pravda* about the French witnesses, Vishnevsky praised Vaillant-Couturier for telling her story "exactly, clearly, and simply." There was "dead silence in the courtroom when she spoke."[69]

The mood in the courtroom remained somber for the rest of the afternoon as the French witnesses continued to relate their experiences of Mauthausen and Buchenwald. The Soviet correspondents were particularly interested in the testimony of another communist, François Boix—a news photographer who had fled his native Spain in the wake of the Republican defeat in the country's civil war. After the German invasion of France, Boix was sent to Mauthausen. His skills as a photographer had kept him alive and had enabled him to collect evidence of camp conditions. The SS men in charge of the camp had put him to work running a photo laboratory. He had developed pictures of his fellow prisoners, as well as pictures of visiting Nazi leaders and of everyday life. He had secretly made duplicate prints of more than 2,000 images and had managed to smuggle hundreds of them out of the camp. Dubost projected some of these images onto a screen and asked Boix to tell the judges what they were seeing. Boix described the camp quarry where prisoners worked and died, as well as the public humiliation, torture, and murder of inmates. He also described a birthday celebration for the camp commander and visits by Kaltenbrunner and Himmler.[70]

When Rudenko had the chance to examine Boix the following morning, he asked him about the murder of Soviet prisoners at Mauthausen. Boix described the arrival of some 7,000 Russian prisoners of war in November 1941. Initially, the Russians "were left to themselves, but with scarcely anything to eat." Several weeks later, when "they were already at the end of their endurance," the "process of elimination" began. "They were made to work under the most horrible conditions; they were beaten, hit, kicked, and insulted." At the end of three months, there were only thirty soldiers left.[71]

Vishnevsky described the scene between Rudenko and Boix for Soviet readers. Boix said that he had kept a photograph of these thirty surviving Russians. When Rudenko asked about this photograph, a copy was presented to the court. Vishnevsky related how "the necks of the defendants," Goering included, "stretched out" to catch a glimpse of the photograph. He then described the image: "In the snow, stripped completely naked, stand 30 Red Army soldiers. They are indescribably thin." The soldiers in the picture are lined up in the bitter cold, barefoot in the snow, waiting for roll call. They know that their deaths are imminent, but they stare defiantly at the camera, "a fire still burning" in their eyes. Not a single one of them, Vishnevsky emphasized, "shows a shadow of submission or degradation."[72] The message was clear: the Soviet people had endured unthinkable suffering and had come through with their dignity intact.

After Boix finished his testimony, Dubost called the Norwegian lawyer Hans Cappelen to the stand. Cappelen had been interned in a Gestapo prison in Norway and then at several concentration camps in Germany, including Gross-Rosen. Vishnevsky described for Soviet readers how this "pale Norwegian" had limped to the witness box as if in a trance and how he had spoken in a whisper about his ordeal at the hands of the Gestapo. Cappelen told the court how the Gestapo had beaten him repeatedly to a state of unconsciousness. He described how one Gestapo agent had scalped him during an interrogation, ripping "the hair from his head with blood and pieces of skin" still attached. Vishnevsky described the way that everyone in the hall involuntarily stared at Cappelen's "strangely whitened bare skull" and saw the "blood vessels pulsing under paper-thin skin." When Cappelen stopped speaking, Vishnevsky noted, the courtroom became eerily still. "In the face of tragedy people shrink inward and fall silent."[73]

The French witness testimony was deeply affecting, though some observers thought that it was gratuitous. British alternate judge Norman Birkett reflected in his diary that the French eyewitnesses had built up "a most terrible and convincing case of complete horror and inhumanity in the concentration camp." Nonetheless, the court, he believed, did not need to hear such details.[74] The Soviets, by contrast, saw the French witness testimony as the most vital part of the entire case presented thus far and appreciated it precisely for its emotional resonance. After the French testimony, Soviet leaders looked at their list of approved witnesses with fresh eyes, giving special consideration to survivors of Nazi war crimes and crimes against humanity—to those who could bring meaning to the numbers by giving voice to individual suffering.

Vishnevsky was doing all he could, in his own way, to bring down the former Nazi leaders. His article about the French witnesses appeared in *Pravda* on February 1, as part of an overall effort to fully educate the Soviet people about the depravity of the "fascist beasts." That same day, Vishnevsky sent Rudenko a letter offering advice about the upcoming Soviet presentations. Vishnevsky had many roles in Nuremberg: star correspondent for the Soviet press, informant for Moscow, and aide to the Soviet prosecution. Some American authorities had noticed Vishnevsky skulking about and concluded that he was doing the bidding of SMERSH or the NKVD.[75] It was not so simple. In the mid-1930s, at the height of the Stalinist Terror, he had indeed denounced numerous colleagues to the NKVD, partly out of loyalty and partly to save his own skin.[76] But in Nuremberg, many of his suggestions for improving the work of the Soviet delegation ran counter to NKVD wishes. While the NKVD prized secrecy, for example, Vishnevsky was encouraging the Soviet prosecutors and correspondents to emulate their Western counterparts—to share evidence and other materials more freely with the international press.[77]

Vishnevsky thought that the Soviet Union could learn valuable lessons from the other delegations. The American, British, and French prosecutors were taking the right approach in releasing documents to the press, he related in his letter to Rudenko—sometimes even circulating evidence that was not presented in open court. Western newspapers had been printing documents that damaged Nazism and helped the prosecution's case, he pointed out. The Soviet prosecution, by contrast, was far less open with the press, a point

FIGURE 7.2 Roman Rudenko chatting with Vsevolod Vishnevsky and other Soviet correspondents during a recess of the court, 1946. From left: Roman Rudenko, Porfiry Krylov, Nikolai Sokolov, Semyon Kirsanov, Mikhail Kuprianov, Vsevolod Vishnevsky.

Credit: Russian State Archive of Literature and Art f. 1038, op. 1, d. 4762, l. 1. Photographer: Viktor Temin.

Vishnevsky made emphatically: "FOR THE MOST PART OUR LEGAL STAFF BY TRADITION HOLDS ALL THE MATERIAL IT HAS UNDER LOCK AND KEY."[78] The tradition was, of course, part and parcel of the Stalinist system, which prized centralization and secrecy and discouraged individual initiative.

Vishnevsky recounted that he had recently asked the Soviet delegation's French translator to provide him with the texts of the testimonies of Vaillant-Couturier and Cappelen to place in the Soviet literary magazine *Znamya.* "These are staggering documents," he noted, which he had hoped to make known quickly to the Soviet people. The young Soviet translator had enthusiastically begun to work on them, according to Vishnevsky, but then "in a very sharp manner was stopped by his boss." Vishnevsky cautioned that if the Soviet delegation did not adopt a different strategy during the Soviet presentations, the international press corps would face tremendous difficulties—which would negatively affect their coverage of the Soviet case. In effect, he was asking the Soviet legal team to buck Stalinist tradition.[79]

Vishnevsky also observed that the Western delegations were using a variety of public relations techniques, including press conferences, informal chats, and dinners, to ensure positive coverage in the international press. The Soviets might do the same, he advised Rudenko. This would enable the Soviet prosecution to introduce the correspondents in advance to the substance of their speeches, witness testimony, and films. He recommended that the Soviet delegation hold daily briefings at the Press Camp in English and French. In addition, the delegation might host informal receptions in order to communicate with the press in what he called a more "lively and spontaneous" manner. Such events would have the added benefit of allowing the Soviets to gauge the reactions of the foreign correspondents. He further deemed it imperative for the Soviets to precirculate summaries of their speeches to the press corps. The Americans, the French, and the British had done this, he noted, "and if we do not manage to do so we will hurt ourselves." He implored Rudenko to remember that a key aim of the Nuremberg Trials was to influence international public opinion.[80]

Not everyone in Nuremberg was as sanguine as Vishnevsky about the relationship between the prosecution and the press—or about circulating documents before they were presented in court. At a February 5 organizational meeting of the Tribunal, all of the chief prosecutors, including Rudenko, voiced alarm at the number of sensitive documents the international press had obtained. A month earlier, Jackson had circulated a memo to his staff banning press interviews with witnesses and defendants. No one had tried to actually enforce this or to stop other members of the U.S. delegation from leaking information to the press. It was generally known that members of Colonel Burton Andrus's staff at the Nuremberg prison were providing a steady stream of stories about the defendants to Western journalists.[81]

With the Soviet presentations coming up, Rudenko directed his assistant prosecutors to keep a strict accounting of all of their evidence. He and Gorshenin had added some new and sensational documents to the Soviet case in recent weeks and had no interest in sharing them ahead of time. These documents included the so-called Bormann memorandum, which outlined Hitler's plans for using the Slavic peoples as slave laborers after the war to make up for Germany's population losses.[82] Jackson learned from an advance copy of Rudenko's opening speech that the Soviets had found Bormann's papers in Germany. He asked Rudenko for permission to look through these papers, which he suspected contained "a good many documents" relevant to the American case.[83] Rudenko ignored this request, just as Jackson had ignored the many requests of the Soviet prosecution.

As the French began to wrap up their case, more intrigue developed in Nuremberg. Rumors spread that Germany's putative "fascist underground"—about which there had been a great deal of speculation—was planning a raid on the Nuremberg prison. On Monday, February 4, American guards with machine guns appeared on the roofs of the Palace of Justice and the Nuremberg prison as well as inside the courthouse, and American troops blockaded the roads leading to the city. As French deputy chief prosecutor Edgar Faure presented evidence on Nazi race policy in Western Europe, members of the Soviet delegation gathered information about the suspected plot. Vishnevsky reported to Moscow that evening that American counterintelligence had discovered a cache of explosives in the Nuremberg region and had concluded that a group of former SS men were plotting to free the Nazi leaders.[84]

Later in the week, the French presented information on the pillaging of art in occupied Western Europe amid continuing talk of an imminent attack on the Palace of Justice. Vishnevsky reported to *Pravda* chief Peter Pospelov that a local newspaper had come out with a different version of the conspiracy story: in this telling, a group of antifascists were planning a raid to kill the defendants.[85] Soon after, the American authorities declared the whole affair to be a false alarm, concluding that the pile of dynamite that had been uncovered in the Nuremberg region had been left over from the war.[86] The Soviets were not sure what to think. Roman Karmen concluded that there may have been the real danger of a raid. He also attributed some of the hype to what he called the American journalists' "penchant for rumors."[87] There was nothing like a little extra drama to put everyone in a state of high alert on the eve of the Soviet case.

Back in Moscow, Stalin and the Politburo Commission were making final preparations for the Soviet presentations. Most significantly, Stalin gave the go-ahead to a proposal from Gorshenin and Kruglov to bring the generals Paulus and Buschenhagen to Nuremberg to testify in person. Having seen how the Americans' use of former Nazis as surprise witnesses had strengthened their case and captured the public's attention, Soviet leaders had resolved to do the same. Rudenko had interrogated these prisoners while he was in Moscow and agreed with the NKVD that they were ready to give "necessary testimony" about the Nazi conspiracy to wage aggressive war. The NKVD would oversee their transportation to Germany.[88]

Stalin also made some personnel changes to the Vyshinsky Commission. Vyshinsky and Gorshenin would continue to run it, with the deputy procurator general Grigory Safonov (who had extensive experience with Soviet military courts) now serving as third in command. The diplomat and propaganda expert Mikhail Kharlamov would replace Lev Kuzmin as the liaison to the press corps. Mankovsky was ousted (after lobbying for a trip to Nuremberg for his daughter, a Moscow lawyer)—leaving Trainin as the sole Soviet international-law expert in Nuremberg.[89]

The French concluded their case against the Nazi leaders on Thursday, February 7. British assistant prosecutor Mervyn Griffith-Jones then stepped in to sum up the charges against Hess (who was now being represented by Frank's attorney, Alfred Seidl) under Counts One and Two. Griffith-Jones focused on Hess's famous flight to Scotland and his claims that he had been on a peacemaking mission to lessen the chance of war. Griffith-Jones presented evidence that, he argued, proved that Hess had proposed a separate peace not out of concern for lives that would be squandered but so that Germany could focus its forces on attacking Russia. There was extensive evidence, he reminded the court, that the defendants were making plans to invade the Soviet Union as early as November 1940. Hess, as Hitler's deputy, could not have been in the dark about these plans.[90] Rudenko would also address the question of German treachery in the Soviet prosecution's opening speech, which was scheduled for the following morning.

It was almost time, at long last, for the Soviet prosecutors to take center stage. While waiting for the French to finish, Vishnevsky had sent Pospelov a flurry of telegrams predicting that the Soviet presentations would "undoubtedly be very interesting and lively." The Soviet and American delegations had recently attended a private preview of the atrocity film put together by Karmen's studio in Moscow, and Vishnevsky told Pospelov that it was the most compelling visual evidence of Nazi crimes to date. He further reported that he had met with key Soviet personnel and had made some progress on the propaganda front. The Soviet journalists were setting up a press bureau; the Soviet legal team had agreed to hold press conferences (though not to precirculate documents); and Rudenko had promised to keep the Soviet press corps fully briefed about the Soviet case.[91]

Over the previous month, the alliance among the countries of the prosecution had continued to fracture in Nuremberg, giving way to a growing divide with the British and the Americans on one side and the Soviets and the French on the other. But this was just part of the story. The Soviets had been learning from the Western powers about how to operate effectively on the international stage and had made critical course corrections. Soviet prosecutors, watching the Western prosecutors present their cases, had seen what kinds of documents, visual evidence, and witnesses made the strongest impressions in court. They had been particularly moved by the testimony of the French survivors—testimony that had caused Ribbentrop, Schacht, Papen, and Doenitz to take off their headphones and look away.[92] The Soviet correspondents, for their part, had brought the ins and outs of the trials to the Soviet people, while also studying the ways of the Western press corps and the public relations techniques of the Americans. Rudenko, meanwhile, had received a critical political education in Moscow and had fully absorbed the complicated history of Soviet-German relations. He was as ready to take on the Nazi leaders in the Nuremberg courtroom as he would ever be.

CHAPTER 8 | Bearing Witness

O N T H E M O R N I N G of Friday, February 8, a crowd filed into the
Palace of Justice. The visitors' gallery was packed, the press box
was overflowing; there were not enough seats even at the tables of the
prosecutors. Roman Karmen observed with satisfaction that the courtroom filled up like this "only on the days of special sensations."[1] Telford
Taylor also took note of the throng. He knew everyone was wondering
the same things: What would the Soviets say about the German-Soviet
Non-Aggression Pact of 1939? Would they address the Soviet-German division of Poland? What about the Soviet invasion of Finland? The Soviets
were finally at center stage, and no one had any idea what to expect. Even
the defendants took note of the boisterous atmosphere in the courtroom.
Goering remarked to the U.S. prison psychologist Gustave Gilbert that the
crowd had come "to see the show."[2]

The question was what kind of show it would be. It certainly would not
be the grand political spectacle Stalin and Vyshinsky had envisioned: the
defendants had able counsel representing them and would not be meekly
reading from a prepared script. But neither would it be the walk-on appearance the Americans were hoping for. The Soviet Union had been devastated
by the war. The Soviet people had suffered immeasurably. This would be
their moment of collective catharsis and reckoning. Though it had taken the
Soviets some time to figure out how to operate effectively on the international stage, they finally had their plans together. They had expanded their
part of the case to cover all four counts facing the Nazis; they had brought
in new evidence that would make their case persuasively; they had lined up

witnesses who could counter the defense's claims about preventive war and who could speak eloquently and movingly of the horrors of the German occupation. They would remind the world of the heroism and the sacrifices of the Soviet people. They would tell their story.

Roman Rudenko stepped up to the rostrum in full military uniform, and the sound of the Russian language began to reverberate in the courtroom. Rudenko took a moment to acknowledge the historical significance of the occasion. He described the IMT as a new institution of international justice, one that had taken long-established principles such as the criminality of aggressive war and codified them into law. He then reminded everyone why they were there. The defendants had seized the German state and made it the instrument of shameful crimes. They had "poisoned the conscience and the mind of an entire generation of Germans." They had launched illegal wars and brought terrible suffering to the "freedom-loving nations" of Europe. Now, Rudenko proclaimed, the time of judgment had arrived.[3] Stalin had chosen Rudenko for this role because of his talents as an orator—and he commanded the room. Boris Polevoi wrote that he felt "as if the great and powerful Soviet people had entered the courtroom" and were "looking over the dock from the rostrum."[4]

In staccato statements Rudenko described how the defendants had organized a criminal conspiracy and waged war with the aim of imperialistic expansion. He emphasized that Germany's aggressive actions from 1938 to 1941 had all been leading up to its "predatory military campaign" against the Soviet Union, which Hitler had always seen as the main source of Lebensraum and food supplies for Germany. Rudenko studiously avoided the topic of the German-Soviet Non-Aggression Pact—except to note that Hitler had not felt "constrained by it." Most critically, Rudenko dismissed the defense's argument about preventive war, declaring that the original documents of the German government and High Command, which the Soviets would present, plainly demonstrated the absurdity of such claims. "Much as the fascist wolf might disguise himself in a sheep's skin, he cannot hide his teeth!"[5]

Turning to war crimes and crimes against humanity, Rudenko spoke of how the defendants had turned war into a "system of militarized banditry" in Eastern Europe and the Soviet Union. He described the razing of villages, the torture of prisoners of war, and the massacre of men, women, and children. He spoke of the intentional destruction of cultural monuments, schools, hospitals, scientific institutions, and churches. "Side by side with the barbarous destruction and looting of villages, towns, and national cultural monuments, the Hitlerites also mocked the religious feelings of the believers among the Soviet population." In one monastery, Soviet forces had discovered

FIGURE 8.1 Roman Rudenko presenting before the Tribunal, 1946.

Credit: United States Holocaust Memorial Museum, courtesy of Robert Kempner. Photographer: Charles Alexander.

"the naked bodies of tortured Red Army prisoners of war, stacked in piles." Rudenko painted a chilling picture of the horrors of the concentration camps, calling Dachau and Buchenwald "anemic prototypes" of Majdanek and the other death camps the Nazis had set up in the occupied East.[6]

Glaring at the defendants in the dock, Rudenko called them out one by one for their roles in these crimes. Rosenberg had overseen a "regime of tyranny and terror" in the East. Goering had declared his intention to "plunder and to plunder thoroughly." Keitel had prescribed "mass extermination and the far-reaching application of the death penalty against the Soviet people."[7] Polevoi watched the defendants react to the charges. Goering angrily removed his earphones and then put them back on and kept readjusting them. Rosenberg, who knew Russian, took his earphones off and cocked his head to listen. Keitel tugged at his coat collar "as though the noose was already squeezing his neck."[8] Rudenko reminded the court that it was not possible to cover in an opening statement all of the ways the defendants had terrorized Europe. Promising a more complete accounting of their crimes in the weeks ahead, he ended with a plea on behalf of the millions of innocent victims. "May justice be done!"[9]

Yuri Pokrovsky closed the day in court with the first Soviet presentation on the Nazi conspiracy and crimes against peace—addressing Counts One and Two, which the Americans and the British thought they had wrapped up a few weeks earlier. Pokrovsky began with a vivid account of how Germany had "lulled" other nations to sleep with nonaggression pacts, waiting for the right moment to strike. When Pokrovsky attempted to introduce newly discovered German Foreign Office documents about the invasion of Czechoslovakia that the Red Army had brought back from Berlin, a commotion ensued about their admissibility. The Soviets had submitted only photocopies of these documents to the Tribunal. In response to Judge Lawrence's request for the originals, Pokrovsky explained that some of the documents were in Moscow. Lawrence insisted that the Tribunal needed the originals in order to ensure that it was evaluating "really genuine evidence"—at which point Pokrovsky took offense. The Soviet prosecution was following precedent, he insisted. The U.S. prosecution had submitted photocopies without incident.[10] Was there a double standard?

The Tribunal called a recess to discuss the matter, and when the judges reconvened they acknowledged that Pokrovsky was right. The Tribunal had in fact accepted photocopies from the other countries of the prosecution. Now on the spot, the judges elaborated guidelines: original documents should be deposited with the Tribunal whenever this was possible. When this proved to be "impossible" or "highly inconvenient," the Tribunal would accept photocopies. But each photocopy needed to be accompanied by a certificate attesting that it was an exact copy and that the original document was authentic. The Tribunal would accept the Soviet photocopies, with the understanding that the certificates would be forthcoming.[11]

Pokrovsky resumed his presentation, but the Soviets were on notice. The Soviet prosecutors knew full well that some of their documents lacked the necessary certificates. Moreover, Lawrence's sudden concern with the provenance of submitted documents had implied that the Tribunal might have concerns about the authenticity of some of the Soviet evidence.

The next morning, a Saturday, Pokrovsky turned to the German invasion of Poland—again highlighting Nazi treachery. He showed how German leaders had issued solemn proclamations of friendship with Poland while secretly preparing for war.[12] Here the Soviets were on especially perilous ground, for it was generally understood that the German-Soviet Non-Aggression Pact had provided the impetus for the Nazi invasion. What's more, the Soviets had invaded Poland from the east two weeks after the Nazis had from the west, on the pretense of protecting the region's Ukrainian and Belorussian minorities. Pokrovsky's presentation nonetheless went without incident.

The start of the Soviet case was a cause for celebration for all of the delegations in Nuremberg, for it meant that they were that much closer to wrapping up the trials. On the night of February 9, the American commandant of the Nuremberg prison, Burton Andrus, hosted a party in honor of the Soviets. Soviet judges Nikitchenko and Volchkov both attended and were treated to a performance of Giuseppe Verdi's *Un Ballo in Maschera*, one of the composer's lesser-known operas, involving a political conspiracy in the eighteenth century against the king of Sweden.[13] It was a night of drinking, dancing, and the kind of fraternizing that Soviet leaders in Moscow frowned on.

That same evening in the Soviet Union, at Moscow's Bolshoi Theater, Stalin made his first major public speech since the end of the war, celebrating the victory over fascism. He spoke of a threatening world; he declared that it was imperative for the Soviet Union to step up its efforts for economic development and military defense. The speech was a reminder to the Soviet people that sacrifice was still necessary. American and British diplomats, including George F. Kennan, the American charge d'affaires in Moscow, interpreted it as a battle cry "for a divided world." American experts on Russia warned of the menaces of Soviet totalitarianism and expansionism and questioned the prospects for peace.[14]

The Soviet prosecutors were eager to resume their case on Monday morning—for they had a surprise in store. Midday on Saturday, Rudenko had privately informed the judges that the Soviet prosecution planned to call two witnesses to testify about German crimes against peace: Field Marshal Friedrich von Paulus and General Erich Buschenhagen.[15] Paulus, an author of the Barbarossa Plan, was the highest-ranking German officer in Soviet custody. He had commanded the Sixth German Army at Stalingrad, surrendering to the Red Army in January 1943. German leaders had kept Paulus's surrender a secret from the German people. They had announced that he had been killed in action, and he had been given a hero's burial; the coffin had in fact been empty. Buschenhagen, the former chief of staff of the German forces in Norway and a former commander of the Fifty-Second Corps of Paulus's army, had been captured by Soviet troops in Romania in September 1944.[16]

Both Paulus and Buschenhagen had cooperated with the NKVD during their confinement in Moscow. Paulus had given the NKVD a statement about German plans to invade the Soviet Union. Buschenhagen had provided the

NKVD with testimony about German-Finnish military collaboration that had just been used as evidence in the Finnish War Responsibility Trial in January.[17] Rudenko had personally interrogated both witnesses during his recent stay in Moscow; not long afterward, Soviet agents had secretly conveyed them to Germany.[18]

On the morning of Monday, February 11, Pokrovsky finished his presentation on crimes against peace. Focusing on Germany's plans to invade Yugoslavia, he presented two critical documents. The first was an affidavit from the German general Alexander Lohr describing his orders from Goering to prepare an air attack against Yugoslavia. The second was a certified copy of Rudenko's interrogation of Paulus in Moscow. Pokrovsky read Paulus's description of how Hitler and Colonel General Franz Halder had entrusted him in March 1941 with coordinating strategic preparations for a joint German-Hungarian attack on Yugoslavia.[19]

Pokrovsky then ceded the spotlight to Nikolai Zorya, whom Stalin had hand-picked to present on the charge of planning and waging an aggressive war. Zorya began with a discussion of the Barbarossa Plan—reading an excerpt from the Soviet interrogation of General Walter Warlimont, which had taken place in November in the Nuremberg prison. Warlimont, who had worked in the Operations Department of the High Command, had attested to learning from General Alfred Jodl in July 1940 that Hitler was preparing for war against Russia.[20] Zorya next introduced a statement from Paulus about his involvement in drafting and carrying out Barbarossa. This was not an excerpt from Rudenko's interrogation of Paulus, from which Pokrovsky had just quoted; rather, it was from the statement Paulus had given to the NKVD. As the Soviets had anticipated, the defense objected to this document on the grounds that it was a photocopy and lacked the required certificate. Zorya agreed to provide the certificate at a later date. Then, without missing a beat, he offered to produce Paulus as a witness.[21] Polevoi watched as everyone initially froze in their places at the sound of Paulus's name and then "snapped into convulsive movement." A huge "racket broke out in the court which was otherwise always so quiet," he later wrote.[22] The Tribunal adjourned for a recess.

When the trial resumed, Zorya received the judges' permission to call Paulus for direct examination by Rudenko. A couple of minutes later a bailiff led Paulus into the courtroom. Karmen observed that he was tall and slim in a dark blue suit, "girded like a soldier." Paulus silently took his seat in the witness box, looking composed and calm. The defendants on the other hand were agitated. Goering shouted something at Hess; Jodl and Keitel shrank in their seats. Paulus, whom Karmen described as "the specter of

FIGURE 8.2 The surprise Soviet witness Field Marshal Friedrich von Paulus during a recess, 1946.

Credit: State Archive of the Russian Federation f. 10140, op. 2, d. 154, l. 3. Photographer: Viktor Temin.

Stalingrad," had come to tell the court "everything, everything he knew."[23] The Soviets had pulled it off. "Except for the Russians, everyone in the courtroom was thunderstruck," Taylor later recalled.[24] Only the judges had known that Paulus was waiting in the wings.

Paulus took the oath and affirmed that he had commanded the Sixth German Army at Stalingrad. Rudenko then asked him to tell what he knew about Germany's preparations for an armed attack on the Soviet Union. Paulus cleared his throat, took a sip of water, and began.[25] He acknowledged that starting in September 1940 he had been directly involved in the development of the Barbarossa Plan. From the very beginning this plan had been aimed at the conquest, colonization, and exploitation of the territories of the Soviet Union, he told the court. German leaders had set their sights on reaching the Volga-Archangelsk line, which stretched from the White Sea in the north all the way southward to the mouth of the Volga River on the Caspian Sea. This would have meant the attainment of vast agricultural areas, the oil of the Caucasus, and Russia's key industrial centers.[26]

Paulus spoke slowly, describing how the Barbarossa Plan was completed in early November 1940 and was followed up with military exercises. He then told how he had traveled through Europe with other members of the General Staff, enlisting Romania, Finland, and Hungary in a future war against the Soviet Union. In March 1941, Halder had summoned him to the Reich Chancellery in Berlin and had advised him of Hitler's plans to attack Yugoslavia as a prelude to invading Russia. When asked by Rudenko who among the defendants were most to blame for the initiation of the war against the Soviet Union, Paulus pointed to Hitler's three main military advisors—Keitel, Jodl, and Goering.[27]

The crowd was riveted by Paulus's testimony. The American journalists "were in such a state that they scribbled and scribbled without stop," Karmen observed.[28] Many correspondents were "breaking pencils in their haste," noted Polevoi. Almost everything Paulus said was "pretty well known from evidence given by other witnesses, or from documents," Polevoi added, but hearing Paulus describe it gave it all "special significance."[29]

Polevoi and Karmen listened to Paulus's testimony with personal interest: both had come face to face with him during the war. Polevoi had witnessed Paulus's surrender in Stalingrad in January 1943. Paulus had been trapped in the basement of a bombed-out department store, and Polevoi had waited outside the building with Soviet soldiers while an officer went down the stairs to deliver an ultimatum to surrender. When the officer reemerged, he announced that Paulus had accepted the ultimatum. A couple of minutes later Paulus himself had appeared "in a military cap and a long fur-lined coat," with his "head held high and tired eyes," Polevoi recalled.[30] Karmen, too, had been in Stalingrad at the time of the Soviet victory and had been the sole war correspondent present for Paulus's first interrogation.[31]

Now they watched Paulus incriminate his former associates. Polevoi noticed that Paulus "framed his sentences concisely" and surmised that this was because "he had thought it all through" during his three years of imprisonment.[32] Some of the Western prosecutors had a different explanation for Paulus's performance, wondering what he had experienced at the hands of the NKVD. U.S. assistant prosecutor Thomas Dodd found the testimony "just a bit too well rehearsed"—which, of course, it had been.[33] The NKVD and Rudenko had carefully prepared Paulus for his appearance before the Tribunal.

A battery of defense attorneys tried to rattle Paulus the next morning, February 12, during their cross-examinations. Keitel's attorney, Otto Nelte, asked Paulus whether he had had "any scruples" about participating in an attack that he now denounced as "criminal." Paulus answered that his understanding of the attack's criminality had only come later. At the time, he had believed that he was doing his duty toward his fatherland. Other defense attorneys attempted to get Paulus to incriminate the Soviet Union in war crimes. Sauckel's lawyer, Robert Servatius, asked Paulus if he knew whether German prisoners of war had been used as forced laborers in the Russian armament industries. Paulus maintained that he did not. Hans Laternser, the counsel for the General Staff and the High Command, asked Paulus to tell the court how German prisoners of war were treated in the Soviet Union—at which point Lawrence reminded the defense that this question had no bearing on the case. Martin Horn, Ribbentrop's attorney since early January, asked Paulus about his involvement in the Free Germany Committee in Russia (an anti-Nazi organization that had been run by the Soviet security police). When asked by Lawrence about the purpose of this question, Horn responded that he wanted to determine the witness's credibility. Lawrence declared that Paulus's thoughts or actions as a Soviet prisoner of war were irrelevant.[34]

Before Paulus left the witness box, Nikitchenko questioned him from the bench about the relationship between the General Staff and the High Command. Paulus testified that the General Staff had faithfully fulfilled all of the High Command's instructions—including instructions for the economic exploitation of the Soviet Union. The goal of such exploitation, he explained, was to win the war and guarantee Germany's "future supremacy in Europe."[35]

Paulus's testimony had simultaneously angered and demoralized the defendants. Prison psychologist Gilbert listened in as Jodl dismissed Paulus as "all washed up" and Ribbentrop judged him to have "disgraced himself." Gilbert found it "ironic to hear the defeated and disgraced Nazi war criminals" sit in judgment of Paulus "as if deciding that they would not hire a man like that for the next war."[36]

Later that afternoon Zorya called the second surprise Soviet witness, Buschenhagen, to testify about Finnish-German collaboration against the Soviet Union. Buschenhagen recounted how, on orders from the High Command, he had traveled to Helsinki to meet with the Finnish General Staff in February 1941. The "sole purpose" of this meeting and subsequent meetings had been to ensure the participation of Finnish troops in the invasion of the Soviet Union, he told the court. Any assertion by the Finnish General Staff that its intentions were defensive was "camouflage"; no one "reckoned with the possibility of a Russian attack on Finland." Zorya then summed up the main point for the court: the Finns had waged war on the Soviet Union at the urging of Germany because they hoped to attain large swaths of the Soviet Union, such as Eastern Karelia and the city and region of

Leningrad.[37] The Soviet invasion of Finland some fifteen months earlier was conveniently missing from this account.

Zorya next used affidavits recently provided by the NKVD and SMERSH to prove that the Germans had also conspired with Romanian and Hungarian leaders to plan the invasion of the Soviet Union. Statements from Ion Antonescu and Constantin Pantazi affirmed that Romania had started preparing for war against the Soviet Union in November 1940 and that the entire Romanian air force and army had been "reorganized and retrained along German lines." A statement from the former chief of intelligence and counterintelligence services of the Hungarian General Staff, Esteban Ujsaazy (also a prisoner of the Soviets), described military collaboration between Germany and Hungary during the same time frame.[38]

The next day, with everyone still talking about the surprise Soviet witnesses, Pokrovsky returned to the rostrum to address Count Three—war crimes. He began by describing the German mistreatment and murder of prisoners of war in the East. It was a topic the Americans had covered in some detail. However, Pokrovsky brought in compelling new evidence: excerpts from the Soviet interrogations of several German officers, including Warlimont, Halder, and Kurt von Osterreich (the commander of the Prisoner of War Section of the Danzig Military District). Pokrovsky used Halder's statement to the NKVD to prove that Hitler, long before invading the USSR, had declared that German forces would employ far harsher methods against the peoples of the Soviet Union than those it was using in Western Europe. He introduced a confession Osterreich had given to his Red Army interrogators to establish that German leaders had ordered the murder of all communists and Jews. Pokrovsky then read from dozens of Extraordinary State Commission reports detailing how internees in Nazi camps were forced to do hard labor, tortured, and ultimately killed. While most prisoners were shot, thousands of others died from disease; one report described how the Germans frequently corralled typhus patients into unventilated rooms with hundreds of healthy prisoners in order to spread the deadly illness.[39]

Finally Pokrovsky brought up the issue that everyone was waiting for: Katyn. It was one of the war crimes listed in the Indictment, and the Soviets remained intent on pinning it on the Germans. Jackson had been worrying for months about how the Soviets would deal with this in court. On Thursday, February 14, he got his answer. Pokrovsky dove into Katyn— and the Soviet case moved from fact to fabrication. Soviet leaders had spent the past several years manufacturing "evidence" of German guilt.[40] Most recently, they had used a Leningrad trial of seven Wehrmacht soldiers to produce more "proof": one of the soldiers, Arno Diere, had confessed under oath (after being threatened and probably tortured) to having participated in the burial of 15,000 to 20,000 Polish soldiers in the Katyn Forest.[41] The main piece of Soviet evidence remained the Burdenko Report of January 1944, which charged German forces, "disguised as the 537th Engineering Battalion," with carrying out the massacre in the fall of 1941. The report named three commanding officers—Ahrens, Rex, and Hodt—as responsible for the murder. It emphasized that the Poles had been killed with "a pistol shot in the nape of the neck," the same method that had been used to kill Soviet citizens in Orel, Krasnodar, and Smolensk.[42] Soviet leaders were certain that Pokrovsky had enough material to make the Katyn charge stick to the Germans for good.

Standing before the Tribunal, Pokrovsky now characterized the Katyn massacre as one of the most heinous Nazi crimes. He read out the conclusions of the Burdenko Report, explaining that they were based on depositions from more than 100 witnesses and forensic evidence from the exhumed graves. Much of his presentation was devoted to exposing a supposed German cover-up of this crime. The Germans in the spring of 1943 had undertaken "a whole series of measures to ascribe their own misdeeds to organizations of the Soviet authorities, in order to make mischief between the Russians and the Poles," he asserted. They had tortured Soviet citizens to obtain false testimony, he charged; they had forced Russian prisoners of war to dig up the mass graves in order to tamper with the evidence. Once the graves had been dug, Pokrovsky concluded, the Germans had shot the Russian prisoners, to make sure they could never talk about what had happened.[43]

Did Pokrovsky know that he was presenting fabricated evidence? Possibly—although it is equally possible that Moscow had left him in the dark. He had no reason to question the evidence he was presenting. The Wehrmacht and the SS had committed numerous mass atrocities in Poland; German occupation authorities had tortured countless Soviet citizens and had forced Russian prisoners of war to dig up mass graves throughout Russia and Ukraine. On the face of things, the Soviet charges about Katyn were completely plausible.

By now, though, the defense attorneys clearly understood that the Western prosecutors were uneasy about the inclusion of Katyn in the Indictment. As Pokrovsky made his case, the defense mobilized to challenge the Soviet evidence. On Friday, February 15, Kaltenbrunner's attorney, Kurt Kauffmann, complained to the Tribunal that all reports from Soviet investigative commissions should be prohibited. They lacked exact information about their sources and their contents could not be verified. Judge Lawrence defended the Soviet right to use these reports, citing Article 21 of the Nuremberg Charter—which stipulated that the Tribunal would automatically accept "the acts and documents of the committees set up in the various allied countries for the investigation of war crimes." If the defense wanted to challenge particular reports, he added, it could do so later.[44]

For the Western powers, Pokrovsky's presentation undoubtedly raised even more questions about the general veracity of Soviet evidence. The American and British governments already had information pointing to Soviet responsibility for Katyn. If the Soviets had fabricated evidence and coerced witness testimony in order to implicate the Nazis in this crime, what did this mean for the rest of their case?[45] The Soviet prosecution had introduced as evidence to the Tribunal not just Soviet war crimes commission reports but also the verdicts of Soviet tribunals held in Krasnodar, Kharkov, Leningrad, Smolensk, and other cities. Could those verdicts be trusted?

The Western powers did not doubt the brutality of the German occupation in the USSR. But Soviet insistence on including Katyn as a Nazi war crime was in equal parts devious and dangerous. British alternate judge Birkett wrote in his diary the day after Pokrovsky's presentation that there was likely "a good deal of exaggeration" in the Soviet presentations. "But no doubt can remain in any dispassionate mind," he added, "that great horrors and cruelties were perpetrated" and that the Nazis had used "calculated cruelty and terror as their usual weapons."[46] Stalin and Vyshinsky, who were accustomed to using trials to shape whatever narrative they wanted, were counting on the Western powers going along with the Soviet story about Katyn. For now, at least, their gamble seemed to be paying off.

From Moscow's perspective, the Soviet case was proceeding well. Articles in the Western press praised the Soviet presentations as "exceedingly well organized" and declared that Russia had sent some of its "most able men to court."[47] Letters to Rudenko, which Soviet leaders carefully reviewed, suggested that the Soviet prosecution's opening speech had evoked an especially powerful response. One woman in Krefeld on the Rhine, in the British zone of occupied Germany, thanked Rudenko for telling the truth about the horrors of Nazism and expressed her disappointment with the slow pace of denazification in her town. "When you follow on the radio or in the newspapers everything that you and your countrymen have presented before the Tribunal, you almost completely lose the courage to continue living as a German," she wrote. "The guilty should be obliterated." Soviet women appealed to Rudenko for help finding information about sons who had not returned from the war. One woman in Ukraine expressed faith that "a compassionate Soviet person" like

Rudenko, who was intimately familiar with the evidence against the German war criminals, would understand "a mother's grief" and render assistance.[48]

One Soviet official in Moscow who did voice concern about the Soviet presentations was Andrei Smirnov, an expert on Germany at the Ministry of Foreign Affairs. On February 14, he complained to Molotov that the Soviet prosecutors were focusing too narrowly on German aggression against the Soviet Union. He pointed out that Rudenko had depicted the Nazi onslaught on Europe as merely preparatory to launching "the main attack" against the Soviet Union; Pokrovsky and Zorya had followed a similar line, describing the German assaults on Czechoslovakia, Poland, and Yugoslavia as steps on the way to the launching of Operation Barbarossa. Smirnov added that even the citations from *Mein Kampf* in the Soviet speeches overly emphasized German aspirations for Lebensraum in the East. All of this could make it possible to conclude that Germany had not been pursuing a broader goal of world domination. He suggested that the Soviet prosecution mirror more closely the narratives about the war that the Western prosecutors had presented.[49] This would make the Soviet Union less vulnerable to separate attacks from the defense.

Smirnov was doing his part in Moscow to strengthen the Soviet case by working behind the scenes with SMERSH and the NKVD to prepare a group of Soviet witnesses, all victims of Nazi crimes, for the trip to Nuremberg. On February 16, he notified Soviet authorities in Berlin that ten witnesses would be arriving in two days.[50] Three of them had lived through the siege of Leningrad and could testify on the German destruction of culture: the Armenian academic and State Hermitage Museum director Joseph Orbeli; Professor Yuri Dmitriev, an expert on ancient Russian art; and the Russian Orthodox priest (and Archdeacon of Leningrad Churches) Nikolai Lomakin. These men had also worked closely with the Extraordinary State Commission to collect evidence of German war crimes.[51] Another two witnesses, Stanislav Tarkovsky and Evgeny Kivelisha, could testify on the mistreatment of Soviet prisoners of war. Four other witnesses had been selected to testify about atrocities against civilians. Liubov Sopilnik, a Ukrainian, had been interned at Auschwitz. Evgeniya Panasiuk, a survivor of Majdanek, had witnessed the mass murder of children from a Belorussian orphanage. David Budnik, a Jew from Kiev in Ukraine, had escaped from Babi Yar—the ravine on the outskirts of the city that had been the site of numerous massacres. Iakov Grigoriev, a forty-seven-year old peasant, had witnessed the razing of his village near Pskov in western Russia.[52]

The final Soviet witness, the Jewish poet Abraham Sutzkever, was a late addition to this group and had not appeared on earlier lists of witnesses. He and his wife, Freydke, had been interned in the ghetto in Vilna, Lithuania, from September 1941 until September 1943, when they fled through the sewers and joined a group of partisans in the forests near Lake Narach in northwestern Belorussia. Before escaping the ghetto, Sutzkever had smuggled out some of his poems, which reached the Jewish Anti-Fascist Committee in Moscow. Ilya Ehrenburg (a member of this committee) had recognized Sutzkever as an ideal "witness-survivor"—and in March 1944 Soviet leaders had airlifted Sutzkever and his wife out of German-occupied territory to Moscow. Soon after this rescue, Ehrenburg profiled Sutzkever and his partisan activities in *Pravda*; he also publicized one of Sutzkever's poems, *Kol Nidre*, about a Jewish father who ends his son's life to save him from being tortured by the Nazis.[53]

Sutzkever had worked with Ehrenburg and the rest of the Jewish Anti-Fascist Committee to prepare evidence for *The Black Book*, a massive compilation documenting German atrocities against the Jews in the occupied Soviet Union. Soviet leaders had been contemplating using *The Black Book* (which had not yet been published) as evidence at Nuremberg. But after the French called concentration camp survivors as witnesses, they decided to send Sutzkever in person, summoning him to Moscow from Vilna.[54] The

FIGURE 8.3 Freydke and Abraham Sutzkever in Moscow soon after their rescue, March 1944.

Credit: Yad Vashem Photo Archive, Jerusalem, 20174/95.

NKVD had vetted the first nine Soviet witnesses in November, but did not interview Sutzkever until February 17, the day before the group left Moscow for Nuremberg.[55] On the evening before his departure, after buying a new suit, Sutzkever confided to his diary that he hoped to testify in Yiddish, "in the language of the people that the accused have attempted to exterminate."[56]

The Soviet witnesses' journey to Nuremberg was not easy. Their plane left as planned on February 18 but was grounded in Minsk because of bad weather. Moreover, the plane was not heated, and Panasiuk fell ill.[57] In his diary, Sutzkever described the stopover in Minsk as a pleasant interlude during which he got to know his travel companions. He admired the way Orbeli, an older gentleman with a thick grey beard, raised his glass during dinner in a toast "to the coexistence of all peoples with the Jewish people." Lomakin on the other hand he dismissed as a lecherous drunk and lout straight out of a Nikolai Gogol story.[58] The bad weather continued. On February 19 Rudenko told the judges that he could not provide a list yet of the Soviet witnesses because there were difficulties in bringing them to Nuremberg.[59]

The Soviet prosecution forged ahead without its witnesses. On February 18 and 19, Lev Smirnov presented evidence on German crimes against civilians, describing the annihilation of the Czechoslovak village of Lidice in all its horror. On June 10, 1942, all of the men and teenage boys of the village were shot. "The murders lasted from early morning until 4 o'clock in the afternoon. Afterwards the executioners were photographed with the corpses at their feet." The village was burned to the ground, and the women and the children were separated and sent to different concentration camps. Smirnov then reminded the court that Lidice was not unique. This kind of sadistic destruction was repeated in villages throughout the Soviet Union, each massacre more brutal than the last. Civilians were routinely burned alive or executed in still more barbarous ways. Smirnov gave special attention to the Germans' slaughter of children, reading evidence collected by the Extraordinary State Commission. Many thousands of children were tortured to death, asphyxiated in the gas vans, shot, drowned, or buried alive. He read the testimony of two Soviet citizens recounting how the Germans had thrown infants into open pits at Babi Yar and buried them with wounded or dead parents: "One could see the surface of the ground moving over the buried people who were still alive." German leaders had specifically targeted children, Smirnov explained, because they "understood that this form of terrorism would be particularly frightful for the survivors."[60]

Smirnov further told how, when defeat seemed near, German occupation forces had tried to conceal their crimes by forcing concentration camp prisoners to dig up and incinerate corpses. At Babi Yar, prisoners had piled up corpses and firewood in many layers; petroleum was poured on top, and then the pile was ignited. In the course of six weeks some 70,000 corpses were destroyed in this way. When it was not possible to burn corpses, German forces camouflaged mass graves. Describing the concealment of execution sites near Lvov, Smirnov invoked Katyn: he quoted an Extraordinary State Commission report stating that the Germans had used "the same methods for concealing their crimes" in the Lisenitz Forest outside Lvov "that they had used in the Katyn Forest."[61]

Even as German forces tried to cover up atrocities, individual German soldiers had photographed grisly scenes and kept the snapshots as souvenirs. The courtroom fell silent as Smirnov projected some of these images on the courtroom screen. One photograph showed Soviet youths being shot in the back of the neck; another showed naked women running past German guards; several others showed bodies hanging from gallows. Several photographs included German soldiers laughing at the victims. A *New York Times* correspondent reported that Ribbentrop turned away when a photograph of "a pile of human heads and grinning executioners flashed on the screen."[62]

Smirnov's final piece of evidence was the atrocity film put together by Karmen's studio in Moscow, *Atrocities Committed by the German Fascist Invaders in the USSR*. The Soviet witnesses still had not arrived in Nuremberg. But as the lights dimmed in the courtroom, Polevoi and the other correspondents watched as "corpses who had long ago been reduced to ashes" took their place in the witness box. The film took viewers down a Rostov street that was littered with bodies, zooming in on a dead child in the snow. It moved from there to a town square where corpses had been arranged "in neat piles like firewood." As the camera moved closer, it became clear that the bodies were those of executed soldiers. The film then took viewers on a journey west, through Latvia, Estonia, and Lithuania—and then to Poland, to the basement of the Danzig Technological Institute, where, the narrator explained, human corpses had been rendered into soap. The camera panned to a pile of decapitated bodies, stacked near large vats; severed heads were heaped nearby in a bin. "You felt like closing your eyes tightly, jumping up and running out of the courtroom," Polevoi wrote of his reaction to this scene. "But you had to pass through all the circles of this hell on earth, peer into the very heart of Nazism." When the film ended and the courtroom light was switched back on, people sat speechless, trying to comprehend what they had just seen.[63]

The American film about the Nazi concentration camps had not shown such "terrible things," Karmen later commented. Many of the horrific scenes in the Soviet documentary had also been omitted from the Soviet newsreels shown at home during the war. "Severed heads, severed arms, terrible camps in which we Soviet cameramen appeared with the first detachments . . . naked skeletons, murdered children. . . . " It hadn't been necessary to show the Soviet people such footage, Karmen noted. But this film was different, for it was "a document of the court." He had remained in the courtroom for the viewing of his film, studying the reactions of the defendants. In the end he was satisfied. Judging from their expressions, the defendants finally grasped the charges against them and "understood that they will not live."[64] The prison psychiatrist Gilbert agreed that the film had hit the mark even more than the one the Americans had shown.[65] New York Times correspondent Drew Middleton reported that the film had been so disturbing that "war-hardened Army guards gasped and swore under their breath." He suggested that it had put to rest any supposition that the stories coming out of the East about the German occupation had been overblown.[66]

The Soviet prosecution continued to present on Count Three, still without its witnesses, on February 20. Lev Sheinin presented on the plunder of the Soviet Union and Eastern Europe, introducing extensive evidence—including a 1942 speech in which Goering had directed the Reich commissioners to "squeeze" the people of the occupied territories to the point of starvation so that Germany might prosper.[67] The next morning, Mark Raginsky addressed the German destruction of national cultures. He read an affidavit from Yuri Dmitriev, one of the witnesses en route, about the destruction of Novgorod. He also presented excerpts of Extraordinary State Commission reports (that the witness Orbeli had helped write) about the looting of Russian palaces. Raginsky gave special attention to the role of the Sonderkommando Ribbentrop, an elite SS task force attached to the German Foreign Office, in confiscating Russian and Ukrainian relics, rare books, and works of art and sending them to Germany.[68] He also presented on the German destruction of churches, describing how the occupying forces vandalized, burned down, or blew up more than 2,000 houses of worship throughout the Soviet Union. He closed the afternoon with a showing of the second evidentiary film produced by Karmen's studio, The German Fascist Destruction of the Cultural Treasures of the Peoples of the USSR.[69] The New York Times called the before and after images shown in the film "a more striking indictment of vandalism than many thousands of words."[70]

On the evening of Thursday, February 21, the ten Soviet witnesses finally arrived by plane in Nuremberg, having been further delayed in Landsberg (Poland) and then Berlin by a blizzard. They checked into the Grand Hotel and waited to see who among them would be called before the Tribunal.

After getting settled in, Sutzkever received a personal visit from Rudenko, who urged him to get some rest. Before going to bed Sutzkever wrote in his diary, reflecting that "the name of Nuremberg would go down in history for eternity: first as the place of the Nuremberg Laws and now as the place of the Nuremberg Trials," where those "who had ordered the extermination of the Jewish people would be judged as criminals." Sutzkever, whose wife had watched the Nazis murder their newborn son, felt called upon to represent the Jewish people. "And I, perhaps the only surviving Yiddish poet of all occupied Europe, come to the Nuremberg Trials, not only to testify, but as a living witness to the immortality of my people."[71]

The next morning, Raginsky returned to the rostrum to present evidence on the German destruction of cities, towns, and villages. He took the court through German military directives to render uninhabitable all regions from which German forces withdrew. One order called for the destruction of all villages, stipulating that all stocks of foodstuffs and hay should be burned and that all stoves (which were used for both cooking and heating in peasant homes) should be blown up with hand grenades. Raginsky ended the morning session with the third Soviet film, *The German Fascist Destruction of Soviet Cities*.[72]

After a recess, Raginsky announced that Joseph Orbeli, who had lived in the Hermitage's Winter Palace (a grand museum filled with cultural treasures) during the siege of Leningrad, would testify about the destruction of the city's monuments of culture and art. The defense attorney Servatius (who represented the Leadership Corps of the Nazi Party in addition to Sauckel) tried to object on the grounds that Leningrad had never been under German occupation—but the Tribunal shut him down. Orbeli, looking worn out and tired, slowly stepped up to the witness box. With his voice shaking, he began to speak of the siege of the city, focusing on the destruction of its buildings.[73]

According to Orbeli, there was no doubt that German forces had targeted the Hermitage during the siege. Damage was caused not by chance but by systematic shelling over the course of months. Servatius, cross-examining Orbeli, asked how someone who was not a professional artilleryman could determine that the German military had not been directing its fire at the nearby Palace Bridge—given that bridges were known strategic targets. It seemed unlikely, Orbeli answered, that if German artillery were aiming at the bridge it would have hit it only once but would have struck the Winter Palace, across the way, with thirty shells. "Within these limits," he added, "I am an artilleryman." When Orbeli finished speaking, the correspondents from Leningrad congratulated him. "You've nailed them down" and "crushed

FIGURE 8.4 Soviet witness Joseph Orbeli in the witness box, February 1946.
Credit: State Archive of the Russian Federation f. 10140, op. 2, d. 153, l. 13.

them," Vishnevsky exulted. "I shake your hand as a Leningrader who lived through the blockade."[74]

The Soviet case was due to wrap up in less than a week. On Saturday, February 23, looking ahead to the next stage of the trials—the defense case—the Tribunal heard defense petitions for witnesses and documents. Otto Stahmer and Martin Horn (representing Goering and Ribbentrop, respectively) protested that the Tribunal's procedures were biased against the accused. The defense was repeatedly faced with surprise witnesses from the prosecution, while the defendants were expected to name their witnesses in advance. Getting nowhere with this argument, the defense attorneys began to list names. Goering wanted Field Marshal Albert Kesselring, Air Field Marshal Erhard Milch, General Karl Bodenschatz, and a number of other military leaders. Stahmer told the judges that Bodenschatz would attest that Goering had tried to stop Hitler from attacking Russia. Goering also requested Birger Dahlerus of Stockholm and Lord Halifax; both would testify that he had wanted peace. At the top of Ribbentrop's list of requested witnesses were his private secretary, Margarete Blank, and former ambassador Friedrich Gaus (who had headed the German Foreign Office's Legal Department). He also requested Winston Churchill, putting forward the theory that a "prewar threat" by the British prime minister might have prompted Hitler "to rearm Germany and plan aggressive wars." Alfred Seidl, who had recently taken over the Hess case, requested several witnesses, including the defendant's brother Alfred, who had been a deputy Gauleiter in the foreign section of the Nazi Party.[75]

The Soviets meanwhile were undecided about which of their other witnesses they should call on. That night, as the Soviet delegation hosted a party in honor of Red Army Day with plenty of vodka and caviar (at which David Maxwell Fyfe danced with several of the Russian interpreters), the Soviet witnesses remained in their quarters at the Grand Hotel, wondering which of them would testify.[76] The next morning, Sutzkever wrote in his diary that he had heard that it was "almost decided" that he, Grigoriev, Lomakin, and Tarkovsky would be called. But on Monday only Grigoriev, Lomakin, and Tarkovsky were confirmed. Sutzkever now speculated that there might be "reservations," as he put it, about his appearance as a witness.[77] He was right. He had asked to testify in Yiddish, and there were problems finding an interpreter. There was possibly also another issue in play. Ehrenburg later wrote that Sutzkever had confided to him his intention "to smuggle a gun into the Palace of Justice to shoot Goering"—and that he had talked Sutzkever out of making such an attempt.[78]

On Monday, February 25, Lev Smirnov gave the main Soviet speech on crimes against humanity. The Nuremberg Charter had defined "crimes against humanity" as "murder, extermination, enslavement, deportation, and other inhumane acts committed against any civilian population" or as "persecutions on political, racial or religious grounds" in connection with any crime within the Tribunal's jurisdiction. Smirnov maintained that the concept also had a broader meaning. The fascists had not just committed inhumane acts, including murder, but had tried to deprive people of that which made them human. The fascists forced their victims "to pass through numerous and agonizing phases, insulting to human dignity," he stated. People were "deprived of their homes, families, and native country," as well as "the right to speak or read in their mother tongue." They were stripped of their names and denied "the right to have children." Finally, "they were deprived of their last right—to live." Those who managed to escape required a prolonged recovery period in order to return to the "conventions of human society."[79]

Later that evening, Smirnov visited Sutzkever and informed him that he would be called on to testify—in Russian, one of the four official languages of the Tribunal. Smirnov impressed on Sutzkever the importance of his testimony as "the first Jewish witness." It would be up to him, Smirnov stressed, to "speak on behalf of millions of victims. You must tell the world how Fascism massacred your brothers."[80]

The next day, however, Sutzkever was not called. He sat in the courtroom all day while two other Soviet witnesses testified about the brutal methods used by the German occupiers. The first was Grigoriev, the peasant from Pskov. Western journalists observed how this witness "scowled and clenched his hands" as he quietly recounted how German soldiers had destroyed his village and massacred his family.[81] "On the memorable day of October 28, 1943, German soldiers suddenly raided our village and started murdering the peaceful citizens, shooting them, chasing them into the houses," Grigoriev began. He, two of his sons, and sixteen other peasants were marched to a house on the outskirts of the village. Shortly after, four armed German soldiers came in, lined them up against a wall, and sprayed them with machine gun fire. Grigoriev told the court that he and his younger son survived and escaped to the nearby forest, where they hid while the soldiers set the village ablaze; he later learned that his wife and middle son had been taken to a different house and murdered. When asked by Smirnov why the Germans had destroyed his village, Grigoriev said that he did not know. The Germans had claimed that the villagers were hiding partisans, but this was false, he testified. The villagers were mostly old people and children and did not even know who these supposed "partisans" were. Grigoriev's testimony made a powerful impression; the international press held him up as a "spokesman" for the "millions of humble persons who suffered under the Nazis."[82]

The next witness, Kivelisha, the Red Army doctor, testified about the abuse and murder of captured Soviet soldiers. Questioned by Pokrovsky, Kivelisha described his experiences in seven prisoner-of-war camps in Ukraine—each more appalling than the last. He had been assigned to work in the infirmaries of some of these camps, but the conditions had made it impossible to give the prisoners medical care. In a camp in Uman, thousands of wounded Soviet soldiers were left outside, "their dust-covered dressings soaked in blood, often in pus." In a camp in Rakovo, prisoners of war were put to work paving roads during the day and crammed into unheated stables at night. When a large number of people in a stable fell ill and became too weak to work, the guards locked the prisoners inside. After a few days, the stable "would be opened and the dead brought out by the hundreds."[83]

Smirnov completed his presentation on crimes against humanity with evidence about the Nazi plan to exterminate the Jews. He presented a report from the commanders of Einzatzgruppe A (which had operated in the Baltic region and Belorussia) that the Red Army had found in the Gestapo archives in Latvia. It covered the period from October 1941 to January 1942 and bragged about having fulfilled the orders to eliminate the Jews "to the fullest possible extent." It noted that this goal had been almost completely realized in Latvia, Lithuania, and Estonia and that those Jews remaining had been concentrated in ghettos.[84] The next morning, February 27, Smirnov quoted from a Polish government report stating that three million Jews had been exterminated in Poland, and spoke about the annihilation of the Jews of Czechoslovakia and Yugoslavia. He then called Sutzkever to the witness box.[85]

Sutzkever had spent a couple of fitful days and sleepless nights nervously waiting to testify. The responsibility of representing the Jewish people weighed on him heavily. "Will I pass the exam? Will I fulfill my mission properly for history, for my people? God only knows!" he had written in his diary. Now, before the courtroom, the poet was visibly overcome with emotion. Unlike the other witnesses, he remained standing in the witness box, as if, he later wrote, it had been a matter of "reciting Kaddish," the Jewish prayer for the dead.[86]

Sutzkever's voice trembled and his body shook as he told the court about the operations of the Einsatzgruppen in Vilna.[87] He described how in the autumn of 1941 the "man hunters" of the SD had barged into Jewish homes day and night, dragging men away to the nearby village of Ponary—most of whom were never heard from again. He also spoke of the pogrom the Germans had initiated in Vilna earlier, in July 1941: blood had "streamed through the street as if a red rain had fallen." Even before the Vilna ghetto was organized that August, half of the city's Jewish population had been murdered, he attested. The Germans used the ghetto "to exterminate the rest of the Jewish population with greater ease." Before the occupation some 80,000 Jews had lived in Vilna, Sutzkever emphasized. At the end of the war, there were only 600 Jews left. Smirnov asked for a clarification: "Thus, 79,400 persons were exterminated?" Sutzkever answered yes.[88]

The most harrowing part of Sutzkever's testimony was his recounting of the murder of his newborn son. An order had been issued in the ghetto in late December 1941 forbidding Jewish women to bear children. Around that time, Sutzkever's wife gave birth to a boy in a ghetto hospital. The Jewish doctors hid the baby and other newborns in one of the rooms, but German soldiers heard their cries and burst in. When Sutzkever's wife heard the commotion, she ran to the room. "She saw one German holding the baby and smearing something under its nose. Afterwards he threw it on the bed and laughed." Sutzkever told the court that when he arrived a short time later his baby was dead. "He was still warm."[89]

Sutzkever had testified for almost forty minutes, and he was spent, "shaken to the core," as he wrote in his diary. He was consumed by both his own suffering and his desire for vengeance—but also strengthened by the knowledge that the Jewish people had survived, heartened by "the ardent, intense feeling . . . that no power of darkness is able to annihilate us." He considered it a matter of "Jewish destiny" that he, a Yiddish poet, had "survived to judge Rosenberg and Frank in Nuremberg" and, through them, all who had adhered to their ideology. Sutzkever had indeed done well, speaking for the Jewish people—and also testifying on behalf of the Soviet people. Smirnov, Sheinin, and Zorya all congratulated him afterward for so ably doing his part.[90] Sutzkever, a Jew and a partisan, served an important role for the Soviet prosecution at this point during the trials. Through his testimony, the Soviets were able to integrate the story of the annihilation of the Jews into the larger narrative about German crimes against humanity and the wartime suffering of the entire Soviet people in the occupied East.

Smirnov's next two witnesses, Seweryna Szmaglewska and Samuel Rajzman, both from Poland, were last-minute additions to the Soviet case. Szmaglewska had been interned at Auschwitz-Birkenau from October 1942 to January 1945, when she escaped from an evacuation transport. Rajzman, a Jew, had been deported from the Warsaw ghetto to Treblinka in September 1942. Eleven months later he had led a group of fighters during the Treblinka uprising and escaped to a nearby forest. After the war, both witnesses had published accounts of the concentration camps.[91] The Polish government had provided these publications as evidence for the prosecution and had brought the two survivors to Nuremberg to have available for questioning in case their accounts were challenged. At some point in February, Soviet leaders had directed the Soviet prosecution to call on them instead of Panasiuk and Sopilnik. These witnesses had especially powerful stories to tell.

Smirnov introduced Szmaglewska as a Polish woman who had witnessed the murder of children. She testified about newborns being seized from their mothers in Auschwitz-Birkenau and spoke of how children born in the camp had numbers tattooed onto their legs because the five digits could not fit "on their tiny arms." She told how in early 1943 the children were "taken away from the camp." When asked by Smirnov where the children had been taken, she cried out that she did not know. "I should like, in the name of all the women of Europe who became mothers in concentration camps, to ask the

Germans today, 'Where are these children?'" Szmaglewska further testified that at a time when great numbers of Jews were being killed in the camp's gas chambers, "an order was issued that the children should be thrown into the crematory ovens or the crematory ditches without previous asphyxiation with gas." Yes, she confirmed when questioned by Smirnov, "the children were thrown in alive. Their cries could be heard all over the camp."[92]

The Soviet jurist Poltorak later recalled how people wept openly at Szmaglewska's testimony. A number of the defense attorneys lowered their heads, while others stared blankly ahead. Even some of the defendants looked at the floor.[93] After a recess, Rajzman testified about the mass extermination of Jews—estimating that at Treblinka the Germans had killed an average of "ten to twelve thousand people" a day. He had remained alive, he explained, only because he knew many languages and could be used as an interpreter.[94]

The last Soviet witness was the Russian Orthodox priest Lomakin, who appeared before the court in long black velvet robes with two large gilt crosses hanging from his neck and a medal for the defense of Leningrad pinned to his chest.[95] He had been called to add to Orbeli's testimony about

FIGURE 8.5 Soviet witness Nikolai Lomakin in the witness box, February 1946.
Credit: Russian State Documentary Film and Photo Archive No. B-3190.
Photographer: Evgeny Khaldei.

the besieged city. Speaking from the witness box, he described the winter of 1941–1942 as particularly grim, with constant shelling and air raids, overflowing sewage, darkness, and terrible starvation. He also recounted the targeted bombing of cemeteries. "Please imagine the scene when people who have found eternal rest—their coffins, bodies, bones, skulls—all this is thrown out on the ground." Leningraders who had just lost relatives had to grieve all over again as exploding shells left giant craters "on the very spot where they had just buried" their kin.[96] The American prosecutors found it striking that the Soviets had called on a priest to testify and saw it as a calculated move for world sympathy and support. "These Russkies are really on their toes!" wrote U.S. assistant prosecutor Dodd in a letter home that evening, adding acerbically that whether or not Lomakin was really a religious leader, he certainly "looked the part."[97]

Following Lomakin's testimony, the Soviets wrapped up their case. Smirnov made a brief final speech, emphasizing the great responsibility of the judges and looking forward to "a just and speedy verdict."[98] Before that, however, each of the defendants would have his day—or much more—in court.

The Soviet presentations, documentary films, and witness testimony had been emotionally wrenching and deeply disturbing. Some American and British observers suspected the Soviet prosecution of exaggeration and in some instances even fabrication—but this did not diminish the power of their case. Taylor later wrote that in spite of some apparent flaws in the Soviet evidence, no one (except for Goering) questioned its overall veracity in painting a picture of Nazism in the occupied East. The Soviets, in his opinion, had done a particularly capable job of presenting evidence on the Nazi extermination of the Jews—something he found to be of great significance given what he knew about the Soviet government's general "reluctance" to recognize the Jews "as a primary and unique victim of Nazism."[99] Sutzkever's testimony had been especially moving and effective. The Soviets had highlighted the role of anti-Semitism in Germany's crimes against humanity, while also emphasizing that other peoples had been victimized as well.

Soviet observers also believed that Rudenko and his assistants had acquitted themselves ably before the court. Vishnevsky sent Vyshinsky an eight-page appraisal of the Soviet case, reporting that it had gone "satisfactorily and in a number of instances very well." A French journalist had complimented the Soviet presentations to him as the most straightforward and powerful, he noted. The Soviet witness testimony had made a particularly strong impression on the Western correspondents, and the surprise appearance of Paulus had been a highlight. Vishnevsky had overheard someone exclaim that after the Soviet prosecutors had produced Paulus, he "wouldn't be surprised if they reveal Hitler here too."[100]

Vishnevsky did pass along some criticism he had heard regarding the Soviet case as well as some observations about its coverage in the international press. Several German newspapers had attempted to discredit Paulus's testimony, and a member of the British delegation had complained that some of the Soviet data had been misleading, combining combat deaths with executions. The London newspapers, he noted, had omitted Soviet statistical data and had given some of the Soviet speeches only cursory mention. Vishnevsky blamed this on international politics, noting the strained Soviet-British negotiations at the United Nations meeting in London. Coverage in the American newsmagazine *Time*, he added, also "has an unfavorable character for us." (The magazine gave scant coverage to the Soviet presentations, focusing instead on the Soviet threat to Europe.)[101]

Though the court had accepted all of the Soviet evidence—including the Burdenko Commission's report about Katyn—Vishnevsky did not think that the Soviets could afford to let their guard down. The German attorneys had increased their efforts during the Soviet case to dismiss the Tribunal as a "court of the victors," he reported. They had attempted to cast doubt on the Soviet witness testimony and were challenging Article 21 of the Nuremberg Charter as an illegality that had allowed the prosecution to introduce unverifiable evidence. Looking ahead to the defense case, he anticipated a fairly intense struggle against the prosecution. The defense attorneys would likely invoke "the Führer principle," he predicted, to argue that the defendants had obediently fulfilled their narrow functions without understanding the bigger picture. He also expected that they would continue to dispute the aggressive war charge.[102]

Vishnevsky therefore called for the mobilization of the entire Soviet apparatus for the defense case and suggested that Rudenko enlist the full services of Soviet experts on Germany. The Soviet prosecution needed "to seize the INITIATIVE," he emphasized, and anticipate the defense's arguments ahead of time. It was also desirable to throw the defense off guard by bringing in new evidence and witnesses if the rules would allow it. Finally, he argued that it was essential to improve the morale of the Soviet delegation. Homesickness was getting to everyone, he wrote, noting brawling among the drivers and "tears and depression" among the translators and typists. Some members of the Soviet delegation were "hanging on the telephone line to Moscow." Others fraternized with locals and had become obsessed with buying goods on the black market. Vishnevsky blamed these problems on the isolation of the Soviets in the American zone.[103] But there were clearly other issues also in play. The witness testimony and graphic images of the Soviet case had taken a toll on everyone in the Nuremberg courtroom, but the Soviet delegation in particular had been unable to look away.

Over the preceding few weeks, the world had come to better understand exactly what the Soviet people had endured. Rumors and generalities became graphic images of horror. The Soviets had successfully presented their evidence against the accused and had received praise and recognition in the international press for their performance in the courtroom and their vital role in the Allied victory. Stalin's interventions in the Soviet case had proven effective. The Soviets had successfully countered the threat of being upstaged by the Americans by bringing in new evidence and compelling witnesses. They had made persuasive arguments to counter the defense's claims about preventive war.

But by late February, the split between the Soviet Union and the West was growing—and American and British leaders were expressing far more concern about a future Soviet threat than about a continuing German one. Kennan, the American diplomat, had galvanized American fears about the Soviet menace to postwar Europe with his "Long Telegram," sent to Secretary of State James Byrnes on February 22 (the same day the Soviet witnesses had begun to take the stand), which portrayed the Soviets as dangerously expansionistic.[104] The issue of repatriation had also reached an emotional peak. At the United Nations meeting in London, Vyshinsky had tried to push through Soviet proposals that would have mandated the repatriation of all Soviet citizens from Europe to the USSR, regardless of circumstance. The Soviet proposals were rejected. Rumors spread nonetheless about the forced deportation of Baltic nationals (Latvians, Lithuanians, and Estonians) from Germany to the Soviet Union.[105]

Going into the next phase of the Nuremberg Trials, the Soviet delegation would face significant challenges from the Western powers as well as from the defense. The defense attorneys would introduce documentary evidence and call witnesses with the explicit aims of challenging key parts of the Soviet case and implicating the Soviet Union in war crimes and crimes against peace. At the same time, growing tensions between the Soviet Union on the one side and the United States and Great Britain on the other—in particular over the fate of Germany and the political and economic orientation of postwar Europe—would spill over into the Nuremberg courtroom. Vishnevsky's letter to Moscow was prescient. The Soviets would need to take the initiative to navigate the challenges ahead.

PART III | The Defense Case

| The Cold War Comes
to Nuremberg

W HEN THE SOVIET lawyer Arkady Poltorak arrived in the Nuremberg
courtroom on Wednesday, March 6, a strange scene met his eyes.
The dock looked like a "disturbed hive," he later wrote, and the faces of the
defendants shone with hope and expectation. Winston Churchill, the former
British prime minister, had delivered his "Iron Curtain" speech in Fulton,
Missouri, the previous day, calling for Anglo-American resistance to Soviet
aggression and tyranny. That morning, the American army newspaper *Stars
and Stripes* had printed the speech under a bannered headline: "Unite to Stop
Russians, Churchill Warns at Fulton."[1] Boris Polevoi now watched as the defense attorneys stood in the courtroom and leafed through their copies of the
newspaper, "as if reading them, but in fact making it possible for their clients
to read Churchill's speech over their shoulders."[2] Goering observed aloud
that "the only Allies who are still allied are the four prosecutors, and they are
only allied against the defendants."[3] The Cold War had come to Nuremberg.

The Soviets had just wrapped up their case against the Nazi leaders,
and the day in court was devoted to reviewing the defense's applications
for witnesses. Everyone was preoccupied, however, with this latest development on the international scene. "Whatever Churchill's anti-Russian speech
sounded like to the outside world, it exploded over the Allied courthouse in
wrecked Nuremberg like a large, postwar bombshell," reflected the American
correspondent Janet Flanner.[4] Writing home that evening, the U.S. assistant
prosecutor Thomas Dodd noted that it had been "a bad day" in Nuremberg

after news spread about the speech and that it would not be too surprising if the Soviets withdrew and the trial broke up. Dodd shared Robert Jackson's hostility toward the Soviets and personally agreed with Churchill that the Russians were "the same breed of cat" as the Nazis. He also knew that the defendants were hoping for a conflict between the Western powers and the Soviets.[5] The Soviets, too, wondered what Churchill's speech would mean for the trials. Polevoi studied the prosecutors, the judges, the defense attorneys, and the defendants, uncertain how the speech would affect their behavior. The "most enterprising reaction to Churchill's speech," Polevoi later noted, came from his favorite American bartender, who introduced a new cocktail called "the Sir Winnie"—a bitter concoction that "stung our mouths from the first sip."[6]

The timing of Churchill's speech was inauspicious for the Soviets. Their prosecutors had done extremely well after many months of preparation, and their witnesses had made a powerful impression. Gorshenin and Trainin, two key members of the Vyshinsky Commission, had returned to Moscow immediately after the Soviets finished their presentations at the end of February. Now the defense case was about to begin, and the trials were moving into unfamiliar territory. The Soviets were still adjusting to the fact that the Nazi defendants were being allowed to launch a defense at all. Rudenko and Nikitchenko were both used to dealing with defendants who had been intimidated or tortured by the NKVD, not hostile and unrepentant defendants who also had the benefit of assertive counsel. The Soviets were hoping to divide the defendants and promote their mutual unmasking. The defense, meanwhile, was intent on broadening the gap between the Soviet Union and the other countries of the prosecution. Churchill's speech, delivered on American soil, pushed existing tensions among the erstwhile allies to the surface and gave the former Nazi leaders and their attorneys an opening.

The defense case began on Friday, March 8. The courtroom was again packed, as it had been during the Soviet opening presentation. Its physical layout had been altered slightly: the witness box had been moved closer to the dock. Many of the defendants would be testifying on their own behalf.

The Goering defense was up first, and Nuremberg was abuzz. There was heightened security everywhere. American military authorities had stationed additional guards throughout the Palace of Justice, fearing a possible raid aimed at freeing the infamous "Nazi no. 2."[7] The Soviet correspondents settled into the overcrowded press box, where the conversation kept returning to Churchill's speech.[8] Roman Karmen, setting up his equipment, looked over at the defense attorneys—noting their resemblance to "sinister birds."[9]

Goering's attorney, Otto Stahmer, began the morning by petitioning the Tribunal for additional witnesses to rebut Soviet charges about German responsibility for the Katyn massacre. According to Stahmer, a number of German soldiers had come forward after the Soviet prosecution's presentation of the Burdenko Report to say that the Soviets were lying. Stahmer asked to summon to Nuremberg the three German officers named in the report (Ahrens, Rex, and Hodt—all in Soviet hands) and two other officers who were in American and British custody (General Eugen Oberhauser and Senior Lieutenant Berg). Stahmer submitted an additional petition to call Professor François Naville, a forensic expert at the University of Geneva who had served on the German-sponsored International Katyn Commission— which had investigated the gravesite in April 1943 and identified the Soviets as the culprits.[10] The Katyn challenge, which Jackson had been dreading almost from the moment the Indictment was filed, had begun.

FIGURE 9.1 Hermann Goering talks with his attorney, Otto Stahmer, in the Nuremberg prison, 1946.

Credit: United States Holocaust Memorial Museum, courtesy of National Archives and Records Administration, College Park. Photographer: Evgeny Khaldei.

Having put the Soviets on alert, Stahmer proceeded to call Goering's first witnesses: General Karl Bodenschatz and General Field Marshal Erhard Milch. Bodenschatz, the former liaison officer between the Luftwaffe (Air Force) and Hitler's headquarters, characterized Goering as a pacifist who had tried to dissuade Hitler from attacking the Soviet Union. He also described him as a "benefactor to all in need" who had not known about the conditions in the concentration camps or the extermination of the Jews. Milch, who had been in charge of German aircraft production, also claimed that Goering opposed war. These improbable descriptions of Goering began to fall apart upon cross-examination. Jackson got Bodenschatz to admit that Goering had known all about the concentration camps and had personally given the orders to exclude Jews from Germany's economic life.[11]

On that first afternoon of the defense case, Jackson warned Rudenko and the French chief prosecutor, Auguste Champetier de Ribes, that trouble lay ahead. He had fresh information that the defense was planning to attack the French treatment of prisoners of war, British policy regarding Norway, and "Soviet policy as constituting aggression in connection with the Finnish, Polish, Balkan and Baltic States situations." Recalling the chief prosecutors' mutual agreement to resist "political attacks" from the defense, Jackson reaffirmed his willingness to "lead the effort to restrict the proof closely to the charges and to try to stop political discussions." But he needed the French and the Soviets to provide those written lists of their governments' wartime policies and actions that could be fodder for the defense's attacks.[12] David Maxwell Fyfe had circulated just such a list in December (noting Britain's wartime relationship with Norway as well as the history of British imperialism more generally), but the French and the Soviets had been less forthcoming.[13] Indeed, while the Vyshinsky Commission had shared such a list with Rudenko and authorized him to communicate its contents, it had still not given him permission to share a physical copy with his Western colleagues.

Jackson now cautioned that he could not "commit the United States to the support of undisclosed positions" which might require consultation with the U.S. State Department or American military authorities. He reminded Rudenko and de Ribes that defense witnesses would likely use their cross-examinations to volunteer information about sensitive questions and that this too could be better dealt with if planned for in advance. Acknowledging that the judges might overrule the prosecution's objections, Jackson also asked the other chief prosecutors to communicate the steps they wished him to take if the defense succeeded in making countercharges against the Allied powers in open court. It would be "embarrassing to all" if the United States were taken by surprise by information revealed in court and found it impossible to come out in support of its wartime allies.[14]

The Soviets were caught between the Scylla and Charybdis of German defense tactics and American ambition. Soviet leaders mistrusted the Americans, but they decided that it was probably in their best interests to take Jackson up on his offer. Moscow gave Rudenko the go-ahead, and on March 11 he shared the Soviet list with Jackson, Maxwell Fyfe, and de Ribes. The list was almost identical to the one that Soviet leaders had put together and the Vyshinsky Commission had discussed back in November. It specified as taboo all questions about Soviet foreign policy, making particular mention of the German-Soviet Non-Aggression Pact, German foreign minister Ribbentrop's visit to Moscow and Soviet foreign minister Molotov's visit to Berlin, Soviet-Polish relations, and Soviet policy regarding the Baltic republics and the Balkans. The list also declared off limits all questions concerning the Soviet political system. Rudenko agreed with Jackson that the prosecutors must stand together to prevent the defense from using the courtroom to examine matters without "direct relevance to the case." He complained that the accused and their attorneys were already spreading misinformation about the actions and policies of the Allied governments.[15]

Even as Rudenko was sharing the Soviet list with Jackson, other challenges were mounting behind the scenes. Stahmer and the other defense attorneys, determined to give their clients a vigorous defense, were submitting thousands of pages of evidence to the Tribunal. This presented a logistical challenge for the IMT's Translation Division. It was a particular nightmare for the Soviet delegation, which, somewhat incredibly, was still woefully short of skilled translators. The Tribunal's attempt to ameliorate this problem created further difficulties for the Soviets. On March 8, the judges announced that to avoid needless translation work, the defense should indicate to the prosecution "the exact passages in all documents" it proposed to use for its case. The prosecution could then object to any evidence it deemed irrelevant before it was fully translated for the court.[16] This was a pragmatic measure—but it meant that the Soviet prosecution would have to quickly screen a mountain of German-language documents.

As the Soviet prosecution geared up to tackle these latest challenges, Stahmer called a parade of witnesses to the stand for Goering. On Tuesday, March 12, former military adjutant Colonel Bernd von Brauchitsch and former Prussian state secretary Paul Koerner contributed their attestations to Goering's upright character. Koerner even maintained that Goering had helped to build up agricultural production in the countries that Germany occupied. When confronted by Rudenko, Koerner insisted that Germany had not practiced "plunder" and that it had been only natural for the occupied territories to contribute to the Wehrmacht's food supply. Goering's final witness of the day, Albert Kesselring, had served as general field marshal of the Luftwaffe before becoming commander-in-chief of the German troops in Italy; he described the Luftwaffe as "purely a weapon of defense" with a straight face.[17]

While cross-examining Kesselring, several defense attorneys attempted to charge that the Allies, too, had committed war crimes. Hans Laternser, counsel for the General Staff and High Command, asked Kesselring if he knew whether the Allied powers had violated international law. As Kesselring began to answer in the affirmative, Rudenko loudly protested that the witness had no right to evaluate the actions of "Germany's enemies." Asked by the judges to state his intentions, Laternser explained that he wanted to determine whether the witness had become more lenient toward his own men's behavior after hearing of Allied war crimes. Jackson jumped in and tried to keep the discussion focused on European Axis crimes. He reminded the court that it was generally established that violations of the rules and customs of international law on one side did not excuse such violations on the other side. After a brief recess, the judges declared Laternser's question inadmissible.[18]

The Tribunal's ruling against Laternser's tu quoque ("you did it too") argument boded well for the prosecution. The Soviets had some cause for hope that the judges might also reject Stahmer's request for witnesses to testify about Katyn. In a March 11 petition to the Tribunal, Rudenko invoked Article 21 of the Nuremberg Charter to assert that the Burdenko Report, as the report of a national war crimes commission, must stand as incontrovertible proof of German guilt for the massacre. When the Tribunal met in closed session the following day, however, the three Western judges disputed the Soviet interpretation of Article 21. They argued that it covered only the initial submission of evidence; it did not prohibit the defense from challenging evidence after it had been submitted. Judge Biddle maintained that a defendant had the right to attempt to refute a document.[19] That night, Poltorak broke the news to Moscow that the Western judges had sided with Stahmer about Article 21 and would allow German witness testimony for Katyn.[20] Soviet counterintelligence agent Vsevolod Siuganov sent his own report to SMERSH a few days later, confirming that the Tribunal had made its decision over Nikitchenko's objections.[21]

On Wednesday afternoon, March 13, Goering himself sauntered into the witness box in jackboots and baggy pants, a bundle of papers tucked under his arm. Expectations were high among the correspondents that Goering would be "a good story"—and it became immediately apparent that he intended to use his testimony to reminisce about his glory days. For the rest of the afternoon Goering gave exhaustive answers to Stahmer's leading questions. He recounted with evident fondness the first time he heard Hitler speak, and he spoke with pride about the role he had played in facilitating Hitler's rise to power. He readily described setting up the Gestapo and using it to conduct mass arrests of German Communists, calling it simply "a question of removing a danger."[22]

The Tribunal seemed to be at a loss for how to deal with Goering. An American journalist noted that the judges did not interrupt even when Goering stated "with suave impertinence and a sly glance" at the Soviet judges "that he had plagiarized the idea of concentration camps from abroad."[23] British alternate judge Birkett fretted over his colleagues' leniency. He reflected in his diary that if all of the defendants were permitted to speak so freely, Nuremberg would "be written down as a failure."[24] Such was of course Goering's intention.

FIGURE 9.2 Hermann Goering in the witness box, March 1946.

Credit: United States Holocaust Memorial Museum, courtesy of Gerald (Gerd) Schwab.

The following day Goering continued to make provocative speeches. He gave an unapologetic account of Nazi foreign policy, arguing that Russia, France, Great Britain, and their allies had "forced" Germany to action. The Soviet Union had begun producing weapons at an alarming rate, he maintained, and so Germany had been compelled to rearm for the "security of the Reich." He similarly described the German occupations of Czechoslovakia and Norway as preventive measures.[25] Writing home that evening, Dodd remarked that Goering was "not cringing or crawling." Dodd also noted that "a certain tenseness" remained in Nuremberg—referring to the continuing fallout from Churchill's speech. A March 12 *Stars and Stripes* headline, "Moscow Calls Churchill 'Warmonger,'" had prompted another groundswell of gossip in the Palace of Justice. The article referred to a recent *Pravda* interview with Stalin in which he had insinuated that Churchill was a fascist—suggesting that Churchill, like Hitler, believed in the superiority of his race and harbored imperialistic ambitions. Stalin had vowed in the interview that Churchill and his friends in England and America would be defeated if they had the temerity to launch a war against the Soviet Union. Poltorak later described how this war of words continued to encourage the defendants, who anticipated each bit of news about the situation between the Soviet Union and the West "the same way a hen dreams of millet."[26]

Andrei Vyshinsky, tracking the trials from Moscow, sprang into action after the Tribunal's decision to permit testimony on Katyn. Goering was a nuisance for the entire prosecution, but Katyn was a special Soviet problem. On March 15, he directed Rudenko to present a letter to the judges (which he attached) insisting on the Soviet interpretation of Article 21 and arguing that the decision to allow German witnesses to testify about Katyn marked a serious breach of the Nuremberg Charter. Rudenko was to seek support for this letter from the other chief prosecutors by arguing that it was unconscionable for the Tribunal to allow "the direct perpetrators" of the Katyn massacre to take the stand as supposed witnesses to this atrocity and by warning that the Tribunal's decision would set a precedent for the rest of the trials. If the judges ultimately refused to change their decision, Rudenko was to demand to call Soviet witnesses and forensic experts on Katyn.[27] Rudenko circulated this letter to Jackson, Maxwell Fyfe, and de Ribes on March 18.[28]

While the Soviets were strategizing about Katyn, Goering continued to use the witness box to elaborate a story about preventive war—asserting that Hitler had become convinced after his meeting with Molotov in 1940 that Russia was preparing to attack Germany. Goering did not pass up an opportunity to make digs at the Soviets. Yes, Germany had used Russian prisoners of war in antiaircraft operations. These were "volunteers," he claimed, who had chosen to fight against the Soviet Union. Yes, Russian agriculture was in ruins. This was because retreating Red Army troops had destroyed the harvest and the seeds, he insisted. He then announced that the German occupation of the Soviet Union had been far less damaging than the subsequent Soviet occupation of Germany.[29] The entire prosecution sat mute while he rattled on. The judges, for their part, seemed intent on letting him say his piece, in hopes of putting to rest potential defense claims about victors' justice.

The Goering show continued through the weekend. On March 16 and 18, fourteen defense attorneys cross-examined him. Many of them probed the question of agency. Could their clients have influenced Hitler to change his policies? Could they have resigned in protest? Goering answered all of these questions in the negative. Responding to Ribbentrop's attorney, Martin Horn, Goering attested that Ribbentrop had wielded "no influence" with Hitler. Other defense counsel asked Goering questions that were intended to further drive a wedge between the Soviets and the Western powers. Raeder's lawyer, Walter Siemers, elicited Goering's testimony about French and English plans to bomb the oil fields of the Caucasus in 1940 in order to cut off the supply of fuel to Germany.[30] While this was old news, it seemed to take on more significance in the wake of the Churchill-Stalin exchange.

On March 18, Jackson began his cross-examination of Goering. The crowd was counting on Jackson to put Goering in his place. They were promptly disappointed. Jackson approached Goering in a "blustering police-court manner," observed Janet Flanner. Jackson tried to lead him through questions about the rise of the Nazi Party, but Goering would not be led.[31] Answering Jackson's questions about the concentration camps, Goering argued that it had been necessary to take certain groups "into protective custody"—and compared Nazi policy with the "protective measures" the Allies were now taking in occupied Germany.[32]

Jackson tried to rein in Goering; the Western judges would not let him. Tribunal president Lawrence stated that the witness should be allowed to answer questions with whatever explanations he deemed right. The other defendants nudged one another, sat back, and enjoyed the spectacle.[33] Birkett noted in his diary that evening that neither the prosecutors nor the judges had been prepared for Goering's "immense ability and knowledge." He blamed the judges primarily, for failing to properly manage the proceedings.[34] Jackson could not have agreed more. Following his disastrous face-off with Goering, he met with his French and British colleagues and vented his frustration with the Tribunal's refusal to control the defendant.[35]

FIGURE 9.3 The Press Room at the Palace of Justice, where the correspondents received briefings, ca. 1945–1946.

Credit: United States Holocaust Memorial Museum, courtesy of Harry S. Truman Library. Photographer: Charles Alexander.

The international press was having a field day covering Goering: he *was* a good story. The Western newspapers carried articles appraising every aspect of his personality, health, and sartorial choices. Soviet journalists, like Polevoi, also found Goering fascinating, though they kept their coverage focused on his crimes.[36] In general, the Western and Soviet journalists took markedly different approaches to Goering's defense. One *New York Times* correspondent noted that many Western journalists, having extensively covered the prosecution's case, now felt obliged to "publish Goering's eulogies of Hitler and his defense of Nazism."[37] The Soviet press was careful not to give the Nazi leaders a platform. On one of the most dramatic "Goering days," *Pravda* succinctly noted that Goering had offered the usual "fascist propaganda."[38]

The local chatter about Churchill's speech, combined with Goering's testimony, made the Soviet correspondents in Nuremberg feel increasingly aggrieved. Life went on. Polevoi and the other Khaldeians continued to frequent

FIGURE 9.4 The American authorities provided buses to transport the correspondents between the Press Camp (the Faber Castle) and the Palace of Justice, 1945.

Credit: Russian State Documentary Film and Photo Archive No. B-3007. Photographer: Evgeny Khaldei.

their favorite bar; Karmen, Vsevolod Vishnevsky, and the other Big Wigs took in the entertainment at the Grand Hotel. Some of the correspondents even went to the occasional soccer match. But the trials were weighing on them, and Nuremberg itself had lost its novelty. On March 19, Vishnevsky complained to *Pravda* chief Peter Pospelov that while Goering was giving his performance, local conditions had become even more "psychologically difficult" for the Soviets. "Everything is very alien, at times hostile," he wrote, noting the fresh onslaught of anti-Soviet articles in the local press. Vishnevsky also believed that the American authorities had become more aggressive in spying on the Soviet delegation. He reported that bugs had been discovered in the buzzers used to ring for maid service and that one had just been found in a table used by Rudenko.[39] (While Vishnevsky assumed that the Americans were to blame, it was also possible—and perhaps even more likely—that SMERSH or the NKVD were eavesdropping on the Soviet delegation.)

Vishnevsky noted that the isolation and the stress of the trials were affecting many of the Soviet correspondents. Polevoi had become so nervous that he had asked to be called back home. After months of emotional strain and loneliness, hearing constantly about terrible crimes and atrocities, such reactions were understandable. Vishnevsky expressed regret that the Party did not seem to grasp this and arrange for even a friendly exchange of telegrams between Moscow and Nuremberg. He had continued to send informational reports to the Party but for many weeks had not received a single reply—and was beginning to question whether his work was even useful. He also wondered what had become of the articles he had recently sent for *Pravda* and whether they had ended up simply dumped in the trash, as he feared. He understood that the Nuremberg Trials were probably of only moderate interest to many Soviet readers. Still, regular communication from Moscow would be appreciated. He added that he had only just received, earlier that day, the week-old issue of *Pravda* with Stalin's interview about the Churchill speech.[40]

The U.S. delegation was having its own troubles at this stage of the trials. When Jackson resumed his cross-examination the following afternoon, he made a gaffe because someone on his staff had mistranslated the minutes from a 1935 meeting of the Reich Defense Council. Jackson quoted a passage with

FIGURE 9.5 Some of the Soviet correspondents take in a soccer match in Nuremberg: Vsevolod Vishnevsky (second to left), Roman Karmen (furthest right), 1946.

Credit: Russian State Archive of Literature and Art f. 1038, op. 1, d. 4762, l. 2.

the intention of proving that Goering had violated the Treaty of Versailles by plotting the "liberation of the Rhineland." Goering eagerly corrected the mistake. The document called not for liberating the Rhineland but for clearing the Rhine River of freighters and tugboats in case of mobilization. Jackson pushed on, asking whether these actions had been intended as part of the plan for rearmament. When Goering insisted that these were general mobilization plans "such as every country makes," Jackson asked why they had been kept secret. At this point Goering remarked that he could not remember having seen any published U.S. mobilization plans. This sent Jackson over the edge. He complained to the judges that Goering had adopted a "contemptuous attitude" toward the IMT, which was "giving him the trial which he never gave a living soul, nor dead ones either." Judge Lawrence suggested that the court adjourn for the day.[41]

The following morning, before continuing his cross-examination, Jackson issued a protest before the Tribunal. In a plea to legality, he invoked Article 18 of the Nuremberg Charter, which obliged the Tribunal to "rule out irrelevant issues and statements." Lawrence agreed that Goering's comments about U.S. mobilization plans had no relevance to the case. However, Lawrence suggested that his hands were tied: the witness was allowed to offer explanations. Jackson made the obvious point that Goering's explanations became part of the trial record before the prosecution had the opportunity to object. In a trial like this one, where propaganda was a key aim of the defendants, striking out answers after they have been made obviously "does no good." At this point Stahmer stepped in and vehemently objected to Jackson's allegation that Goering was trying "to make propaganda" in court. Lawrence calmly tried to move things along. He agreed that Goering should not have referred to the United States, suggesting, a little feebly, that this was a matter that everyone "might well ignore."[42] Lawrence's response was a defeat for the prosecution—and both Jackson and Goering knew it. Turning back to the witness box, Jackson confronted Goering with evidence about his role in the extermination of the Jews. Everyone watched as Goering puffed himself up and shouted denial after denial.[43] When the cross-examination, such as it was, concluded, he strode back to the dock, and the other defendants roundly congratulated him. Flanner was reminded of "a gladiator who has just won his fight."[44]

For the next day and a half, Maxwell Fyfe took his turn questioning Goering. He succeeded in rattling Goering with evidence of the Luftwaffe's involvement in the murder of fifty Royal Air Force officers. Nevertheless, Goering never wavered in his assertions that the extermination of the Jews and the details of the concentration camps had been hidden from him. When Maxwell Fyfe presented an August 1942 document stating that "only a few Jews" were "left alive," Goering claimed that this, too, had been mistranslated. It stated that Jews were "left in small numbers," he insisted. They could have "gone away" somewhere.[45] Overall, Maxwell Fyfe was pleased with his cross-examination—especially when comparing himself with Jackson, who he thought had "built up the fat boy further." Writing home, he told his wife that he had knocked Goering down a peg or two.[46]

Goering still had a lot of fight in him, as the Soviets were about to discover. On Thursday afternoon, March 21, Rudenko began his cross-examination of Goering as the Western prosecutors looked on. These "two men understood each other well and fought with heavy clubs rather than rapiers," noted Telford Taylor.[47] Rudenko spoke softly but forcefully, challenging Goering's claims about preventive war.[48] Goering responded with obvious scorn, insisting yet again that Operation Barbarossa had been enacted to preclude a Russian attack. His denials continued when Rudenko presented him with the notes from the June 1941 conference at which German leaders had discussed the future annexation of the Crimea, the Caucasus, the Volga region, and the Baltic territories. These notes were "exaggerated," Goering maintained: "As an old hunter, I acted according to the principle of not dividing the bear's skin before the bear was shot." "Luckily, this did not happen," Rudenko responded. "Luckily for you," Goering retorted.[49]

Goering visibly enjoyed this repartee. When Rudenko referred to an August 1942 order to "squeeze out" everything possible from the occupied territories of the East, Goering again found fault with the translation, arguing that the word in question should have been translated as "obtain." There was a huge difference in German between "obtain" and "squeeze out," he insisted loudly. Soon after, he conceded that Germany had used forced labor—but suggested that not all of the people missing from Eastern Europe had been brought to Germany. The Soviets had deported some 1,680,000 Poles and Ukrainians from Poland to the Far East, he charged.[50] Rudenko directed him back to the topic of German forced labor—but did not refute the allegations. Later that evening, Goering bragged to prison psychologist Gustave Gilbert about having "slipped in that one" about the Poles and Ukrainians. "Hoho! I bet he gets a hot wire from Old Joe on that one!"[51]

By this point the entire prosecution was frustrated by the Tribunal's refusal to restrain Goering. Jackson was feeling particularly betrayed by his old friend Biddle.[52] At the same time, the Soviet prosecutors recognized that in important ways they were on their own. Jackson, Maxwell Fyfe, and de Ribes had all refused to add their names to Rudenko's letter of protest to the

Tribunal about Article 21—letting the Soviets know in no uncertain terms that when it came to Katyn they would have to fend for themselves.[53]

In Moscow, Vyshinsky convened a meeting of the Politburo Commission for the Nuremberg Trials on March 21 to discuss the Katyn situation. When the Soviets had decided to add Katyn to the Indictment in September, they had never imagined that the Tribunal would allow the defense to call witnesses to testify about the massacre. The Politburo Commission now set out to find and prepare its own witnesses to support the Soviet charges. Gorshenin would round up witnesses from Poland; Viktor Abakumov, chief of SMERSH, would send agents to Sofia to speak with Bulgarian witnesses; NKGB chief Vsevolod Merkulov would recruit witnesses from Germany and the Soviet Union. Merkulov would also interview Soviet forensic experts and gather "certified documents" about the corpses, including the protocols of the forensic examinations. This was of course an elaborate sham: much of this evidence was or would be fabricated. Vyshinsky directed Rudenko to learn more about the requested defense witnesses. Who were Oberhauser and Berg and what did they know about Katyn?[54]

Vyshinsky also instructed officials at the Ministry of Foreign Affairs to compile a list of the Tribunal's violations of procedure. He wanted this list as ammunition in case the Katyn situation veered further out of control. The officials completed this task quickly, finding numerous violations to cite. The Tribunal had breached the Nuremberg Charter early on, they argued, by allowing the U.S. prosecution to call witnesses before the other chief prosecutors had given their opening speeches. The Tribunal had also failed to stop the defendants from giving interviews to the press. Here they called out Goering's December interview with *Die Neue Zeitung* lauding fascism. Turning to recent concerns, the officials argued that the judges were failing to heed not just Article 21 but also Article 19, which stated that the Tribunal would not be "bound by technical rules of evidence" when dealing with generally known facts.[55] The Soviets continued to argue that German responsibility for Katyn was one such fact.

When Rudenko resumed his cross-examination of Goering on March 22, Goering tried to call attention to Soviet wartime atrocities. In an increasingly rare moment of American-Soviet cooperation, Jackson joined Rudenko in objecting to Goering's accusations—and the court struck a number of Goering's statements from the record. Dodd wrote home about the incident, describing how "Rudenko came over to our table" and thanked Jackson for his assistance.[56] Rudenko wrapped up his cross-examination before the midday break. De Ribes, who was tired of Goering holding forth, announced that the French had no questions for him.[57]

It had been a very long two weeks of Goering, and Stahmer had yet to present his client's documentary evidence to the Tribunal. Jackson was troubled by the thought of the defense attorneys reading document after document into the trial record, shifting the focus even more to the former Nazi leaders and weakening the impact of the prosecution's case. Anxious to avoid such a scenario and hoping to speed things along, Jackson approached Stahmer and the judges that afternoon with a proposal. The Translation Division had finished rendering Goering's documents into the four languages of the trial. Perhaps Stahmer could submit them in bulk to the Tribunal, without reading them aloud in court. If Stahmer agreed, Jackson continued, the U.S. prosecution would not challenge the relevance of individual documents. Maxwell Fyfe expressed support for Jackson's proposal, but Rudenko and de Ribes were taken completely by surprise and balked. Both had been planning to challenge a number of Stahmer's documents—including excerpts from the White Books of the German Foreign Office, which purported to chronicle Soviet and French breaches of international law. (After most military campaigns, the German government had issued a White Book or White Paper containing selected diplomatic documents that they claimed justified their actions.)

Stahmer and his colleagues, for their part, criticized what Jackson was proposing as unfair. The prosecution had read its evidence in court; they were entitled to do so as well. None of the defense attorneys were willing to forgo the chance to explain the significance of each document to the public. Jackson took offense at the suggestion that the prosecution was being anything less than "completely fair" to the defendants. To make his point, he noted that the Translation Division had already printed 250 copies of the full set of Stahmer's evidence for Goering—including documents the Tribunal had ruled inadmissible. Once Stahmer submitted his evidence to the Tribunal, these copies could be handed off to the press.[58] The defense attorneys were not reassured. Neither were Rudenko and de Ribes. Yes, Jackson's proposal would save time and cut down on the reading of inflammatory materials in open court (and into the Tribunal's stenographic record). But it would also channel irrelevant and provocative materials to the press for wider distribution.

After a recess, the judges announced a compromise. Documents that had been translated could be submitted to the Tribunal without being read aloud—but the defense could sum them up, read out short passages, or describe their relevance before the court. When each piece of evidence was presented, the Tribunal would hear any objections from the prosecution.[59] Lawrence then turned toward the dock and made a belated attempt to assert control over the trials. He warned the defendants and their counsel that the judges would not tolerate any more speeches praising Hitler and the Third Reich. The Tribunal had allowed Goering, who went first and was generally regarded as Hitler's second in command, to narrate the entire history of Nazism. Going forward, the Tribunal would not permit other defendants to cover this same ground unless it was clearly essential for their defense.[60]

The day's drama was not over. Stahmer began to present his evidence to the court—including some of the White Book materials, which, as expected, prompted immediate challenges from the prosecution. Rudenko objected vociferously to a White Book from 1941 called "Bolshevist Crimes against the Laws of War and Humanity," denouncing it as propaganda designed to justify or hide Nazi crimes. Stahmer maintained that this evidence was authentic. The German Foreign Office had investigated reports of Russian atrocities and had recorded them in White Papers that had then been forwarded to the Red Cross in Geneva. According to Stahmer, this evidence was vital for the defense case, for it showed that any German "excesses" (as he put it) had been prompted by "similar violations . . . on the other side" and thus "must be judged more leniently."[61]

Lawrence reminded Stahmer that the Tribunal had not convened to try the countries of the prosecution. The judges ruled out this White Book, as well as a document about the French abuse of German prisoners of war and a document describing British air raids against nonmilitary targets. The Tribunal did not dismiss the possibility that the Allied powers had committed war crimes, but reiterated that such matters were outside its scope. As Lawrence noted, if the Tribunal were to try the actions of the countries of the prosecution, there would be no end to the proceedings.[62]

The Soviets, meanwhile, were continuing to prepare their own evidence and witnesses for the anticipated showdown over Katyn. On the night of March 21, the Soviet ambassador to Bulgaria, Stepan Kirsanov, notified Vyshinsky that the photocopies he had requested involving the "Katyn affair" were ready—and bore all the required stamps, seals, and signatures attesting to their authenticity. The bulk of the documents concerned Dr. Marko Markov, a professor of forensic medicine at Sofia University who had served on the German-sponsored International Katyn Commission. A couple of nights later, Kirsanov sent Vyshinsky another telegram, recommending that the Soviet prosecution use Markov as a witness. According to Kirsanov, Markov would give testimony that exposed the Katyn "provocation." The other Bulgarian witnesses he had interviewed were far less reliable, he added. The three priests on Abakumov's list had all appeared on the German-Bulgarian broadcast station Radio Donau, spewing "anti-Soviet slander."[63]

As the Soviets were fighting one fire, another one ignited. On Monday, March 25, the Hess defense began. That morning, Alfred Seidl (who had recently signed on as Hess's attorney) attempted to introduce an affidavit from Friedrich Gaus, the former ambassador and former head of the German Foreign Office's Legal Department, concerning the secret protocols to the German-Soviet Non-Aggression Pact. Gaus had accompanied Ribbentrop to Moscow in 1939, and his affidavit described the Moscow negotiations and the contents of the secret protocols, which he had helped to draft. Seidl, noting that Hess was charged with "conspiring to wage aggressive war," argued that this affidavit would describe the events that had led to the outbreak of hostilities. The excerpts he intended to read were short, he added, and could be translated on the spot by the courtroom interpreters.[64]

Seidl's move blindsided Rudenko, who stood speechless until Lawrence asked if the prosecution had any objections to this document. This was "a completely unknown document," Rudenko piped up, stressing that the prosecution would need time to look it over. He added that he had no idea what "secret agreements" Seidl could be referring to. Seidl retorted that if Rudenko really claimed ignorance of the secret protocols then his client would have to petition for Molotov as a witness. Lawrence advised Seidl that he would need to have the affidavit translated into English and Russian before the Tribunal would hear him on it. He instructed him to furnish his copy to the prosecution to send to the Translation Division, after which the Tribunal would consider the matter. Later that afternoon, Seidl attempted to call Gaus himself to the witness box. The Tribunal refused, on the grounds that Gaus had been brought to Nuremberg to testify for Ribbentrop. Seidl would need to submit a separate petition requesting him as a witness for Hess.[65]

When the Hess defense continued the next day, Seidl addressed the charge that his client had helped the Nazi Party seize power. He argued that the Nazi Party had become wildly popular as a result of the conditions imposed on Germany in the peace settlement that ended the First World War. When Maxwell Fyfe protested that the Treaty of Versailles had no relevance to the case, Seidl disagreed, reiterating that the treaty's harsh terms had led to economic disaster and were a direct cause of the Nazi Party's rapid growth. He further alleged that the Western powers and Russia had not met their obligations under the treaty, leading the defendants to "infer the right to rearm." After briefly adjourning, the judges declared this evidence inadmissible. Seidl then announced that Hess (whom everyone understood to be mentally unstable) would not testify, as a result of his lack of faith in "the competency of this Court."[66]

With Ribbentrop up next, the Soviets were on edge. Rudenko understood all too well that the former German foreign minister had carried on secret negotiations with both Stalin and Molotov and knew more than anyone else in Nuremberg about Soviet-German collaboration. Most of the items on the Vyshinsky Commission's list of taboo topics dealt with matters Ribbentrop had been personally involved with—including, of course, the negotiation of the secret protocols. Stalin had sent Nikolai Zorya to Nuremberg with instructions to prevent Soviet secrets from coming to light. But neither Zorya nor Rudenko nor any other Soviet prosecutor could keep Ribbentrop from talking.

Ribbentrop's defense, which got under way on the afternoon of March 26, began predictably enough, with his attorney, Horn, emphasizing that Ribbentrop had been compelled to follow the "lines laid down by Hitler" in foreign policy. Horn's first witness, former secretary of state Gustav Adolf von Steengracht, added to the picture of Ribbentrop's lack of influence by testifying that Hitler had generally ignored Ribbentrop's suggestions. Steengracht also asserted that Ribbentrop was not a "typical Nazi"—a statement that U.S. assistant prosecutor John Amen followed up on the next morning by asking which of the defendants were "typical Nazis." Steengracht promptly named Goering, Hess, Sauckel, Rosenberg, Frank, and Streicher.[67]

When Steengracht left the witness box, Horn began to introduce his evidence to the Tribunal. His first batch of documents concerned German foreign policy of the 1930s. Germany had acted in self-defense, Horn maintained, referencing memoranda relating to the Franco-Russian and Russo-Czechoslovak mutual assistance pacts. Pokrovsky interrupted this presentation to complain that many of these documents still had not been made available to the Soviet prosecution. Horn replied that he had delivered his documents to the Translation Division but had been told that it was short on Russian and French translators. Lawrence, wanting to avoid a delay, suggested that Horn go ahead and submit the documents now, subject to "any objection being taken to them" once the translations were available.[68]

Pokrovsky was exasperated. Horn had dumped an enormous pile of documents on the Translation Division in the past few days with almost no notice. Of those documents that had been translated, Pokrovsky told the Tribunal, many were outrageously provocative and irrelevant to the case. Lawrence assured Pokrovsky that the Tribunal would evaluate the admissibility of individual documents later. But Pokrovsky would not back down. He reiterated Jackson's complaint that as soon a document was mentioned in the trial transcript it became part of the official record. It also became fair game for the press. Lawrence acknowledged this concern and admonished the defense counsel and the prosecutors not to share documents with the press until after the Tribunal had approved them. Lawrence also conceded that the judges had little control over this situation. Their efforts thus far to shut down the pipeline to the press had been a failure.[69]

The defense was now making a concerted effort to introduce the secret protocols in open court. On the morning of March 28 it looked like success was imminent. When Ribbentrop's former secretary, Margarete Blank, took the stand, Horn went in for the kill. He asked her whether she was aware that in addition to the nonaggression pact and trade agreement, yet another agreement had been concluded in Moscow. "Yes," Blank replied, "there was an additional secret agreement."[70] This was the moment that Jackson had warned of and that the Soviet prosecution had long feared.

An agitated Rudenko tried to object that Blank, a secretary, was not competent to testify on foreign policy issues. At this point Lawrence asked Horn whether this secret agreement had been put into writing. Horn replied in the affirmative, though he admitted that he did not have a copy. Seidl broke in to explain that there were only two copies of the secret protocols. One copy had remained in Moscow, and Ribbentrop had taken the other copy to Berlin. Seidl reminded everyone that according to the press, the archives of the German Foreign Office had been seized by Soviet troops. He then suggested coyly that the Soviet government might provide the Tribunal with "the original of the agreement."[71]

As the Tribunal adjourned to discuss the admissibility of Horn's question to Blank, some of the defendants became giddy over the prospect of the secret protocols coming to light. The prison psychologist Gilbert watched the scene unfold in the dock: "Jodl was grinning like a fox," and "Frank and Rosenberg enjoyed themselves over the anticipated Russian embarrassment." Frank even "laughed out loud" as he anticipated the unveiling of the conspiracy between Stalin and Hitler. Speer gnomically remarked: "History is history, there is no use hiding it."[72]

The Tribunal reconvened and announced that it would allow the question. After all the buildup, it turned out that Blank did not know much about the secret protocols after all. Due to illness she had not accompanied Ribbentrop on his two trips to Russia, she explained. She had learned that a secret agreement existed only after Ribbentrop's return, when she was told to file a sealed envelope that had been labeled something like "German-Russian secret or additional agreement."[73] Blank's testimony did not go anywhere. Nonetheless, by allowing it, the Western judges had signaled their willingness to hear evidence that incriminated the Soviet Union. The defendants were keenly attuned to the changing dynamics in the courtroom, according to Gilbert. Reliving the incident over lunch, Hans Fritzsche noted how Biddle's face had dropped when Blank's testimony turned out to be a bust; Karl Doenitz agreed that the American judge had "wanted that thing brought out, and he was disappointed when it did not come out."[74]

Ribbentrop, too, took note of the Tribunal's apparent shift in position. Settling into the witness box that afternoon to testify in his own defense, Ribbentrop—whom the political cartoonist Boris Efimov had caricatured as a rat-like hyena—launched into an intimate history of Soviet-German friendship. He recounted how Hitler had gradually warmed to Stalin's proposal for a meeting, dispatching him to Moscow for that purpose in August 1939. According to Ribbentrop, he had found Stalin and Molotov quite congenial, and they had all talked "frankly," as he put it, about Poland. Their discussions bore fruit in a nonaggression pact and a secret agreement, which, as Ribbentrop now explained, ensured that "German and Russian interests in the Polish theater could and would not collide." Elaborating on the secret agreement, Ribbentrop described how a line of demarcation was drawn through Poland along the Vistula, San, and Bug rivers. In the event of a war between Germany and Poland, the territories to the west would be in the "German sphere of interest," while the territories to the east would be in the "Russian sphere of interest." Ribbentrop added that he had gleaned at the meeting that Germany and Russia had lost these territories "after an unfortunate war" (by which he meant the First World War). The leaders had also discussed the division of Finland, Bessarabia, and the Baltic states between Russia and Germany, Ribbentrop noted.[75] Just like that, the details of the secret protocols had become part of the record of the Nuremberg Trials.

The next day the Soviets watched impotently as Ribbentrop told the court that he and Hitler had broken agreements with deep regret and had reluctantly started "a preventive war against Russia." Ribbentrop took his time elaborating the details of his talks with Molotov and Stalin. His second trip to Moscow in September 1939 had gone well; the nonaggression pact was "politically amplified into a treaty of friendship." The friendship had started to sour, Ribbentrop suggested, with the Soviet occupation of the Baltic states, Bessarabia, and northern Bukovina. This, together with the Soviet-Finnish war, had made Hitler question Stalin's intentions. When Molotov visited Berlin in November 1940 he had spoken of Russia's "vital interests in Finland" and had told Hitler that Stalin also wanted military bases in Bulgaria. The Soviets seemed insatiable, Ribbentrop told the court, and Hitler soon became convinced that they were preparing for a war against

FIGURE 9.6 Boris Efimov's caricature of Joachim von Ribbentrop, part of the artist's series "Fascist Beasts (from the Hall of Justice)." The caricature was published in *Krasnaia zvezda* on December 15, 1945.

Credit: Reproduced courtesy of Boris Efimov and the Ne Boltai! Collection.

Germany. The Soviet-Yugoslav Non-Aggression Pact of April 1941, which the Soviets signed with the new antifascist Yugoslav regime, was the last straw, Ribbentrop added, for it confirmed to Hitler that Stalin could not be trusted.[76]

British alternate judge Birkett lamented that with Ribbentrop's testimony the trial had gotten "completely out of hand."[77] There was no reeling things back in. Discussion of the secret protocols continued, much to the Soviets' chagrin. On April 1, while cross-examining Ribbentrop, Seidl read a paragraph aloud and asked him whether the secret part of the German-Soviet Non-Aggression Pact "had approximately that wording." Ribbentrop replied in the affirmative. Seidl then asked again for permission to introduce the Gaus affidavit, which by now had been translated into English and Russian. Rudenko fiercely objected—again—that the Tribunal had not been convened to discuss the policies of the Allied powers and that Seidl's questions to Ribbentrop had no relevance to the case. The Western prosecutors, despite their vow to do everything possible to keep the trials focused on Axis crimes, remained silent. The judges privately conferred and overruled Rudenko's objection, outvoting Nikitchenko.[78]

Seidl began to read from Gaus's affidavit, which, as expected, described negotiations on a "secret document" aimed at demarcating "spheres of interest" in the territories situated between Germany and Russia. When Seidl looked up from the document, Ribbentrop confirmed that an agreement had been reached in August 1939 and that soon thereafter, in keeping with its terms, Soviet and German troops had occupied Poland and the Baltic states. Ribbentrop then got to the point: if Germany was guilty of planning and waging an "aggressive war" against Poland, then surely the Soviets were "guilty of it" too.[79]

Rudenko, Zorya, and other key members of the Soviet prosecution had been in the know about the secret protocols before Ribbentrop testified. Other members of the Soviet delegation had not been privy to such information and were therefore taken aback by Ribbentrop's courtroom revelations. The Soviet interpreter Tatiana Stupnikova—who was translating Ribbentrop's testimony into Russian as he gave it—later wrote about how shocking it was for her to be made aware of the secret protocols and their contents in court and how she had struggled to maintain her composure.[80] Outside the courtroom, the Soviets continued to put on a good face. That evening, Nikitchenko and Volchkov attended a dinner party with Dodd and poured on the charm—prompting Dodd to write in a letter home that some of the Russians "as individuals" were "really very likeable."[81] The next morning, the "alleged Russian-German agreement to split up Poland" was reported on widely in the international press.[82]

Rudenko took a turn cross-examining Ribbentrop on April 2. Unsurprisingly, he could not get him to admit that Germany had waged "aggressive war" against any states. Ribbentrop insisted that the Anschluss had been the realization of Austrian and German wishes for national unity and that the annexation of the Sudetenland was also a matter of national self-determination. The invasion of Poland had been made "inevitable," he insisted, by the actions and attitudes of the Western powers. As far as the Soviet Union was concerned, Ribbentrop repeated the argument that Germany had engaged in a "preventive intervention" and not an act of "aggression in the literal sense of the word." Pressed by Rudenko on his understanding of "aggression," Ribbentrop cagily replied that aggression was "a very complicated concept, which even today the world at large cannot readily define."[83] This was precisely the scenario Jackson had been worrying about at the London Conference when he had pushed, unsuccessfully, to get a definition of "aggression" into the Nuremberg Charter.

Ribbentrop then added that he had hoped that matters with the Soviet Union could have been settled "differently, diplomatically," but that Soviet actions in 1940 and 1941 had convinced Hitler that Russia and England were conspiring to attack Germany. Rudenko followed up as if Ribbentrop had just confessed: "You admitted just now that all these acts of aggression on the part of Germany were justified." Ribbentrop flatly denied this, launching into a long speech reiterating that Germany had not acted aggressively and that the outbreak of war had been "caused by circumstances" outside Hitler's control. Rudenko, faced with a defendant who could not be rattled, was at a loss for how to respond without making the situation worse. "This is clear," he finally stated, before moving on to his next question.[84]

Rudenko's cross-examination went downhill from there. Ribbentrop denied every accusation and claimed ignorance even of documents he had obviously authored. Other lines of questioning were short-circuited by Lawrence. Finally, in exasperation, Rudenko turned to Ribbentrop. "How can you explain the fact that even now, when the entire panorama of the bloody crimes of the Hitler regime has been unfolded before your eyes, when you fully realize the complete crash of that Hitlerite policy which has brought you to the dock—how can we explain that you are still defending this regime; and, furthermore, that you are still praising Hitler?" he thundered. Lawrence deemed this not "a proper question to put to the witness."[85]

When Ribbentrop left the witness box there was still the question of some of his documentary evidence. At a meeting of the Tribunal that evening the prosecution continued to protest the inclusion of White Book documents, arguing that they were forgeries. The prosecutors also noted that much of the evidence submitted for Ribbentrop was "cumulative" (corroborating evidence that had been put forward earlier) and thus a waste of the Tribunal's time. Horn agreed to withdraw the cumulative documents but continued to push for the admission of the White Books.[86] Meeting again the following day, the judges rejected more than half of Horn's documents. Still, much controversial evidence remained. Most ominously for the Soviets, the Tribunal rejected most of Ribbentrop's documents about the Munich Pact (on the grounds that the negotiations leading up to the conclusion of this treaty were irrelevant to the case) but allowed in key evidence relating to the German-Soviet Non-Aggression Pact.[87]

The Nuremberg Trials had taken a bad turn for the Soviets as soon as the defense started to make its case. Yet again the narrative of the war had gotten away from them. On April 4, Soviet diplomat Mikhail Kharlamov (a member of the Vyshinsky Commission) sent his superiors at the Party's propaganda department a secret report describing the struggles the Soviet prosecution was facing at what he referred to as "this new stage of the trial." Earlier, during the prosecution's case, the wartime allies had formed a united front. This was no longer true, Kharlamov wrote. The situation had shifted most dramatically with the judges' recent decision to dismiss most evidence relating to the Munich Pact: Rudenko had lost important leverage. In spite of the "gentleman's agreement" among the prosecutors to keep the IMT focused on Nazi crimes, Rudenko could no longer count on support from his Western colleagues to keep "the events of 1939" out of the courtroom.[88]

According to Kharlamov, the Soviet prosecution, having failed to "split the defense," was increasingly finding itself under attack. The defendants were ignoring the French and "cringing" before the British and the Americans, while persistently challenging Soviet evidence, he reported. This was weakening the impact of the Soviet presentations. What's more, the defense was broadening the split between the USSR and the West by focusing on the "Polish problem." He described how the Tribunal had allowed Hess's attorney to read out Gaus's testimony and how Ribbentrop had testified that the Soviet Union had been prepared to go to war on Germany's side "in certain circumstances." He also related that the British newspaper the *Daily Mail* had printed Gaus's affidavit even before the judges had ruled on whether or not to allow it to be read in court.[89]

Kharlamov reported that the Gaus affidavit was just the most recent of a series of attacks on the Soviet Union in the Nuremberg courtroom—and that Rudenko and Pokrovsky were not doing enough to protect Soviet interests. In particular, they had not stood down the defense's petition to summon German witnesses about Katyn. Kharlamov complained that the "fascist abominators" who had carried out the Katyn massacre would now appear in court and "chatter to the whole world." For Kharlamov the situation in Nuremberg was scandalous. The Soviet Union—a "country of victors"—had gone to Nuremberg to prosecute the fascists and had instead become "the object of their provocative attacks."[90]

These most recent Soviet difficulties were a result of "the particularities of this stage of the trial" combined with the tense international situation, Kharlamov speculated. The amicable relationship among the prosecutors early on had led the Soviets to underestimate potential difficulties. Even now, Rudenko continued to "groundlessly trust" the Western prosecutors to defend the Soviet Union's interests, he maintained. Making matters worse, after the presentation of the Soviet case, everyone seemed to think that the main business of the trial was over. Gorshenin and Trainin had even been allowed to return to Moscow.[91]

Kharlamov's astute analysis of the situation in Nuremberg got immediate attention in Moscow. The Party's propaganda department agreed that the lack of competent people able to make quick decisions on the spot was undermining the Soviet case. It sent Kharlamov's report on to Malenkov and advised the Party to immediately send Gorshenin and Trainin back to Nuremberg along with a political advisor from the Ministry of Foreign Affairs. Malenkov quickly forwarded these materials to Molotov, explaining that they set forth serious "blunders in the work of the Soviet prosecution." Molotov read through the report and wrote on top: "Comrade Kharlamov is fundamentally correct."[92]

Even as Soviet leaders were taking action, the situation in Nuremberg continued to deteriorate. On April 6, the judges, meeting in closed session, stood by their ruling to allow the defense to call witnesses to testify about Katyn. Further, Biddle had taken offense at Rudenko's letter, which had accused the Tribunal of "misconstruing" the Nuremberg Charter and "violating its duty" by allowing the defense to challenge Soviet evidence. (Rudenko had submitted the letter on his own to the Tribunal, on Moscow's orders, after the other chief prosecutors refused to sign on.) Fulminating before his fellow judges in closed session, Biddle condemned the letter as a "slanderous, arrogant, and unwarranted attack on the Tribunal" and threatened to have Rudenko censured or even arrested for contempt. Biddle further complained that Rudenko's argument about Article 21 completely echoed Nikitchenko's argument on the topic, speculating that the two were in cahoots. (Rudenko and Nikitchenko were of course both taking instructions from Vyshinsky.) Biddle pushed for the Tribunal to issue a statement declaring that the Soviet understanding of Article 21 was "mistaken." Rudenko's petition was turned down, but on Nikitchenko's strong insistence, no such statement was publicly issued.[93] The dispute would stay out of the press, but the Soviet understanding of Article 21 as prohibiting defense challenges to the evidence would not stand. The Katyn charge would be subject to scrutiny in open court.

A Cold War chill had swept through the courtroom, emboldening the accused and creating still greater distance between the Soviets and their wartime allies. Nikitchenko was increasingly finding himself outvoted by the other judges, especially on issues affecting the Soviet Union. Rudenko was countering defense provocations increasingly on his own. The first few defendants and their attorneys had successfully introduced incriminating evidence about Soviet war crimes and crimes against peace. The defense's story about Hitler launching a preventive war against an aggressive Soviet state was not dismissed out of hand. As the Soviets prepared new witnesses and new evidence to address mounting challenges from the defense, they found themselves isolated from the other victors. This isolation would only deepen in the weeks and months ahead, leaving Vishnevsky, Polevoi, and the other Soviet correspondents desperately yearning for home. "To tell the truth, I didn't want to think about the trial any more," Polevoi later wrote of this juncture. "But what could I do? I was committed to it for a long, long time."

CHAPTER 10 | In the Name of a Fair Trial

T HE MONTH OF March had gone badly for the prosecution in the Palace of Justice. The unexpected drama of the defense case—the self-righteous speeches of the defendants, the unending attacks on the Allied governments, the repeated challenges to the Tribunal's legitimacy—had profoundly shifted the mood in the courtroom and threatened to alter the trajectory of the trials. As April got under way and the days grew longer, Konstantin Gorshenin headed back to Nuremberg to assess the situation for Molotov and Stalin. Gorshenin had spent a hectic few weeks in Moscow, attending to his duties in the procurator general's office and weighing in on Soviet plans to participate in the Tokyo War Crimes Trial, which was being convened by eleven Allied nations in May to try the former leaders of the Empire of Japan. He had also conferred with the NKVD about the selection of witnesses to support the Soviet charges of German guilt for Katyn.[1]

Gorshenin, the deputy head of the Vyshinsky Commission, was the ideal Soviet bureaucrat: steadfast, unquestioning, hardworking, and loyal. The son of a railway worker from western Russia, he had risen through the Soviet system by virtue of his class background, intelligence, and grit. He had begun his career as a mechanic for the Kazan Railway in 1925, at age eighteen, and had thrown himself into Communist Party politics. In 1929, at a time of tremendous upward mobility for Soviet young people with pro-letarian backgrounds, he had studied labor law at Moscow University; a few years later he became deputy director for research at the Kazan Institute of Soviet Law. In 1937, at the height of the Stalinist Terror, he was nominated to a post in the Ministry of Justice—and his career took off. He was named procurator general of the USSR in 1943 and launched a wartime campaign for labor discipline.[2]

As the designated problem-solver for the Soviet delegation in Nuremberg, Gorshenin had his work cut out for him. The first few weeks of the defense case had been hard on the whole prosecution; nobody had fared well against Goering. David Maxwell Fyfe later acknowledged that "Goering's appearance and vanity had been such a gift to the cartoonists that we had been inclined to underestimate his ability."[3] The Ribbentrop defense, however, had highlighted the shortcomings of Soviet trial techniques outside the controlled environment of a Soviet courtroom. Rudenko's method of cross-examination was a blunt instrument that did little to shatter the defendant's composure and produced not much more than disdainful denials. The Soviets had no experience with Western-style cross-examination, no sense of how to use its give-and-take to trip up a defendant or to produce a compelling narrative. Unused to having to convince anyone, including the judge, of a defendant's guilt, they had anticipated cross-examinations as little more than guided public confessions—and had difficulty adapting when a defendant flatly denied his guilt or otherwise tried to throw things off track.[4]

Gorshenin had gotten his orders to return to Nuremberg from the highest levels of the Party. He was to buck up the Soviet prosecution and protect Soviet interests—doing everything possible to keep the defendants from making "provocative attacks" against the Soviet Union in court. But when it came to practical matters like how to cross-examine a brazenly unrepentant witness, Gorshenin, too, was at a loss. His education and years of experience in the Soviet bureaucracy had not equipped him for a Western-style trial.

While Gorshenin was wrapping up his business in Moscow, the defense case was gaining further momentum. On April 3, Wilhelm Keitel, the former head of the Wehrmacht's High Command, attempted to clear the entire German military of the charge of planning and waging a "war of aggression." Eleven months earlier, Keitel had surrendered to General Georgy Zhukov in Berlin. Now he sat ramrod straight in the witness box, asserting that the idea of "aggressive war" was purely a "political concept." It had not been the Wehrmacht's responsibility to assess the character of its military operations, he argued in response to questions from his attorney, Otto Nelte. The Soviet correspondents looked at Keitel with curiosity, surprised that this man who had called for the brutalization of the East had such a "respectable appearance."[5]

Rudenko faced off against Keitel on Friday, April 5, and did not score many points. Keitel was evasive when asked whether the High Command had drawn up plans to invade the Soviet Union in September 1940. Who could say whether or not Field Marshal Paulus had told the truth on the stand, he blustered. Truth was subjective. Questioned about Hitler's plans to seize and colonize Soviet territories, Keitel claimed ignorance. When reminded that he was under oath, he equivocated, though only slightly: "It is true that I believed that the Baltic provinces should be made dependents of the Reich, and that the Ukraine should come into a closer connection," he admitted, "but concrete plans for conquest are not known to me." Rudenko let Keitel's response pass unchallenged and moved on to the next question on his list, about Hitler's plans to raze the city of Leningrad. He similarly got nowhere.[6]

The following morning Rudenko confronted Keitel with the most damning evidence he had: the reprisal order for the occupied East. Asserting that human life had "no value" in the Soviet Union, the order stipulated that fifty to one hundred communists should be shot for each German soldier killed by partisans. Keitel admitted to signing this order but asserted that it initially had called for the shooting of five to ten communists for every German; Hitler had changed the numbers. Again Rudenko did not press the point. He turned instead to a second order, this one authorizing German troops to take brutal measures against women and children in the fight against the partisans—and asked whether this included murder. Keitel responded that no German soldier or officer had ever thought of killing women and children. Incredulous, Rudenko mustered a follow-up question—which only got Keitel to deny any direct or secondhand knowledge of such atrocities. Closing his cross-examination, Rudenko suggested that Keitel had served Hitler not just out of duty but because he was a devout Nazi. At this point Keitel raised his voice: "I was a loyal and obedient soldier to my Führer. I do not think there are generals in Russia who do not give Marshal Stalin implicit obedience." Rudenko snapped back: "I have finished with my questions."[7]

Maxwell Fyfe returned to the theme of loyalty in his cross-examination of Keitel that morning—and, unlike Rudenko, managed to elicit a confession. Maxwell Fyfe had a sense of how best to play to the psychology of this defendant. Invoking the honor of the soldier, he asked Keitel why he had lacked the courage to stand up to Hitler and oppose cold-blooded murder. Keitel muttered that he had done much that went "against the inner voice" of his conscience. Seeing an opportunity, Maxwell Fyfe asked him to elaborate. Keitel admitted that he had issued orders in the East that violated the rules of war. He also spoke of the murder of British Royal Air Force officers and of his "Night and Fog" (Nacht und Nebel) decree of December 1941, which called for the secret deportation of civilians who resisted the Nazi occupiers to concentration camps.[8] Rebecca West, covering the trials for the *New Yorker*, praised Maxwell Fyfe's ability to take each witness to "the edge of some moral abyss" where the truth comes out. "The Nazis seem not to care when a Russian lawyer cross-examines them, because they see he does not know how to do it. . . . But they are ashamed when Sir David proves them liars."[9]

The Keitel case wrapped up on April 9 after the appearance of several witnesses, including General Adolf Westhoff, who had served in the High Command's prisoner-of-war section. Yuri Pokrovsky's berating of this witness during his cross-examination made a strong impression on the Americans. Confronting a general who had dealt with Soviet prisoners of war, Pokrovsky "was loaded for bear," Telford Taylor later wrote. Pokrovsky produced fresh evidence about the murder of millions of Russian soldiers by cold and starvation in unheated boxcars. As the Tribunal recessed for lunch, Alfred Jodl suddenly shouted wildly from the dock: "Goddamit. . . . Of course thousands of Russian prisoners came in transports frozen to death! So did our own soldiers!" Jodl vowed that when his own turn came to testify, he would give the court "a belly-full!"[10] If the IMT continued at its current pace, Jodl would have a long wait ahead of him.

Gorshenin arrived in Nuremberg on April 8 and was greeted with the sobering news that the Western judges had reaffirmed their decision to allow the defense to call witnesses to testify about Katyn. They had rejected Rudenko's letter.[11] He also saw immediately that the judges and the prosecutors—faced with the unanticipated challenges of the defense case—were at odds over the very notion of what constituted a fair trial. It was a moment of existential crisis for the IMT. The prosecutors were complaining that the judges were giving too much leeway to the defendants in court and approving too many of their petitions for witnesses. The judges were censuring the prosecution for their lengthy cross-examinations and asking whether so many prosecutors really needed to question each witness. Pressed, the prosecutors agreed to try to limit their cross-examinations. But they were not about to sit back if a defendant attacked their governments' wartime policies or practices. Too much was at stake to look away.[12]

The Allied representatives had agreed at the London Conference back in August that the defendants were entitled to a robust defense. Each of the indicted Nazi leaders had been allowed to select the attorney of his choice and to request any witnesses who might help his case. Each had been granted the right to testify on his own behalf in open court. Before the IMT convened, the Western judges and prosecutors had agreed with one another—over strong Soviet objections—that these were the prerequisites for a fair trial. What Jackson and the other Western prosecutors had not expected was for the defendants to spend weeks on the stand dissembling, making long circuitous digressions, and taking repeated jabs at the prosecution. All of the prosecutors thought that the judges were betraying the cause of justice by giving the defendants such free rein.

The Western judges on the other hand were determined to prove their impartiality to the world. It was not lost on them that the defendants were taking advantage of the Tribunal's rules to stage a spectacle—but they saw no way to clamp down on this without evoking outraged cries of "victors' justice." Rebecca West (who had an affair with Judge Biddle during her time in Nuremberg) later wrote that the Western judges were terribly self-conscious about the victors trying the vanquished and thus bent over backward to ensure that each defendant was seen as receiving a fair trial. This, they believed, was necessary for the world to trust the Tribunal's ultimate judgments.[13] That Nikitchenko hardly seemed impartial as a judge greatly troubled Biddle and Lawrence and may well have led them to be even more solicitous of the defendants.

Tensions between the judges and the prosecutors remained high on April 11, when the court moved on to the defense of Ernst von Kaltenbrunner, former chief of the Reich Central Security Office (RSHA), who had served directly under SS chief Heinrich Himmler. Just looking at Kaltenbrunner gave the Soviet interpreter Tatiana Stupnikova a strong feeling of revulsion: his elongated skull, scar-covered face, and "cold, hateful" eyes suggested a "merciless executioner," she later wrote.[14] Thomas Dodd also thought him "really an evil-looking man."[15] Kaltenbrunner's attorney, Kurt Kauffmann (another former Nazi), began his defense by trying to dispel these impressions, reading affidavits from former Gestapo chiefs and SS men attesting to his client's decency.[16]

The courtroom fell quiet as Kaltenbrunner entered the witness box. "I know the hatred of the world is directed against me," he began. "I realize that I shall have to tell the truth in this courtroom" so that the Tribunal and the world might understand what happened during the war and "judge it with fairness."[17] This sounded like the beginning of a confession—but it was not. Kaltenbrunner would spend the next three days denying that he had wielded either power or influence.[18] The Soviet lawyer Arkady Poltorak thought that Kaltenbrunner was perhaps the most challenging defendant of all, despite the fact that his name "was associated with Auschwitz and Majdanek, with

Treblinka and Dachau." It was clear to Poltorak that he would "clutch at any straw" of denial.[19] Kaltenbrunner breezily dismissed the fact that his signature appeared on hundreds of directives for the execution of Soviet civilians and prisoners of war and on thousands of orders sending people to the concentration camps. He insisted that others must have forged his name.[20]

Kaltenbrunner also testified that Himmler and Hitler had kept him in the dark about their plans to exterminate the Jews. He claimed not to have learned until February or March 1944 that Auschwitz was an extermination camp, and he pleaded similar ignorance about Mauthausen. The U.S. prosecution challenged these and other statements, one by one. On Friday, April 12, assistant prosecutor John Amen produced affidavits from survivors of Mauthausen describing Kaltenbrunner's visits to the concentration camp. One survivor recalled how Kaltenbrunner had started laughing during an inspection of the gas chamber.[21]

When Amen concluded his cross-examination, Judge Lawrence told Kaltenbrunner that he could return to his seat. At that moment Soviet assistant prosecutor Lev Smirnov's voice rang out: "Just a minute, stay!" He, too, wanted to question this defendant. When Lawrence reminded Smirnov that the prosecution had agreed to limit its cross-examination, Charles Dubost stood up for the Soviets. The prosecutors represented four governments with their own interests, he protested. While they had agreed to economize on time where possible, they ought to be able to intervene as needed on behalf of their countries. Smirnov claimed to have groundbreaking evidence that had just arrived. Lawrence allowed him to proceed.[22]

Smirnov did not in fact have any such evidence. He did have a list of questions from the Vyshinsky Commission to ask the defendant—and could not let the former SS leader leave the witness box without confronting him. Smirnov made a fuss of presenting an entry from one of Hans Frank's diaries that suggested that Kaltenbrunner had helped carry out the operations against Poland's Jews. The entry noted that Friedrich-Wilhelm Krüger, the Higher SS and Police Leader in the General Government of occupied Poland, had asked Kaltenbrunner to tell Himmler that some of the Jews slated for "removal" were specialists who could not be easily replaced. Kaltenbrunner retorted that this diary entry only proved that Krüger had asked him to appeal to Himmler—and implied that he had used this information to save these particular Jews.[23] Even Poltorak admitted that the cross-examination had been a bust.[24]

The Tribunal was less accommodating a few days later when the Soviets demanded the right to question Kaltenbrunner's chief witness, Rudolf Hoess. The former commandant of Auschwitz, Hoess marginally helped

Kaltenbrunner's case by corroborating the claim that he had never visited Auschwitz.[25] What made Hoess's testimony unforgettable was how casually he confessed to supervising the deaths of millions of people, and how he boasted about his success in maximizing the efficiency of the notorious death factory. The Americans had chief responsibility for cross-examining Hoess. Amen confronted him with an affidavit he had signed earlier, explaining his efforts to "improve upon" (as he put it) the methods used at Treblinka by using fast-acting Zyklon B instead of monoxide gas and by building gas chambers that could contain 2,000 people at one time.

The courtroom was silent as Amen finished up with Hoess. The somber mood was broken only when Amen told the Tribunal that the Soviets and the French also had questions for the witness. Lawrence refused. Rudenko angrily protested that the prosecutors were entitled to question witnesses on matters pertinent to their own countries. Pokrovsky announced that his questions dealt with the death of millions of Soviet citizens. Lawrence stood his ground: he would not allow the Soviets or the French to question Hoess. There was nothing in the Nuremberg Charter stating that each delegation was entitled to cross-examine a defense witness, he maintained. On the contrary, Article 18 directed the Tribunal to take firm measures to prevent an "unreasonable delay."[26] The Soviet prosecution reluctantly backed down.

Alfred Rosenberg's defense, which began on April 15, was of special concern to the Soviet prosecution. The former Reich minister of the Occupied Eastern Territories and a Baltic German, Rosenberg had been born in Reval (now Tallinn, Estonia) in the Russian Empire in 1893. He spoke fluent Russian, prompting the Soviet translators to refer to him sarcastically as "our fellow countryman." During the First World War he had been evacuated to Moscow, and shortly after the Bolshevik Revolution of 1917 he had emigrated to Germany. He told the court that his experiences in revolutionary Russia had strengthened his resolve to prevent "Germany from backsliding into Bolshevism." National Socialism, he maintained, was a response to the specter of Soviet socialism.[27]

Rosenberg, whom Boris Efimov had caricatured for the Soviet press as a hideous rodent, spent much of his time in the witness box defending German occupation policies and insisting that the Soviets had misrepresented his good intentions. What the Soviets described as the theft of cultural treasures, he argued, had been a program to protect valuable Russian icons from destruction in the war. Rosenberg similarly presented himself as a champion of national self-determination, citing excerpts from speeches in which he had called for a revival of Ukrainian historical consciousness. Turning to his birthplace of Estonia, Rosenberg argued that there was no basis for Soviet claims that the German occupiers had tried to destroy the independence of the Estonian people. It was the Soviets, he insisted, who had ended Estonian independence in 1940, with "the marching in of the Red Army!" Rudenko interjected to denounce this remark as nothing but fascist propaganda and demanded that Rosenberg answer Soviet charges as to his criminal activity. Rosenberg instead gave a counter-narrative of his efforts to foster culture and science in Latvia, Lithuania, and Estonia.[28]

The prosecution had the opportunity to cross-examine Rosenberg on April 17. Dodd got him to admit that he had recruited forced labor for Germany, but had less success showing his complicity in the extermination of the Jews. The Soviets were also intent on cross-examining Rosenberg, and this time the Tribunal did not stand in their way. Rudenko approached Rosenberg with a stack of evidence and a list of questions but had no luck extracting a confession. When Rudenko introduced a report calling for the elimination of "undesirable elements" in Estonia, Latvia, Lithuania, and Belorussia, Rosenberg began exclaiming about problems with the Russian translation.[29] Prison psychologist Gustave Gilbert later speculated that Rosenberg was following Goering's lead and trying to obstruct Rudenko's cross-examination.[30]

Ignoring Rosenberg's outburst, Rudenko called out the absurdity of his professed concern for the peoples of Ukraine. He read from a July 1942 report in which Rosenberg called for Germany's seizure of Ukrainian grain. Rosenberg did not deny this but argued that it was tied to his aspirations to integrate Ukraine along with the Caucasus into "the total economic system" of the continent. The cross-examination grew only more heated from there. When Rudenko brought in evidence of the brutal police methods used in the occupied East, Rosenberg argued that such an approach had been needed to put down the partisans, who, he claimed, had been murdering German policemen and officials and Soviet farmers "by the thousands." Calling the partisans "bandits" was a typical Nazi strategy, Rudenko retorted, and hardly explained the German murder of old men, women, and children.[31]

While Rudenko was cross-examining Rosenberg, Gorshenin was quietly fielding other defense challenges. Alfred Seidl (the attorney for Hess and Frank) was doing his utmost to turn the court's attention back to Soviet crimes. Since the start of the defense case he had been requesting witnesses who could shed light on the history of Soviet-German relations. Earlier in the week Seidl had lodged a petition with the Tribunal asking permission to introduce more evidence for the Hess defense: copies of the secret protocols of the German-Soviet Non-Aggression Pact of August 1939 and of the German-Soviet Friendship Treaty of September 1939, along with a second affidavit from Gaus attesting to these documents' authenticity. A couple of days later Seidl had submitted another petition, this one asking to call Gaus as a witness. Recognizing that Seidl was preparing an ambush, Gorshenin sent urgent messages to Vyshinsky.[32]

The Tribunal considered a number of Seidl's petitions after the Rosenberg case concluded on April 17. The judges began with an earlier petition he had submitted requesting two witnesses who could testify about Soviet-German collaboration: Gustav Hilger and Ernst von Weizsacker. Hilger had worked in the German embassy in Moscow; Weizsacker had served as state secretary at the German Foreign Office. Both had participated in the August 1939 talks that led to the German-Soviet Non-Aggression Pact. Maxwell Fyfe, speaking for the entire prosecution, questioned Seidl's motives in calling witnesses who had no relation to either of his clients. It was obvious that Seidl wanted them to speak about the discussions that had prepared the ground for the drafting of the secret protocols—but the court had ruled earlier (in relation

FIGURE 10.1 Alfred Seidl, defense attorney for Hans Frank and Rudolf Hess, launched a campaign to introduce the secret protocols to the German-Soviet Non-Aggression Pact in court, ca. 1945-1946.

Credit: United States Holocaust Memorial Museum, courtesy of National Archives and Records Administration, College Park.

to the Munich Pact) that it would not hear testimony about these sorts of "antecedent negotiations." Besides, Maxwell Fyfe added, Seidl had already examined Ribbentrop himself in open court; allowing "secondary witnesses" to testify would needlessly draw out the proceedings.[33]

After hearing Maxwell Fyfe out, the Tribunal turned to Seidl's request to introduce the secret protocols as evidence. Seidl explained to the judges that he had recently come into possession of a copy of the protocols. He did not name his source. Lawrence asked Maxwell Fyfe if he objected to Seidl producing these materials for the Tribunal's consideration. Maxwell Fyfe replied that he had no grounds on which to object, since the Tribunal had already rejected the prosecution's argument (made at the time of the Ribbentrop defense) that the secret protocols were not relevant to the case. Rudenko and Pokrovsky did object but did not cite their reasons in court. With Gorshenin's assistance, and Vyshinsky's input from afar, they had just submitted a letter for the Tribunal to consider in private; Pokrovsky now stated that this letter elaborated the Soviet position on a number of issues connected with the nonaggression pact. Lawrence assured him that the Tribunal would take it under consideration.[34]

Later that evening, the Committee of Chief Prosecutors met and discussed the Tribunal's decision to restrict the number of cross-examinations. The prosecutors penned a joint letter protesting the Tribunal's recent refusal to let Pokrovsky cross-examine Hoess. Reiterating the arguments Dubost and Rudenko had made in court, they reminded the judges that the prosecution was "united but not indivisible." Each prosecutor had an obligation to act on behalf of his own country and in support of its interests. Yes, the prosecutors had agreed to try to shorten the trial—but that did not mean that they could automatically assume responsibility for representing one another's concerns. One member of the prosecution would take the lead for each cross-examination, but the others had not forfeited their right to speak if the defense touched on matters of importance to their countries. And in any case, Pokrovsky's questions for Hoess had been prompted by the witness's responses to Amen's questions and could not have been anticipated ahead of time.[35]

Rudenko was pleased to get this support from his Western colleagues. However, Jackson, Maxwell Fyfe, and Dubost had their own motivations for speaking up. The letter made it absolutely clear that the four countries of the prosecution would not always stand together. With questions about Katyn still unsettled, the Western prosecutors wanted to establish as much distance between themselves and the Soviets as possible. Jackson was especially determined to do so. Bitterly disappointed by his cross-examination of Goering,

Jackson had recently turned some of his energy away from the trials to focus on the struggle against the Soviet threat in Europe. During the previous couple of weeks, he had given talks in Paris, Vienna, and Prague warning of a coming "Continent-wide conflict" between those forces who favored "Communism and a Russian alliance" and those who favored "their own political independence and our way of life." In a report to Truman, Jackson wrote of giving anticommunist forces a "visible sign" of American interest and support.[36]

The court's focus turned back to Poland on April 18, as Hans Frank, the former governor-general of occupied Poland, took the stand. Frank, unlike the defendants who had preceded him, immediately admitted to "a deep sense of guilt." Yet he also claimed innocence of the particular charges leveled against him. He vigorously denied any direct involvement in the concentration camps and argued that he had lacked power over the local police and SS. He also countered Soviet accusations that he had "plundered" Poland, arguing that he had tried to revitalize local agriculture under the German occupation and that partisans had undermined his efforts. He completed his testimony in a brief two hours and fifteen minutes. Smirnov led Frank's cross-examination and countered many of his assertions—including the claim that he had not even heard the name "Majdanek" until 1944. Smirnov introduced a May 1943 police report Frank had forwarded to Hitler: it stated that Polish intellectuals and workers had not been stirred up by German reports of Soviet atrocities at Katyn because they knew that Poles were "likewise" being murdered in German "concentration camps at Auschwitz and Majdanek." This was a double-edged piece of evidence for Smirnov to present, as it brought more attention to the charge of Soviet responsibility for Katyn. It did, however, prove that Frank was lying about Majdanek.[37]

On April 19 the Tribunal went into recess for Easter. The Soviet judges Nikitchenko and Volchkov left for Prague as the guests of Czechoslovakia's minister of defense, Ludvik Svoboda, whom they had met in Nuremberg.[38] A large group of Soviet correspondents also headed to Prague with their Czech colleagues, with whom, Polevoi noted, they had struck up a "warm friendship."[39] Gorshenin remained in Nuremberg and got down to work, using the long weekend to coordinate with Moscow. He sent Molotov transcripts of the Tribunal's closed—and private—meetings. He also sent an update to Vyshinsky, assuring him that he had taken "the agreed-on steps" to improve the work of the Soviet delegation—helping them get out in front of some of the defense's challenges. Gorshenin predicted, however, that the defense would continue to attack the Soviet Union in open court, given that the Western judges were responding "quite favorably," as he put it, to such efforts.[40]

Soviet leaders took heed of Gorshenin's warnings and also considered Mikhail Kharlamov's earlier recommendation to introduce new evidence and witnesses in order to throw off the defense. NKGB chief Vsevolod Merkulov sent Gorshenin a list of new documents from the German Foreign Office.[41] Vyshinsky sent Gorshenin information about another potential blockbuster witness: Professor Walter Schreiber, from Germany's Military Medical Academy. Schreiber, who was being held in an NKVD prison, had just given his interrogators a statement describing German preparations after their defeat at Stalingrad for bacteriological warfare. According to his statement, Hitler, Goering, and Keitel had ordered the establishment of scientific institutes in Saxony and Posen where experiments with plague, typhus, and other pathogens were performed on Soviet prisoners of war. Gorshenin mulled over the possibility of bringing Schreiber to Nuremberg.[42]

When the Nuremberg Trials resumed on Tuesday, April 23, the Soviet correspondents lamented that, with fifteen defendants still to go, no end was in sight.[43] The next defendant, Wilhelm Frick, former Reich minister of the interior, was of lesser interest to the Soviets. Taciturn and aloof, he remained in the dock, choosing not to testify in his defense.[44] The sole witness for the Frick case, Hans Bernd Gisevius, a former Gestapo officer who had participated in the July 1944 bomb plot against Hitler, was on the other hand of exceptional interest to everyone in the courtroom. To Western journalists, Gisevius was a heroic figure of the German Resistance. Soviet correspondents and jurists, by contrast, derided him as a "vulture" and friend of the American "monopoly bourgeoisie."[45] The Soviets resented Gisevius for his undercover efforts to forge an alliance during the war between the German Resistance and the Western powers, which would have shut out the Soviet Union.

Frick's attorney, Otto Pannenbecker, called Gisevius to the witness box on April 24 to affirm that his client had held no sway over the police. Then, with the indulgence of the Tribunal, Gisevius told a gripping story about the anti-Hitler conspiracy. He recounted how he had broken with the Gestapo and joined up with a group of conspirators. These conspirators had tried to convince the Wehrmacht to stage a coup, while repeatedly warning the British and French governments of Hitler's intentions in Eastern Europe. During the Munich crisis of September 1938, they told their Western contacts that Hitler was planning to invade all of Czechoslovakia. Then, as the Polish crisis deepened in the spring of 1939, they cautioned that Hitler wanted all of Poland and Ukraine. While Gisevius did not use the word "appeasement," he was clearly outraged by the British and French lack of action.[46]

Gisevius remained in the witness box to testify for Hjalmar Schacht, former president of the Reichsbank. Schacht's attorney, Rudolph Dix, had also requested Gisevius as a witness—for good reason. Gisevius had just published a memoir in which he described Schacht as a member of the Resistance.[47] Responding to questions from Dix and from Jackson, Gisevius argued that the march toward war had turned Schacht from a faithful follower of Hitler into an opponent of the Nazi regime. According to Gisevius, Schacht had attempted to convince Walther von Brauchitsch, commander-in-chief of the German army, to overthrow Hitler, and had tried to prevent the launching of Operation Barbarossa.[48]

The Soviets were intent on hanging Schacht as an industrialist who had enabled Germany's rearmament. Gisevius's description of him as a pacifist was too much to bear. On April 26, Georgy Alexandrov asked for the chance to cross-examine the witness. The judges grumbled but allowed it on the grounds that the Soviets had a special interest in the Schacht case. Alexandrov approached Gisevius and barraged him with questions: What role had Schacht played in Hitler's seizure of power? Hadn't Schacht arranged a meeting between Hitler and a group of industrialists in February 1933? Gisevius replied that he had not met Schacht until 1934 and had no knowledge of any such meeting. When Alexandrov presented a January 1939 letter in which Hitler thanked Schacht for his central role in Germany's rearmament, Gisevius retorted that he had never considered anything that Hitler said to be true.[49] The Western press reported the next day that Gisevius had helped exculpate Schacht.[50] The Soviet press, by contrast, praised Alexandrov's cross-examination and treated Hitler's letter to Schacht as a smoking gun.[51]

Schacht himself would soon take the stand. First, however, the Tribunal moved on to Julius Streicher, the publisher of the anti-Semitic tabloid *Der Stürmer*. The interpreter Stupnikova later recalled that Streicher looked at first glance like a harmless "little old man"—but his wild eyes, gesticulating mouth, and vile reputation quickly evoked a feeling of "disgust."[52] Streicher trumpeted his contributions to the Nazi cause while denying responsibility for, or even knowledge of, Nazi atrocities. He dismissed the idea that he had been part of a conspiracy, noting that he had met most of his codefendants for the first time in the Nuremberg prison. Most of all, he disputed the charge that *Der Stürmer* had incited people to violence. The Soviets remained on high alert during Streicher's testimony, for he had a great deal to say about

Bolshevism. At one point he testified that Hitler saw Stalin "as a man of action" who was unfortunately surrounded by Jews. Rudenko, who had become increasingly comfortable interrupting the defendants, demanded that the Tribunal stop Streicher from making these speeches.[53]

British assistant prosecutor Mervyn Griffith-Jones used his cross-examination to challenge Streicher's claim that he had not known about the extermination of the Jews. To prove his point, he submitted bundles of a Swiss Jewish newspaper to which Streicher was known to have subscribed. Griffith-Jones read excerpts aloud. A December 1941 article noted reports that thousands of Jews had been executed in Odessa, Kiev, and other Soviet cities. A November 1942 article warned that if the Nazis were not stopped, then "only 2 million" of Europe's "6 or 7 million" Jews would be left. Streicher responded by claiming that he could not remember reading such articles—and that if he had come across them, he would have dismissed them as unbelievable. Griffith-Jones then introduced some of Streicher's own articles, one of which anticipated the annihilation of Judaism "down to the last man."[54]

The defense testimony was tedious, the cross-examinations often pointless. After two days of Streicher, the Tribunal called another closed meeting with the prosecutors to again discuss how to speed the defense case along. The Western judges reiterated that it was the prosecutors' responsibility to keep things moving. They would have to limit their cross-examinations. Dodd volunteered that the U.S. prosecution would only examine those defendants and witnesses for whom it had "primary responsibility." From the Soviet perspective, this was disingenuous. The Americans, who had interrogated all of the defendants and witnesses in the Nuremberg prison before the trials had even started, had claimed "primary responsibility" for most of them.[55] After prolonged negotiation, the prosecutors settled on a plan. The Americans would take the lead in cross-examining Schacht, Walther Funk, Baldur von Schirach, and Albert Speer. The British would take on Karl Doenitz, Erich Raeder, Alfred Jodl, and Konstantin von Neurath. In all of these cases, the Soviets would follow up if needed. The French would conduct the main cross-examination of Fritz Sauckel, with the Soviets and the Americans potentially joining in. The French and the Americans would split the cross-examination of Arthur Seyss-Inquart; the British would take sole responsibility for Franz von Papen; and the Soviets would take sole responsibility for Hans Fritzsche. Regardless of this arrangement, the prosecutors were willing to cede only so much to the Tribunal. All four delegations continued to insist on their right to ask questions if issues arose that were critical for their countries.[56] It was only fair.

By this point in the trials, each country had developed its own areas of focus. For the British, crimes at sea and the treatment of prisoners of war were of special interest. For the French it was the Nazi policies of plunder and enslavement; for the Americans it was the conspiracy. For the Soviets, a primary point of concern remained the criminal responsibility of the German financiers and industrialists who had bankrolled the Nazis.

The Soviets had been bitterly disappointed when the Krupp case had been put aside in November. Schacht was not a fat cat like the Krupps, but Moscow saw him and Funk as acceptable proxies—capitalists who had served as middlemen between the industrialists and Hitler. The Soviets, who were continuing to clash with the Americans outside the courtroom about the total reparations due to them—and who were determined to highlight the links between fascism and capitalism—saw a great deal at stake in demonstrating the criminal responsibility of German capitalists for Nazi crimes. Jackson, too, wanted to convict Schacht and Funk, but other members of the U.S. prosecution worried about the so-called economics case and questioned Schacht's guilt.[57] The danger was real: American businesses (including IBM) had also supported Hitler. There was no telling where a more general economics case might end.

Schacht played to these American reservations as his defense began on April 30. He testified that he had not seen any criminal intentions in the Nazi Party program and that he had entered the Ministry of Economics in 1934 hoping to exert a moderating influence on policy. He further maintained that he had advocated rearmament only to the point of parity with other states— and that he was dismissed as Reichsbank president in 1939 because of his efforts to "apply the brakes."[58] He then tried to shift the blame for the rise of Hitler onto the Western powers and their reparations policy after the First World War. He further alleged that the respect shown by Western statesmen to the Nazi elite from 1935 through 1938 had made it harder to convince the German people of Hitler's true intentions. Jackson and Rudenko both objected that Schacht's speeches were irrelevant and were prolonging the trials—and for once the judges agreed with them and cut him off. Schacht got in some additional digs at Britain and France before finishing up, however, declaring that Hitler had gotten more at Munich than he had hoped for when the Allies gave him the Sudetenland "on a silver platter."[59]

Both Jackson and Alexandrov cross-examined Schacht—without much success. Questioned by Jackson, Schacht denied that he had used his banking connections to further Hitler's aggressive goals. He expressed satisfaction at having helped along Germany's rearmament but voiced regret that Hitler had not "made different use of it."[60] Alexandrov quizzed Schacht about his early association with Nazi Party leaders. Why had he agreed to meet with Hitler and Goering in 1931? Didn't he realize that they intended "to inveigle him" into joining the fascist movement? Schacht would only confess to curiosity; he had wanted to see "what kind of people" the Party leaders were. The Soviets were desperate to prove that Schacht had avidly supported Hitler's most radical programs, but they lacked compelling evidence. Alexandrov presented a November 1932 entry from Goebbels's diary describing Schacht as one of the "few" who fully agreed with Hitler's position. He also read an affidavit from Schacht's biographer (Franz Renter) stating that Schacht had helped Hitler rise to power. Schacht rejected these statements as incorrect. Alexandrov asked why Schacht had organized a meeting between the industrialists and Hitler in 1933. Lawrence intervened to remind Alexandrov that Schacht's role as middleman had been sufficiently plumbed.[61]

Economic questions remained paramount when the Funk defense began on May 3. In life as well as in court, Funk had followed in Schacht's footsteps, holding the posts of Reichsbank president, minister of economics, and plenipotentiary of the war economy in the late 1930s.[62] Like many of his codefendants, Funk had chosen a strategy of asserting his own insignificance—arguing that he had not been important enough to participate in "political and military discussions." Asked by Dodd whether he admitted to guilt for the persecution of the Jews, Funk seemed to waffle. He admitted to "moral guilt" about the fate of Germany's Jews while denying personal responsibility for any specific "crimes against humanity."[63] Unable to elicit a true confession, Dodd used the rest of his cross-examination to prove that Funk had collaborated with the SS to enrich Germany. He presented film footage shot by the U.S. Army in Frankfurt showing the loot that had been discovered in the vaults of the Reichsbank: bags stuffed with diamonds, jewelry, watches, eyeglass frames, and dental gold. Dodd then read from an affidavit given by Emil Puhl, Funk's former assistant at the Reichsbank, about these shipments. According to Puhl, Funk had told him that these valuables had been confiscated in "the Eastern Occupied Territories" and had advised him to ask no further questions. Confronted by Dodd, Funk offered vehement denials.[64]

Mark Raginsky cross-examined Funk on Tuesday, May 7, and tried to get him to confess that he had masterminded a plan to plunder the occupied territories to support the German war economy. The cross-examination started off well enough: Raginsky got Funk to admit that one of the "special departments" of the Ministry of Economics had overseen the removal of Jews from Germany's economic life. However, Raginsky ran aground when he asked Funk about another "special department" of the Ministry of Economics that had collaborated with the overseas branch of the Nazi Party (the Auslands Organization). He appeared genuinely confused when Funk insisted that this had been only a small liaison office whose purpose had been to facilitate connections between German and foreign economists. Raginsky, who had been planning to connect this department to Nazi occupation policies in the East, announced that he would return to this question. He never did.[65]

FIGURE 10.2 Mark Raginsky, like the rest of the Soviet prosecution, struggled with cross-examination, 1946.

Credit: Russian State Documentary Film and Photo Archive No. B-3025. Photographer: Evgeny Khaldei.

Raginsky instead presented Funk with a series of leading questions about the economic despoliation of Eastern Europe—and came up against a wall of denials. Funk would not admit that Germany had exploited the countries it occupied by confiscating property or by depreciating the currency. "You do not admit this?" Raginsky tried one last time. "In no way whatsoever," Funk responded.[66] Taylor, for one, thought that Raginsky had been too easy on Funk and that Raginsky did not understand even the basics of cross-examination.[67] Raginsky, for his part, believed that the judges had seen through Funk's efforts to dodge his questions.[68] Taylor and Raginsky were both right. The Soviets were still struggling with their cross-examinations; and the judges had realized that Funk had taken advantage of Raginsky's clumsiness to avoid giving straight answers.

The Soviet prosecutors were not the only ones having difficulties during this second month of the defense case. British alternate judge Birkett thought that Jackson had bungled the cross-examinations of both Goering and Schacht.[69] The defendants were giving the Soviets and the Americans the run-around, albeit in different ways. The Soviets were flailing because of their near-total inexperience; Dodd thought that the Soviets had learned something about cross-examination since the trials started but still lacked any "sense of timing or restraint—or of the real purposes of the practice."[70] Regarding Jackson's difficulties, it was less clear what was going wrong. Biddle thought that Jackson was relying too much on his notes and that this made him look unprepared.[71] Birkett agreed that Jackson lacked spontaneity but considered this merely an effect of his surprising lack of command of the evidence. Birkett reflected in his diary that a cross-examiner needed a "complete grasp" of all of the material "so that he may attack the witness whenever a weak place appears, with the knowledge he carries in his head." Jackson's uncertainty and hesitation had cost him the advantage time and time again.[72] Others, including Taylor and Maxwell Fyfe, thought that the unexpected leniency Biddle and Lawrence were showing the defendants had thrown Jackson off his game.[73]

The fact was that no one had expected the Tribunal to allow the defendants so much leeway in the name of a fair trial. Jackson and Maxwell Fyfe had been worried at the outset about the defendants litigating the causes of the war—but they had never anticipated a scenario in which the defendants were allowed to hold forth for weeks on end, belligerently denying their guilt and trying to undermine the prosecution. Nikitchenko had assumed that the judges would work together to keep the trials focused on European Axis crimes. Every passing day reinforced how wrong he had been.

The U.S. prosecution was starting to learn from its mistakes. Jackson and his assistants had learned that the defendants could not be led and would seize any opportunity to make lengthy speeches—and so they tried to at least avoid asking open-ended questions. The Soviets were having a harder time, in part because they were working from a set of cross-examination questions prepared months beforehand. Though the Vyshinsky Commission had originally suggested that the questions could be adjusted based on a defendant's responses, the Soviet prosecutors had persistently stuck close to the script; they had little experience and less comfort changing strategies on the fly and were not even sure how far they could take a new line of inquiry without incurring Moscow's wrath. Gorshenin was no help here. He had gotten as far as he had in life by following the Party line.

As the defense case crawled along in Nuremberg, Vyshinsky and Molotov went to France for a meeting of the Council of Foreign Ministers. On Sunday, May 5, the Soviet foreign ministers dined with James Byrnes, the U.S. secretary of state, at the Soviet consulate in Paris—and, unsurprisingly, the IMT became a topic of conversation. Byrnes complained about the slow pace of the trials and expressed hope that things might be wrapped up more quickly. Vyshinsky agreed that things were dragging along, placing the blame on Lawrence for being "too scrupulous." Lawrence wanted the court to study "each hair on the head of the accused from all sides when it would be sufficient just to study the head."[74]

The men then turned to the topic of Churchill's speech in Fulton two months earlier. Molotov and Vyshinsky lambasted it as "nothing less than an appeal for a new war" and asked why it had been delivered in the United States. Byrnes assured Vyshinsky that Churchill had spoken under his own authority and not as a member of the British government—and that neither he nor Truman had seen the speech beforehand. Unconvinced, Molotov accused Churchill of proclaiming "a new race theory, a theory of Anglo-Saxon dominance over the world." The discussion quickly deteriorated. Molotov and Byrnes expressed sharply divergent views about American and Soviet military presence in other countries and traded accusations of expansionism.[75]

Underneath it all was the question of the future of Germany. At stake here, too, were questions of justice. The Soviet Union and France wanted Germany to remain divided and weak to ensure it would not reemerge as a threat. They insisted on all of the reparations that were due them as a result of the occupation and plunder of their countries. The Americans and British saw this perspective as being clouded by vengefulness—and had their own concerns about the future of Europe. Lucius Clay, the deputy head of the U.S. military government in Germany, warned that Germany was being bled dry and that any further deterioration of its economy would give rise to increased political unrest and the spread of communism. In early May, he announced that the U.S. government was halting the shipment of dismantled industrial plants (part of the reparations plan agreed to at Potsdam) from the American zone of Germany to the Soviet Union and other countries pending a decision about whether or not Germany would be treated as a single economic unit. Soviet leaders saw this announcement as proof that the United States felt no compunction to keep its international obligations if its interest lay elsewhere. The suspicion of course was mutual.[76]

A couple of days later in Paris, Vyshinsky received a parcel from Nuremberg. It contained what was identified as a transcript of the German-Soviet secret protocols from August and September 1939. Included was a note from a Soviet informant explaining that these were translations of the materials Seidl had submitted to the Tribunal a few weeks earlier. The informant passed on Gorshenin's assurances that the Soviet prosecution had solid ground on which to object that these materials lacked judicial authority. An "unknown person" had given the text of the protocols to Seidl, and Gaus had confirmed its accuracy based on his memory. The Soviet prosecution could easily question Gaus's reliability, the informant relayed, for earlier in the trials Ribbentrop's attorney had asked to substitute another witness for Gaus on the grounds that the former ambassador had "a weak memory and cannot report exactly on events."[77]

The Soviet informant also speculated as to whether Seidl was bluffing. He reported that Seidl had attempted to initiate a conversation with Rudenko about the Soviet-German agreements and wondered what kind of fishing expedition he was on. Perhaps Seidl had not seen an actual copy of the secret protocols and had generated a text relying on Gaus's memory alone. Or perhaps he had a copy of the original documents but was afraid to name the person who had passed them along to him. The informant told Vyshinsky that Gorshenin would do everything in his power to prevent Seidl's petition from being approved—but also warned that the majority of the judges seemed to favor Seidl.[78]

On May 8 the Tribunal marked the first anniversary of the victory against the Nazis. The prosecutors and the judges put their differences aside and gathered for a luncheon. Nikitchenko raised his glass in a toast to President Truman in honor of his sixty-second birthday.[79] Looking at the dock in the Nuremberg courtroom, the prosecutors and judges had something tangible to cheer about: two months after the start of the defense case, they had finally moved on to the second row of defendants. That morning Karl Doenitz, former commander-in-chief of the German navy and briefly Hitler's successor, had begun his defense. It was Doenitz who had secretly negotiated Germany's initial surrender a year ago, through an emissary in Reims, France. Doenitz, like Keitel, presented himself to the Tribunal as a professional soldier who had not been concerned with "political questions"—such as whether or not a war was "aggressive." Responding to the accusation that he had violated the laws of naval warfare, he insisted that all of the combatants had acted in an identical manner.[80] This would become a refrain.

The defense was continuing to ramp up its courtroom campaign. Doenitz's attorney, Otto Kranzbuehler, had submitted documents alleging that the Allies had shot at the survivors of sinking ships and had attacked German hospital ships. Maxwell Fyfe had protested that these materials had no relevance to the case. Now returning to this matter, the judges ruled out evidence dealing directly with the Allies' treatment of Axis survivors at sea. They remained open, however, to the claim that the German navy had behaved no differently from the American admiralty in its submarine warfare and gave Kranzbuehler permission to seek an affidavit from the commander of the U.S. Pacific Fleet, Admiral Chester Nimitz. Notably, Kranzbuehler did not claim that Doenitz's policies were justified because the American admiralty had also broken the law (tu quoque). Instead he argued that neither American nor German policies were illegal. The "universality" of their actions showed that the laws of naval warfare had evolved.[81]

That evening some of the Americans hosted a raucous V-E Day celebration. Maxwell Fyfe wrote home that he had retired before 10 p.m. in order to prepare for his cross-examination of Doenitz—but the secretaries had danced until 3 a.m. The after-hours merrymaking continued the next night. Biddle's wife, Katherine, who was in town visiting, hosted a dinner party for her husband's sixtieth birthday at the Villa Schickedanz, a mansion the Americans sometimes used for entertaining. The invitees gathered around the large swimming pool, enjoying plenty of food and drink. Taylor later recalled that the atmosphere was unusually "warm and playful." Nikitchenko apparently drank heavily and flirted with the hostess, pretending to throw her into the pool. Several women from the French delegation made a stir by appearing in what would later that summer become known as bikinis.[82] For the Soviets, May 9 had special meaning—it was the date Stalin had chosen as Victory Day. As Nikitchenko enjoyed himself in Nuremberg, a somber commemoration was taking place in Russia. Thirty-gun salvoes went off in Soviet cities, and Stalin admonished the Soviet people to "struggle selflessly and enthusiastically" toward the goal of building socialism.[83]

Sandwiched between the festivities, the Doenitz case had continued. On May 9 Doenitz had testified that he had refused to capitulate in the early spring of 1945 because he had feared the Soviet "extermination" of German soldiers and civilians, including women and children. German nationals could be more easily evacuated from the Soviet-controlled East in May 1945, and this, he had told the court, had allowed him to surrender.[84] He stood his ground the following day when cross-examined by Maxwell Fyfe and Pokrovsky. He admitted to Maxwell Fyfe that the German sinking of the *Athenia*, a British passenger liner, in September 1939 had been a mistake, but insisted that sinking ships that were behaving like warships was legal under international law. He similarly rebutted Pokrovsky's charge that he had prolonged the war because he was a fanatical Nazi and spoke again of the viciousness of the Red Army. Pokrovsky denounced the defendant's "idea of truth."[85]

May 11 saw stepped-up security in the Palace of Justice amid concerns about the safety of the court. The night before, a sharpshooter lying in wait on a residential street had killed two American soldiers riding by in a jeep with three women. News of the shooting created a panic and inspired a frenzied hunt for the killer, who was presumed to be German.[86] (It was later determined that an American GI was responsible for the shooting.) The Soviets were preoccupied with other concerns. That morning, the Tribunal formally considered Seidl's petitions from mid-April to introduce the secret protocols and to call Gaus as a witness. Maxwell Fyfe, a sometime friend of the Soviets, supported Pokrovsky in an attempt to shut this matter down once and for all; he argued that the substance of the secret protocols was already in evidence and that delving into them any further was a waste of the Tribunal's time. Lawrence seemed to disagree, signaling that the Tribunal might be favorably disposed toward the admission of Seidl's documents. If the Tribunal admitted a copy of the secret protocols as evidence, there would be no reason to call Gaus as a witness, Lawrence mused aloud. Seidl continued to press his argument. Yes, the Tribunal had heard testimony outlining the secret Soviet-German agreements, he acknowledged. But this did not mean that the defense should not be allowed to refer to the documents themselves. He continued to insist that the secret agreements were indeed relevant to the Hess case.[87]

Further destabilizing the Soviet prosecution, the Tribunal announced during this same session that it would soon reach its decision about the applications from Goering's attorney, Otto Stahmer, for the additional witnesses he had requested back in March to testify about Katyn. Stahmer had asked for several officers with the Wehrmacht's Army Group Center who had been stationed near Katyn, including the telephone expert Reinhard von Eichborn. Stahmer wanted them to attest that the Burdenko Report was full of lies. Hans Laternser, the attorney for the High Command, spoke in support of Stahmer's petition, explaining that the Katyn case was important to his clients as well.[88] Pokrovsky protested Stahmer's request. The Soviet prosecution had assumed that German responsibility for Katyn was "common knowledge," he maintained, and had thus introduced into the court record "only a few short excerpts" from the Burdenko Report. If the Tribunal doubted the credibility of some of the witnesses or documents accepted as evidence—and especially if the defense were allowed to call witnesses about Katyn—the Soviet prosecution would be compelled to read the entire Burdenko Report into the record, to present additional evidence, and to call new witnesses of its own. All of this would extend the trials by many days, he warned.[89]

The Tribunal met in closed session that afternoon. Nikitchenko did his best to fight these latest defense requests. He insisted that the secret protocols were irrelevant to the case and that Seidl clearly had other aims in introducing them. What's more, the document in question—which Seidl was calling "a copy"—had unknown origins and had not been properly certified; Gaus had verified the text by memory alone. Nikitchenko admonished his fellow judges for even considering accepting such shaky evidence. He pointed out (following Gorshenin's advice) that Ribbentrop's attorney had earlier asked to replace Gaus as a witness due to his "significant loss of memory."

The Western judges were not receptive to Nikitchenko's arguments. They countered that the secret protocols were the addenda to a nonaggression pact that the prosecution itself had introduced as evidence—and thus did in fact have bearing on the case. Biddle added dryly that if the Soviet prosecution disputed the accuracy of the defense's copy of the secret protocols then it should present the Tribunal with the originals, which were surely in the possession of the Soviet government.[90] Biddle's disdain for the Soviets was palpable.

Nikitchenko stood firm. Yes, the nonaggression pact related to the case, but only because Germany had violated its provisions; any addenda, he insisted, were irrelevant. He reminded his fellow judges that the Tribunal had recently ruled to disallow a discussion of the Munich Pact, determining that its details had no bearing on the case. He deemed the issue of the secret protocols "analogous." Recognizing that he might not get far with this argument, he then focused in on the juridical shortcomings of the document in question. If the transcript Seidl had submitted to the Tribunal was "a copy" of the secret protocols, what had it been copied from? In the end a compromise of sorts was reached. The Western judges stood by their ruling that the secret protocols were germane to the case. But they told Seidl that he would need to present the original document.[91]

The Tribunal's focus next turned to Katyn—and the Western judges stood by their previous decision to allow the defense to summon witnesses to contest the Burdenko Report.[92] This did not bode well, and Gorshenin knew it. By now it had become clear to him that the Soviets had overplayed their hand by including Katyn in the Indictment. These witnesses were likely to bring one of the Soviet Union's greatest wartime secrets out into the open. The Soviets were left to figure out their next move.

Meanwhile, the Americans and the Soviets continued to exchange niceties. A few days after the judges affirmed their decision about Katyn, a member of Jackson's staff reminded Rudenko that Truman wished to award him, Pokrovsky, and Alexandrov the Legion of Merit, one of the U.S. military's most prestigious honors, for their work at Nuremberg.[93] The wartime alliance was strained but not yet completely broken.

April and the first half of May had been a difficult period for the entire prosecution in Nuremberg. Continuing disagreements with the judges about what it meant to give the defendants a fair trial, combined with a determined effort on the part of the defense to make countercharges against the Allied powers, had frustrated all four delegations. The Soviets continued to face their own particular difficulties: the further unraveling of the wartime alliance, along with the challenges of cross-examining recalcitrant witnesses and parrying the strategies of energetic defense counsel, had knocked the Soviet prosecution back on its heels. Gorshenin and Rudenko had worked feverishly behind the scenes to keep the secret protocols and the defense's countercharges about Katyn out of the courtroom. The challenges to the Soviets at Nuremberg were mounting from all directions. As the defense case continued, some jurists and politicians—Soviet as well as Western—continued to idealize Nuremberg as the place where the Allied powers had voluntarily "stayed the hand of vengeance" in order to create a new postwar order based on international cooperation and justice. Others began to see it primarily as the site of a heated propaganda war between former allies.

CHAPTER 11 | Accusations and
Counter-accusations

D AY TO DAY in Nuremberg most of the participants found it easy to
get weighed down by the tedium of the trials, the horrific descriptions
of atrocities, and the latest intrigues. The afternoon of May 18 provided a
rare moment for the judges and the prosecutors to remember that they had
gathered for a higher purpose and that the IMT's findings—about the Nazi
conspiracy, crimes against peace, war crimes, and crimes against humanity—
could have real significance for the future of international law. The Palace of
Justice was hosting the first postwar session of the International Association
of Penal Law. The French judge on the Tribunal, Henri Donnedieu de
Vabres, the author of numerous books on international and criminal law
and a longtime advocate of an international criminal court, had organized
this gathering. He had personally invited his fellow Nuremberg judges and
prosecutors to attend. They were joined by other international-law experts
who had come to Nuremberg expressly for this occasion.[1]

It was a chance to step back and take things in. The attendees discussed
the postwar peace and the creation of a new organization of criminologists.[2]
De Vabres believed passionately that Nuremberg had provided a unique opportunity for lawyers from all over the world to compare their legal traditions
and to think about extending their cooperation into the future. Before the war,
the International Association of Penal Law had been limited to Francophone
countries. The postwar world, de Vabres maintained, needed a "global collaboration of criminologists" that could work toward the development of

an international criminal code. The new system of simultaneous translation that was being successfully utilized in Nuremberg, he added, made such collaboration possible. He noted that he had spoken with Soviet, British, French, and American jurists, and all had expressed support for the idea. Aron Trainin had even suggested Moscow as the site for a future congress.[3]

Iona Nikitchenko and Alexander Volchkov were uncertain how to position themselves at this meeting. They had learned a good number of lessons over the previous six months in Nuremberg; by now they understood that Moscow would want them to be diplomatic without committing the Soviet government to anything specific. Nikitchenko reminded those assembled that he did not officially represent the Soviet Union but was a guest of the meeting's organizers. Asked to say a few words, he expressed confidence that "every supporter of human progress" would welcome the creation of an association dedicated to "the strengthening of world peace." He then suggested that the organizers draft a statute to communicate their association's goals far and wide. This was received enthusiastically.[4]

It was a brief moment of unanimity—perhaps especially appreciated by the Soviets, who had become increasingly isolated in the Nuremberg courtroom. This gathering was permeated with the spirit of cooperation and goodwill. The Romanian jurist Vespasian Pella (whose writings on international law were known to everyone in the room) praised the IMT as an important step toward the creation of international criminal law that would safeguard the postwar peace. He called special attention to Robert Jackson's November 1945 opening speech, which described "the peacekeeping mission" of criminal law, and to Roman Rudenko's "remarkable opening speech" of February 1946. He also praised Andrei Vyshinsky's preface to Trainin's "very important" book *The Criminal Responsibility of the Hitlerites*. "Criminal law is called on to advance the cause of peace," Pella declared, quoting Vyshinsky, "and must be mobilized against war and against those who foment it." Before the meeting closed, the participants established a commission to work up a draft statute; they agreed that Trainin would represent the USSR, pending Moscow's approval.[5]

Trainin, who was in Moscow while his name was being invoked in Nuremberg, had of course been calling for a new codification of international criminal law for more than a decade. At the moment, though, he had his hands full with the more urgent problem of countering the defense's latest challenges to the Soviet prosecution. Trainin's and Nikitchenko's efforts many months earlier in London to get the Nuremberg Charter to explicitly prohibit Nazi propaganda during the trials had been shut down by Jackson and others. As a result, Trainin was now fighting a rear-guard action alongside members of the Soviet security apparatus. He moved between his roles as international jurist and Soviet legal strategist with relative ease, simultaneously calling for new international legal institutions to promote world peace and working to secure the Soviet narrative about the Second World War as a Soviet-led triumph over a relentlessly expansionist Germany. Soviet atrocities and crimes against peace had no place in that narrative.

As the Nuremberg Trials entered their sixth month, each of the four wartime Allies remained committed to using the case against the Nazis to put forward its own history of the war. Everyone understood that the way the events of the previous decade were presented in the Nuremberg courtroom had tremendous implications—not just for the verdicts but for the entire postwar order. Justice was at stake; so was realpolitik. While the Soviets positioned themselves as inveterate antifascists and as the saviors of Europe, Great Britain and France were attempting to present themselves as the defenders of small countries and national minorities—arguing that they had gone to war to defend Poland and the rest of Europe from German tyranny. Keeping to this narrative was no small feat for either the British or the French given their histories of colonialism and their appeasement of Hitler at Munich. For its part, the United States, which had experienced neither the horrors nor the indignities of the Nazi occupation, was making the claim that it had rescued Europe from itself. The defendants, meanwhile, had their own counter-narratives to put forth. They continued to protest that they had behaved no differently from the Allied powers and were on trial only because Germany had been defeated.

The struggle over the narrative of the war resumed at the Palace of Justice on Monday morning, May 20, with the cross-examination of Erich Raeder, one of the two defendants the Soviets had brought to Nuremberg. Raeder, now seventy, had served as commander-in-chief of the German navy from 1928 until his resignation in January 1943. Captured by Soviet forces in Berlin during the last days of the war, he had been interned in an NKVD prisoner-of-war camp before being moved with his wife to an NKVD mansion outside Moscow. Raeder, who spoke Russian, had offered the Soviets his services as a naval advisor and strategist. In August 1945 he had produced a lengthy memorandum for the NKVD cataloguing the flaws of the Nazi leadership; Soviet officials took to calling it his "Moscow statement." On October 15, several SMERSH officers had escorted Raeder to Berlin, assuring him that he would soon return to Moscow. He learned on October 18 that he had been indicted as a war criminal. A few days later he was driven to the American zone and interned in the Nuremberg prison.[6]

The prosecution had charged Raeder with violating the Treaty of Versailles by rebuilding the German navy, as well as with conspiring in the plan to invade Norway and with planning and carrying out a war at sea against the Soviet Union. He had begun his defense on May 15 by attesting that German naval construction had been defensive and that any violation of the Versailles Treaty had been "minor." His attorney, Walter Siemers, had insisted that not every treaty violation was a war crime. The decisive factor was whether violations were motivated by the aim of waging aggressive war. Siemers had further argued that Allied as well as German policies had aimed at "national preservation"—and that this was a valid principle in international law. To prove Allied intentions, he had introduced into evidence a White Book with captured Allied documents showing that Britain and France had contemplated invading Norway and other neutral countries. In spite of the prosecution's objections, many of these documents were accepted into the court record. Raeder had also used his first days in the witness box to distance himself from Hitler's actions. He told the court that he had tried to dissuade Hitler from invading Russia by arguing that "it would be morally wrong" to break the German-Soviet Non-Aggression Pact.[7]

Raeder had been neither broken nor cowed by his months in Soviet custody; on the contrary, he was proud and defiant. Questioned by David Maxwell Fyfe about Germany's plans to violate Belgium's neutrality, Raeder responded with counter-accusations. He attested that Hitler had received intelligence in the early spring of 1940 that Belgium was preparing to welcome British and French troops and would not remain neutral—and that this was what had precipitated the German invasion. Raeder was equally unyielding when Maxwell Fyfe asked incredulously if he had really thought that Great Britain planned to occupy Norway. Certainly, he responded: "We had so much information about it that I could have no doubt whatever." Maxwell Fyfe undoubtedly knew that the British government had in fact been considering an occupation of Norway, given its inclusion on the list of taboo topics he had shared with Jackson, Rudenko, and Charles Dubost. His goal was to discount the defense's claims by making them seem outlandish. Raeder's confident assertions stymied this approach.[8]

Yuri Pokrovsky was similarly frustrated when challenging Raeder's claims to have favored a peaceful relationship with the Soviet Union. Hadn't Raeder known in 1940 that Hitler was planning to attack Russia? No, Raeder responded. Hitler had not said that he wanted to go to war, just that the German military must "be prepared." Pokrovsky then handed Raeder part of his Moscow statement and asked him to read it aloud. In the highlighted passage, Raeder had dismissed as "propaganda" official statements by the

German Foreign Office and High Command blaming Moscow for breaching the German-Soviet Non-Aggression Pact and thus precipitating the war. If Raeder had seen through these lies, and had disagreed with Hitler's foreign policy to boot, then why hadn't he resigned earlier? Raeder responded that even though Operation Barbarossa had troubled him morally, "as the highest man in the Navy" he could not have walked away at the start of the war. Doing so would have been "unsoldierly."[9]

The Soviet prosecution had long been eager to use Raeder's Moscow statement to embarrass and split the defense. Pokrovsky now submitted to the Tribunal a pile of excerpts in which Raeder had described some of his codefendants in unflattering terms. Pokrovsky read aloud a section concerning Goering: "unimaginable vanity and immeasurable ambition were his main peculiarities." He next read Raeder's characterization of Doenitz as having a "strong political inclination to the Party." At this point Judge Lawrence interrupted. The judges might read the remaining passages themselves, he suggested, if Raeder confirmed having written them. Pokrovsky tried to skip ahead to Raeder's descriptions of Keitel and Jodl, but Siemers asked that the entire document be submitted to the Tribunal for private review. The judges agreed.

Pokrovsky was visibly disappointed; U.S. assistant prosecutor Thomas Dodd was too. Both had been anticipating a spectacle. Dodd attempted to salvage the situation by suggesting that the Tribunal distribute copies of Raeder's statement to all of the defense attorneys. The other defendants "might be surprised" by its contents, he noted provocatively. The judges gave their assent. Later that evening Raeder admitted to U.S. prison psychologist Gustave Gilbert that he had never imagined that his personal reflections would be used in a war crimes trial, let alone one in which he was a defendant.[10]

The following morning Pokrovsky again asked the Tribunal for permission to read into the record the parts of Raeder's statement that concerned Doenitz, Keitel, and Jodl. Siemers emphatically opposed this. He had read the entire statement, he said, and was not intending to put any questions about it to his client. The prosecution pushed back. The statement must be read while Raeder was on the stand, Dodd argued, so that the other defendants mentioned in it could have their attorneys examine him immediately. This, of course, was exactly what the defense wanted to avoid. Siemers assured the judges that none of the defense counsel wished to question Raeder about the document. Dodd and Pokrovsky persisted. Dodd claimed sympathy for the defendants' wishes not to have the statement shared in public but warned that questions raised about it later would hold up the trials.

Pokrovsky maintained that the Soviet prosecution considered this document to be of great significance and did not see why it should not be read publicly. Lawrence, who understood that the statement was only marginally relevant to the prosecution's case, was firm: if the defense had no plans to challenge the statement, the rest of it would not be read in open court.[11]

The defense could feel the sympathies of the Western judges swinging further against the Soviets. Alfred Seidl saw an opportunity—and took it—later that day when Siemers called Ernst von Weizsaecker, former state secretary of the German Foreign Office, to the stand as a witness for Raeder. Siemers questioned Weizsaecker about the sinking of the *Athenia* in September 1939 and its political ramifications. At the conclusion of Weizsaecker's direct examination, when the other defense attorneys were given the chance to question the witness, Seidl stepped forward, brandishing a handful of papers. He asked Weizsaecker whether any other agreements besides the nonaggression pact had been concluded between Germany and the Soviet Union in August 1939. Rudenko loudly objected that Weizsaecker had been called as a witness to answer specific questions regarding Raeder. Insisting that Seidl's question was not germane to the Raeder case, he demanded that it be excluded.[12]

The Soviet prosecutors, though furious about this latest gambit to bring in the secret protocols, were not exactly surprised. They had known that Seidl was up to something; he had visited their offices earlier in the day, making veiled references to new information he had obtained. Rudenko had refused to talk with him. Nikolai Zorya had briefly humored him before shooing him away, declaring that there was "no point in having such a conversation."[13] Now, overruling Rudenko's objections—and in spite of Nikitchenko's opposition—the Tribunal allowed Seidl to pose his question. Weizsaecker responded in the affirmative, and explained that certain agreements were contained in "a secret protocol" he had read in his role as state secretary of the German Foreign Office.[14]

Seidl attempted to hand Weizsaecker the papers he was holding, explaining that former ambassador Friedrich Gaus was completely certain that the agreements in question were accurately set out in this text. Asked by Lawrence to identify this document, Seidl stated that it was the text of the secret protocols. Wasn't this the same document he had already attempted to present to the Tribunal? Lawrence asked. Seidl admitted that it was; the Tribunal had refused to accept it because he had been unwilling to divulge its "origin and source." Seidl explained that he was no longer asking to submit the document as evidence. Instead, he wanted to use it to prod the memory of the witness and to ask if the secret agreements were in fact accurately reproduced in it.[15]

Rudenko again protested that the court had no business examining the foreign policies of the Allied powers, and dismissed the document in Seidl's possession as "forged." Seidl retorted that this document was an essential part of the German-Soviet Non-Aggression Pact and that he did not see why it could not be presented to the witness for comment; the prosecution had similarly put documents before witnesses during its cross-examinations. The plot thickened when the Tribunal pressed Seidl to reveal where the document in question had come from. Seidl replied that he had received it a few weeks earlier from someone on the Allied side who appeared "absolutely reliable" and that he had promised this man not to reveal his identity.[16]

At this point, Dodd joined Rudenko in objecting to the introduction of the document, on the grounds that its source was not known. Before Rudenko understood what was happening, however, Dodd made a further suggestion. Why not simply allow Seidl to ask Weizsaecker directly about the contents of the "purported agreement"?[17] While making a show of supporting Rudenko, Dodd had just opened the door to yet another discussion of Soviet-German collaboration. This was clearly intentional. Dodd cooperated with the Soviet prosecution when he felt that it suited American interests—but he was also eager to expose Soviet hypocrisy.

The Tribunal could have shut this matter down but chose not to. Instead Lawrence gave Seidl the go-ahead to ask Weizsaecker what he remembered of the treaty. And Seidl did just that. Weizsaecker held everyone's attention as he described "a very far-reaching secret addendum to the non-aggression pact" that drew a line of demarcation between Soviet and German spheres of influence. He next told the court that the original secret agreement from August 1939 was amended a month or two later. Most of Lithuania now fell into the Soviet sphere of interest, while considerably more of Poland now fell into the German sphere. Did the secret protocols determine the future of Poland? Seidl asked, anticipating the answer. Weizsaecker replied that they did.[18]

Lawrence then asked Weizsaecker if he had seen the original of the secret treaty. Weizsaecker explained that he had seen a photostat of the original and quite possibly the original as well. He still had the photostat locked up in his personal safe. Would he recognize a copy of the secret treaty if it was shown to him? Lawrence asked. "I definitely think so," Weizsaecker replied. The Tribunal called a recess, and the Soviet prosecutors waited for a tense forty-five minutes while the judges held a private consultation. Finally, the Tribunal announced its decision: Seidl could not put the document to the witness. The Tribunal's reasons were twofold. First, Seidl was still refusing to reveal his source. Second, the document itself was now superfluous, as its contents had been discussed in open court several times over. Nikitchenko had prevailed, but by this point it was very much a pyrrhic victory.[19]

Thwarted in introducing his copy of the secret protocols as evidence for the defense, Seidl brought it to the international press. On May 22 the *St. Louis Post-Dispatch* published a full transcript of the secret protocols alongside an article by the paper's Nuremberg correspondent, Richard L. Stokes. The article also included Ribbentrop's account of subsequent German-Russian negotiations as to a possible military alliance—describing how things fell apart when Hitler flatly refused Stalin's demands for the Soviet occupation of Finland, Soviet domination in Bulgaria, and Soviet control of the Dardanelles.

How had the text of the secret protocols made its way to an American newspaper? In the article Stokes revealed his source: Dodd. According to Stokes, Dodd had obtained a copy of Seidl's German-language text and had arranged for its translation into English.[20] A key member of the U.S. prosecution had gone out of his way to enable the publication of a document implicating the Soviet Union in crimes against peace.

Whether or not Dodd's action of leaking the secret protocols to an American journalist was part of a larger U.S. effort to sound the alarm about communist treachery and aggression is unclear. Also unclear is whether Jackson, who had been giving talks around Europe with the expressed aim of supporting America's allies against the spread of communism, knew what Dodd was up to. Dodd's political ambitions were likely in play, as was his moral outrage at the Soviets, whom he privately denounced in his letters home as "no different from the Nazis."[21] The Soviets, for their part, saw an Anglo-American anti-Soviet conspiracy at work.

The publication of the secret protocols was yet another serious blow to the Soviet prosecution. It was bad enough that the Tribunal had allowed the accused and their witnesses to reveal details of the secret German-Soviet agreement in the courtroom and that these details had become part of the public record. Now, due to the maneuverings of a member of the U.S. prosecution, the actual text of the secret protocols had appeared in the American press. It is hard to know what Rudenko and Zorya could have done to make things turn out differently, but they had every reason to fear Stalin's wrath.

Zorya was notably absent from the Soviet prosecution's table in the courtroom the following morning when the next defendant, former Hitler Youth leader Baldur von Schirach, began his testimony. A SMERSH officer approached a member of the Soviet delegation and informed him that he had found the assistant prosecutor in his hotel room—with a bullet in his head.

FIGURE 11.1 Nikolai Zorya and his colleagues during better days in the Palace of Justice, 1946. Nikolai Zorya is front right; Lev Sheinin is second to right; Mark Raginsky is on the other side of Sheinin; Lev Smirnov is in back of Raginsky; Yuri Pokrovsky is front left.

Credit: Russian State Documentary Film and Photo Archive No. 0-359141. Photographer: Viktor Temin.

Gorshenin phoned Moscow and reported that Zorya had committed suicide. In Nuremberg, the Soviets put forward another story: Zorya had accidentally shot himself while cleaning his gun. Rudenko personally told Jackson about the death and requested permission to move the body to the Soviet zone of Germany.[22]

No one believed that Zorya's death was an accident. The interpreter Tatiana Stupnikova speculated that it was either a murder or a suicide and later recalled how she and other members of the Soviet delegation had "silently mulled over" the possibilities.[23] Some members of the U.S. prosecution blamed the Soviet secret police. Dodd speculated that Zorya had gotten too friendly with the Americans and the British and that the NKVD had "removed" him.[24] It was certainly possible that the NKVD had been involved in Zorya's death, although it would have been more typical for Stalin to call someone back to Moscow and then have him arrested and shot. Zorya may have ended his own life in anticipation of such a fate. It is also possible that other factors beyond the revelation of the secret protocols prompted his immediate "removal." Zorya's son later maintained that his father had grown uneasy about the Katyn case and had asked to return to Moscow to talk to Vyshinsky about flaws in the Soviet evidence—which might have concerned someone enough to order his execution.[25]

Suspecting foul play and anxious to avoid an international scandal, Jackson bypassed the U.S. military's Criminal Investigation Division and had one of his own people quietly investigate the story. Word came back that it was not likely that a Russian general would be cleaning his own gun, especially while it was loaded and pointed at his forehead. Jackson, who wanted to keep the trials moving along, kept this quiet. Pokrovsky escorted the body to Leipzig, in the Soviet zone, where it was buried in an unmarked grave.[26]

Seidl, emboldened by his success in leaking the secret protocols to the press, redoubled his efforts to introduce them as defense evidence. The day after Zorya's death, Seidl submitted another petition to the Tribunal, again insisting that the agreements were a sine qua non condition for the German-Soviet Non-Aggression Pact and thus key evidence for the Hess defense. He related in this petition that he had learned the details of the secret protocols from Gaus, with whom he had spoken for the first time on March 11 in the presence of an American soldier in the interview room of the Nuremberg courthouse. Since Gaus could precisely recall the secret protocols' contents, Seidl had asked him to make an affidavit based on what he remembered. According to Seidl, Gaus had drafted this affidavit alone in his cell in the witnesses' section of the Nuremberg prison.[27]

Seidl's petition read in parts like a spy thriller, telling the dramatic story of how he had come to obtain a copy of the secret protocols. He described how in early April 1946 a U.S. Army serviceman had surreptitiously handed him two documents—which turned out to be the secret protocols of August and September 1939. Seidl had asked his interlocutor about the origin of the documents and was told that they were copies of photostats "captured by the armies of the Western powers." A few days later he had shown these documents to Gaus, who had said that he had absolutely no doubt that these were the real thing. Soon after that, Gaus had prepared a second affidavit, which Seidl had given to the Tribunal on April 13 along with the documents themselves. Seidl disputed the Soviet prosecution's claim that Gaus had a weak memory and suggested that Gaus be heard as a witness in order to remove any doubt.[28]

The exposure of the secret protocols had put Soviet leaders on edge. The day after Zorya's death, Vyshinsky called an urgent meeting of the Politburo Commission for the Nuremberg Trials to strategize about Katyn. The commission composed a statement for Nikitchenko to circulate to the Western judges in his name, denouncing the Tribunal's interpretation of Article 21 of the Nuremberg Charter as well as its decision to allow the defense to call witnesses to testify about Katyn. Recognizing that this was not likely to change the situation, the commission further discussed the selection of Soviet witnesses to counter German witness testimony. Vyshinsky, Trainin, NKVD chief Sergei Kruglov, and other commission members put together an initial list of three witnesses for the Soviet prosecution: Metropolitan Nikolai (who had been a member of the Burdenko Commission); Boris Bazilevsky, a Soviet astronomy professor who had served as Smolensk's deputy mayor during the German occupation (and who was one of the "witnesses" Western journalists had met during their Soviet-sponsored trip to the Katyn Forest in January 1944); and Sergei Kolesnikov, the president of the Soviet Red Cross and a coauthor of the Burdenko Report.[29]

The Politburo Commission also created a Katyn subcommission made up of Trainin, assistant prosecutor Lev Sheinin, and NKVD officer Leonid Raikhman—directing it to review all of the Soviet materials about the massacre and select those documents that would best "expose" German guilt. The subcommission was given five days to carry out this task. Trainin and Sheinin (the head of the Evidence Department in the procurator general's office) probably knew that much of the evidence that they were looking at had been fabricated, and certainly understood the politics that were in play. Raikhman was completely in the know about all aspects of Katyn and had been instrumental in the Soviet cover-up. As the head of the NKVD's Polish office, he had signed off on the order for the massacre. He had also participated in the fabrication of evidence for the Burdenko Report.[30]

In Nuremberg, amid gossip about the secret protocols and rumors circulating about Zorya's death, the Schirach defense was proceeding with its own quiet drama. Schirach followed what was now standard defense practice by challenging Soviet evidence—including an Extraordinary State Commission report that accused the Germans of using the same methods to cover up their crimes in the Lvov region that they had allegedly used in Katyn. Schirach disputed the eyewitness testimony in this report, including an affidavit from a French witness, Ida Vasseau, who attested that the Hitler Youth in Lvov had shot at Jewish children for target practice. Schirach insisted that this was impossible, as the only weapon carried by the Hitler Youth was a camping knife similar to those carried by Boy Scouts.[31]

The Soviets had been anticipating a challenge to Vasseau's testimony. A month earlier, the Tribunal had granted Schirach's attorney, Fritz Sauter, permission to send Vasseau an interrogatory (a list of questions) concerning her affidavit. The Soviet prosecution, perhaps heeding Vsevolod Vishnevsky's advice to take the initiative, had a countermove prepared. Georgy Alexandrov announced during his cross-examination of Schirach on May 27 that he had just received a second affidavit from Vasseau, whom the Soviet prosecution had located in Lvov. Alexandrov read aloud Vasseau's description of the brutal atrocities the Hitler Youth had perpetrated during the summer of 1941. Young Germans in uniform, armed not just with knives but also with heavy sticks and pistols, had hunted down and murdered anyone they thought was Jewish. Many of these victims, Vasseau had added, were Russians, Ukrainians, and Poles.[32]

Schirach denounced Vasseau's second affidavit as a lie, wondering aloud how the Soviets had obtained it while Vasseau had not even replied to Sauter's interrogatory. Alexandrov maintained that the Soviet prosecution had only just discovered her whereabouts. The Tribunal put the second affidavit on hold and directed the Soviets to ensure that Vasseau received Sauter's questions. Alexandrov's cross-examination went downhill from there, partly due to the sort of translation problems that continued to vex the Soviets. He grilled Schirach over his purported prison confession to have worshiped Hitler as "a deity," only for it to be revealed that this was a mistranslation of the defendant's words. Schirach had in fact said only that he considered Hitler's writings "a manifestation of truth."[33]

The attacks on the Soviet Union continued with the next defendant, Fritz Sauckel, the former head of the Nazi labor program. Testifying on May 28, Sauckel admitted that he had brought foreigners into Germany's war industries in order to free up German citizens for military service. Asked by his attorney, Robert Servatius, if he had worried that he was breaking international law, Sauckel answered no—especially as far as Soviet workers were concerned. "I was told that Russia had not joined the Geneva Convention, and so Germany for her part was not bound by it." Besides, he added, the Soviets had themselves "claimed workers" from the Baltic countries as well as about three million from China.[34]

French assistant prosecutor Jacques Herzog led off the cross-examination of Sauckel with questions about Germany's foreign policy. There was a clamor when Herzog produced a confession Sauckel had signed in prison in which he affirmed that he had believed in the "superior racial level" of the German people and had thus worked to execute Hitler's plan for Lebensraum. Sauckel now recanted this confession—claiming that it had been presented to him in its finished form and that a "Russian or Polish officer" had threatened to hand him, his wife, and his ten children over to Soviet authorities unless he cooperated. After a tense exchange with the judges, the prosecution agreed to withdraw Sauckel's statement. It was lost on no one that the head of the Nazi deportation program had managed to present himself as a husband and father fearing for the lives of his family at the hands of the Soviets.[35]

Alexandrov began his cross-examination of Sauckel on May 30 by trying to establish how many foreigners had been brought to Germany during the war to do forced labor. Citing figures from several documents, he proposed a number of "ten million." Sauckel denied that the forced labor program had been so large. When Alexandrov returned to this question the following morning, Lawrence grew impatient. It made no difference to the case, Lawrence finally exclaimed, whether "5 million or 6 million or 7 million workers came to Germany." Alexandrov disagreed but moved on to questions about Germany's war industry. When Sauckel acknowledged that the entire German economy had been reoriented toward the war, Alexandrov moved in for the kill. Was not all of this manpower used to conduct Germany's "war of aggression?" Sauckel insisted that his own view excluded the word "aggression" (echoing Ribbentrop and other defendants), prompting Alexandrov to lose his temper: "Your role in organizing the mass enslavement of the peaceful population of the occupied territories is sufficiently clear!"[36] This kind of accusatory outburst would have earned Alexandrov points in a Soviet show trial of the 1930s. At Nuremberg in May 1946 it fell flat.

The Soviets had already established a reputation for ham-fistedness in their cross-examinations. Even so, Alexandrov's approach to Sauckel confounded the Western judges. When Alexandrov asked Sauckel to describe Goering's criminal role in deporting and enslaving the peoples of the occupied East, Lawrence cut him off: it would be preferable not to allege that certain activities were criminal, he advised. When Alexandrov asked Sauckel whether Ribbentrop had sanctioned the violation of international conventions regarding the use of prisoners of war, Lawrence again intervened. The defendant had already asserted that international law was not violated, he reminded Alexandrov. After a couple of unsuccessful attempts to rephrase the question, Alexandrov simply asked Sauckel to comment on Ribbentrop's role in the allocation of labor. Sauckel sang Ribbentrop's praises, telling the court how the German foreign minister had worked to secure the best conditions he could for foreign workers.[37]

As Alexandrov and Sauckel engaged in a shouting match, Rudenko was figuring out his next move. At a meeting of the Committee of Chief Prosecutors on the evening of May 30, he asked Dodd, Maxwell Fyfe, and Dubost for their support in appealing the Tribunal's decision to allow the defense to challenge the Burdenko Report (which the Soviets continued to insist was incontrovertible evidence under Article 21). The Western prosecutors refused. They did suggest that if the defense called witnesses to testify about Katyn, the Soviet prosecution should also be allowed to do so. The message was clear: the battle over Katyn would be the Soviets' to fight alone.[38]

Disappointed but not surprised, Rudenko took a new tack and tried calling on the prosecution's common interests. The defense was trying to sow discord among the prosecution, he charged. Why else would Seidl claim to have received a copy of the secret protocols from "an American Army man?" Rudenko also noted a recent defense petition to introduce a deposition from the German politician and industrialist Arnold Rechberg, who claimed that Stalin had channeled funds to Hitler in 1933 in order to foster a Soviet-German alliance against the West. Rudenko further suggested that the defense was submitting White Book documents elaborating British and French plans from 1940 to bomb the oil fields of the Caucasus with the intention of stirring things up among the Allies. Invoking the prosecutors' "gentlemen's agreement" to keep the case focused on Axis crimes, Rudenko urged his colleagues to form a united front against the defense's tactics. He offered to pen a joint letter to the Tribunal complaining about these latest attacks on the prosecution.[39]

The Western prosecutors were outwardly sympathetic. Maxwell Fyfe agreed with Rudenko that Seidl's campaign to introduce the secret protocols was "ill-intentioned," and Dodd threw in his opinion that Seidl's claim to have received the secret protocols from an American Army officer was "malicious" (though if Rudenko knew of Dodd's role in getting the secret protocols to the press, his support must have rung hollow). Dubost added that the French shared the Soviet view that Rechberg's aim was to split the prosecution. The prosecutors supported the idea of a joint letter to the Tribunal about Seidl, but encouraged Rudenko to leave the other matters alone.[40]

Rudenko went ahead and put together a draft (with input from the Vyshinsky Commission). It maintained that Seidl's recent petitions about the secret protocols should be denied—not only because the documents he submitted could not be trusted and lacked relevance for his clients but also because they were part of a defense scheme to divert the Tribunal's attention away from the defendants' guilt and toward the actions of the Allied governments. The letter also denounced Seidl's claim to have received secret documents from a "U.S. serviceman" as "plainly provocative."[41] The finalized letter, which the Committee of Chief Prosecutors approved on June 5, was promptly submitted to the Tribunal.

The Soviet prosecution also continued, on its own, to oppose the calling of German defense witnesses to testify about Katyn. On June 3, when the Tribunal considered Otto Stahmer's most recent list of proposed witnesses,

Rudenko repeated the Soviet argument about Article 21 one more time. The Burdenko Report—the report of an official war crimes commission—had definitively established German guilt for the massacre, he maintained, and furthermore had shown it to be "but a link in the chain of many bestial crimes perpetrated by the Hitlerites." Rudenko then elaborated his objections to specific witnesses. Captain Gerhard Böhmert had been part of the Wehrmacht battalion which had allegedly carried out the executions; if he knew about the atrocities it was because of his own role in them. Reinhard von Eichborn had been a telephone expert on the staff of Army Group Center (one of the three German army groups that had participated in the invasion of the Soviet Union) and similarly could not give an unbiased account of events. Stahmer defended his choice of witnesses. The Burdenko Report did not name Böhmert and Eichborn as perpetrators, and in any case one could not prevent testimony from a witness by saying that he was involved in the crime. The Tribunal would take up these matters in closed session.[42]

The defense of Alfred Jodl, the former chief of the Operations Staff of the German Armed Forces High Command, began on June 3 and continued the trend of publicizing Soviet aggression against Poland. The Soviets were determined to hang Jodl for transmitting Hitler's orders to conduct the war with "barbarism" in the East.[43] An unapologetic Jodl, however, used his time in the witness box to recount how the Red Army and the Wehrmacht had coordinated their invasions of Poland in September 1939. Questioned by his attorney, Franz Exner, Jodl recalled his surprise on learning that the two armies would jointly occupy Poland. German troops were a three-day march from the Vistula River when the German Foreign Office informed him that the Red Army would meet the Wehrmacht at an agreed-on demarcation line. This line, which was shown to him on a map, followed the Prussian-Lithuanian border along the Narew, Vistula, and San rivers. The judges allowed Jodl to describe some of the Soviet-German difficulties near the San—the Red Army "shot at everything," including fleeing civilians and German soldiers—before abruptly announcing that such details were a waste of the Tribunal's time.[44]

Jodl also furthered the defense's claims about preventive war. The German military had taken note of the unusual strength of the forces the Soviets had marshaled against Poland, Bessarabia, and the Baltic states, he maintained. Then, in the summer of 1940, German intelligence had noted a spike in the deployment of Soviet troops along the USSR's western border. This was around the same time, Jodl added, that Hitler received information about Soviet designs on Romania's oil fields. According to Jodl, Hitler had tried to clear the air with Stalin and Molotov but had become convinced that Russia and England were conspiring and that Germany would either "become the victim of cold-blooded political extortion" or be attacked. Jodl attested that Hitler had been right to preemptively attack the Soviet Union: "If we had waited until the invasion, and a Russian attack had caught us in a pincer movement, simultaneously, we certainly would have been lost."[45]

It was perhaps some consolation to the Soviets that Jodl also accused the British of crimes against peace. He, like Raeder, described Germany's invasion of Norway as a defensive move. The occupation of Norway had been "a terribly weighty decision" for the German leadership, Jodl asserted, for it involved putting the entire German fleet at risk. He insisted that German leaders had given their orders only after the receipt of reliable information confirming British plans to attack. Addressing the charge of war crimes, he again made counter-accusations against the British, asserting that Hitler's Commando Order (which threatened Allied special-forces soldiers with execution) had been prompted by British violations of the Geneva Convention. Jodl claimed to have seen eyewitness testimony and photographs from the Dieppe Raid of August 1942 (a failed British raid on the German-occupied French town) proving that the British had intentionally shackled German prisoners of war in such a way that they would strangle themselves. He began to rattle off a list of other British war crimes but was stopped by Lawrence.[46]

The British and Soviet prosecutors, put on the defensive, responded to Jodl's accusations with more accusations of their own. The British assistant prosecutor G. D. Roberts alleged that German motives regarding Norway had been aggressive from the start. "You wanted air bases and U-boat bases, didn't you?" he asked. Jodl stood his ground. When Roberts cross-examined Jodl about the Commando Order, Jodl began to rant about victors' justice. If Germany had won the war everyone would have learned about "the strangled at Dieppe" in a similar trial, he proclaimed. Victors' justice surfaced again when Roberts suggested that Germany's surprise attack on Russia would "dishonor" the German nation "for centuries to come." Jodl retorted that such was not the case—for an investigation of Russian documents was sure to prove that the Soviet Union had been planning its own attack.[47]

When Pokrovsky cross-examined Jodl on Friday, June 7, he challenged the defense's claim of preventive war by presenting evidence of a plan Himmler had outlined prior to the invasion calling for the annihilation of ten million Slavs and Jews in the East. Didn't this prove that Germany had waged a predatory war against the Soviet Union, aiming to wipe out local populations and create living space for Germans? Jodl refused to concede anything of the sort, insisting again that Germany had acted only because of the threat of an imminent Soviet attack.[48] He was giving Pokrovsky the "belly-full" he had promised several months earlier. While the prosecution's evidence was comprehensive and powerful, Jodl had used his time in the witness box to put forward an alternative narrative of the origins and course of the war. And that, too, was proving to be compelling.

Outside the courtroom, Rudenko continued to appeal to the Western prosecutors to jointly protest the defense's "counterattacks" on the Allies. He asked them to sign a second letter, this one denouncing the White Books as "dubious sources" filled with propaganda.[49] Jackson declined and urged Rudenko to leave the White Books alone. Privately, Jackson was similarly exasperated by the tactics of the defense; he had complained to Truman a few weeks earlier about the defense's attempts "to throw all the propaganda that is possible into the case."[50] But he also believed that the prosecution "did not stand one chance in a thousand" of getting the Tribunal's support on this matter. Tactically, he determined, the best approach was to turn a blind eye.[51]

The pattern of the trial had been set early on, Jackson mused in a June 7 letter to Rudenko, Dubost, and Maxwell Fyfe, and altering it would not be possible. The Tribunal's ruling regarding Goering back in March had been catastrophic, he wrote, allowing a defendant the freedom to offer whatever explanation he wanted during his cross-examination. It had led to serious wasting of time and was making the Tribunal lose control of the proceedings. It had also hurt the prosecution, as the defense had been able to toss "all manner of irrelevant issues" into the case with no chance for the prosecution to object before they became part of the trial record. Because of the latitude given to the defendants, the entire prosecution had set aside much of its planned cross-examination, Jackson observed, and still had not managed to keep the case focused on the crimes committed by the defendants and their organizations. He worried that the defense's case was leaving the impression that the prosecution was trying the Nazi leaders for their politics and ideology rather than for their crimes. He expressed confidence nevertheless that the case the prosecution had made was "so strong that nothing can destroy it now."[52] Rudenko was less optimistic. Even if the prosecution's case withstood the defense's attacks, the Soviet Union's reputation might not. And after the death of Zorya, Rudenko had to be wondering about his own future.

The Soviets experienced one victory after the Jodl case ended on June 8. The Tribunal rejected Seidl's petitions to introduce the second Gaus affidavit and to call Gaus as a witness. It ruled that the affidavit lacked legal weight, and that Gaus's testimony would add nothing to the evidence the Tribunal had already heard about the secret protocols. The Western press reported on the ruling, proclaiming that the Tribunal had finally put to rest a defense campaign to bring into evidence a so-called secret treaty between the Soviet Union and Germany to divide Europe up into spheres of influence. The Soviets took heart at this decision, though they were well aware of its limits. Thanks to all of the press coverage, the details of the secret protocols were already common knowledge.[53]

Following the Tribunal's announcement about the secret protocols, Rudenko appealed to the Western prosecutors a third time, imploring them to collectively oppose the defense's attacks against the countries of the prosecution. Jackson demurred, doubtful that the remaining five defendants (Seyss-Inquart, Papen, Speer, Neurath, and Fritzsche) would be as much trouble as those who had preceded them.[54] The British, who were now taking a beating over Norway, were more receptive. Maxwell Fyfe suggested that each chief prosecutor present the judge from his country with a memorandum objecting to the defense tactic of making countercharges against the Allied powers.[55]

The Soviets received a bit of a reprieve during the Seyss-Inquart and Papen defenses, which took place during the week of June 10. Both of these defendants blamed the Western powers for abandoning Germany and Austria to the forces of political radicalism. The Soviet prosecution played a limited part in these two cases, having agreed to leave the cross-examinations to the Western prosecutors. Rudenko had assured Moscow that Soviet interests would nonetheless not be overlooked. Before Seyss-Inquart took the stand, Rudenko gave Jackson a list of questions focused on the defendant's stint as the deputy to Hans Frank, the governor-general of Poland. In true Soviet style, the document was scripted, with anticipated answers and follow-up questions.[56] Jackson politely accepted it and put it aside.

The Seyss-Inquart defense focused mostly on the defendant's time as chancellor of Austria, touching only briefly on Poland. Seyss-Inquart did not try to refute the charge that the German occupation government of Poland had carried out the sweeping arrest, incarceration, and murder of tens of thousands of Polish intellectuals. He instead argued that this had been a measured response to the Polish resistance. Asked by Dodd if he accepted responsibility along with Frank "for whatever went on in Poland," Seyss-Inquart answered that he did not deny anything.[57]

Papen, by contrast, denied all personal criminal responsibility, arguing that during his time as vice chancellor of Germany he had tried to exert a moderating influence on policy. Asked by Maxwell Fyfe why it had taken him so long to learn the "obvious truth" about Hitler, Papen turned the tables. British and French leaders had been willing to work with Hitler through the Munich crisis right up to the Polish campaign, he pointed out, even though "they knew everything that was going on." Papen then pleasantly surprised the Soviets by denouncing Germany's invasion of Russia as a terrible crime.[58]

The Katyn confrontation remained on the horizon, growing closer each day. In Moscow, the Politburo Commission spent the week finalizing plans for the anticipated witness testimony. Vyshinsky, Trainin, Kruglov, Minister of Justice Nikolai Rychkov, and others met on June 11 and came up with a new list of eight potential witnesses. It included the astronomy professor Bazilevsky as well as three other Soviet citizens who had served the German occupiers in the Katyn area (two night watchmen and a maid). The list also included a Soviet engineer who had been interned in a German prisoner-of-war camp in Smolensk and a German soldier who had been captured by the Soviets. The remaining two witnesses were forensic experts. Dr. Marko Markov, who had served on the German-sponsored International Katyn Commission, had already confessed before a People's Tribunal in Soviet-occupied Bulgaria to having signed the German-sponsored report under duress. He was expected to give a repeat performance in Nuremberg. Professor Viktor Prozorovsky, a member of the Burdenko Commission, had headed the team of Soviet forensic experts who had investigated the gravesite in January 1944. Like Bazilevsky, he had met with the Western journalists during their trip to Katyn.[59]

Soviet plans regarding Katyn now moved ahead quickly. The Politburo Commission directed its Katyn subcommission (Trainin, Sheinin, and Raikhman) to secure the dispatch of the Soviet witnesses from Moscow to Berlin the next day, June 12. They were to be escorted by Soviet state security agents. Rychkov would monitor events in Nuremberg from Moscow while Vyshinsky was in Paris with Molotov for a meeting of the Council of Foreign Ministers to discuss the peace treaties for Romania, Bulgaria, Italy, Hungary, and Finland.[60]

Things went awry almost immediately. On the evening of June 13 the Soviet diplomat Mikhail Kharlamov informed Vyshinsky that the witnesses, following their arrival in Berlin, had been stranded at the Dalhoff Aerodrome for more than seven hours. The Soviet agents responsible for meeting their plane had been mistakenly sent to another aerodrome, and it had taken everyone several hours to figure out what had happened. While Kharlamov assured Vyshinsky that everything had now been taken care of, such carelessness did not bode well.[61]

In Nuremberg, Rudenko and Nikitchenko were doing their best to prevent what now looked like the inevitable. Rudenko continued to protest Stahmer's applications for witnesses. He also challenged various pieces of evidence, such as Josef Czapski's 1944 *Reminiscences of Starobielsk*, a firsthand account of what Polish officers had experienced in Soviet prisoner-of-war and labor camps. Rudenko maintained that Czapski's book could not be accepted as evidence since it was a work of literature, "published with a particular purpose in view."[62] Nikitchenko suggested at a closed judges' meeting on June 19 that there was no need to bring the Katyn witnesses to Nuremberg. All evidence—German and Soviet—could be presented in written form. The Soviet witnesses had been in Berlin for almost a week at this point and were ready to go, but Moscow still hoped to avoid a showdown that would be widely reported on in the press. The Western judges agreed to bring Nikitchenko's suggestion to the defense.[63]

With the details of the Katyn contest still being worked out, the Tribunal turned to Albert Speer's defense. Speer had first gained fame as Hitler's personal architect; he had designed the Nazi Party Rally Grounds, which the filmmaker Roman Karmen had seen filled with goose-stepping troops in 1930s newsreels. In early 1942, Speer became minister of armaments and war production, using his technical prowess to sustain Germany's war effort.[64] Now, speaking before the court, he blithely admitted to having used forced foreign labor, including concentration camp internees and Russian prisoners of war, to keep the German war industry on track. He insisted, however, that the foreigners had only been used to produce nonmilitary items such as textiles and engine parts. He knew that he was splitting hairs: challenged by Jackson, he acknowledged that every article produced in Germany at that time, from shoes to coal, had been a part of the war effort.[65]

Speer riveted the international press as he recounted his ill-fated attempt to assassinate Hitler, Goebbels, Martin Bormann, and Robert Ley after realizing in 1945 that Hitler planned to continue the war "at all costs." His plan to introduce poison gas into the ventilation system of Hitler's bunker had been foiled, he explained, when on Hitler's orders the ground-level ventilation shaft was suddenly replaced with a tall and inaccessible chimney. During Jackson's cross-examination, Speer further trumpeted his resistance to Hitler, claiming that he had personally blocked the manufacture of chemicals needed to make chemical weapons in November 1944. He asserted that he had wanted to prevent Hitler from committing war crimes that might be held against the German people. Speer also told Jackson that Germany had not gotten very far in atomic research because its finest experts in this field had emigrated to America.[66] The Soviet interpreter Stupnikova recalled how "something resembling a moan" had passed through the courtroom at this moment as everyone imagined the atomic bomb deployed in support of Nazism.[67]

Mark Raginsky began his cross-examination of Speer on June 21 by trying to get him to admit to participating in the conspiracy to wage aggressive war. He reminded Speer of his admission to Soviet interrogators that he had learned about Hitler's plans against the USSR by reading *Mein Kampf*. Speer now maintained that he had lied, too ashamed to admit that he had not read the whole of Hitler's book. A surprised Raginsky suggested that Speer, as a member of the inner circle, must have known of Hitler's plans in any case. Speer answered that he had seen no indication of such plans, and any concerns he might have had about Germany's relationship to Russia were allayed in 1939 with the signing of the nonaggression pact. Speer then wondered aloud why Russian diplomats, who themselves must have read *Mein Kampf*, had signed this agreement.

Raginsky had more success with the rest of his cross-examination, despite the fact that Speer repeatedly deflected questions by finding fault with their wording. Speer admitted to extracting metals and raw materials from the countries Germany occupied but took offense at the term "plundering." He conceded to acquiring labor through a policy of "compulsory recruitment" but rejected the suggestion that his employees had been "enslaved."[68] He succeeded in muddying the waters. British alternate judge Birkett, who had grown to expect Soviet translation problems, complained in his diary that evening that Raginsky's cross-examination had been "mangled" by "the worst interpretation the world has ever known."[69] In this case, at least, many of the supposed errors were not actually questions of language but matters of historical interpretation.

After another month of the defense case, the prosecutors and the judges felt little of the hope and idealism that had marked the May meeting of the International Association of Penal Law. The Soviets were exhausted. The continued attention to the secret protocols, the death of Zorya, and the worry over Katyn must have had them wondering why they had come to Nuremberg in the first place. It seemed to matter little now that the Soviets had been the ones out in front calling for a special international tribunal or that Aron Trainin's arguments about Nazi criminality had been vital to the development of the case. The prosecution's efforts to keep the trials focused on European Axis crimes had collapsed: the defendants had spent the past four months using Trainin's idea of "crimes against peace" to make one counter-accusation after another against the Soviet Union. The language of international law was proving to be a double-edged sword.

That language was about to come back into the spotlight. The defense of Konstantin von Neurath, the former Reich Protector of Bohemia and

Moravia, began on June 22 and ignited a discussion about the meaning of the term "genocide" that would reverberate far beyond Nuremberg. Maxwell Fyfe had submitted as evidence a memorandum Neurath had sent to Hitler in August 1940 outlining the policies that he had introduced to suppress the Czech population. The memorandum, Maxwell Fyfe wrote to his wife, was "one of the worst documents of the trial."[70] He found it to be a shockingly clear elaboration of the Nazi policy of genocide.

Neurath, an older man with an aristocratic bearing, began his defense by testifying that he had planned to win over the Czechs with moderate policies but more radical forces had intervened. He made the implausible claim that he had not even known about the thousands of arrests that took place on the day the war broke out. Maxwell Fyfe had primary responsibility for cross-examining Neurath and was ready to challenge these claims. He brought forward damning excerpts from the memorandum—showing that Neurath had effectively sought to wipe out the Czech nation. Neurath had advised the expulsion of all Czechs from Bohemia and Moravia who were not "suitable for Germanization," including the entire educated class. He had also proposed measures such as "the extermination of the Czech historical myth" and a campaign against the use of the Czech language in order to erase Czech culture. He had recommended retaining only those Czechs who were deemed suitable for "Germanization by individual selective breeding," since there were not enough Germans to repopulate the country were they to "evacuate all Czechs completely."[71]

Maxwell Fyfe reminded Neurath that the prosecution was charging him and many of his fellow defendants with genocide, "which we say is the extermination of racial or national groups." He then cited Raphael Lemkin's definition of genocide as "a coordinated plan" aimed at destroying the "essential foundations of the life of national groups" with the intention of "annihilating the groups themselves."[72] As a result of Lemkin's efforts in the summer and fall of 1945, the Indictment had listed "genocide" as a war crime—defining it as the intentional destruction of "particular races and classes of people and national, racial, or religious groups."[73]

The term "genocide" had not been mentioned in court since the reading of the Indictment on the first day of the trials. Maxwell Fyfe now not only reintroduced it but also expanded its definition to include forced assimilation. This in fact corresponded with Lemkin's original conceptualization of the term as set out in his 1944 work *Axis Rule in Occupied Europe*. Lemkin had argued that "genocide" entailed a wide range of techniques for group destruction, including attacking the intelligentsia, banning the use of native language in education, and siphoning off a group's economic resources.[74] "You meant to destroy the Czech people as a national entity with their own language, history, and traditions, and assimilate them into the Greater German Reich," Maxwell Fyfe charged. "To make the Czechs disappear as a nation was altogether impossible," Neurath replied. "But they were to incorporate themselves more closely into the Reich."[75]

The British prosecution raised the matter of genocide partly at the instigation of Bohuslav Ečer, the UNWCC member and special Czech envoy to the IMT. He and the Polish and Yugoslav envoys (Stanisław Piotrowski and Albert Weiss) had for months been asking the prosecution to broaden its use and definition of the term.[76] Lemkin himself had arrived in Nuremberg in early June and had been buttonholing the prosecutors, imploring them to use "genocide" in reference to the Nazis' destruction of national, racial, or religious groups through the destruction of their cultures. He had also circulated a paper, "The Necessity to Develop the Concept of Genocide in the Proceedings," in which he argued that terms such as "mass extermination" could not capture the true nature of Nazi crimes.[77] Ečer and the other envoys agreed with Lemkin that the evidence presented thus far in court showed that genocide had been committed not just against the Jews, Poles, and Gypsies but also against "particular classes" in Czechoslovakia and Yugoslavia, including the intelligentsia and the clergy. Both Ečer and Lemkin were delighted with Maxwell Fyfe's cross-examination of Neurath; Ečer offered Maxwell Fyfe his hearty congratulations, and Lemkin sent a personal note of appreciation and thanks.[78]

The Soviet prosecutors, who had been watching the gap widen between themselves and the Western prosecutors since the start of the defense case, were uncertain how to respond to the discussion about genocide given the broader definition Maxwell Fyfe was now attaching to the term. During the war, Ečer and Trainin had both called for the creation of a permanent international criminal court to judge individuals charged with war crimes. But Ečer and the Soviets now found themselves to be further apart. Ečer, along with Lemkin and many others, wanted to see the international legal concepts introduced at Nuremberg used not just to prosecute those who had acted on behalf of the European Axis powers but also to protect human rights throughout the world.[79] He had been recommending that the prosecution's closing speeches and the judgment address the full scope of the crime of "genocide," not only for immediate justice but also to set a precedent that could ensure the "peaceful development of future populations."[80] The Soviets meanwhile were coming to understand that the language of human rights— like the language of war crimes—could be harnessed for all sorts of political ends. It could just as easily be used against them and their interests.

Even as the Soviets continued to send lawyers and diplomats to participate in international organizations devoted to peace, security, and international law, they were becoming aware that these organizations could become forums for criticizing or interfering with Moscow's policies in Eastern Europe. The Soviets had been taken aback in mid-June when the Economic and Social Council of the United Nations proposed that provisions guaranteeing human rights be included in the peace treaties that the foreign ministers of the Allied powers were drafting in Paris. The Soviet lawyer Nikolai Orlov had responded that the former European Axis countries needed to be "made ready for human liberties before they received them."[81] The Soviets were setting up puppet governments in Romania, Hungary, and Bulgaria. They did not want anyone telling them how to run things.

With the defense case nearing its conclusion, the Soviets were still wrestling with the possibilities and the perils of international law. During the German occupation, Stalin and Molotov had anticipated the propaganda value of a special international tribunal to try the former Nazi leaders, hoping to bring world attention to the enormity of Soviet wartime losses and to further the Soviet claim for reparations. Even as the reparations question took on a political life of its own, the Soviets had continued to call for a tribunal, envisioning it as a means to fully establish the Soviet Union's position as an international power. They had come a long way toward achieving this goal at Nuremberg. But all had not gone as planned for the Soviets. The defendants and their witnesses had repeatedly raised the possibility that Soviet leaders and organizations were themselves guilty of war crimes and crimes against peace. Seidl and other defense attorneys, seemingly with the acquiescence of the Western judges, were using the courtroom to bring the secret history of Soviet-German collaboration to light. They were also using the press to try the Soviets in the court of international public opinion. Soviet leaders had learned the hard way that even those international institutions that they had helped to organize could be used against them. And Katyn loomed just ahead.

CHAPTER 12 | The Katyn Showdown

D EPUTY FOREIGN MINISTER Solomon Lozovsky, the head of the Soviet Information Bureau, was a seasoned propagandist. He had directed the Soviet press campaign throughout the war, filtering the news from the fronts. Lozovsky had a way with words and a wry sense of humor. The American photographer Margaret Bourke-White, who was in Moscow when the city came under heavy bombardment in the summer of 1941, later wrote of his ease with foreign correspondents: "Witty, clever, he was always ready with a joke when the questions of the press got too explicit." He especially enjoyed taking apart German propaganda. "His favorite pastime," she recalled, "was to disprove German claims and call them 'just some more lies out of the gossip factory.'"[1]

Throughout the war, Lozovsky's daily briefings were a regular feature in Soviet broadcasts and were also repackaged for the Western press.[2] It was rumored that he and Nazi propaganda chief Joseph Goebbels closely studied each other's official statements, each attempting to read between the other's lines. Lozovsky's role in the war effort had gone far beyond the press. He had played a significant part in the creation of the Extraordinary State Commission and had been a key organizer of the Jewish Anti-Fascist Committee, which had disseminated evidence abroad of German atrocities and raised funds for the Red Army.[3]

Lozovsky knew all too well that the Soviets were struggling on the propaganda front at Nuremberg—and that Katyn was the most dangerous of all the propaganda problems they were facing. He had played an active part in the original Soviet cover-up of Katyn and had overseen the press campaign to publicize the Soviet version of events. It was Lozovsky who had organized the train trip for the Western correspondents to the Katyn Forest in January 1944.[4] The "Katyn junket" had served as a test run for the evidence and witness statements that were then included in the Burdenko Report. The press coverage, which had taken the Soviet evidence at face value, had given Soviet leaders the confidence to charge the Nazis with the atrocity before the IMT.[5] After the Allied victory, Lozovsky had assumed that the Soviet narrative about Katyn was safe from further challenges. This was only the latest Soviet assumption to be upended at Nuremberg. Ever since the defense had successfully petitioned the Tribunal to allow witness testimony about Katyn, he had been awaiting word on when these hearings would begin.[6]

The topic of propaganda took center stage at the Palace of Justice on the afternoon of June 26 with the testimony of Hans Fritzsche, the last defendant in the dock. Fritzsche, the Nazis' chief of radio propaganda, had been taken into Soviet custody in Berlin on May 2, 1945, after appearing at Red Army headquarters and offering to make a radio broadcast urging German troops to surrender. A Red Army general had taken Fritzsche up on his offer—and had then turned him over to SMERSH. Fritzsche had spent the next couple of months in a Soviet-run prison in Berlin. In late July, he was put on a plane to Moscow and interned in the notorious Lubyanka prison, in the basement of NKVD headquarters.[7] In mid-August, as the list of Nuremberg defendants was coming together, SMERSH had informed Vyshinsky that Fritzsche had pled guilty to directing the "fascist propaganda efforts that slandered the Soviet Union, England, and America."[8] On October 15, Fritzsche was put on another plane—this one taking him back to Germany to stand trial before the IMT.

The Western prosecutors had been reluctant to add Fritzsche, who was not a member of Hitler's inner circle, to the list of defendants. But the Soviets had insisted that with Goebbels dead, Fritzsche was needed to illuminate the workings of the Nazi propaganda machine. He had been the head of the German Press Division of Goebbels's propaganda ministry when war broke out; he later took over the ministry's Radio Division, which, among other things, had presented the Katyn massacre as an atrocity committed by the "Jewish-Bolshevik secret police."[9] Fritzsche had worked with Goebbels to spread information about the atrocity abroad, circulating photographs of the unearthed corpses with the aim of creating a schism between the Soviets and the Western powers.[10]

Fritzsche's voice was familiar in Germany; his nightly radio broadcasts had narrated the war for the German people.[11] That voice, live, now filled the Nuremberg courtroom. Fritzsche spoke proudly of his work for Goebbels's ministry. He differentiated between the official propaganda he had helped disseminate and the "radical agitation" practiced by anti-Semites such as Julius Streicher—endeavoring to distance himself from the latter. Asked by his attorney, Heinz Fritz, about his repeated denunciations of Jews and Bolsheviks, Fritzsche explained that he had blamed these groups and their anti-Nazi agitation for precipitating the war.[12]

Fritzsche further told the court that he had been unaware of Hitler's plans to exterminate the Jews—insisting that he too had been a victim of Nazi disinformation. Goebbels had assured him, he attested, that the gas vans mentioned at the Soviet Union's Kharkov Trial in 1943 were "pure invention."[13] Fritzsche matter-of-factly recounted his wartime efforts to win the European people over to what he called "the German cause." When asked by his attorney if he had used propaganda to try to split the Allies, he responded forthrightly. "Of course I attempted to do that," he said. "I considered that a permissible method of waging war."[14] It could not have been lost on the Soviets that the defense was employing a similar technique to great effect at Nuremberg.

Rudenko began his cross-examination of Fritzsche on June 28 and encountered difficulties from the start. When Rudenko read from an affidavit that Fritzsche had signed during his Moscow imprisonment, Fritzsche objected strongly to a line in which he had described himself as a confidant of Goebbels. Rudenko pointed out his signature—at which point Fritzsche acknowledged that he had signed the document but continued to protest that those were not his words. Tribunal president Lawrence broke in: What was Fritzsche trying to say? Fritzsche answered that the affidavit was a rough summary of the answers he had given to his interrogators over many days and weeks of questioning, often late at night. He had signed it under duress, he maintained, after a "very severe solitary confinement which had lasted for several months." Rudenko looked at him with disbelief. "Of course, you never thought, Defendant Fritzsche, that after all you had done you would be sent to a sanatorium?"[15]

Unable to get Fritzsche to verify his Moscow confession, Rudenko presented evidence from his radio broadcasts in order to establish his role in laying the groundwork for the war. Hadn't Fritzsche tried in an August 1939 speech to convince the German people of the necessity of the attack on Poland? Rudenko asked. Fritzsche insisted that Poland had pushed Hitler to action. He then added that it had been "a matter of great satisfaction" for

FIGURE 12.1 Hans Fritzsche was one of the two defendants the Soviets brought to Nuremberg, ca. 1945-1946.

Credit: United States Holocaust Memorial Museum, courtesy of Harry S. Truman Library. Photographer: Charles Alexander.

him to read in the Soviet press soon afterward that the Soviet government agreed with his interpretation. Telford Taylor later described Rudenko's line of questioning as reckless, given what everyone knew at this point about Soviet-German collaboration against Poland. (The strategy was of course not Rudenko's own; the Vyshinsky Commission had determined his approach.) Staying on the topic of Germany's war plans, Rudenko pressed Fritzsche about his ministry's interactions with the German Foreign Office, which had published a White Book depicting Operation Barbarossa as a preventive assault. Fritzsche admitted that the evidence in this White Book had been "meager." Nonetheless, he claimed to have believed it, for it would have been "nonsensical" for Germany to choose to initiate a war against the Soviet Union while already fighting the Western powers.[16]

To counter Fritzsche's claims that he had not incited the German people to violence, Rudenko presented depositions from three high-ranking German officers: Field Marshal Ferdinand Schörner, Vice Admiral Hans-Erich Voss, and Lieutenant General Reiner Stahel. All three had been (along with Fritzsche) on the list of war criminals Molotov and Vyshinsky had originally proposed sending to Nuremberg; they were still prisoners in Moscow.[17] Voss, the former naval liaison officer at Hitler's headquarters, attested that Fritzsche had riled up the German people after the defeat at Stalingrad with reports of Soviet intentions to wipe out the German nation. Stahel, one of Hitler's most ruthless generals, corroborated these claims and stated that Fritzsche had incited German soldiers to commit atrocities against Soviet civilians. Schörner, who had headed the National Socialist Political Guidance Staff of the Armed Forces (which was concerned with questions of ideology), maintained that Fritzsche had used his radio broadcasts to intentionally deceive the German people. Fritzsche dismissed these depositions as "nonsense." His attorney pointed out that the statements were riddled with Soviet jargon, implicitly questioning their authenticity.[18]

The international press gave Rudenko's cross-examination of Fritzsche little coverage. Soviet newspapers on the other hand quoted at length from Fritzsche's confession and from the officers' depositions.[19] Even as the Soviet prosecution encountered difficulties in Nuremberg, a highly censored press made it possible for Moscow to control the story that was brought to the Soviet people back home. This was perhaps some consolation to Soviet leaders as they braced themselves for the struggle ahead.

On Saturday, June 29, as the Fritzsche defense was wrapping up, Judge Lawrence announced that starting on Monday morning the Tribunal would hear three defense witnesses and three Soviet witnesses on the topic of Katyn. He explained that the Tribunal was limiting the number of witnesses and would not review any other evidence from either side because Katyn was "only a subsidiary allegation of fact" and should not be allowed to take up too much time.[20] Gorshenin sent an urgent memo to Lozovsky in Moscow asking him to make arrangements for the immediate transfer of the Soviet witnesses from Berlin to Nuremberg by military plane.[21] The Katyn showdown was about to begin.

FIGURE 12.2 Lev Smirnov represented the Soviet prosecution in the courtroom showdown over Katyn, ca. 1945-1946.

Credit: United States Holocaust Memorial Museum, courtesy of National Archives and Records Administration, College Park.

Lev Smirnov would be representing the Soviet prosecution in the courtroom confrontation over Katyn. Reputed to be one of the Soviet Union's most able courtroom orators, he had joined the Soviet delegation in Nuremberg in December after impressing Soviet leaders with his work prosecuting a Soviet war crimes trial in Smolensk.[22] In February, he had presented critical parts of the Soviet case before the IMT, giving a stirring speech on crimes against humanity. Of all the Soviet prosecutors, he was the best at thinking on his feet. Even so, he had rarely faced off against a true adversary like Otto Stahmer in open court. Smirnov appreciated the importance as well as the dangers of this particular moment of the trials, fully aware that the Soviets would be on their own. The Western prosecutors, who had bristled from the start about including Katyn in the Indictment, would watch this part of the case from the sidelines.

The Soviet prosecution and the German defense had chosen different strategies to make their case, as illustrated by their choices of witnesses. Stahmer's three witnesses were all officers who had been stationed near the Katyn Forest in the fall of 1941: Colonel Friedrich Ahrens (who had been named in the Burdenko Report as a perpetrator of the massacre) as well as Lieutenant Reinhard von Eichborn and Lieutenant General Eugen Oberhauser. The Politburo Commission for the Nuremberg Trials, by contrast, had decided to go with three professionals. Boris Bazilevsky, the astronomy professor and deputy mayor of Smolensk, had come across well when Lozovsky had presented him to Western journalists in January 1944. Dr. Marko Markov (a forensic expert with the German-sponsored International Katyn Commission) and Professor Viktor Prozorovsky (a forensic expert with the Burdenko Commission) could speak to the competing evidence about the timing of the massacre.[23]

For both sides, nearly everything hinged on establishing when the crime took place. The International Katyn Commission, whose report Markov was being called on to discredit, had dated the massacre to March or April 1940, before German forces had invaded the Soviet Union and taken the region. The Burdenko Commission had dated it to the autumn of 1941, pinning the blame on the 537th Engineering Battalion of the Wehrmacht's Army Group Center.

On Monday morning, July 1, Stahmer called his first witness. The Soviet interpreter Tatiana Stupnikova later remembered being filled with anxiety, knowing that even a small mistranslation could bring disaster.[24] Ahrens, a tall and elegant-looking middle-aged man, began his testimony by acknowledging that he had commanded Signal Regiment 537, which had been misidentified as "Engineering Battalion 537" in the Burdenko Report. The regiment had been responsible for maintaining communications between Army Group Center and neighboring units. Ahrens's regimental staff had been stationed in the "little Katyn wood" within the Katyn Forest beginning in September 1941—and the Dnieper Castle, at the southern edge of the wood, had served as their headquarters. With these facts established, Stahmer quickly refuted Soviet charges about Ahrens's role by revealing that he had not assumed his command in the Katyn region until late November 1941—well after the alleged date of the massacre. Ahrens then attested that he had neither heard of orders from Berlin to shoot Polish prisoners of war nor issued such orders himself. When Stahmer asked him about Soviet claims that there had been frequent gunfire in the Katyn wood that fall, Ahrens had a ready reply: the regiment had often practiced defensive maneuvers.[25]

Ahrens then told the court how he had discovered the graves in the Katyn wood. That winter, "in late December 1941 or early January 1942," one of his soldiers had pointed out to him a snow-covered mound in the distance with a birch cross on it. In the months that followed he heard rumors from his men about a mass shooting that was said to have taken place in the woods, but he had dismissed this as improbable. Then in early 1943, while tracking a wolf through the woods, he came upon the mound; there were wolf scratchings on top and bones nearby that were ultimately determined to be human. Shortly after he reported this discovery, a German forensic expert made exhumations and uncovered "conclusive evidence" proving that a

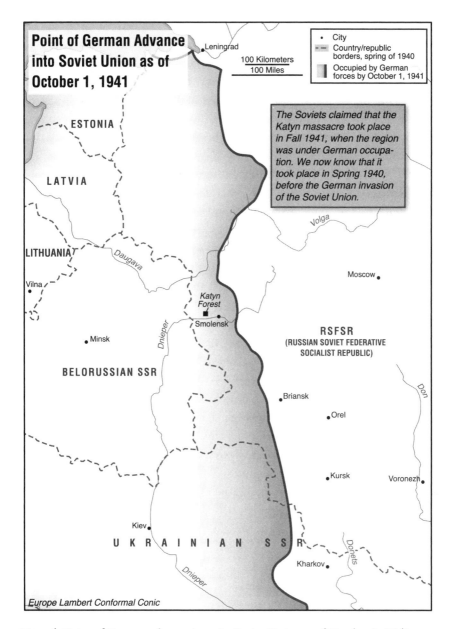

Point of German Advance into Soviet Union as of October 1, 1941

100 Kilometers
100 Miles

- City
- Country/republic borders, spring of 1940
- Occupied by German forces by October 1, 1941

The Soviets claimed that the Katyn massacre took place in Fall 1941, when the region was under German occupation. We now know that it took place in Spring 1940, before the German invasion of the Soviet Union.

Leningrad

ESTONIA

LATVIA

LITHUANIA

Daugava

Vilna

Volga

Moscow

Katyn Forest

Smolensk

Dnieper

Minsk

BELORUSSIAN SSR

RSFSR
(RUSSIAN SOVIET FEDERATIVE SOCIALIST REPUBLIC)

Briansk

Orel

Don

Kursk

Voronezh

Kiev

UKRAINIAN SSR

Dnieper

Donets

Kharkov

Europe Lambert Conformal Conic

MAP 4 Point of German advance into the Soviet Union as of October 1, 1941.

shooting had occurred in the spring of 1940. This evidence included a Polish officer's diary that ended abruptly at that time, expressing in one of its final entries the fear that "something horrible was going to happen."[26]

Smirnov began his cross-examination of Ahrens by addressing Stahmer's revelation that Ahrens had not arrived at Katyn until November 1941.

Given this timing, could Ahrens really know what had happened in the Katyn Forest earlier in the fall? When Ahrens conceded the point, Smirnov declared that this witness had no business testifying about the shootings at all.[27] Taylor appreciated Smirnov's strategy. The Germans had invaded the region in July 1941, leaving a span of several months during which they could have massacred the Poles without Ahrens having known about it.[28] Stahmer may have made a persuasive argument for Ahrens's personal innocence, but Smirnov had made clear that there was life in the Soviet case.

Smirnov also challenged Ahrens's testimony about the gravesite, asking whether he had personally seen the Katyn graves. Yes, Ahrens replied, explaining that he had driven past them repeatedly while the exhumations were taking place. Could he say how deep the bodies were buried? Ahrens replied that he could not, for the smell had been so sickening that he had sped by as quickly as possible. The Burdenko Commission had established that the graves were between one-and-a-half and two meters deep, Smirnov revealed, wondering aloud how a wolf could have tunneled that far into the earth. Nikitchenko followed up from the bench with a sharply pointed question for the witness: Had Ahrens been present when the diary and other material evidence were found? No, Ahrens admitted. He could not attest to their provenance.[29]

Stahmer's next witness, Eichborn, had been stationed near the Katyn Forest starting in mid-September 1941. It was out of the question, Eichborn told the court, that the execution and burial of 11,000 Polish officers could have taken place that fall near the regimental headquarters without him having heard of it. As the regiment's telephone expert, it had been his job to relay all orders and information, and he testified that no directive to shoot Polish prisoners of war had been issued.[30]

Smirnov was ready to counter the assumption that the order for the massacre had gone through official channels. Had Eichborn seen any telegrams from Einsatzgruppe B or from Special Command Moscow? Both of these units had been in Smolensk at this time, Smirnov noted, and both had been assigned to exterminate prisoners of war. Eichborn demurred, explaining that these kinds of special detachments had run "their own wireless stations." This was exactly the answer Smirnov had been waiting for. How then could Eichborn say for certain that there were no orders or reports about the Poles? Didn't he know that the killing of the Polish officers had also been "a special action"? Stahmer asked to summon a fourth witness to respond to Smirnov's charge. The Tribunal refused.[31]

Instead, Stahmer ended his case with Oberhauser, the chief signal officer of Army Group Center and Ahrens's commanding officer. Oberhauser, who had reached the Katyn region with his staff in September 1941, attested that he had not heard anything about the shooting until 1943, "when the graves were opened." He corroborated much of Ahrens's testimony, reiterating that no order had come from Berlin to shoot Polish officers; such an order would have had to go through him, he explained, as the direct superior of the regiment. Even if such an order had been sent to the regiment via "some obscure channel," the commanders would have told him about it. Asked whether he thought it possible that 11,000 Poles could have been shot and buried in the Katyn wood between June and September 1941, he appealed to reason. The commander of the regiment's advance party would never have decided to locate his headquarters next to a mass grave containing 11,000 bodies.[32]

Much of Oberhauser's testimony focused on establishing that Signal Regiment 537 had not been equipped with the weapons and ammunition to carry out a massacre.[33] Smirnov homed in on this point during his cross-examination. Exactly what weapons did the regiment have? Oberhauser answered that the regiment had pistols and carbines but not automatic weapons; noncommissioned officers generally had only small pistols, such as a Walther or a Mauser. Questioned further, Oberhauser added things up: if each of the regiment's noncommissioned officers had a pistol, that would amount to fifteen per company, making a total of 150. Smirnov pushed on. Why, he asked, did Oberhauser think that 150 pistols would be insufficient to carry out shootings on a large scale? Oberhauser responded by attempting to explain the work of a signal regiment, whose men were deployed over a very large area. There were never "150 pistols in one and the same place."[34]

The end of Oberhauser's testimony marked the completion of the defense's presentation about Katyn. Stahmer's approach had on the whole been successful. His witnesses had sown doubt about the timing of the massacre, throwing the Soviet charges of German guilt into question. Smirnov had done an able job of cross-examination but had been unable to fully counter the impression that there was something off about the Soviet version of events. Taylor, for one, believed that he had heard strong evidence that the killings had not taken place while Ahrens's regiment was headquartered near the forest. Stupnikova later remembered July 1 as "a black day." The technical job of translating the German witness testimony had been straightforward; the difficulties had sprung from the content, which differed profoundly from the official Soviet version of events promulgated by Lozovsky and his Soviet Information Bureau.[35]

The day was not yet over. Determined to move things along, Lawrence asked Smirnov to call his first witness. Bazilevsky, a longtime resident of Smolensk, told the court that the German occupiers had forced him to serve as the city's deputy mayor in July 1941. He had learned of the massacre because of his position. According to Bazilevsky, in September 1941 the German-appointed mayor, Boris Menschagin, had told him about a secret German proposal to "exterminate" prisoners of war. A couple of weeks later, Menschagin had informed him that the deed was done: the Polish officers had been shot in the vicinity of Smolensk. Bazilevsky's testimony was all hearsay—and Lawrence called out this weakness. Did Bazilevsky know whether Menschagin had direct knowledge of the massacre? Bazilevsky answered that he had "understood quite definitely" that Menschagin had gotten his information at German headquarters.[36]

Cross-examined by Stahmer, Bazilevsky admitted that his knowledge of the massacre was based on rumors. When Stahmer asked if he could name an eyewitness who had been present at the shooting, Bazilevsky was scornful. This atrocity had been carried out under such circumstances that it was "scarcely possible" for Soviet witnesses to be present, he answered. Surprising everyone in court, Stahmer suddenly accused Bazilevsky of reading his responses from a script. "How can you explain the fact that the interpreter already had your answers?" A flustered Bazilevsky protested that he had not read anything and did not know how the interpreter could possibly have known his answers ahead of time. At this point the U.S. prosecution decided that it could not remain silent. Thomas Dodd sent a note to the interpreters and then announced to the court that none of them had had any prior knowledge of either questions or answers. Lawrence warned Stahmer to watch his step.[37]

The day finished with testimony from the second Soviet witness, the Bulgarian forensic expert Markov. As a member of the German-sponsored commission that had investigated the gravesite in April 1943, Markov had signed the report that dated the massacre to the spring of 1940 and blamed it on the Soviets. Speaking now through a Bulgarian interpreter, Markov told the court that he had tried to refuse serving on the commission, to no avail. Bulgarian officials had reminded him that their country was at war and that he could be sent wherever they wanted. They had assured him that he would not be gone for long, for the Germans had already exhumed many corpses and drafted a report. He had only to see what had been done and sign. Markov and the other commission members had met in Berlin and then set off for Smolensk.[38]

Answering Smirnov's questions, Markov described the commission's visit to Katyn as "superficial and rushed." The commission members had spent two afternoons in the Katyn wood, for three or four hours at a stretch. The Germans gave them a brief tour and showed them the open graves; the exhumed corpses had been laid out and were waiting for them. The commission members were then brought to a small house outside the Katyn wood where they were shown papers said to have been found in the clothing of the corpses—dated letters and receipts that ended abruptly in April 1940. Smirnov asked Markov whether he had been permitted to inspect the papers, to see, for example, if they "were impregnated with any acids which had developed by the decay of the corpses." No, Markov replied. These items had been in glass cases and the commission members had not been allowed to handle them.[39]

According to Markov, the only part of the commission's work that could even remotely be considered "scientific" were the autopsies carried out by some of its members. But of the 11,000 corpses found in the forest, the commission had been allowed to examine only eight, all chosen ahead of time by the Germans. Markov had personally examined just one corpse. Asked by Smirnov if the forensic investigation indicated that the corpses had already been buried for three years, Markov gave a careful no. He believed that the corpse he had dissected had been buried for only a year or eighteen months. Returning to this question the following morning, Smirnov got Markov to declare definitively that the murders could not have been committed in 1940.[40]

The rest of Markov's testimony focused on the skulls of the exhumed corpses. The German forensic report had hinged on the finding of something called "pseudocallus" inside the craniums. Markov told the court that he had heard this term for the first time at a meeting of the commission in Smolensk in late April 1943. A Hungarian commission member, Professor Ferenc Orsos, had described pseudocallus as a sediment of salts that forms inside the cranium after a corpse has been buried for a minimum of three years. Showing the rest of the commission what he called a pseudocallus within one of the skulls, Orsos had claimed to be able to date the massacre. Markov now heaped doubt on this evidence. The skull in question was taken from a corpse marked with the number 526, he recounted. From this he speculated that it had been exhumed well before the commission's arrival in Katyn, given that the corpses they had autopsied bore numbers over 800. Markov told the court that he and the other commission members had not noticed any sediment on the skulls they had examined. Since the skull shown by Professor Orsos was the only one with such traits, he continued, the commission had been mistaken to arrive at a definite conclusion about the age of all of the corpses in the Katyn graves.[41]

Prompted by Smirnov, Markov also challenged the eyewitness testimony the commission had included in its report about Katyn. He told the Tribunal that he and the other commission members had been prevented from speaking with any witnesses to the massacre. On their arrival in Smolensk, they were handed typed depositions. Later, when they were in the Katyn wood, several Russians were brought to the gravesite "under German escort" and identified as the witnesses who had given the depositions. Professor Orsos had asked each witness several questions; the other commission members were not permitted to address them at all. Markov reminded the court that the depositions, the papers supposedly found on the corpses, and the skull produced by Professor Orsos were the entire basis for the commission's conclusion that the massacre had taken place in 1940. Real forensic data, he argued, was lacking.[42]

Smirnov then asked Markov the obvious question: Why had he signed the commission's report if he believed that it was inaccurate? Markov replied that he had had no choice. He described how the official protocol had been presented to the group during a stop at an isolated military airfield on the way back to Berlin, with a significant number of German military personnel present. All of the commission members had signed; Markov suggested that doing so had been understood to be a "condition of takeoff." Stahmer, during his cross-examination, asked Markov several times why he and the other commission members did not take steps later on to challenge or rectify the report. Markov stood firm. All of the members of the commission had been intimidated, he declared.[43]

Introducing the official protocol into evidence, Stahmer tried to shake Markov's allegation that it contained "few scientific details." He read a description of the decomposition of the bodies. It ended with the observation that "insects or remains of insects" were absent among the corpses, leading to the supposition that the victims had been killed and buried during "a season which was cold and free from insects." Markov stood by his assertion that concrete details about the condition of the corpses were scant. He further argued that the statement about the lack of insect remains was untrue. Some of the forensic experts, he explained, had indeed found insect remains and larvae in the mouths of the corpses. Stahmer asked Markov about the protocol's statement that the scientists had examined a large number of skulls. No, Markov insisted, the commission had only been shown a single skull. It was doubtful that Professor Orsos had examined a large number of skulls on his own, he added, "for he came with us and left with us."[44]

Markov had been convincing as a witness. As he left the witness box, Smirnov could relax a little. His first two witnesses had done exactly what was expected of them. The final Soviet witness, Prozorovsky, had signed the forensic report for the Burdenko Commission. Unlike Markov and

Bazilevsky, he had never collaborated with the Germans and his testimony could be counted on completely.

Once in the witness box, Prozorovsky told the court how he had worked with other Soviet physicians to exhume and examine 925 corpses in the Katyn wood in January 1944, soon after Soviet forces retook the area. His group had brought corpses from two large graves to the town of Smolensk and had thoroughly inspected them, with special attention given to their clothing. The corpses were then subjected to a complete forensic dissection of the skull, the chest, and the abdomen, in addition to the inner organs. The commission's findings, he testified, indicated that the corpses had been buried in the fall of 1941, when the Germans had control over the Katyn area.[45]

Prozorovsky reaffirmed the Soviet arguments about Katyn. He maintained that he had found letters and receipts in the pockets of the some of the corpses with dates from the summer of 1941, after the Soviets had left the region. He also told the court that the bullets that had killed the Polish officers were from German weapons. The Burdenko Commission had found cartridge cases embossed with the name of a German firm (Geco) during its exhumations. He explained that while he had only recently become acquainted with the term "pseudocallus," none of the experts who examined the 925 corpses had observed mineral deposits on any part of any of the skulls. Prozorovsky then gave a full accounting of the condition of the bodies and their vital organs (prompting Dodd to complain in a letter home that his testimony "sounded like a coroner's inquest"). Summing up, Prozorovsky stated that the forensic examinations, combined with the material evidence, had led to the commission's conclusion that the bodies could not have been buried before the fall of 1941. "The year 1940 is out of the question?" Smirnov asked. "Yes," Prozorovsky answered. "It is completely excluded."[46]

Determined to draw a link between Katyn and "other" Nazi atrocities, Smirnov asked Prozorovsky to relate his experiences as a forensic expert in other regions that had endured German occupation. Prozorovsky explained that in and around Smolensk he and his assistants had exhumed and examined 1,173 corpses in addition to those from Katyn. They had also exhumed more than 5,000 bodies in territories liberated from German occupation in and around Krasnodar, Kharkov, and Smolensk, as well as at Majdanek. The cause of death, according to Prozorovsky, was almost always the same: "a shot in the nape of the neck, at point-blank range," with an exit wound "on the forehead or in the face." During his cross-examination, Stahmer tried to get Prozorovsky to admit to even a small bit of uncertainty regarding the date of the shooting, but he was unshakable. When Prozorovsky stepped out of the witness box, both Stahmer and Smirnov asked to call additional witnesses. The judges turned them down. They had heard enough.[47]

The Soviets had done reasonably well in this contest with the defense, especially given the fact that they were engaging in an elaborate charade. The *New York Times* reported on each side's witness testimony as if it were all perfectly credible.[48] The *Times* of London concluded that the defense had failed to prove its innocence of the crime and reported in detail on the testimony of the Soviet forensic witnesses, Markov and Prozorovsky.[49] The Politburo Commission's fabrication of documentary evidence and careful preparation of witnesses had paid off. Furthermore, the Americans had ultimately come to the aid of the Soviets for the sake of the IMT, shutting down Stahmer's effort to challenge the Soviet witness testimony as scripted.

For anyone hoping for a huge public scandal, the two days in court would have felt anticlimactic. But for many members of the Soviet delegation, the German witnesses' testimony was eye-opening, making them question what they thought they knew about the war. The German witnesses had thrown reasonable doubt on the Soviet charges about Katyn, and the Soviet witnesses had not been able to fully undo the damage. In the eyes of most observers, the showdown had been a draw—which for all intents and purposes amounted to a Soviet loss.[50]

While we now have definitive evidence from the former Soviet archives of the NKVD's responsibility for the massacre, many questions still remain about who knew what when. How much did the Soviet prosecution know when its witnesses took the stand? It is all but certain that Rudenko and Smirnov both knew the truth, and Lev Sheinin (who was part of the Politburo Commission's Katyn subcommission) likely did as well. It is not clear, however, what the rest of the delegation knew about the Soviet fabrication of evidence. How much did the three Soviet witnesses know? The NKVD and the NKGB had tampered with the gravesites before the Soviet forensic experts arrived on the scene.[51] While Prozorovsky, a skilled forensic scientist, must have suspected the truth about the Soviet evidence, there is no proof that he was personally involved in generating it. Markov, who was a prisoner of the Soviets, probably knew with some degree of certainty that the NKVD had carried out the crime. As for Bazilevsky, his testimony was based on rumors and hearsay in any case—and German forces were responsible for many other atrocities committed against the Poles in the same region. Bazilevsky and Markov, both Nazi collaborators, had testified under duress; their ability to offer compelling testimony supporting the Soviet case was the only thing that was keeping them alive.

The American and British governments, even at this stage, had more reliable intelligence about the Katyn massacre than did some members of the Soviet prosecution in Nuremberg. Robert Jackson had long been in possession of evidence from the OSS that pointed to Soviet guilt. Given what the Americans almost certainly knew, their responses to the Katyn witness testimony come across as misleading and coy. Dodd reasoned in a letter to his wife that the Soviets and the Germans both "had motive" and speculated that they had "jointly" murdered the officers.[52] Taylor went out of his way in his memoir (published decades later) to give the Soviets the benefit of the doubt. "Circumstantially, the guilt for Katyn leaned heavily on the Soviet Union," he noted. However, he also reminded his readers that Hitler had used the SD to exterminate "the Polish intelligentsia, the nobility, the clergy, and in fact all elements which could be regarded as leaders of a national resistance" and that Katyn "was right in line with such purposes."[53] For the sake of appearances, and to preserve the legitimacy of the IMT, the American prosecutors clouded the question of guilt for the massacre. An acknowledgment of the Soviet lie about Katyn would have prompted challenges to the rest of the Soviet evidence and could have done irreparable damage to the credibility of the IMT as a whole.[54] It would also have raised uncomfortable questions about why the Western prosecutors had let the Soviets add the charge to the Indictment to begin with.[55]

In the wake of the Nuremberg Trials, the Poles, as well as Western critics of Nuremberg, would blame the Western governments for not holding the Soviets responsible for Katyn. And indeed, the Soviets never did stand trial for this atrocity. But in permitting the German defense to call witnesses about Katyn, and in allowing those witnesses to paint a picture of Soviet guilt in open court, the Western judges had taken the Soviets to task within the parameters the Tribunal would allow—and the Soviets knew it. The Soviet Union had suffered more devastation as a result of the war and the German occupation than the Western powers could truly imagine: it was impossible to fully grasp the idea of 27 million dead. The Soviets could also legitimately claim to have saved the world from Nazism. However, Soviet suffering, bravery, and sacrifice were far from everyone's minds during the Katyn testimony. As the Soviets struggled to prove that they had not murdered thousands of Polish prisoners of war, the characterization that settled on them was the one the defense had put forth: that of unindicted criminals.

The hearing of defense witnesses about Katyn did not, as the Western judges had hoped, put to rest arguments about victors' justice. On the contrary, questions about what constituted a fair trial were front and center as the defense began its closing arguments on July 4. Hermann Jahrreiss, assistant counsel for Alfred Jodl and an accomplished professor of international law, spoke for the defense as a whole—and asserted that the victors could not possibly reach a fair verdict so soon after the war. He further argued that the prosecution was trying to create law retroactively. There was no international law on the books "penalizing aggressive war," he maintained (repeating an argument that Goering and his attorney had made on the eve of the trials), and it was unheard of to prosecute individuals, even government and military leaders, for breaching "the peace between states."[56]

Stahmer and Martin Horn hit upon these same themes in their summations for Goering and Ribbentrop that afternoon and the following morning. Stahmer argued that a court of the victors violated the very notion of justice. Horn criticized what he called the Tribunal's double standard; he insisted that the IMT needed to consider the Soviet Union's partnership with Germany. Stahmer, not surprisingly, also used much of his summation to revisit the evidence about Katyn, dismissing the Soviet testimony as "worthless." He belatedly argued that the gravesite discovery of bullets "for pistols of German make" did not prove that Germans had carried out the massacre, for the factory that manufactured this ammunition had also shipped to other countries. Arguing that the Soviet prosecution had failed to prove its case about Katyn, Stahmer insisted that the charge "be struck from the Indictment."[57]

As the defense attorneys criticized the IMT, the Soviet Union and the United States were ramping up their propaganda campaigns against each other's foreign policies. The July 4 edition of *Izvestiia* accused the United States of embarking on a program of "economic penetration and military expansion." *Krasnaya zvezda* denounced the American atomic bomb tests in the Pacific as a "stimulus to an arms race" and accused the U.S. government of attempting "to dictate to the peoples of the world." The *New York Times* reported on the rise of anti-American feelings in the Soviet Union. It also continued its coverage of the Soviet takeover of governments in Eastern Europe.[58] The Americans and the Soviets in Nuremberg continued to socialize after hours, but the two sides were less indulgent of each other. During a muted Independence Day celebration, Francis Biddle joked to his Soviet colleagues that the Russians were new to making revolutions compared with the other countries of the prosecution and that they might come to the Americans to learn "how to do it right." Nikitchenko was not amused.[59]

Over the next three weeks the defense attorneys continued their summations, challenging the prosecution's evidence while repeatedly condemning the wartime policies of the Allied powers. Wilhelm Keitel's lawyer, Otto Nelte, argued that the USSR's Extraordinary State Commission reports contained eyewitness statements in which "hatred finds its clear expression" and thus could not be considered impartial. Fritz Sauckel's attorney, Robert Servatius, also questioned Soviet evidence when rebutting the charge that his client was responsible for the deaths of hundreds of thousands of Soviet prisoners of war. The case of Katyn, he argued, had demonstrated just how challenging it could be to determine the truth when such events were used as "weapons of propaganda."[60] Summing up for Ernst von Kaltenbrunner, Kurt Kauffman similarly alleged that "error and truth" were "mysteriously mixed" in the prosecution's evidence. He also reproached all the countries of the prosecution for shrugging off responsibility for killing millions of noncombatant women and children in air raids. Even in a defensive war, he argued, the victorious side should not try to excuse such actions.[61]

Alfred Seidl added to this chorus in his closing for Hans Frank, declaring that "considerably more than a million" civilians had died as a result of Allied bombing raids over Germany. He also pointed to the U.S. use of atomic bombs against Japan, which had "razed Hiroshima and Nagasaki to the ground and killed hundreds of thousands of people." In an attempt to refute the prosecution's characterization of German deportations as criminal, Seidl called out the postwar policies of the victors. More than ten million Germans had been deported from their "ancestral" homes in Silesia and the Sudetenland alone in keeping with an Allied resolution from Potsdam, he noted. Rudenko protested once more that Allied policy had no relevance to the case. His objection was upheld by the judges—even as other defense counsel continued to revisit this topic.[62] The resettlement question was particularly sensitive for the Soviets, who were themselves carrying out deportations throughout Eastern Europe and were in the process of expelling tens of thousands of Poles from the Soviet Union, whose borders now included former parts of Poland.[63]

In its summations, the defense was keen to highlight the hypocrisies of all four countries of the prosecution. Arthur Seyss-Inquart's lawyer, Gustav Steinbauer, noted that the recent French Constitution (which had been submitted to the National Assembly in April 1946) had ruled against retroactive law. Could there really be different "Rights of Man" for the French than for the Germans? Jodl's main attorney, Franz Exner, declared that it was ridiculous for the prosecution to accuse his client of participating in a conspiracy against Poland considering what everyone now knew about the "German-Russian Secret Treaty."[64] Seidl, too, invoked the secret protocols in his summation for Hess.[65]

The summations came to a close on Thursday afternoon, July 25. That evening the Soviets hosted a dinner party for the prosecutors and the judges "with all kinds of vodka and plenty of it," as Dodd noted in a letter home.[66]

All four delegations welcomed the end of the defense case, which had lasted far longer than anyone had anticipated and had repeatedly challenged the legitimacy of the trials. Everyone was weary. The prosecutors and the judges were also all too aware of the dispute among their governments about the fate of postwar Germany. The U.S. and British governments were taking steps toward the merger of their occupation zones. The Soviets and the French, fearing a resurgent Germany, opposed this—pointing out that the process of denazification had only just gotten under way. Moscow was accusing the British and the Americans of harboring "Gestapo executioners and SS men" in their parts of Germany.[67] The wartime alliance was on its last legs. It seemed high time to finish the trials and go home.

Of course, a great deal of work remained to be done, including the hearing of the defense witnesses for the indicted organizations. First, though, the prosecution would step back in to make its final arguments against the former Nazi leaders. The order and the scope of these speeches had been the subject of negotiations among the prosecutors over the past month, some of them quite tense. Rudenko wanted the Soviets to have the last word here, but also worried about the Americans and the British once again stealing his thunder. He had suggested that the closing speeches follow the same order as the opening speeches, with the stipulation that each prosecutor only recap the arguments and evidence presented by his own delegation.[68] Maxwell Fyfe had assured Rudenko that the British "would not for a moment contemplate infringing" on the Soviet delegation's part of the case. He had also solicited Rudenko's support for his own proposal to give Hartley Shawcross the first closing speech. Rudenko had agreed—but Jackson had balked at this idea. Ultimately, Jackson prevailed on all fronts: the closing speeches would follow the same order as the opening speeches, and each chief prosecutor could speak to any or even all of the charges.[69]

On the morning of July 26, Jackson was still making revisions to his speech. He continued to hone the text on the drive to the Palace of Justice.[70] Every sentence had to resonate; it had to be perfect. On arriving he saw that the courtroom was packed and the atmosphere expectant.

Jackson was in his element—a trial lawyer about to deliver his closing on the case of a lifetime. He strode to the rostrum and boldly defended the right of the victors to judge the vanquished. Germany had surrendered, "but no peace treaty had been signed," he declared. The IMT, as a military tribunal, marked the final phase of the Allied war effort. At the same time, Jackson trumpeted the righteousness of the victors, who, he again reminded everyone, had given the defendants "the kind of a trial which, they, in the days of their pomp and power, never gave to any man." Future generations would never have to wonder what the Nazis could have said in their defense, he continued. "History will know that whatever could be said, they were allowed to say."

As expected, Jackson focused much of his address on the conspiracy charge (Count One of the Indictment), describing how each defendant had played his part to advance a "common plan" to transform Europe. Jackson characterized crimes against peace as the chief crimes of the defendants—and argued that war crimes and crimes against humanity were subordinate to, but also essential to, Hitler's plans to wage war. The slave labor program had served industry and agriculture, and these in turn had supported the military machine; the concentration camps, which were supplied by the Gestapo, had buoyed the war industry. He also argued that the persecution of the Jews had been integral to Nazi war plans. Initially, Hitler used anti-Semitism to stir up the German people; later, the Jews were used as slave labor for the war effort.[71]

Jackson, who believed that the United States had an essential role to play in postwar Europe, did not spare the feelings of his British and French colleagues in his speech. He blamed European policies of the 1920s and 1930s for spurring the rise of the Nazi Party. At the same time, he insisted that this was irrelevant, for the Tribunal had not been convened to try "the motives, hopes, or frustrations" that may have led Germany to invade its neighbors. The victors could admit that the Treaty of Versailles had created terrible problems for Germany; they could even acknowledge that the world had not provided Germany with solutions that were "honorable and acceptable alternatives to war." But this did not change the criminality of "aggressive war," he argued, making an argument very similar to the one put forward by Aron Trainin years earlier. Jackson again invoked the 1930s when dismissing the defense's claims about preventive war. Germany had faced a Europe that not only was "unwilling to attack," he noted, but had gone to the "verge of dishonor, if not beyond, to buy its peace."[72]

After addressing the crimes and moral failings of the individual defendants—giving them Homeric epithets such as "the duplicitous Ribbentrop," "the fanatical Frank," "Kaltenbrunner, the grand inquisitor," "Rosenberg, the intellectual high priest of the 'master race,'" and so on—Jackson closed his speech on a note intended to remind everyone what was at stake. The Tribunal must find the defendants guilty. To do otherwise would be as if to declare "that there has been no war, there are no slain, there has been no crime."[73] His words had their desired effect. British officer Airey Neave, who had thought Jackson "ineffectual" as a cross-examiner, found the speech "magnificent." Complimenting it but also acknowledging its deliberate the-atricality, he remarked on how it evoked "the atmosphere of a Hollywood trial."[74]

Shawcross began the British closing speech later that afternoon by taking pains to distance Great Britain from the other countries of the prosecution. He told the court that each delegation had prepared its remarks independ-ently so that the Tribunal and their own countries "might know exactly the grounds on which we seek the condemnation of these men." The British and the Americans, in spite of their close relationship, had different ideas about the core aims of Nazism. Whereas Jackson emphasized the unpro-voked military assault on Europe as the main offense, Shawcross argued that the defendants' gravest crime was their "cold, calculated, deliberate attempt to destroy nations and races." Here he spoke of murder committed in the manner of "some mass production industry" in the concentration camps. He also condemned the revival of slavery in Europe, whereby civilians were "taken from their homes, treated as beasts, starved, beaten, and murdered."[75]

Answering the appeals made by Raphael Lemkin, Bohuslav Ečer, and other Eastern European jurists—and elaborating on the argument Maxwell Fyfe had made when cross-examining Konstantin von Neurath—Shawcross used the term "genocide" to describe the Nazis' "deliberate and systematic plan" to wipe out peoples and cultures. He revisited the evidence about the Einsatzgruppen and about Auschwitz. But he also reminded the Tribunal that genocide had not been limited to the murder of Jews and Gypsies. (This was a point that the Soviets had been making since before the start of the trials—minus the term "genocide.") Shawcross emphasized that the Nazis had pursued genocide "in different forms" in Poland, the Soviet Union, Yugoslavia, Czechoslovakia, and Alsace-Lorraine. The method applied to the Polish intelligentsia, he noted, was "outright annihilation," whereas in Alsace, deportation was the program of choice. In the German-occupied Soviet Union, the technique was death by starvation; in Bohemia and Moravia, the Nazis embarked on a policy of forced Germanization.[76]

Jackson and Shawcross had shifted world attention back to the sheer enormity of Nazi crimes. The *Times* of London reported that the IMT would be remembered for its "examination of the crime of 'genocide,' the new conception in law of which Nuremberg will remain the fount."[77] Concerns about victors' justice nonetheless remained. It did not help that over the past several days the international press had been filled with accounts of the Soviet pillaging of Eastern Europe; one article reported that the Red Army was systematically stripping Hungary "of essential food and indus-trial materials."[78] Dodd noted in a letter home that during the first two closing speeches he had found himself mulling over not just Soviet but also British hypocrisy, thinking about what had happened in Ireland in the recent past as well as in other British colonies, and "what is probably still happening in India."[79] Dodd, like many other Americans, was enamored of the idea of American exceptionalism—conveniently forgetting his own country's history of slavery and imperialism, as well as its treatment of Native Americans.

On Monday, July 29, the French prosecution delivered its closing remarks in Nuremberg, just as the Paris Peace Conference was getting under way in France. Auguste Champetier de Ribes confronted the accusations of victors' justice directly, emphasizing that the Tribunal had excluded anything that "might have appeared to be dictated by a spirit of vengeance." In the name of historical truth, it had chronicled not just Nazi crimes but also "the ir-resolution, the weaknesses, the omissions of the peace-loving democracies." Like Shawcross, he highlighted the crime of genocide, but he stayed closer to the definition in the Indictment—emphasizing the "scientific and system-atic" nature of the Nazis' efforts to exterminate those groups whose existence "hampered the hegemony of the Germanic race." This attempt to eliminate entire peoples was a crime "so monstrous," he added, that a new term had been required in order to describe it.[80]

Charles Dubost gave the rest of the French summation, elaborating on the role of genocide in the Nazi conspiracy. The defendants had participated in the crime of "genocide" with the goal of Lebensraum, he argued, and all of their other crimes were a means to this end. He then addressed each de-fendant, explaining how his crimes fit into the united criminal plan. Goering had not only prepared the way for war but had also founded the concentra-tion camps, where "genocide was almost totally achieved." Ribbentrop had pursued German living space through conquest and through "acts of ter-rorism and extermination" in the countries Germany had occupied. Dubost, who like de Vabres was envisioning a leading role for France in the postwar development of international criminal law, then waxed philosophical about law and politics. Those who had attempted to dispute the Tribunal's legit-imacy had forgotten that jurisprudence evolves over time, he argued. Here he put forward a passionate plea for the creation of new international law as well as a "superstate organization" that could check state sovereignty and thus protect the rights of individuals.[81] Dubost's vision received a mixed re-ception in the international community. However, it deeply resonated with international-law experts at the conference in Paris who wanted to see a more expansive role for the new United Nations and new legislation on human rights.

Rudenko began his closing address that afternoon, delivering a speech that had been carefully prepared with the help of the Vyshinsky Commission. During the previous few months, Gorshenin and Vyshinsky had corresponded via secret channels about the speech's content.[82] Now, speaking before the court, Rudenko proclaimed "aggressive war" to be the chief crime of the former Nazi leaders. He, like Jackson—and in contrast to Shawcross and Dubost—argued that all of the defendants' criminal activities had been directed toward this aim.

Whereas Shawcross had tried to establish distance between the victors, Rudenko spoke of their shared values as "peace-loving" and "freedom-loving" nations. This was a strategic move on the part of the Soviets, an attempt to counter their previous isolation and shift the focus away from their collaboration with Germany. Rudenko (again echoing Jackson) then emphasized the justness of the trial, which had given the defendants every opportunity to defend themselves. Showing solidarity with the British and French prosecutions and with jurists like Ečer, Rudenko used the term "genocide" in his presentation—needless to say, a deliberate choice on the part of Soviet leaders. He referenced it just once, when upholding the right of the Allied nations "to punish those who made enslavement and genocide their aim."[83] (Debate about the meaning and usefulness of the term "genocide" would soon take place at the USSR's Ministry of Foreign Affairs behind closed doors.)

Rudenko hit hard at the defense's legal challenges, calling them a "smoke screen" for the terrible truth about the defendants' crimes. He also dismissed the defense's assertion that the prosecution, in calling out the defendants for not standing up to Hitler, did not understand the nature of the Nazi state. The authors of the Nuremberg Charter had learned all about Hitler's Germany as a result of the Kharkov Trial and other war crimes trials, he emphasized, and this was why they had specified that obeying a superior's orders "does not exonerate one from criminal responsibility." Regarding the defense's attempt to portray the invasion of the Soviet Union as a preventive attack, Rudenko declared this too absurd to further waste the Tribunal's time. Rudenko also threw out the defense's claims that individuals could not be held responsible for state crimes. Paraphrasing Trainin, who had explored this question in depth in *The Criminal Responsibility of the Hitlerites*, he noted that individuals always acted on behalf of the state in international relations and thus could be found "guilty of the most varied offenses."[84]

The most notable aspect of Rudenko's speech was its almost complete omission of Katyn. An earlier draft of the speech had included a long passage about the massacre, reasserting German responsibility for it and condemning the defense's efforts to cover it up. In the end, Moscow had deleted this section altogether.[85] Rudenko did briefly invoke Katyn, but only in passing, when summing up the evidence against Hans Frank.[86]

Much of Rudenko's speech, like Jackson's and Dubost's, was spent explicating the role of each defendant in the fascist conspiracy—but here the focus was specifically on the war in the East. Rudenko highlighted Ribbentrop's "primary part" in preparing the invasion of the Soviet Union. He also detailed the roles of the defendants in crimes against humanity and war crimes that were carried out in Soviet or Eastern European territories. Seyss-Inquart and Frank had personally conducted a campaign of terror in Poland; Walther Funk had turned the Reichbank's vaults into "depositories for the treasures plundered by the SS men" in the East. Rudenko gave special attention to Sauckel, who had insisted that the Germans had recruited only voluntary labor. This was a terrible slander against the millions of people who had been forcibly deported to labor in Hitler's Germany, he argued. Rudenko concluded his speech on Tuesday morning, July 30, by asking the Tribunal to sentence all of the defendants to death.[87]

Rudenko's speech ended a challenging month for the Soviets at Nuremberg. Now, just as the cases of the individual defendants were wrapping up, Dubost passed on to Rudenko a curious document supporting Soviet charges of German guilt for Katyn: the May 1946 interrogation of a Dutch mechanic, relating his wartime conversations with an Austrian soldier. In December 1944, the soldier, who supposedly had connections in high places, had told the mechanic that the murders had been committed by the Germans.[88] This latest Katyn document was too little too late—and, as hearsay, it would not have helped the Soviets press their claims in any case. In sharing it with Rudenko, Dubost was signaling French sympathy and support.

As the fates of the defendants remained undetermined, the balance of the postwar order did as well. Ideas and arguments about victors' justice, genocide, and human rights that were articulated in the Palace of Justice would soon shape discussions at the United Nations about "the Nuremberg principles" (as they would come to be called) and the future of international law. Soviet frustration with the IMT would affect Moscow's feelings about the efficacy of international courts and other international institutions well into the future. The Soviet Union's difficulties managing its message on the international stage would prompt Soviet leaders, including Vyshinsky and Lozovsky, to deliberate on how best to transform the Soviet Union's legal, propaganda, and foreign-policy institutions to meet the challenges of the Cold War.

All of this was yet to come. The Tribunal still had to reach its judgment and decide on the verdicts. And even before that it had another critical matter to assess: the question of organizational guilt.

PART IV | Last Words and Judgments

CHAPTER 13 | Collective Guilt and the Fate
of Postwar Europe

B Y THE END of July, just about everyone in Nuremberg had grown impatient with the pace of the trials. Rebecca West reflected that the courtroom by the ninth month had become "a citadel of boredom"—not because the work of the Tribunal was unimportant but because the lawyers, the judges, the guards, and the interpreters had all become exhausted by their "perpetual confrontation" with a terrible episode of history that "everyone wants to forget."[1] The Soviet interpreter Tatiana Stupnikova and her colleagues spent idle moments composing and quietly singing little ditties on this theme: "It's time to finish, we want to go home!"[2]

After many months focused on individual defendants with oversized personalities such as Hermann Goering and Albert Speer, the Tribunal had returned to the organizations case. Over the next couple of weeks it would hear defense witnesses and closing arguments for the Leadership Corps of the Nazi Party, the Gestapo, the SD, the SA, the SS, the Reich Cabinet, and the military's General Staff and High Command. The organizations case felt like an afterthought to many in Nuremberg. Nonetheless, it went to the heart of the IMT—and its outcome had the potential to affect postwar Europe far more than did the individual verdicts against the former Nazi leaders. For each organization, a finding of criminal responsibility by the Tribunal would open the door to national trials of its members, ultimately touching many millions of lives.[3]

From Moscow's perspective, the hearing of defense witnesses for the organizations carried risks without rewards. The Soviets took it as a given that the Nazi organizations were guilty; they had long been arresting former SS members and Gestapo agents in their occupation zone of Germany and conscripting them for forced labor. At the London Conference a year earlier, Nikitchenko and Trainin had reluctantly agreed to the American plan to try organizations, won over by Jackson's argument that this was the most efficient way to proceed against as many war criminals as possible. But there had been a wrinkle. The Nuremberg Charter had stipulated, also at American insistence, that former members of these organizations could request a hearing before the Tribunal—and to everyone's astonishment, thousands of Germans had petitioned to testify in court.[4]

The idea of collective guilt had become a hot political issue in America and Europe over the course of the winter, after the U.S. prosecution had finished presenting its evidence against the indicted organizations before the Tribunal. The realization that the Tribunal could issue blanket rulings of guilt had shocked many people. Rumors had spread that the Soviets were planning to use declarations of organizational guilt at Nuremberg to justify mass reprisals in their zone of Germany and throughout Eastern Europe.[5] Playing to these fears, the defense had pressed the Tribunal to dismiss the organizations case—making the argument that trying organizations was unheard of in international law.

In late February and early March the Tribunal had considered the defense's request. The entire prosecution had stood together to insist that the trial of the organizations go forward. The Soviets had never liked the organizations case, but they understood that tossing it out at this late stage of the trials would be a tremendous victory for the defense. Jackson, speaking for the four chief prosecutors, had argued that the indicted organizations were a "continuing menace" to peace and that it would be a "far greater catastrophe" to let them off the hook than to acquit the individual Nazi leaders. Putting aside his own worries about the unleashing of a Soviet reign of terror, he had assured the judges that large numbers of Germans and Eastern Europeans would not be summarily rounded up and put behind bars if the Tribunal declared an organization to be guilty. National courts would still have to try individuals for their alleged membership and participation.

The defense had countered that it was disingenuous to suggest that the members of an organization would be able to exonerate themselves following a declaration of organizational guilt. Millions of people would stand trial with only the remotest chance of clearing their names. Ludwig Babel, one of the lawyers for the SS, had warned that Germany would be devastated.

Former members of these organizations and their families would be ruined, personally and financially.[6]

The judges had probed the prosecutors about the relationship between collective guilt and individual criminal responsibility. Were all members of an organization equally guilty? Could an individual claim before a national court that he did not know the true aims of a criminal organization and was thus innocent of its crimes? Rudenko had allowed that there could be individuals who had been tricked or forced into joining an organization and that this might be grounds for their exoneration. He had emphasized that it would be up to the national courts to decide. Jackson, who understood the Western judges' concerns and was anxious to get this matter settled, had suggested that the Tribunal could itself narrow the circle of guilt in its rulings by applying the finding of criminality to only those subsets of each organization that had actively furthered its goals. His proposal had infuriated Rudenko. Moscow was strongly opposed to the Tribunal preemptively limiting the scope of collective guilt or putting any restrictions on the national courts. Babel and his colleagues, on the other hand, took heart; Jackson had inadvertently helped them to formulate their defense.

The organizations case had turned into a legal and logistical nightmare. Abandoning it, however, would have invalidated part of the Nuremberg Charter and thrown into question one of the main premises of the trials, an even more terrifying scenario. Instead, the Tribunal had pushed ahead that spring and called for the screening of witnesses to testify in defense of the organizations. Defense counsel visited eighty Allied internment camps in Germany and selected 603 people to consider bringing to Nuremberg for further questioning. (They did not visit Soviet internment camps, having received only a couple of applications from the Soviet zone—where identifying oneself as a former Nazi would have meant certain arrest.[7]) The Tribunal organized two four-power commissions, which interviewed witnesses in side rooms of the Palace of Justice while the defense case proceeded in the primary courtroom.[8] By late July, these commissions had heard over a hundred witnesses and had reviewed summaries of some 50,000 affidavits. The judges and the defense ultimately settled on a list of twenty-two witnesses to be called on in open court. The Western judges wanted to demonstrate to the German people that they would be dealt with fairly. From the Soviet perspective, though, the Tribunal was being dangerously indulgent toward war criminals.[9] August would be a long month.

Given the stakes for Europe's future, the hearing of defense witnesses for the Leadership Corps of the Nazi Party began with remarkably little ado on the morning of July 30, immediately after Rudenko concluded the prosecution's case against the individual defendants. With Rudenko's cry for justice still ringing in people's ears, Tribunal president Lawrence quietly signaled for the organizations case to resume.

Defense attorney Robert Servatius (who was also representing Sauckel) called the first of his five witnesses for the Leadership Corps of the Nazi Party. The organization had included between 600,000 and two million members, depending on which subgroups were counted. Servatius was well aware that the Western judges had reservations about sweeping verdicts—and he was aiming to narrow the circle of guilt to as small a subset of the organization as possible. His witnesses testified that the Leadership Corps had not been the tightly knit group the prosecution described. They further maintained that the so-called lower Party leaders, such as the Kreisleiter and Blockleiter (district and neighborhood leaders), had lacked any kind of political or police authority and had focused primarily on improving the welfare of the local population.[10]

The British had sole responsibility for cross-examining these witnesses. Maxwell Fyfe confronted them with fresh evidence of the Leadership Corps's responsibility for war crimes, including the murder of Allied parachutists who landed on German soil. Assistant prosecutor Mervyn Griffith-Jones challenged the notion that the lower Party leaders had devoted themselves to social work, presenting proof that Kreisleiter had informed on their neighbors and attacked members of the political opposition in the early 1930s, facilitating Hitler's rise to power. Before this part of the case wrapped up, Soviet assistant prosecutor Mark Raginsky received permission from the Tribunal to further rebut the witness testimony with new documents from Yugoslavia's war crimes commission showing the role of Kreisleiter in forcefully Germanizing Northern Slovenia—a crime that (if the Tribunal accepted Maxwell Fyfe's courtroom argument of a few months earlier) could fall under the heading of genocide.[11]

Stupnikova and the other Soviet interpreters struggled to translate the witness testimony for the Leadership Corps, uncertain how to render the names of the different ranks—Gauleiter, Kreisleiter, Ortsgruppenleiter, Zellenleiter, and Blockleiter. There were simply no equivalents in Russian. Yet in other respects the Leadership Corps reminded them uncomfortably of the Communist Party of the USSR. "None of us, finding ourselves in a foreign country . . . at the Nuremberg Trials, wanted to make this comparison," Stupnikova later wrote. "This comparison sprang up of its own accord." Soviet leaders, for their part, had wanted to make it crystal clear that there were no similarities between the Soviet Union and Nazi Germany and had forbidden the interpreters from using the word "socialist" to refer to the Nazi Party. Whenever the term "national-socialist" sounded in the interpreters' headphones, they were obliged to translate it using a different term, such as "German-fascist."[12] This was not simply paranoia on the part of the Soviets. American policymakers, journalists, and academics were by now characterizing the political systems of both countries as "totalitarian."[13]

Connections between the Soviet Union and Nazi Germany—and similarities between Soviet and Nazi organizations—remained on everybody's mind as the Tribunal turned next to the Gestapo, Hitler's secret police. Those members of the Soviet delegation who were in the know about the joint Soviet-German invasion of Poland in 1939 had extra reason to be on edge during the Gestapo defense. After the Wehrmacht and the Red Army had moved in, the Gestapo and the NKVD had both acted to crush Polish resistance.[14]

Beginning on Wednesday, July 31, defense attorney Rudolf Merkel questioned two witnesses in court: Werner Best (who had run the Gestapo office on legal affairs) and Karl Hoffmann (who had headed the Gestapo in Denmark). Both emphasized the compulsory nature of Gestapo membership, arguing that police officials and administrators from all over Germany had been conscripted and forced to serve. Hoffmann tried to clear the Gestapo of blame for some of the most heinous crimes associated with its name: he argued that Adolf Eichmann's Department for Jewish Affairs, which had overseen the extermination of Europe's Jews, had operated apart from the rest of the organization. Best admitted that the Gestapo had carried out executions and deportations, but—reaching toward a defense of "superior orders"—he told the court that any Gestapo member who did not follow directives risked being court-martialed and sentenced to death. Both witnesses stressed, in their own efforts to narrow the circle of guilt, that only some Gestapo members had worked as agents; according to Best, the Gestapo's technical personnel (drivers, typists, janitors, and the like) had been completely in the dark as to the "facts and reasons" behind their work.[15]

To the relief of the Soviets, the topic of Soviet-German collaboration was not broached during the Gestapo defense. Instead, the prosecution's cross-examinations of Best and Hoffman brought into the court record new evidence of the Gestapo's crimes against Soviet prisoners of war. The U.S. prosecution confronted Best with documents proving that Gestapo agents had sought out Soviet prisoners of war who were officers, communists, or Jews, declared them "intolerable," and consigned them to die in Dachau.[16]

When the Gestapo case wrapped up on August 1, defense attorney Hans Gawlik (another former Nazi) called witnesses for the SD, which from 1931 onward had served as the main intelligence and security agency of the SS and the Nazi Party. The prosecution had initially treated the Gestapo and the SD as a single organization, but Gawlik had convinced the Tribunal to (at least temporarily) uncouple them. His witnesses now strove to depict the SD as a benign organization whose role had been limited to collecting public-opinion data. Former SD official Rolf-Heinz Hoeppner testifed that, unlike the Gestapo, the SD had not conducted brutal interrogations or used police methods to gather information. He further insisted that the SD had no connection to paramilitary organizations like the SS or the Einsatzgruppen.[17]

Lev Smirnov took a crack at Hoeppner the following morning, determined to prove that the SD had been deeply involved in Hitler's plans to take over Europe. He introduced documents captured by the Red Army showing that in June 1938, three months before the Munich Pact, Hitler had drawn up directives for the SD to participate in the military assault on Czechoslovakia by fighting partisans in the rear. These orders were so specific that they included provisions for Czech language training and dictionaries. Wasn't this proof that the SD had taken part in planning for the invasion? Hoeppner would not agree, insisting that any SD members who were assigned to Einsatzgruppen had ceased to be members of the SD itself.[18]

The march of the German witnesses, with their attestations of ignorance, innocence, and duress, continued that afternoon as the Tribunal turned to the Reich Cabinet. This was the smallest of the indicted organizations, made up of only thirty to forty members, mostly government ministers. Defense attorney Egon Kubuschok (who was also representing Papen) called just one witness, former minister of justice Franz Schlegelberger, who testified that from March 1933 onward the Reich Cabinet had completely lacked agency. U.S. assistant prosecutor Robert Kempner successfully refuted this claim by getting Schlegelberger to admit that the Reich ministers had continued to pass legislation even without formal sessions. Kempner then produced a legislative proposal Schlegelberger had personally signed in 1942 calling for the sterilization of "all half-Jews in Germany and the occupied territories." Schlegelberger claimed that his motive had been a noble one: to save part-Jews from being sent to labor camps in Poland. Lawrence intervened and immediately cut to the point: "What I understand is that the conditions in the working camps in Poland were, in your opinion, such that it would be preferable for half-Jews to be sterilized?" Schlegelberger replied yes.[19] It looked like a victory for the prosecution.

The Soviet press gave little coverage to this first week of witness testimony for the organizations case, seeing no reason to bring the defense's arguments to the Soviet people. *Pravda* and *Izvestiia* used the space to reprint Rudenko's July 30 closing speech and to recap the charges against all of the individual defendants. The Soviet newspapers also gave front-page coverage to the Paris Peace Conference, where Molotov and Vyshinsky were participating in deliberations about the future of Italy, Hungary, Finland, Bulgaria, and Romania.[20] France's president, Georges Bidault (the former foreign minister), had opened the conference by calling for "an effective peace" to guard against future aggression.[21] It was still unclear to everyone what that peace would look like. The former wartime allies continued to have conflicting ideas about all kinds of issues, from denazification—which presumably would be furthered via declarations of guilt in the organizations case—to the postwar balance of power. These issues were on everyone's minds during the conference, given that Hungary, Bulgaria, and Romania were all under Soviet occupation.

It was by now abundantly clear that the four-power alliance was under considerable strain at Nuremberg. As the Soviet Union, France, Great Britain, and the United States tried to conclude the organizations case, plans for subsequent four-power trials of German war criminals collapsed. Back in November, and sporadically since then, there had been talk of convening a second international tribunal in Europe to bring the German industrialists to justice. Jackson, who could not stomach the thought of further cooperation with the Soviets, vehemently opposed such a trial. Meeting with Secretary of State Byrnes in Paris, he warned that the different economic philosophies and policies of the Soviet Union and the West would present an insurmountable hurdle.[22] The *New York Times*, covering the American change of heart about a four-power trial of industrialists, reported that the Soviets were already expropriating "large enterprises and large fortunes" in their zone of Germany "on the assumption that the owners must be Fascist."[23] The implication was clear: the Soviets would not approach an industrialists' trial in good faith.

The U.S. occupation government in Germany shared Jackson's opposition to future four-power trials, recommending instead separate "zonal trials" under agreed-on policies.[24] By now all of the Allied powers were conducting their own trials of rank-and-file war criminals and collaborators, and the Americans were actively preparing for a trial of Nazi medical doctors. But from Moscow's perspective, the industrialists' case was different. Most of the German industrialists who had backed Hitler were in American and British custody, and the Soviets as well as the French had been expecting to have a role in bringing them to justice.[25] The Soviets also remained eager to use an industrialists' case to make a bigger point about the capitalist underpinnings of fascism.

In reaction to this shift in the American position, the Soviets again invoked the specter of a capitalist conspiracy, denouncing the U.S. government for attempting to prevent a "full revelation of the ties" between Nazi and American industrialists.[26] They also charged American and British authorities with illegally stripping enterprises in their own occupation zones, including aviation plants that the Allied Control Council had designated for joint reparations.[27] The latter charge was just the latest volley in the escalating dispute between the Soviet Union and the Americans about reparations, with each side accusing the other of not living up to the terms set out in the Potsdam Agreement. Moscow was still angry about the American refusal to release promised reparations deliveries from its occupation zone until questions about Germany's economic and political future were settled.[28] The Truman administration, in turn, charged the Soviets with failing to provide for the most basic needs of the Germans living in their zone.

The international press trumpeted the story of the disintegrating Soviet-American relationship as the SS defense began on Saturday August 3. The Soviet correspondents, meanwhile, refocused their attention on the action in the courtroom, hopeful that there would be a story to bring back to the Soviet people. The SS, a paramilitary force and a bureaucracy unto itself, was the most notorious of the Nazi organizations on trial. The prosecution had provided overwhelming evidence against the SS back in December and January. Rumors had spread that another witness for the prosecution was now waiting in the wings.

Defense attorney Horst Pelckmann, a Berlin lawyer, called the first of the six witnesses he had selected from the many thousands of SS men who had asked to speak for their organization in court. Adopting a now-familiar defense strategy, he attempted to refute the prosecution's characterization of the SS as a unified whole, hoping to provide an opening for parts of the organization to escape the umbrella of collective guilt. His first witness, SS Gruppenführer Friedrich von Eberstein, testified that the General SS had been completely separate from the Waffen-SS and had had nothing to do with running the concentration camps. Eberstein was adamant that the General SS was innocent of atrocities; he even claimed to have used his own position to end Dr. Sigmund Rascher's notorious biological experiments at Dachau. British assistant prosecutor Frederick Elwyn Jones took apart Eberstein's story, presenting evidence that Rascher's experiments had continued through the end of the war. He then introduced a pile of new documents implicating the General SS in war crimes and crimes against humanity. One of the documents described how SS men had guarded secret labor camps where tens of thousands of Jews were put to work manufacturing armaments. Eberstein feebly claimed ignorance.[29]

The next two defense witnesses spoke for the Waffen-SS and similarly argued for its separation from the rest of the SS—but on the grounds that it had been a regular military division that had answered to the Wehrmacht. It was unjust, they insisted, to treat Waffen-SS men more harshly than rank-and-file soldiers. Smirnov demolished this claim by producing evidence of the deep level of Waffen-SS involvement in the concentration camps. He read from a Waffen-SS directive detailing the "proper way" to shave and process the hair of inmates to produce felt for the German navy.[30] Smirnov and Elwyn Jones both questioned one of the Waffen-SS witnesses, Generaloberst Paul Hauser, about the Prinz Eugen Division, which had gained infamy for its role in the destruction of Lidice. They also confronted Hauser with graphic evidence of atrocities carried out by this division during another campaign, in Croatia. Smirnov produced a photograph of the severed heads of Slovene partisans and announced that the victims had been decapitated by the SS. Such images still had the ability to shock. Pelckmann fell back on the tu quoque ("you did it too") defense, asking Hauser if he had heard about similar atrocities being carried out by the Red Army. Rudenko strenuously objected and berated the defense for continuing to spread fascist propaganda and lies. The Tribunal declared Pelckmann's question inadmissible.[31]

The SS defense seemed to go on forever. In a letter home on August 6, Thomas Dodd, who was filling in for Jackson in Nuremberg, blamed the British prosecution for having "slowed things down."[32] That same day, Maxwell Fyfe related in a letter to his wife that "the happy thought" of wrapping things up by August 17 was "not going to work out."[33] All four delegations were desperate to leave Nuremberg. But, as in earlier parts of the trials, they were each unwilling to cut short their own cross-examinations, acting on the premise that every defense claim—no matter how absurd—must be refuted for the historical record.

The remaining SS defense witnesses, meanwhile, took up another day and a half spinning such fantastical stories of their innocence and of the superb conditions at Buchenwald (complete with a cinema, a library, gardens, and even a brothel) that some of the prosecutors burst out laughing.[34] Aron Trainin watched the SS case from the Soviet prosecution's table. One wonders what was going through his mind as one SS witness after another entered the witness box. Did his thoughts go back to the London Conference of August 1945 and to his and Nikitchenko's efforts to prevent such witness testimony? Did he recall Jackson's and Maxwell Fyfe's assurances that no SS witness would dare come forward to testify for fear of arrest? No doubt there was little that surprised Trainin by this point in the trials—but even so, the audacity of these witnesses must have been shocking.

On Thursday, August 8, the prosecution finally had a chance to re-assert some control over the proceedings. The British called Wolfram Sievers, who had headed a Nazi research institute (the SS-Ahnenerbe or Ancestral Heritage Research Institute). While testifying before one of the

FIGURE 13.1 Aron Trainin sat with Roman Rudenko and other members of the Soviet prosecution during the organizations case, August 1946. Trainin is second from the front on the left side of the table; Rudenko is at the corner of the table, front right; Lev Smirnov is to Rudenko's right.

Credit: United States Holocaust Memorial Museum, courtesy of National Archives and Records Administration, College Park.

four-power commissions in the spring, Sievers had claimed ignorance about Rascher's experiments on concentration camp inmates. The British had since received documents from Himmler's files revealing that Sievers had lied, and the Tribunal had agreed to his reexamination in court. Sievers, nicknamed the "Nazi Bluebeard" by the international press because of his fierce countenance (and ink-black beard), betrayed no emotion in the witness box.[35] He stared straight ahead even as Elwyn Jones produced his diary—which described vaccine research, blood coagulation studies, and attempts to freeze and thaw living human beings. Elwyn Jones got Sievers to admit that the scientists who conducted these experiments at Dachau were SS men; he then used other evidence to connect the scientists to Goering, who had headed the Reich Research Council. Elwyn Jones also questioned Sievers about his part in procuring the skulls of "Jewish-Bolshevik commissars" for Nazi research, meeting his denials with letters between Himmler and Eichmann implicating him as a middleman.[36] The major Soviet newspapers printed long excerpts of Sievers's testimony verbatim. There was no need for commentary; the lurid details spoke for themselves.

When the Soviet lawyer Arkady Poltorak arrived at the Palace of Justice on the morning of August 8 he immediately noticed that there were more American soldiers and officers in the courtroom than usual. The U.S. secretary of war, Robert P. Patterson, occupied a prime seat in the visitors' gallery, surrounded by a small group of generals. The General Staff and High Command of the Wehrmacht was the next organization on the docket—and the case against it was highly controversial.[37]

Poltorak knew that Rudenko and his team faced a formidable challenge. While Stalin was demanding guilty verdicts for all of the organizations, he was especially intent on seeing Germany's military leaders labeled as war criminals. Soviet leaders blamed the General Staff and High Command as much as they blamed Hitler for the devastation that had been wrought on the Soviet Union. A guilty verdict, they believed, would lay the groundwork for the punishment of more than 100 field marshals and generals—nearly all of whom were otherwise out of reach, in U.S. and British prisons—and would serve as a bulwark against a revival of German militarism. The trouble was that convicting military personnel for waging war was a radical notion. A number of U.S. policymakers and military leaders opposed this part of the case, wary of its implications for future wars.[38] Telford Taylor, who had taken charge of this part of the case for the Americans, was no doubt reminded of this every time he glanced up at the visitors' gallery.

Over the next several days, Hans Laternser (a former Nazi Party leader and Wehrmacht officer himself) called three of Nazi Germany's most prominent field marshals as witnesses. Walther von Brauchitsch had served as commander-in-chief of the Wehrmacht from 1939 until 1941; Gerd von Rundstedt had commanded Army Group South during the invasions of Poland and the Soviet Union; Erich von Manstein had served as Rundstedt's chief of staff. The three men had a great deal in common. They had all come from military families and had served in the First World War. Their careers had been well established long before the Nazis came to power. They each exuded quiet self-confidence as they took their turns testifying in the witness box.[39]

The three also adopted the same lines of defense. First, they stressed the military's lack of influence with Hitler. Manstein told the court that Hitler had ignored his generals and commanders when making any important military decision; Brauchitsch made a similar claim and further attested that none of the German generals had played any role in politics. Next, they repeated the now-familiar argument that Germany's wars from 1939 through 1945 had been "preventive" and "defensive." Brauchitsch gave the preventive-war story a special twist in the context of Operation Barbarossa: Hitler had assured him, he told the court, that Soviet rule was so unpopular that the locals would welcome German forces.

Addressing the prosecution's charges of war crimes and crimes against humanity, all three witnesses earnestly insisted that they had obeyed the rules of warfare and international law set out in the Geneva and Hague Conventions and had demanded the same from those under their command. Brauchitsch denied any knowledge of the Wehrmacht's collaboration with the Einsatzkommandos. Rundstedt maintained that the General Staff had ordered its soldiers to fight "chivalrously." Manstein protested the accusation that the Wehrmacht had carried out destruction that had not been militarily necessary. He blamed the devastation of the Soviet Union on the orders issued by both Stalin and Hitler "to fight for every foot of ground"; this made it inevitable, he argued, that cities like Stalingrad would be reduced to "heaps of rubble."[40]

Soviet assistant prosecutor Georgy Alexandrov shared responsibility for cross-examining these witnesses with Taylor. With Nikolai Zorya gone, he was the member of the Soviet prosecution most familiar with the evidence against the German military. He was eager to catch Brauchitsch in a lie. Alexandrov challenged Brauchitsch's claim that Hitler had not informed his generals in advance of any plans for invasion and conquest. Hadn't Hitler's decree of May 30, 1938 vowed to shatter Czechoslovakia with an armed invasion? Yes, Brauchitsch acknowledged, but it had been impossible to know when to take Hitler seriously.[41] Alexandrov also skeptically asked the former commander-in-chief how he could possibly not have known that the Einsatzgruppen and the Wehrmacht were working together. When Brauchitsch gave an unsatisfactory reply, Alexandrov presented evidence of close cooperation between Army Group North (which had operated in northern Russia and the Baltic territories) and Einsatzgruppe A.

Taylor returned to the connection between the Wehrmacht and the Einsatzgruppen in his cross-examination of Manstein. He introduced an October 1941 report discussing the success of Einsatzgruppe D—which had been attached to Manstein's Eleventh Army—in murdering communists and Jews. When Manstein denied all knowledge of such things, Taylor produced a November 1941 order with Manstein's stamp on it stating that the "Jewish-Bolshevist system must be exterminated once and for all." Manstein claimed that he did not remember this order, even as he acknowledged his signature. Trying vainly to exculpate himself, he pointed out that it called for the extermination of a "system," not of people.[42]

Alexandrov approached Manstein in the witness box on August 12, nursing a secret. He began his cross-examination predictably enough, challenging Manstein's professed ignorance of the connection between his Eleventh Army and Einsatzgruppe D. He then posed the question he had been holding close to his chest: Did Manstein know what measures the High Command had undertaken with the aim of waging biological warfare? When Manstein said no, Alexandrov presented an affidavit from Major General Walter P. Schreiber, the well-known German army scientist whose whereabouts were unknown. Schreiber had worked during the war at the headquarters of the High Command and had overseen the science and health departments in the Army Medical Inspectorate. His area of specialization had been vaccine research.[43]

Unbeknownst to the defense or even to the Western prosecutors, Schreiber had been captured by the Red Army in Berlin in April 1945 and had spent the past sixteen months in NKVD custody. In his affidavit, which Alexandrov began to read aloud, Schreiber attested that a large part of the guilt for Nazi crimes was borne by German scientists and doctors, who had been working on a new kind of weapon that would have put remarkable scientific discoveries to an "evil use." Laternser, after overcoming his surprise, objected that this affidavit leveled serious charges and demanded the right to cross-examine Schreiber. The Tribunal, on learning that Schreiber was alive, directed Alexandrov to withdraw the affidavit until he could be produced in person.

Alexandrov promised that the Soviets would take the necessary steps to bring Schreiber to Nuremberg, but reminded the court that the distance from Moscow was considerable.[44] In fact, Soviet leaders had been ready and eager to dispatch Schreiber to Nuremberg for several months now and had worked with Gorshenin and Rudenko to orchestrate a situation in which he might be produced in court.[45] They were hoping to cap the trial with a stir similar to the one they had made back in February by producing Field Marshal Friedrich von Paulus.

Everyone took solace from the fact that there was just one more organization to go—the SA, whose defense began that very afternoon. The SA had achieved notoriety as a violent paramilitary force during Hitler's early years in power but was stripped of its influence in 1934, when its leaders were murdered on Hitler's orders as part of the so-called Night of the Long Knives. The SA's attorney, Georg Boehm, now argued that the organization, even in its most active years, had been primarily a sporting club. His first witness, Franz Bock of the SA Supreme Staff, rejected the prosecution's suggestion that sport had been a means to a more nefarious end. According to Bock, the SA had drilled in order to appear disciplined, "like all sport organizations," and had chosen exercises similar to the Olympic pentathlon. Boehm did not try to dispute the charge that the SA had guarded concentration camps for a short period between 1933 and 1934—but his next witness, Werner Schaefer (the former camp commandant for Oranienburg), insisted that the inmates had lived in "humanly dignified" conditions and that the situation had deteriorated only when the SS took over the camps.[46]

As the SA witnesses continued their testimony over the rest of the week, the Soviets were planning their endgame. The prosecution would be giving a second set of closing speeches for the organizations case. On Thursday, August 15, Gorshenin sent a draft of Rudenko's speech from Nuremberg to Vyshinsky in Paris. Vyshinsky returned a marked-up document five days later. Many of his edits dealt with word choice: for example, he replaced the term "Party comrades" with "members of the Fascist Party" whenever it appeared. Vyshinsky also crossed out a line criticizing the Nazis for banning other political parties in Germany. As earlier, this hit far too close to home. Still other edits placed greater emphasis on certain aspects of an organization's crimes—highlighting, for example, the Gestapo's role "in the destruction of the Jews."[47] Work on Rudenko's speech was just beginning. In the days that followed, Gorshenin forwarded copies of the text to Stalin, Zhdanov, and other Party leaders for their review.[48]

The Palace of Justice saw a brief return to the animation of the earlier part of the trials on Tuesday, August 20, with Goering's reappearance in the witness box. The Tribunal was allowing him to respond to the prosecution's charge that he bore responsibility for medical experiments on inmates at Dachau. With an attitude of bored disinterest, he acknowledged that he had established the Reich Research Council to conduct scientific research to meet "the necessities of war." But he denied involvement in, or even knowledge of, experiments on prisoners. He also denied having received from Hitler any kind of authority to plan for bacteriological warfare of the kind mentioned by General Schreiber. When Maxwell Fyfe challenged the notion that this research could have happened without Goering's authorization, Goering insisted with improbable modesty that he had been merely a figurehead.[49]

Goering's reappearance seemed to revitalize the entire defense. Over the next couple of days, defense counsel for the organizations logged in new documentary evidence making additional accusations against the Soviets. Boehm's attempt to submit an affidavit for the SA from the German politician Arnold Rechberg was denounced by Yuri Pokrovsky as yet another fascist provocation. Rechberg had attested that more than 20,000 communists backed by Moscow had "infiltrated" the SA in the 1930s and had instigated its turn to violence. Pokrovsky reminded the Tribunal that Rechberg was a known source of "anti-Soviet inventions." The judges supported Pokrovsky.[50] A small pile of Laternser's affidavits for the General Staff and High Command posed an even greater challenge to the Soviet case. Disputing evidence from the Extraordinary State Commission, they contended that not German but Soviet forces had plundered, ransacked, or destroyed major cultural and religious sites in Leningrad, Novgorod, and other cities (including Leo Tolstoy's estate in Yasnaya Polyana near Tula). Rudenko was caught off guard and did not even try to challenge these affidavits. They thus became part of the court record and would fuel decades of speculation about Soviet versus German responsibility for these acts of destruction.[51]

The broader question of collective guilt again took center stage in the Nuremberg courtroom as the defense began its closing arguments for the organizations on August 22. The attorneys tried to clear each organization of criminal responsibility to as great a degree as possible—while simultaneously urging the judges to reject the very idea of collective guilt for the sake of postwar Europe. Servatius reminded the court that the Allied Control Council had made "mere membership" in a criminal organization a punishable offense. In the case of the Leadership Corps alone more than two million persons would be condemned by a declaration of criminality, Servatius blustered (intentionally inflating the numbers). He argued that the Tribunal should circumscribe its ruling to those Party leaders who had wielded the greatest authority. Merkel took a similar tack in his closing for the Gestapo. Playing to the concerns of the Western judges, he warned that findings of collective guilt would shake the world's faith in what he referred to as "fundamental human rights."[52] By strategically using the language of the Paris Peace Conference and the United Nations, the defense was trying to turn the tables on the prosecution—reframing the organizations case as an assault on the rights of the German people.

The Soviet prosecution brought the court's attention back to Nazi atrocities on Monday, August 26, with the announcement that Schreiber had arrived in Nuremberg. The Tribunal put the defense closings on hold and called the fifty-three-year old Nazi scientist, a short and stocky man with thinning hair, to testify. The Soviets were pleased with themselves and it showed. Alexandrov boldly approached Schreiber and peppered him with questions about the High Command's preparations for bacteriological warfare. Schreiber described a secret conference in Berlin that the High Command had called in July 1943. He had taken part as a representative of the Army Medical Inspectorate and had learned that as a result of the defeat at Stalingrad the High Command had agreed to support the use of bacteria as a weapon in warfare. Goering, whom Hitler had put in charge of the preparations, had directed Kurt Blome (the deputy chief of the Reich Physicians League) to set up an institute in Posen for mass-producing bacterial cultures.[53]

Why hadn't the German High Command put these plans for biological warfare into effect? Alexandrov asked, already knowing the answer. Schreiber responded that it was only the Red Army's advance on Posen that had halted the execution of these plans. Blome had been forced to evacuate, and although he had resumed his work in Sachsenburg, valuable time had been lost; it had not been possible to create a serum to inoculate German troops and civilians. Alexandrov, satisfied with this response, next asked Schreiber what he knew about the experiments German doctors had carried out on prisoners. Schreiber described learning in October 1943 about research on the typhus vaccine at Buchenwald; these experiments had been of "no scientific value," he added, and had led to numerous inmate deaths. Schreiber also described experiments at Dachau that had been carried out for the Luftwaffe High Command. The stated purpose had been to obtain data that could be used for producing protective garments for pilots. Prisoners had been immersed in freezing water, and measurements had been taken of their declining body temperatures. Goering had ordered this research, he emphasized, and Himmler had supplied the subjects.[54]

Laternser began his cross-examination by suggesting that Schreiber's testimony could not be trusted because he had been a Soviet prisoner. He asked Schreiber if his answers to the prosecution's questions had been "previously determined." Schreiber denied this; he assured the Tribunal that he had not been promised any special privileges for appearing in court. Laternser next asked him why he had not protested the alleged plans for biological warfare. Schreiber maintained that he had told his superiors that bacteria were dangerous and unreliable but had quickly understood that he was facing "a fait accompli." Did Schreiber know whether the High Command had issued a positive order that bacteriological warfare should actually be carried out? He admitted that he had not seen any such order. Wasn't it possible, Laternser asked, that this form of warfare had been abandoned because the High Command had come to realize its danger? No, Schreiber insisted, this had not been a concern.[55] Schreiber's testimony was chilling. On the heels of these revelations, Gorshenin added a paragraph to the Soviet closing speech reminding the world that only the advance of the Red Army had stopped the General Staff and High Command from using the plague bacillus as a weapon and threatening Europe with unimaginable "calamities and devastation."[56]

As the organizations case neared its conclusion, the world continued to grapple with the nature of Nazi crimes. The same day that Schreiber appeared in court, the *New York Times* published an editorial asserting that the Nuremberg defendants should be found guilty of the crime of genocide. The editorial further argued that incorporating this concept into international law was necessary because "no state would prosecute a crime instigated and committed by itself."[57] Soviet leaders, meanwhile, doubled down on the idea that Nazi crimes, including genocide, were very specifically a manifestation of fascism (which they defined as an "ideology of misanthropy and racial hatred") and could not be generalized to any other political system. The Party's propaganda department reminded Gorshenin that the Soviet prosecutors, in their closing speech for the organizations case, would need to underline the relationship between Nazi race theory and "the imperialist politics of German fascism" (the drive for Lebensraum) in order to hit the right political notes.[58]

By this point, the Nuremberg Trials had become a laboratory for the articulation and development of a new language about human rights. The organizations case unmistakably illustrated to everyone that this language cut both ways: both the prosecution and the defense made use of it to support their arguments for or against the idea of collective guilt. When the defense attorneys resumed their closings after Schreiber's testimony, they issued repeated warnings about the Tribunal's potential to commit what Pelckmann called "mass injustice in legal form." Kubuschok, Gawlik, and Boehm, in their closings for the Reich Cabinet, the SD, and the SA, echoed Merkel's argument of a few days earlier that verdicts of organizational guilt would violate a basic human right. Gawlik stressed the injustice of including the "simple members" of an organization in a sweeping verdict based solely on the presumption that they had been in the know about its crimes.[59] Kubuschok warned that such verdicts would perpetuate the "feeling of legal insecurity" that Germans had experienced under the Nazis and claimed that this in and of itself was a violation of their human rights.[60]

The prosecution also invoked the topic of human rights—here interwoven with the theme of criminal responsibility—when it began its closing arguments for the organizations case on August 28. The British, American, French, and Soviet prosecutors reiterated the purpose of the trials, the charges that had been set out in the Indictment, and the connections between the individual defendants and the indicted organizations. For two and a half days, they recapped the most compelling and gruesome evidence of each organization's crimes, rebutted the defense's protests of innocence and ignorance, and warned that only declarations of organizational guilt could free Europe from the scourge of Nazism.

Maxwell Fyfe began his presentation by differentiating between so-called ordinary Germans and the "disciples of the Führer's creed of hate and cruelty." The ultimate aim of the organizations case, he argued, was to protect the former from those elements of the latter who remained in their midst. Maxwell Fyfe focused his remarks on the Leadership Corps of the Nazi Party, the SA, and the SS—what he described as the "dangerous core" of Nazism. He called out the SS as the most abominable organization of all, using the term "genocide" to describe its "demonic plan" to wipe out entire nations, peoples, and races. Countering the defense's arguments, he argued that the entire SS had worked in unison, with the Waffen-SS providing personnel to the various Nazi "genocide organizations" that operated as part of and on behalf of the SS.[61]

Dodd, continuing to act as Jackson's proxy, began the U.S. closing presentation the next day by describing the Nazi state as a "political Frankenstein" and detailing the role each organization had played to accomplish the common aims of the criminal conspiracy. He did not use the term "genocide," but he gave special attention to the crimes committed against Europe's Jews—painting a picture of how the organizations had conspired to perpetrate six million murders. The demise of Hitler's Germany did not mean that the world was out of danger, he warned, for the Nazis had "piped" their ideological poison throughout Europe and other parts of the world. Declarations of organizational guilt were necessary lest Nazism revive and threaten civilization again.[62]

Taylor followed up on this warning in a second American speech on August 30, this one focused on the dangers of German militarism. He reminded the court that there was overpowering evidence of collaboration between the military and the Einsatzgruppen. The General Staff and High Command bore responsibility not just for waging a criminal war but also for terrible crimes against civilians. The idea that death squads had "flitted through Russia," murdering Jews and communists on a huge scale, without the Wehrmacht's awareness was "utterly preposterous." A declaration of criminality against the General Staff and High Command was needed in order to safeguard Europe's future, for militarism held no regard for "the rights of others."[63]

Later that morning, de Ribes reflected on the importance of human rights for Europe's future. He reminded the court that the constitutions of "all civilized nations" spoke of "inalienable rights" and that the Charter of the United Nations (signed at the San Francisco Conference) had proclaimed its signatories' faith in the fundamental rights of man. Nazism had been so monstrous, he argued, precisely because it had held no regard for the "humanity of individuals" and had sought to impose biological ideas such as "natural selection" and the "struggle for existence" on human communities. Deportations, concentration camps, gas chambers, and finally genocide had all been consequences of this murderous ideology. Declarations of organizational guilt were essential for the work of postwar peace, he proclaimed, for they would remind the world that there is such a thing as "a moral law."[64]

Rudenko, once again going last, concluded the organizations case that afternoon by urging a severe judgment. He, too, recapped each organization's major crimes as he stressed their service to the fascist conspiracy. In a booming voice, he denounced the "false testimony" of numerous defense witnesses. If their accounts were true, who had murdered twelve million peaceful civilians? He became especially irate as he described how Manstein, Brauchitsch, and Rundstedt had come to Nuremberg to spread lies. The prosecution had proved beyond any doubt, he argued, that Germany's military leaders were responsible for preparing and waging aggressive war. Here he recapped the key details of Paulus's earlier testimony as well as Schreiber's account of the High Command's role in planning for biological warfare.[65]

Rudenko, like Maxwell Fyfe and de Ribes, used the term "genocide" as he discussed the crimes of the SS—but, following Moscow's directives, he emphasized that genocide was a crime specifically tied to fascism. The German fascists, as "imperialists," had aimed to seize other countries and further the spread of "militant German capitalism," Rudenko told the court. They had called themselves socialists in order to conceal their true ambitions. His obvious implication was that the Nazis had more in common with the capitalist countries of the West than with the Soviet Union.

The matter of unpaid reparations remained a sore spot for Moscow, and Rudenko made sure to remind the court that in the Soviet Union alone the Nazis had inflicted material damage totaling nearly 680 billion rubles (128 billion dollars).[66] He ended his speech with a paean to international cooperation—without mentioning the degree to which it was currently under strain.[67]

After ten long and difficult months, the prosecution rested its case. There was one last order of business to attend to, however, before the judges went into deliberation: the individual defendants would be allowed to make short final statements. When the Soviet correspondents arrived back at the Palace of Justice the following morning, the last day of August 1946, they found a packed courtroom tense with anticipation. For the first time in weeks no one complained about boredom. The twenty-one defendants, in freshly pressed suits, were in their usual places in the dock when the IMT was called into session. Boris Polevoi thought that in spite of their spiffed-up appearances they looked "quiet, miserable, and servile"—especially as compared with how "insolent, smug, pompous, and frenzied" they had appeared in photographs from their glory days.[68] The Tribunal was giving the defendants the last word. Everyone's attention was trained on them as, one by one, they rose in their places with papers in hand and addressed the court.

Most of the defendants stuck to familiar themes, reiterating points they had made earlier in the trials. Goering, Hess, and Ribbentrop all used the occasion to give short speeches on victors' justice. Goering complained that the court had treated the defendants unfairly. Hess spoke semicoherently about British imperialism of the late nineteenth century. Ribbentrop called out the hypocrisy of the Allied powers. The victors certainly held "different views about international law" before the war than they did at present, he noted sardonically. When he had gone to Moscow in 1939, Stalin had not raised the possibility of peacefully settling "the German-Polish conflict within the framework of the Kellogg-Briand Pact" but instead had laid claim to the Baltic countries and half of Poland. Invoking Churchill's "Iron Curtain" speech of March 1946, Ribbentrop declared that the United States and Great Britain currently faced the same questions Germany had faced in 1939 regarding Soviet territorial ambitions. Would they be able to stop Soviet incursions "at the Elbe, at the Adriatic coast, and at the Dardanelles?"[69]

Most of the remaining defendants' statements proceeded less dramatically but just as predictably. Fritzsche, Kaltenbrunner, and Funk repeated their earlier claims to have been hoodwinked by Hitler. Papen and Neurath reiterated that they had cooperated with Hitler's government with the hope of moderating his policies. Raeder, Seyss-Inquart, and Frick proclaimed their eternal devotion to Germany and the German people. Schacht, playing to the sympathy of the court, portrayed himself as an enemy of the Nazi regime whose resistance to Hitler "was known at home and abroad." Doenitz, Jodl, and Keitel used their last words to defend the actions of the military. Doenitz restated his belief that German submarine warfare had been legal; Jodl argued again that the Wehrmacht had been justified in using what he called "harsh measures" against partisans.[70]

Several defendants, picking up on the themes that had dominated the courtroom over the past few weeks, used their closings to express concern for Germany's future. Frank urged the German people to return to God. Rosenberg, after declaring his own innocence, welcomed the news that "a crime of genocide" would be outlawed by international agreement, with the understanding that "neither now nor in the future shall genocide be permitted in any way against the German people either." Speer took a different approach and used his final words to warn of the danger that modern weapons posed to all of humankind.[71]

After the last defendant spoke, the Tribunal adjourned. The fates of the individual defendants, and of the millions of Germans who had belonged to the indicted organizations, would soon be decided. The prosecutors had spent the previous few evenings holding a final round of parties and packing to go home.[72] On Sunday, September 1, the Soviet prosecutors played host and broke bread with their Western colleagues in Nuremberg one last time. All of the prosecutors and their support staffs were in equal measure exhausted, hopeful, and nervous. After months of intensive work they would now step back and wait, while the judges considered the evidence and the testimony and ultimately rendered their judgments. What verdicts would the Tribunal reach about the former Nazi leaders and their organizations—and what would its decisions mean for the shape of postwar Europe? The members of the Soviet delegation had an additional concern: How would Stalin judge their performances in the Nuremberg Trials?

CHAPTER 14 | Judgment

A FTER THE TRIBUNAL adjourned in early September, the Palace of
Justice went quiet. The prosecutors and their staffs, along with much
of the press corps, had vacated Nuremberg, and the judges had moved from
the courtroom to a small conference room for their final deliberations. For
Iona Nikitchenko and Alexander Volchkov, the most difficult part of the
trial was now beginning. The Soviet judges had instructions from Moscow
to secure nothing less than guilty verdicts for all twenty-two defendants and
declarations of criminality for all of the indicted organizations. The Western
judges, meanwhile, harbored doubts about the very legality of some of
the charges. The verdicts and the sentences were still highly uncertain. As
Nuremberg itself grew quieter, Soviet informants and political advisors engaged in a flurry of behind-the-scenes activity.

The four judges were a study in contrasts. Henri Donnedieu de Vabres was
a quiet man who could talk endlessly about the intricacies of the law. He was
a strong advocate for the creation of a permanent international criminal court
and wanted to ensure that all aspects of the Tribunal's decisions rested on
firm legal ground. Francis Biddle, FDR's last attorney general, was in equal
parts suspicious of the Soviets and impatient with the French. However, he
shared with de Vabres a deep concern that the Tribunal's accomplishment
might later be dismissed as victors' justice. Geoffrey Lawrence, a British
High Court judge, had served as the voice of the Tribunal over the preceding
ten months; as its presiding judge, he had delivered its rulings from the
bench. He had maintained his reputation for evenhandedness throughout.
His insistence on allowing each defendant to say his piece, even for days or

weeks on end, had been a never-ending source of frustration to the prosecution. Nikitchenko, with his provincial background, blunt manner, and lack of familiarity with the finer points of international law, was the odd man out. The fact that Stalin had picked Nikitchenko to serve as the Soviet judge at Nuremberg illustrated the kind of trial Moscow had initially been expecting. Nearly everything that had happened over the past ten months had confounded these expectations.

The Tribunal began its final deliberations on September 2, though preparations had started months earlier. That spring, while the defense was presenting its case, the judges had begun their analyses of the evidence and had started to discuss the verdicts.[1] Nikitchenko and de Vabres had initially suggested that

FIGURE 14.1 The judges and their alternates, ca. 1945-1946. From left to right: Soviet alternate judge Alexander Volchkov, Soviet judge Iona Nikitchenko, British alternate judge Norman Birkett, British judge and Tribunal president Geoffrey Lawrence, U.S. judge Francis Biddle, U.S. alternate judge John Parker, French judge Henri Donnedieu de Vabres, French alternate judge Robert Falco.

Credit: United States Holocaust Memorial Museum, courtesy of Tade Wolfe. Photographer: Charles Alexander.

the four judges each write a part of the judgment, focusing on the crimes committed against his country. Biddle and Lawrence, hoping to exercise American and British influence on the crafting of the entire document, had opposed this idea on the grounds that it was customary for the presiding judge (in this case Lawrence) to pen the first draft himself. Nikitchenko and de Vabres had reluctantly agreed—after which Lawrence, who disliked any kind of legal paperwork, had quietly delegated much of this task to Biddle and British alternate judge Norman Birkett.[2]

In late June, the Tribunal had held its first official meeting to discuss the judgment. Lawrence had circulated a partial draft that he, Biddle, and Birkett had prepared over the preceding couple of months. It was a huge document—the size of a novella—detailing the history of the Nazi regime and its assault on Europe, the road to the Nuremberg Trials, and the prosecution's case against the individual defendants and the indicted organizations. It outlined the four counts agreed to in London a year earlier: participation in a conspiracy, crimes against peace, war crimes, and crimes against humanity. Nikitchenko had perfunctorily complimented the document's structure before launching into his criticisms: it was far too long and went off on too many tangents. It would be better to get straight to the point. De Vabres had then surprised his fellow judges by suggesting that they drop Count One, the conspiracy charge, from the judgment altogether. It was not only ex post facto; it was also unnecessary, he had argued, for the prosecution had proven beyond a doubt that the defendants had committed "actual crimes."[3] The idea that the Nazi Party had from its founding been a conspiracy seeking world domination seemed to him highly improbable. Nikitchenko's alarmed report on this meeting had quickly found its way to the Politburo Commission for the Nuremberg Trials and to Moscow's Institute of Law—Aron Trainin's home institution.[4]

For the rest of the summer the Soviets had tried to shape the still inchoate judgment, with mixed results. At a closed Tribunal meeting on July 11, Nikitchenko had suggested that the judgment address the role of German industrialists and diplomats in Germany's preparations for war. This had fallen flat.[5] A week later, he had recommended that the judgment devote more space to Germany's invasion of the Soviet Union—not for reasons of national loyalty, he had explained, but because this was one of the "clearest cases of aggression." Nikitchenko, in keeping with Moscow's emphasis on the suffering of the entire Soviet people, had also recommended that the judgment make clear that the Nazis had persecuted other groups in addition to the Jews. The Western judges had agreed to the latter suggestion.[6] At a meeting on August 8, Nikitchenko had demanded the deletion of a reference to the secret protocols of the German-Soviet Non-Aggression Pact as well as the deletion of a line (a quote from one of Hitler's speeches) implying that the pact had ensured the isolation and destruction of Poland.[7] The Western judges had been unmoved.[8]

Nikitchenko and Volchkov had also mobilized, with the help of Trainin and the rest of the Vyshinsky Commission, to protect Count One from de Vabres and keep it in the judgment. The Soviets had not forgiven Robert Jackson for using the conspiracy charge to take over the lion's share of the case. They had nonetheless come to recognize the importance of this charge for securing guilty verdicts. Nikitchenko had elaborated the Soviet position in a July 17 memorandum to the Tribunal. The Nuremberg Charter was "the first and as yet the only act of international law" to include the charge of conspiracy, the memorandum acknowledged, but the Nazi plot had been so sweeping that this charge fit the crime. The heart of the memorandum drew directly from the description of "complicity" in Trainin's *The Criminal Responsibility of the Hitlerites* (and was likely written by Trainin himself). The possibility that some of the conspirators may have been ignorant of their compatriots' crimes did not diminish their own responsibility, it emphasized, for they had all been working toward a common goal. The memorandum also disputed the notion that the Führer's absolute authority was incompatible with the idea of a conspiracy, arguing that all conspiratorial bands have a "gang leader" driving them forward.[9] Nikitchenko had circulated a second memorandum a few weeks later addressing lingering concerns about treating war as a criminal act. This time, he played down the novelty of the Nuremberg Charter—reminding the other judges that it was based on earlier international agreements, like the Kellogg-Briand Pact, that had renounced war as an instrument of foreign policy.[10]

The debate over the conspiracy charge had continued through the summer. At a couple of mid-August meetings, de Vabres reiterated his wish to do away with Count One. Nikitchenko had stood firm—and Lawrence and Birkett had backed him. It didn't matter whether the conspiracy charge was retroactive, Lawrence had declared; occupying powers can write a charter "in any way they want."[11] Biddle, finding this argument distasteful, had thrown his support behind de Vabres. An exasperated Nikitchenko had reminded his colleagues that they were supposed to be a "practical" group, "not a discussion club." Could they really be so bothered by ex post facto convictions that served a noble end? Far more troubling, he had warned (sounding less like a judge than a prosecutor), was the possibility of defendants going free. Hans Fritzsche, for one, could not be convicted without the conspiracy charge. Giving speeches on the radio was not in itself a crime. Birkett, agreeing with Nikitchenko, had reminded his colleagues that the purpose of Count One was to show that "war arose from a common plan," not "out of a clear sky." If Count One were eliminated, he warned, the trial's "whole value" would go.[12]

By late August, the British, American, and French judges had reached a compromise on Count One. Lawrence and Biddle had proposed limiting the charge of conspiracy in the judgment to cover only "crimes against peace"—effectively redefining it as strictly a conspiracy to wage aggressive war, which they felt was all that had been conclusively proven by the evidence. They had further suggested dating the start of this conspiracy to sometime after Hitler's consolidation of power, probably in the mid- to late 1930s, thereby rejecting the prosecution's argument that it had originated in the early days of the Nazi Party. De Vabres had agreed, and Lawrence had given Biddle the job of redrafting this part of the judgment.[13] This turn of events boded poorly for Nikitchenko and for Soviet concerns more generally. It seemed unlikely that the conspiracy charge would remain robust enough to result in convictions of all the defendants.

By now the Soviets had also experienced a defeat on another front. The defense had thrown enough doubt on Soviet claims about German responsibility for Katyn that the Western judges had essentially set aside the Soviet charges. The judgment would contain no mention of the Katyn massacre. There would be no official finding of German guilt for the crime.[14]

When the court went into recess on Monday, September 2, the Tribunal turned its full attention to the judgment and the verdicts. The judges spent their first week in the locked conference room reviewing the cases against the individual defendants and holding informal polls on the question of their guilt.[15] They were aided by two interpreters, one of whom was Oleg Troyanovsky—the Swarthmore graduate who had been at Nikitchenko's side at the London Conference the previous summer.

The judges worked down the list of the accused according to their seats in the dock, row by row, postponing discussions about the more challenging or contentious cases (such as Erich Raeder and Rudolf Hess) for later. The four judges and four alternates all shared their opinions at this early stage—but the four primary judges alone would participate in the final votes. Nikitchenko, predictably, demanded guilty verdicts and death sentences for each and every defendant; the Western judges were more tempered. Early in the week, Biddle distributed his redraft of Count One for consideration. As expected, it linked the conspiracy exclusively to the planning of the Nazi assault on Europe: it proposed November 5, 1937—the date of the Hossbach

Conference, at which Hitler had revealed to his generals his plans for war—as the date the conspiracy had begun.[16]

The judges also expressed divergent opinions on the organizations case. Biddle continued to voice strong discomfort with the idea of collective guilt, troubled by the possibility that millions of Germans would get caught up in sweeping declarations of criminality. The potential consequences were serious: if the Allied Control Council (the four-power occupation government) had its way, mere membership in an organization deemed criminal by the

FIGURE 14.2 Mikhail Cheremnykh, "The Fascist Bandits in Their Circle," TASS propaganda poster, ca. 1945-1946. Stalin wanted to see guilty verdicts for all of the defendants and all of the indicted organizations.

Credit: Courtesy of the Library of Congress.

Tribunal would be punishable, with sentences ranging from a loss of civil rights to the death penalty. Nikitchenko, echoing the prosecution's earlier arguments, dismissed as unfounded any concerns about convicting the innocent. But Biddle and U.S. alternate judge John Parker advised strict limitations for a finding of criminality, such as clear evidence that most of an organization's members had willingly participated in its criminal activities.[17]

The Palace of Justice was eerily quiet as the judges carried on these discussions. The American authorities had disconnected the telephone lines to ensure that the judges were sequestered. Other security measures had been taken as well: the contents of the wastepaper baskets were burned every evening.[18] None of this, however, prevented Nikitchenko from keeping Soviet leaders apprised of the Tribunal's confidential deliberations about the verdicts—or from smuggling to Moscow sections of the judgment-in-progress.

On September 4 the judges discussed Biddle's reformulation of Count One, which spoke of the existence of "many separate plans" for individual military actions. Nikitchenko roundly criticized it, insisting that the judgment highlight the conspirators' overarching plan to take over the world. Concerned that the Western judges were losing their focus, Nikitchenko pushed for the inclusion of some of the most gruesome details of Nazi crimes that had been described before the Tribunal, such as the rendering of corpses into soap. He also argued that all mention of partisan warfare in the occupied Soviet Union should emphasize the extreme brutality of the German response.[19] On September 7, the judges revisited the sections of the judgment dealing with the start of the war. An aggrieved Nikitchenko again objected to the line about the secret protocols as well as to the line linking the German-Soviet Non-Aggression Pact to the conquest of Poland. This time the Western judges relented, and both lines were eliminated.[20]

On September 6 and 7, the judges also resumed their discussions about the individual verdicts. They reached a quick consensus that Hermann Goering, Joachim von Ribbentrop, Wilhelm Keitel, Alfred Jodl, Alfred Rosenberg, Wilhelm Frick, Fritz Sauckel, and Arthur Seyss-Inquart should hang. Then, to Nikitchenko's consternation, the Western judges suggested leniency for some of the other defendants. Lawrence and Birkett argued for an acquittal of the banker Hjalmar Schacht on the grounds of reasonable doubt. De Vabres responded that he did not want to acquit anyone, but that Schacht should receive a mild sentence. Nikitchenko insisted—to no avail— that Schacht be convicted on Counts One and Two since he had "certainly prepared Germany for war." Lawrence and Biddle then voiced misgivings about convicting Franz von Papen, who had been dismissed from his post as Germany's ambassador to Austria before the Anschluss. De Vabres argued that Papen was "somewhat similar to Schacht" but that his guilt was greater, for he had remained loyal to Hitler.[21]

As the second week of deliberations began, Nikitchenko made a desperate bid to avert these acquittals. He put forward the argument that in keeping with the Nuremberg Charter all decisions on guilt or innocence must be made by a majority vote of three to one. The other judges countered his interpretation. The Charter had stipulated only that there must be a three-to-one vote to convict. A split vote would result in an acquittal. Nikitchenko gained still further cause for concern that afternoon when de Vabres urged a light sentence for Karl Doenitz and Biddle called for an acquittal. Biddle argued that it would be ridiculous to convict Doenitz for sinking ships without warning when doing otherwise would have made submarine use impossible; he reminded the group that U.S. admiral Chester Nimitz had acted similarly. Nikitchenko retorted that letting Doenitz go free "would be saying that his submarine warfare was legal and proper." Lawrence joined Nikitchenko in pushing for a conviction. He called Doenitz's actions "typically national socialist—harsh and inhumane"—and suggested that Nimitz had adopted "similar methods" only in response (basically offering up a tu quoque defense for the U.S. admiral, who was of course not on trial).[22]

The discussion the following day about Fritzsche was equally fraught. De Vabres characterized Fritzsche as the "least guilty" of the defendants, and Biddle agreed that he was a "small man" with whom "Hitler wouldn't have wasted five minutes." Parker, the U.S. alternate judge, added his opinion that Fritzsche had only been indicted because Goebbels was dead, as a kind of "vicarious sacrifice." Again Nikitchenko and Lawrence argued for a conviction, with Volchkov chiming in that Fritzsche's ideas about German racial superiority had led to the extermination of more than ten million people.[23]

Disputes about the verdicts carried over to the discussions about sentencing. The Hess sentence provoked the sharpest debate. Biddle and de Vabres dismissed Nikitchenko's assertion that Hess's signature on the Nuremberg Laws of 1935 had made him responsible for the deaths of millions of Jews. They also questioned the long-standing Soviet claim that the chief purpose of Hess's flight to Scotland in May 1941 had been to double-cross the Soviet Union. At a meeting on September 10, de Vabres voted for a twenty-year prison term, Biddle and Lawrence for a life sentence, and Nikitchenko for the death penalty. Worried that Biddle and Lawrence might join de Vabres, Nikitchenko reluctantly agreed to life.[24] The judges were also strongly divided about the architect-turned-armaments-minister Albert Speer. De Vabres and Lawrence, arguing that his belated efforts to oppose Hitler mitigated his guilt, suggested a fifteen-year prison term.

Nikitchenko and Biddle demanded the death penalty—until Biddle (who later characterized Speer as the "most humane and decent of the defendants") switched sides, agreeing to fifteen years. The sentence for Hitler Youth leader Baldur von Schirach similarly sparked disagreement. Nikitchenko again argued that only death would do, but de Vabres and Biddle deemed this too harsh. The judges settled on twenty years.[25]

The gap between Nikitchenko and the Western judges widened further in mid-September, when Biddle and Lawrence both insisted on an acquittal for Papen. De Vabres responded by proposing that Fritzsche and Schacht also be acquitted. These three defendants bore similar degrees of responsibility, he argued. Nikitchenko, reading the signs, retracted his demand that Papen be hanged and announced that he would settle for a ten-year sentence. It was too late. Biddle, who had been supporting Schacht's conviction, did another turnabout, declaring that the "old man" was mainly guilty of "imprudence" and that it would be cruel to sentence him. Nikitchenko, after being outvoted yet again, threatened to dissent from the judgment. Biddle urged him to reconsider, insisting that the judges must never go public with what he called their "frank private discussions."[26]

These deliberations were not going well for Nikitchenko. And from his perspective the organizations case was also skidding off the rails. In an effort to narrow the net of guilt, Parker had proposed that membership in an indicted organization should be considered "criminal" only from the time of the outbreak of the war—a restriction similar (but not identical) to the one the Tribunal had placed on the conspiracy charge. The other Western judges had supported this idea. Even more serious, though, was the suggestion that the prosecution had failed to fully prove the guilt of some of the indicted groups. Biddle, de Vabres, and Lawrence all questioned the prosecution's assertion that the General Staff and High Command had constituted a discrete organization and remained unconvinced that it had exerted meaningful influence over Nazi policies. They also asserted that the Reich Cabinet was not large enough to warrant a general declaration of criminality. Finally, they pointed out that the SA had lost its influence after 1934.[27]

By September 17 the judges had realized that they needed more time to finish their deliberations. The Tribunal announced that it would not reconvene in the Palace of Justice on September 23 as planned but would take an additional week.[28] While the judges were close to finalizing many of their decisions, there was still much to discuss. Nikitchenko could already tell that he stood absolutely no chance of securing guilty verdicts down the line.

Work on the judgment had been moving forward more slowly than the judges would have liked, but more quickly than Soviet leaders seemed to be expecting. While the judges were hammering out the verdicts and sentences, Soviet leaders and international-law experts, as well as members of the Soviet prosecution, all back in Moscow, were reviewing a two-week-old, significantly outdated draft of the judgment. Of course, they were not supposed to have seen the work in progress at all.

The Soviet personnel in Moscow were slow to understand the gravity and the finality of what was happening in Nuremberg. The assistant prosecutors Lev Sheinin and Dmitry Karev did not send Konstantin Gorshenin their comments on the draft judgment's "crimes against peace" section until September 14. They advised the deletion of a paragraph stating that Germans and Austrians shared "common traits" and that the Anschluss had been "achieved without bloodshed," on the grounds that these details were irrelevant. They also called for the removal of the reference to the secret protocols of the German-Soviet Non-Aggression Pact, as well as the line noting the pact's role in diplomatically isolating Poland. (Nikitchenko had anticipated the objections relating to the nonaggression pact and had already convinced the other judges to agree to these changes.)

At the same time, Grigory Safonov, Gorshenin's assistant on the Vyshinsky Commission, registered concern about the judgment's "crimes against humanity" section (Count Four). He argued that the Soviet judges must prevent the judgment from excluding Germany's persecution of the Jews prior to the war.[29] This would in fact be extremely difficult to do. The Tribunal's recent reformulation of the conspiracy charge (Count One), combined with the original language of the Nuremberg Charter (which had circumscribed "crimes against humanity" to crimes committed "in execution of or in connection with" another crime within the Tribunal's jurisdiction), posed a formidable obstacle. The Tribunal would need to find that the violence against Germany's Jews before the war had been directly related to the conspiracy to invade and conquer Europe that had been set out at the Hossbach Conference.

On September 17, the day the Tribunal announced its delay, Gorshenin asked Stalin to review instructions for Nikitchenko that the Vyshinsky Commission had written up (and that Molotov had already approved) relating to the verdicts and sentences. Time was of the essence, Gorshenin informed Stalin, for the Tribunal would soon be finalizing its decisions. It made no difference to Soviet leaders that Nikitchenko was supposed to be deliberating with the other judges in complete isolation. They neither trusted Nikitchenko nor wanted him to act of his own volition. They were more intent than ever on stage-managing what they could of the Tribunal from afar. Stalin verified the instructions, and they were sent to Nikitchenko as a ciphered telegram on September 19.[30]

One can almost hear Nikitchenko sigh heavily on reading his marching orders. The Vyshinsky Commission agreed only with the anticipated verdicts on Goering, Ribbentrop, Keitel, Rosenberg, Frick, Jodl, and Bormann, all of whom would be found guilty on all four counts and hanged. (The missing Bormann was in fact already dead.) The commission insisted that Hess, Speer, and Frank receive the same verdict and death sentence—and gave Nikitchenko advice on how to win the other judges over to this position. He was to remind them, for example, that the doctors had found Hess to be sane, and he was to emphasize Hess's role as Hitler's deputy in planning unprovoked military attacks, including Operation Barbarossa. He was to make a case for Frank's guilt on Counts One and Two (in addition to Counts Three and Four, which the four judges had already agreed on) by highlighting Frank's role in elaborating a policy of "fascist imperialism" in Eastern Europe.[31]

Moscow was most worried about the possible acquittals, and here the Vyshinsky Commission advised Nikitchenko to use a mixture of persuasion, bluffing, and conciliation. He was to convince the other judges that Fritzsche deserved the death penalty by reminding them that this defendant had acted as Goebbels's "right arm," kindling Germany's "imperialistic strivings" and inciting atrocities in the occupied territories. If the other judges refused to move, however, Nikitchenko could agree to life imprisonment. Nikitchenko was to push for the death penalty for Papen on the grounds that the former German chancellor had helped Hitler to seize power. Nikitchenko had the firmest orders regarding Schacht: he was to demand death and not back down, reminding the other judges that Schacht had financed Hitler's rise to power and Germany's invasion of many countries.[32]

The instructions about Julius Streicher and Konstantin von Neurath were complicated, for Moscow envisioned using these defendants as bargaining chips. For Streicher, Nikitchenko could agree to a finding of guilt on Count Four alone, as long as the death penalty was guaranteed. But he was to "make a gift" of his agreement, presenting it as a concession in return for which the Western judges would need to compromise on other defendants such as Schacht. Regarding Neurath, Nikitchenko was also to call for a death sentence but could, if necessary, agree to a fifteen-year prison term. This, too, Nikitchenko was to present as gesture of goodwill with the "gentle hint" (as the instructions put it) that he expected the Western judges to offer a similar compromise in return.[33]

Nikitchenko was to continue to insist on death sentences for the remaining defendants, even if they were found guilty on only one or two counts. The instructions provided specific advice here too. He was to "win Biddle over" on a death sentence for Walther Funk, the former economics minister, by reminding Biddle that Funk had turned plundering into an official policy. Nikitchenko was to make sure that the Tribunal did not try to soften Doenitz's sentence on the grounds that he had given the order for a ceasefire in May 1945, for by then Germany was "already defeated." Turning to the organizations case, the commission instructed Nikitchenko to insist on declarations of guilt for the Reich Cabinet as well as the General Staff and High Command, which the Western judges were proposing to exclude from their findings of criminal responsibility. (The commission did not comment on the anticipated ruling for the SA.)[34]

The Vyshinsky Commission concluded its instructions with a plan of action. Nikitchenko was to do everything possible to get the other judges to accept Moscow's position. He was to appeal in particular to Lawrence, who, as the presiding judge, should be made to understand that the world would not accept a "softhearted judgment" after the defendants' crimes had been so thoroughly proven before the court. If it turned out to be impossible to come to an acceptable agreement with the Western judges about the verdicts and sentences, Nikitchenko was to threaten to withhold his signature from the judgment. If this did not yield the desired results, he was to present his dissenting opinion in written form, demand that it be attached to the judgment, and insist that Lawrence share its contents in open court. The commission signed off by reminding Nikitchenko that its instructions were just an outline: it was up to him and Volchkov to make irrefutable arguments against acquittals and light sentences by making use of the evidence.[35]

The clock had almost run down and the moment for making irrefutable arguments had passed. By the time that Nikitchenko received these instructions on September 20, the verdicts and judgment were close to being finalized. On September 21, Safonov suggested to Molotov that Trainin, who had remained in Nuremberg after the organizations case to secretly assist the Soviet judges, fly to Paris to brief Vyshinsky in person on "the situation taking shape in the Tribunal." On Molotov's orders, Safonov went instead. He delivered the bad news that Nikitchenko's arguments against acquittals and light sentences were falling on deaf ears.[36]

The Tribunal finalized its judgment over the next few days without conceding to any of Nikitchenko's demands about the verdicts and the sentences. Instead, the Western judges added even more limits and exclusions to the organizations case. While all four judges agreed that the SS, the

Leadership Corps of the Nazi Party, and the Gestapo and SD (considered again as one organization) were criminal, Lawrence, Biddle, and de Vabres voted to exclude various subgroups, such as lower-level Party leaders.[37] The three Western judges also called for "uniformity of sentencing" for the members of these criminal organizations throughout the four occupation zones of Germany. Nikitchenko objected that the Tribunal had no right to make any such exclusions or stipulations; questions of this sort were supposed to be left to the national courts. His protests proved futile. The other judges repeatedly voted him down three to one—or really three to zero, for he refused to vote on matters that he thought fell outside the Tribunal's proper reach.[38]

These final deliberations about the judgment took place amid an ever-intensifying propaganda war between the Soviet Union and the United States.[39] Yet the international press was expecting unanimity from the Tribunal when it went back into session on September 30. That morning, the *Times* of London announced as much, celebrating the anticipated unanimous judgment as "an outstanding example of international solidarity." This was not to be. The night before, Nikitchenko had informed Biddle that he would be issuing a dissenting opinion: objecting to the three acquittals, to Hess's light sentence, and to the Tribunal's refusal to declare the Reich Cabinet and the General Staff and High Command criminal organizations.[40] Airey Neave later speculated that the Soviet judge had felt "embarrassed" about doing Moscow's bidding.[41] This is unlikely. Nikitchenko had understood from the start what his job would be in Nuremberg. He had loudly proclaimed the guilt of the defendants before the trials had even begun.

The Palace of Justice was a hub of activity as September 30 dawned. It was a bright, crisp day, and the rising sun revealed a thousand American soldiers stationed around and on top of the building and its adjoining prison.[42] Arriving that morning, the jurists and correspondents encountered tight security and throngs of people. "All the checkpoints were reinforced," observed Arkady Poltorak. "The guards inspected the contents of briefcases, looked closely at the passes and compared them with the proffered passports." Entering the courtroom, Poltorak recognized people he had not seen in Nuremberg since the start of the trial the previous November; he once again heard "a babel of voices."[43] Boris Polevoi was among the crowd of journalists looking for a place to sit. "The press box was so full that one could hardly breathe there," he later wrote. The courtroom was so packed that latecomers were forced to run up to the visitors' gallery.[44]

The prosecutors had assembled back at their old tables in the courtroom. Robert Jackson had returned to Nuremberg and had arrived at the

Palace of Justice with Thomas Dodd, Telford Taylor, Robert Kempner, and other members of his staff.[45] Roman Rudenko, Yuri Pokrovsky, and the rest of the Soviet team were also present in full force. The British and French prosecutions were well represented as well. Tensions between the prosecutors and the judges had been high at various points during the trials, and rumors of acquittals had started to circulate; the prosecution teams waited apprehensively, not knowing what lay ahead.[46] Thanks to the covert efforts of Nikitchenko, some of the Soviet prosecutors had seen an earlier draft of the judgment, but without the final verdicts and sentences.

The four judges and their alternates were sequestered in a side room of the Palace of Justice. They had arrived earlier in the morning in black bullet-proof sedans, each escorted by military jeeps with sirens. The judges waited for the appointed hour, their work almost done. The Western judges put on their robes. Nikitchenko and Volchkov adjusted their freshly pressed military uniforms.[47] Judgment day had at long last arrived. The Soviet judges were tired and anxious. Nikitchenko had been in secret communication with Soviet leaders about his dissenting opinion—and still did not have Moscow's final approval on the wording of the document.[48]

By 9:30 a.m., the defense counsel had settled into their places in the courtroom. Soon afterward the defendants were led in one by one; the crowd watched in silence as they filed into the dock. Suddenly the bailiff cried out: "Rise, the court is in session!" Everyone rose as the eight judges strode in. Lawrence carried a thick folder that drew everyone's attention. It was obvious that it held the judgment.[49] The judges took their place, the crowd was seated, and the proceedings began.

The four judges and their alternates took turns reading from the judgment. Lawrence led off, describing the origins of the Nuremberg Charter and the main charges against the twenty-two defendants. He then recounted the history of Nazism, from the founding of the Nazi Party to Hitler's ascension. Norman Birkett next read a long section about Hitler's consolidation of power. He described how the Nazi Party had removed all political opposition and had attacked churches, trade unions, and the Jews. He also told how the Nazi government and the military had pursued rearmament. He then turned to the charge of crimes against peace. He explained that Counts One and Two both concerned the waging of aggressive war, which the Tribunal considered the "supreme international crime." "Aggression" was an "essential part of Nazi foreign policy" aimed in part at the creation of a "Greater Germany," he declared, recapping evidence about the secret meetings at which Hitler had revealed his plans for war against Europe.[50]

The two French judges went next. De Vabres detailed Germany's initial crimes against peace, beginning with the Anschluss. Whether or not the Germans and the Austrians shared common characteristics was "immaterial," as was the question of whether or not the annexation had been accomplished "without bloodshed," he read, as the evidence had shown that the methods were "those of an aggressor." (This wording neatly addressed Soviet concerns.) He next described the German invasion of Czechoslovakia and Poland. The facts, he stated, had clearly established that Hitler had attacked Poland in September 1939 with the aim of enlarging Germany's "living space" and securing food and other resources. This section carefully avoided the topic of Soviet-German collaboration, noting only that Hitler had sent Ribbentrop to Moscow "to negotiate a non-aggression pact."[51]

French alternate judge Robert Falco then covered the German invasion of Denmark and Norway. Proof was lacking, Falco announced, to support the defense's claim that Germany had invaded Norway, the Netherlands, Belgium, and Luxembourg in order to forestall Allied invasions. After reading the judgment's sections about Greece and Yugoslavia, he addressed Hitler's betrayal of Stalin. Though the Soviets had abided by the terms of the German-Soviet Non-Aggression Pact, the Nazis had nonetheless begun preparing in the summer of 1940 for an attack on the Soviet Union. Their plans for mass deportations, the murder of local leaders, and the economic exploitation of conquered territory, he continued, had all been part of a carefully constructed plot. He concluded with an account of Germany's declaration of war against the United States.[52]

There was still much to cover, and when the court went back into session after lunch Biddle detailed Germany's violations of international treaties. It was impossible to imagine that the defendants had not known that they were defying international law when they "carried out their designs of invasion and aggression," he read. It fell to Biddle to elaborate the Tribunal's reformulation of the conspiracy charge—and a stir went through the courtroom as he revealed where the judges had parted ways with the prosecution. The Tribunal had rejected the prosecution's argument that the conspiracy had begun with the creation of the Nazi Party and had instead dated its start to November 5, 1937, by which point Hitler's plans to invade neighboring countries had "been established beyond doubt." The judges had also decided that the conspiracy charge did not extend to war crimes or crimes against humanity.[53]

The courtroom quieted when John Parker introduced the judgment's sections on Counts Three and Four. The Nazis had committed war crimes on an unprecedented scale, he began. Many had been planned long before the start of hostilities. Turning to the "crimes against humanity" charge, he related the Tribunal's finding that the German occupiers had imposed a regime of systematic violence and terror throughout Europe. In the occupied Soviet Union and Poland, the abuse and murder of civilians had "reached its height," he read. The Einsatzgruppen had exterminated Jews, communists, and other groups in order to clear the way for the colonization of their territories by Germans.[54]

It was midafternoon when Nikitchenko stepped in to describe how Soviet citizens had been forced to support the German war economy by working as slave laborers on military fortifications. Then, turning to the crimes against the Jews, he announced the Tribunal's finding that the defendants had acted with "consistent and systematic inhumanity." The methods of annihilating the Jews took many forms, he read: in some cases, Jews were murdered in concentration camps, while in others the Einsatzgruppen did the work of extermination. All in all, Nazi policies had resulted in the murder of six million Jews. Nikitchenko was now forced to go against Moscow's instructions and explain why atrocities committed against the Jews before 1939 would not be considered crimes against humanity for the purposes of the judgment. As "revolting and horrible" as these earlier crimes may have been, he read, the prosecution did not prove that they had been committed "in execution of, or in connection with, the aggressive war."[55]

By late afternoon, the audience had become restless.[56] Around 4 p.m. the judges finally turned to the first part of the verdict: the findings for the organizations case. Volchkov now took his turn at the microphone. Betraying no emotion, he elaborated the provisions the Tribunal had introduced, also against Soviet wishes, to limit the web of guilt. He then announced the Tribunal's rulings. The Leadership Corps of the Nazi Party, the SS, and the Gestapo and SD had all been found "criminal." However, they were deemed culpable only for crimes committed after the start of the war. Individuals who had left these organizations before September 1, 1939 (the day Germany invaded Poland) were thus exempted from responsibility. The Tribunal also exempted some technical workers and subgroups, including the Secret Field Police of the Gestapo and the lower Party leaders (the Blockleiter and the Zellenleiter).[57]

It also fell to Volchkov to announce the Tribunal's findings of "not guilty" for the SA, the Reich Cabinet, and the General Staff and High Command. This must have felt like a cruel joke to the Soviet judges, given Stalin's insistence on guilty verdicts. The SA had played a fundamental part in establishing a "Nazi reign of terror over Germany" and had participated in "violence against the Jews," he read. But the prosecution had not proven that these activities were related to the planning or waging of the war. The Reich Cabinet had ceased to exist in any meaningful way before the war and was small enough for its members to stand trial individually. Volchkov also related the Tribunal's finding (which the Soviet judges had hotly disputed) that the General Staff and High Command was not an "organization" as defined by the Charter. This did not mean that Wehrmacht officers were not responsible for crimes against peace or for war crimes and crimes against humanity, he explained, for many of them had either participated in or silently acquiesced to these crimes.[58] But there would be no declaration of the military's collective guilt.

The most anticipated part of the judgment—the verdicts against the individual defendants—would wait until morning. When the court adjourned, Polevoi and some of the other Soviet correspondents headed to the local bar, where a knot of Western journalists was making wagers on the fate of the defendants: "Hanging? Shooting? Life imprisonment? Acquittal?" Polevoi later remembered how the bartender recorded the bets, as if they had been at the racetrack.[59]

There was no rest for the Soviet delegation. Late that night, members of the Vyshinsky Commission finalized Nikitchenko's dissenting opinion. At 2:10 a.m. Moscow time, a Soviet diplomat (Enver Mamedov) passed on a secret message to the deputy foreign minister Vladimir Dekanozov: Minister of Justice Nikolai Rychkov and Ivan Goliakov, the chairman of the Soviet Union's Supreme Court, had approved the dissent, and SMERSH chief Viktor Abakumov was expected to give a positive appraisal as well. Dekanozov phoned Vyshinsky in Paris with this news. Vyshinsky added his own approval, and the document was sent immediately to Nuremberg.[60]

The Palace of Justice was again packed on the morning of October 1. For the very last time, the defendants were back in their usual places in the dock as they awaited word of their fates. Goering looked around through dark glasses, a hint of a grin on his face; Hess sat rifling through a pile of papers; Keitel sat rigidly in his military uniform, staring straight ahead.[61] As the court went into session, Lawrence announced that the Tribunal would begin by delivering the verdicts and would follow later with the sentencing.

Lawrence read the verdicts against the first several defendants. He turned first to Goering, summing up the evidence of his crimes. Goering's guilt was "unique in its enormity" and there was "nothing to be said in mitigation." He was guilty on all four counts. Hess was next, and the verdict was mixed. While the prosecution had shown that he might have known about war crimes committed in the East and that his subordinates in the Party had distributed orders that led to the commission of these crimes, the Tribunal had deemed such evidence insufficient for findings of guilt. The proof of his participation in Hitler's planning for war, however, was incontrovertible; he was guilty on Counts One and Two. Lawrence moved on to Ribbentrop—whose participation in Nazi crimes was found to be "whole-hearted." He was guilty on all four counts.[62] The verdict against Keitel was the same. He might have personally opposed the war against the Soviet Union, but he had initialed the invasion plan, organized the attack, and passed down directives that had resulted in the commission of atrocities. Next came Ernst von Kaltenbrunner, whom the Tribunal had found guilty on Counts Three and Four.[63]

Nikitchenko stepped in to deliver the verdict against Rosenberg. This defendant had set up a "system of organized plunder" in the occupied Soviet Union and had been fully aware of the cruel mistreatment of the Soviet people. He was guilty on all four counts. Biddle then read the verdict against Frank. The prosecution had not proven that Frank was guilty of conspiracy, Biddle stated. Counts Three and Four stood, however, for Frank had knowingly participated in the deportation and enslavement of "over a million Poles" and the murder of "at least three million Jews." De Vabres then turned to Frick, announcing that the Tribunal had found him guilty on Counts Two, Three, and Four. Lawrence read the verdict against Streicher, declaring him guilty on Count Four. Next, Nikitchenko presented the Funk verdict. While Funk had not played a leading role in the conspiracy, he had made economic preparations for the invasion and looting of other countries; later, as head of the Reichsbank, he had collected truckloads of currency, jewelry, and gold teeth from concentration camp victims. He was guilty on Counts Two, Three, and Four.[64]

After a brief recess, Biddle moved on to Schacht, describing his critical part in facilitating Germany's rearmament and military resurgence. However, rearmament itself was not a criminal act, Biddle explained, and the prosecution had failed to prove that Schacht had known of Hitler's plans for war. The Tribunal found him not guilty and ordered his release.[65] Poltorak later recounted how a "rumble mounted in the courtroom" with this announcement, with some people expressing approval and others anger and disappointment.[66] The correspondents, who had been uncertain about the likelihood of acquittals, instantly adjusted their expectations. Anything now seemed possible.

The two admirals, Doenitz and Raeder, were next in the dock, and de Vabres and Lawrence read their verdicts. Both were found guilty of crimes against peace and war crimes; Raeder was also found guilty of conspiracy for his role in the invasion of Norway. The ruling on war crimes, however, contained an important caveat for both defendants: for the purposes of sentencing, the Tribunal would not consider their practice of sinking ships without warning, given that the U.S. Navy had waged war in a similar manner in the Pacific. The next two verdicts, read by Nikitchenko and Biddle, were also mixed. Schirach was found guilty only on Count Four, for deporting the Jews from Vienna. Sauckel was found guilty on Counts Three and Four, for his role in overseeing the deportation of more than five million people for slave labor. Jodl was next, and here the verdict was unequivocal. The Tribunal had disallowed his plea of "superior orders," de Vabres announced, and had found him guilty on all four counts.[67]

The Papen verdict was the second big sensation of the day. The Tribunal had found the evidence against this defendant lacking, Lawrence explained. Papen had used "intrigue and bullying" to bolster the Nazi Party in Austria in an effort to bring about the Anschluss. But this was not a crime under the Nuremberg Charter, and the prosecution had not established that he had been involved in any war plans. He was acquitted. After the crowd settled down, Nikitchenko presented the Seyss-Inquart verdict: guilty on Counts Two, Three, and Four. Biddle read the Speer and Neurath verdicts. While Speer had run the armaments industry to support the German war effort, the Tribunal did not find that this was tantamount to planning or waging war. The Tribunal did find him guilty on Counts Three and Four, largely for his use of forced labor; but the Tribunal noted mitigating factors for his sentencing, such as his resistance to Hitler near the war's end. Neurath by contrast was found guilty on all four counts.[68]

Fritzsche was next, and Nikitchenko sat stoically as Lawrence read the verdict. Fritzsche had instructed the German press how to write about the wars against Poland and the Soviet Union. He had not, however, been one of the key formulators of Germany's propaganda policies. He had not even been important enough to be included in the conferences that developed the plans for the war. As such, Lawrence continued, his activities did not fit the Tribunal's definition of conspiracy. Nor would the Tribunal hold him responsible for inciting Germans to carry out atrocities. While he had spewed anti-Semitism, he had not directly called for the persecution or murder of the Jews. He was acquitted on all counts. The Bormann verdict was last, and Nikitchenko announced his guilt (in absentia) on Counts Three and Four.[69]

In the end, Counts Three and Four proved to be the most robust. Just two of the eighteen defendants charged with war crimes and two of the seventeen defendants charged with crimes against humanity (in both cases, Hess and Fritzsche) were acquitted of these charges. Count Two also fared reasonably well. Twelve of the sixteen defendants charged with crimes against peace—all but Speer, Papen, Schacht, and Sauckel—were found guilty on this count. Only the conspiracy charge, which Jackson had deemed so necessary to illustrate the breadth and depth of Nazi criminality, proved to be a bust. All twenty-two defendants had been charged under Count One. In the end, after narrowing the charge, the Tribunal found only eight of them guilty of conspiracy. Even here, the conspiracy charge had little effect on the outcome of the trial—for those eight were all also convicted of crimes against peace.[70]

The court went into recess, and the bailiff immediately released the three men who had been fully acquitted. Polevoi, watching them closely, noted that Fritzsche cheerfully bid farewell to the other defendants, "unable to contain his sheer animal joy." Papen "took leave only of the military and naval officers and Goering." Schacht walked right past the other defendants with "an expression of disdain on his bulldog face."[71] The three freed defendants headed to the pressroom to give interviews, followed closely by Western reporters. The Soviet journalists stayed behind.[72]

At 2:50 p.m. the court reconvened for the last time. The feeling in the courtroom was now entirely different. The lights had been dimmed: there would be no photography or filming of this final session. The dock was empty, for the defendants would enter the courtroom one by one to hear their sentences. The journalists and other observers who crowded the press box and the visitors' gallery sat expectant and still. They rose as the judges entered the courtroom, then took their seats again and continued to wait in silence.[73]

A few minutes passed, and then Judge Lawrence looked out over the courtroom and nodded. A sliding door behind the dock quietly opened and Goering walked through, flanked by two military policemen. Lawrence read his sentence: "death by hanging." Goering glanced at the judges before turning and leaving the courtroom. Hess was led in a few seconds later and heard his sentence of life imprisonment. He exited, and an ashen-faced Ribbentrop entered the courtroom. "Death by hanging." And so the procession continued. Keitel, Kaltenbrunner, Rosenberg, Frank, Frick, and Streicher all stood before the Tribunal, one after another, and heard the same three words: "death by hanging." The next four defendants would be spared the hangman's noose. Funk and Raeder were sentenced to life imprisonment; Doenitz received a ten-year prison term; and Schirach was sentenced to twenty years. Sauckel, Jodl, and Seyss-Inquart, on the other hand, would hang. Speer received twenty years, and Neurath fifteen. Bormann received a death sentence in absentia. In less than an hour all of the sentences were read.[74]

Before the crowd dispersed, Lawrence announced that Nikitchenko wished to record his dissent from the verdicts in the cases of Schacht, Papen, and Fritzsche. "He is of the opinion that they should have been convicted and not acquitted," Lawrence stated. Nikitchenko also dissented from the Tribunal's findings about the Reich Cabinet and the General Staff and High Command, "being of the opinion that they should have been declared to be criminal organizations." And he dissented from the Tribunal's decision about Hess, arguing that his sentence "should have been death, and not life imprisonment." Lawrence noted that this dissenting opinion would be attached to the final judgment, which would soon be published. With this, the Nuremberg Trials came to an end.[75]

The acquittals did not sit well with many Germans. By the time the court adjourned, an angry crowd had already gathered outside the Palace of Justice, upset at the idea of Papen, Schacht, and Fritzsche going free.[76] The Soviets were more than ready to seize on this outrage and immediately launched a plan of action. In Berlin, Soviet diplomat Vladimir Semenov met with Walter Ulbricht and other German politicians, giving them directions for conducting a protest campaign in the press and on the radio and for organizing demonstrations aimed at showing the support of the German people for Nikitchenko's dissenting opinion. On October 2, Semenov informed the Ministry of Foreign Affairs that this plan was under way. In keeping with Moscow's instructions, demonstrations had been held in Berlin immediately after the verdicts were revealed, and protests were now occurring all throughout the Soviet zone.[77]

These demonstrations made a strong impression on observers. Poltorak later remembered that "a hundred thousand people demonstrated" in Leipzig alone, waving banners stating: "Death to the War Criminals!" "We Want Lasting Peace!" and "A People's Trial for von Papen, Schacht and Fritzsche!"[78] Lucius Clay (the U.S. deputy military governor in Germany) also noted the widespread discontent about the acquittals. Writing to the adjutant general's office of the U.S. War Department on October 7, he reported that both the Social Democratic Party and the Socialist Unity (Communist) Party had organized mass protests in Berlin on October 2 and that the latter had also held demonstrations in many other cities in the Soviet zone. Local leaders as well as ordinary Germans were calling for Schacht, Papen, and Fritzsche to be tried by German national courts for crimes against the German people.[79]

Clay further elaborated on the public reactions of German politicians. Alfred Kubel, the prime minister of Braunschweig, called the acquittals "surprising," noting that Papen "could not have been ignorant of Nazi intentions." Kurt Schumacher, the national chairman of the Social Democratic Party, also criticized Papen's acquittal and suggested that the verdicts clearly showed that the victors had failed to understand "the essence of Nazism." Jakob Kaiser, the national chairman of the Christian Democratic Union, privately expressed his disapproval of the acquittals—and of a judgment determined by the victors. The politicians were clearly aware that it was politically advantageous to express "anti-Nazi sentiments at this moment," Clay wrote. He also observed "considerable genuine indignation" along with the widespread wish to purge Germany "once and for all" of Nazism.[80]

Moscow facilitated the publication of Nikitchenko's dissenting opinion at home and abroad, and Soviet leaders monitored the responses in the world press. Semenov informed the Ministry of Foreign Affairs that "progressive newspapers" throughout the world were expressing "shock and anger" about the acquittals and also disapproval of the light sentences given to some of the other defendants, declaring their support for Nikitchenko. According to Semenov, the Argentinean paper La Ora had even reported that Schacht had been acquitted because the Anglo-American imperialists needed him to reorganize German industry and finance. The British press, by contrast, had defended the judgment and had questioned the right of German national courts to try men who had been acquitted in Nuremberg, as this would suggest that they had more authority than the Tribunal.[81]

On October 9 and 10, the Allied Control Council denied petitions for pardons, and plans began to move ahead for carrying out the death sentences.[82] The executions were scheduled for just after midnight on October 16 and would take place in a small gymnasium in the Nuremberg prison courtyard. Meanwhile, Clay forwarded a memo from the U.S. State Department to American occupation authorities reflecting continuing concerns about the trials being perceived as an act of victors' justice. It advised American officials to present the Nuremberg judgment to the German people as the legal redress of the terrible wrongs that the war criminals had "inflicted on civilization"—and to stress that the prosecution's main evidence had come from the Nazi regime itself. They were to underscore that the verdict was not an act of vengeance but the result of an impartial trial, which had reaffirmed existing international law.[83]

On the evening of October 15, the Press Camp was a hive of expectation and excitement. Polevoi reflected that if "it were only a matter of wishing, everyone would have instantly dashed off to the prison courtyard" to witness the executions for themselves. Each of the four countries of the prosecution had been given just two slots for the press: one for a reporter and one for a photographer. The Soviet slots went to the TASS correspondent Boris Afanasyev and the *Pravda* photographer Viktor Temin, whose images of the German capitulation in Berlin were already iconic.[84]

At around 8:00 p.m., the chosen correspondents arrived at the Palace of Justice. They were directed to a meeting room, where U.S. commandant Colonel Burton Andrus directed them not to communicate with anyone on the outside until after the sentences were carried out. Andrus then gave them a tour of the prison, leading them down a narrow stairway and into a dimly lit corridor. There were doors on both sides with sturdy locks. Afanasyev observed that lamps burned over eleven doors and understood that these were the cells of the men sentenced to die. Stopping by these cells, the correspondents peered through small eyeholes to look inside. Some of the prisoners were reading or writing; Ribbentrop was talking with a priest. Around 9:30 p.m., Andrus led the correspondents out into the night air and then into a small building, an empty gymnasium that had been used just a few days earlier by American security guards for a basketball game. Three scaffolds, painted forest green, took up most of the room; a staircase of thirteen steps led up to each of them, and thick ropes hung from a crossbeam supported by two posts. Four tables with chairs had been set before the scaffolds for the press and other official observers. The correspondents looked things over, and Andrus then ushered them outside.[85]

At 11:00 p.m. Andrus brought the correspondents back to the meeting room where they had first assembled. They sat, waiting, for almost two hours, hearing activity and raised voices outside and beginning to wonder about the apparent delay. Finally, at about 1:00 a.m., they were brought back to the gym and took their seats in front of the scaffolds along with medical experts and a member of the military command from each of the four Allied powers.[86] Temin and Afanasyev noticed that Andrus was agitated, and it soon became obvious that something was wrong. People were whispering Goering's name, but no one would say what had happened. A moment later Ribbentrop was led out to the scaffold and mounted the stairs. A priest approached him and whispered a short prayer. The executioner placed a noose and a black hood over Ribbentrop's head. A lever was pulled, a trap door opened, and Ribbentrop disappeared. All that was visible was a taut rope swinging back and forth.[87]

The American sergeant who performed the executions worked quickly and efficiently. He alternated between two of the scaffolds, holding the third in reserve. In "an hour and a half he disposed of the ten condemned men," Afanasyev observed. The bodies were placed in black boxes behind a curtain, and the correspondents were allowed to photograph them. Although ten men had been hanged, eleven boxes lay side by side—the eleventh containing

Goering's body. The correspondents learned that he had ingested cyanide a few hours earlier in his cell. How he had obtained the poison was a question that none of those present could answer.[88] Following the executions, the bodies were secretly transported to Munich. They were burned in a crematorium there, and their ashes were scattered into a stream that ran into the nearby Isar River.[89] Hess, Funk, Doenitz, Raeder, Schirach, Speer, and Neurath were brought to Spandau Prison in western Berlin, where they would serve their sentences.[90]

After the judgment, the Palace of Justice again grew quiet. The Soviet interpreters and translators had already left for Leipzig, in the Soviet zone. They would spend the next three months there, correcting the Russian-language text of the stenographic record of the trial.[91] With the sentences now carried out, the Press Camp evaporated too. Polevoi and his colleagues bid farewell to the many international correspondents they had gotten to know over the preceding months and boarded a military transport plane for the first leg of the trip back to Moscow.[92] There they would join Roman Karmen, whose documentary about Nuremberg, *Judgment of the Peoples* (*Sud narodov*), was almost ready for release.[93] Nikitchenko and Volchkov also left for Moscow. Trainin, too, returned to Moscow, where he would prepare for an upcoming trip to Paris to attend the International Congress of Jurists.[94] In Paris he would gather with de Vabres, René Cassin, and other international-law experts to discuss Nuremberg's triumphs and failures.

In the wake of the judgment, the Soviet Union, the United States, France, and Great Britain would compete with one another to define the legacy of Nuremberg through new postwar institutions, including the United Nations. They would also discuss the possible creation of a permanent international criminal court. Soviet leaders had been dissatisfied with parts of the judgment: they had not gotten all of the guilty verdicts or death sentences they had sought. Yet the judgment had ratified some of the Soviet Union's key contributions to the IMT—most notably the rejection of the defense of superior orders and the concept of a crime against peace. Going forward, Soviet leaders would render their own judgment on the successes and failures of the Nuremberg Trials and on the Soviet Union's role in international institutions more generally. They would deliberate on what lessons to take from Nuremberg about politics, propaganda, and international law. All of this would acquire acute importance for the Soviet Union in the months and years ahead.

CHAPTER 15 | Beyond Nuremberg

A S THE EUPHORIA of the victory over Nazi Germany faded, and as the IMT carried out its sentences in mid-October 1946, the Soviet Union was still digging out from the ruins of war. Shortages of housing and food had become only more acute as Red Army soldiers demobilized and returned home. Driving the Soviet people forward, Stalin warned of an inevitable clash with the capitalist West and intensified the internal hunt for Nazi collaborators, both real and imagined. He also continued to demand recognition and respect for the Soviet Union as an international power.[1]

Aron Trainin brought a heavy sense of purpose to Paris a week later as he headed to the first International Congress of Jurists. The Congress was dedicated to the theme "Law and Peace," and topics on the agenda included Nazi crimes against humanity and the defense of democratic freedoms. Plans for the Congress had been hatched the previous May, when Henri Donnedieu de Vabres had convened the first postwar meeting of the International Association of Criminal Law in Nuremberg's Palace of Justice. The recently established United Nations had provided a further impetus with its call for the "progressive development of international law." The United Nations, too, would be discussing Nuremberg and its legacy. While Trainin prepared for his Paris debut, Vyacheslav Molotov and Andrei Vyshinsky flew to New York, where they would represent Soviet interests at the United Nations General Assembly in Flushing Meadows, Queens. New international institutions were becoming visible sites of power and diplomacy, and the Soviets were determined to have a hand in shaping them.

Paris was bleak in the autumn of 1946.[2] The war had left its mark on all of Europe's cities and its people—described by former prime minister Winston Churchill that September as a "quivering mass of tormented, hungry, careworn and bewildered human beings."[3] The Nazi rampage across the continent—the mass atrocities and senseless destruction—had brought civilization to its knees. Yet in the wake of Nuremberg there was also hope. By introducing concepts such as "crimes against peace," "crimes against humanity," and "genocide" into global discourse, the IMT had opened up a wide-ranging conversation about how international law might be expanded to protect humankind from its worst impulses.

Arriving in Paris on October 24, Trainin joined some 200 other lawyers and judges from twenty-four countries. He had been planning to use the Congress to protest the Nuremberg acquittals and to present the Soviet Union as a world leader in the burgeoning postwar movement for peace and human rights. Upon his arrival, he was taken aback to discover how dramatically France's political environment had changed after the June elections. The left had lost significant ground. How would this affect the Congress? Would any of the Western lawyers put him on the spot by attacking the new "socialist democracies" of Eastern Europe? To Trainin's relief, the Congress proceeded smoothly enough—although, as he reported to Moscow, the attendees disagreed over the meaning of the term "democracy." A major theme of the Congress was the unfinished business of Nuremberg, and here there was much agreement. The delegates expressed their collective disapproval of the acquittals of Hjalmar Schacht and Franz von Papen. They also declared the Tribunal's understanding of "crimes against humanity," restricted to crimes carried out on behalf of an aggressor state during wartime, to be unnecessarily narrow. Addressing the Congress, Trainin added his own critique, lambasting the Tribunal for allowing the German industrialists who had supported Hitler to escape trial.[4]

The Congress passed three resolutions that together set out an ambitious agenda for the development of international law. The first called on the United Nations to draft an international bill of human rights. The second defined crimes against humanity as the persecution or extermination of individuals or groups on account of nationality, race, religion, or opinions and declared that Nazi mass murder based on these criteria could be defined as genocide. This resolution also recommended the creation of an international criminal court to try such crimes. Thus began the process of reclassifying genocide, which had been listed as a war crime at Nuremberg, as a crime against humanity—and as a punishable criminal offense outside the context of war. The third resolution, initiated by Trainin, demanded the convening of a second international military tribunal to bring the German industrialists to justice. Before dispersing, the Congress voted to create a new organization: the International Association of Democratic Lawyers. It nominated Trainin and the French lawyer René Cassin to two of its top positions.[5]

Trainin had used his time in Paris to create momentum for an international trial of industrialists. Telford Taylor, who had remained in Nuremberg to prepare for an American trial of the German doctors who had carried out the Nazi "euthanasia" program, was troubled by this development. He knew that nobody on the American side had any interest in further collaborating with the Soviets. On October 30, Taylor wrote to Robert Jackson, who had just returned to the Supreme Court. The industrialists' trial had "erroneously become tied up in everyone's mind with the question of an international trial," Taylor noted. President Truman could help the situation by announcing that the Americans would be trying the industrialists in Germany—on their own, without the other Allied powers. Taylor further suggested that Truman make it clear that industrialists were not the only ones who would stand trial. American trials in Germany would cover "representatives of all the important segments of the Third Reich," including Reich Cabinet ministers, militarists, and SS and police officials. Finally, Taylor urged diplomacy. Should Truman go further and declare that the U.S. government would not participate in any more four-power war crimes trials, he should phrase this in such a way "so as to do no damage to the prestige of the London Agreement" of August 1945, which had set out the framework for Nuremberg and still had great significance for "the development of international law with respect to war crimes."[6]

Nuremberg was on everyone's mind. It had been an extraordinary event. Did it also have implications for the future of international law?[7] If so, what were they? While the International Congress of Jurists was setting out its agenda in Paris, the United Nations General Assembly had been discussing the codification of international law. At the General Assembly's opening session on October 23, Truman had praised the Nuremberg Charter for showing the way to prevent future wars. The following day, Secretary-General Trygve Lie (who had served until recently as the foreign minister of the Norwegian government-in-exile) had urged that the principles underlying Nuremberg be made into permanent international law "as quickly as possible."[8] The General Assembly had also taken under consideration a proposal from China, India, and Cuba to prepare a resolution condemning the "crime of genocide." Calling out a major failing of the Nuremberg judgment, they had declared it outrageous that a state's massacre of its own citizens had been deemed to fall outside the realm of international concern.[9] A few weeks later, the British delegate to the United Nations—the former Nuremberg prosecutor Hartley Shawcross—suggested that the General Assembly declare genocide "an international crime for the commission of which principals and accessories, as well as states, are individually responsible."[10]

In London, the United Nations War Crimes Commission (UNWCC), which had continued over the previous year with its work of investigating lower-level war crimes, was having its own discussions about Nuremberg and what it meant. At a November 8 meeting, the Yugoslav lawyer Radomir Živković, who had recently returned from the International Congress of Jurists, reported positively on the Congress's resolution to push for the inclusion of "crimes against humanity" in a new international-law code to protect human rights.[11] The members of the UNWCC also supported the idea that Nuremberg's definition of "crimes against humanity" deserved rethinking. The fact that the Nuremberg judgment had considered this charge restrictively, as a by-product of war, need not serve as a precedent, the UNWCC concluded—for the IMT had been an occupation court with jurisdiction only over Germany.[12]

Francis Biddle, who had also returned to Washington and was trying to figure out his next career move, was embarking on his own campaign to shape Nuremberg's legacy. He considered the Nuremberg judgment, as written, a suitable precedent for the future development of international law. In a November 9 letter to Truman, he advised that the U.S. government take the lead and ask the United Nations to codify the main principles set out in Article 6 of the Nuremberg Charter, either on their own or as part of a broader "codification of offenses against the peace and security of mankind."[13]

For Biddle, a "crime against peace" was and always would be the fundamental crime. A "war to conquer territory and subdue populations," he later wrote, "necessarily resulted in the kind of savagery in which the German leaders indulged, the torture rooms of the Gestapo and the concentration camps." Unlike the delegates to the International Congress of Jurists and the members of the UNWCC, Biddle held fast to the view that crimes against humanity—including the persecution, deportation, enslavement, and extermination of civilians—were tightly bound up with state-sponsored warfare. He had Truman's support. In a November 12 response to Biddle, Truman endorsed the call to codify what would soon be called the "Nuremberg principles" in a new code of international criminal law to deal with "all who wage aggressive war."[14]

Biddle's letter and Truman's response were made public and served as a prompt to action.[15] On November 15, the U.S. delegation to the United

Nations introduced a draft resolution to the General Assembly, asking it to reaffirm the principles of international law recognized by the Nuremberg Charter and by the judgment of the Tribunal. The U.S. delegation further suggested that the General Assembly ask the newly established Committee on the Progressive Development of International Law and its Codification (the Codification Committee) to write these principles into any new law adopted by the United Nations.[16]

Not everyone was on board with the idea of making the Nuremberg principles a permanent part of international law. In an editorial on November 14, the *New York Times* warned that the concept of "crimes against peace" was much too vague.[17] Perhaps the biggest critic, though, was Robert Jackson. In a November 16 letter to Secretary of State James Byrnes, Jackson expressed concern about the effort to get the United Nations to adopt the principles underlying the Nuremberg Trials. Jackson acknowledged that "if this could be done, and in a way that we would all like to see it done, it would be a great forward step." But he was certain that politics would get in the way. The Allied nations had agreed to the Nuremberg Charter in August 1945 only because of the timing, he noted. The war had just ended, and the governments had pledged to their own citizens that they would punish the Nazi war criminals. The process had been helped along because the politicians had left the lawyers to work "without interference," which would certainly not happen now. Even so, it had been impossible "to get a definition of 'aggressive warfare'" into the Charter. Today, there was "far less unity of purpose and spirit," he reflected, and the Allied nations had become too "sovereignty-conscious" to back a meaningful codification project. Not much more than a year earlier, Jackson had hoped to use the IMT to shape international law. He now feared that a failed effort by the United Nations to codify the Nuremberg principles would undermine everything Nuremberg had achieved, giving the "next aggressor," as he put it, an excuse for its actions.[18] Ever a realist, Jackson understood perhaps better than anyone else the political challenges this endeavor would face.

In the Soviet Union, Stalin was tracking these discussions about the Nuremberg principles from his villa in Sochi on the Black Sea. On November 14, TASS's Secret Department presented him with a memorandum, "Biddle's Letter and Truman's Response," which reported that the White House had approved Biddle's recommendation that the United Nations draft a new international-law code criminalizing "aggressive war." The memorandum pointed out that Biddle's letter had noted the Soviet dissent from parts of the Nuremberg judgment while affirming the four nations' general accord regarding the principles set out in the Nuremberg Charter's Article 6.[19]

Aron Trainin—who had of course introduced the idea of a "crime against peace" even before helping to write the Nuremberg Charter—had after Paris become only more convinced that the Soviet Union was destined to play a leading role in the progressive development of international law. On his return to Moscow he briefed the Institute of Law about the International Congress of Jurists and communicated his belief that the Nuremberg Charter and the Nuremberg judgment had great significance as sources of a universal international criminal law. He also anticipated the expansion of the Soviet criminal code to include a new section on international crimes against peace and humanity, taking it as a point of pride that the Soviet Union, "the most progressive country," would be out in front in this effort.[20]

Even as Trainin struck an optimistic chord about Soviet leadership in the realm of international law, other Soviet lawyers were warning of danger. In a November lecture in Moscow, Evgeny Korovin (an early skeptic of legal universalism whose career had stalled while Trainin's took off in the 1930s) spoke soberly of international law as a struggle between what he called "progressive democratic" forces and "reactionary imperialistic" forces. He agreed with Trainin that international law could be a force for peace. But he cautioned that "the political cooks of the capitalists" were already serving up "warmed-over scraps from the fascist kitchen" by envisioning the Anglo-Saxons as a "chosen race" destined "to lead the world." Korovin complained that the Americans and the British were posing as "defenders of human rights . . . for some reason never on their own continents, but on the opposite side of the globe." He also called out the U.S. government for failing to honor its treaty obligations, most significantly for halting reparations payments from its zone of Germany earlier in the year.[21] For Korovin, international law was dangerous, and international agreements were only as reliable as their signatories.

Trainin's and Korovin's opposing views captured Moscow's ambivalence about how Nuremberg had gone. The Second World War had catapulted the Soviet Union into the world of international law and international institutions. The Soviets had played a leading role in organizing the IMT and developing its legal framework. They had used Nuremberg to seek justice and pursue reparations—and to make their presence felt as a world power. But Nuremberg had also exposed Soviet vulnerabilities, as well as probable Soviet culpability for war crimes and crimes against peace. The Soviets had gotten something very different from the show trial they had anticipated (quick decision, quick punishment) when Molotov had first pressed for a special international tribunal during the war.

The question now was how to go forward. Could the Soviets use international institutions to their advantage? Could they use what they had learned at Nuremberg to be better prepared and to prevent being outmaneuvered in the future? Given the important role these institutions were certain to play in the postwar context, did they even have a choice?

In spite of the disappointments of Nuremberg, Stalin and Molotov had not given up on international justice. There was no other way to pursue a group they wanted to see hang: the German industrialists who had supported Hitler. Most of these men were in American or British custody. Thus, even as Trainin and Korovin were debating the possibilities and perils of international law, Soviet diplomats in Paris were gauging the chances of a second inter-Allied trial. On November 14, the Soviet ambassador K. F. Starikov spoke privately with French lawyer and former Nuremberg prosecutor Charles Dubost and broached this topic. Dubost, as Starikov knew, was a longtime proponent of an industrialists' trial and was actively gathering evidence for one. Reporting back to the Ministry of Foreign Affairs, Starikov relayed Dubost's opinion that the Americans had gotten cold feet about trying the industrialists because they were loath to expose the connections between American and German industrialist circles. Starikov passed on Dubost's assurances that the French government remained interested in four-power cooperation and was actively looking into the idea of a second international trial.[22]

While Soviet leaders were discussing Starikov's report, the French government passed a diplomatic note to the Soviet embassy in Paris expressing the view that by dropping the industrialists' case the IMT had not lived up to the promise of the Nuremberg Charter. The French government proposed that the Committee of Chief Prosecutors be convened anew, "the sooner the better," possibly in Paris. The Soviet government replied to the French on December 7, asking for clarification on several questions. Did the French anticipate indicting additional industrialists? What kind of trial did they hope to organize? Had they also approached the American and British governments?[23]

Meeting again in Paris a week later, Dubost told Starikov that the French government wanted to try not just the Krupps but also other German industrialists who had "committed colossal injury to the French people"— and that it was envisioning another four-power tribunal on the order of Nuremberg. Regarding the Soviet government's third question, he admitted that neither the Americans nor the British had responded to the French government's inquiry. He repeated his belief that the Americans were anxious to conceal their German business connections. He also told Starikov that his recent trip to Germany had made "a gloomy impression." Denazification had petered out in the Western zone, and all kinds of "political criminals" were "walking about in freedom" and engaging in political activities. Dubost suggested that the Americans were preparing for a trial of Nazi doctors in order to "divert attention," as he put it, from the current state of affairs.[24]

While pursuing a four-power trial of German industrialists, the Soviets threw their support behind the United Nations' effort to codify the Nuremberg principles. On December 11, 1946, the General Assembly (which did not include any of the former Axis powers) unanimously passed a resolution affirming "the principles recognized in the Charter of the Nuremberg Tribunal and in the judgment of the Tribunal" and directed the Codification Committee to commence with its assignment.[25] In the same session the General Assembly unanimously passed a resolution declaring genocide an international crime and asked the United Nations Economic and Social Council to draft a genocide convention. The resolution defined genocide as "a denial of the right to existence of entire human groups" and noted that this crime occurred when "racial, religious, political and other groups" were "destroyed, entirely or in part." On Vyshinsky's instructions, the Soviet delegates voted for both resolutions.[26]

Moscow understood that it could not decline to participate in the efforts of the United Nations to promote peace and human rights without damaging Soviet claims to world leadership. The Soviet Union was already enmeshed in a propaganda battle with the United States for the hearts and minds of Europe. Leading Soviet artists and writers who had until recently been at Nuremberg had been enlisted for the struggle, including Ilya Ehrenburg, Boris Polevoi, Boris Efimov, and Roman Karmen (whose film *Judgment of the Peoples* had just opened in New York to mixed reviews). At a mid-December meeting of the Soviet Information Bureau, Solomon Lozovsky summed up what was at stake. During wartime, he explained, the Anglo-American campaign against the USSR had been "tamped down" so as not to "impede the joint struggle against Germany." But with the crushing of fascism, the Soviet Union had become the only force standing against British and American imperialism—and so the anti-Soviet campaign had been launched anew. He blamed "reactionaries" in the West for playing down the Soviet role in defeating Germany and for sowing doubt about the Soviet Union's commitment to democracy.[27]

As Trainin had seen in Paris, however, the Soviet Union and the Western powers had different understandings of democracy. At the United Nations, Valentin Tepliakov, the Soviet representative to the new Human Rights Commission, quickly ran into trouble trying to influence the conversation about democratic freedoms and human rights. The eighteen-member commission held its first meeting in Lake Success, New York, in January 1947. The main item on the agenda was the creation of a human rights bill. Eleanor Roosevelt chaired the meeting, and René Cassin assumed a leading role. Tepliakov saw at once that there was little support for the Soviet position that social and economic rights such as the right to work (which could only be guaranteed by the state) were more important than individual civil rights such as freedom of religion and expression. The Soviet Union's highly centralized command structure also limited his effectiveness. Soviet leaders had not authorized him to make any decisions on his own, forcing him to stall for time while awaiting responses from Moscow.[28] The same kinds of difficulties that had plagued Roman Rudenko and Iona Nikitchenko in London and Nuremberg had followed the Soviets to the United Nations. Though the Soviet representatives at Nuremberg had learned a great deal about the work of international organizations, Stalin himself continued to prize top-down control.

Cold War politics were about to intrude further into international organizations' efforts to codify and expand international law to protect human rights. On March 5, 1947 (exactly a year after Churchill delivered his "Iron Curtain" speech), the U.S. government announced what soon became known as the "Truman Doctrine," pledging economic and military support to people "resisting attempted subjugation by armed minorities or by outside pressure." Its chief purpose was to prevent the spread of communism. Barely a month later, the Soviet Union and the Western powers hit an impasse in their negotiations about Germany's future.[29] At the same time, the United States announced that it would begin its own trials of German industrialists in Nuremberg. The Soviet-French efforts to launch a second international trial had come to a dead end. The postwar experiment with four-power justice in Europe was officially over. Over the next nine months, the Americans would hold three industrialist trials: the Flick Trial, the Farben Trial, and the Krupp Trial.[30] Meanwhile, Dubost worked toward the prosecution of French businessmen who had collaborated with Hitler.[31]

The United Nations moved forward with its international-law projects that spring and summer, but with increasing mistrust among many of its members.[32] A proposal from the French brought this discord out into the open. In May, the Soviets sent the seasoned international-law expert Vladimir Koretsky (from the Ministry of Foreign Affairs) to serve on the Codification Committee at Lake Success. Henri Donnedieu de Vabres was representing the French—and at the opening meeting he suggested incorporating the

Nuremberg principles into a new international criminal code, to be enforced through a fifteen-member international criminal court. De Vabres, a long-time proponent of such a court, now touted it as a remedy for victors' justice, explaining that he had keenly felt the criticism of the Nuremberg judgment for having been decided only by representatives of victor countries.[33]

The Soviets balked at de Vabres's proposal. A decade earlier and seem-ingly a lifetime ago, Trainin and Vyshinsky had themselves advocated the creation of an international criminal court to try "persons violating peace." More recently Trainin had supported the call by the International Congress of Jurists for a court to try crimes against humanity. But Trainin had under-stood that such a court's mandate would be strictly to punish fascist aggres-sion. De Vabres, by contrast, was envisioning a court of fifteen judges that would operate in wartime and peacetime—and that could hear evidence of crimes committed by the citizens or by the leaders of a state. An explicit goal of the French proposal was to put a check on state sovereignty.

It was not clear to many of the delegates how a permanent international criminal court would work. It seemed improbable that a state would will-ingly hand its citizens over to such a body—or that leaders accused of abuses would submit themselves to such a body's jurisdiction.[34] The Soviets were not the only ones with misgivings about de Vabres's proposal but were the most direct and absolute in their opposition to it. The U.S. representative to the Codification Committee, Philip Jessup, shrewdly framed American objections in technical terms. He argued that the committee's charge had been only to study plans for the development of international law—and that the United Nations would need to create a separate commission to draft ac-tual legislation.[35] The Codification Committee was not deterred. It promptly asked the General Assembly to create an international-law commission, which might prepare two documents for consideration: a draft convention laying out the Nuremberg principles and a broader draft code of Offenses Against the Peace and Security of Mankind. The committee also advised the General Assembly that the implementation of the Nuremberg principles might make the creation of an international court desirable. The delegates from Poland, Yugoslavia, Egypt, and Great Britain joined the Soviet del-egate, Koretsky, in dissenting from these recommendations—all of them signaling concerns about state sovereignty.[36]

The sovereignty issue also weighed upon United Nations deliberations that summer about the international bill of rights and about the genocide convention. When Koretsky, who had replaced Tepliakov on the Human Rights Commission, opposed all articles allowing interference in another country's domestic affairs, Cassin took him on. Cassin argued that the chief purpose of the project was to prevent a repeat of 1933, when Germany began to murder its own citizens and no one intervened. Koretsky warned Moscow afterward that the human rights bill in its current form was intended to allow governments to interfere in one another's business.[37] Soviet leaders also recognized that the draft genocide convention (which the United Nations Secretariat had drawn up in June after conferring with de Vabres, Raphael Lemkin, and Vespasian Pella) posed an even more direct challenge to state sovereignty. The convention defined genocide broadly—as intentionally destroying or impeding the development of "racial, national, linguistic, religious, or political groups of human beings." It required signees to submit offenders to an international criminal court when genocidal acts were committed on behalf of or with the tolerance of the state.[38]

Unhappy with the direction things were taking in the United Nations, the Soviets looked to influence the conversation about international law through the International Association of Democratic Lawyers (IADL), which Trainin had helped to establish in October. In July 1947 Trainin headed to Brussels for the IADL's first Congress. Cassin attended, too, but the Congress's focus on antifascism provided common ground. The Congress called for the extradition of war criminals and for restitution by all states found guilty of waging wars of invasion and conquest—what everyone was by now calling "wars of aggression," adopting the terminology of Nuremberg. The Congress also appealed to the United Nations to draw up an international bill of rights that incorporated social and economic rights such as the right to work and the right to security in old age. Trainin enthusiastically supported these measures and ushered through a resolution urging all governments to keep up the fight against "the remnants of Fascism and Nazism," which were, as he put it, "obstructing the free exercise of human rights."[39]

The IADL Congress was a diplomatic success for the Soviets. In its wake the United Nations recognized the IADL as a consultative agency of its Economic and Social Council, which was moving forward on the genocide convention. Experts from around the world declared that the Congress had shown that cooperation between capitalist and socialist states still remained possible. The American Bar Association was less enthusiastic about the IADL, criticizing "the ascendancy of Marxist-collectivist ideologies" in many of its participating countries.[40]

Soviet diplomats and lawyers at the United Nations, meanwhile, continued to oppose an international criminal court as permitting "fantastic and dangerous" interference in a state's domestic affairs.[41] In late 1947 it was looking like Moscow's concerns were well founded: a number of émigré groups based in the United States publicly accused the Soviet Union of genocide and asked the United Nations for assistance. The Ukrainian Congress Committee of America asked the General Assembly to investigate Soviet genocide in western Ukraine. The Lithuanian delegation in Washington, D.C. appealed to the United Nations to protect the Lithuanian people from "enslavement and extermination" by the Soviets. Representatives from the former Estonian and Latvian governments also accused Moscow of committing genocide in the Baltic republics.[42] These groups were already using the language of human rights to demand action against the Soviet Union. An international criminal court would give them an official channel for pursuing their claims.

The fact was that the Soviets, who had insisted on narrowing the Nuremberg Charter to address only the crimes of the Axis powers, had a good deal to be concerned about. Soviet forces were conducting mass arrests, deportations, and population transfers throughout the Soviet Union and Eastern Europe. They had intervened in local elections in Poland, Hungary, Romania, and Bulgaria, pressuring voters and stuffing ballot boxes in order to ensure the establishment of communist governments. And they were using military tribunals and show trials to support the imprisonment and execution of all kinds of political opponents, sometimes on trumped-up charges of wartime collaboration with the Nazis.[43] Trainin, Korovin, Koretsky, and other Soviet lawyers did not publicly defend these policies, but it is hard to imagine that they did not know about them. In the months ahead they would intensify their efforts to circumscribe the language of Nuremberg to apply only to the actions of the Nazis and other fascists—giving the Soviet regime cover.

In 1948, with the Nuremberg Trials fading into the past and Cold War tensions growing, the Soviets and the Americans continued their battle over the history of the Second World War with a new vehemence. In January, the U.S. State Department published the secret protocols to the German-Soviet Non-Aggression Pact, along with other evidence of Soviet-German collaboration, in a 350-page document collection titled *Soviet-Nazi Relations, 1939-1941: Documents from the Archives of the German Foreign Office.*[44] Soviet leaders—who continued to claim that the secret protocols were a slanderous invention of the Nazi defendants—were outraged. Lozovsky and the Sovinformburo struck back a few weeks later with the publication of *Falsifiers of History*, a short English-language book that denounced this attempt to malign the Soviet Union and charged the Western powers with facilitating Hitler's rise to power. The book accused American industrialists of financing Germany's war industry and implied that the United States was holding its own trials of German industrialists in order to cover up American complicity in Nazi war crimes. It also described the Munich Pact of 1938, which had handed the Sudetenland to Hitler, as an agreement aimed primarily at "goading" the Nazis to strike against the Soviet Union.[45]

In February 1948, local communists backed by the Soviet Union seized power in Czechoslovakia, and the American, British, and French governments moved toward the establishment of a West German state. These developments, perhaps inevitably, further politicized ongoing discussions about democracy, sovereignty, and human rights. The Soviets continued to participate in United Nations codification projects—but now with an unabashed commitment to limiting their scope. That March the lawyer Platon Morozov, the Soviet representative to the United Nations Ad Hoc Committee on Genocide, disputed that the destruction of "political groups" was a form of genocide. He further insisted that genocide was "organically bound up with Fascism-Nazism" and that if the convention's scope extended further, some term other than "genocide" would have to be found.[46] A couple of months later the diplomat Alexei Pavlov, the new Soviet representative to the Human Rights Commission, rejected a draft human rights bill on the grounds that it violated state sovereignty and gave insufficient attention to the ongoing struggle against Nazism. Soviet objections were noted even as both documents moved forward, eventually reaching the General Assembly's Sixth (Legal) Committee for further evaluation.[47]

In Moscow, Trainin again entered the fray—this time to explain the Soviet objection to an international criminal court. "Of course the struggle against genocide as a crime directed toward the extermination of peoples and nations has the staunch support of the entire Soviet people," Trainin maintained in one public lecture (later circulated as a pamphlet). But under current international conditions an international criminal court would be a dangerous weapon in the hands of the United States, which had launched a "slanderous campaign against the USSR" and was attempting "to trample the sovereignty" of countries throughout the world. Recommending caution toward the international movement coalescing around the term "genocide," he invoked the politics of the 1920s, when the League of Nations and lawyers such as Raphael Lemkin had rallied around the term "terrorism" in order to push back against the growing influence of communism. Trainin predicted that in the current political climate, the term "genocide" would be similarly wielded by anti-Soviet forces against the USSR. In the "interest of justice," he concluded, only national courts should hear cases about genocide.[48]

Trainin understood as well as anyone that the campaign for human rights had become hopelessly entangled with the politics of the Cold War. As always, he was highly attuned to the demands of the moment. In September 1948, he went to Prague for the IADL's second Congress. Arriving in communist Czechoslovakia at the height of the Berlin Blockade, Trainin delivered a fiery speech denouncing the American and British governments for breaking with the Yalta and Potsdam agreements and the ideals proclaimed at Nuremberg.[49]

Representatives from the socialist bloc now dominated the IADL. Cassin was put on the defensive as the delegates passed a resolution criticizing the United Nations Human Rights Commission's draft bill of rights, which he had played a major role in crafting. The resolution asserted that human rights could only be protected and secured within the state and not via supranational institutions. The Congress addressed the crime of genocide in a separate resolution, defining it as the "annihilation of communities" or "collective groups" during peacetime or wartime "for reasons of race, religion, or nationality." This definition of genocide differed notably from the one under discussion at the United Nations: it did not cover the destruction of "political groups." In another resolution, the Congress censured American and British occupation authorities for failing to follow through on the denazification of Germany and proclaimed that the light sentences handed down in the Farben, Krupp, Flick, and List trials in 1947 and 1948 (acquittals and short prison terms) were incompatible with the Nuremberg Charter. The *New York Times* reported on the Congress under the headline "Lawyers Take Red Line." In an article for the Soviet press, Trainin reported that the Congress had revealed the "intensifying struggle of two camps, the imperialist and the democratic," with the Soviet Union leading the latter.[50]

While Trainin was in Prague, the United Nations General Assembly convened in Paris. Vyshinsky, representing the Soviet Union, launched into a tirade against the United States for using the Marshall Plan—a massive aid program that was providing billions of dollars to rebuild the European economy—to stage an economic and political takeover of Europe. According to Vyshinsky, all of the "pompous and grandiloquent speeches about international co-operation, peace, the independence of peoples, human rights and democracy" being delivered in the General Assembly were completely hypocritical. Behind the scenes, the United States and its allies were unabashedly pursuing "world domination."[51]

For a while, even as the United Nations became a forum for vitriolic speeches, it continued to move forward on its international-law projects. On December 9, 1948, the General Assembly unanimously approved the genocide convention—affirming that genocide, whether committed during war or in peacetime, was a crime under international law. The Soviets threw in their support after "political groups" was cut from the definition, but only because the convention also stepped carefully around the idea of enforcement.

Figure 15.1 Boris Efimov's political cartoon of President Harry S. Truman, "Amicable American Pressure," 1948. During the Cold War Efimov turned his talent to caricaturing American leaders and U.S. foreign policy.

Credit: INTERFOTO/Alamy.

The convention mentioned the possibility of trying perpetrators before a national tribunal or an international criminal court but made clear that any such court's jurisdiction would depend on the consent of the convention's signatories—leaving open the possibility of opting out later.[52]

The Human Rights Commission had shown less willingness to compromise, and Vyshinsky tried to sink its bill of rights. A "universal declaration of human rights should be worthy of its lofty purposes," he declared before the General Assembly at its December 9 session. According to Vyshinsky, this one gave fascists too many protections, including freedom of speech, while threatening state sovereignty—which he declared to be a prerequisite for international cooperation. He publicly repudiated Cassin's claim that the "doctrine of national sovereignty" had enabled Germany to commit crimes against its own people with impunity and had ultimately led to world war. The cause of the war, he retorted, had been French and British appeasement of Hitler. Vyshinsky's speech made a stir but did not delay the vote or change its outcome. The General Assembly adopted the Universal Declaration of Human Rights on December 10, with the USSR, the Ukrainian SSR, the Belorussian SSR, Poland, Czechoslovakia, Yugoslavia, South Africa, and Saudi Arabia abstaining.[53]

Vyshinsky and Trainin had traveled a long way together since their initial collaboration in the 1930s. Their paths were now about to diverge. By the time Trainin traveled to Prague in 1948, Stalin had already launched a virulent anti-Western campaign—turning still further away from the United States and Western Europe and targeting so-called cosmopolitanism in the Soviet Union. Soviet experts in all fields were told to excise all "bourgeois" influences from their disciplines and to stop bowing and scraping before the West.[54] Trainin had seen this coming, and his speech at the IADL Congress had neatly reflected the Party line. But this would not be enough to protect him. In January 1949 the anticosmopolitan campaign took on a definite anti-Jewish character as Solomon Lozovsky and other members of the Jewish Anti-Fascist Committee, which had served the Soviet Union so well during the war, were arrested on trumped-up charges of espionage and other anti-Soviet activity. Soviet Jews in positions of authority, especially those such as Trainin with ties to the West, fell under increasing suspicion.[55]

As Vyshinsky's star continued to rise—in March 1949 Stalin tapped him to replace Molotov as foreign minister—Trainin's was rapidly falling. That same month, the Institute of Law held a meeting to denounce "rootless cosmopolitans" among Soviet lawyers. Korovin, who had just become the Institute's director, led the charge. Opening the meeting, he criticized Soviet international-law experts for having been taken in by Western lies: they had failed to see that the "Anglo-American imperialists" were aspiring to suppress people throughout the world by introducing a "world government" by means of the United Nations. The accusations were convoluted, but the message was clear: the Soviet Union's experiment with legal universalism had come to an end. A number of Trainin's colleagues at the Institute of Law and at Moscow University were publicly rebuked for their ideological shortcomings. Trainin, who by now was well known in the West, continued to publish—but he came under closer surveillance and was prohibited from traveling abroad.[56]

Later that spring, as Stalin's anticosmopolitan campaign continued to gather momentum, Vladimir Koretsky returned to Lake Success for the first session of the United Nations International Law Commission. The fifteen-member commission set out to write up the Nuremberg principles as well as a more general Code of Offenses Against the Peace and Security of Mankind.[57] The commission would also consider the possibility of establishing an international criminal court. Prior to leaving Moscow, Koretsky had prepared for the meeting by consulting with Iona Nikitchenko, Mark Raginsky, Korovin, and other Soviet lawyers.[58] Nikitchenko had returned to his position on the Soviet Union's Supreme Court after Nuremberg but was currently under investigation for several alleged offenses, including that of fraternizing with "a female German acquaintance" at the time of the trials.[59] Vyshinsky, from his new perch as foreign minister, instructed Koretsky to check back in with him about all key decisions during the session and to firmly oppose the creation of an international criminal court.[60]

Koretsky strove to follow Vyshinsky's orders at Lake Success. He flatly rejected a list of possible offenses presented by the United Nations Secretariat for inclusion in the Code of Offenses Against the Peace and Security of Mankind, proposing instead that the delegates confer with their governments to define the scope of the proposed project. He was overruled.[61] The commission selected fourteen topics for possible codification, including the fomenting of civil unrest in another state and the use of force in violation of international law. It also discussed the controversial questions of extradition and forced repatriation. Koretsky offered to compose a different list of codification topics reflecting what he described as more pressing concerns, most notably the struggle against fascism. The others turned him down.[62]

The International Law Commission turned to the Nuremberg principles on May 9—and here Koretsky played a significant role in shaping the outcome of the discussion. When some of the delegates suggested that the draft declare the supremacy of international law over national law, he protested that this would open the door to a world government.[63] When the commission turned to the relationship between the Nuremberg principles and the Code of Offenses Against the Peace and Security of Mankind, he insisted that these two projects be kept separate. Formulating the Nuremberg principles would be relatively straightforward, he maintained, but a broader international criminal code was more contentious—and combining the two would delay things considerably. The commission heeded his warning and resolved to proceed at least in the short term with two separate documents. It would complete its draft of the Nuremberg principles and discuss the possibility of establishing an international criminal court at its next session, in 1950.[64]

Soviet leaders were no longer interested in building bridges to the West. When the third IADL Congress was held in Rome in the fall of 1949, Trainin was not among the delegates. Stalin sent Roman Rudenko in his place. The substitution of Rudenko (who had returned to his post as procurator general of the Ukrainian SSR) for Trainin represented a turning point in the Soviet relationship with international institutions. Trainin had been the Soviet Union's face to the West in the context of international law; Rudenko, even after Nuremberg, was still associated abroad with the Soviet Union's ends-justify-the-means show-trial history. The IADL now had a decisive communist majority—Cassin had left the organization earlier in the year, and other Western lawyers had followed suit—and Trainin's ability to find common ground with international-law experts from all over Europe was no longer needed.

International law, like Europe itself, was fracturing into socialist and Western camps. Rudenko's lectern-thumping speeches denouncing the recently established North Atlantic Treaty Organization as a breach of international agreements found an appreciative audience at the Congress—but not in other circles.[65] Soon after this meeting, the United Nations revoked the status of the IADL as a consultative body of the Economic and Social Council. The IADL would continue to wield influence going forward, as a Communist Party front organization.

Meanwhile, Western European lawyers and politicians were creating another organization—the European Assembly, which would have its own human rights charter and court of justice. This Assembly held its first session in Paris in November 1949, just a few weeks after the IADL met in Rome. David Maxwell Fyfe chaired the Assembly's legal committee and oversaw the drafting of a European Convention on Human Rights, which he personally envisioned both as a complement to the United Nations' Universal Declaration of Human Rights and as a bulwark against communism. He expressed the hope that this convention might "stop the progress of totalitarianism" and serve as "a beacon to the peoples behind the Iron Curtain."[66]

Back in Moscow, behind that proverbial Iron Curtain, Korovin was continuing to call for a "patriotic Soviet science of law."[67] Trainin and others had been attempting to redeem themselves by writing articles about the fallacies of bourgeois justice.[68] But by now fear and uncertainty had settled over the entire Soviet legal profession. The Institute of Law urgently tried to interpret Stalin's writings for clues about his views on jurisprudence, to little avail.[69] Soviet international-law experts were especially vulnerable because of their close association with Western jurists. Koretsky therefore had much to fear in June 1950 when he headed to Geneva for the second session of the United

Nations International Law Commission. In the end, he played the politics brilliantly—walking out of the deliberations after the commission rebuffed his demand to replace the Kuomintang representative with one from the new Chinese People's Republic.[70]

It was thus in Koretsky's absence that the International Law Commission finished elaborating the Nuremberg principles. The final document was relatively straightforward and hewed closely to the Nuremberg Charter. It stipulated that crimes against peace, war crimes, and crimes against humanity were all punishable crimes under international law. It also held that complicity in any of these acts was similarly punishable—here going farther than the Nuremberg judgment, which had limited the complicity charge to crimes against peace. It established that heads of state could bear criminal responsibility and it dismissed the defense of superior orders. Much of this closely followed Trainin's original arguments from *The Criminal Responsibility of the Hitlerites*. Trainin's ideas about crimes against peace and complicity were continuing to shape the discussion about international law even as Trainin himself had fallen out of favor in the Soviet Union.

In its formulation of the Nuremberg principles, the International Law Commission had decided at least in the short term to follow the example of Nuremberg in leaving the term "aggression" undefined. But the commission had expanded the concept of "crimes against humanity"—which it defined as "persecution on political, racial, or religious grounds"—to specifically include acts that leaders committed against their own populations.[71] This went far beyond both the Nuremberg Charter and the Nuremberg judgment.

The International Law Commission's discussions about enforcement went much more smoothly without Koretsky in the room. Most of the delegates spoke in favor of the creation of an international criminal court. They understood, however, that the IMT had come together only because of the total surrender of the Axis powers—and that in the current environment, getting countries to agree to an international criminal court with binding jurisdiction would be, to say the least, a difficult proposition. In the end, the commission concluded that the establishment of such a court was desirable, even if it faced formidable challenges. The commission sent its findings and its formulation of the Nuremberg principles to the Sixth (Legal) Committee of the United Nations, which approved them and sent them on to the General Assembly. In December 1950 the General Assembly forwarded the Nuremberg principles to the governments with a vital question: should these principles stand alone or be inserted into the Code of Offenses Against the Peace and Security of Mankind? The General Assembly also resolved to create yet another committee, this one to consider the creation of an international criminal court.[72]

By now, the language of human rights was regularly being mobilized as a political weapon in the Cold War. Soviet leaders, writers, and lawyers frequently called out examples of alleged Western aggression and crimes against humanity worldwide.[73] Trainin, because he was well known among Western lawyers and diplomats, continued to play an important propaganda role for the Soviet Union—even as he remained grounded in Moscow. After the start of the Korean War in the summer of 1950, he had crafted reports and articles accusing the United States of committing genocide in Korea and throughout the developing world and of preparing for a "third world war" against the Soviet Union and the "peoples' democracies" of Eastern Europe.[74] In response, U.S. officials had charged the Soviets with attempting to "hamstring the United Nations and confuse world opinion" by claiming to support peace while supporting and encouraging communist takeovers in Europe and Asia.[75] American journalists were also invoking the Nuremberg principles to call for sanctions against the Soviet Union. In July 1951 an editorial in Washington's *Evening Star* charged that "the same Russia whose representative sat in judgment on the court at Nuremberg" had planned the invasion of South Korea and should be held responsible for "crimes against peace."[76]

Even as Soviet lawyers participated in these exchanges, they floundered in their efforts to define a specifically Soviet approach to international law. Korovin made a valiant attempt to do so in 1951 with the publication of a new textbook that differentiated between "bourgeois" and "socialist" international law, but came under fire when the Ministry of Foreign Affairs challenged his formulation as counter to "the diplomatic practice of the Soviet state." He became the focus of a Party-led meeting at the Academy of Sciences in 1952 that affirmed that there was only "one system of international law"—but two opposing political systems, socialist and imperialist. Soviet lawyers were expected to expose the international-law violations of the states in the imperialist camp.[77] For his heresy, Korovin was removed from his post as director at the Institute of Law, but emerged otherwise unscathed.

Trainin, meanwhile, had fallen under increasing scrutiny. Over the course of the next year he was accused at meetings and in the Soviet press of advancing "politically dangerous theories," failing to support the Party and the building of communism, and leading Korovin and other international-law experts down the wrong path.[78] This last charge must have rankled him the most.

Trainin was not the only Soviet participant in the Nuremberg Trials who was targeted as part of Stalin's anticosmopolitan campaign. The prosecutor and writer Lev Sheinin and the NKVD officer Leonid Raikhman were both arrested and imprisoned in 1951. Viktor Abakumov, former chief of SMERSH, was arrested soon thereafter on charges of treason and shot. Trainin, Sheinin, Raikhman, and Abakumov, along with Lozovsky (who was executed in August 1952), had all been involved in the Katyn cover-up. All but Abakumov were Jewish—and the accusations leveled at him included participation in a "Jewish conspiracy."[79] The irony of this turn of events could not have been lost on Trainin, who had formulated the Soviet idea of conspiracy during the Moscow Trials in the 1930s and who, along with other Soviet lawyers and writers, had spent the war years emphasizing the Soviet identity of the Jewish victims of the Nazis in order to highlight the solidarity of the Soviet people.

As Trainin faded from the international scene, Vyshinsky remained the face of Soviet foreign relations. Now more than ever Vyshinsky used his appearances at the United Nations to trumpet the Soviet commitment to world peace. The advisor to the U.S. Mission to the United Nations, Thomas J. Cory, was struck by Vyshinsky's new attitude of "sweet reasonableness," observing that the Soviet delegation was doing more entertaining than usual. Intent on the United States maintaining the upper hand, he advised the U.S. delegation to exploit Soviet weaknesses such as the inability to react quickly to change. It would be possible to throw the Soviets off balance, he suggested, by being unpredictable: "by insulting Stalin, pointing to contradictions in Stalin's statements . . . or comparing the Communists and Nazis." The Soviet delegates would have to tear up their prepared speeches in order to come to Stalin's defense.[80]

By 1952 the United Nations had become a forum for showboating and political one-upmanship and had drifted far from its original ideals. It is thus not particularly surprising that deliberations over the Code of Offenses Against the Peace and Security of Mankind broke down over the course of that year. What is perhaps surprising is what ultimately did it in: the effort—and ultimately the inability—to define a term that diplomats, lawyers, and politicians had been using matter-of-factly for years: aggression.

What was "aggression"? The International Law Commission proposed a definition that characterized it as one state's use of force against another state for any purpose other than "national or collective self-defense." Moscow and Washington both objected to this formulation. Soviet leaders and lawyers argued that the United Nations needed to revise the definition to distinguish between "just" and "unjust" wars: a war of liberation was different from a war of conquest.[81] The U.S. State Department agreed that the proposed language was too vague, but also insisted that it would be impossible to find a mutually acceptable definition of "aggression" and that it would be preferable to leave the term undefined. The State Department acknowledged that its position was similar to the one taken by the Soviets at the London Conference in August 1945—and argued that the current Soviet effort to define the term was "fundamentally opportunistic." A definition, it warned in one confidential memorandum, would "merely serve as a propaganda tool" for those governments that wanted "to label others aggressors" or hide behind "the loopholes inevitably offered by any definition."[82]

Stalin's death in March 1953 brought an era to its end. It also saved Trainin's life. At the start of the year the political situation in the Soviet Union had turned even more treacherous for Trainin. In January the Soviet press had published supposed revelations about a "Doctors' Plot" among Jewish physicians to murder Soviet leaders. The following month officials at Moscow University's Law Faculty publicly announced that there were "saboteur jurists" in their midst and accused Trainin of supporting international Zionism. Trainin, now seventy and in ill health (he had just suffered a heart attack), was fired from his positions; the supposed evidence against him was turned over to the secret police.[83] With Stalin's death, the charges against the jurists were dropped. Trainin returned to his academic posts and continued to write about international law, though he never again represented the Soviet Union abroad. Stalin's death also affected Vyshinsky's fate, by prompting another reshuffling of positions at the Ministry of Foreign Affairs. Molotov was reappointed foreign minister. Vyshinsky, demoted back to deputy foreign minister, became the Soviet Union's permanent representative to the United Nations—remaining in that role until his death in November 1954.[84]

Trainin outlived Vyshinsky, Stalin, and the anticosmopolitan campaign and got the chance to publicly commemorate the ten-year anniversary of the Nuremberg verdicts before his death in February 1957. In October 1956, he wrote a retrospective for *Pravda* celebrating the Nuremberg principles as a powerful force for the future peace and security of all nations—for what the new Soviet leader, Nikita Khrushchev, was calling "peaceful coexistence." Trainin reminded his readers that the Nuremberg prosecutors, despite coming from states with very different political and legal systems, had all agreed that the IMT was necessary both to punish the former Nazi leaders and to ensure that their crimes would never be repeated. He lamented that further work on the codification of international law had become "completely frozen in the ice of the Cold War."[85]

FIGURE 15.2 Andrei Vyshinsky, the Soviet representative to the United Nations, serving as president of the UN Security Council, April 1954.

Credit: United Nations Photo Archive.

In the years that followed, the Nuremberg principles became part of the corpus of international law as a set of guidelines for assessing what constituted a war crime, even as the larger projects to create a Code of Offenses Against the Peace and Security of Mankind and an international criminal court to punish such offenses stalled, not to be revived until after the Soviet Union's demise in the 1990s. Robert Jackson had been prescient: concerns about sovereignty ruled the day. The Universal Declaration of Human Rights and the Genocide Convention continued to prompt wide-ranging discussions about war crimes and human rights, but both lacked the capacity for enforcement. The Soviets ratified the Genocide Convention in May 1954 only after filing a reservation rejecting the jurisdiction of an international criminal court; the U.S. government did not fully sign on to the convention until decades later.[86]

The postwar turn to international law did have a powerful impact on international politics during the Cold War—but in ways far from those originally envisioned by Henri Donnedieu de Vabres (who died in early 1952). In the decades after Stalin's death, the United States and the USSR each continued to invoke the Nuremberg-inspired language of human rights to take the other to task. In 1960, when the new procurator general of the USSR—none other than Roman Rudenko—tried the American U-2 pilot Francis Gary Powers for violating Soviet airspace, he denounced the U.S. government for organizing a terrible crime against peace.[87] In the chilly climate of the late 1960s and the 1970s, the Soviet and U.S. governments regularly criticized each other's domestic policies—including the Soviet suppression of religion and American practices of racial segregation—as crimes against humanity. The language of law and rights continued to have a moral as well as a political power. Dissident groups in the USSR and civil rights organizations in the United States increasingly used this language, sometimes to great effect, to wage struggles for political and social reform in their own countries.[88]

It was during these same years of the Cold War that a popular mythology took hold in the United States that celebrated Nuremberg as the birthplace of postwar human rights and Robert Jackson (who died in October 1954, while still in his prime) posthumously as a key founding father. Minimizing the Soviet Union's role in the IMT and in the story of the postwar development of international law was part of a larger effort to produce an uplifting and usable myth of the Nuremberg Moment. By the time that the Cold War ended and the United Nations revisited the idea of an international criminal court—ratifying the Code of Crimes Against the Peace and Security of Mankind in 1996 and creating the International Criminal Court in The Hague in 1998—it had long been forgotten in the West that Stalin's Soviet Union had played a key part in organizing the Nuremberg Trials and in bringing the ideals of the Nuremberg principles into existence.

The myth of the Nuremberg Moment celebrated the power of American leadership and Western liberal ideals. It gave meaning to the war and to the triumph over Nazism. But it told only part of the Nuremberg story.

What do we get by putting the Soviet Union back into the history of the Nuremberg Trials? We get a story about the Katyn massacre and the secret protocols of the German-Soviet Non-Aggression Pact—and the Soviet Union overplaying its hand. But we also get an unexpected story about the Soviet contribution to the postwar development of international law. We get a history of international cooperation and a history of international rivalry—and we are reminded that they are simultaneously true. There are liberators and there are perpetrators, but these categories sometimes blur. There are moments of dark comedy: we see the surprising weaknesses of Stalin's Soviet Union on the international stage. But this impression, too, is tempered—by the strength and humanity of witnesses like Abraham Sutzkever and by the brilliance of artists like Roman Karmen and Boris Efimov. We see how Soviet lawyers and diplomats used the language of the law both to justify domestic show trials and to usher in an international movement for human rights.

And we consider the legacy of someone like Aron Trainin, who was central to both efforts.

Putting the Soviet Union back into the Nuremberg story gives us a far richer understanding of the IMT and the postwar movement for human rights. We are directly confronted with all of Nuremberg's contradictions, and we come face to face with all of the ways international justice is an inherently political process. We see how concepts like "genocide," "crimes against humanity," "aggressive war," and "crimes against peace" gained meaning. We are reminded that these terms have political as well as humanitarian origins—and that they have been used at different moments by different actors for different ends. None of this undermines the revolutionary nature of the Nuremberg Trials. It does remind us, though, not to idealize a mythical Nuremberg Moment.

The real story of Nuremberg is messy—filled with intrigue, back-room negotiation, and compromise—and there is actually a great deal of hope in this. Representatives from the Soviet Union, the United States, France, and Great Britain, with their different ideas about the meaning of justice and their competing visions for the postwar future, somehow found enough common ground to move forward. They drew up a set of principles that became the foundation for new international law—principles that, however flawed in practice, still provide a set of ideals toward which states and their citizens can aspire.

ACKNOWLEDGMENTS

THIS BOOK HAS been fifteen years in the making. I am grateful to the many institutions and individuals who provided assistance and support along the way. The International Research and Exchanges Board (IREX), the Kennan Institute of the Woodrow Wilson Center, the Global Legal Studies Initiative of the University of Wisconsin–Madison, the Trustees of the William F. Vilas Estate, and the Office of the Vice Chancellor for Research and Graduate Education (OVCRGE) at the University of Wisconsin funded my initial research in Russia and in the United States. The American Council of Learned Societies (ACLS), the Institute for Research in the Humanities at the University of Wisconsin, and OVCRGE provided me with the time and the funding to do additional research and to write.

For the duration of this project I have been lucky to call the University of Wisconsin–Madison my intellectual home. It has been a privilege to be surrounded by talented colleagues and students; it has been a blessing to be in such a creative, supportive, and stimulating environment. I would like to thank those History Department colleagues and friends who have generously engaged with earlier drafts of this book. Tony Michels, Jennifer Ratner-Rosenhagen, David McDonald, Laird Boswell, Leonora Neville, Kathryn Ciancia, and Amos Bitzan all read chapters or large parts of the manuscript and gave thoughtful feedback on the arguments as well as on the writing. Mary Louise Roberts read the entire manuscript and offered incisive suggestions as well as encouragement at a key point in my revising process. Our conversations helped me to hone the narrative and to better situate the Soviet story in a larger European framework. Sarah Thal read multiple chapters in their almost-final form. Her suggestions and keen eye for detail helped me to clarify key points; our many walks around the neighborhood have helped in ways that are impossible to express. I have been incredibly fortunate to have David McDonald as my Russian history colleague at Wisconsin; I am grateful to him for sharing his knowledge as well as his wisdom, and for his friendship. Coteaching a graduate seminar with Laird Boswell on postwar Europe deepened my understanding of the Second World War and its impact.

I would also like to thank those colleagues at the University of Wisconsin who helped in other ways in the making of this book. Tanya Buckingham of the Cartography Lab expertly made the maps. Mike Burmeister, John Persike, Jana Valeo, and Todd Anderson provided critical technical and administrative support. Karl Shoemaker and Alexandra Huneeus answered my many questions about international and comparative law; Heinz Klug welcomed my participation in workshops at the Law School. Slavic Bibliographer Andy Spencer and Memorial Library Reference Librarian Beth Harper shared their expertise and helped me track down sources. Emily Lobenstein, Benjamin Raiklin, David Houston, Marin Cerchez, Sean Gillen, Ayten Kilic, and Chad Gibbs provided research assistance at various stages of the project.

Other historian friends and colleagues, in the United States and in Russia, have also provided invaluable support. Laura Engelstein, my former graduate advisor, has been a wonderful friend and colleague. She read all of the chapters (in some cases more than once) and provided encouragement as well as honest feedback; our many conversations over the years have helped me to sharpen my arguments and have inspired me. James Heinzen and Charles Steinwedel read large sections of the manuscript and asked the kinds of insightful questions that helped me to clarify my arguments. Marina Sorokina introduced me to key collections at the Archive of the Russian Academy of Sciences, generously shared her extensive knowledge of Soviet history and sources, and enriched my time in Moscow with her friendship. Peter Solomon offered helpful comments on early chapters and served as a fount of knowledge on the history of Soviet law. He and Benjamin Nathans provided advice and support as I was getting this project under way. John Q. Barrett answered my many questions about the life and career of Robert H. Jackson. Peter Holquist, Stephen Kotkin, Joshua Rubenstein, and Amir Weiner provided helpful answers to various queries about the Second World War, the history of international law, and Stalinism. Michael Geyer and Warren Rosenblum answered questions about German history and geography.

Other friends have also generously shared their time and insights. Arthur McKee, a former Russian historian, read the entire manuscript twice from the perspective of an interested general reader. His comments on an early version helped me figure out what to cut and where to add further explanation. I am grateful to him for his keen editorial eye and his intellectual generosity. Ingrid Klass read the beginning chapters and made wonderful suggestions for opening them up to a more general audience. The Torinus family and the Goldman-Gundersen family took an interest in Nuremberg; our conversations helped me to believe that the Soviet story could be of interest to a broader audience.

Archivists and librarians in Moscow and Washington, D.C., also helped in key ways. I am especially grateful to Nataliia Vladimirovna Borodina and Sergei Vitalevich Pavlov at the Archive of the Foreign Policy of the Russian Federation (AVPRF); Galina Raufovna Zlobina and Kseniia Viktorovna Iakovleva at the Russian State Archive of Literature and Art (RGALI); and Vadim Altskan at the United States Holocaust Memorial Museum Archive (USHMMA) for their kind assistance. Vladislav Rybakov, a graduate student at the Higher School of Economics in Moscow, helped me to obtain photographs and permissions from the State Archive of the Russian Federation (GARF).

I am grateful to the late Boris Efimov for giving me permission to use his brilliant caricatures of the Nazi defendants and to Anna Loginova, the curator of the Ne Boltai! Collection, for providing me with high-quality scans. I would also like to thank Anna Khaldei for allowing me to use her late father's powerful photographs of the Nuremberg Trials. Tom Blackmore kindly shared copies of the letters exchanged between his grandparents David and Sylvia Maxwell Fyfe. Darya Vassina helped me with some questions of translation; Bella Kulakova identified Roman Karmen (whom she had met in Moscow) in the photographs.

Timothy Bent at Oxford University Press has been an outstanding intellectual interlocutor and editor. I thank him for taking on this project and for sharing his time and talent. I have learned a tremendous amount from him about the art of storytelling; his astute insights and editorial suggestions have improved this book immeasurably. I also thank Mariah White, who oversaw numerous details, graciously answered my questions about the editorial and production processes, and guided my manuscript into production. I am grateful to Martha Ramsey for her careful copyediting. Gwen Colvin was an excellent production editor. I thank her for her patience and her guidance through the copyediting and production processes.

Writing a book can be lonely work, especially a book that deals with the horrors and atrocities of the Second World War. I am deeply grateful to my family for their support. My parents, Mark and Lois Hirsch, have always believed in me; their love has been a great source of strength. My brother, David Hirschwerk, and my in-laws, Erika Hessman and the late Lawrence Hessman, took an interest in this project and in my work as a historian and have cheered me on from afar. My children, Isaac and Elena, have kept my life in balance and have graced it with their curiosity and their laughter. Finally, my husband, Mark Hessman, has been my rock; his love, companionship, and cooking have sustained me. He read numerous drafts of this manuscript over the years and fully engaged with its ideas. His substantive and stylistic suggestions have made this a better book; his steadfast support made it possible for me to finish writing it. It is to him that I dedicate this book.

This book incorporates some material that also appeared in the following articles: "The Soviets at Nuremberg: International Law, Propaganda, and the Making of the Postwar Order," *American Historical Review* 113, no. 3 (2008): 701–730; "The Nuremberg Trials as Cold War Competition," in *Memory and Postwar Memorials: Confronting the Past as Violence*, ed. Marc Silberman and Florence Vatan (New York: Palgrave MacMillan, 2013), 17–40; "The Politics of the Nuremberg Trials and the Postwar Moment," in *Political Trials in Theory and History*, ed. Devin Pendas and Jens Meierhenrich (Cambridge: Cambridge University Press, 2017), 157–183; "The Soviet Union at the Palace of Justice: Law, Intrigue, and International Rivalry in the Nuremberg Trials," in *Stalin's Soviet Justice: "Show" Trials, War Crimes Trials, and Nuremberg*, ed. David Crowe (London: Bloomsbury Press, 2019), 171–198.

ARCHIVES CONSULTED

T HIS BOOK COULD not have been written without the opening of the former Soviet archives and the generosity of Russian archivists. It is based in large part on a close reading of thousands of telegrams, letters, memoranda, secret reports, unpublished diaries, meeting transcripts, and other sources from five Moscow archives. These materials shed light on all aspects of the Soviet Union's role in the Nuremberg Trials. They also show the human side of the story: how Soviet lawyers, judges, writers, filmmakers, and other personnel navigated the challenges of the trial and of daily life in the international setting of Nuremberg.

Materials consulted from the Archive of the Foreign Ministry of the Russian Federation (Arkhiv vneshnei politiki Rossiiskoi Federatsii; AVPRF) include diplomatic correspondence and secret Soviet memoranda about reparations, war crimes, and postwar justice. Some of the most interesting documents are the working drafts of Soviet memoranda marked up by Joseph Stalin, Vyacheslav Molotov, Andrei Vyshinsky, and other Soviet leaders. Materials from the Archive of the Russian Academy of Sciences (Arkhiv Rossiiskoi Akademii nauk; ARAN) include the transcripts of meetings of the Institute of Law, which illuminate the important work that Soviet international-law experts such as Aron Trainin were doing for the Ministry of Foreign Affairs. Materials from the Russian State Archive of Literature and Art (Rossiiskii gosudarstvennyi arkhiv literatury i iskusstva; RGALI) include the unpublished diaries and professional correspondence of the writer Vsevolod Vishnevsky and the papers of the filmmaker Roman Karmen.

Materials consulted from the Russian State Archive of Socio-Political History (Rossiiskii gosudarstvennyi arkhiv sotsial'no-politicheskoi istorii; RGASPI) include the files of the Central Committee of the Communist Party, the files of Joseph Stalin, and the files of *Pravda* editor Peter Pospelov. Key documents from these collections proved essential for understanding Soviet aims and actions at Nuremberg. Materials from the State Archive of the Russian Federation (Gosudarstvennyi arkhiv Rossiiskoi Federatsii; GARF) include the official Soviet transcript of the Nuremberg Trials as well as Soviet memoranda relating to the Indictment, the cross-examination of witnesses, the speeches of the Soviet prosecution, and the verdict. Correspondence between Moscow and Soviet headquarters in Berlin reveals some of the finer details of Soviet logistical planning.

Archives in the United States were also critical for this project. Materials accessed at United States Holocaust Memorial Museum Archives (USHMMA) include copies of reports and witness depositions from the Soviet Union's Extraordinary State Commission, as well as film footage shot by Roman Karmen at the end of the war. Materials consulted at the Library of Congress (LOC) include Robert H. Jackson's unpublished diaries; Office of Strategic Services reports about the Soviet position on war crimes and about the interrogation of war criminals; and correspondence relating to the early United Nations. Materials consulted at the National Archives and Records Administration—College Park (NARA) include reports from the U.S. occupation government in Germany, State Department documents relating to the Nuremberg principles, and the transcripts of the meetings of the London-based United Nations War Crimes Commission.

Several other archival collections were consulted remotely. Archivists from the American Heritage Center of the University of Wyoming (home to the Murray Bernays Collection) and from Syracuse University's Special Collections Research Center (home to the Francis Biddle Collection) helped me to order documents by phone and email. I accessed key materials from the Harry S. Truman Presidential Library and Museum and from Cornell University's Donovan Nuremberg Trials Collection online. Finally, the grandson of Sir David Maxwell Fyfe shared copies of letters between his grandparents before they were otherwise accessible to researchers. These letters are now available at the Churchill Archives Centre at Churchill College in Cambridge, England, and also online.

List of Key Archival Collections

RUSSIAN STATE ARCHIVE OF LITERATURE AND ART,
MOSCOW (ROSSIISKII GOSUDARSTVENNYI ARKHIV
LITERATURY I ISKUSSTVA; RGALI)

    f. 1038   Vsevolod Vishnevsky
    f. 2989   Roman Karmen

RUSSIAN STATE ARCHIVE OF SOCIO-POLITICAL HISTORY,
MOSCOW (ROSSIISKII GOSUDARSTVENNYI ARKHIV
SOTSIAL'NO-POLITICHESKOI ISTORII; RGASPI)

    f. 17   Central Committee of the Communist Party of the
           Soviet Union
    f. 558   Joseph Stalin
    f. 629   Peter Pospelov

ARCHIVE OF THE FOREIGN POLICY OF THE RUSSIAN
FEDERATION, MOSCOW (ARKHIV VNESHNEI POLITIKI
ROSSIISKOI FEDERATSII; AVPRF)

    f. 06   Secretariat of Foreign Minister Vyacheslav Molotov
    f. 07   Secretariat of Deputy Foreign Minister Andrei Vyshinsky
    f. 012   Secretariat of Deputy Foreign Minister Vladimir Dekanozov
    f. 059   Encrypted Telegrams
    f. 082   Germany
    f. 192   Embassy of the USSR in the USA

ARCHIVE OF THE RUSSIAN ACADEMY OF SCIENCES,
MOSCOW (ARKHIV AKADEMII NAUK SSSR; ARAN)

    f. 360   Institute of Soviet Construction and Law of the Communist
           Academy of the Central Executive Committee (TsIK) of
           the USSR

f. 499   Department of Economic, Philosophical, and Legal Sciences of
          the Academy of Sciences of the USSR
f. 586   Il'ya Trainin
f. 1711   Aron Trainin

STATE ARCHIVE OF THE RUSSIAN FEDERATION, MOSCOW (GOSUDARSTVENNYI ARKHIV ROSSIISKOI FEDERATSII; GARF)

f. 7445   International Military Tribunal, Nuremberg
f. 7523   USSR Supreme Court
f. 8131   Procuracy of the USSR
f. 8581   Soviet Information Bureau
f. 9492   Ministry of Justice of the USSR

NATIONAL ARCHIVES AND RECORDS ADMINISTRATION— COLLEGE PARK, MARYLAND (NARA)

RG 59   Department of State Central Files
RG 84   U.S. Embassies, Legations, Consulates General, Consulates, and
         Missions
RG 238   War Crimes Records
RG 260   Records of U.S. Occupation Headquarters, World War II
         (OMGUS)

LIBRARY OF CONGRESS, MANUSCRIPT DIVISION, WASHINGTON, D.C. (LOC)

Robert H. Jackson Collection (RHJ)

HARRY S. TRUMAN PRESIDENTIAL LIBRARY AND MUSEUM, INDEPENDENCE, MO (HSTPLM)

Harry S. Truman Papers
Samuel I. Rosenman Papers

George M. Elsey Papers
The War Crimes Trial at Nuremberg

UNITED STATES HOLOCAUST MEMORIAL MUSEUM ARCHIVE, WASHINGTON, D.C. (USHMMA)

RG-22.002M	Extraordinary State Commission to Investigate German-Fascist Crimes Committed on Soviet Territory from the USSR
RG-22.002M, Reel 27	International Military Tribunal at Nuremberg

UNIVERSITY OF WYOMING, AMERICAN HERITAGE CENTER, LARAMIE, WY (AHC)

Murray Bernays Collection (3817)

SYRACUSE UNIVERSITY SPECIAL COLLECTIONS RESEARCH CENTER, SYRACUSE, NY (SCRC)

Francis Biddle Collection (FBC)

CORNELL UNIVERSITY LAW LIBRARY, ITHACA, NY (CULL)

Donovan Nuremberg Trials Collection (DNTC)

CHURCHILL ARCHIVES CENTRE AT CHURCHILL COLLEGE IN CAMBRIDGE, ENGLAND

The Papers of Lord Kilmuir (KLMR Acc 1485)

NOTES

Note on Transliteration

In transliterating Russian titles and authors' names in the notes, I have used the Library of Congress system.

Introduction

1. Russian State Archive of Literature and Art (RGALI) f. 2989, op. 1, d. 190, ll. 4–6. Karmen's impressions and reflections are gleaned from notes he wrote up during the trials. These notes became the basis for lectures he delivered in Moscow in 1946.
2. RGALI f. 2989, op. 1, d. 190, ll. 5–6, 36.
3. Ibid. For descriptions of the building also see A. Poltorak, *The Nuremberg Epilogue* (Moscow: Progress Publishers, 1971), 22–28; Boris Polevoi, *The Final Reckoning: Nuremberg Diaries* (Moscow: Progress Publishers, 1978), 73, 81–82.
4. Roman Karmen, "Lublin Extermination Camp Called 'Worst Yet' by Writer," *Daily Worker*, August 14, 1944, 8; Roman Karmen, "Writer Describes Nazi Murder Plant in Poland," *Los Angeles Times*, August 13, 1944, 5. On Karmen's articles see David Shneer, *Through Soviet Jewish Eyes: Photography, War, and the Holocaust* (New Brunswick: Rutgers University Press, 2012), 164–165.
5. RGALI f. 2989, op. 1, d. 190, l. 44.
6. On Karmen's reactions and descriptions of the defendants and their claims see RGALI f. 2989, op. 1, d. 190, ll. 31–52. On Karmen's method see N. Kolesnikova, G. Senchakova, and T. Slepneva, *Roman Karmen* (Moscow: Iskusstvo, 1959), and Jeremy Hicks, *First Films of*

the Holocaust: Soviet Cinema and the Genocide of the Jews, 1938–1946 (Pittsburgh: University of Pittsburgh Press, 2012).

7. Bosley Crowther, "Goering, with Swagger Lacking, in 'Nuremberg Trials,' at Stanley," *New York Times*, May 26, 1947, 24.

8. J.P., "'The Nuremberg Trials'—Stanley," *New York Herald Tribune*, May 26, 1947, 16; Hicks, *First Films of the Holocaust*, 209–210, on the reception and forgetting of Karmen's film.

9. See for example Lawrence Douglas, *The Memory of Judgment: Making Law and History in the Trials of the Holocaust* (New Haven: Yale University Press, 2001). On Soviet involvement as "the Achilles' heel" see Christopher J. Dodd with Lary Bloom, *Letters from Nuremberg: My Father's Narrative of a Quest for Justice* (New York: Crown, 2007), 341. Also see Gary Jonathan Bass, *Stay the Hand of Vengeance: The Politics of War Crimes Tribunals* (Princeton: Princeton University Press, 2000), 147–205. Bass argues that "Soviet vengeance was utterly unhindered by liberal legalistic norms" (p. 196). For a discussion of some of the different ways Nuremberg has been invoked as a "human rights moment," see Elizabeth Borgwardt, "Commerce and Complicity: Human Rights and the Legacy of Nuremberg," in *Making the American Century: Essays in the Political Culture of Twentieth Century America*, ed. Bruce J. Schulman (New York: Oxford University Press, 2014), 92–108.

10. The 1961 film focuses on one of the subsequent Nuremberg Trials, the Justice Case of 1947 (The United States of America vs. Josef Altstötter et al.)—which was prosecuted solely by the United States. The 2000 film focuses on the original four-power Tribunal of 1945–1946. Also notable is the PBS American Experience documentary *The Nuremberg Trials*, which aired in 2006—and which also celebrated Nuremberg as the triumph of Jackson.

11. Joseph E. Persico, *Nuremberg: Infamy on Trial* (New York: Penguin Books, 1994). These published accounts include Francis Biddle, *In Brief Authority* (New York: Doubleday, 1962); G. M. Gilbert, *Nuremberg Diary* (New York: Farrar, Straus, 1947); Whitney R. Harris, *Tyranny on Trial* (Dallas: Southern Methodist University Press, 1954); Burton C. Andrus, *I Was the Nuremberg Jailer* (New York: Coward-McCann, 1969); Airey Neave, *On Trial at Nuremberg* (Boston: Little, Brown, 1979); and Telford Taylor, *The Anatomy of the Nuremberg Trials* (Boston: Knopf, 1992). For a somewhat more balanced popular account based primarily on the British archives and on memoirs and told from an Anglo-American perspective, see Ann Tusa and John Tusa, *The Nuremberg Trial* (London: Atheneum, 1983).

12. See for example Norman M. Naimark, *The Russians in Germany: A History of the Soviet Zone of Occupation, 1945–1949* (Cambridge, MA: Harvard University Press, 1997); Timothy Snyder, *Bloodlands: Europe Between Hitler and Stalin* (New York: Basic Books, 2010); Anne Applebaum, *Iron Curtain: The Crushing of Eastern Europe, 1945–1956* (New York: Doubleday,

2012); Antony Beevor, *The Fall of Berlin 1945* (New York: Penguin Books, 2003).

13. Philippe Sands, *East West Street: On the Origins of "Genocide" and "Crimes Against Humanity"* (New York: Knopf, 2016). The third major figure of Sands's work is the Nazi Hans Frank.

14. On Trainin, Lemkin, and Lauterpacht see Michelle Jean Penn, "The Extermination of Peaceful Soviet Citizens: Aron Trainin and International Law" (PhD diss., University of Colorado at Boulder, 2017). Penn critiques Sands's book from a similar perspective and places Trainin in dialogue with Lemkin and Lauterpacht.

15. On this revolution see for example Norbert Ehrenfreund, *The Nuremberg Legacy: How the Nazi War Crimes Trials Changed the Course of History* (New York: Palgrave Macmillan, 2007).

16. Historians as well as legal scholars tend to assume the liberal origins of human rights and international law. See for example Oona A. Hathaway and Scott J. Shapiro, *The Internationalists: How a Radical Plan to Outlaw War Remade the World* (New York: Simon and Schuster, 2017). On the Russian contribution to international law see the work of Peter Holquist, who is completing a book on the Russian Empire's role in extending and codifying the international law of war. On illiberal justice and Soviet law also see Franziska Exeler, "Nazi Atrocities, International Criminal Law, and Soviet War Crimes Trials: The Soviet Union and the Global Movement of Post-Second World War Justice," in *The New Histories of International Criminal Law: Retrials*, ed. Immi Tallgren and Thomas Skouteris (Oxford: Oxford University Press, 2019), 189-219.

17. Trainin's role in the trials had until recently gone underappreciated in the Western literature. An important exception was George Ginsburgs, *Moscow's Road to Nuremberg: The Soviet Background to the Trial* (The Hague: Martinus Nijhoff, 1996). Trainin is starting to get his due. See especially Kirsten Sellars, *"Crimes against Peace" and International Law* (Cambridge: Cambridge University Press, 2015), and Penn, "The Extermination of Peaceful Soviet Citizens."

18. The Soviet term for show trial, *pokazatel'nyi protsess*, referred to a trial with explicit educational goals. On political trials and didactic legalism, see Judith N. Shklar, *Legalism: Law, Moralism, and Political Trials* (Cambridge, MA: Harvard University Press, 1964).

19. Its full name was the Commission for Directing the Work of the Soviet Representatives in the International Tribunal and the Committee of Chief Prosecutors in Nuremberg.

20. RGALI f. 2989, op. 1, d. 190, l. 33.

21. Rebecca West, *A Train of Powder* (New York: Viking Press, 1955), 8.

22. Also see Tusa and Tusa, *Nuremberg Trial,* 230. There were 300–400 journalists in Nuremberg at peak times of the trial. Less than half that number could be accommodated in the courtroom at one time.

23. These correspondents included filmmakers, photographers, and artists.

24. RGALI f. 2989, op. 1, d. 190, l. 33.

25. Russian State Archive of Socio-Political History (RGASPI) f. 629, op. 1, d. 109, ll. 84–85ob.

26. On SMERSH and the NKVD see Vadim J. Birstein, *SMERSH: Stalin's Secret Weapon* (London: Biteback, 2011).

27. Polevoi, *Final Reckoning,* 73.

28. Robert H. Jackson, "Opening Speech for the United States of America," November 21, 1945, *International Military Tribunal—Major War Criminals,* https://digitalcommons.law.uga.edu/imt/11 (accessed April 30, 2019).

29. RGALI f. 2989, op. 1, d. 253, ll. 39–40.

Chapter 1

1. J. V. Stalin, "Order of the Day," February 23, 1942, Marxists Internet Archive, https://www.marxists.org/reference/archive/stalin/works/1942/02/23.htm (accessed June 21, 2018).

2. Richard Overy, *Russia's War: A History of the Soviet War Effort, 1941–1945* (New York: Penguin Books, 1997), 117; Catherine Merridale, *Ivan's War: Life and Death in the Red Army, 1939–1943* (New York: Picador, 2006), 146–147; Rodric Braithwaite, *Moscow 1941: A City and Its People at War* (New York: Knopf, 2006), 273–274.

3. Merridale, *Ivan's War,* 127–129. The first two notes were published in London in 1942 as "Molotov Notes on German Atrocities."

4. Library of Congress, Manuscript Division, Robert H. Jackson Collection (LOC-RHJ) b. 95, f. 3, "Note Sent by M. Molotov on April 17, 1942." For NKVD and other reports about Nazi atrocities see Archive of the Foreign Policy of the Russian Federation (AVPRF) f. 06, op. 4, p. 7, d. 73, ll. 17–39.

5. AVPRF f. 06, op. 4, p. 7, d. 69, ll. 1–9; Marina Sorokina, "People and Procedures: Toward a History of the Investigation of Nazi Crimes in the USSR," *Kritika: Explorations in Russian and Eurasian History* 6, no. 4 (2005): 797–831.

6. The Great Terror was a deadly campaign of political repression from 1936 to 1938.

7. Archive of the Russian Academy of Sciences (ARAN) f. 586, op. 4, d. 6, ll. 1–3. Vyshinsky corresponded with the director Ilya Trainin—soliciting the help of Aron Trainin and others.

8. Arkady Vaksberg, *Stalin's Prosecutor: The Life of Andrei Vyshinsky,* trans. Jan Butler (New York: Grove Weidenfeld, 1991), 13–31; Donald

Rayfield, *Stalin and His Hangmen: The Tyrant and Those Who Killed for Him* (New York: Random House, 2004), 162.

9. Stephen Kotkin, *Stalin: Paradoxes of Power, 1878–1928* (New York: Penguin, 2014), 702–705.

10. Vaksberg, *Stalin's Prosecutor*, 51–54, 62.

11. ARAN f. 360, op. 4, d. 400, ll. 1–14; Evgeny Pashukanis, "Selections from the Encyclopedia of State and Law: International Law," in *Selected Writings on Marxism and Law,* ed. Piers Beirne and Robert Sharlet (London: Academic Press, 1980), 171–172.

12. A. Ia. Vyshinskii, *K polozheniiu na fronte pravovoi teorii* (Moscow: Iuridicheskoe izdatel'stvo NKIu, 1937). Also Peter H. Solomon Jr., "Soviet Criminology— Its Demise and Rebirth, 1928–1963," in *Crime, Criminology and Public Policy: Essays in Honour of Sir Leon Radzinowicz,* ed. Roger Hood (New York: Free Press, 1975), 571–593.

13. A. N. Trainin, "Ia zhil za chertoi," *Molodaia gvardiia* 93, no. 8 (1937): 42– 44; A. N. Trainin, "Vospominaniia o Moskovskom universitete," *Vestnik Moskovskogo universiteta,* ser. 11, *Pravo* (1991), no. 2: 56–63, 3: 40–48, 4: 32– 39, 5: 39–46. Also Mira Traynina, "A. N. Traynin: A Legal Scholar under Tsar and Soviets," *Soviet Jewish Affairs* 13, no. 3 (1983): 45–54. On Trainin's work as a criminologist see Joan Neuberger, *Hooliganism: Crime, Culture, and Power in St. Petersburg, 1900–1914* (Berkeley: University of California Press, 1993), and Laura Engelstein, *The Keys to Happiness: Sex and the Search for Modernity in Fin-de-Siecle Russia* (Ithaca: Cornell University Press, 1992).

14. *Ugolovnoe pravo RSFSR. Chast' osobennaia* (Moscow: Iuridicheskoe izdatel'stvo NKIu, 1925). In 1925 Trainin returned to Berlin to study new developments in German criminal law. A. N. Trainin, *Krizis nauki ugolovnogo prava* (Moscow: Pravo i zhizn', 1926).

15. A. N. Trainin, *Ugolovnaia interventsiia: Dvizhenie po unifikatsii ugolovnogo zakonodatel'stva kapitalisticheskikh stran* (Moscow: Sovetskoe zakonodatel'stvo, 1935), 18–21, 44–46. Also see George Ginsburgs, *Moscow's Road to Nuremberg: The Soviet Background to the Trial* (The Hague: Martinus Nijhoff, 1996), 19.

16. A. Trainin, *Zashchita mira i ugolovnyi zakon* (Moscow: Iuridicheskoe izdatel'stvo NKIIu, 1937), 21–32; Ginsburgs, *Moscow's Road to Nuremberg,* 20–23; "Kellogg-Briand Pact 1928," Avalon Project at Yale University Law School, http://avalon.law.yale.edu/20th_century/kbpact.asp (accessed May 5, 2019). On Kellogg-Briand also see Oona A. Hathaway and Scott J. Shapiro, *The Internationalists: How a Radical Plan to Outlaw War Remade the World* (New York: Simon and Schuster, 2017), 121–130.

17. Vyshinsky, introduction to Trainin, *Zashchita mira i ugolovnyi zakon,* 4.

18. In this context, "Trotskyist" was a slanderous term used to denounce supposed followers of Leon Trotsky, whom Stalin had falsely accused of conspiring with foreign governments against the USSR. Vyshinskii, *K*

polozheniiu na fronte pravovoi teorii, 5; Vaksberg, *Stalin's Prosecutor,* 70, 79; Peter H. Solomon Jr., *Soviet Criminal Justice under Stalin* (Cambridge: Cambridge University Press, 1996).

19. A. N. Trainin, "Iz knigi *Uchenie o souchastii* (1941)," in *A. N. Trainin: Izbrannye trudy,* ed. N. F. Kuznetsova (St. Petersburg: Iuridicheskii tsentr Press, 2004), 247–368. While Trainin focused on domestic crimes in this book, he would soon apply the idea of complicity to the international context.

20. ARAN f. 499, op. 1, d. 24, ll. 1–9, 20–39 (on partisans esp. 37–39).

21. ARAN f. 499, op. 1, d. 42, ll. 19–40; A. N. Trainin, *Ob ugolovnoi otvetstvennosti gitlerovtsev: Stenogramma publichnoi lektsii* (Moscow: Sovnarkom SSSR, 1943), 3. The public lecture was initially delivered on September 10, 1943 at the House of Unions in Moscow. See ARAN f. 1711,op. 1, d. 1, l. 1.

22. Inter-Allied Information Committee, *The Inter-Allied Declaration Signed at St. James Palace, London, on 13th January, 1942, and Relative Documents* (London: HMSO, 1942); Ginsburgs, *Moscow's Road to Nuremberg,* 34; Arieh J. Kochavi, *Prelude to Nuremberg: Allied War Crimes Policy and the Question of Punishment* (Chapel Hill: University of North Carolina Press, 1998), 17–20.

23. Kochavi, *Prelude to Nuremberg,* 21–28; "Memorandum Prepared by Mr. Harry L. Hopkins for President Roosevelt," September 24, 1942, *Foreign Relations of the United States (FRUS),* 1942, vol. 1, 56–57.

24. Kochavi, *Prelude to Nuremberg,* 28–31.

25. Ibid., 33–34; Franklin D. Roosevelt, "Statement Warning Against Axis Crimes in Occupied Countries," in *The Public Papers and Addresses of Franklin D. Roosevelt,* 1942 volume, Humanity on the Defensive (New York: Harper, 1950), 329–330.

26. AVPRF f. 06, op. 4, p. 14, d. 137, ll. 1–2; Kochavi, *Prelude to Nuremberg,* 33–34; Sorokina, "People and Procedures," 814–815.

27. AVPRF f. 06, op. 4, p. 14, d. 137, ll. 5–8, 13–17, 21–23.

28. On Stalin's concerns about Hess see AVPRF f. 06, op. 4, p. 1, d. 14, ll. 57–61. On Stalin's suspicion of the British and anger about the failure to open a second front see Overy, *Russia's War,* 70, 167–169.

29. AVPRF f. 06, op. 4, p. 4, d. 35, ll. 42–49; p. 6, d. 65, ll. 42–57; Russian State Archive of Socio-Political History (RGASPI) f. 17, op. 3, d. 1045, ll. 2, 60, 82.

30. "Zaiavlenie Sovetskogo pravitel'stva ob otvetstvennosti gitlerovskikh zakhvatchikov i ikh soobshchnikov za zlodeianiia sovershaemye imi v okkupirovannykh stranakh Evropy," *Pravda,* October 15, 1942, 1.

31. "Prestupnuiu gitlerovskuiu kliku k otvetu," *Pravda,* October 19, 1942, 1. It was reprinted in *Soviet War News* (a publication of the Soviet embassy). For the original see AVPRF f. 06, op. 4, p. 14, d. 137, l. 19.

32. AVPRF f. 06, op. 4, p. 7, d. 69, ll. 12–14, 17–30. The file contains the decree of November 2, 1942. The full name was The Extraordinary State

Commission for Ascertaining and Investigating Crimes Perpetrated by the German-Fascist Invaders and their Accomplices and the Damage Inflicted by Them on the Citizens, Collective Farms, Social Organizations, State Enterprises and Institutions of the USSR.

33. Ibid. Also State Archive of the Russian Federation (GARF) f. 7523, op. 4, d. 113, ll. 5–6; RGASPI f. 17, op. 125, d. 79, ll. 9–14; Sorokina, "People and Procedures," 804–805, 815–824. Katyn is the clearest example of fabrication. Sorokina argues that it was "far from being the only such case." For an argument about the Soviet fabrication of data on war crimes in the Cherek region of Kabardino-Balkariia in the North Caucasus see K. G. Azamatov, M. O. Temirzhanov, B. B. Temukuev, A. I. Tetuev, and M. Chechenov, ed., *Cherekskaia tragediia* (Nal'chik: El'brus, 1994).

34. Kochavi, *Prelude to Nuremberg*, 39.

35. AVPRF f. 06, op. 4, p. 14, d. 137, ll. 5–17.

36. RGASPI f. 558, op. 11, d. 284, ll. 11–21, 34–36; AVPRF f. 06, op. 4, p. 1, d. 14, ll. 57–61.

37. A. Y. Vyshinsky, *Traitors Accused: Indictment of the Piatakov-Radek Trotskyite Group* (New York: Workers Library, 1937), 6.

38. RGASPI f. 558, op. 11, d. 284, ll. 34–36.

39. AVPRF f. 06, op. 4, p. 1, d. 14, ll. 60–61.

40. "11 Allies Condemn Nazi War on Jews: United Nations Issue Joint Declaration of Protest on 'Cold Blooded Extermination,'" *New York Times*, December 18, 1942, 1.

41. "Ob osushchestvlenii gitlerovskimi vlastiami plana istrebleniia evreiskogo naseleniia Evropy," *Izvestiia*, December 19, 1942, 1; "Russia Issues Statement," *New York Times*, December 20, 1942, 23. For the Soviet original see AVPRF f. 06, op. 4, p. 7, d. 67, ll. 53–67. The Soviet Union's Jewish Anti-Fascist Committee had been publicizing the Nazi murder of Jews in the German-occupied USSR, but this was the first such statement issued by the Ministry of Foreign Affairs.

42. Karel C. Berkhoff, "Total Annihilation of the Jewish Population: The Holocaust in the Soviet Media, 1941–45," in *The Holocaust in the East: Local Perpetrators and Soviet Responses*, ed. Michael David-Fox, Peter Holquist, and Alexander M. Martin (Pittsburgh: University of Pittsburgh Press, 2014), 83–117. Berkhoff argues (against other scholars of the Holocaust) that it is not true that the Soviets suppressed information about the targeted killing of Jews.

43. AVPRF f. 06, op. 5, p. 20, d. 221, ll. 14–15.

44. Kiril Feferman, "Soviet Investigation of Nazi Crimes in the USSR: Documenting the Holocaust," *Journal of Genocide Research* 5, no. 4 (2003): 587–602; David Shneer, *Through Soviet Jewish Eyes: Photography, War, and the Holocaust* (New Brunswick: Rutgers University Press, 2012), 140–143; Alexander Werth, *Russia at War, 1941–1945* (New York: Carroll and Graf, 1964), 609–618.

45. AVPRF f. 06, op. 5, p. 17, d. 166, ll. 1–7.
46. "Radio Communiqué on the Discovery of Graves of Polish Officers in the Smolensk Area, April 13, 1943, Berlin, 9:15 a.m.," "Communiqué Issued by the Sovinformburo Attacking the German 'Fabrications' about the Graves of Polish Officers in Katyn Forest, April 15, 1943, Moscow," and "Statement of the Polish Government Concerning the Discovery of the Graves of Polish Officers Near Smolensk, April 17, 1943, London," in *Katyn: A Crime Without Punishment,* ed. Anna M. Cienciala, Natalia S. Lebedeva, and Wojciech Materski (New Haven: Yale University Press, 2007), 305–309. Also GARF f. 8581, op. 2, d. 132, ll. 56–61.
47. "Records Relating to the Katyn Forest Massacre at the National Archives," National Archives and Records Administration, https://www.archives.gov/research/foreign-policy/katyn-massacre (accessed June 15, 2017).
48. Christian Lowe, "Wartime Allies Hushed Up Katyn Massacre of Poles: Documents," Reuters, September 11, 2012, https://www.reuters.com/article/us-usa-poland-katyn/war-time-allies-hushed-up-katyn-massacre-of-poles-documents-idUSBRE88A0O020120911 (accessed June 21, 2018).
49. The "proposal" to murder the Poles originated with Lavrenty Beria and was accepted by the Politburo on March 5, 1940. See "Beria Memorandum to Joseph Stalin Proposing the Execution of the Polish Officers, Gendarmes, Police, Military Settlers, and Others in the Three Special POW Camps, Along with Those Held in the Prisons of the Western Regions of Ukraine and Belorussia, Accepted by the Politburo March 5, 1940, Moscow," in Cienciala et al., *Katyn*, 118-120. For the editors' discussion of the Soviet crime and cover-up see 121-148, 318–319. Also see Allen Paul, *Katyn: Stalin's Massacre and the Triumph of Truth* (De Kalb: Northern Illinois University Press, 1991).
50. Sorokina, "People and Procedures," 826–830; Witold Wasilewski, "The Birth and Persistence of the Katyn Lie," *Case Western Reserve Journal of International Law* 45, no. 3 (2012): 671–693.
51. Sorokina, "People and Procedures," 826–830; Ilya Bourtman, " 'Blood for Blood, Death for Death,' The Soviet Military Tribunal in Krasnodar, 1943," *Holocaust and Genocide Studies* 22, no. 2 (2008); Tanja Penter, "Local Collaborators on Trial: Soviet War Crimes Trials under Stalin (1943–1953)," *Cahiers du monde russe* 49, no. 2–3 (2008): 341–364; Sergey Kudryashov and Vanessa Voisin, "The Early Stages of 'Legal Purges' in Soviet Russia (1941–1945)," *Cahiers du monde russe* 49, no. 2–3 (2008): 263–296; Alexander V. Prusin, " 'Fascist Criminals to the Gallows!': The Holocaust and Soviet War Crimes Trials, December 1945–February 1946," *Holocaust and Genocide Studies* 17, no. 1 (2003): 1–30. The figure of 7,000 is from Penter.
52. Jeremy Hicks, " 'Soul Destroyers': Soviet Reporting of Nazi Genocide and Its Perpetrators at the Krasnodar and Khar'kov Trials," *History* 98, no. 4 (2013): 530–547; Shneer, *Through Soviet Jewish Eyes*, 142.

53. AVPRF f. 06, op. 5, p. 17, d. 166, ll. 14–15.
54. AVPRF f. 06, op. 7, p. 20, d. 208, ll. 1–3. They were annexed in 1940.
55. AVPRF f. 06, op. 5, p. 17, d. 166, ll. 34–35, 39–44.
56. These were the Geneva Convention of 1864 and the Hague Conventions of 1899 and 1907.
57. National Archives and Records Administration—College Park (NARA) Record Group (RG) 238, entry 52, b. 7, "United Nations Commission for the Investigation of War Crimes, Notes of Unofficial Preliminary Meeting," October 26, 1943; LOC-RHJ b. 118, f. 8, Dr. B. Ečer, "Contribution to the History of the UNWCC," January 19, 1948. On Hurst also see Mark Lewis, *The Birth of the New Justice: The Internationalization of Crime and Punishment, 1919–1950* (Oxford: Oxford University Press, 2014), 161–162.
58. LOC-RHJ b. 118, f. 8, Dr. B. Ečer, "Contribution to the History of the UNWCC."
59. ARAN f. 499, op. 1, d. 32, ll. 20, 27–50. It was discussed at the meeting on September 23, 1943. Vyshinsky attended some of the Institute of Law's meetings in September. Also ARAN f. 499, op. 1, d. 39, ll. 11, 20; d. 50, ll. 2–8.
60. A. Farrin [Trainin], "The Responsibility for Nazi Crimes," *Central European Observer*, September 17, 1943, 281–282; A. Farrin [Trainin], "The Responsibility for Nazi Crimes," *Information Bulletin* (Embassy of the USSR), October 2, 1943, 5–7; Trainin, "Ob ugolovnoi otvetstvennosti gitlerovtsev." Also Kirsten Sellars, *"Crimes against Peace" and International Law* (Cambridge: Cambridge University Press, 2015).
61. Farrin [Trainin], "The Responsibility for Nazi Crimes," *Central European Observer*; Farrin [Trainin], "The Responsibility for Nazi Crimes," *Information Bulletin*; Trainin, "Ob ugolovnoi otvetstvennosti gitlerovtsev."
62. AVPRF f. 3b, op. 1, p. 19, d. 227, ll. 1–2, 6–8.
63. Ibid.
64. Debra J. Allen, *The Oder-Neisse Line: The United States, Poland, and Germany in the Cold War* (Westport: Praeger, 2003).
65. "The Tehran Conference, Proceedings of the Conference," Monday, November 29, 1943, Tripartite dinner meeting, 8:30 (Document 368), Bohlen Minutes, *FRUS, 1943,* Diplomatic Papers, The Conferences at Cairo and Tehran, https://history.state.gov/historicaldocuments/frus1943CairoTehran/d368 (accessed June 12, 2017); William Manchester and Paul Reid, *The Last Lion: Winston Spencer Churchill, Defender of the Realm, 1940–1965* (New York: Bantam, 2012), 765–766.
66. Peter Whitewood, *The Red Army and the Great Terror: Stalin's Purge of the Soviet Military* (Lawrence: University Press of Kansas, 2015), 264. This purge took place from June 1937 to November 1938.

67. Ginsburgs, *Moscow's Road to Nuremberg*, 52–57; Greg Dawson, *Judgment Before Nuremberg: The Holocaust in the Ukraine and the First Nazi War Crimes Trial* (New York: Pegasus, 2012); Hicks, " 'Soul Destroyers,' " 543–544. Ehrenburg's article also noted the murder of Russians, Ukrainians, and others.

68. A. Trainin, "Ob ugolovnoi otvetstvennosti gitlerovskikh prestupnikov," *Voina i rabochii klass*, no. 1 (1944): 19–21 (quoted from p. 20).

69. "Kharkov Trial: First Pictures from Russian Movie Show Legal Trial and Death of Nazi War Criminals," *Life* 17, no. 2 (July 10, 1944): 94, 97; Dawson, *Judgment Before Nuremberg*, 343–344.

70. "The Kharkov Trial: A Grim Newsreel Record," *Times* (London), July 7, 1944, 6. Ečer and the OSS both studied the Kharkov Trial. B. Etcher, *The Lessons of the Kharkov Trial* (London: Russia Today Society, 1944); LOC-RHJ b. 111, f. 10, Office of Strategic Services Research and Analysis Branch, no. 1988.1, "Soviet Intentions to Punish War Criminals," April 30, 1945, 38–41. Also see Jeremy Hicks, *First Films of the Holocaust: Soviet Cinema and the Genocide of the Jews, 1938–1946* (Pittsburgh: University of Pittsburgh Press, 2012), 196. The Russian is sometimes translated as "Justice is Coming!"

71. Wasilewski, "The Birth and Persistence of the Katyn Lie," 677–682.

72. Ibid. Also "The Burdenko Commission Report, January 24, 1944, Moscow," in Cienciala et al., *Katyn*, 319-326. The full name was The Special State Commission for Ascertaining and Investigating the Circumstances of the Shooting of the Polish Prisoners of War by the German Fascist Invaders in the Katyn Forest.

73. AVPRF f. 06, op. 5, p. 17, d. 166, ll. 83–84. The USSR adopted this amendment on February 2, 1944.

74. LOC-RHJ b. 118, f. 8, Dr. B. Ečer, "Contribution to the History of the UNWCC," 7–8, 26–32; Michael S. Blayney, "Herbert Pell, War Crimes, and the Jews," *American Historical Jewish Quarterly* 65, no. 4 (1976): 335–352. Also Kirsten von Lingen, "Defining Crimes against Humanity: The Contribution of the United Nations War Crimes Commission to International Criminal Law, 1944–1947," in *The Historical Origins of International Criminal Law*, ed. Morten Bergsmo, Wui Ling Cheah, and Ping Yi, vol. 1 (Oslo: TOAEP, 2014), 475–505.

75. A. N. Trainin, *Ugolovnaia otvetstvennost' gitlerovtsev*, ed. A. Ia. Vyshinskii (Moscow: Iuridicheskoe izdatel'stvo, 1944), 12–13, 35–41, 45–70, 99–106.

76. Ibid., 78–91 (quoted from p. 91).

77. A. N. Trainin, "Judging the War Criminals" and "Judging the War Criminals II," *New Masses*, September 12, 1944, 3–6, and September 19, 1944, 10–12; A. Trainin, "Certain Lessons of Versailles," *Information Bulletin* (Embassy of the USSR), September 26, 1944, 1–2.

78. NARA RG 238, entry 52, b. 7, "UNWCC, Supplement to the Minority Report Presented by Dr. B. Ecer," October 6, 1944.

79. NARA RG 238, entry 52, b. 7, "UNWCC, Minutes of the 35th Meeting," October 10, 1944.

80. Ibid., and NARA RG 238, entry 52, b. 7, "UNWCC, Minutes of the 36th Meeting," October 17, 1944. The term was underlined in the original.

81. NARA RG 238, entry 52, b. 7, "UNWCC, Report Made by Dr. Ečer on Professor Trainin's Book 'The Criminal Responsibility of the Hitlerites' at the Commission's Meeting of October 31, 1944," November 11, 1944. (A copy of this report can also be found at University of Wyoming, American Heritage Center, Murray Bernays Collection (3817) b. 4, f. 1.)

82. Harry S. Truman Presidential Library and Museum (HSTPLM), Samuel I. Rosenman Papers, War Crimes File, "Memorandum from the United Nations War Crimes Commission, 'Report Made by Dr. Ečer on Professor Trainin's Book,'" November 11, 1944.

83. The Soviets had the work translated into English in 1944. A. N. Trainin, *The Criminal Responsibility of the Hitlerites* (Moscow: Legal Publishing House NKU, 1944). The book was also published in French, Arabic, and other languages.

84. HSTPLM, Rosenman Papers, War Crimes File, "Memorandum from Murray C. Bernays and D. W. Brown," January 4, 1945. A copy can also be found in the Murray Bernays Collection (3817) b. 4, f. 5.

85. Sellars, *"Crimes against Peace" and International Law*, 65–66; Gary Jonathan Bass, *Stay the Hand of Vengeance: The Politics of War Crimes Tribunals* (Princeton: Princeton University Press, 2000), 157–169.

86. Sellars, *"Crimes against Peace" and International Law*, 67–70; Bass, *Stay the Hand of Vengeance*, 170; "Subject: Trial of European War Criminals (By Colonel Murray C. Bernays, G-1)," September 15, 1944, in Bradley F. Smith, ed., *American Road to Nuremberg: The Documentary Record. 1944-1945* (Stanford: Hoover Institution Press, 1982), 33–37.

87. The Bernays archive includes an abridged copy of Trainin's "Criminal Responsibility of the Hitlerites" and Ečer's analysis of it. Murray Bernays Collection (3817) b. 4, f. 1, "Memorandum for General Berry from M.C.B.," December 18, 1944; "Memorandum for the Judge Advocate General," [after November 24,] 1944; "Summary of 'The Criminal Responsibility of the Hitlerites' by Professor A. N. Trainin," n.d.; "Report Made by Dr. Ečer on Professor Trainin's Book," November 11, 1944.

88. HSTPLM, Rosenman Papers, War Crimes File, "Memorandum from Murray C. Bernays and D. W. Brown."

89. A. Trainin, "The Strategy of 'Mercy,'" *Communist*, December 1944, 1073–1077.

90. AVPRF f. 06, op. 7, p. 20, d. 208, ll. 1–3.

91. AVPRF f. 06, op. 7, p. 206, d. 8, ll. 1–3.

92. LOC-RHJ b. 95, f. 5, "Memorandum for the President: Trial and Punishment of Nazi War Criminals," January 22, 1945. A copy can be found in the Murray Bernays Collection (3817) b. 4, f. 1.

93. Ibid.

94. Ibid.

95. S. M. Plokhy, *Yalta: The Price of Peace* (New York: Penguin, 2010), 69–79. The quote (p. 77) is from Major General Laurence S. Kuter of the U.S. Army Air Force, who was with the U.S. delegation.

96. Ibid.; "Protocol of Proceedings of Crimea Conference," February 11, 1945, Avalon Project at Yale University Law School, http://avalon.law.yale.edu/wwii/yalta.asp (accessed June 15, 2017). Lavrenty Beria was also part of the Soviet delegation.

97. "Protocol of Proceedings of Crimea Conference," February 11, 1945.

98. Soviet economists had been arguing for labor reparations. Bruno Suviranta, *The Way to War Indemnities in Kind* (Helsinki: Acta Forestalia Fennica, 1954).

99. NARA RG 238, entry 52, b. 7, "UNWCC, Minutes of 52nd Meeting," March 14, 1945, and "UNWCC, Second Progress Report, Draft," March 20, 1945.

100. Kochavi, *Prelude to Nuremberg*, 212.

101. They also noted that joint Allied military tribunals might be convened in countries where there were obstacles to holding national trials. NARA RG 260, AG 000.5, b. 3, f. 1, "Memorandum: War Crimes and Atrocities," April 6, 1945.

102. NARA RG 260, AG 000.5, b. 3, f. 1, "Memorandum of Meeting," April 4, 1945.

103. NARA RG 260, AG 000.5, b. 3, f. 1, Simon to Rosenman, April 6, 1945. Also "The Ambassador of the United Kingdom to the Secretary of State," April 7, 1945, *FRUS, 1945*, Diplomatic Papers, European Advisory Commission, Austria, Germany, vol. 3, https://history.state.gov/historicaldocuments/frus1945v03/d877 (accessed June 15, 2017); Ann Tusa and John Tusa, *The Nuremberg Trial* (London: Atheneum, 1983), 65.

104. Kochavi, *Prelude to Nuremberg*, 164.

105. HSTPLM, Rosenman Papers, War Crimes File, "Draft of statement from James Byrnes to Soviet Ambassador," April 13, 1945.

106. Ibid.

Chapter 2

1. Stephen C. Schlesinger, *Act of Creation: The Founding of the United Nations* (New York: Basic Books, 2004), 115–119.

2. William Lee Miller, *Two Americans: Truman, Eisenhower and a Dangerous World* (New York: Knopf, 2012), 160; Geoffrey Roberts, "Sexing Up the

Cold War: New Evidence on the Molotov-Truman Talks of April 1945," *Cold War History* 4, no. 3 (2004): 105–125; D. Watson, *Molotov: A Biography* (New York: Palgrave Macmillan, 2005).

3. National Archives and Records Administration—College Park (NARA) RG 59, entry 1560, b. 4, "Memorandum of Conversation," April 24, 1945, 4.

4. On the fall of the city see Antony Beevor, *The Fall of Berlin 1945* (New York: Penguin Books, 2003), 386–405.

5. Harry S. Truman, "The President's News Conference," May 2, 1945, The American Presidency Project, ed. Gerhard Peters and John T. Woolley, http://www.presidency.ucsb.edu/ws/?pid=12258 (accessed June 7, 2017).

6. NARA RG 59, entry 1560, b. 4, "Memorandum of Conversation," May 3, 1945. For the Soviet transcript see Archive of the Foreign Policy of the Russian Federation (AVPRF) f. 06, op. 7, p. 20, d. 209, ll. 1–4.

7. Ibid.

8. AVPRF f. 06, op. 7, p. 20, d. 209, ll. 14–20.

9. Library of Congress, Manuscript Division, Robert H. Jackson Collection (LOC-RHJ) b. 95, f. 5, Robert H. Jackson (RHJ) Diary, May 10, 1945.

10. LOC-RHJ b. 95, f. 5, "Rosenman to Jackson, with Mimeographed Copy of the Agreement," May 6, 1945, and RHJ Diary, May 7, 1945.

11. Beevor, *Fall of Berlin*, 402–405.

12. AVPRF f. 07, op. 13, p. 41, d. 3, ll. 34–36.

13. LOC-RHJ b. 95, f. 5, "Memorandum re Document Entitled 'Punishment of War Criminals,'" draft, April 29, 1945.

14. This was the 1944 case of *Korematsu v. United States*. Jackson never officially took a leave from the Supreme Court but absented himself from June 1945 until the IMT's close. John Q. Barrett, "The Nuremberg Roles of Justice Robert H. Jackson," *Washington University Global Studies Law Review* 6 (2007): 511–525. For more on Jackson's early years see Eugene C. Gerhart, *America's Advocate: Robert H. Jackson* (Indianapolis: Bobbs-Merrill, 1958).

15. LOC-RHJ b. 95, f. 5, RHJ Diary, May 10, 1945. (He noted this after working through the evidence, a week later.)

16. LOC-RHJ b. 95, f. 5, RHJ Diary, May 4, 1945.

17. LOC-RHJ b. 95, f. 5, RHJ Diary, May 4, 1945, 7 p.m.

18. LOC-RHJ b. 95, f. 5, "Informal Policy Committee on Germany: Instructions for the U.S. Representative on the Reparation Commission," May 3, 1945.

19. LOC-RHJ b. 95, f. 5, RHJ Diary, May 12, 1945.

20. LOC-RHJ b. 95, f. 5, "Memorandum for Edwin W. Pauley from Robert Jackson," n.d., and "Draft Statement on Labor Reparations," May 2, 1945.

21. LOC-RHJ b. 95, f. 5, RHJ Diary, May 15, 1945; Douglas Waller, *Wild Bill Donovan: The Spymaster Who Created the OSS and Modern American Espionage* (New York: Free Press, 2011), 324–325. On the Donovan-Jackson partnership also see Kim Christian Priemel, *The Betrayal: The Nuremberg Trials and German Divergence* (Oxford: Oxford University Press, 2016), 72-74.

22. LOC-RHJ b. 95, f. 5, RHJ Diary, May 15, 1945.
23. LOC-RHJ b. 111, f. 10, Office of Strategic Services Research and Analysis Branch, no. 1988.1, "Soviet Intentions to Punish War Criminals," April 30, 1945.
24. LOC-RHJ b. 95, f. 5, RHJ Diary, May 17, 1945.
25. LOC-RHJ b. 95, f. 5, RHJ Diary, May 18, 1945.
26. Drew Pearson, "The Washington Merry-Go-Round," *Washington Post*, May 23, 1945, in LOC-RHJ b. 95, f. 5.
27. Quoted in LOC-RHJ b. 107, f. 1, Office of War Information, Bureau of Overseas Intelligence, European Comment on War Criminals, June 1, 1945.
28. Pavel Polian, *Against Their Will: The History and Geography of Forced Migrations in the USSR* (Budapest: Central European University Press, 2003), 241–275.
29. For example, A. Trainin, "Trudovye reparatsii (Po stranitsam inostrannoi pechati)," *Voina i rabochii klass*, no. 2 (May 1, 1945): 14–16.
30. AVPRF f. 06, op. 7, p. 45, d. 711, l. 2.
31. LOC-RHJ b. 95, f. 5, RHJ Diary, May 22–27, 1945.
32. Walker, *Wild Bill Donovan*, 323–326.
33. LOC-RHJ b. 95, f. 5, RHJ Diary, May 28, 1945.
34. Ibid.
35. LOC-RHJ b. 95, f. 5, "Meeting at House of Lords," May 29, 1945.
36. LOC-RHJ b. 95, f. 5, RHJ Diary, May 24, 1945.
37. LOC-RHJ b. 95, f. 5, "Meeting at House of Lords," May 29, 1945.
38. LOC-RHJ b. 95, f. 6, "Memorandum from the British Embassy: The Use of German Labour as Reparation," May 27, 1945.
39. LOC-RHJ b. 95, f. 5, RHJ Diary, May 30, 1945.
40. LOC-RHJ b. 95, f. 4, RHJ Diary, June 7, 1945, and "Memorandum for Mr. McCloy from Robert H. Jackson," June 8, 1945.
41. NARA RG 238, entry 52, b. 7, "Report to the President of the United States by Mr. Justice Robert H. Jackson," *Radio Bulletin,* no. 136, Washington, DC, June 7, 1946.
42. AVPRF f. 07, op. 13, p. 41, d. 3, ll. 3, 112–114, 117–118; f. 06, op. 7, p. 20, d. 209, ll. 60–61.
43. AVPRF f. 07, op. 13, p. 41, d. 3, ll. 1–2.
44. LOC-RHJ b. 95, f. 4, RHJ Diary, June 14, 1945.
45. Ibid.
46. Arieh J. Kochavi, *Prelude to Nuremberg: Allied War Crimes Policy and the Question of Punishment* (Chapel Hill: University of North Carolina Press, 1998), 192–193.
47. AVPRF f. 192, op. 12a, p. 84, d. 1a, ll. 78–81, in *SSSR i germanskii vopros, 1941–1949: Dokumenty iz Arkhiva vneshnei politiki Rossiiskoi Federatsii,* ed. Georgii P. Kynin and Jochen Laufer, vol. 2 (Moscow: Mezhdunarodnye otnosheniia, 2000), 722.

48. LOC-RHJ b. 95, f. 4, RHJ Diary, June 14, 1945.

49. Ibid.

50. Ibid.

51. The numbers are from Donald J. Raleigh, *Soviet Baby Boomers: An Oral History of Russia's Cold War Generation* (New York: Oxford University Press, 2012), 7; William C. Fuller Jr., "The Great Fatherland War and Late Stalinism, 1941–1953," in *Russia: A History,* ed. Gregory L. Freeze (Oxford: Oxford University Press, 2009), 392.

52. AVPRF f. 07, op. 13, p. 41, d. 3, ll. 51–52.

53. A. Poltorak, *The Nuremberg Epilogue* (Moscow: Progress Publishers, 1971), 153–155.

54. Telford Taylor, *The Anatomy of the Nuremberg Trials* (Boston: Knopf, 1992), 59; George Ginsburgs, *Moscow's Road to Nuremberg: The Soviet Background to the Trial* (The Hague: Martinus Nijhoff, 1996), 93.

55. AVPRF f. 06, op. 7, p. 24, d. 278, ll. 3, 6.

56. LOC-RHJ b. 95, f. 4, RHJ Diary, June 22, 23, and 25, 1945.

57. Philippe Sands, *East West Street: On the Origins of "Genocide" and "Crimes Against Humanity"* (New York: Knopf, 2016), 271.

58. NARA RG 260, AG 000.5, b. 3, f. 4, Jackson to U.S. Group Control Council, cable, June 22, 1945, and U.S. Group Control Council to Jackson, cable, June 24, 1945.

59. On Jackson and his relationship to Truman see Barrett, "The Nuremberg Roles of Justice Robert H. Jackson."

60. AVPRF f. 07, op. 13, p. 41, d. 3, ll. 70–75.

61. Ibid., l. 4.

62. LOC-RHJ b. 95, f. 4, RHJ Diary, June 26, 1945.

63. David Patrick Maxwell Fyfe, *Political Adventure: The Memoirs of the Earl of Kilmuir* (London: Weidenfeld and Nicolson, 1964), 83.

64. Taylor, *Anatomy of the Nuremberg Trials*, 59.

65. "Minutes of Conference Session of June 26, 1945," International Conference on Military Trials: London, 1945 (ICMT), Avalon Project at Yale University Law School, http://avalon.law.yale.edu/imt/jack13.asp (accessed June 9, 2017), and LOC-RHJ b. 95, f. 4, RHJ Diary, June 26, 1945.

66. "Minutes of Conference Session of June 26, 1945."

67. Ibid.; Maxwell Fyfe, *Political Adventure*, 88; Taylor, *Anatomy of the Nuremberg Trials*, 59.

68. Vadim J. Birstein, *SMERSH: Stalin's Secret Weapon* (London: Biteback, 2011), 374–375.

69. AVPRF f. 07, op. 13, p. 41, d. 3, l. 4; LOC-RHJ b. 93, f. 2, "Basic Questions for Inclusion in the Statute on the International Military Tribunal, June 28, 1945."

70. "Minutes of Conference Session of June 29, 1945," ICMT, http://avalon.law.yale.edu/imt/jack17.asp (accessed July 9, 2017).

71. Maxwell Fyfe, *Political Adventure*, 88.

72. Taylor, *Anatomy of the Nuremberg Trials*, 59.

73. "Minutes of Conference Session of June 29, 1945."

74. Ibid.

75. LOC-RHJ b. 95, f. 4, RHJ Diary, June 29, 1945.

76. "Revised Draft of Agreement and Memorandum Submitted by American Delegation, June 30, 1945," ICMT, http://avalon.law.yale.edu/imt/jack18. asp (accessed July 9, 2017). For the Russian-language draft see AVPRF f. 07, op. 13, p. 41, d. 3, ll. 76–88.

77. "Minutes of Conference Session of July 2, 1945," ICMT, http://avalon.law. yale.edu/imt/jack20.asp (accessed July 9, 2017).

78. Ibid.

79. "Minutes of Conference Session of July 4, 1945," ICMT, http://avalon.law. yale.edu/imt/jack22.asp (accessed July 9, 2017).

80. LOC-RHJ b. 95, f. 4, RHJ Diary, July 4, 1945.

81. LOC-RHJ b. 95, f. 4, RHJ Diary, July 6, 1945.

82. LOC-RHJ b. 110, f. 2, Byrnes to Jackson, cable, July 3, 1945, and Jackson to Byrnes, cable, July 4, 1945.

83. LOC-RHJ b. 93, f. 2, "4-Power Conference—Church House, July 5, 1945." Also "Report of American Member of Drafting Subcommittee, July 11, 1945," ICMT, http://avalon.law.yale.edu/imt/jack24.asp (accessed July 10, 2017).

84. Ibid.

85. LOC-RHJ b. 95, f. 4, RHJ Diary, July 7, 1945. The meeting was subsequently named after Hitler's military adjutant, Friedrich Hossbach, who wrote up the minutes.

86. LOC-RHJ b. 95, f. 4, RHJ Diary, July 8, 1945; NARA RG 260, AG 000.5, b. 3, f. 4, Clay to Jackson, cable, July 9, 1945. Clay was also commander of the U.S. Group Control Council.

87. "Minutes of Conference Session of July 13, 1945," ICMT, http://avalon.law. yale.edu/imt/jack27.asp (accessed July 9, 2017).

88. Ibid.

89. Ibid.

90. "Minutes of Conference Session of July 16, 1945," ICMT, http://avalon.law. yale.edu/imt/jack30.asp (accessed July 9, 2017). Also Ann Tusa and John Tusa, *The Nuremberg Trial* (London: Atheneum, 1983), 79–80.

91. "Minutes of Conference Sessions of July 17, 1945" and "Minutes of Conference Session of July 18, 1945," ICMT, http://avalon.law.yale.edu/imt/ jack32.asp and http://avalon.law.yale.edu/imt/jack33.asp (accessed July 10, 2017). Also University of Wyoming, American Heritage Center, Murray Bernays Collection (3817) b. 4, f. 5, "Definition of Aggression Memo for Mr.

Alderman," July 9, 1945, and "Protocol—The Charge of Launching a War of Aggression."

92. LOC-RHJ b. 93, f. 2, "Transcript of July 19th Meeting." Also "Minutes of Conference Session of July 19, 1945," ICMT, http://avalon.law.yale.edu/imt/jack37.asp (accessed July 10, 2017).

93. Ibid.

94. Taylor, *Anatomy of the Nuremberg Trials*, 64-65; LOC-RHJ b. 95, f. 4, RHJ Diary, July 20, 1945; LOC-RHJ b. 112, f. 4, Sidney S. Alderman, "The London Negotiations for War Crimes Prosecutions," n.d.

95. Maxwell Fyfe, *Political Adventure*, 90.

96. LOC-RHJ b. 95, f. 4, RHJ Diary, July 21, 1945.

97. State Archive of the Russian Federation (GARF) f. 8581, op. 2, d. 136, ll. 61–64.

98. On the Soviet occupation of Berlin see Norman M. Naimark, *The Russians in Germany: A History of the Soviet Zone of Occupation, 1945–1949* (Cambridge, MA: Harvard University Press, 1997).

99. "Redraft of Definition of 'Crimes,' Submitted by Soviet Delegation, July 23, 1945" and "Minutes of Conference Session of July 23, 1945," ICMT, http://avalon.law.yale.edu/imt/jack43.asp and http://avalon.law.yale.edu/imt/jack44.asp (accessed July 10, 2017).

100. "Minutes of Conference Session of July 23, 1945" and "Minutes of Conference Session of July 24, 1945," ICMT, http://avalon.law.yale.edu/imt/jack47.asp (accessed July 10, 2017).

101. "Minutes of Conference Session of July 23, 1945" and "Minutes of Conference Session of July 24, 1945." The Soviets would switch positions on this later.

102. "Redraft of Definition of 'Crimes,' Submitted by American Delegation, July 25, 1945" and "Minutes of Conference Session of July 25, 1945," ICMT, http://avalon.law.yale.edu/imt/jack49.asp and http://avalon.law.yale.edu/imt/jack51.asp (accessed July 10, 2017).

103. "Minutes of Conference Session of July 25, 1945."

104. AVPRF f. 07, op. 10, p. 8, d. 83, ll. 44–45.

105. Ibid.; AVPRF f. 07, op. 13, p. 41, d. 3, ll. 121–123.

106. LOC-RHJ b. 95, f. 4, RHJ Diary, July 26, 1945.

107. LOC-RHJ b. 95, f. 4, RHJ Diary, July 27, 1945.

108. AVPRF f. 0639, op. 3, p. 12, d. 12, ll. 1, 4, in *SSSR i Niurnbergskii protsess. Neizvestnye i maloizvestnye stranitsy istorii: Dokumenty*, ed. N. S. Lebedeva (Moscow: MFD, 2012), 214 (n. 1 to document no. 66); Ginsburgs, *Moscow's Road to Nuremberg*, 106.

109. Chris Tudda, *Cold War Summits: A History from Potsdam to Malta* (New York: Bloomsbury Academic, 2015), 29–30.

110. "The Berlin (Potsdam) Conference, July 17–August 2, 1945," A Decade of American Foreign Policy, Avalon Project at Yale University Law School, http://avalon.law.yale.edu/20th_century/decade17.asp (accessed May 25, 2019).

111. LOC-RHJ b. 95, f. 4, RHJ Diary, August 2, 1945.

112. AVPRF f. 06, op. 7, p. 20, d. 208, ll. 14–15.

113. "Minutes of Conference Session of August 2, 1945," ICMT, http://avalon.law.yale.edu/imt/jack59.asp (accessed July 19, 2017).

114. The Soviets would have liked a statement on rank-and-file war criminals as well but settled on an affirmation that nothing in the agreement would interfere with the Moscow Declarations of October 1943.

115. Philippe Sands writes that Lauterpacht suggested the use of the term "crimes against humanity" to Jackson. Sands, *East West Street*, 113. Lauterpacht would have known that the UNWCC had been using this term in its discussions.

116. "London Agreement of August 8th 1945" and "Charter of the International Military Tribunal," Nuremberg Trial Proceedings (NTP), vol. 1, Avalon Project at Yale University Law School, http://avalon.law.yale.edu/imt/imtchart.asp and http://avalon.law.yale.edu/imt/imtconst.asp (accessed July 10, 2017).

117. LOC-RHJ b. 95, f. 4, RHJ Diary, August 8, 1945. Gros does not in fact end up serving on the French delegation.

118. GARF f. 8131, op. 37, d. 2219, l. 1.

119. AVPRF f. 06, op. 7, p. 20, d. 210, ll. 1–3. Fritzsche was actually the chief of the propaganda ministry's Radio Division. The Soviets either overestimated or overstated his importance.

120. GARF f. 7445, op. 2, d. 6, ll. 203–204, in Lebedeva, *SSSR i Niurnbergskii protsess*, 234–236.

121. AVPRF f. 06, op. 7, p. 20, d. 210, ll. 4–10. The others on the NKVD list of possible defendants were: Martin Mutschmann, Johann-Georg Richert, Wilhelm Robert Oksmann, Hans Julius Traut, Friedrich Gustav Bernhardt, and Günther Walter Klammt.

122. Ibid.

123. Taylor, *Anatomy of the Nuremberg Trials*, 89–90.

124. "Trial of Major War Criminals: Goering Heads First List of 24," *Times* (London), August 30, 1945, 4.

125. AVPRF f. 07, op. 13, p. 41, d. 9, ll. 1–6.

126. Russian State Archive of Socio-Political History (RGASPI) f. 17, op. 163, d. 1463, l. 105; AVPRF f. 07, op. 13, p. 41, d. 4, l. 1.

127. LOC-RHJ b. 107, f. 1, Office of War Information, Research and Analysis Section, "Weekly Report on European Radio Output on War Crimes and War Criminals," no. 11: August 5–August 12, 1945.

Chapter 3

1. Aleksandr Zviagintsev, *Rudenko* (Moscow: Molodaia gvardiia, 2008), 64–65. Also Hiroaki Kuromiya, *Freedom and Terror in the Donbas: A Ukrainian-Russian Borderland, 1870s–1990s* (Cambridge: Cambridge University Press, 1998).

2. Aleksandr Zviagintsev and Iurii Orlov, *Prokurory dvukh epokh: Andrei Vyshinskii i Roman Rudenko* (Moscow: Olma Press, 2001), 212–213; Vadim J. Birstein, *SMERSH: Stalin's Secret Weapon* (London: Biteback, 2011), 375.

3. Birstein, *SMERSH*, 375; Matthew E. Lenoe, *The Kirov Murder and Soviet History* (New Haven: Yale University Press, 2010), 559.

4. Library of Congress, Manuscript Division, Robert H. Jackson Collection (LOC-RHJ) b. 95, f. 4, Robert H. Jackson (RHJ) Diary, September 13, 1945.

5. Telford Taylor, *The Anatomy of the Nuremberg Trials* (Boston: Knopf, 1992), 100.

6. LOC-RHJ b. 95, f. 4, RHJ Diary, September 16, 1945.

7. Russian State Archive of Socio-Political History (RGASPI) f. 17, op. 3, d. 1053, l. 52.

8. LOC-RHJ b. 95, f. 5, RHJ Diary, April 27, 1945.

9. RGASPI f. 17, op. 3, d. 1053, l. 52. Also RGASPI f. 17, op. 163, d. 1463, ll. 104–105, in *SSSR i Niurnbergskii protsess. Neizvestnye i maloizvestnye stranitsy istorii: Dokumenty*, ed. N. S. Lebedeva (Moscow: MFD, 2012), 238. The shorthand "Politburo Four" was occasionally used in Soviet telegrams.

10. Taylor, *Anatomy of the Nuremberg Trials*, 100–101.

11. David Patrick Maxwell Fyfe, *Political Adventure: The Memoirs of the Earl of Kilmuir* (London: Weidenfeld and Nicolson, 1964), 102.

12. LOC-RHJ b. 107, f. 1, "Outgoing Cable, August 14, 1945." Each committee was supposed to include members of all four delegations. In fact, the Soviets and the French did not contribute much to the committees headed by the Americans and the British.

13. For a fuller account see Taylor, *Anatomy of the Nuremberg Trials*, 78–115.

14. Taylor, *Anatomy of the Nuremberg Trials*, 100–101; Archive of the Foreign Policy of the Russian Federation (AVPRF) f. 07, op. 13, p. 41, d. 9, ll. 10–13.

15. AVPRF f. 07, op. 13, p. 41, d. 10, ll. 10–11.

16. Ibid.

17. Ibid.

18. Taylor, *Anatomy of the Nuremberg Trials*, 101. On Jackson's departure for Nuremberg see LOC-RHJ b. 95, f. 4, RHJ Diary, September 13, 1945. Alderman's official title was associate trial counsel.

19. AVPRF f. 07, op. 13, p. 41, d. 9, ll. 14–16.

20. LOC-RHJ b. 95, f. 4, RHJ Diary, September 18 to October 5, 1945. Also Ann Tusa and John Tusa, *The Nuremberg Trial* (London: Atheneum, 1983), 105, and Francesca Gaiba, *The Origins of Simultaneous Translation: The Nuremberg Trial* (Ottawa: University of Ottawa Press, 1998), 41–42.

21. Gaiba, *Origins of Simultaneous Translation*, 41–42.

22. State Archive of the Russian Federation (GARF) f. 8131, op. 37, d. 2219, l. 19; AVPRF f. 07, op. 13, p. 41, d. 4, l. 2.

23. AVPRF f. 07, op. 13, p. 41, d. 4, l. 3.

24. GARF f. 8131, op. 38, d. 238, ll. 13–15.

25. AVPRF f. 07, op. 13, p. 41, d. 10, ll. 12–35.

26. Ibid., ll. 37–39.

27. Ibid., ll. 40–43, 71–72.

28. Ibid. He recommended tapping Sergei Golunsky, who was in London, to help with this translation. For a Russian-language version of this part of the Indictment, covering "war crimes" and "crimes against humanity," see GARF f. 8131, op. 38, d. 238, ll. 94–141. Katyn is mentioned at l. 135.

29. R. B. Cockett, " 'In Wartime Every Objective Reporter Should Be Shot.' The Experience of British Press Correspondents in Moscow, 1941–5," *Journal of Contemporary History* 4, no. 3 (2004): 105–125.

30. AVPRF f. 0122, op. 27a, p. 206, d. 3, ll. 59–60, in Lebedeva, *SSSR i Niurnbergskii protsess*, 227–229.

31. On the 925 corpses see "The Burdenko Commission Report, January 24, 1944, Moscow," in *Katyn: A Crime Without Punishment*, ed. Anna M. Cienciala, Natalia S. Lebedeva, and Wojciech Materski (New Haven: Yale University Press, 2007), 319–326.

32. AVPRF f. 07, op. 13, p. 41, d. 10, l. 43.

33. Taylor, *Anatomy of the Nuremberg Trials*, 102.

34. Ibid., 99; Tusa and Tusa, *Nuremberg Trial*, 103.

35. Taylor, *Anatomy of the Nuremberg Trials*, 102; Tusa and Tusa, *Nuremberg Trial*, 112–113.

36. On Ivanov's earlier post see Lebedeva, *SSSR i Niurnbergskii protsess*, 553.

37. AVPRF f. 082, op. 27, p. 122, d. 23, ll. 16–18.

38. Ibid. Ivanov noted that the British and French delegations included historians and legal experts.

39. Ibid.

40. Ibid.

41. Taylor, *Anatomy of the Nuremberg Trials*, 100–102.

42. AVPRF f. 082, op. 27, p. 122, d. 23, ll. 16–18.

43. On the Ministry of Foreign Affairs and the purges see Alastair Kocho-Williams, "The Soviet Diplomatic Corps and Stalin's Purges," *Slavonic and East European Review* 86, no. 1 (2008): 90–110, and Teddy J. Uldricks, "The Impact of the Great Purges on the People's Commissariat of Foreign Affairs," *Slavic Review* 36, no. 2 (1977): 187–204.

44. AVPRF f. 07, op. 13, p. 41, d. 4, ll. 5–6.

45. GARF f. 7445, op. 2, d. 1, ll. 124–125.

46. AVPRF f. 07, op. 13, p. 41, d. 10, ll. 45–47.

47. GARF f. 7445, op. 2, d. 1, l. 409.

48. Taylor, *Anatomy of the Nuremberg Trials*, 103–104.

49. LOC-RHJ b. 95, f. 4, RHJ Diary, September 18 to October 5, 1945; Taylor, *Anatomy of the Nuremberg Trials*, 104; Tusa and Tusa, *Nuremberg Trial*, 113.

50. Tusa and Tusa, *Nuremberg Trial*, 114.

51. The full title was *Axis Rule in Occupied Europe: Laws of Occupation, Analysis of Government, Proposals for Redress.* Also see Raphael Lemkin, *Totally Unofficial: The Autobiography of Raphael Lemkin*, ed. Donna-Lee Frieze (New Haven: Yale University Press, 2013). On Lemkin and his ideas see Douglas Irvin-Erickson, *Raphael Lemkin and the Concept of Genocide* (Philadelphia: University of Pennsylvania Press, 2017). On Lemkin's lobbying efforts see Anton Weiss-Wendt, *The Soviet Union and the Gutting of the UN Genocide Convention* (Madison: University of Wisconsin Press, 2017), 22.

52. See Chapter 15.

53. LOC-RHJ b. 95, f. 4, RHJ Diary, September 18 to October 5, 1945. Jackson later sent formal notes to his fellow prosecutors attesting that nothing in the Indictment could be "construed as recognition of Russian sovereignty" over Latvia, Lithuania, and Estonia. GARF f. 7445, op. 2, d. 8, l. 500.

54. As remembered by Maxwell Fyfe, *Political Adventure*, 96. Also Tusa and Tusa, *Nuremberg Trial*, 113.

55. Taylor, *Anatomy of the Nuremberg Trials*, 117.

56. LOC-RHJ b. 95, f. 4, RHJ Diary, September 18 to October 5, 1945.

57. A. Poltorak, *The Nuremberg Epilogue* (Moscow: Progress Publishers, 1971), 121–122.

58. G. N. Aleksandrov, *Niurnberg vchera i segodnia* (Moscow: Izdatel'stvo politicheskoi literatury, 1971), 48–49; George Ginsburgs, *Moscow's Road to Nuremberg: The Soviet Background to the Trial* (The Hague: Martinus Nijhoff, 1996), 113, n. 36.

59. AVPRF f. 07, op. 13, p. 41, d. 9, ll. 7–8, 18–20, in *SSSR i germanskii vopros, 1941–1949: Dokumenty iz Arkhiva vneshnei politiki Rossiiskoi Federatsii*, ed. Georgii P. Kynin and Jochen Laufer, vol. 2 (Moscow: Mezhdunarodnye otnosheniia, 2000), 258–259. Also Tusa and Tusa, *Nuremberg Trial*, 109, and AVPRF f. 07, op. 13, p. 41, d. 4, l. 14.

60. Taylor, *Anatomy of the Nuremberg Trials*, 117–118.

61. Maxwell Fyfe, *Political Adventure*, 95.

62. AVPRF f. 06, op. 7, p. 20, d. 208, l. 16.

63. Taylor, *Anatomy of the Nuremberg Trials*, 118.

64. Ibid.

65. AVPRF f. 07, op. 13, p. 41, d. 10, ll. 60–61.

66. AVPRF f. 07, op. 7, p. 24, d. 278, ll. 5–8; LOC-RHJ b. 95, f. 4, RHJ Diary, October 8, 1945.

67. Poltorak, *Nuremberg Epilogue*, 155.

68. LOC-RHJ b. 95, f. 4, RHJ Diary, October 9, 1945.

69. AVPRF f. 06, op. 7, p. 20, d. 208, l. 21.

70. AVPRF f. 07, op. 13, p. 41, d. 10, ll. 60–61.

71. Taylor, *Anatomy of the Nuremberg Trials*, 121.

72. LOC-RHJ b. 95, f. 4, RHJ Diary, October 10, 1945.

73. AVPRF f. 07, op. 13, p. 41, d. 10, ll. 48–49.

74. It's not exactly clear who besides Dmitrieva was working on it at this point—but Soviet diplomats in London (including Golunsky) were likely pitching in.

75. AVPRF f. 07, op. 13, p. 41, d. 10, ll. 48–49.

76. Taylor, *Anatomy of the Nuremberg Trials*, 122–123.

77. Ibid.

78. AVPRF f. 07, op. 13, p. 41, d. 10, ll. 60–61.

79. AVPRF f. 07, op. 13, p. 41, d. 9, l. 24.

80. AVPRF f. 06, op. 7, p. 20, d. 208, l. 21.

81. AVPRF f. 07, op. 13, p. 41, d. 9, ll. 24–24ob, in Lebedeva, *SSSR i Niurnbergskii protsess*, 255.

82. AVPRF f. 07, op. 13, p. 41, d. 8, ll. 3–9; Taylor, *Anatomy of the Nuremberg Trials*, 122–125.

83. Harry S. Truman Presidential Library and Museum (HSTPLM), Harry S. Truman Papers, President's Secretary's File, Robert Jackson to Harry S. Truman, October 12, 1945, 3, https://www.trumanlibrary.gov/library/research-files/letter-robert-jackson-harry-s-truman?documentid=3&pagenumber=1 (accessed June 3, 2018). American and British forces had captured the vast majority of the Nazi leaders who ended up on the list of defendants. Fifteen of the defendants had been in American custody at "Ashcan" (Central Continental Prisoner of War Enclosure 32) in Mondorf-les-Bains, Luxembourg before being transferred to the Nuremberg prison in mid August: Doenitz, Frank, Frick, Funk, Goering, Kaltenbrunner, Keitel, Jodl, Ley, Papen, Ribbentrop, Rosenberg, Sauckel, Seyss-Inquart, Streicher. Two of the defendants, Schacht and Speer, had been in British custody at another camp, codenamed "Dustbin," in Frankfurt. See Steven David Schrag, "ASHCAN: Nazis, Generals and Bureaucrats as Guests at the Palace Hotel, Mondorf les Bains, Luxembourg, May–August 1945," (PhD diss., University of Toledo, 2015), and Kim Christian Priemel, *The Betrayal: The Nuremberg Trials and German Divergence* (Oxford: Oxford University Press, 2016), 81–82.

84. AVPRF f. 07, op. 13, p. 41, d. 8, ll. 3–9; Taylor, *Anatomy of the Nuremberg Trials*, 122–125.

85. GARF f. 8131, op. 38, d. 238, l. 71; AVPRF f. 07, op. 13, p. 41, d. 10, ll. 57, 58.

448 | NOTES

86. Joshua Rubenstein, *The Last Days of Stalin* (New Haven: Yale University Press, 2017), 4.

87. On Stalin in Sochi see Vladimir O. Pechatnov, "'The Allies Are Pressing on You to Break Your Will . . .' Foreign Policy Correspondence between Stalin and Molotov and Other Politburo Members, September 1945–December 1946," Working Paper no. 26, Cold War International History Project (Washington, DC, 1999).

88. AVPRF f. 07, op. 13, p. 41, d. 10, ll. 50–51, 56–57.

89. GARF f. 8131, op. 38, d. 238, ll. 67–70.

90. Ibid. (l. 69 on Katyn).

91. Ibid., ll. 67–70.

92. AVPRF f. 06, op. 7, p. 20, d. 208, ll. 10–13.

93. Ibid. See for example Clifton Daniel, "Churchill Warns against Socialism: Says Labor Party Rule Means Totalitarian State with Some Sort of 'Gestapo,'" *New York Times*, June 5, 1945, 1; Herbert L. Matthews, "British Left Leaders Are Firm with Russia: Foreign Minister Bevin Takes a Line Which Closely Follows Churchill," *New York Times*, August 26, 1945, E4.

94. AVPRF f. 06, op. 7, p. 20, d. 208, ll. 6–9.

95. National Archives and Records Administration—College Park (NARA) RG 260, AG 773.1, b. 112, f. 9, Transcript of Judges' Meeting, Sunday, October 14, 1945, 61–78.

96. Taylor, *Anatomy of the Nuremberg Trials*, 124; Tusa and Tusa, *Nuremberg Trial*, 119; LOC-RHJ b. 95, f. 4, RHJ Diary, October 14, 1945.

97. LOC-RHJ b. 95, f. 4, RHJ Diary, October 14, 1945.

98. Taylor, *Anatomy of the Nuremberg Trials*, 124.

99. NARA RG 260, AG 773.1, b. 112, f. 9, Transcript of Judges' Meeting, Sunday, October 14, 1945, 78–95.

100. Taylor, *Anatomy of the Nuremberg Trials*, 125; Tusa and Tusa, *Nuremberg Trial*, 119–120.

101. Taylor, *Anatomy of the Nuremberg Trials*, 125–126.

102. Ibid.,, 125.

103. AVPRF f. 06, op. 7, p. 20, d. 208, l. 16.

104. AVPRF f. 07, op. 13, p. 41, d. 10, ll. 62–65.

105. Ibid.

106. Ibid. Soviet leaders had removed the earlier reference to the Poles and the Gypsies.

107. Ibid.

108. AVPRF f. 06, op. 7, p. 20, d. 208, ll. 27–31.

109. Ibid., l. 22.

110. Taylor, *Anatomy of the Nuremberg Trials*, 126.

111. I have not found an explanation for this change. "Indictment: Count One," Nuremberg Trial Proceedings (NTP), vol. 1, Avalon Project at Yale

University Law School, http://avalon.law.yale.edu/imt/count1.asp (accessed June 9, 2018).

112. Ibid.

113. Ibid.

114. "Indictment: Count Three," NTP, vol. 1, http://avalon.law.yale.edu/imt/count3.asp (accessed June 9, 2018).

115. Taylor, *Anatomy of the Nuremberg Trials*, 126. Also GARF f. 7445, op. 1, d. 2608, ll. 41-42, in Lebedeva, *SSSR i Niurnbergskii protsess*, 263. The representatives were Rudenko, Dubost, Shawcross, and Shea.

116. Airey Neave, *On Trial at Nuremberg* (Boston: Little, Brown, 1979), 32–62.

117. AVPRF f. 07, op. 13, p. 41, d. 8, l. 22. Lawrence, who had returned to London, phoned in his approval.

Chapter 4

1. Archive of the Foreign Policy of the Russian Federation (AVPRF) f. 07, op. 13, p. 41, d. 8, ll. 23–24.

2. For the list see Russian State Archive of Socio-Political History (RGASPI) f. 17, op. 3, d. 1054, l. 15. TASS was the Soviet Telegraph Agency. The list of twenty-four correspondents included the political cartoonists Mikhail Kupriyanov, Porfiry Krylov, and Nikolai Sokolov (known as the Kukryniksy), as well as special TASS correspondents, such as the journalists Daniil Kraminov and Boris Afanasyev, legal experts Lev Sheinin and Arkady Poltorak, and Georgy Bespalov from the Soviet Military Administration's Information Bureau. Sheinin was also a writer of detective fiction.

3. RGASPI f. 17, op. 125, d. 316, ll. 100, 102.

4. AVPRF f. 06, op. 7, p. 20, d. 208, ll. 34–35. Also AVPRF f. 082, op. 32, p. 18, d. 1, ll. 100–101, in *SSSR i Niurnbergskii protsess. Neizvestnye i maloizvestnye stranitsy istorii: Dokumenty*, ed. N. S. Lebedeva (Moscow: MFD, 2012), 278–279.

5. AVPRF f. 07, op. 13, p. 41, d. 8, l. 31.

6. Ibid., ll. 28–30. Some of the Americans claimed that Gustav instead of Alfried had been named in the Indictment in error. Ann Tusa and John Tusa, *The Nuremberg Trial* (London: Atheneum, 1983), 94, and Telford Taylor, *The Anatomy of the Nuremberg Trials* (Boston: Knopf, 1992), 89.

7. AVPRF f. 07, op. 13, p. 41, d. 8, l. 33.

8. G. M. Gilbert, *Nuremberg Diary* (New York: Farrar, Straus, 1947), 7–8. Soviet leaders discussed the suicide of Ley on October 26. AVPRF f. 082, op. 32, p. 178, d. 5, ll. 22–25, in Lebedeva, *SSSR i Niurnbergskii protsess*, 268–270.

9. AVPRF f. 07, op. 13, p. 41, d. 8, l. 32.

10. Ibid., l. 34.

11. Taylor, *Anatomy of the Nuremberg Trials,* 140–143; Tusa and Tusa, *Nuremberg Trial,* 134.

12. Churchill Archives Centre, Churchill College, Cambridge, The Papers of Lord Kilmuir, KLMR Acc 1485, Sir David Maxwell Fyfe to Sylvia Maxwell Fyfe, October 28, 1945, available at http://www.kilmuirpapers.org/letters/4579523443.

13. Taylor, *Anatomy of the Nuremberg Trials,* 152; AVPRF f. 07, op. 13, p. 41, d. 4, ll. 8–9. The Soviet experts were Evgeny Sepp, professor of neurology, Evgeny Krasnushkin, professor of psychiatry, and Professor Nikolai Kurshakov, chief internist at the Ministry of Health.

14. Airey Neave, *On Trial at Nuremberg* (Boston: Little, Brown, 1979), 227–230.

15. Ibid.; Joseph E. Persico, *Nuremberg: Infamy on Trial* (New York: Penguin Books, 1994), 93–96.

16. AVPRF f. 07, op. 13, p. 41, d. 8, ll. 26–27, 37–46. Each country of the prosecution would advance funds to pay the defense attorneys and would later be reimbursed from funds seized from the defendants.

17. Edwin Black, *IBM and the Holocaust: The Strategic Alliance between Nazi Germany and America's Most Powerful Corporation* (New York: Crown, 2001).

18. AVPRF f. 07, op. 13, p. 41, d. 8, ll. 44–45. Also Francesca Gaiba, *The Origins of Simultaneous Translation: The Nuremberg Trial* (Ottawa: University of Ottawa Press, 1998), 37–45.

19. Harry S. Truman Presidential Library and Museum (HSTPLM), Harry S. Truman Papers, President's Secretary's File, Robert Jackson to Harry S. Truman, October 12, 1945, 4.

20. Douglas Waller, *Wild Bill Donovan: The Spymaster Who Created the OSS and Modern American Espionage* (New York: Free Press, 2011), 343–344.

21. Cornell University Law Library, Donovan Nuremberg Trials Collection (CULL-DNTC), "Memorandum for Mr. Justice Jackson from General Donovan," October 20, 1945, and "Literal Translation of Opinion on Indictment No. 1 before the International Military Tribunal by Fabian von Schlabrendorff," n. d., http://lawcollections.library.cornell.edu/nuremberg/catalog/nur:02066 and http://lawcollections.library.cornell.edu/nuremberg/catalog/nur:02060 (accessed June 6, 2018).

22. CULL-DNTC, "Memorandum from Dr. A. Pathy to General Donovan," October 19, 1945, http://lawcollections.library.cornell.edu/nuremberg/catalog/nur:02073 (accessed June 6, 2018). The OSS had been closed down on October 1. Donovan flew to Nuremberg two days later. Waller, *Wild Bill Donovan,* 343.

23. The Papers of Lord Kilmuir, KLMR Acc 1485, Sir David Maxwell Fyfe to Sylvia Maxwell Fyfe, November 1, 1945, available at http://www.kilmuirpapers.org/letters/4579523443.

24. Library of Congress, Manuscript Division, Robert H. Jackson Collection (LOC-RHJ) b. 103, f. 8, "Report of Interrogation, Hilger," October 17, 1945.

25. CULL-DNTC, "Memorandum from Lt. Col. John W. Griggs to Justice Jackson: German Nationals as Potential Witnesses: Secret," October 5, 1945, http://lawcollections.library.cornell.edu/nuremberg/catalog/nur:02124 (accessed June 6, 2018).

26. AVPRF f. 06, op. 7, p. 20, d. 208, ll. 10–11.

27. AVPRF f. 07, op. 13, p. 41, d. 8, l. 46.

28. Tusa and Tusa, *Nuremberg Trial*, 135; Taylor, *Anatomy of the Nuremberg Trials*, 145.

29. AVPRF f. 07, op. 13, p. 41, d. 8, ll. 48–49; "Report of Medical Commission Appointed to Examine Defendant Gustav Krupp von Bohlen," Nuremberg Trial Proceedings (NTP), vol. 1, Avalon Project at Yale University Law School, http://avalon.law.yale.edu/imt/v1-10.asp (accessed June 6, 2018); Taylor, *Anatomy of the Nuremberg Trials*, 145.

30. The Papers of Lord Kilmuir, KLMR Acc 1485, Sir David Maxwell Fyfe to Sylvia Maxwell Fyfe, November 8, 1945, available at http://www. kilmuirpapers.org/letters/4579523443; State Archive of the Russian Federation (GARF) f. 7445, op. 2, d. 7, ll. 83, 84; Taylor, *Anatomy of the Nuremberg Trials*, 210.

31. GARF f. 8131, op. 38, d. 238, ll. 17–21.

32. Ibid.

33. Ibid.

34. AVPRF f. 07, op. 13, p. 41, d. 8, ll. 48–49.

35. GARF f. 8131, op. 38, d. 238, ll. 20–21, 26.

36. Ibid. Also AVPRF f. 082, op. 32, p. 178, d. 1, ll. 100–101, in Lebedeva, *SSSR i Niurnbergskii protsess*, 278–279.

37. The other members of the subcommission were Gorshenin, Commissar of Justice Nikolai Rychkov, and the chairman of the Supreme Court of the USSR, Ivan Goliakov.

38. GARF f. 8131, op. 38, d. 238, l. 20. For more on the selection of witnesses see ll. 210–215, 222–226.

39. AVPRF f. 07, op. 13, p. 41, d. 4, l. 15.

40. AVPRF f. 07, op. 13, p. 41, d. 8, l. 50.

41. CULL-DNTC, Donovan to Jackson, November 6, 1945, http:// lawcollections.library.cornell.edu/nuremberg/catalog/nur:02146 (accessed June 5, 2018); LOC-RHJ b. 95, f. 4, "The Right to Resort to War," November 6, 1945.

42. Noted in GARF f. 7445, op. 2, d. 8, l. 394.

43. National Archives and Records Administration—College Park (NARA) RG 59, entry 1560, b. 4, "Memorandum from Charles E. Bohlen," October 18, 1945. This marked a shift from wartime, when the Soviets had celebrated the "Anglo-Soviet-American" coalition.

44. NARA RG 260, AG 014.33, b. 20, f. 2, "Memorandum Concerning the Repatriation of Soviet Citizens from the American Zone of Occupation in Germany," October 19, 1945. In some cases the Soviets were correct.

45. AVPRF f. 07, op. 13, p. 41, d. 8, l. 57. (Vyshinsky's reply is added in handwriting.)

46. AVPRF f. 07, op. 13, p. 41, d. 10, ll. 70–72.

47. Taylor, *Anatomy of the Nuremberg Trials*, 155.

48. "Preliminary Hearing, Wednesday, November 14, 1945," NTP, vol. 2, http://avalon.law.yale.edu/imt/11-14-45.asp (accessed June 6, 2018).

49. Taylor, *Anatomy of the Nuremberg Trials*, 157–158.

50. Telephoned telegrams reprinted in A. G. Zviagintsev, *Glavnyi protsess chelovechestva. Niurnberg: Dokumenty, issledovaniia, vospominaniia* (Moscow: Olma Media Grupp, 2011), 33–34.

51. "Preliminary Hearing, Thursday, November 15, 1945," NTP, vol. 2, http://avalon.law.yale.edu/imt/11-15-45.asp#krupp (accessed June 6, 2018).

52. AVPRF f. 07, op. 13, p. 41, d. 8, ll. 59–61.

53. Ibid.

54. GARF f. 7445, op. 2, d. 391, ll. 55–56.

55. AVPRF f. 07, op. 13, p. 41, d. 4, ll. 11, 16.

56. AVPRF f. 07, op. 13, p. 41, d. 9, l. 56.

57. AVPRF f. 07, op. 13, p. 41, d. 8, l. 62.

58. Ibid.

59. I am grateful to Charles Steinwedel for information about the disease cycle of malaria. On malaria's spread during the war see Leonard J. Bruce-Chwatt, "Malaria Research and Eradication in the USSR: A Review of Soviet Achievements in the Field of Malariology," *Bulletin of the World Health Organization* 21 (1959): 737–772.

60. AVPRF f. 07, op. 13, p. 41, d. 8, l. 58.

61. GARF f. 7445, op. 2, d. 6, l. 225.

62. "Preliminary Hearing, Saturday, November 17, 1945," NTP, vol. 2, http://avalon.law.yale.edu/imt/11-17-45.asp (accessed June 6, 2018).

63. AVPRF f. 07, op. 13, p. 41, d. 8, ll. 69–70. Krasnushkin, Sepp, and Kurshakov had concluded their report, finding that Hess's "loss of memory" was the result not of mental illness but of "hysterical amnesia," which would likely disappear with the start of the trial. NARA RG 260, AG 773.2, b. 111, f. 12, "Protokol obsledovaniia Rudol'fa Gess," November 17, 1945.

64. AVPRF f. 07, op. 13, p. 41, d. 8, ll. 69–70.

65. RGASPI f. 558, op. 11, d. 99, ll. 13–20. Poltorak was a lawyer and a writer who would later write a memoir about the Nuremberg Trials.

66. Ibid.

67. RGASPI f. 558, op. 11, d. 99, ll. 13–15.

68. Ibid., ll. 15–17.

69. Ibid., ll. 18–19.

70. Cited in Tusa and Tusa, *Nuremberg Trial*, 144.

71. AVPRF f. 07, op. 13, p. 41, d. 8, l. 63; "Allies' Prosecutors Will Confer Today," *New York Times*, November 19, 1945, 6.

72. Taylor, *Anatomy of the Nuremberg Trials*, 144, 150; Neave, *On Trial at Nuremberg*, 95.

73. AVPRF f. 07, op. 13, p. 41, d. 8, l. 68.

74. Ibid.

75. GARF f. 7445, op. 2, d. 391, l. 57.

76. Ibid., l. 58.

77. Ibid., l. 58.

78. Ibid., l. 59.

79. Taylor, *Anatomy of the Nuremberg Trials*, 158–162.

80. AVPRF f. 06, op. 7, p. 20, d. 208, ll. 36–37.

81. LOC-RHJ b. 95, f. 4, Robert H. Jackson (RHJ) Diary, November 19, 1945; Taylor, *Anatomy of the Nuremberg Trials*, 161.

82. LOC-RHJ b. 95, f. 4, RHJ Diary, November 19, 1945.

83. AVPRF f. 07, op. 13, p. 41, d. 8, l. 74; Taylor, *Anatomy of the Nuremberg Trials*, 160–161.

84. Taylor, *Anatomy of the Nuremberg Trials*, 162–163.

85. AVPRF f. 06, op. 7, p. 20, d. 208, ll. 36–37.

86. AVPRF f. 07, op. 13, p. 41, d. 8, l. 79; LOC-RHJ b. 95, f. 4, RHJ Diary, November 19, 1945; Taylor, *Anatomy of the Nuremberg Trials*, 161–163.

87. AVPRF f. 06, op. 7, p. 20, d. 208, l. 38.

Chapter 5

1. Russian State Archive of Literature and Art (RGALI) f. 2989, op. 1, d. 190, ll. 1–3.

2. Ibid. Also RGALI f. 1038, op. 2, d. 243, l. 1.

3. RGALI f. 1038, op. 2, d. 243, ll. 1–2; RGALI f. 2989, op. 1, d. 190, l. 1. The *Tägliche Rundschau* was a Soviet-run newspaper.

4. He made this film with Boris Makadeev. Antony Beevor, *The Battle for Spain: The Spanish Civil War 1936–1939* (New York: Penguin, 2006), 249.

5. RGALI f. 2989, op. 1, d. 190, ll. 31–33; K. Slavin, *Roman Karmen: 'Igraiu s ognem!..'* (Moscow: Soiuz kino, 1989); Roman Karmen, *No pasaran!* (Moscow: Sovetskaia Rossiia, 1972); A. L. Vinogradova, ed., *Roman Karmen v vospominaniiakh sovremennikov* (Moscow: Iskusstvo, 1983).

6. For Vishnevsky's biography see the introduction to his archival fond: RGALI f. 1038. Vishnevsky wrote *Trial of the Kronstadt Mutineers* in 1921. Elizabeth Wood, *Performing Justice: Agitation Trials in Early Soviet Russia* (Ithaca: Cornell University Press, 2005), 52–55. Also see Leonid Trofimov, "Soviet Reporters at the Nuremberg Trial: Agenda, Attitudes, and Encounters, 1945–46," *Cahiers d'histoire* 28, no. 2 (2010): 45–70. Among those present were the

satirists Mikhail Kupriyanov, Porfiry Krylov, and Nikolai Sokolov (known collectively as the Kukryniksy). On the Kukryniksy see Peter Kort Zegers and Douglas Druick, eds., *Windows on the War: Soviet TASS Posters at Home and Abroad, 1941–1945* (Chicago: Art Institute of Chicago, 2011).

7. Boris Efimov, *Forced Laughter: An Exhibition of 105 Cartoons by Boris Efimov* (Prague: Galerie Nova sin, 2005), and *Desiat' desiatiletii: O tom, chto videl, perezhil, zapomnil* (Moscow: Vagrius, 2000).

8. RGALI f. 2989, op. 1, d. 190, ll. 2–6; RGALI f. 1038, op. 2, d. 243, ll. 2–3. On the Press Camp also see Boris Polevoi, *The Final Reckoning: Nuremberg Diaries* (Moscow: Progress Publishers, 1978), 69–70.

9. "1st Day, Tuesday, November 20, 1945," Nuremberg Trial Proceedings (NTP), vol. 2, Avalon Project at Yale University Law School, http://avalon.law.yale.edu/imt/11-20-45.asp (accessed June 5, 2018). Also Ann Tusa and John Tusa, *The Nuremberg Trial* (London: Atheneum, 1983), 147–150.

10. "1st Day, Tuesday, November 20, 1945."

11. On the defendants see A. Poltorak, *The Nuremberg Epilogue* (Moscow: Progress Publishers, 1971), 44–61. On the opening see D. Zaslavskii, "Germanskii fashizm pered sudom narodov," *Pravda*, November 22, 1945, in *Sud istorii: Reportazhi s Niurnbergskogo protsessa*, ed. V. Velichko and G. N. Aleksandrov (Moscow: Izdatel'stvo politicheskoi literatury, 1966), 13–17.

12. Archive of the Foreign Policy of the Russian Federation (AVPRF) f. 07, op. 13, p. 41, d. 8, l. 77.

13. State Archive of the Russian Federation (GARF) f. 7445, op. 2, d. 8, ll. 10–13. Also Telford Taylor, *The Anatomy of the Nuremberg Trials* (Boston: Knopf, 1992), 166. Some Western lawyers shared this opinion. On Stahmer see Joseph E. Persico, *Nuremberg: Infamy on Trial* (New York: Penguin Books, 1994), 94.

14. AVPRF f. 07, op. 13, p. 41, d. 7, l. 1.

15. Taylor, *Anatomy of the Nuremberg Trials*, 166–167; "2nd Day, Wednesday, November 21, 1945," NTP, vol. 2, http://avalon.law.yale.edu/imt/11-21-45.asp (accessed June 4, 2018); "Goering's Statement," *New York Times*, November 22, 1945, 3.

16. "2nd Day, Wednesday, November 21, 1945"; Tusa and Tusa, *Nuremberg Trial*, 150–158; Eugene C. Gerhart, *America's Advocate: Robert H. Jackson* (Indianapolis: Bobbs-Merrill, 1958), 22–23.

17. "2nd Day, Wednesday, November 21, 1945."

18. Ibid.

19. Ibid.

20. AVPRF f. 07, op. 13, p. 41, d. 8, l. 83.

21. "Rech' glavnogo obviniteliia ot SShA Dzheksona," *Pravda*, November 24, 1945, 4. "Rech' glavnogo obviniteliia ot SShA Dzheksona," *Izvestiia*, November 24, 1945, 4.

22. AVPRF f. 07, op. 13, p. 41, d. 8, ll. 81–82. On the food see RGALI f. 1038, op. 2, d. 243, l. 3. On accommodations, also see Trofimov, "Soviet Reporters at the Nuremberg Trial," and Lara Feigel, *The Bitter Taste of Victory: Life, Love and Art in the Ruins of the Reich* (London: Bloomsbury, 2016).

23. AVPRF f. 07, op. 13, p. 41, d. 8, ll. 81–82.

24. AVPRF f. 07, op. 13, p. 41, d. 9, l. 33. For another copy see Russian State Archive of Socio-Political History (RGASPI) f. 17, op. 162, d. 37, l. 158.

25. Ibid. The full name of the propaganda department was the Department of Agitation and Propaganda.

26. Ibid.

27. GARF f. 8131, op. 38, d. 238, ll. 158–159. Its full name was the Politburo Commission for Preparing to Conduct the Nuremberg Trials. The Indictment Commission was officially dissolved with the start of the trials.

28. In early 1946 Andrei Zhdanov was added to this group.

29. See Vladimir O. Pechatnov, "'The Allies Are Pressing on You to Break Your Will . . .' Foreign Policy Correspondence between Stalin and Molotov and Other Politburo Members, September 1945–December 1946," Working Paper no. 26, Cold War International History Project (Washington, DC, 1999).

30. AVPRF f. 07, op. 13, p. 41, d. 4, l. 12.

31. Arkady Vaksberg, *Stalin's Prosecutor: The Life of Andrei Vyshinsky*, trans. Jan Butler (New York: Grove Weidenfeld, 1991), 101.

32. "3rd Day, Thursday, November 22, 1945," NTP, vol. 2, http://avalon.law. yale.edu/imt/11-22-45.asp (accessed June 4, 2018).

33. RGALI f. 2989, op. 1, d. 190, ll. 4–6.

34. Ibid.

35. Joshua Rubenstein, *Tangled Loyalties: The Life and Times of Ilya Ehrenburg* (New York: Basic Books, 1996), 229–230.

36. Polevoi, *Final Reckoning*, 69–70.

37. GARF f. 7445, op. 2, d. 407, ll. 1–2.

38. Ilya Ehrenburg, *Post-War Years: 1945–54* (Cleveland: World, 1967), 33.

39. RGALI f. 1038, op. 2, d. 243, l. 10.

40. Ibid., ll. 3–9. Also "4th Day, Friday, November 23, 1945," NTP, vol. 2, http://avalon.law.yale.edu/imt/11-23-45.asp (accessed June 4, 2018).

41. Ehrenburg, *Post-War Years*, 33.

42. RGASPI f. 629, op. 1, d. 109, l. 84.

43. Ehrenburg, *Post-War Years*, 33.

44. RGALI f. 1038, op. 2, d. 243, l. 9.

45. Polevoi, *Final Reckoning*, 75.

46. RGALI f. 1038, op. 2, d. 243, l. 7.

47. RGASPI f. 629, op. 1, d. 109, ll. 84–85ob.

48. Ibid.

49. Discussed in Feigel, *Bitter Taste of Victory*, 146.

50. RGASPI f. 629, op. 1, d. 109, ll. 84–85ob.

51. RGALI f. 1038, op. 2, d. 243, l. 8.

52. On Soviet informing see, for example, James W. Heinzen, "Informers and the State under Late Socialism: Informant Networks and Crimes against 'Socialist Property,' 1940–1953," *Kritika: Explorations in Russian and Eurasian History* 8, no. 4 (2007): 789–815, and V. I. Kozlov, "Denunciation and Its Functions in Soviet Governance: A Study of Denunciations and Their Bureaucratic Handling from Soviet Police Archives, 1944–1953," *Journal of Modern History* 68, no. 4 (1996): 867–898. On the practice of schoolchildren informing on their parents see Catriona Kelly, *Comrade Pavlik: The Rise and Fall of a Soviet Boy Hero* (London: Granta Books, 2005).

53. RGASPI f. 629, op. 1, d. 109, l. 84ob; Trofimov, "Soviet Reporters at the Nuremberg Trial," 67.

54. Taylor, *Anatomy of the Nuremberg Trials*, 211.

55. Vaksberg, *Stalin's Prosecutor*, 259.

56. AVPRF f. 059, op. 25, p. 58, d. 339, ll. 3-14, in *SSSR i germanskii vopros, 1941–1949: Dokumenty iz Arkhiva vneshnei politiki Rossiiskoi Federatsii*, ed. Georgii P. Kynin and Jochen Laufer, vol. 2 (Moscow: Mezhdunarodnye otnosheniia, 2000), 750–751 (n. 140). Also see the editors' introduction to the volume, esp. p. 84.

57. AVPRF f. 07, op. 13, p. 41, d. 9, l. 33.

58. Vaksberg, *Stalin's Prosecutor*, 255–258.

59. RGASPI f. 17, op. 162, d. 37, ll. 159–160.

60. "5th Day, Monday, November 26, 1945," NTP, vol. 2, http://avalon.law.yale.edu/imt/11-26-45.asp (accessed June 5, 2018); Tusa and Tusa, *Nuremberg Trial*, 159.

61. AVPRF f. 07, op. 13, p. 41, d. 7, ll. 2–4.

62. Polevoi, *Final Reckoning*, 127. Emphasis in the original. For Vishnevsky's reaction see RGALI f. 1038, op. 2, d. 243, ll. 13–14.

63. AVPRF f. 07, op. 13, p. 41, d. 7, ll. 2–4. They also petitioned for Ambassador Emil von Rintelen.

64. GARF f. 7445, op. 2, d. 391, ll. 43–46. Sheinin also served as a special correspondent with the press corps. On his career see Sheila Fitzpatrick, *Tear Off the Masks!: Identity and Imposture in Twentieth-Century Russia* (Princeton: Princeton University Press, 2005), 21.

65. GARF f. 7445, op. 2, d. 391, ll. 44–45; Taylor, *Anatomy of the Nuremberg Trials*, 151.

66. GARF f. 7445, op. 2, d. 391, ll. 43–44. On the length of the speeches see ll. 57–58.

67. GARF f. 7445, op. 2, d. 7, l. 81.

68. GARF f. 7445, op. 2, d. 391, ll. 45–46.

69. Ibid.

70. Ibid., l. 47. Also Iu. Zoria, "'Prokurorskaia diplomatiia' Vyshinskogo," in *Inkvizitor. Stalinskii prokuror Vyshinskii*, ed. O. E. Kutafin (Moscow: Respublika, 1992), 268–288, and Yuri Zorya and Natalia Lebedeva, "The Year 1939 in the Nuremberg Files," *International Affairs* (Moscow) 10 (October 1989): 117–129.

71. GARF f. 7445, op. 2, d. 391, ll. 45–46.

72. Taylor, *Anatomy of the Nuremberg Trials*, 211–212.

73. Vaskberg, *Stalin's Prosecutor*, 261.

74. RGALI f. 1038, op. 2, d. 243, l. 16.

75. Taylor, *Anatomy of the Nuremberg Trials*, 210–211.

76. Ibid.; Churchill Archives Centre, Churchill College, Cambridge, The Papers of Lord Kilmuir, KLMR Acc 1485, Sir David Maxwell Fyfe to Sylvia Maxwell Fyfe, December 4, 1945, available at http://www.kilmuirpapers.org/letters/4579523443.

77. Taylor, *Anatomy of the Nuremberg Trials*, 211–212.

78. H. Montgomery Hyde, *Norman Birkett* (London: Hamish Hamilton, 1964), 500–501.

79. AVPRF f. 059, op. 25, p. 58, d. 339, ll. 3-14, in Kynin and Laufer, *SSSR i germanskii vopros*, vol. 2, 750–751 (n. 140).

80. Taylor, *Anatomy of the Nuremberg Trials*, 186–187.

81. RGALI f. 2989, op. 1, d. 190, ll. 15–16.

82. AVPRF f. 07, op. 13, p. 41, d. 7, ll. 8–10.

83. RGALI f. 2989, op. 1, d. 190, l. 16.

84. Taylor, *Anatomy of the Nuremberg Trials*, 189; Tusa and Tusa, *Nuremberg Trial*, 163–165; "9th Day, Friday, November 30, 1945," NTP, vol. 2, http://avalon.law.yale.edu/imt/11-30-45.asp (accessed July 3, 2013).

85. AVPRF f. 07, op. 13, p. 41, d. 7, ll. 11–16.

86. Taylor, *Anatomy of the Nuremberg Trials*, 177–178.

87. Polevoi, *Final Reckoning*, 89; "9th Day, Friday, November 30, 1945."

88. Polevoi, *Final Reckoning*, 89–92; Taylor, *Anatomy of the Nuremberg Trials*, 177–179.

89. AVPRF f. 07, op. 13, p. 41, d. 7, ll. 17–19.

90. GARF f. 7445, op. 2, d. 391, ll. 39–42.

91. Ibid.

92. Ibid.

93. GARF f. 8131, op. 38, d. 238, ll. 52–64.

94. Ibid., ll. 213–214.

95. Ibid., ll. 205–206.

96. Ibid., l. 59; GARF f. 9492, op. 1a, d. 468, l. 101, in *SSSR i Niurnbergskii protsess. Neizvestnye i maloizvestnye stranitsy istorii: Dokumenty*, ed. N. S. Lebedeva (Moscow: MFD, 2012), 321. For the protocol of his deposition see United States Holocaust Memorial Museum Archives, RG-22:002M, reel 27 (GARF f. 7445, op. 2, d. 75, ll. 96-106).

97. GARF f. 8131, op. 38, d. 238, ll. 212–213.
98. GARF f. 7445, op. 2, d. 391, ll. 44–45.
99. GARF f. 8131, op. 38, d. 238, ll. 158–159. The commission had also resolved to identify and select additional eyewitnesses to Nazi atrocities in Latvia, Lithuania, Estonia, Belorussia, Ukraine, and the North Caucasus.
100. GARF f. 7445, op. 2, d. 391, ll. 39–42. Vyshinsky suggested that the Politburo Commission immediately prepare "ten to twelve witnesses" from its list.
101. For example GARF f. 8131, op. 37, d. 2823, l. 63.
102. GARF f. 7445, op. 2, d. 391, ll. 41–42.
103. Ibid., ll. 32–35.
104. AVPRF f. 07, op. 13, p. 41, d. 9, ll. 76–77, 79–81. Vyshinsky signed it at the top on December 6.
105. Ibid.
106. Ibid.
107. GARF f. 7445, op. 2, d. 391, ll. 28–32.
108. AVPRF f. 07, op. 13, p. 41, d. 8, ll. 88–89.
109. Ibid.
110. AVPRF f. 07, op. 13, p. 41, d. 4, l. 17.
111. GARF f. 7445, op. 2, d. 391, l. 60. Alexandrov related that there had been one "incident" of note, when the defendant Hans Frank had called U.S. Lieutenant Colonel Thomas Hinkel "a swine," but insisted that no slurs had been made against the USSR.
112. RGALI f. 2989, op. 1, d. 190, l. 14.

Chapter 6

1. Boris Efimov, *Rabota, vospominaniia, vstrechi* (Moscow: Sovetskii khudozhnik, 1963), 167.
2. Maya Balakirsky Katz, *Drawing the Iron Curtain: Jews and the Golden Age of Soviet Animation* (New Brunswick: Rutgers University Press, 2016), 162–163; Stephen M. Norris, "The Sharp Weapon of Soviet Laughter: Boris Efimov and Visual Humor," *Russian Literature* 74, no. 1–2 (2013): 31–62; Tim Benson, "Boris Efimov: Stalin's Favourite Cartoonist," Political Cartoon Society, n.d., http://www.original-political-cartoon.com/cartoon-history/boris-efimov-stalins-favourite-cartoonist/; Boris Efimov, *Forced Laughter: An Exhibition of 105 Cartoons by Boris Efimov* (Prague: Galerie Nova sin, 2005).
3. Boris Efimov, *Desiat' desiatiletii: O tom, chto videl, perezhil, zapomnil* (Moscow: Vagrius, 2000), 378–383.
4. Efimov, *Rabota, vospominaniia, vstrechi*, 186–187; Bor. Efimov, "Fashistskii zverinets (Iz zala suda)," *Izvestiia*, December 9, 1945, 4; Bor. Efimov, "Fashistskii zverinets (Iz zala suda)," *Izvestiia*, December 17, 1945, 4.

5. Efimov, *Rabota, vospominaniia, vstrechi*, 183. On the Soviet portrayal of the Nazis as "fascist beasts" see Karel C. Berkhoff, *Motherland in Danger: Soviet Propaganda during World War II* (Cambridge, MA: Harvard University Press, 2012).

6. "12th Day, Tuesday, December 4, 1945," Nuremberg Trial Proceedings (NTP), vol. 3, Avalon Project at Yale University Law School, http://avalon. law.yale.edu/imt/12-04-45.asp (accessed May 31, 2018).

7. Ibid.; Ann Tusa and John Tusa, *The Nuremberg Trial* (London: Atheneum, 1983), 175–180; Telford Taylor, *The Anatomy of the Nuremberg Trials* (Boston: Knopf, 1992), 193.

8. "12th Day, Tuesday, December 4, 1945"; Taylor, *Anatomy of the Nuremberg Trials*, 192–193.

9. Tusa and Tusa, *Nuremberg Trial*, 176; Churchill Archives Centre, Churchill College, Cambridge, The Papers of Lord Kilmuir, KLMR Acc 1485, Sir David Maxwell Fyfe to Sylvia Maxwell Fyfe, November 25, 1945, available at http://www.kilmuirpapers.org/letters/4579523443.

10. Taylor, *Anatomy of the Nuremberg Trials*, 194–196; Tusa and Tusa, *Nuremberg Trial*, 181–182.

11. "15th Day, Friday, December 7, 1945," NTP, vol. 3, http://avalon.law.yale. edu/imt/12-07-45.asp (accessed May 31, 2018).

12. State Archive of the Russian Federation (GARF) f. 7445, op. 2, d. 391, ll. 22–23.

13. Ibid. On the Alexandrov investigation see GARF f. 7445, op. 2, d. 391, l. 60.

14. GARF f. 7445, op. 2, d. 391, ll. 16–18, 22–23, 37, 68.

15. "Goering Reaffirms Belief in Nazism," *New York Times*, December 2, 1945, 1; Wes Gallagher and Louis P. Lochner, "Goering Declares He's Still Nazi and Would Support Fuehrer Again," *Los Angeles Times,* December 2, 1945, 2.

16. "Nazis Beat Reds to Punch, Keitel Says, Justifying Attack," *Zanesville (OH) Signal*, December 4, 1945, 1; Daniel De Luce and Nolard Norgaard, "Keitel Terms Invasion of Russia Defensive," *Los Angeles Times*, December 5, 1945, 5.

17. Russian State Archive of Socio-Political History (RGASPI) f. 558, op. 11, d. 99, ll. 111–112.

18. A. Poltorak, *The Nuremberg Epilogue* (Moscow: Progress Publishers, 1971), 24–25. The Secretariat received all documents addressed to the Tribunal, maintained the Tribunal's records, and provided clerical services to the Tribunal.

19. GARF f. 7445, op. 2, d. 6, ll. 242–243. "Interview mit Göring," *Die Neue Zeitung,* December 7, 1945, 4. An excerpt of the interview with Hess was published on December 10, 1945.

20. The U.S. military government in Germany had rejected suggestions that it use the newspaper as a mouthpiece of U.S. occupation authorities. Jessica C. E. Gienow-Hecht, *Transmission Impossible: American Journalism as Cultural*

Diplomacy in Postwar Germany, 1945–1955 (Baton Rouge: Louisiana State University Press, 1999), 45–47.

21. Russian State Archive of Literature and Art (RGALI) f. 2989, op. 1, d. 190, l. 25.

22. RGASPI f. 558, op. 11, d. 99, ll. 84–85, 124–126. For the article see Selkirk Panton, "Sir Hartley Cuts Out Bits of His Speech; Russians said: 'Do You Mind?'" *Daily Express*, December 5, 1945, 4.

23. RGASPI f. 558, op. 11, d. 99, ll. 124–126.

24. RGASPI f. 629, op. 1, d. 109, l. 88.

25. RGASPI f. 558, op. 11, d. 99, ll. 124–126.

26. RGASPI f. 558, op. 11, d. 99, ll. 84–85, 101–102, 124–126.

27. On Stalin's time in Sochi and his anger about the press see Yoram Gorlizki and Oleg Khlevniuk, *Cold Peace: Stalin and the Soviet Ruling Circle, 1945–1953* (Oxford: Oxford University Press, 2004), 21–23, and Vladimir O. Pechatnov, "'The Allies Are Pressing on You to Break Your Will . . .' Foreign Policy Correspondence between Stalin and Molotov and Other Politburo Members, September 1945–December 1946," Working Paper no. 26, Cold War International History Project (Washington, DC, 1999). For Stalin's secret telegram about Molotov see RGASPI f. 558, op. 11, d. 99, ll. 96–97, in *SSSR i Niurnbergskii protsess. Neizvestnye i maloizvestnye stranitsy istorii: Dokumenty,* ed. N. S. Lebedeva (Moscow: MFD, 2012), 340–341.

28. Archive of the Foreign Policy of the Russian Federation (AVPRF) f. 07, op. 13, p. 41, d. 9, l. 82.

29. AVPRF f. 082, op. 12, p. 178, d. 5, l. 37.

30. GARF f. 7445, op. 2, d. 391, ll. 9–10.

31. Harold Burson interview in *Witnesses to Nuremberg: An Oral History of American Participants at the War Crimes Trials*, ed. Bruce M. Stave, Michele Palmer, and Leslie Frank (New York: Twayne, 1998), 187–188; Leonid Trofimov, "Soviet Reporters at the Nuremberg Trial: Agenda, Attitudes, and Encounters, 1945–46," *Cahiers d'histoire* 28, no. 2 (2010): 45–70.

32. Boris Polevoi, *The Final Reckoning: Nuremberg Diaries* (Moscow: Progress Publishers, 1978), 166–173.

33. Harold Burson interview in *Witnesses to Nuremberg*, 187–188. Also Trofimov, "Soviet Reporters at the Nuremberg Trial," 66.

34. Efimov, *Desiat' desiatiletii*, 415–432, esp. 428–429. On Soviet nightlife also see Polevoi, *Final Reckoning,* and Trofimov, "Soviet Reporters at the Nuremberg Trial."

35. Efimov, *Rabota, vospominania, vstrechi*, 172.

36. RGASPI f. 558, op. 11, d. 99, ll. 139–141; Library of Congress, Manuscript Division, Robert H. Jackson Collection (LOC-RHJ) b. 111, f. 10, Rudenko to Jackson, December 9, 1945.

37. RGASPI f. 558, op. 11, d. 99, ll. 139–141. This report also circulated among Vyshinsky, the Politburo Four, and Vladimir Dekanozov.

38. LOC-RHJ b. 111, f. 10, Rudenko to Jackson, December 9, 1945.

39. GARF f. 7445, op. 2, d. 8, l. 234.

40. Vladimir Abarinov, "V kuluarakh dvortsa iustitsii," *Gorizont*, no. 9 (1989): 42–52, esp. 48; Vadim J. Birstein, *SMERSH: Stalin's Secret Weapon* (London: Biteback, 2011), 389–390. The make of the car was Horch.

41. Polevoi, *Final Reckoning*, 165–166.

42. RGASPI f. 558, op. 11, d. 99, ll. 139–141.

43. Aleksandr Zviagintsev and Iurii Orlov, *Prokurory dvukh epokh: Andrei Vyshinskii i Roman Rudenko* (Moscow: Olma Press, 2001), 215. According to Zviagintsev and Orlov, Gorshenin appealed to the Party and to Abakumov (chief of SMERSH) to deal with Likhachev. Likhachev returned to Moscow sometime after December 12 and spent ten days under arrest.

44. "16th Day, Monday, December 10, 1945," NTP, vol. 3, http://avalon.law. yale.edu/imt/12-10-45.asp (accessed May 31, 2018). Also Taylor, *Anatomy of the Nuremberg Trials*, 197–198.

45. Efimov, *Desiat' desiatiletii*, 427–428.

46. RGALI f. 2989, op. 1, d. 190, ll. 13–16.

47. Polevoi, *Final Reckoning*, 127.

48. Taylor, *Anatomy of the Nuremberg Trials*, 200; G. M. Gilbert, *Nuremberg Diary* (New York: Farrar, Straus, 1947), 65–67.

49. Valerie Hartouni, *Visualizing Atrocity: Arendt, Evil, and the Optics of Thoughtlessness* (New York: New York University Press, 2012).

50. Taylor, *Anatomy of the Nuremberg Trials*, 200.

51. See Vsevolod Ivanov, "Prizraki, istochaiushchie iad," *Izvestiia*, December 16, 1945.

52. GARF f. 8131, op. 38, d. 238, l. 193.

53. AVPRF f. 07, op. 13, p. 41, d. 9, l. 21.

54. AVPRF f. 07, op. 13, p. 41, d. 8, ll. 26–27, 31–32ob.

55. Ibid. The other filmmakers included Elizaveta Svilova, Maria Slavinskaya, Irina Setkina-Nesterova, and Samuil Bubrik.

56. Poltorak, *Final Reckoning*, 180.

57. "18th Day, Wednesday, December 12, 1945," "19th Day, Thursday, December 13, 1945," and "20th Day, Friday, December 14, 1945," NTP, vol. 3, http://avalon.law.yale.edu/imt/12-12-45.asp, http://avalon.law.yale.edu/imt/12-13-45.asp, and http://avalon.law.yale.edu/imt/12-14-45.asp (accessed May 31, 2018).

58. Ibid.

59. Tusa and Tusa, *Nuremberg Trial*, 175.

60. GARF f. 7445, op. 2, d. 391, ll. 14–17.

61. See chapters 3 and 4.

62. On the legal problem of "crimes against humanity" see Harry S. Truman Presidential Library and Museum (HSTPLM), The War Crimes Trial at Nuremberg, Records of the World Jewish Congress, Report by Gerhard

Jacoby, "Some Preliminary Remarks on Legal Problems of the Crimes against Humanity," December 13, 1945, https://www.trumanlibrary.gov/library/research-files/report-gerhard-jacoby-some-preliminary-remarks-legal-problems-crimes-against (accessed June 3, 2018).

63. GARF f. 7445, op. 2, d. 391, ll. 14–18. Also AVPRF f. 082, op. 12, p. 178, d. 5, l. 26.

64. AVPRF f. 07, op. 13, p. 41, d. 8, ll. 26–27, 37–46.

65. The IMT's Secretariat was made up of a general secretary, four secretaries, and their assistants. The general secretary was William L. Mitchell, a U.S. Army lawyer.

66. GARF f. 7445, op. 2, d. 391, ll. 9–10.

67. Ibid., ll. 16–18.

68. RGASPI f. 629, op. 1, d. 109, ll. 86–87. The emphasis is in the original.

69. GARF f. 7445, op. 2, d. 391, ll. 14–15.

70. Taylor, *Anatomy of the Nuremberg Trials*, 172–177.

71. GARF f. 7445, op. 2, d. 6, l. 275.

72. GARF f. 7445, op. 2, d. 391, ll. 11–13.

73. RGALI f. 2989, op. 1, d. 190, ll. 11–12.

74. RGALI f. 1038, op. 2, d. 243, l. 9.

75. Efimov, *Rabota, vospominaniia, vstrechi*, 184.

76. AVPRF f. 07, op. 13, p. 41, d. 8, ll. 93–95; GARF f. 7445, op. 2, d. 391, ll. 11–15.

77. GARF f. 7445, op. 2, d. 6, ll. 241–243.

78. GARF f. 7445, op. 2, d. 8, ll. 227–228.

79. GARF f. 7445, op. 2, d. 391, ll. 9–10.

80. "21st Day, Monday, December 17, 1945," NTP, vol. 4, http://avalon.law.yale.edu/imt/12-17-45.asp (accessed May 31, 2014).

81. "Protsess glavnykh nemetskikh voennykh prestupnikov v Niurnberge: Utrennee zasedanie 17 dekabria," *Izvestiia*, December 18, 1945.

82. RGASPI f. 629, op. 1, d. 109, ll. 88–88ob.

83. "21st Day, Monday, December 17, 1945"; AVPRF f. 082, op. 12, p. 178, d. 5, ll. 102–104.

84. "21st Day, Monday, December 17, 1945."

85. Polevoi, *Final Reckoning*, 128–129.

86. Tusa and Tusa, *Nuremberg Trial*, 169–171; GARF f. 8131, op. 37, d. 2823, l. 14.

87. Polevoi, *Final Reckoning*, 137–139.

88. GARF f. 7445, op. 2, d. 391, ll. 1–5.

89. Ibid. Poltorak was soon brought into the work of this Tribunal subcommission.

90. Polevoi, *Final Reckoning*, 131.

91. Ibid., 143; RGASPI f. 629, op. 1, d. 109, ll. 86–87.

92. GARF f. 8131, op. 38, d. 238, l. 235.

93. GARF f. 7445, op. 2, d. 407, ll. 1–6.

94. Ibid.

95. Ibid.

96. RGALI f. 2989, op. 1, d. 190, l. 17. Also Francesca Gaiba, *The Origins of Simultaneous Translation: The Nuremberg Trial* (Ottawa: University of Ottawa Press, 1998).

97. GARF f. 7445, op. 2, d. 407, ll. 1–6.

98. Ibid.

99. Ibid.

100. Anna Holian, *Between National Socialism and Soviet Communism: Displaced Persons in Postwar Germany* (Ann Arbor: University of Michigan Press, 2011), 99.

101. GARF f. 7445, op. 2, d. 407, l. 6.

102. Ibid., l. 1. Added in handwriting.

Chapter 7

1. Boris Polevoi, *The Final Reckoning: Nuremberg Diaries* (Moscow: Progress Publishers, 1978), 143.

2. Ibid., 131. Also Telford Taylor, *The Anatomy of the Nuremberg Trials* (Boston: Knopf, 1992), 244–245.

3. Russian State Archive of Socio-Political History (RGASPI) f. 629, op. 1, d. 109, l. 87.

4. Vsevolod Vishnevsky, "Frank," *Pravda*, December 24, 1945, and "Baron fon Neurat," *Pravda*, December 26, 1945.

5. Katerina Clark, *Moscow: The Fourth Rome: Stalinism, Cosmopolitanism, and the Evolution of Soviet Culture, 1931–1941* (Cambridge, MA: Harvard University Press, 2011), 267–269; John Garrard and Carol Garrard, *Inside the Soviet Writers' Union* (London: Free Press, 1990), 32.

6. Ilya Ehrenburg, *Memoirs: 1921–1941*, trans. Tatania Shebunina (New York: Grosset and Dunlap, 1966), 411.

7. Harrison Salisbury, *The 900 Days: The Siege of Leningrad* (New York: Harper and Row, 1969).

8. "25th Day, Wednesday, January 2, 1946," Nuremberg Trial Proceedings (NTP), vol. 4, Avalon Project at Yale University Law School, http://avalon. law.yale.edu/imt/01-02-46.asp (accessed May 28, 2018); Taylor, *Anatomy of the Nuremberg Trials*, 244–246.

9. "26th Day, Thursday, January 3, 1946," NTP, vol. 4, http://avalon.law.yale. edu/imt/01-03-46.asp (accessed May 28, 2018); Tania Long, "Mass-Killing Chief Describes His Task: Testifying at Nuremberg Yesterday," *New York Times*, January 4, 1946, 4; Joseph E. Persico, *Nuremberg: Infamy on Trial* (New York: Penguin Books, 1994), 200–201. Amen was the head of the Interrogation Division of the U.S. prosecution.

10. "26th Day, Thursday, January 3, 1946."

11. Ibid.

12. Ibid. The letter from Himmler had been dated April 1942.

13. "27th Day, Friday, January 4, 1946," NTP, vol. 4, http://avalon.law.yale.edu/imt/01-04-46.asp (accessed May 28, 2018).

14. Ibid.; A. Poltorak, *The Nuremberg Epilogue* (Moscow: Progress Publishers, 1971), 96–97.

15. State Archive of the Russian Federation (GARF) f. 8131, op. 37, d. 2823, l. 53.

16. Keith Hitchens, *Romania 1866–1947* (New York: Clarendon Press, 1994); Sydney Gruson, "UNO Dinner Marks Eve of Assembly," *New York Times*, January 9, 1946, 10.

17. On Andrei Smirnov see *SSSR i Niurnbergskii protsess. Neizvestnye i maloizvestnye stranitsy istorii: Dokumenty*, ed. N. S. Lebedeva (Moscow: MFD, 2012), 580.

18. GARF f. 8131, op. 37, d. 2823, l. 3; d. 2196, ll. 12–13; RGASPI f. 17, op. 125, d. 410, ll. 1–76; Archive of the Foreign Policy of the Russian Federation (AVPRF) f. 082, op. 32, p. 178, d. 2, l. 29.

19. "Iz zhurnala posetitelei kremlevskogo kabineta I. V. Stalina, 6 ianvariia 1946," *Istoricheskii arkhiv*, no. 3 (1996): 115, in Lebedeva, *SSSR i Niurnbergskii protsess*, 379–380.

20. Noted in Lebedeva, *SSSR i Niurnbergskii protsess*, 380.

21. Merkulov was Kobulov's boss.

22. RGASPI f. 17, op. 162, d. 38, ll. 1–2, in Lebedeva, *SSSR i Niurnbergskii protsess*, 380–381.

23. For example GARF f. 8131, op. 37, d. 2196, ll. 11, 14, 17.

24. GARF f. 7445, op. 2, d. 373, ll. 84–85.

25. GARF f. 8131, op. 37, d. 2823, ll. 51–52, 54. On Smirnov, see Poltorak, *Nuremberg Epilogue*, 138.

26. GARF f. 7445, op. 2, d. 404, l. 27, in Lebedeva, *SSSR i Niurnbergskii protsess*, 381–382.

27. GARF f. 8131, op. 37, d. 2823, l. 53.

28. GARF f. 8131, op. 37, d. 2196, ll. 62, 67.

29. Ibid., ll. 16, 25, 36–54, 56–61.

30. GARF f. 7445, op. 2, d. 6, l. 300.

31. GARF f. 7445, op. 2, d. 8, ll. 418–419.

32. "28th Day, Monday, January 7, 1946," NTP, vol. 4, http://avalon.law.yale.edu/imt/01-07-46.asp (accessed May 28, 2018).

33. Ibid.

34. Ibid.; Taylor, *Anatomy of the Nuremberg Trials*, 258–261; Poltorak, *Nuremberg Epilogue*, 125–126.

35. "29th Day, Tuesday, January 8, 1946," NTP, vol. 4, http://avalon.law.yale.edu/imt/01-08-46.asp (accessed May 28, 2018).

36. Taylor, *Anatomy of the Nuremberg Trials*, 262–263.

37. Harry S. Truman Presidential Library and Museum (HSTPLM), Harry S. Truman Papers, President's Secretary's Files, President Harry S. Truman to Secretary of State James Byrnes, January 5, 1946, 11, https://www. trumanlibrary.org/whistlestop/study_collections/trumanpapers/psf/longhand/ index.php?documentVersion=both&documentid=hst-psf_naid735237-01 (accessed May 28, 2018).

38. Ann Tusa and John Tusa, *The Nuremberg Trial* (London: Atheneum, 1983), 182–183. The Americans took on Goering, Kaltenbrunner, Rosenberg, Hans Frank, Fritz Sauckel, Albert Speer, Hans Frank, and the economists Hjalmar Schacht and Walther Funk; the British took on Ribbentrop, Julius Streicher, and the generals Wilhelm Keitel and Alfred Jodl.

39. "31st Day, Thursday, January 10, 1946," NTP, vol. 5, http://avalon.law.yale. edu/imt/01-10-46.asp (accessed May 28, 2018).

40. Polevoi, *Final Reckoning*, 148–151; "32nd Day, Friday, January 11, 1946," NTP, vol. 5, http://avalon.law.yale.edu/imt/01-11-46.asp (accessed May 28, 2018); "Protsess glavnykh nemetskikh voennykh prestupnikov v Niurnberge: Vechernee zasedanie 11 ianvaria," *Izvestiia*, January 13, 1946.

41. GARF f. 8131, op. 37, d. 2823, ll. 28–50. The draft of the speech was also sent to others, including Andrei Smirnov.

42. Ibid., ll. 29–38.

43. Ibid., ll. 38–50.

44. For summaries of the films see ibid., ll. 64–71, 86–88. The original cut of the atrocity film was eighty-five minutes. On the approval of the films see RGASPI f. 17, op. 125, d. 373, ll. 235–237.

45. "Iz zhurnala posetitelei kremlevskogo kabineta I. V. Stalina, 13 ianvariia 1946," *Istoricheskii arkhiv*, no. 4 (1996): 115, in Lebedeva, *SSSR i Niurnbergskii protsess*, 386. Stalin met with Molotov, Beria, Zhdanov, and Mikoyan immediately after this meeting.

46. GARF f. 8131, op. 37, d. 2823, ll. 55–58.

47. Ibid., ll. 59–60.

48. "34th Day, Tuesday, January 15, 1946," NTP, vol. 5, http://avalon.law. yale.edu/imt/01-15-46.asp (accessed May 18, 2018). The British also called witnesses about German crimes at sea. On January 16 they summed up the evidence against Baldur von Schirach, Martin Bormann, Arthur Seyss-Inquart, and Wilhelm Frick.

49. Antonin Tisseron, *La France et le procès de Nuremberg: Inventer le droit international* (Paris: Les Prairies ordinaires, 2014), 138–139.

50. "36th Day, Thursday, January 17, 1946," NTP, vol. 5, http://avalon.law.yale. edu/imt/01-17-46.asp (accessed May 28, 2018).

51. Ibid. Also Taylor, *Anatomy of the Nuremberg Trials*, 293–298; "Protsess glavnykh nemetskikh voennykh prestupnikov v Niurnberge: Vechernee zasedanie 17 ianvariia," *Pravda*, January 19, 1946. On the French and

collective guilt see Lara Feigel, *The Bitter Taste of Victory: Life, Love and Art in the Ruins of the Reich* (London: Bloomsbury, 2016), 160–164.

52. National Archives and Records Administration—College Park (NARA) RG 238, entry 52, b. 5, "R. M. W. Kempner, Memorandum for Mr. Justice Jackson: Indictment of Organizations," January 23, 1946.

53. NARA RG 260, AG 000.5, b. 3, f. 2, "From OMGUS for Jackson," January 21, 1946. The Soviets were well aware of these rumors. GARF f. 8581, op. 2, d. 132, ll. 49–51.

54. Library of Congress, Manuscript Division, Robert H. Jackson Collection (LOC-RHJ) b. 111, f. 9, "The Anti-Soviet Defense Line of Ribbentrop," January 25, 1946. Ribbentrop had fired Sauter around January 5.

55. GARF f. 7445, op. 2, d. 6, ll. 304–305.

56. These included documents from the Latvian archives about the branding and execution of Soviet soldiers, as well as a statement from Imre Ruszkiczay-Rüdiger, Hungary's former deputy minister of war, about Hungarian-German collaboration. GARF f. 8131, op. 37, d. 2823, ll. 98–99; d. 2196, ll. 73, 84–89.

57. Taylor, *Anatomy of the Nuremberg Trials*, 299.

58. Churchill Archives Centre, Churchill College, Cambridge, The Papers of Lord Kilmuir, KLMR Acc 1485, Sir David Maxwell Fyfe to Sylvia Maxwell Fyfe, January 20, 1946, available at http://www.kilmuirpapers.org/letters/4579523443.

59. "39th Day, Monday, January 21, 1946," NTP, vol. 5, and "40th Day, Tuesday, January 22, 1946," NTP, vol. 6, http://avalon.law.yale.edu/imt/01-21-46.asp and http://avalon.law.yale.edu/imt/01-22-46.asp (accessed May 28, 2018); "Starvation Policy Charged to Nazis," *New York Times*, January 23, 1946, 14.

60. "41st Day, Wednesday, January 23, 1946," NTP, vol. 6, http://avalon.law.yale.edu/imt/01-23-46.asp (accessed May 28, 2018).

61. On Fritzsche and the Soviets see Vadim J. Birstein, *SMERSH: Stalin's Secret Weapon* (London: Biteback, 2011), 383–385.

62. Taylor, *Anatomy of the Nuremberg Trials*, 102-103.

63. David Patrick Maxwell Fyfe, *Political Adventure: The Memoirs of the Earl of Kilmuir* (London: Weidenfeld and Nicolson, 1964), 102.

64. Tusa and Tusa, *Nuremberg Trial*, 191.

65. "43rd Day, Friday, January 25, 1946," NTP, vol. 6, http://avalon.law.yale.edu/imt/01-25-46.asp (accessed May 28, 2018).

66. Ibid.

67. Poltorak, *Nuremberg Epilogue*, 301.

68. "44th Day, Monday, January 28, 1946," NTP, vol. 6, http://avalon.law.yale.edu/imt/01-28-46.asp (accessed May 28, 2018); Poltorak, *Nuremberg Epilogue*, 130–133; Persico, *Nuremberg*, 236–237; "Protsess glavnykh nemetskikh

voennykh prestupnikov v Niurnberg: Utrennee zasedanie 28 ianvaria," *Izvestiia*, January 29, 1946.

69. V. Vishnevskii, "Govoriat svideteli, govoriat ochevidtsy," *Pravda*, February 1, 1946, in *Sud istorii: Reportazhi s Niurnbergskogo protsessa*, ed. V. Velichko and G. N. Aleksandrov (Moscow: Izdatel'stvo politicheskoi literatury, 1966), 218-222, esp. 220.

70. "44th Day, Monday, January 28, 1946"; Persico, *Nuremberg*, 238–239. On Boix see Donald Kahn, *Photography: A Concise History* (Bloomington: XLIBRIS, 2014), 87–88.

71. "45th Day, Tuesday, January 29, 1946," NTP, vol. 6, http://avalon.law.yale.edu/imt/01-29-46.asp (accessed May 18, 2018).

72. Vishnevskii, "Govoriat svideteli, govoriat ochevidtsy," 220.

73. Ibid., 220–221. Also "45th Day, Tuesday, January 29, 1946."

74. H. Montgomery Hyde, *Norman Birkett* (London: Hamish Hamilton, 1964), 505.

75. Birstein, *SMERSH,* 391. The biographical information that Vishnevsky put together for the Soviet prosecution included notes from a *Life* article about Albert Speer by John Kenneth Galbraith and George Ball. According to the authors, Speer considered Goering "incompetent," regarded Ribbentrop as "a clown," and detested Sauckel, Funk, and Jodl. Russian State Archive of Literature and Art (RGALI) f. 1038, op. 1, d. 2439, ll. 9–11.

76. Garrard and Garrard, *Inside the Soviet Writers' Union*, 40, 51.

77. RGALI f. 1038, op. 1, d. 2439, ll. 1–6.

78. Ibid. The original is capitalized for emphasis.

79. Ibid.

80. Ibid.

81. Tusa and Tusa, *Nuremberg Trial*, 214.

82. GARF f. 7445, op. 2, d. 6, l. 315.

83. GARF f. 7445, op. 2, d. 8, l. 49; LOC-RHJ b. 110, f. 2, Jackson to Rudenko, February 7, 1946, and "Message for Byrnes from Jackson," February 7, 1946.

84. RGASPI f. 629, op. 1, d. 109, l. 91.

85. Ibid., l. 93.

86. The Papers of Lord Kilmuir, KLMR Acc 1485, Sir David Maxwell Fyfe to Sylvia Maxwell Fyfe, February 5, 1946, available at http://www.kilmuirpapers.org/letters/4579523443. Also Tusa and Tusa, *Nuremberg Trial*, 227–228.

87. RGALI f. 2829, op. 1, d. 190, l. 39.

88. GARF f. 8131, op. 37, d. 2823, ll. 63, 98–99; d. 2196, ll. 73, 84–89.

89. GARF f. 8131, op. 37, d. 2823, ll. 141, 169.

90. "53rd Day, Thursday, February 7, 1946," NTP, vol. 7, http://avalon.law.yale.edu/imt/02-07-46.asp (accessed May 28, 2018).

91. RGASPI f. 629, op. 1, d. 109, ll. 91–94 (quoted from l. 93).

92. "Witness Depicts German Tortures," *New York Times*, January 26, 1946, 8.

Chapter 8

1. Russian State Archive of Literature and Art (RGALI) f. 1038, op. 1, d. 190, l. 17.
2. Telford Taylor, *The Anatomy of the Nuremberg Trials* (Boston: Knopf, 1992), 307.
3. RGALI f. 1038, op. 1, d. 190, ll. 18–21; "54th Day, Friday, February 8, 1946," Nuremberg Trial Proceedings (NTP), vol. 7, Avalon Project at Yale University Law School, http://avalon.law.yale.edu/imt/02-08-46.asp (accessed May 28, 2018).
4. Boris Polevoi, *The Final Reckoning: Nuremberg Diaries* (Moscow: Progress Publishers, 1978), 175.
5. Taylor, *Anatomy of the Nuremberg Trials*, 307; "54th Day, Friday, February 8, 1946."
6. "54th Day, Friday, February 8, 1946."
7. Ibid.
8. Polevoi, *Final Reckoning,* 179.
9. "54th Day, Friday, February 8, 1946."
10. Ibid. Pokrovsky was preceded by Soviet assistant prosecutor Dmitry Karev, who gave an overview of the Soviet evidence.
11. Ibid. Such certificates were to note the origins of the document and its current location. These guidelines were retroactive and would be applied to all of the countries of the prosecution.
12. "55th Day, Saturday, February 9, 1946," NTP, vol. 7, http://avalon.law.yale.edu/imt/02-09-46.asp (accessed May 28, 2018).
13. Joseph E. Persico, *Nuremberg: Infamy on Trial* (New York: Penguin Books, 1994), 243.
14. J. Stalin, "Speech Delivered by J. V. Stalin at a Meeting of Voters of the Stalin Electoral District, Moscow," February 9, 1946, in *Speeches Delivered at Meetings of Voters of the Stalin Electoral District* (Moscow: Foreign Languages Publishing House, 1950), 19–44; Michael Cassella-Blackburn, *The Donkey, the Carrot and the Club: William C. Bullitt and Soviet-American Relations, 1917–1948* (Westport: Praeger, 2004), 236; Michael Karpovich, "Examining the Political Evolution of the USSR," *New York Times*, February 10, 1946, 115. Karpovich was a well-known historian.
15. State Archive of the Russian Federation (GARF) f. 7445, op. 2, d. 6, l. 269.
16. Vadim J. Birstein, *SMERSH: Stalin's Secret Weapon* (London: Biteback, 2011), 238; Persico, *Nuremberg*, 244–245; Samuel W. Mitcham Jr., *Crumbling Empire, The German Defeat in the East, 1944* (Westport: Praeger, 2001), 186.
17. Patrycja Grzebyk, *Criminal Responsibility of the Crime of Aggression* (Abingdon, England: CRC Press, 2013), 190.

18. GARF f. 8131, op. 37, d. 2823, l. 63; Birstein, *SMERSH,* 388.

19. "56th Day, Monday, February 11, 1946," NTP, vol. 7, http://avalon.law.yale.edu/imt/02-11-46.asp (accessed May 28, 2018).

20. Ibid. Soviet investigator Alexandrov had carried out the interrogation of Warlimont. Zorya noted that Warlimont was still in Nuremberg if the defense wished to cross-examine him.

21. Ibid. On the astonishment see Polevoi, *Final Reckoning,* 195–196, and Ann Tusa and John Tusa, *The Nuremberg Trial* (London: Atheneum, 1983), 195–196.

22. Polevoi, *Final Reckoning,* 195–198.

23. Ibid.; RGALI f. 2989, op. 1, d. 190, l. 23.

24. Taylor, *Anatomy of the Nuremberg Trials,* 309.

25. RGALI f. 2989, op. 1, d. 190, l. 24.

26. Polevoi, *Final Reckoning,* 198–199; "56th Day, Monday, February 11, 1946."

27. "56th Day, Monday, February 11, 1946"; Polevoi, *Final Reckoning,* 200; G. M. Gilbert, *Nuremberg Diary* (New York: Farrar, Straus, 1947), 146–148.

28. RGALI f. 2989, op. 1, d. 190, l. 24.

29. Polevoi, *Final Reckoning,* 199.

30. Ibid., 197; Persico, *Nuremberg,* 245–246.

31. RGALI f. 2989, op. 1, d. 190, l. 47.

32. Polevoi, *Final Reckoning,* 199.

33. Christopher J. Dodd with Lary Bloom, *Letters from Nuremberg: My Father's Narrative of a Quest for Justice* (New York: Crown, 2007), 231–232.

34. "57th Day, Tuesday, February 12, 1946," NTP, vol. 7, http://avalon.law.yale.edu/imt/02-12-46.asp (accessed May 28, 2018).

35. Ibid.

36. Gilbert, *Nuremberg Diary,* 149.

37. "57th Day, Tuesday, February 12, 1946," and RGALI f. 2989, op. 1, d. 190, ll. 25–26.

38. "57th Day, Tuesday, February 12, 1946."

39. "58th Day, Wednesday, February 13, 1946," NTP, vol. 7, http://avalon.law.yale.edu/imt/02-13-46.asp (accessed May 28, 2018).

40. On the fabrication see Marina Sorokina, "People and Procedures: Toward a History of the Investigation of Nazi Crimes in the USSR," *Kritika: Explorations in Russian and Eurasian History* 6, no. 4 (2005): 797–831.

41. Inessa Iazhborovskaiia, Anatolii Iablokov, and Valentina Parsadanova, *Katynskii sindrom v Sovetsko-Pol'skikh i Rossiisko-Pol'skikh otnosheniiakh* (Moscow: ROSSPEN, 2009), 336–337. The Soviets did not bring Diere to Nuremberg.

42. "59th Day, Thursday, February 14, 1946," NTP, vol. 7, http://avalon.law.yale.edu/imt/02-14-46.asp (accessed May 28, 2018). Also see "The Burdenko Commission Report, January 24, 1944, Moscow," in *Katyn: A Crime Without Punishment,* ed. Anna M. Cienciala, Natalia S. Lebedeva, and Wojciech

Materski (New Haven: Yale University Press, 2007), 319-226. The editors of the volume discuss the report on pp. 226–229.

43. "59th Day, Thursday, February 14, 1946."

44. "60th Day, Friday, February 15, 1946," NTP, vol. 7, http://avalon.law. yale.edu/imt/02-15-46.asp (accessed May 28, 2018). Also "Charter of the International Military Tribunal," NTP, vol. 1, https://avalon.law.yale.edu/ imt/imtconst.asp#art21 (accessed June 21, 2019).

45. On the Soviet evidence see Sorokina, "People and Procedures"; Pavel N. Knyshevskii, *Dobycha: Tainy germanskikh reparatsii* (Moscow: Soratnik, 1994); K. G. Azamatov, M. O. Temirzhanov, B. B. Temukuev, A. I. Tetuev, and M. Chechenov, ed., *Cherekskaia tragediia* (Nal'chik: Elbrus, 1994), and I. M. Malinin, "Massovye ubiistva NKVD (Vinnitsa)," ed. M. Iu. Sorokina, in *Ezhegodnik Doma russkogo zarubezh'ia imeni Aleksandra Solzhenitsyna* 2012 (Moscow: Dom russkogo zarubezh'ia, 2013), 179–203.

46. H. Montgomery Hyde, *Norman Birkett* (London: Hamish Hamilton, 1964), 507.

47. "Abroad: Nuremberg Looks East," *New York Times,* February 17, 1946, 68.

48. GARF f. 7445, op. 2. d. 7, ll. 126–131, 137–138.

49. Archive of the Foreign Policy of the Russian Federation (AVPRF) f. 06, op. 8, p. 33, d. 508, l. 3.

50. AVPRF f. 082, op. 32, p. 178, d. 2, l. 68, in *SSSR i Niurnbergskii protsess. Neizvestnye i maloizvestnye stranitsy istorii: Dokumenty*, ed. N. S. Lebedeva (Moscow: MFD, 2012), 395, n. 1.

51. GARF f. 8131, op. 38, d. 238, ll. 64, 158–159, 215. For the list from late November see GARF f. 9492, op. 1a, d. 468, ll. 93–101, in Lebedeva, *SSSR i Niurnbergskii protsess*, 318–321.

52. GARF f. 8131, op. 38, d. 238, ll. 59, 210–211, 223, 224. Also GARF f. 9492, op. 1a, d. 468, ll. 93–101, in Lebedeva, *SSSR i Niurnbergskii protsess*, 318–321.

53. Joshua A. Rubenstein, "The War and the Final Solution on the Russian Front," in *The Unknown Black Book: The Holocaust in the German Occupied Soviet Territories,* ed. Joshua Rubenstein and Ilya Altman (Bloomington: Indiana University Press, 2008), 22; Susanne Klingenstein, *Enlarging America: The Cultural Work of Jewish Literary Scholars, 1930–1990,* 320; Ruth R. Wisse, "Abrom Sutzkever," in *The Yivo Encyclopedia of Jews in Eastern Europe*, http:// www.yivoencyclopedia.org/article.aspx/Sutzkever_Avrom (accessed May 28, 2018).

54. Rubenstein, "The War and the Final Solution on the Russian Front," 32.

55. United States Holocaust Memorial Museum Archives, RG-22:002M, reel 27 (GARF f. 7445, op. 2, d. 75, ll. 188-198).

56. Avrom Sutzkever, "Mon témoignage au procès de Nuremberg," trans. Gilles Rozier, *Europe*, special issue (August-September 1995), 141–142.

57. Panasiuk recovered and continued with the group. AVPRF f. 082, op. 32, p. 178, d. 2, ll. 68, 89, in Lebedeva, *SSSR i Niurnbergskii protsess*, 395 n. 1, 396.

58. Sutzkever, "Mon témoignage au procès de Nuremberg," 41.

59. "62nd Day, Tuesday, February 19, 1946," NTP, vol. 7, http://avalon.law.yale.edu/imt/02-19-46.asp (accessed May 28, 2018).

60. "61st Day, Monday, February 18, 1946," NTP, vol. 7, http://avalon.law.yale.edu/imt/02-18-46.asp (accessed May 28, 2018).

61. "62nd Day, Tuesday, February 19, 1946." It was also called the Lissenitzach Forest.

62. "61st Day, Monday, February 18, 1946"; Drew Middleton, "War on Children Charged to Nazis," *New York Times*, February 19, 1946, 8.

63. "62nd Day, Tuesday, February 19, 1946"; Polevoi, *Final Reckoning*, 180–184.

64. RGALI f. 2989, op. 1, d. 190, ll. 27–29.

65. Gilbert, *Nuremberg Diary*, 161.

66. Drew Middleton, "Films Back Charge of German Crimes," *New York Times*, February 20, 1946, 6.

67. "63rd Day, Wednesday, February 20, 1946," NTP, vol. 8, http://avalon.law.yale.edu/imt/02-20-46.asp (accessed May 28, 2018); Drew Middleton, "Goering Is Called Worst Despoiler," *New York Times*, February 21, 1946, 6.

68. "64th Day, Thursday, February 21, 1946," NTP, vol. 8, http://avalon.law.yale.edu/imt/02-21-46.asp (accessed May 28, 2018). On the Soviet evidence see GARF f. 8131, op. 37, d. 2196, l. 157.

69. "64th Day, Thursday, February 21, 1946." On the churches see Aleksandr Formozov, *Russkie arkheologi v period totalitarizma* (Moscow: Znak, 2004).

70. Drew Middleton, "Cultural Crimes of Germans Cited," *New York Times*, February 22, 1946, 6.

71. Sutzkever, "Mon témoignage au procès de Nuremberg," 144. On the weather see Churchill Archives Centre, Churchill College, Cambridge, The Papers of Lord Kilmuir, KLMR Acc 1485, Sir David Maxwell Fyfe to Sylvia Maxwell Fyfe, February 20, 1946, available at http://www.kilmuirpapers.org/letters/4579523443.

72. "65th Day Friday, February 22, 1946," NTP, vol. 8, http://avalon.law.yale.edu/imt/02-22-46.asp (accessed May 28, 2018) .

73. Ibid.; Polevoi, *Final Reckoning*, 162–163; A. Poltorak, *The Nuremberg Epilogue* (Moscow: Progress Publishers, 1971), 135–137.

74. "65th Day, Friday, February 22, 1946"; Polevoi, *Final Reckoning*, 162–163.

75. "66th Day, Saturday, February 23, 1946," NTP, vol. 8, http://avalon.law.yale.edu/imt/02-23-46.asp (accessed May 28, 2018).

76. The Papers of Lord Kilmuir, KLMR Acc 1485, Sir David Maxwell Fyfe to Sylvia Maxwell Fyfe, February 25, 1946, available at http://www.kilmuirpapers.org/letters/4579523443.

77. Sutzkever, "Mon témoignage au procès de Nuremberg," 146–148.

78. Rubenstein, "The War and the Final Solution on the Russian Front," 32, n. 101, citing Joseph Leftwich, *Abraham Sutzkever: Partisan Poet* (New York: T. Yoseloff, 1971), 10, 51.

79. "67th Day, Monday, February 25, 1946," NTP, vol. 8, http://avalon.law. yale.edu/imt/02-25-46.asp (accessed May 28, 2018). For the Russian-language version see GARF f. 7445, op. 1, d. 1682, ll. 1–2. In Russian this was the difference between crimes against *chelovechestvo* and crimes against *chelovechnost'*. Also Nathalie Moine and John Angell, "Defining 'War Crimes against Humanity' in the Soviet Union: Nazi Arson of Soviet Villages and the Soviet Narrative on Jewish and Non-Jewish Soviet War Victims, 1941–1947," *Cahiers du monde russe* 52, no. 2 (2011): 441–473.

80. Sutzkever, "Mon témoignage au procès de Nuremberg," 149.

81. "Nazi Sadism Shown in War Trial Film," *New York Times*, February 27, 1946, 14.

82. Ibid.; "68th Day, Tuesday, February 26, 1946," NTP, vol. 8, http://avalon. law.yale.edu/imt/02-26-46.asp (accessed May 28, 2018); Polevoi, *Final Reckoning*, 157–158.

83. "68th Day, Tuesday, February 26, 1946."

84. Ibid.

85. "69th Day, Wednesday, February 27, 1946," NTP, vol. 8, http://avalon.law. yale.edu/imt/02-27-46.asp (accessed May 28, 2018).

86. Sutzkever, "Mon témoignage au procès de Nuremberg," 149–150.

87. Polevoi, *Final Reckoning*, 159.

88. "69th Day, Wednesday, February 27, 1946."

89. Ibid.

90. Sutzkever, "Mon témoignage au procès de Nuremberg," 149–151.

91. "69th Day, Wednesday, February 27, 1946"; Seweryna Szmaglewska, *Smoke over Birkenau*, trans. Jadwiga Rynas (New York: Holt, 1947); Robert Pick, "Memoir of Hell," *Saturday Review* 30 (1947), 13. Rajzman's "Uprising in Treblinka" had served as evidence at a March 1945 hearing of the U.S. House Committee on Foreign Affairs about German war crimes. Samuel Rajzman, "Uprising in Treblinka," in *Punishment of War Criminals*, United States Congress, House Committee on Foreign Affairs, 79th Congress, 1st session (Washington, DC: 1945): 120–125. He had also testified before Poland's Central Commission for the Investigation of German Crimes, which had prepared evidence for Nuremberg.

92. "69th Day, Wednesday, February 27, 1946."

93. Poltorak, *Nuremberg Epilogue*, 134.

94. "69th Day, Wednesday, February 27, 1946."

95. Sutzkever, "Mon témoignage au procès de Nuremberg," 151–152.

96. "69th Day, Wednesday, February 27, 1946."

97. Dodd, *Letters from Nuremberg*, 246.

98. "69th Day, Wednesday, February 27, 1946."

99. Taylor, *Anatomy of the Nuremberg Trials,* 315, 317.

100. GARF f. 8131, op. 37, d. 2196, ll. 158–166. He sent a copy to Gorshenin.

101. Ibid. See the issues from February 1946.

102. Ibid.

103. Ibid.

104. Harry S. Truman Presidential Library and Museum (HSTPLM), Harry S. Truman Administration File, George M. Elsey Papers, Telegram, George Kennan to George Marshall [Long Telegram], February 22, 1946, https://www.trumanlibrary.gov/library/research-files/telegram-george-kennan-james-byrnes-long-telegram (accessed December 3, 2014).

105. National Archives and Records Administration—College Park (NARA) RG 260, AG 000.5, b. 4, f. 2, "International News Service Dispatch Regarding Balts," February 20, 1946.

Chapter 9

1. A. Poltorak, *The Nuremberg Epilogue* (Moscow: Progress Publishers, 1971), 90; "Unite to Stop Russians, Churchill Warns at Fulton," *Stars and Stripes,* March 6, 1946, 1, 8; Winston Churchill, "The Sinews of Peace," in Churchill, *Winston S. Churchill: His Complete Speeches, 1897–1963,* ed. Robert Rhodes James, vol. 7 (New York: Chelsea House Publishers, 1974), 7285–7293.

2. Boris Polevoi, *The Final Reckoning: Nuremberg Diaries* (Moscow: Progress Publishers, 1978), 210–211.

3. Poltorak, *Nuremberg Epilogue,* 91.

4. Janet Flanner, "Letters from Nuremberg," in *Janet Flanner's World: Uncollected Writings, 1932–1975,* ed. Irving Drutman (New York: Harcourt Brace Jovanovich, 1979), 109.

5. Christopher J. Dodd with Lary Bloom, *Letters from Nuremberg: My Father's Narrative of a Quest for Justice* (New York: Crown, 2007), 260–261.

6. Polevoi, *Final Reckoning,* 210–213.

7. Ann Tusa and John Tusa, *The Nuremberg Trial* (London: Atheneum, 1983), 270.

8. Russian State Archive of Literature and Art (RGALI) f. 1038, op. 1, d. 2134, l. 2.

9. RGALI f. 2989, op. 1, d. 190, l. 12.

10. "77th Day, Friday, March 8, 1946," Nuremberg Trial Proceedings (NTP), vol. 9, Avalon Project at Yale University Law School, http://avalon.law.yale.edu/imt/03-08-46.asp (accessed March 23, 2015). Also Joseph E. Persico, *Nuremberg: Infamy on Trial* (New York: Penguin Books, 1994), 269. The first names of Ahrens, Rex, Hodt, and Berg are not given in the documents.

11. "77th Day, Friday, March 8, 1946"; Tusa and Tusa, *Nuremberg Trial,* 270–272.

12. State Archive of the Russian Federation (GARF) f. 7445, op. 2, d. 8, l. 47–47, 394.
13. GARF f. 7445, op. 2, d. 404, ll. 12–14, in Yuri Zorya and Natalia Lebedeva, "The Year 1939 in the Nuremberg Files," *International Affairs* (Moscow) 10 (October 1989), 120–121.
14. GARF f. 7445, op. 2, d. 8, ll. 47–48, 394.
15. GARF f. 7445, op. 2, d. 8, l. 170. This list omitted Versailles, which had already been disqualified as a defense. It also omitted mention of "the Soviet-German agreement about the exchange of the German population of Lithuania, Latvia, and Estonia with Germany."
16. "77th Day, Friday, March 8, 1946." The Tribunal would then adjudicate.
17. Taylor, *Anatomy of the Nuremberg Trials*, 327; "79th Day, Tuesday, March 12, 1946," NTP, vol. 9, http://avalon.law.yale.edu/imt/03-12-46.asp (accessed March 23, 2015).
18. Ibid. Also Tusa and Tusa, *Nuremberg Trial*, 274. This was reported triumphantly in the Soviet press. "Protsess glavnykh nemetskikh voennykh prestupnikov v Niurnberge: Vechernee zasedanie 12 marta," *Pravda*, March 14, 1946, 4.
19. GARF f. 7445, op. 1, d. 2625, ll. 166–176, in *SSSR i Niurnbergskii protsess. Neizvestnye i maloizvestnye stranitsy istorii: Dokumenty*, ed. N. S. Lebedeva (Moscow: MFD, 2012), 412–418.
20. GARF f. 7445, op. 2, d. 400, l. 30.
21. GARF f. 8131, op. 37, d. 2196, ll. 173–175.
22. H. Montgomery Hyde, *Norman Birkett* (London: Hamish Hamilton, 1964), 508; Dodd, *Letters from Nuremberg*, 252; "80th Day, Wednesday, March 13, 1946," NTP, vol. 9, http://avalon.law.yale.edu/imt/03-13-46.asp (accessed March 23, 2015).
23. Raymond Daniell, "Goering Defends Nazi Suppression from Witness Stand in Nuremberg," *New York Times*, March 14, 1946, 1.
24. Hyde, *Norman Birkett*, 508.
25. "81st Day, Thursday, March 14, 1946," NTP, vol. 9, http://avalon.law.yale.edu/imt/03-14-46.asp (accessed March 23, 2015).
26. Dodd, *Letters from Nuremberg*, 263; Poltorak, *Nuremberg Epilogue*, 89. The *Pravda* article was translated and printed in the *New York Times*. Joseph Stalin, "Reply to Churchill," *New York Times*, March 14, 1946, 4.
27. GARF f. 7445, op. 2, d. 391, ll. 61–63.
28. GARF f. 7445, op. 2, d. 6, ll. 255–257.
29. "82nd Day, Friday, March 15, 1946," NTP, vol. 9, http://avalon.law.yale.edu/imt/03-15-46.asp (accessed March 23, 2015).
30. "83rd Day, Saturday, March 16, 1946" and "84th Day, Monday, March 18, 1946," NTP, vol. 9, http://avalon.law.yale.edu/imt/03-16-46.asp and http://avalon.law.yale.edu/imt/03-18-46.asp (accessed March 23, 2015); Poltorak, *Nuremberg Epilogue*, 90–93.

31. Flanner, "Letters from Nuremberg," 117–118; Tusa and Tusa, *Nuremberg Trial*, 279–281.

32. "84th Day, Monday, March 18, 1946."

33. Ibid.; Raymond Daniell, "Goering Says He Denied Defeat until Ardennes Drive Collapsed," *New York Times*, March 19, 1946, 10.

34. Hyde, *Norman Birkett*, 509–512.

35. Dodd, *Letters from Nuremberg*, 265.

36. Polevoi, *Final Reckoning*, 213.

37. Raymond Daniell, "Nuremberg Trial Used as a Forum of Nazism," *New York Times*, March 24, 1946, 76.

38. "Protsess glavnykh nemetskikh voennykh prestupnikov v Niurnberge: Utrennee zasedanie 14 marta," *Pravda*, March 15, 1946, 4.

39. Russian State Archive of Socio-Political History (RGASPI) f. 629, op. 1, d. 109, ll. 98–102.

40. Ibid.

41. "85th Day, Tuesday, March 19, 1946," NTP, vol. 9, http://avalon.law.yale.edu/imt/03-19-46.asp (accessed March 23, 2015); Tusa and Tusa, *Nuremberg Trial*, 281–282.

42. "86th Day, Wednesday, March 20, 1946," NTP, vol. 9, http://avalon.law.yale.edu/imt/03-20-46.asp (accessed March 23, 2015).

43. Harold Burson, script of radio report from Nuremberg, broadcast on American Forces Network, March 20, 1946, http://www.haroldburson.com (accessed March 23, 2015).

44. Flanner, "Letters from Nuremberg," 117.

45. "87th Day, Thursday, March 21, 1946," NTP, vol. 9, http://avalon.law.yale.edu/imt/03-21-46.asp (accessed March 23, 2015).

46. Churchill Archives Centre, Churchill College, Cambridge, The Papers of Lord Kilmuir, KLMR Acc 1485, Sir David Maxwell Fyfe to Sylvia Maxwell Fyfe, March 21, 1946, available at http://www.kilmuirpapers.org/letters/4579523443.

47. Taylor, *Anatomy of the Nuremberg Trials*, 211–212, 345.

48. Tusa and Tusa, *Nuremberg Trial*, 288.

49. "87th Day, Thursday, March 21, 1946."

50. Ibid.

51. G. M. Gilbert, *Nuremberg Diary* (New York: Farrar, Straus, 1947), 209.

52. In Washington, Jackson had been Biddle's patron; in Nuremberg their relationship became much more complicated. John Q. Barrett, "Doing TV Justice to Nuremberg," *FindLaw*, https://supreme.findlaw.com/legal-commentary/doing-tv-justice-to-nuremberg.html (accessed July 31, 2018).

53. Lebedeva, *SSSR i Niurnbergskii protsess*, 421 (n. 1 to document no. 217).

54. GARF f. 7445, op. 2, d. 391, ll. 49, 63. Rychkov, Goliakov, and Ivan Lavrov (from the Ministry of Foreign Affairs) were also in attendance.

On the fabrication of these documents see Marina Sorokina, "People and Procedures: Toward a History of the Investigation of Nazi Crimes in the USSR," *Kritika: Explorations in Russian and Eurasian History* 6, no. 4 (2005): 797–831, and Witold Wasilewski, "The Birth and Persistence of the Katyn Lie," *Case Western Reserve Journal of International Law* 45, no. 3 (2012): 671–693.

55. Archive of the Foreign Policy of the Russian Federation (AVPRF) f. 082, op. 12, p. 178, d. 5, ll. 102–104.
56. Dodd, *Letters from Nuremberg*, 267–269.
57. "88th Day, Friday, March 22, 1946," NTP, vol. 9, http://avalon.law.yale.edu/imt/03-22-46.asp (accessed March 23, 2015).
58. Ibid.
59. Ibid. Some of the White Books contained captured Allied documents.
60. Ibid. Lawrence also advised that the Tribunal would not accept as defense evidence excerpts of books and articles by academics or public figures on matters of ethics or history—for example, works by historians about the Treaty of Versailles.
61. Ibid.
62. Ibid.
63. AVPRF f. 07, op. 13, p. 41, d. 8, ll. 106, 107.
64. "90th Day, Monday, March 25, 1946," NTP, vol. 10, http://avalon.law.yale.edu/imt/03-25-46.asp (accessed January, 5, 2015).
65. Ibid.
66. "91st Day, Tuesday, March 26, 1946," NTP, vol. 10, http://avalon.law.yale.edu/imt/03-26-46.asp (accessed March 23, 2015).
67. Ibid.; "92nd Day, Wednesday, March 27, 1946," NTP, vol. 10, http://avalon.law.yale.edu/imt/03-27-46.asp (accessed March 23, 2015).
68. "92nd Day, Wednesday, March 27, 1946."
69. Ibid. Also GARF f. 7445, op. 2, d. 6, ll. 263–264, in Lebedeva, *SSSR i Niurnbergskii protsess,* 412.
70. "93rd Day, Thursday, March 28, 1946," NTP, vol. 10, http://avalon.law.yale.edu/imt/03-28-46.asp (accessed March 23, 2015).
71. Ibid.
72. Gilbert, *Nuremberg Diary*, 223–224.
73. "93rd Day, Thursday, March 28, 1946."
74. Gilbert, *Nuremberg Diary*, 224.
75. "94th Day, Friday, March 29, 1946," NTP, vol. 10, http://avalon.law.yale.edu/imt/03-29-46.asp (accessed March 23, 2015).
76. Gilbert, *Nuremberg Diary*, 227–228; "95th Day, Saturday, March 30, 1946," NTP, vol. 10, http://avalon.law.yale.edu/imt/03-30-46.asp (accessed March 23, 2015).
77. Hyde, *Norman Birkett*, 512–513.

78. "96th Day, Monday, April 1, 1946," NTP, vol. 10, http://avalon.law.yale.edu/imt/04-01-46.asp (accessed January 5, 2015); Taylor, *Anatomy of the Nuremberg Trials*, 350.

79. "96th Day, Monday, April 1, 1946."

80. Tat'iana Stupnikova, *Nichego krome pravdy: Niurnbergskii protsess. Vospominaniia perevodchika* (Moscow: Vozvrashchenie, 2003), 97.

81. Dodd, *Letters from Nuremberg*, 275.

82. See for example "Tells of Russo-German Accord," *New York Times*, April 2, 1946, 12.

83. "97th Day, Tuesday, April 2, 1946," NTP, vol. 10, http://avalon.law.yale.edu/imt/04-02-46.asp (accessed March 23, 2015).

84. Ibid.

85. Ibid.

86. Ibid.

87. "98th Day, Wednesday, April 3, 1946," NTP, vol. 10, http://avalon.law.yale.edu/imt/04-03-46.asp (accessed March 23, 2015).

88. AVPRF f. 07, op. 13, p. 41, d. 9, ll. 112–116.

89. Ibid. He is referring to "War Eve Pact Revealed at Hess Trial," *Daily Mail*, March 26, 1946, 1.

90. AVPRF f. 07, op. 13, p. 41, d. 9, ll. 112–116.

91. Ibid.

92. Ibid.

93. GARF f. 7445, op. 1, d. 2610, ll. 103–109, in Lebedeva, *SSSR i Niurnbergskii protsess*, 428–431; Taylor, *Anatomy of the Nuremberg Trials*, 469; Francis Biddle, *In Brief Authority* (New York: Doubleday, 1962), 415.

Chapter 10

1. State Archive of the Russian Federation (GARF) f. 7445, op. 2, d. 391, l. 49. On Soviet plans for the Tokyo Trial see Russian State Archive of Socio-Political History (RGASPI) f. 17, op. 162, d. 38, ll. 36, 39–40, in *SSSR i Niurnbergskii protsess. Neizvestnye i maloizvestnye stranitsy istorii: Dokumenty*, ed. N. S. Lebedeva (Moscow: MFD, 2012), 420–424.

2. A. G. Zviagintsev and Iu. G. Orlov, *Prigovorennye vremenem: Rossiiskie i sovetskie prokurory XX vek 1937–1953* (Moscow: ROSSPEN, 2001), 289–292. He studied at Moscow University's Institute of Soviet Law. He had served between 1940 and 1943 as minister of justice of the RSFSR.

3. David Patrick Maxwell Fyfe, *Political Adventure: The Memoirs of the Earl of Kilmuir* (London: Weidenfeld and Nicolson, 1964), 111.

4. Francis Biddle, *In Brief Authority* (New York: Doubleday, 1962), 413.

5. Joseph E. Persico, *Nuremberg: Infamy on Trial* (New York: Penguin Books, 1994), 306–307; Boris Polevoi, *The Final Reckoning: Nuremberg Diaries* (Moscow: Progress Publishers, 1978), 253; "98th Day, Wednesday, April 3,

1946," Nuremberg Trial Proceedings (NTP), vol. 10, Avalon Project at Yale University Law School, http://avalon.law.yale.edu/imt/04-03-46.asp (accessed June 19, 2017).

6. "100th Day, Friday, April 5, 1946," NTP, vol. 10, http://avalon.law.yale.edu/imt/04-05-46.asp (accessed June 19, 2017).

7. "101st Day, Saturday, April 6, 1946," NTP, vol. 10, http://avalon.law.yale.edu/imt/04-06-46.asp (accessed June 19, 2017); Raymond Daniell, "Keitel Arrogance Wilts under Fire," *New York Times*, April 7, 1946, 11.

8. "101st Day, Saturday, April 6, 1946"; Persico, *Nuremberg*, 308–309.

9. Rebecca West, "Extraordinary Exile," September 7, 1946, https://www.newyorker.com/magazine/1946/09/07/extraordinary-exile (accessed June 29, 2018).

10. Telford Taylor, *The Anatomy of the Nuremberg Trials* (Boston: Knopf, 1992), 357–358; G. M. Gilbert, *Nuremberg Diary* (New York: Farrar, Straus, 1947), 252.

11. GARF f. 8131, op. 37, d. 2196, ll. 172–172ob; Aleksandr Zviagintsev, *Rudenko* (Moscow: Molodaia gvardiia, 2008), 136.

12. Taylor, *Anatomy of the Nuremberg Trials*, 358; Ann Tusa and John Tusa, *The Nuremberg Trial* (London: Atheneum, 1983), 312–314; Christopher J. Dodd with Lary Bloom, *Letters from Nuremberg: My Father's Narrative of a Quest for Justice* (New York: Crown, 2007), 281–282.

13. West, "Extraordinary Exile."

14. Tat'iana Stupnikova, *Nichego krome pravdy: Niurnbergskii protsess. Vospominaniia perevodchika* (Moscow: Vozvrashchenie, 2003), 35.

15. Dodd, *Letters from Nuremberg*, 284.

16. "105th Day, Thursday, April 11, 1946," NTP, vol. 11, http://avalon.law.yale.edu/imt/04-11-46.asp (accessed June 19, 2017).

17. Ibid.

18. H. Montgomery Hyde, *Norman Birkett* (London: Hamish Hamilton, 1964), 513–514.

19. A. Poltorak, *The Nuremberg Epilogue* (Moscow: Progress Publishers, 1971), 334–335.

20. "105th Day, Thursday, April 11, 1946"; B. Polevoi, "Gimmler i ego podruchnyi," *Pravda*, April 14, 1946.

21. "105th Day, Thursday, April 11, 1946"; "106th Day, Thursday, April 12, 1946," NTP, vol. 11, http://avalon.law.yale.edu/imt/04-12-46.asp (accessed June 19, 2017). Also Tusa and Tusa, *Nuremberg Trial*, 318–319.

22. "107th Day, Saturday, April 13, 1946," NTP, vol. 11, http://avalon.law.yale.edu/imt/04-13-46.asp (accessed June 19, 2017).

23. Ibid.

24. Poltorak, *Nuremberg Epilogue*, 342.

25. Sydney Gruson, "Nazi Race Theorist Pleads Innocence," *New York Times*, April 16, 1946, 10.

26. "108th Day, Monday, April 15, 1946," NTP, vol. 11, http://avalon.law.yale.edu/imt/04-15-46.asp (accessed June 19, 2017).

27. "108th Day, Monday, April 15, 1946"; Stupnikova, *Nichego krome pravdy*, 119-122; S. Krushinskii, "Gitler i ego podruchnye," *Pravda*, April 22, 1946.

28. 108th Day, Monday, April 15, 1946"; "109th Day, Tuesday, April 16, 1946," NTP, vol. 11, http://avalon.law.yale.edu/imt/04-16-46.asp (accessed June 19, 2017).

29. "110th Day, Wednesday, April 17, 1946," NTP, vol. 11, http://avalon.law.yale.edu/imt/04-17-46.asp (accessed June 19, 2017).

30. Gilbert, *Nuremberg Diary*, 274.

31. "110th Day, Wednesday, April 17, 1946." French assistant prosecutor Henri Monneray followed Rudenko, briefly questioning Rosenberg about the seizure of valuables belonging to French Jews.

32. Ibid., and Archive of the Foreign Policy of the Russian Federation (AVPRF) f. 07, op. 13, p. 41, d. 9, l. 122.

33. "110th Day, Wednesday, April 17, 1946."

34. Ibid., and AVPRF f. 07, op. 13, p. 41, d. 9, l. 122.

35. GARF f. 7445, op. 2, d. 8, ll. 5-7, in Lebedeva, *SSSR i Niurnbergskii protsess*, 434–435.

36. Library of Congress, Manuscript Division, Robert H. Jackson Collection (LOC-RHJ) b. 111, f. 10, Jackson to President Truman, May 13, 1946.

37. "111th Day, Wednesday, April 18, 1946," NTP, vol. 12, http://avalon.law.yale.edu/imt/04-18-46.asp (accessed June 19, 2017).

38. AVPRF f. 07, op. 13, p. 41, d. 8, l. 108.

39. Polevoi, *Final Reckoning*, 227–236.

40. AVPRF f. 07, op. 13, p. 41, d. 8, l. 109.

41. GARF f. 8131, op. 37, d. 2196, ll. 180–186.

42. Ibid., l. 179, and AVPRF f. 07, op. 13, p. 41, d. 9, ll. 119–120.

43. Polevoi, *Final Reckoning*, 236.

44. "113th Day, Wednesday, April 24, 1946," NTP, vol. 12, http://avalon.law.yale.edu/imt/04-24-46.asp (accessed June 19, 2017); Stupnikova, *Nichego krome pravdy*, 129.

45. See for example Poltorak, *Nuremberg Epilogue*, 417; John H. Waller, *The Unseen War in Europe: Espionage and Conspiracy in the Second World War* (New York: Random House, 1996), 364–365.

46. "113th Day, Wednesday, April 24, 1946"; Tusa and Tusa, *Nuremberg Trial*, 329–332; Joseph E. Persico, *Roosevelt's Secret War: FDR and World War II Espionage* (New York: Random House, 2001), 322–323.

47. Tusa and Tusa, *Nuremberg Trial*, 330; Hans Bernd Gisevius, *To the Bitter End: An Insider's Account of the Plot to Kill Hitler, 1933–1944* (Cambridge, MA: Harvard University Press, 1998).

48. "113th Day, Wednesday, April 24, 1946"; "114th Day, Thursday, April 25, 1946" and "115th Day, Friday, April 26, 1946," NTP, vol. 12, http://avalon.

law.yale.edu/imt/04-25-46.asp and http://avalon.law.yale.edu/imt/04-26-46.asp (accessed June 19, 2017).

49. "115th Day, Friday, April 26, 1946."

50. "Witness for the Defense," *New York Times*, April 27, 1946, 16.

51. "Protsess glavnykh nemetskikh voennykh prestupnikov v Niurnberge," *Pravda*, April 28, 1946.

52. Stupnikova, *Nichego krome pravdy,* 35.

53. "115th Day, Friday, April 26, 1946"; "116th Day, Monday, April 29, 1946," NTP, vol. 12, http://avalon.law.yale.edu/imt/04-29-46.asp (accessed June 19, 2017).

54. "116th Day, Monday, April 29, 1946"; Taylor, *Anatomy of the Nuremberg Trials*, 380.

55. Dodd, *Letters from Nuremberg*, 295; Tusa and Tusa, *Nuremberg Trial*, 335.

56. GARF f. 7445, op. 2, d. 6, ll. 63–65, in Lebedeva, *SSSR i Niurnbergskii protsess,* 437–439.

57. Taylor, *Anatomy of the Nuremberg Trials*, 386–387; Tusa and Tusa, *Nuremberg Trial*, 337–338.

58. "117th Day, Tuesday, April 30, 1946" and "118th Day, Wednesday, May 1, 1946," NTP, vol. 12, http://avalon.law.yale.edu/imt/04-30-46.asp and http://avalon.law.yale.edu/imt/05-01-46.asp (accessed June 19, 2017).

59. "119th Day, Thursday, May 2, 1946," NTP, vol. 12, http://avalon.law.yale.edu/imt/05-02-46.asp (accessed June 19, 2017).

60. Ibid.

61. "120th Day, Friday, May 3, 1946," NTP, vol. 13, http://avalon.law.yale.edu/imt/05-03-46.asp (accessed June 19, 2017).

62. Ibid.; "121st Day, Saturday, May 4, 1946," NTP, vol. 13, http://avalon.law.yale.edu/imt/05-04-46.asp (accessed June 19, 2017).

63. "122nd Day, Monday, May 6, 1946," NTP, vol. 13, http://avalon.law.yale.edu/imt/05-06-46.asp (accessed June 19, 2017); "Funk Bases Defense on His 'Insignificance,'" *New York Times*, May 5, 1946, 32.

64. "123rd Day, Tuesday, May 7, 1946," NTP, vol. 13, http://avalon.law.yale.edu/imt/05-07-46.asp (accessed June 19, 2017).

65. Ibid.

66. Ibid.

67. Taylor, *Anatomy of the Nuremberg Trials*, 396–397.

68. M. Iu. Raginskii, *Niurnberg: Pered sudom istorii* (Moscow: Izdatel'stvo politicheskoi literatury, 1986), 100–105.

69. Hyde, *Norman Birkett*, 516.

70. Dodd, *Letters from Nuremberg*, 287.

71. Biddle, *In Brief Authority*, 410.

72. Hyde, *Norman Birkett*, 516.

73. Taylor, *Anatomy of the Nuremberg Trials*, 387–388; Maxwell Fyfe, *Political Adventure*, 113.

74. AVPRF f. 06, op. 8, p. 1, d. 8, ll. 29–34, in *SSSR i germanskii vopros, 1941–1949: Dokumenty iz Arkhiva vneshnei politiki Rossiiskoi Federatsii*, ed. Georgii P. Kynin and Jochen Laufer, vol. 2 (Moscow: Mezhdunarodnye otnosheniia, 2000), 475–479.

75. Ibid.

76. John Gimbel, "The American Reparations Stop in Germany: An Essay on the Political Uses of History," *Historian* 37, no. 2 (1975): 276–296; Jean Edward Smith, *Lucius D. Clay: An American Life* (New York: Holt, 1990); John Lewis Gaddis, *Russia, the Soviet Union, and the United States: An Interpretive History* (New York: McGraw-Hill, 1990), 44-45.

77. AVPRF f. 07, op. 13, p. 41, d. 9, l. 122 and attachment. The informant was named or codenamed "Apitanov."

78. Ibid.

79. Dodd, *Letters from Nuremberg*, 300.

80. "124th Day, Wednesday, May 8, 1946," NTP, vol. 13, http://avalon.law.yale.edu/imt/05-08-46.asp (accessed January 31, 2016); Tusa and Tusa, *Nuremberg Trial*, 354–357.

81. Ibid.; "123rd Day, Tuesday, May 7, 1946"; Taylor, *Anatomy of the Nuremberg Trials*, 398–401; Airey Neave, *On Trial at Nuremberg* (Boston: Little, Brown, 1979), 200–213.

82. Taylor, *Anatomy of the Nuremberg Trials,* 398.

83. Jeffrey Brooks, *Thank You, Comrade Stalin!: Soviet Public Culture from Revolution to Cold War* (Princeton: Princeton University Press, 2001), 201.

84. "125th Day, Thursday, May 9, 1946," NTP, vol. 13, http://avalon.law.yale.edu/imt/05-09-46.asp (accessed January 31, 2016). Also "Doenitz Defends Prolonging War: Says It Saved 'Millions' of Germans from Death at Hands of Russians," *New York Times*, May 10, 1946, 12.

85. "126th Day, Friday, May 10, 1946," NTP, vol. 13, http://avalon.law.yale.edu/imt/05-10-46.asp (accessed January 31, 2016).

86. "Two GI's Murdered in German Ambush: Sharpshooter Finds His Mark with Two of Three Shots in Nuremberg Street," *New York Times*, May 12, 1946, 16.

87. "127th Day, Saturday, May 11, 1946," NTP, vol. 13, http://avalon.law.yale.edu/imt/05-11-46.asp (accessed January 31, 2016).

88. Ibid.; GARF f. 7445, op. 1, d. 2619, ll. 19–25, in Lebedeva, *SSSR i Niurnbergskii protsess*, 445–449.

89. "127th Day, Saturday, May 11, 1946"; GARF f. 7445, op. 2, d. 400, ll. 28–29, 36–38.

90. GARF f. 7445, op. 1, d. 2625, ll. 177–188, in Lebedeva, *SSSR i Niurnbergskii protsess*, 442–445.

91. Ibid. Nikitchenko requested that his dissenting opinion be noted in the protocol of the meeting.

92. GARF f. 7445, op. 2, d. 400, ll. 36–38.

93. GARF f. 7445, op. 2, d. 8, l. 397.

Chapter 11

1. Nikitchenko, Volchkov, Lawrence, Biddle, Maxwell Fyfe, and Falco all attended. State Archive of the Russian Federation (GARF) f. 7445, op. 2, d. 8, ll. 537, 538; Archive of the Foreign Policy of the Russian Federation (AVPRF) f. 07, op. 13, p. 41, d. 9, ll. 125–127; "Procès-verbal de la réunion de l'AIDP siège du Tribunal Militaire International (Nuremberg) 18 mai 1946," *Revue internationale de droit pénal* 73, no. 1–2 (2002): 321–335, https://www.cairn.info/revue-internationale-de-droit-penal-2002-1-page-321.htm. The AIDP was the International Association of Penal Law. Biddle officially presided at the meeting.

2. They referred to the organization in passing as an international association of democratic lawyers—a name that would later stick.

3. "Procès-verbal de la réunion de l'AIDP siège du Tribunal Militaire International."

4. Ibid.

5. Ibid.

6. Vadim J. Birstein, *SMERSH: Stalin's Secret Weapon* (London: Biteback, 2011), 376–387; Erich Raeder, *My Life* (Annapolis: United States Naval Institute Press, 1960), 384–386.

7. "130th Day, Wednesday, May 15, 1946," "131st Day, Thursday, May 16, 1946," "132nd Day, Friday, May 17, 1946," and "133rd Day, Saturday, May 18, 1946," Nuremberg Trial Proceedings (NTP), vol. 14, Avalon Project at Yale University Law School, http://avalon.law.yale.edu/imt/05-15-46.asp, http://avalon.law.yale.edu/imt/05-16-46.asp, http://avalon.law.yale.edu/imt/05-17-46.asp, and http://avalon.law.yale.edu/imt/05-18-46.asp (accessed February 3, 2016). Also Patrick Salmon, "Crimes against Peace: The Case of the Invasion of Norway at the Nuremberg Trials," in *Diplomacy and Intelligence during the Second World War: Essays in Honour of F. H. Hinsley*, ed. Richard Langhorne (Cambridge: Cambridge University Press, 1985), 245–320; G. M. Gilbert, *Nuremberg Diary* (New York: Farrar, Straus, 1947), 336.

8. "134th Day, Monday, May 20, 1946," NTP, vol. 14, http://avalon.law.yale.edu/imt/05-20-46.asp (accessed January 31, 2016); Gilbert, *Nuremberg Diary*, 338. The extent of Britain's plans for the invasion would come out several years later with the publication of Winston Churchill's war memoirs. Salmon, "Crimes against Peace," 245–246.

9. "134th Day, Monday, May 20, 1946."

10. Ibid.; Gilbert, *Nuremberg Diary*, 339–340.

11. "135th Day, Tuesday, May 21, 1946," NTP, vol. 14, http://avalon.law.yale.edu/imt/05-21-46.asp (accessed January 31, 2016).

12. Ibid. Weizsaecker had served in the Foreign Office under both Neurath and Ribbentrop.

13. Yuri Zorya and Natalia Lebedeva, "The Year 1939 in the Nuremberg Files," *International Affairs* (Moscow) 10 (October 1989), 124–125. They quote Alfred Seidl, *Der Fall Rudolf Hess 1941–1987: Dokumentation des Verteidigers* (Munich: Universitas Verlag, 1988), 179. Seidl claims that he first went to see Maxwell Fyfe, who told him that he too "had such a copy and recommended that he acquaint Rudenko" with it. Also Vladimir Abarinov, "V kuluarakh dvortsa iustitsii," *Gorizont*, no. 9 (1989), 46, and Birstein, *SMERSH*, 392.

14. "135th Day, Tuesday, May 21, 1946"; Zorya and Lebedeva, "The Year 1939 in the Nuremberg Files," 117–129.

15. "135th Day, Tuesday, May 21, 1946."

16. Ibid.; Richard L. Stokes, "Secret Soviet-Nazi Pacts on Eastern Europe Aired," *St. Louis Post Dispatch*, May 22, 1946, 1, 6.

17. "135th Day, Tuesday, May 21, 1946."

18. Ibid.

19. Ibid.

20. Stokes, "Secret Soviet-Nazi Pacts on Eastern Europe Aired." Stokes cites his source in the article.

21. Christopher J. Dodd with Lary Bloom, *Letters from Nuremberg: My Father's Narrative of a Quest for Justice* (New York: Crown, 2007), 251.

22. The SMERSH officer was Gennady Samoilov. Birstein, *SMERSH*, 393–394; Joseph E. Persico, *Nuremberg: Infamy on Trial* (New York: Penguin Books, 1994), 343–344; Abarinov, "V kuluarakh dvortsa iustitsii," 51. For Rudenko's correspondence with Moscow see GARF f. 7445, op. 2, d. 6, l. 328. The *New York Times* kept to the sanitized version of events. "Russian Prosecution Aide Slain While Cleaning Gun," *New York Times*, May 25, 1946, 10.

23. Tat'iana Stupnikova, *Nichego krome pravdy: Niurnbergskii protsess. Vospominaniia perevodchika* (Moscow: Vozvrashchenie, 2003), 103.

24. Dodd, *Letters from Nuremberg*, 322.

25. Discussed in Krystyna Kurchab-Redlikh, "Doklad Zori," *Novaia Pol'sha*, no. 9 (2000), Pravda o Katyn: Nezavisimoe rassledovanie, http://www.katyn.ru/index.php?go=Pages&in=view&id=457 (accessed February 2, 2016).

26. Persico, *Nuremberg*, 344; Birstein, *SMERSH*, 393–394; Stupnikova, *Nichego krome pravdy*, 102–105.

27. GARF f. 7445, op. 2, d. 400, ll. 58–61.

28. Ibid. Seidl later speculated that the mysterious man was from "the US prosecution or an American secret service." Seidl, *Der Fall Rudolf Hess*, 170–176, cited in Zorya and Lebedeva, "The Year 1939 in the Nuremberg Files," 124–125.

29. GARF f. 7445, op. 2, d. 391, ll. 50–51. The meeting transcript makes no mention of Zorya's death.

30. On Raikhman see Tennent H. Bagley, *Spymaster: Startling Cold War Revelations of a Soviet KGB Chief* (New York: Skyhorse, 2013), 66–67, and Witold Wasilewski, "The Birth and Persistence of the Katyn Lie," *Case Western Reserve Journal of International Law* 45, no. 3 (2012): 671–693.

31. "137th Day, Thursday, May 23, 1946" and "138th Day, Friday, May 24, 1946," NTP, vol. 14, http://avalon.law.yale.edu/imt/05-23-46.asp and http://avalon.law.yale.edu/imt/05-24-46.asp (accessed January 31, 2016). On Lvov see Tarik Cyril Amar, "A Disturbed Silence: Discourse on the Holocaust in the Soviet West as an Anti-Site of Memory," in *The Holocaust in the East: Local Perpetrators and Soviet Responses*, ed. Michael David-Fox, Peter Holquist, and Alexander M. Martin (Pittsburgh: University of Pittsburgh Press, 2014), 158–184.

32. "139th Day, Monday, May 27, 1946," NTP, vol. 14, http://avalon.law.yale.edu/imt/05-27-46.asp (accessed February 4, 2016). The second affidavit was dated May 16, 1946.

33. Ibid.

34. "140th Day, Tuesday, May 28, 1946," NTP, vol. 15, http://avalon.law.yale.edu/imt/05-28-46.asp (accessed February 4, 2016).

35. "141st Day, Wednesday, May 29, 1946" and "142nd Day, Thursday, May 30, 1946," NTP, vol. 15, http://avalon.law.yale.edu/imt/05-29-46.asp and http://avalon.law.yale.edu/imt/05-30-46.asp (accessed February 5, 2016).

36. "142nd Day, Thursday, May 30, 1946"; "143rd Day, Friday, May 31, 1946," NTP, vol. 15, http://avalon.law.yale.edu/imt/05-31-46.asp (accessed January, 31, 2016).

37. Ibid. Maxwell Fyfe wrote about Alexandrov's cross-examination in a letter home, complaining that Alexandrov was "letting . . . Sauckel recover from the effect of a quite good French cross-examination." Churchill Archives Centre, Churchill College, Cambridge, The Papers of Lord Kilmuir, KLMR Acc 1485, Sir David Maxwell Fyfe to Sylvia Maxwell Fyfe, May 31, 1946, available at http://www.kilmuirpapers.org/letters/4579523443.

38. GARF f. 7445, op. 2. d. 8, ll. 18–20; Dodd, *Letters from Nuremberg*, 311–312. On reports of the cross-examination as a shouting match see Ann Tusa and John Tusa, *The Nuremberg Trial* (London: Atheneum, 1983), 380.

39. GARF f. 7445, op. 2. d. 8, ll. 18–20.

40. Ibid.

41. GARF f. 7445, op. 2, d. 6, ll. 9–10.

42. "145th Day, Monday, June 3, 1946," NTP, vol. 15, http://avalon.law.yale.edu/imt/06-03-46.asp (accessed February 6, 2016). For Rudenko's petition, see GARF f. 7445, op. 2, d. 400, ll. 28–29.

43. Persico, *Nuremberg*, 247.

44. "147th Day, Wednesday, June 5, 1946," NTP, vol. 15, http://avalon.law.yale.edu/imt/06-05-46.asp (accessed May 9, 2016).

45. Ibid.

46. Ibid.; "146th Day, Tuesday, June 4, 1946," NTP, vol. 15, http://avalon.law.yale.edu/imt/06-04-46.asp (accessed May 9, 2016).

47. "148th Day, Thursday, June 6, 1946," NTP, vol. 15, http://avalon.law.yale.edu/imt/06-06-46.asp (accessed May 9, 2016). Roberts's official position was leading counsel.

48. "149th Day, Friday, June 7, 1946," NTP, vol. 15, http://avalon.law.yale.edu/imt/06-07-46.asp (accessed May 9, 2016).

49. GARF f. 7445, op. 2, d. 6, l. 5.

50. Library of Congress, Manuscript Division, Robert H. Jackson Collection (LOC-RHJ) b. 111, f. 10, Robert H. Jackson to President Harry Truman, May 13, 1946.

51. GARF f. 7445, op. 2, d. 8, ll. 390–393.

52. Ibid.

53. "150th Day, Saturday, June 8, 1946," NTP, vol. 15, http://avalon.law.yale.edu/imt/06-08-46.asp (accessed May 9, 2016). "Germans' Charges on Soviet Blocked: Tribunal Refuses to Admit Data Alleging Preparations to Divide Up Europe," *New York Times*, June 9, 1946, 34.

54. GARF f. 7445, op. 2, d. 8, ll. 390–393.

55. GARF f. 7445, op. 2, d. 6, ll. 6–8.

56. GARF f. 7445, op. 2, d. 6, ll. 245–249, in *SSSR i Niurnbergskii protsess. Neizvestnye i maloizvestnye stranitsy istorii: Dokumenty*, ed. N. S. Lebedeva (Moscow: MFD, 2012), 462–465.

57. This campaign in Poland was the "AB Operation." "151st Day, Monday, June 10, 1946," NTP, vol. 15 and "153rd Day, Wednesday, June 12, 1946," NTP, vol. 16, http://avalon.law.yale.edu/imt/06-10-46.asp and http://avalon.law.yale.edu/imt/06-12-46.asp (accessed May 11, 2016).

58. "155th Day, Friday, June 14, 1946," "156th Day, Monday, June 17, 1946," "157th Day, Tuesday, June 18, 1946," and "158th Day, Wednesday, June 19, 1946," NTP, vol. 16, http://avalon.law.yale.edu/imt/06-14-46.asp, http://avalon.law.yale.edu/imt/06-17-46.asp, http://avalon.law.yale.edu/imt/06-18-46.asp, and http://avalon.law.yale.edu/imt/06-19-46.asp (accessed May 11, 2016). For Raginsky's notes about Papen, see GARF f. 7445, op. 2, d. 404, ll. 75–77, in Lebedeva, *SSSR i Niurnbergskii protsess*, 475–476.

59. GARF f. 7445, op. 2, d. 391, ll. 52–53. The names of the other witnesses were Sergei Ivanov, Ivan Savateev, Anna Alekseevna, Pavel Sukharev, and Ludwig Schneider. Markov had been arrested by Soviet forces after the war and spent several months in prison before testifying in Sofia. Prozorovsky was chief forensic medicine expert at the USSR's Scientific-Research Institute of Forensic Medicine. Also see Victor Zaslavsky, *Class Cleansing: The Massacre*

at Katyn (New York: Telos, 2008), 62–63. Kolesnikov and Metropolitan Nikolai did not make it onto this final list.

60. GARF f. 7445, op. 2, d. 391, ll. 52–53.

61. AVPRF f. 07, op. 13, p. 41, d. 8, l. 114.

62. GARF f. 7445, op. 2, d. 400, ll. 4, 51–52. Czapski, a Polish artist and author, had served as an officer in the Polish army in 1939 before being captured by the Red Army. In 1941, after the German invasion of the USSR and the signing of a Soviet-Polish peace treaty, Czapski joined the Soviet-organized Polish army under General Wladyslaw Anders. He had been assigned by Anders to investigate the whereabouts of the missing Polish officers who had been held by the NKVD—and had come up empty-handed. Zaslavsky, *Class Cleansing*, 34; Joseph Czapski, *The Inhuman Land*, trans. Gerard Hopkins (Ann Arbor: University of Michigan Press, 1951).

63. GARF f. 7445, op. 1, d. 2610, ll. 149–150, 151–156, in Lebedeva, *SSSR i Niurnbergskii protsess*, 474, 479–480. At a meeting earlier that week Nikitchenko had asked that the Tribunal remind the defense that the IMT should not be used for criticizing the actions of the Allied countries. The Western judges were non-committal—but did agree to throw out the Rechberg affidavit, deeming it to be groundless.

64. Norman J. W. Goda, *Tales from Spandau: Nazi Criminals and the Cold War* (Cambridge: Cambridge University Press, 2007), chap. 5.

65. "159th Day, Wednesday, June 20, 1946" and "160th Day, Friday, June 21, 1946," NTP, vol. 16, http://avalon.law.yale.edu/imt/06-20-46.asp and http://avalon.law.yale.edu/imt/06-21-46.asp (accessed May 12, 2016).

66. Ibid.

67. Stupnikova, *Nichego krome pravdy*, 141.

68. "160th Day, Friday, June 21, 1946."

69. Cited in H. Montgomery Hyde, *Norman Birkett* (London: Hamish Hamilton, 1964), 520.

70. The Papers of Lord Kilmuir, KLMR Acc 1485, Sir David Maxwell Fyfe to Sylvia Maxwell Fyfe, June 26, 1946, available at http://www.kilmuirpapers.org/letters/4579523443.

71. "163rd Day, Tuesday, June 25, 1946" and "164th Day, Wednesday, June 26, 1946," NTP, vol. 17, http://avalon.law.yale.edu/imt/06-25-46.asp and http://avalon.law.yale.edu/imt/06-26-46.asp (accessed May 10, 2016).

72. "163rd Day, Tuesday, June 25, 1946."

73. "Indictment: Count Three—War Crimes," NTP, vol. 1, http://avalon.law.yale.edu/imt/count3.asp (accessed May 10, 2016).

74. Raphael Lemkin, *Axis Rule in Occupied Europe: Laws of Occupation, Analysis of Government, Proposals for Redress* (Concord, NH: Carnegie Endowment, 1944), chap. 9. Lemkin's definition included "measures for weakening or destroying political, social, and cultural elements in national groups." See A. Dirk Moses, "Raphael Lemkin, Culture, and the Concept of Genocide," in *The*

Oxford Handbook of Genocide Studies, ed. Donald Bloxham and A. Dirk Moses (Oxford: Oxford University Press, 2010), 19–42.

75. "163rd Day, Tuesday, June 25, 1946."

76. GARF f. 7445, op. 2, d. 8, l. 110; f. 8131, op. 37, d. 2196, ll. 202–203.

77. Philippe Sands, *East West Street: On the Origins of "Genocide" and "Crimes Against Humanity"* (New York: Knopf, 2016), 322–325.

78. On Ečer see The Papers of Lord Kilmuir, KLMR Acc 1485, Sir David Maxwell Fyfe to Sylvia Maxwell Fyfe, June 26, 1946, 9:45 p.m., available at http://www.kilmuirpapers.org/letters/4579523443. On the note from Lemkin see Sands, *East-West Street*, 325.

79. Eduard Stehlík, "Bohuslav Ečer and the Prosecution of War Crimes," in *European Conscience and Communism,* Proceedings of the International Conference, Prague, June 2-3, 2008, 52–63.

80. GARF f. 7445, op. 2, d. 8, l. 110; f. 8131, op. 37, d. 2196, ll. 202–203.

81. "Human Rights Bill Proposed in Pacts: U.N. Committee Urges Inclusion before International Code Is Drawn," *New York Times*, June 15, 1946, 5.

Chapter 12

1. Margaret Bourke-White, *Shooting the Russian War* (New York: Simon and Schuster, 1943), 69, cited in *Stalin's Secret Pogrom: The Postwar Inquisition of the Jewish Anti-Fascist Committee,* abr. ed., ed. Joshua Rubenstein and Vladimir P. Naumov (New Haven: Yale University Press, 2005), 178-179. Rubenstein and Naumov provide useful information and commentary throughout this edited volume. Lozovsky had been vice chairman of Sovinformburo during the war. He became its chairman in 1945.

2. Harrison E. Salisbury, *The 900 Days: The Siege of Leningrad* (Cambridge, MA: Harvard University Press, 1969), 450; Phillip Knightley, *The First Casualty: The War Correspondent as Hero and Myth Maker from the Crimea to Iraq* (Baltimore: John Hopkins University Press, 2004), 270.

3. Rubenstein and Naumov, eds., *Stalin's Secret Pogrom*, 179; Marina Sorokina, "People and Procedures: Toward a History of the Investigation of Nazi Crimes in the USSR," *Kritika: Explorations in Russian and Eurasian History* 6, no. 4 (2005): 797–831.

4. R. B. Cockett, " 'In Wartime Every Objective Reporter Should Be Shot': The Experience of British Press Correspondents in Moscow, 1941–5," *Journal of Contemporary History* 23, no. 4 (1988): 515–539.

5. Witold Wasilewski, "The Birth and Persistence of the Katyn Lie," *Case Western Reserve Journal of International Law* 45, no. 3 (2012): 671–693; W. H. Lawrence, "Soviet Blames Foe in Killing of Foes: Commission Reports on the Katyn Incident; Finds Plot to Hurt Russian Prestige," *New York Times*, January 27, 1944, 3.

6. Lozovsky was involved in making the travel arrangements for the Soviet prosecution's three "Katyn witnesses." Archive of the Foreign Policy of the Russian Federation (AVPRF) f. 082, op. 32, p. 178, d. 2, l. 152, in *SSSR i Niurnbergskii protsess. Neizvestnye i maloizvestnye stranitsy istorii: Dokumenty*, ed. N. S. Lebedeva (Moscow: MFD, 2012), 482-483.

7. The general was Vasily Chuikov, who had led Soviet forces in Stalingrad. Vadim J. Birstein, *SMERSH: Stalin's Secret Weapon* (London: Biteback, 2011), 383–384. For Fritzsche's own description see Konrad Heiden, "Why They Confess: The Remarkable Case of Hans Fritzsche," *Life*, June 1949, 92–94, 96, 99–100, 102, 105.

8. AVPRF f. 06, op. 7, p. 20, d. 210, ll. 1–3.

9. Keith Somerville, *Radio Propaganda and the Broadcasting of Hatred: Historical Development and Definitions* (London: Palgrave Macmillan, 2012), 149.

10. Goebbels notes this aim in his diary. *Die Tagebücher von Joseph Goebbels*, ed. Elke Fröhlich, vol. 8, part 2, April-June 1943 (Munich: K. G. Saur, 1993), 104. Cited and discussed in Claudia Weber, "Stalin's Trap: The Katyn Forest Massacre between Propaganda and Taboo," in *Theatres of Violence: Massacre, Mass Killing and Atrocity throughout History*, ed. Philip G. Dwyer and Lyndall Ryan (New York: Berghahn, 2015), 171-172.

11. State Archive of the Russian Federation (GARF) f. 8131, op. 37, d. 2196, l. 197.

12. "165th Day, Thursday, June 27, 1946," Nuremberg Trial Proceedings (NTP), vol. 17, Avalon Project at Yale University Law School, http://avalon.law.yale.edu/imt/06-27-46.asp (accessed May 12, 2016).

13. Ibid.; "164th Day, Wednesday, June 26, 1946" and "166th Day, Friday, June 28, 1946," NTP, vol. 17, http://avalon.law.yale.edu/imt/06-26-46.asp and http://avalon.law.yale.edu/imt/06-28-46.asp (accessed May 10, 2016).

14. "165th Day, Thursday, June 27, 1946."

15. "166th Day, Friday, June 28, 1946."

16. Ibid.; Telford Taylor, *The Anatomy of the Nuremberg Trials* (Boston: Knopf, 1992), 463.

17. AVPRF f. 06, op. 7, p. 20, d. 210, ll. 1–3.

18. "166th Day, Friday, June 28, 1946"; Birstein, *SMERSH*, 386. No doubt SMERSH had a hand in producing them.

19. "Protsess glavnykh nemetskikh voennykh prestupnikov v Niurnberge, Vechernee zasedanie 28 iuniia," *Izvestiia*, June 30, 1946, 4.

20. "167th Day, Saturday, June 29, 1946," NTP, vol. 17, http://avalon.law.yale.edu/imt/06-29-46.asp (accessed May 12, 2016).

21. AVPRF f. 082, op. 32, p. 178, d. 2, l. 152, in Lebedeva, *SSSR i Niurnbergskii protsess*, 482-483.

22. A. Poltorak, *The Nuremberg Epilogue* (Moscow: Progress Publishers, 1971), 138. On Smirnov also see Valentyna Polunina, "The Khabarovsk Trial: The Soviet Riposte to the Tokyo Tribunal," in *Trials for International Crimes in*

Asia, ed. Kirsten Sellars (Cambridge: Cambridge University Press, 2016), 130–131.

23. For a discussion of these witnesses see *Katyn: A Crime Without Punishment,* ed. Anna M. Cienciala, Natalia S. Lebedeva, and Wojciech Materski (New Haven: Yale University Press, 2007), 229-239.

24. Tat'iana Stupnikova, *Nichego krome pravdy: Niurnbergskii protsess. Vospominaniia perevodchika* (Moscow: Vozvrashchenie, 2003), 107.

25. "168th Day, Monday, July 1, 1946," NTP, vol. 17, http://avalon.law.yale.edu/imt/07-01-46.asp (accessed July 25, 2016). Ahrens had reported personally to Oberhauser, the liaison chief of Army Group Center in Smolensk. On Ahrens also see Christiane Kohl, *The Witness House: Nazis and Holocaust Survivors Sharing a Villa during the Nuremberg Trials,* trans. Anthea Bell (New York: Other Press, 2010), 144–149.

26. "168th Day, Monday, July 1, 1946."

27. Ibid.

28. Taylor, *Anatomy of the Nuremberg Trials,* 470.

29. "168th Day, Monday, July 1, 1946."

30. Ibid.

31. Ibid.; Taylor, *Anatomy of the Nuremberg Trials,* 470.

32. "168th Day, Monday, July 1, 1946."

33. Taylor, *Anatomy of the Nuremberg Trials,* 470.

34. "168th Day, Monday, July 1, 1946."

35. Taylor, *Anatomy of the Nuremberg Trials,* 471; Stupnikova, *Nichego krome pravdy,* 112.

36. "168th Day, Monday, July 1, 1946."

37. Ibid.

38. Ibid. The German-sponsored commission's report was published as a White Book.

39. Ibid.

40. Ibid.; "169th Day, Tuesday, July 2, 1946," NTP, vol. 17, http://avalon.law.yale.edu/imt/07-02-46.asp (accessed July 25, 2016); Taylor, *Anatomy of the Nuremberg Trials,* 471.

41. "169th Day, Tuesday, July 2, 1946."

42. Ibid.

43. Ibid. Also Ann Tusa and John Tusa, *The Nuremberg Trial* (London: Atheneum, 1983), 411. Stahmer had requested another commission member, Professor François Naville, as a witness. Naville, an ardent anti-Nazi, had refused to testify. George Sanford, *Katyn and the Soviet Massacre of 1940: Truth, Justice, and Memory* (New York: Routledge, 2005), 130–131.

44. "169th Day, Tuesday, July 2, 1946."

45. Ibid.; "Protsess glavnykh nemetskikh voennykh prestupnikov v Niurnberg," *Izvestiia,* July 3, 1946."

46. "169th Day, Tuesday, July 2, 1946"; Christopher J. Dodd with Lary Bloom, *Letters from Nuremberg: My Father's Narrative of a Quest for Justice* (New York: Crown, 2007), 333.

47. "169th Day, Tuesday, July 2, 1946."

48. "Katyn Forest Issue Revived by Germans," *New York Times*, July 2, 1946, 15; "Germans Forced Katyn Testimony: Report on Polish Massacre Faked and Signed under Duress, Court Hears," *New York Times*, July 3, 1946, 4.

49. "Katyn Forest Crime: Nuremberg Defense Refuted," *Times* (London), July 2, 1946, 3; "Murder of Polish Officers: Medical Conclusions at Nuremberg," *Times* (London), July 3, 1946, 3.

50. That said, it was far from the "embarrassing disaster" that some scholars suggest. On Katyn as an "embarrassing disaster," see Claudia Weber, "The Export of Terror—On the Impact of the Stalinist Culture of Terror on Soviet Foreign Policy during and after World War II," *Journal of Genocide Research* 11, no. 2–3 (2009): 285–306, esp. 303.

51. Wasilewski, "The Birth and Persistence of the Katyn Lie," 677–678. Also see the discussion of the report in Cienciala et al., *Katyn*, 226–228.

52. Dodd, *Letters from Nuremberg*, 333.

53. Taylor, *Anatomy of the Nuremberg Trials*, 472.

54. Also see Weber, "Stalin's Trap," 174–176.

55. These questions did come up in 1951 and 1952 when a U.S. House of Representatives select committee headed by Ray J. Madden investigated the question of Soviet responsibility for Katyn and the U.S. government's role in suppressing information about the massacre. See Benjamin B. Fischer, "The Katyn Controversy: Stalin's Killing Field," *Studies in Intelligence* (Winter 1999-2000), https://www.cia.gov/library/center-for-the-study-of-intelligence/csi-publications/csi-studies/studies/winter99-00/art6.html (accessed August 6, 2019).

56. "171st Day, Thursday, July 4, 1946," NTP, vol. 17, http://avalon.law.yale.edu/imt/07-04-46.asp (accessed July 25, 2016); Taylor, *Anatomy of the Nuremberg Trials*, 474–475; Tusa and Tusa, *Nuremberg Trial*, 414–416.

57. "172nd Day, Friday, July 5, 1946" and "173rd Day, Monday, July 8, 1946," NTP, vol. 17, http://avalon.law.yale.edu/imt/07-05-46.asp and http://avalon.law.yale.edu/imt/07-08-46.asp (accessed July 25, 2016).

58. "U.S. Is Belligerent, Soviet Paper Says," *New York Times*, July 5, 1946, 3.

59. Francis Biddle, *In Brief Authority* (New York: Doubleday, 1962), 423–424.

60. "181st Day, Thursday, July 18, 1946," NTP, vol. 18, http://avalon.law.yale.edu/imt/07-18-46.asp (accessed July 25, 2016).

61. "174th Day, Tuesday, July 9, 1946," NTP, vol. 18, http://avalon.law.yale.edu/imt/07-09-46.asp (accessed July 25, 2016).

62. "176th Day, Thursday, July 11, 1946," NTP, vol. 18, http://avalon.law.yale.edu/imt/07-11-46.asp (accessed July 25, 2016). The actual number of victims of the bombing raids is closer to 600,000. See W. G. Sebald, *On the*

Natural History of Destruction, trans. Anthea Bell (New York: Modern Library, 2004), 4.

63. See for example "Russians Deport German Residents of Austrian Zone: 54,000 Reported Ordered Out by 6 a.m. Today," *New York Times*, July 8, 1946, 1. The Poles were deported from the parts of Ukraine and Belorussia that had been part of Poland before the 1939 Soviet invasion.

64. "182nd Day, Friday, July 19, 1946," NTP, vol. 19, http://avalon.law.yale.edu/imt/07-19-46.asp (accessed July 25, 2016).

65. "186th Day, Thursday, July 25, 1946," NTP, vol. 19, http://avalon.law.yale.edu/imt/07-25-46.asp (accessed July 25, 2016).

66. Dodd, *Letters from Nuremberg*, 340.

67. "Reds Link Fascists with American Zone," *New York Times*, July 24, 1946, 4. National Archives and Records Administration—College Park (NARA) RG 260, AG 000.5, b. 4, f. 2, "P. Troyanovsky's report, 'In the American Zone of Occupation in Germany,'" August 5, 1946.

68. GARF f. 7445, op. 2, d. 6, ll. 252–254.

69. GARF f. 7445, op. 2, d. 8, ll. 14–16, 302–304. The prosecutors agreed to share their speeches in advance. GARF f. 7445, op. 2, d. 8, ll. 105, 106, 298, 387–388.

70. Joseph E. Persico, *Nuremberg: Infamy on Trial* (New York: Penguin Books, 1994), 364.

71. "187th Day, Friday, July 26, 1946," NTP, vol. 19, http://avalon.law.yale.edu/imt/07-26-46.asp (accessed July 25, 2016).

72. Ibid.; "Protsess glavnykh nemetskikh voennykh prestupnikov v Niurnberge," *Pravda*, July 27, 1946.

73. "187th Day, Friday, July 26, 1946"; Taylor, *Anatomy of the Nuremberg Trials*, 490–494.

74. Airey Neave, *On Trial at Nuremberg* (Boston: Little, Brown, 1979), 296.

75. "187th Day, Friday, July 26, 1946."

76. "188th Day, Saturday, July 27, 1946," NTP, vol. 19, http://avalon.law.yale.edu/imt/07-27-46.asp (accessed July 25, 2016).

77. "Nazi Leaders' Crimes: France and Russia Speak," *Times* (London), July 29, 1946, 3. The article noted that the American delegation to the upcoming Paris Peace Conference would be sponsoring the insertion of clauses on "genocide" in treaties with Romania, Hungary, and all other former Axis powers. This particular proposal, which was sponsored by Lemkin, never got off the ground.

78. "Text of U.S. Note to Soviet on Hungary," *New York Times*, July 27, 1946, 11; "Austria Protests Red Army Seizure," *New York Times*, July 24, 1946, 8.

79. Dodd, *Letters from Nuremberg*, 340–341.

80. "189th Day, Monday, July 29, 1946," NTP, vol. 19, http://avalon.law.yale.edu/imt/07-29-46.asp (accessed July 25, 2016).

81. Ibid. Dubost delivered the rest of the French closing speech because de Ribes was ill.

82. Lebedeva, *SSSR i Niurnbergskii protsess*, 489; GARF f. 7445, op. 1, d. 2810, ll. 1–189.

83. "189th Day, Monday, July 29, 1946."

84. Ibid.

85. GARF f. 9492, op. 1a, d. 468, ll. 234–235, in Lebedeva, *SSSR i Niurnbergskii protsess*, 489.

86. "189th Day, Monday, July 29, 1946." Referring to Frank, he repeated Frank's comment that Polish intellectuals and workers had not been stirred up by German reports of Soviet atrocities at Katyn due to their awareness that there were German "concentration camps at Auschwitz and Majdanek" where the "mass murder of the Poles was carried out on assembly lines."

87. Ibid.; "190th Day, Tuesday, July 30, 1946," NTP, vol. 20, http://avalon.law. yale.edu/imt/07-30-46.asp (accessed July 26, 2016).

88. GARF f. 7445, op. 2, d. 7, ll. 181–183, 183a; d. 8, ll. 90–93. The mechanic was Franz Joseph Khervers.

Chapter 13

1. Rebecca West, "Extraordinary Exile," September 7, 1946, https://www. newyorker.com/magazine/1946/09/07/extraordinary-exile (accessed June 29, 2018).

2. Tat'iana Stupnikova, *Nichego krome pravdy: Niurnbergskii protsess. Vospominaniia perevodchika* (Moscow: Vozvrashchenie, 2003), 146–147.

3. Archive of the Foreign Policy of the Russian Federation (AVPRF) f. 07, op. 13, p. 41, d. 3, ll. 1–2, 112–114, 117–118.

4. Airey Neave, *On Trial at Nuremberg* (Boston: Little, Brown, 1978), 274–276.

5. National Archives and Records Administration—College Park (NARA) RG 238, entry 52, b. 5, "R. M. W. Kempner, Memorandum for Mr. Justice Jackson," January 23, 1946.

6. Ibid.; "71st Day, Friday, March 1, 1946" and "72nd Day, Saturday, March 2, 1946," Nuremberg Trial Proceedings (NTP), vol. 8, Avalon Project at Yale University Law School, http://avalon.law.yale.edu/imt/03-01-46.asp and http://avalon.law.yale.edu/imt/03-02-46.asp (accessed November 28, 2016).

7. "70th Day, Thursday, February 28, 1946," NTP, vol. 8, http://avalon. law.yale.edu/imt/02-28-46.asp (accessed November 28, 2016); Telford Taylor, *The Anatomy of the Nuremberg Trials* (Boston: Knopf, 1992), 502–503; "Colonel Neave Report," NTP, vol. 42, http://avalon.law. yale.edu/imt/neave.asp (accessed December 1, 2016); Neave, *On Trial at Nuremberg*, 276; Dana Adams Schmidt, "Germans Await Nuremberg Verdict," *New York Times*, August 4, 1946, 75. Servatius later visited the Soviet zone.

8. Neave, *On Trial at Nuremberg*, chap. 24; State Archive of the Russian Federation (GARF) f. 7445, op. 1, d. 2618, l. 27.

9. Taylor, *Anatomy of the Nuremberg Trials*, 503; Filip Slaveski, *The Soviet Occupation of Germany: Hunger, Mass Violence, and the Struggle for Peace, 1945–1947* (Cambridge: Cambridge University Press, 2013), 127–146.

10. "190th Day, Tuesday, July 30, 1946," NTP, vol. 20, http://avalon.law.yale.edu/imt/07-30-46.asp (accessed November 28, 2016).

11. Ibid.; "191st Day, Wednesday, July 31, 1946," NTP, vol. 20, http://avalon.law.yale.edu/imt/07-31-46.asp (accessed November 28, 2016).

12. Stupnikova, *Nichego krome pravdy*, 148–150.

13. For examples see Herbert L. Matthews, "Socialism vs. Communism—The Stake: Europe: Two Radical Movements," *New York Times*, February 17, 1946, 88; Orville Prescott, "Books of the Times: He Held Important Soviet Posts," *New York Times*, April 16, 1946, 23.

14. Discussed in Margarete Buber-Neumann, *Under Two Dictators: Prisoner of Stalin and Hitler*, trans. Edward Fitzgerald (London: Random House, 2009).

15. "191st Day, Wednesday, July 31, 1946" and "192nd Day, Thursday, August 1, 1946," NTP, vol. 20, http://avalon.law.yale.edu/imt/08-01-46.asp (accessed November 28, 2016).

16. "192nd Day, Thursday, August 1, 1946."

17. Ibid.

18. "193rd Day, Friday, August 2, 1946," NTP, vol. 20, http://avalon.law.yale.edu/imt/08-02-46.asp (accessed November 28, 2016).

19. Ibid.; "194th Day, Saturday, August 3, 1946," NTP, vol. 20, http://avalon.law.yale.edu/imt/08-03-46.asp (accessed November 28, 2016).

20. *Pravda*, August 1, 1946, 1.

21. "Second Plenary Meeting, 4 pm," Tuesday, July 30, 1946, *Foreign Relations of the United States*, 1946, Paris Peace Conference: Proceedings, vol. 3, 334–335.

22. NARA RG 260, AG 000.5, b. 3, f. 1, "OMGUS Incoming Message," July 30, 1946.

23. Dana Adams Schmidt, "U.S. Would Cease 4-Power Trials," *New York Times*, August 3, 1946, 5.

24. NARA RG 260, AG 000.5, b. 2, f. 7, "OMGUS Outgoing Cable," August 5, 1946.

25. GARF f. 7445, op. 1, d. 2810b, ll. 1–16.

26. A. Poltorak, *The Nuremberg Epilogue* (Moscow: Progress Publishers, 1971), 428.

27. NARA RG 260, AG 000.7, b. 4, f. 6, "Note from U.S. Political Adviser Robert Murphy to Lieutenant General Lucius D. Clay," August 5, 1946.

28. Slaveski, *Soviet Occupation of Germany*, 127–146.

29. "194th Day, Saturday, August 3, 1946" and "195th Day, Monday, August 5, 1946," NTP, vol. 20, http://avalon.law.yale.edu/imt/08-05-46.asp (accessed November 28, 2016).

30. "195th Day, Monday, August 5, 1946."
31. "196th Day, Tuesday, August 6, 1946," NTP, vol. 20, http://avalon.law.yale.edu/imt/08-06-46.asp (accessed November 28, 2016).
32. Christopher J. Dodd with Lary Bloom, *Letters from Nuremberg: My Father's Narrative of a Quest for Justice* (New York: Crown, 2007), 343.
33. Churchill Archives Centre, Churchill College, Cambridge, The Papers of Lord Kilmuir, KLMR Acc 1485, Sir David Maxwell Fyfe to Sylvia Maxwell Fyfe, August 17, 1946, available at http://www.kilmuirpapers.org/letters/4579523443.
34. "197th Day, Wednesday, August 7, 1946" and "198th Day, Thursday, August 8, 1946," NTP, vol. 20, http://avalon.law.yale.edu/imt/08-07-46.asp and http://avalon.law.yale.edu/imt/08-08-46.asp (accessed November 28, 2016).
35. William L. Shirer, *The Rise and Fall of the Third Reich: A History of Nazi Germany* (New York: Simon and Schuster, 2011), 980.
36. "194th Day, Saturday, August 3, 1946" and "198th Day, Thursday, August 8, 1946."
37. Poltorak, *Nuremberg Epilogue*, 430–452.
38. Ibid.
39. Ibid.
40. "199th Day, Friday, August 9, 1946," NTP, vol. 20, http://avalon.law.yale.edu/imt/08-09-46.asp (accessed November 28, 2016).
41. "200th Day, Saturday, August 10, 1946," NTP, vol. 20, http://avalon.law.yale.edu/imt/08-10-46.asp (accessed November 28, 2016). The myth of the "clean Wehrmacht" has been taken apart by scholars of Nazi Germany. See for example Wolfram Wette, *The Wehrmacht: History, Myth, Reality*, trans. Deborah Lucas Schneider (Cambridge, MA: Harvard University Press, 2007).
42. "200th Day, Saturday, August 10, 1946."
43. "201st Day, Monday, August 12, 1946," NTP, vol. 21, http://avalon.law.yale.edu/imt/08-12-46.asp (accessed November 28, 2016).
44. Ibid.
45. AVPRF f. 07, op. 13, p. 41, d. 9, ll. 119–129.
46. "202nd Day, Tuesday, August 13, 1946," NTP, vol. 21, http://avalon.law.yale.edu/imt/08-13-46.asp (accessed November 28, 2016).
47. GARF f. 7445, op. 2, d. 373, ll. 1–15, 86, 87, 94–97.
48. Russian State Archive of Socio-Political History (RGASPI) f. 17, op. 125, d. 410, l. 156; GARF f. 8131, op. 37, d. 2826, ll. 28, 74, 90.
49. "207th Day, Tuesday, August 20, 1946," NTP, vol. 21, http://avalon.law.yale.edu/imt/08-20-46.asp (accessed November 29, 2016). Funk also returned to the stand to answer the prosecution's charges, on August 16, 1946.
50. "209th Day, Thursday, August 22, 1946," NTP, vol. 21, http://avalon.law.yale.edu/imt/08-22-46.asp (accessed November 29, 2016).

51. "208th Day, Wednesday, August 21, 1946," NTP, vol. 21, http://avalon. law.yale.edu/imt/08-21-46.asp (accessed November 29, 2016). On Nazi plundering in the Soviet Union see Anders Rydell, *The Book Thieves: The Nazi Looting of Europe's Libraries and the Race to Return a Library Inheritance*, trans. Henning Koch (New York: Penguin, 2017). Patricia Kennedy Grimsted has been researching competing Soviet and Nazi claims about the destruction of churches.

52. "209th Day, Thursday, August 22, 1946"; "210th Day, Friday, August 23, 1946, NTP, vol. 21, http://avalon.law.yale.edu/imt/08-23-46.asp (accessed November 29, 2016).

53. "211th Day, Monday, August 26, 1946," NTP, vol. 21, http://avalon. law.yale.edu/imt/08-26-46.asp (accessed November 29, 2016); G. N. Aleksandrov, *Niurnberg vchera i segodnia* (Moscow: Izdatel'stvo politicheskoi literatury, 1971), 103–112.

54. "211th Day, Monday, August 26, 1946."

55. Ibid.

56. GARF f. 7445, op. 2, d. 373, ll. 81–83.

57. "Genocide," *New York Times*, August 26, 1946, 17.

58. GARF f. 7445, op. 2, d. 373, ll. 88–90.

59. "211th Day, Monday, August 26, 1946."

60. "213th Day, Wednesday, August 28, 1946," NTP, vol. 22, http://avalon.law. yale.edu/imt/08-28-46.asp (accessed November 28, 2016).

61. Ibid.; "214th Day, Thursday, August 29, 1946," NTP, vol. 22, http://avalon. law.yale.edu/imt/08-29-46.asp (accessed November 28, 2016).

62. "214th Day, Thursday, August 29, 1946."

63. "215th Day, Friday, August 30, 1946," NTP, vol. 22, http://avalon.law.yale. edu/imt/08-30-46.asp (accessed November 29, 2016).

64. Ibid.

65. Ibid.

66. I am grateful to Paula Chan for pointing me to the historical exchange rate information. Central Bank of Russia: Tsentral'nyi bank Rossisskoi Federatsii, "Dollar SShA," Kursy valiut za period do 01.07.1992, http://cbr.ru/Content/ Document/File/41420/USD.xls (accessed August 7, 2019). That is the equivalent of approximately $1.7 trillion today.

67. "215th Day, Friday, August 30, 1946."

68. Boris Polevoi, *The Final Reckoning: Nuremberg Diaries* (Moscow: Progress Publishers, 1978), 306.

69. "216th Day, Saturday, August 31, 1946, NTP, vol. 22, http://avalon.law.yale. edu/imt/08-31-46.asp (accessed November 29, 2016).

70. Ibid.

71. Ibid.

72. Dodd, *Letters from Nuremberg*, 349–350.

Chapter 14

1. Airey Neave, *On Trial at Nuremberg* (Boston: Little, Brown, 1978), 306–308; Telford Taylor, *The Anatomy of the Nuremberg Trials* (Boston: Knopf, 1992), 549. For Soviet communications with Moscow about some of these deliberations see Archive of the Foreign Policy of the Russian Federation (AVPRF) f. 082, op. 12, p. 178, d. 5, ll. 105–107; f. 07, op. 13, p. 41, d. 8, ll. 110–112.

2. Francis Biddle, *In Brief Authority* (New York: Doubleday, 1962), 464–465; Bradley F. Smith, *Reaching Judgment at Nuremberg: The Untold Story of How the Nazi War Criminals Were Judged* (New York: Basic Books, 1977), 118.

3. Some twenty meetings were held between June 27 and September 17. Syracuse University Special Collections Research Center, Francis Biddle Collection (FBC) b. 14, "First Meeting to Discuss the Opinion," June 27, 1946, 1–3. Also Smith, *Reaching Judgment at Nuremberg*, 121–123.

4. State Archive of the Russian Federation (GARF) f. 9492, op. 1a, d. 468, ll. 109–119, 212, in *SSSR i Niurnbergskii protsess. Neizvestnye i maloizvestnye stranitsy istorii: Dokumenty*, ed. N. S. Lebedeva (Moscow: MFD, 2012), 482.

5. FBC b. 14, "Second Meeting re Draft of Opinion," July 11, 1946, 4.

6. FBC b. 14, "Third Conference of Opinion," July 17, 1946, 5–7.

7. FBC b. 14, "Conference," August 8, 1946, 10–11.

8. Smith, *Reaching Judgment at Nuremberg*, 148.

9. FBC b. 14, "Memorandum of Soviet Member IMT," July 17, 1946; Smith, *Reaching Judgment at Nuremberg*, 128; Ann Tusa and John Tusa, *The Nuremberg Trial* (London: Atheneum, 1983), 448.

10. FBC b. 14, "Memorandum of Soviet Member [I. T. Nikitchenko] of International Military Tribunal," August 14, 1946.

11. FBC b. 14, "Session on Opinion—Conspiracy," August 14, 1946, 12–16.

12. FBC b. 14, "Session on Opinion—Conspiracy," August 15, 1946, 17–18.

13. FBC b. 14, "Meeting on Opinion," August 19, 1946, 19–20.

14. It is not clear when exactly this decision was made.

15. Kim Christian Priemel, *The Betrayal: The Nuremberg Trials and German Divergence* (Oxford: Oxford University Press, 2016), 143.

16. FBC b. 14, "Meeting on Defendants," September 2, 1946, 21–25; Taylor, *Anatomy of the Nuremberg Trials*, 559; Smith, *Reaching Judgment at Nuremberg*, 130–135. Biddle received assistance from Herbert Wechsler.

17. FBC b. 14, "Meeting on Organizations," September 3, 1946, 21–25; Tusa and Tusa, *Nuremberg Trial*, 451–452; Biddle, *In Brief Authority*, 469.

18. H. Montgomery Hyde, *Norman Birkett* (London: Hamish Hamilton, 1964), 523–524; Joseph E. Persico, *Nuremberg: Infamy on Trial* (New York: Penguin Books, 1994), 383.

19. FBC b. 14, "Meeting on Organizations," September 4, 1946, 29–30.

20. FBC b. 14, "Conference on Judgment," September 7, 1946, 37; Smith, *Reaching Judgment at Nuremberg*, 148.

21. FBC b. 14, "Meeting," September 6, 1946, and "Conference on Judgment," September 7, 1946, 32–37.

22. FBC b. 14, "Meeting," September 9, 1946, 38, 43.

23. Ibid., 38–41; FBC b. 14, "Final Vote on Individuals," September 10, 1946, 44–45.

24. FBC b. 14, "Final Vote on Individuals," September 10, 1946, 47; Taylor, *Anatomy of the Nuremberg Trials*, 560; Tusa and Tusa, *Nuremberg Trial*, 460–461.

25. FBC b. 14, "Final Vote on Individuals," September 10, 1946, and September 11, 1946, 50–52. Also Smith, *Reaching Judgment at Nuremberg*, 218–223; Persico, *Nuremberg*, 391; Biddle, *In Brief Authority*, 443.

26. FBC b. 14, "Final Vote on Individuals," September 12, 1946, and September 13, 1946, 54–59.

27. FBC, b. 14, "Organizations," September 13, 1946, 59–63; Tusa and Tusa, *Nuremberg Trial*, 451–452.

28. FBC b. 14, "Final Vote on Individuals," September 17, 1946, 65.

29. GARF f. 8131, op. 37, d. 2196, ll. 219–223.

30. AVPRF f. 012, op. 7, p. 107, d. 186, ll. 10–19.

31. Ibid.

32. Ibid.

33. Ibid.

34. Ibid.

35. Ibid.

36. AVPRF f. 07, op. 13, p. 41, d. 9, l. 139.

37. The Tribunal would consider the Gestapo and the SD as one organization in its ruling in keeping with the Indictment.

38. Taylor, *Anatomy of the Nuremberg Trials*, 558–559; Smith, *Reaching Judgment at Nuremberg*, 165–169; Neave, *On Trial at Nuremberg*, 308–309.

39. Cold War tensions were high behind the scenes, too: on September 27, the Soviet ambassador to the United States, Nikolai Novikov, sent a telegram to Stalin warning of the American will "to establish world dominance." "Telegram from Nikolai Novikov, Soviet Ambassador to the US, to the Soviet Leadership," September 27, 1946, Cold War International History Project, Wilson Center Digital Archive, http://digitalarchive.wilsoncenter.org/document/110808 (accessed September 28, 2018).

40. "Judgment at Nuremberg Delivery Today. Unanimity of Decision," *Times* (London), September 30, 1946, 4. Also Tusa and Tusa, *Nuremberg Trial*, 465–466.

41. Neave, *On Trial at Nuremberg*, 308–309.

42. Joseph W. Grigg, "Nuremberg Isolated and Tense on Eve of War Trial Verdict," United Press International, September 29, 1946; Lara Feigel,

The Bitter Taste of Victory: Life, Love and Art in the Ruins of the Reich (London: Bloomsbury, 2016), 201–202; Persico, *Nuremberg*, 395.

43. A. Poltorak, *The Nuremberg Epilogue* (Moscow: Progress Publishers, 1971), 458–460.

44. Boris Polevoi, *The Final Reckoning: Nuremberg Diaries* (Moscow: Progress Publishers, 1978), 311–312.

45. Taylor, *Anatomy of the Nuremberg Trials*, 574.

46. On rumors about acquittals see Priemel, *Betrayal*, 142.

47. Persico, *Nuremberg*, 395; Hyde, *Norman Birkett*, 524–524; Grigg, "Nuremberg Isolated and Tense on Eve of War Trial Verdict."

48. For a sense of the late-stage communications see AVPRF f. 07, op. 7, p. 107, d. 186, l. 10, in Lebedeva, *SSSR i Niurnbergskii protsess*, 505 n. 1.

49. Polevoi, *Final Reckoning*, 312; Poltorak, *Nuremberg Epilogue*, 459.

50. "217th Day, Monday, September 30, 1946," Nuremberg Trial Proceedings (NTP), vol. 22, Avalon Project at Yale University Law School, http://avalon.law.yale.edu/imt/09-30-46.asp (accessed September 24, 2018).

51. Ibid.

52. Ibid.

53. Ibid. On the change of mood in the courtroom see Taylor, *Anatomy of the Nuremberg Trials*, 575.

54. "217th Day, Monday, September 30, 1946."

55. Ibid.

56. Persico, *Nuremberg*, 396.

57. "217th Day, Monday, September 30, 1946."

58. Ibid.

59. Polevoi, *Final Reckoning*, 312.

60. AVPRF f. 012, op. 7, p. 107, d. 186, l. 21.

61. Poltorak, *Nuremberg Epilogue*, 459–460. Also film footage of the trial, "Nuremberg Day 218 Judgments," posted by the Robert H. Jackson Center to YouTube, https://www.youtube.com/watch?v=8MGZoipBcW0 (accessed September 24, 2018).

62. "218th Day, Tuesday, October 1, 1946," NTP, vol. 22, http://avalon.law.yale.edu/imt/10-01-46.asp (accessed September 25, 2018).

63. Ibid.

64. Ibid.

65. Ibid.

66. Poltorak, *Nuremberg Epilogue*, 460.

67. "218th Day, Tuesday, October 1, 1946."

68. Ibid.

69. Ibid.

70. Smith, *Reaching Judgment at Nuremberg*, 13–19.

71. Poltorak, *Nuremberg Epilogue*, 462.

72. Polevoi, *Final Reckoning*, 313–314.

73. Poltorak, *Nuremberg Epilogue*, 463; Feigel, *Bitter Taste of Victory*, 203.

74. Poltorak, *Nuremberg Epilogue*, 464–465; Polevoi, *Final Reckoning*, 314–315; "218th Day, Tuesday, October 1, 1946." The Soviets saw death by hanging (as opposed to death by firing squad) as the most appropriate punishment for war criminals.

75. "218th Day, Tuesday, October 1, 1946"; "Judgment: Dissenting Opinion," NTP, http://avalon.law.yale.edu/imt/juddiss.asp (accessed February 9, 2017).

76. Neave, *On Trial at Nuremberg*, 311; Burton C. Andrus, *I Was the Nuremberg Jailer* (New York: Coward-McCann, 1969), 178.

77. AVPRF f. 012, op. 7, p. 106, d. 178, l. 49, in *SSSR i germanskii vopros, 1941–1949: Dokumenty iz Arkhiva vneshnei politiki Rossiiskoi Federatsii*, ed. Georgii P. Kynin and Jochen Laufer, vol. 2 (Moscow: Mezhdunarodnye otnosheniia, 2000), 712–713.

78. Poltorak, *Nuremberg Epilogue*, 462–463.

79. National Archives and Records Administration—College Park (NARA) RG 260, AG 000.5, b. 3, f. 1, "OMGUS Outgoing Message from Clay to AGWAR," October 7, 1946.

80. Ibid. The international press similarly noted the combination of actual indignation and playing the situation for political advantage. See for example "Nuremberg Acquittals," *Spectator*, October 11, 1946, 2, http://archive.spectator.co.uk/article/11th-october-1946/2/the-nuremberg-acquittals (accessed August 10, 2019).

81. Russian State Archive of Socio-Political History (RGASPI) f. 17, op. 125, d. 410, ll. 161–162; AVPRF f. 082, op. 12, p. 178, d. 5, ll. 105–107.

82. Poltorak, *Nuremberg Epilogue*, 467.

83. NARA RG 260, AG 000.5, b. 3, f. 1, "OMGUS Outgoing Message from Clay," October 9, 1946.

84. Polevoi, *Final Reckoning*, 317–318. Viktor Temin's account of these events is quoted from at length in Polevoi, *Final Reckoning*, 318–320.

85. Ibid., 319; Poltorak, *Nuremberg Epilogue*, 467–468. Poltorak recounts a conversation he had with Afanasyev about these events. Also Kingsbury Smith, "The Execution of Nazi War Criminals," International News Service, October 16, 1946.

86. Poltorak, *Nuremberg Epilogue*, 468; Russian State Archive of Literature and Art (RGALI) f. 2989, op. 1, d. 190, ll. 19–20.

87. Polevoi, *Final Reckoning*, 319–321; Andrus, *I Was the Nuremberg Jailer*, 194–195.

88. Polevoi, *Final Reckoning*, 319–321. In 2005, a U.S. guard confessed to having smuggled a vial of liquid into Goering's cell. He said it had been hidden in a fountain pen. "U.S. Guard Tells How Nazi Girlfriend Duped Him into Helping Goering Evade Hangman," *Guardian*, February 8, 2005, https://www.theguardian.com/world/2005/feb/08/usa.secondworldwar (accessed July 24, 2019). Law professor Donald E. Wilkes Jr. has argued

that some of the executions were botched—that some of the defendants
fell from the gallows without enough force to break their necks. See Tom
Zeller Jr., "The Nuremberg Hangings—Not So Smooth Either," *New York
Times Blog, The Lede,* January 17, 2007, https://thelede.blogs.nytimes.com/
2007/01/17/the-nuremburg-hangings-not-so-smooth-either/ (accessed July
31, 2019).

89. Richard Overy, *Interrogations: The Nazi Elite in Allied Hands, 1945*
    (New York: Penguin, 2001), 205.
90. Poltorak, *Nuremberg Epilogue*, 469; Polevoi, *Final Reckoning*, 321; GARF
    f. 7445, op. 1, d. 2850, ll. 199, 126, 203–213.
91. Tat'iana Stupnikova, *Nichego krome pravdy: Niurnbergskii protsess. Vospominaniia
    perevodchika* (Moscow: Vozvrashchenie, 2003), 190–191.
92. Polevoi, *Final Reckoning*, 321.
93. RGALI f. 1038, op. 1, d. 2135, l. 97.
94. Archive of the Russian Academy of Sciences (ARAN) f. 1781, op. 1,
    d. 1, l. 17.

Chapter 15

1. On the postwar Soviet Union see Elena Zubkova, *Russia After the War: Hopes,
   Illusions, and Disappointments, 1945–1957,* trans. Hugh Ragsdale (Armonk,
   NY: M. E. Sharpe, 1998).
2. On the "resigned, doom-laden mood" in Paris and other cities see Tony Judt,
   Postwar: A History of Europe Since 1945 (New York: Penguin, 2005), 90.
3. Winston Churchill, "Winston Churchill's Speech [on a Council of Europe],"
   Zurich, September 19, 1946, Archive of European Integration, University of
   Pittsburgh, http://aei.pitt.edu/14362/ (accessed May 21, 2019).
4. State Archive of the Russian Federation (GARF) f. 7445, op. 2, d. 8, ll.
   537–538; d. 391, ll. 66–67. Trainin attended with his colleague Mikhail
   Strogovich. Also Russian State Archive of Socio-Political History (RGASPI)
   f. 17, op. 125, d. 395, ll. 121–125, and A. N. Trainin, "Mezhdunarodnyi
   kongress iuristov," *Sovetskoe gosudarstvo i pravo,* no. 11–12 (1946): 53–54.
   They did not address the acquittal of Hans Fritzsche, likely seeing it as a
   lost cause.
5. RGASPI f. 17, op. 125, d. 395, ll. 121–125; A. N. Trainin,
   "Mezhdunarodnyi kongress iuristov"; "War-Crimes Code Urged: Jurists at
   Paris Parley Seek to Punish Nazi Sponsors," *New York Times,* October 26,
   1946, 5; Vladimir Kabes and Alfons Sergot, *Blueprint of Deception: Character
   and Record of the International Association of Democratic Lawyers* (The
   Hague: Mouton, 1957), 15–29. Cassin was president; Trainin was among the
   six vice presidents.
6. Library of Congress, Manuscript Division, Robert H. Jackson Collection
   (LOC-RHJ) b. 108, f. 7, "Memorandum to Jackson from Taylor," October
   30, 1946. On the role of Nazi doctors in carrying out genocide see Robert

Jay Lifton, *The Nazi Doctors: Medical Killing and the Psychology of Genocide* (New York: Basic Books, 2017). The term "euthanasia" was, of course, a euphemism.

7. Mark Lewis, *The Birth of the New Justice: The Internationalization of Crime and Punishment, 1919–1950* (Oxford: Oxford University Press, 2014), 200.

8. UN document A/Res/95(1), "Affirmation of the Principles of International Law recognized by the Charter of the Nürnberg Tribunal," December 11, 1946.

9. William A. Schabas, "Origins of the Genocide Convention: From Nuremberg to Paris," *Case Western Reserve Journal of International Law* 35 (2008): 35–55.

10. "Law on Genocide Put to Assembly: Briton Asks That Entire U.N. Outlaw Group Murder by Individuals and States," *New York Times*, November 23, 1946, 7.

11. LOC-RHJ b. 118, f. 7, UNWCC, "Establishment of an International Association of Democratic Lawyers and Resolutions," November 8, 1946.

12. LOC-RHJ b. 118, f. 7, UNWCC, Egon Schwelb, "The Bearing of the Nuremberg Judgment on the Interpretation of the Term 'Crimes against Humanity,'" November 11, 1946. The UNWCC continued to function until March 1948.

13. Harry S. Truman Presidential Library and Museum (HSTPLM), Harry S. Truman Papers, Official File (OF) 325b: IMT—Nuremberg, "Correspondence between Harry S. Truman and Francis Biddle," November 12, 1946, 1–16.

14. Ibid.; Francis Biddle, *In Brief Authority* (New York: Doubleday, 1962), 477–478.

15. HSTPLM, Truman Papers, OF 325b: IMT—Nuremberg, "Press Release of Correspondence between Harry S. Truman and Francis Biddle, November 12, 1946, 1–4. Also "Text of Biddle's Report on Nuremberg and Truman's Reply," *New York Times*, November 13, 1946, 14.

16. LOC-RHJ b. 112, f. 4, "Memorandum: Codification of the Principles of International Law of the Nürnberg Charter and Judgment," September 12, 1947; "U.S. For Nuremberg Code," *New York Times*, November 16, 1946, 6.

17. "The Law against War," *New York Times*, November 14, 1946, 28.

18. LOC-RHJ b. 108, f. 7, Robert H. Jackson to James F. Byrnes and Warren Austin, November 16, 1946.

19. Archive of the Foreign Policy of the Russian Federation (AVPRF) f. 082, op. 12, p. 178, d. 5, ll. 134–136.

20. Archive of the Russian Academy of Sciences (ARAN) f. 499, op. 1, d. 71, ll. 74–99. The Soviet criminal code project indeed got off the ground—but was later dropped.

21. E. A. Korovin, *Mezhdunarodnoe pravo na sovremennom etape: Stenogramma publichnoi lektsii* (Moscow: Pravda, 1946).

22. GARF f. 8131, op. 37, d. 2196, ll. 304–307.

23. GARF f. 8131, op. 37, d. 3420, ll. 2–6.

24. Ibid.

25. UN document A/Res/95(1), "Affirmation of the Principles of International Law recognized by the Charter of the Nürnberg Tribunal," December 11, 1946. The Belorussian SSR and Ukrainian SSR had their own seats even though they were part of the Soviet Union.

26. UN document A/Res/96(1), "The Crime of Genocide," December 11, 1946. Also Douglas Irvin-Erickson, *Raphael Lemkin and the Concept of Genocide* (Philadelphia: University of Pennsylvania Press, 2017), and Anton Weiss-Wendt, *The Soviet Union and the Gutting of the UN Genocide Convention* (Madison: University of Wisconsin Press, 2017).

27. GARF f. 8581, op. 1, d. 178, ll. 13–24.

28. Mary Ann Glendon, *A World Made New: Eleanor Roosevelt and the Universal Declaration of Human Rights* (New York: Random House, 2001), 40–49. Glendon worked with files from AVPRF.

29. John Lewis Gaddis, *Russia, the Soviet Union, and the United States* (New York: McGraw-Hill, 1990), 181–191.

30. Peter Maguire, *Law and War: International Law and American History*, rev. ed. (New York: Columbia University Press, 2010), chap. 4. In April 1947, Schacht was tried by a German denazification court and sentenced to eight years of hard labor. His sentence was commuted soon afterward.

31. See the introductory page to the Charles Dubost archive collection. Centre d'histoire de Sciences Po, Archives d'histoire contemporaine, fonds Charles Dubost, Paris, http://chsp.sciences-po.fr/en/fond-archive/dubost-charles (accessed August 10, 2019). The Tokyo War Crimes Trials, which involved eleven Allied powers but just one chief prosecutor—from the United States—would not wrap up for another year and a half.

32. Ilya V. Gaiduk, *Divided Together: The United States and the Soviet Union in the United Nations, 1945–1965* (Washington, DC: Woodrow Wilson Center Press, 2013).

33. UN document A/AC.10/21, "Memorandum Submitted by the Delegate of France, Draft Proposal for the Establishment of an International Court of Criminal Jurisdiction," May 13, 1947; UN document A/AC.10/34, "Commission for the Study of the Progressive Development of International Law and Its Codification: Memorandum by the Delegate for France," May 27, 1947; UN document A/CN.4/5, *The Charter and Judgment of the Nürnberg Tribunal: History and Analysis* (*Memorandum Submitted by the Secretary-General*) (Lake Success, NY: United Nations, 1949), 23–25. Also Laurent Barcelo, "Aux origines de la cour pénale internationale: Le projet français de chambre criminelle internationale (hiver 1946–printemps 1947)," *Guerres mondiales et conflits contemporains* 2, no. 2 (2006): 103–109.

34. On the first point see Lewis, *Birth of the New Justice*, 199–201.

35. *The Charter and Judgment of the Nürnberg Tribunal*, 15–30; Yuen-Li Liang, "The General Assembly and the Progressive Development and Codification of International Law," *American Journal of International Law* 42, no. 1 (1948): 66–97.

36. UN document A/332, "Plans for the Formulation of the Principles of the Nürnberg Charter and Judgment: Report of the Committee on the Progressive Development of International Law and Its Codification," July 21, 1947; UN document A/CN.4/7Rev.1, *Historical Survey of the Question of International Criminal Jurisdiction (Memorandum Submitted by the Secretary-General)* (Lake Success, NY: 1949).

37. Glendon, *World Made New*, 58–72.

38. It also conferred with the Romanian jurist Vespasian Pella. UN document E447, Economic and Social Council, "Draft Convention on the Crime of Genocide," June 26, 1947. Also David L. Nersessian, *Genocide and Political Groups* (Oxford: Oxford University Press, 2010), 76–90.

39. A. Trainin, "Vtoroi Mezhdunarodnyi kongress iuristov-demokratov," *Sovetskoe gosudarstvo i pravo*, no. 9 (1947): 62–67; Kabes and Sergot, *Blueprint of Deception*, 32–42. The participants called this the second IADL Congress (calling the 1946 Congress of Jurists the first).

40. Kabes and Sergot, *Blueprint of Deception*, 41–42.

41. Glendon, *World Made New*, 93–97.

42. "Ukraine Groups Urge U.N. Check on Soviet," *New York Times*, November 19, 1947, 18; "Genocide Survey Urged: Ukrainian Group Here Asks U.N. to Make Inquiry in Europe," *New York Times*, November 23, 1947, 21; "Appeal from Lithuania," *New York Times*, November 22, 1947, C14; "Lay Genocide to Soviet: Three Baltic Exiles Accuse Russia in Appeal to U.N.," *New York Times*, November 25, 1947, 11. Also Weiss-Wendt, *The Soviet Union and the Gutting of the UN Genocide Convention,* 58–59.

43. See for example Rain Liivoja, "Competing Histories: Soviet War Crimes in the Baltic States," in *The Hidden Histories of War Crimes Trials,* ed. Kevin Heller and Gerry Simpson (Oxford: Oxford University Press, 2013), 248–266.

44. From Weiss-Wendt, *The Soviet Union and the Gutting of the UN Genocide Convention,* 61–62. *Nazi Soviet Relations 1939–1941: Documents from the Archives of the German Foreign Office,* ed. Raymond James Sontag and James Stuart Beddle (Washington, DC: Department of State, 1948).

45. Soviet Information Bureau, *Falsifiers of History (An Historical Note)* (Moscow: Soviet Information Bureau, 1948); E. A. Korovin, "Vazhnyi istoricheskii dokument (Po povody spravki Sovinformbiuro 'Fal'sifikatory istorii')," *Sovetskoe gosudarstvo i pravo*, no. 4 (1948): 1–7.

46. National Archives and Records Administration—College Park (NARA) RG 59, entry 1238, b. 43, "Position on Genocide Convention Prepared by

the Ad Hoc Committee on Genocide." Also UN document AC.6/SR.74, "74th Meeting," October 14, 1948, in *The Genocide Convention: The Travaux Préparatoires*, ed. Hirad Abtahi and Philippa Webb, vol. 2 (Leiden: Brill, 2008), 1401.

47. The Ukrainian, Belorussian, and Yugoslav representatives joined Pavlov in abstaining from the vote. Glendon, *World Made New*, 110–121. On the Sixth Committee's discussion about the genocide convention see Weiss-Wendt, *The Soviet Union and the Gutting of the Genocide Convention*, chap. 6.

48. A. N. Trainin, *Bor'ba progressivnykh sil protiv unichtozheniia natsional'nykh grupp i ras: Stenogramma publichnoi lektsii* (Moscow: Pravda, 1948). Also A. N. Trainin, "Bor'ba s genotsidom kak mezhdunarodnym prestupleniem," *Sovetskoe gosudarstvo i pravo*, no. 5 (1948): 1–16.

49. Kabes and Sergot, *Blueprint of Deception*, 46–65; Trainin, "Tretii Mezhdunarodnyi kongress iuristov-demokratov," *Sovetskoe gosudarstvo i pravo*, no. 11 (1948): 55–60.

50. Ibid.; "Lawyers Take Red Line: 16 Nation Group, Meeting in Prague, Attacks 'Warmongers,'" *New York Times*, September 12, 1948, 30.

51. UN document A/PV.143, "143rd Plenary Meeting," September 25, 1948, Official Records of the Third Session of the General Assembly, 118–136.

52. "United States Delegation Position Paper," December 6, 1948, *Foreign Relations of the United States*, 1948, General, The United States, vol. 1, part 1, https://history.state.gov/historicaldocuments/frus1948v01p1/d186; UN document A/RES/260(III), "Convention on the Prevention and Punishment of the Crime of Genocide," December 9, 1948, United Nations Human Rights Office of the High Commissioner, http://www.ohchr.org/EN/ProfessionalInterest/Pages/CrimeOfGenocide.aspx. It entered into international law on January 9, 1951.

53. UN document A/PV.180, "180th Plenary Meeting," December 9, 1948, Official Records of the Third Session of the General Assembly, 854–857. It passed by a vote of forty-eight to zero.

54. On the anticosmopolitan campaign, see Konstantin Azadovskii and Boris Egorov, "From Anti-Westernism to Anti-Semitism," *Journal of Cold War Studies* 4, no. 1 (2002): 66–80.

55. On the fate of Solomon Lozovsky and the Jewish Anti-Fascist Committee, see *Stalin's Secret Pogrom: The Postwar Inquisition of the Jewish Anti-Fascist Committee*, abr. ed., ed. Joshua Rubenstein and Vladimir P. Naumov (New Haven: Yale University Press, 2005), 177-232.

56. Mira Traynina, "A. N. Traynin: A Legal Scholar under Tsar and Soviets," *Soviet Jewish Affairs* 13, no. 3 (1983), 51–52; Mira Trainina and Grigorii Kravchik, "The 'Lawyers' Plot': An Unknown Chapter of Stalin's Last Repressions," *Soviet Union/Union Sovietique* 13, no. 2 (1986): 217–233. Mira Trainina (sometimes spelled Traynina) was Aron Trainin's daughter.

57. "Agenda of the First Session," in *Yearbook of the International Law Commission 1949* (New York: United Nations, 1956), vi.

58. Weiss-Wendt, *The Soviet Union and the Gutting of the UN Genocide Convention*, 46.

59. On Nikitchenko see James Heinzen, *The Art of the Bribe: Corruption Under Stalin, 1943–1953* (New Haven: Yale University Press, 2016), 220, 350 n. 61. In June 1949 Nikitchenko was removed from his position on the Supreme Court but was not arrested.

60. Weiss-Wendt, *The Soviet Union and the Gutting of the UN Genocide Convention*, 46.

61. "1st Meeting of the ILC" and "2nd Meeting of the ILC," April 12 and 13, 1949, in *Yearbook of the International Law Commission 1949*, 9–22.

62. "4th Meeting of the ILC," "5th Meeting of the ILC," "6th Meeting of the ILC," and "7th Meeting of the ILC," April 18, 19, 20, and 21, 1949, in *Yearbook of the International Law Commission 1949*, 32–62.

63. "17th Meeting of the ILC," "26th Meeting of the ILC," and "29th Meeting of the ILC," May 9, 24, and 27, 1949, in *Yearbook of the International Law Commission 1949*, 129–134, 192–199, 206–212.

64. "30th Meeting of the ILC," May 31, 1949, in *Yearbook of the International Law Commission 1949*, 214–221.

65. Kabes and Sergot, *Blueprint of Deception*, 78–91.

66. David Patrick Maxwell Fyfe, *Political Adventure: The Memoirs of the Earl of Kilmuir* (London: Weidenfeld and Nicolson, 1964), 174–189.

67. Kabes and Sergot, *Blueprint of Deception*, 74–75, and E. A. Korovin, "Za sovetskuiu patrioticheskuiu nauku prava," *Sovetskoe gosudarstvo i pravo*, no. 7 (1949): 6–12.

68. For example A. Trainin, "Mezhdunarodnye otnosheniia. Zhizn' za rubezhom. Za delo mira!" (Knizhnoe obozrenie), *Novyi mir* 26, no. 10 (October 1950): 264–265.

69. For example I. T. Goliakov, "Iosif Vissarionovich Stalin i sotsialisticheskoe pravosudie," *Sovetskoe gosudarstvo i pravo*, no. 1 (1950): 1–19.

70. "39th Meeting of the ILC," June 5, 1950, in *Yearbook of the International Law Commission 1950*, vol. 1 (New York: United Nations, 1957), 1–2.

71. UN document A/1316, "Report of the International Law Commission to the General Assembly," July 1950, pts. 4–5, in *Yearbook of the International Law Commission 1950*, vol. 2 (New York: United Nations, 1957), 374–379. Because the General Assembly had already affirmed the Nuremberg principles in December 1946, the International Law Commission's role had been simply to formulate them.

72. Ibid.; "Formulation of the Nürnberg Principles," in *Yearbook of the United Nations 1950* (New York: United Nations and Columbia University Press, 1951), 852–862.

73. Kabes and Sergot, *Blueprint of Deception*, 134–154; "The Soviet Peace Campaign," *Australian Quarterly* 24, no. 2 (June 1952): 16–20.

74. ARAN f. 499, op. 1, d. 502, ll. 1–4; A. Trainin, "Mezhdunarodnoe pravo ob agressii," *Izvestiia*, August 15, 1950, 3. Also Michelle Penn, "The Extermination of Peaceful Soviet Citizens: Aron Trainin and International Law" (PhD diss., University of Colorado at Boulder, 2017), 209–212.

75. NARA RG 84, entry 1030D, b. 68, "Soviet Offenses against Charter Principles and Responsibilities," n.d., and "Soviet Tactics in the General Assembly," September 15, 1950.

76. LOC-RHJ b. 112, f. 4, "The Crime of Aggression," *Evening Star*, July 7, 1951.

77. William E. Butler, introduction to Grigory Ivanovich Tunkin, *Theory of International Law* (Cambridge, MA: Harvard University Press, 1974), xix. Also Tarja Langstrom, *Transformation in Russia and International Law* (Leiden: Martinus Nijhoff, 2003), 85–87.

78. RGASPI f. 17, op. 133, d. 287, ll. 28, 29, 54–58, 113–116; Trainina and Kravchik, "The 'Lawyers' Plot,'" 221–223; "Preodolet' otstavanie pravovoi nauki," *Izvestiia,* January 23, 1953, 2–3; Penn, "Extermination of Peaceful Soviet Citizens," 213–216.

79. Jonathan Brent, "Doctors' Plot," in *The YIVO Encyclopedia of Jews in Eastern Europe*, http://www.yivoencyclopedia.org/article.aspx/Doctors_Plot (accessed December 3, 2018). The year 1952 also brought a major show trial of Jewish communists in Czechoslovakia (the Slansky Trial), which was modeled on the Moscow Trials of 1936–1938.

80. NARA RG 84, entry 1030D, b. 89, "Secret Security Information, Memorandum by Thomas J. Cory on New Soviet Tactic of Conciliation and Moderation in the General Assembly and What May Be Done to Counter It," November 4, 1952, and "Secret Security Information, Memorandum by Thomas J. Cory, Some Personal Observations on Soviet Performance in the United Nations and What We Might Do to Make It Worse," January 29, 1953.

81. UN document A/CN.4/44, "Draft Code of Offenses against the Peace and Security of Mankind," in *Yearbook of the International Law Commission 1951*, vol. 2 (New York: United Nations 1957), 43–69. Also NARA RG 59, entry 1238, b. 34, SD/A/C.6/127, "State Department, Confidential Position Paper, Draft Declaration of the Rights and Duties of States," October 19, 1951; SD/A/C.6/134, "State Department, Analysis of Resolution 559 (VI) of January 31, 1952"; and SD/A/C.6/138, "State Department, Confidential Position Paper, Draft Code of Offenses against the Peace and Security of Mankind," October 8, 1952.

82. NARA RG 59, entry 1238, box 34, SD/A/C.6/121, "State Department, Position Paper, Definition of Aggression: Report of the International Law

Commission," October 11, 1951" and "Annex A—History of Definition of
Aggression."

83. Trainina and Kravchik, "The 'Lawyers' Plot,'" 230–231.
84. Ibid.; Arkady Vaksberg, *Stalin's Prosecutor: The Life of Andrei Vyshinsky*, trans. Jan Butler (New York: Grove Weidenfeld, 1991), 309–310.
85. A. Trainin, "Desiat' let spustiia," *Pravda*, October 3, 1956, 3.
86. Weiss-Wendt, *The Soviet Union and the Gutting of the Genocide Convention*; Samantha Power, *"A Problem from Hell": America and the Age of Genocide* (New York: Basic Books, 2002).
87. Rudenko assumed this post after Stalin's death in 1953. "1960: Moscow Jails American U-2 Spy Pilot," BBC News, *On This Day,* August 19, 1960, http://news.bbc.co.uk/onthisday/hi/dates/stories/august/19/newsid_2962000/2962600.stm (accessed December 3, 2018).
88. For examples see Mary Dudziak, *Cold War Civil Rights: Race and the Image of American Democracy* (Princeton: Princeton University Press, 1994), and Benjamin Nathans, "Soviet Rights-Talk in the Post-Stalin Era," in *Human Rights in the Twentieth Century,* ed. Stefan-Ludwig Hoffmann (Cambridge: Cambridge University Press, 2011), 166–190.

BIBLIOGRAPHICAL ESSAY

The vast English-language literature on the Nuremberg Trials provided a critical starting point for this book. Some of the best secondary works are Robert E. Conot, *Justice at Nuremberg* (New York: Harper and Row, 1983); Ann Tusa and John Tusa, *The Nuremberg Trial* (London: Macmillan, 1983); and Bradley F. Smith, *Reaching Judgment at Nuremberg* (New York: Basic Books, 1977). Joseph E. Persico, *Nuremberg: Infamy on Trial* (New York: Penguin, 1994), and Whitney R. Harris, *Tyranny on Trial: The Evidence at Nuremberg* (Dallas: Southern Methodist University Press, 1954) are also important contributions.

For a more recent treatment of the American experience of Nuremberg, see Elizabeth Borgwardt, "Re-examining Nuremberg as a New Deal Institution: Politics, Culture and the Limits of Law in Generating Human Rights Law," *Berkeley Journal of International Law* 23, no. 2 (2005): 401–462. For an excellent new history of Nuremberg based on American, British, and French sources, see Kim Christian Priemel, *The Betrayal: The Nuremberg Trials and German Divergence* (Oxford: Oxford University Press, 2016). On the French role in the trials see Antonin Tisseron, *La France et le procès de Nuremberg: Inventer le droit international* (Paris: Les Prairies ordinaires, 2014). For a riveting account of Nuremberg and postwar Germany as seen through the eyes of British and American writers see Lara Feigel, *The Bitter Taste of Victory: Life, Love and Art in the Ruins of the Reich* (London: Bloomsbury, 2016). The best book on the negotiations leading up to Nuremberg is Arieh J. Kochavi, *Prelude to Nuremberg: Allied War Crimes Policy and the Question of Punishment* (Chapel Hill: University of North Carolina Press, 1998).

For thoughtful critiques of Nuremberg and its legacy see Judith N. Shklar, *Legalism: Law, Morals, and Political Trials* (Cambridge, MA: Harvard University Press, 1986); Donald Bloxham, *Genocide on Trial: War Crimes Trials and the Formation of Holocaust History and Memory* (Oxford: Oxford University Press, 2001); and Danilo

Zolo, *Victors' Justice: From Nuremberg to Baghdad*, trans. M. W. Weir (London: Verso, 2009). In some accounts, Soviet participation is held up as Nuremberg's main flaw. See for example Gary Jonathan Bass, *Stay the Hand of Vengeance: The Politics of War Crimes Tribunals* (Princeton: Princeton University Press, 2000).

For more on the defendants and their witnesses see Norman J. W. Goda, *Tales from Spandau: Nazi Criminals and the Cold War* (New York: Cambridge University Press, 2007), and Leon Goldensohn, *The Nuremberg Interviews: An American Psychiatrist's Conversations with the Defendants and Witnesses* (New York: Vintage Books, 2005). Also see Christiane Kohl, *The Witness House: Nazis and Holocaust Survivors Sharing a Villa during the Nuremberg Trials*, trans. Anthea Bell (New York: Other Press, 2010).

American and British participants in the Nuremberg Trials have written a number of engaging memoirs about their experiences. See in particular Telford Taylor, *The Anatomy of the Nuremberg Trials: A Personal Memoir* (New York: Knopf, 1992); G. M. Gilbert, *Nuremberg Diary* (New York: Farrar, Straus, 1947); Airey Neave, *On Trial at Nuremberg* (Boston: Little, Brown, 1979); Francis Biddle, *In Brief Authority* (Garden City, NY; Doubleday, 1962); and David Patrick Maxwell Fyfe, *Political Adventure: The Memoirs of the Earl of Kilmuir* (London: Weidenfeld and Nicolson, 1964). Also see Rebecca West, *A Train of Powder* (New York: Viking Press, 1955). Letters home by U.S. assistant prosecutor Thomas Dodd have been published in Christopher J. Dodd with Lary Bloom, *Letters from Nuremberg: My Father's Narrative of a Quest for Justice* (New York: Three Rivers Press, 2007). For a fascinating collection of interviews with American journalists, translators, and other observer-participants see *Witnesses to Nuremberg: An Oral History of American Participants at the War Crimes Trials*, ed. Bruce M. Stave and Michele Palmer with Leslie Frank (New York: Twayne Publishers, 1998).

Two of the best English-language Soviet memoirs of Nuremberg are Boris Polevoi, *The Final Reckoning: Nuremberg Diaries*, trans. Janet Butler and Doris Bradbury (Moscow: Progress Publishers, 1978), and Arkady Poltorak, *The Nuremberg Epilogue*, trans. David Skvirsky (Moscow: Progress Publishers, 1971). Those who read Russian will also want to look at G. N. Aleksandrov, *Niurnberg vchera i segodnia* [Nuremberg Yesterday and Today] (Moscow: Izdatel'stvo politicheskoi literatury, 1971), and M. Iu. Raginskii, *Niurnberg: Pered sudom istorii* [Nuremberg: Before the Court of History] (Moscow: Izdatel'stvo politicheskoi literatury, 1986). Of special interest is Tat'iana Stupnikova, *Nichego krome pravdy: Niurnbergskii protsess. Vospominaniia perevodchika* [Nothing but the Truth: The Nuremberg Trials. The Memoirs of a Translator] (Moscow: Vozvrashchenie, 2003).

When I began research for this project, there were few scholarly books about the Soviet role in the Nuremberg Trials. Natalya Lebedeva, *Podgotovka Niurnbergskogo protsessa* [The Preparation of the Nuremberg Trials] (Moscow: Nauka, 1975) remains the best Soviet-era book on the subject. Lebedeva had been granted special, albeit restricted, access to the archives. Also see the volume of essays Lebedeva coedited in 2007: N. S. Lebedeva, V. I. Ishchenko, and I. Iu. Korshunov, eds., *Niurnbergskii protsess: Uroki istorii: Materialy mezhdunarodnoi nauchnoi konferentsii.* [The Nuremberg

Trials: Lessons of History: Proceedings from an International Conference] (Moscow: Institut vseobshchei istorii RAN, 2007). George Ginsburgs and Marina Sorokina have also done pathbreaking work on the Soviet contribution to postwar justice. See George Ginsburgs, *Moscow's Road to Nuremberg: The Soviet Background to the Trial* (The Hague: Martinus Nijhoff, 1996), and Marina Sorokina, "People and Procedures: Toward a History of the Investigation of Nazi Crimes in the USSR," *Kritika: Explorations in Russian and Eurasian History* 6, no. 4 (2005): 797–831. Also see Michael J. Bazyler, "The Role of the Soviet Union in the International Military Tribunal at Nuremberg," in *Die Nürnberger Prozesse: Völkerstrafrecht seit 1945* [The Nuremberg Trials: International Criminal Law since 1945], ed. Herbert R. Reginbogin, Christoph J. M. Safferling, and Walter R. Hippel (Munich: KG Saur, 2006), 45–52.

More recently, scholars have investigated different aspects of the Soviet role at Nuremberg in articles and book chapters. Vadim J. Birstein's discussion of Soviet counterespionage agents in Nuremberg and Jeremy Hicks's analysis of Roman Karmen's film *Sud narodov (Judgment of the Peoples)* are major contributions. See Vadim J. Birstein, *SMERSH: Stalin's Secret Weapon* (London: Biteback, 2011), and Jeremy Hicks, *First Films of the Holocaust: Soviet Cinema and the Genocide of the Jews, 1938-46* (Pittsburgh: University of Pittsburgh Press, 2012). On Soviet journalists in Nuremberg see Leonid Trofimov, "Soviet Reporters at the Nuremberg Trial: Agenda, Attitudes, and Encounters, 1945-46," *Cahiers d'histoire* 28, no. 2 (2010): 45–70.

German scholars are also revisiting the Soviet role at Nuremberg. See Irina Schulmeister-André's deeply researched *Internationale Strafgerichtsbarkeit unter sowjetischem Einfluss: Der Beitrag der UdSSR zum Nürnberger Hauptkriegsverbrecherprozess* [International Criminal Jurisdiction under Soviet Influence: The USSR's Contribution to the Nuremberg Trial of Major War Criminals] (Berlin: Duncker & Humblot, 2016). Also see Claudia Weber's reflection on Katyn, "Stalin's Trap: The Katyn Forest Massacre between Propaganda and Taboo," in *Theaters of Violence: Massacre, Mass Killing and Atrocity throughout History*, ed. Philip G. Dwyer and Lyndall Ryan (New York: Berghahn, 2012): 170–185.

Document collections about Nuremberg published by the historians Natalya Lebedeva and Aleksandr Zviagintsev will be of interest to those who read Russian. See *SSSR i Niurnbergskii protsess. Neizvestnye i maloizvestnye stranitsy istorii: Dokumenty* [The USSR and the Nuremberg Trials. An Unknown and Little-Known History: Documents], ed. N. S. Lebedeva (Moscow: Mezhdunarodnyi fond Demokratiia, 2012), and A. G. Zviagintsev, *Glavnyi protsess chelovechestva. Niurnberg: Dokumenty, issledovaniia, vospominaniia* [The Major Trial of Humanity. Nuremberg: Documents, Research, Reminiscences] (Moscow: Olma Media Grupp, 2011). These excellent collections are all the more important given that archival access in Russia has constricted in recent years. Lebedeva's coedited English-language document collection on Katyn is also an invaluable source: *Katyn: A Crime Without Punishment,* ed. Anna M. Cienciala, Natalia S. Lebedeva, and Wojciech Materski (New Haven: Yale University Press, 2007).

There are a number of useful studies on the Soviet war crimes trials that preceded Nuremberg. See for example Greg Dawson, *Judgment Before Nuremberg: The Holocaust in the Ukraine and the First Nazi War Crimes Trial* (New York: Pegasus Books, 2012); Tanja Penter, "Local Collaborators on Trial: Soviet War Crimes Trials under Stalin (1943-1953)," *Cahiers du monde russe* 49, no. 2-3 (2008): 341–364; Ilya Bourtman, " 'Blood for Blood, Death for Death,' The Soviet Military Tribunal in Krasnodar, 1943," *Holocaust and Genocide Studies* 22, no. 2 (2008): 246–265; and Alexander V. Prusin, " 'Fascist Criminals to the Gallows!': The Holocaust and Soviet War Crimes Trials, December 1945–February 1946," *Holocaust and Genocide Studies* 17, no. 1 (2003): 1–30.

In writing this book I have drawn inspiration from the flourishing new literature on the history of human rights, which looks at the interplay of politics and ideas. See for example Samuel Moyn, *The Last Utopia: Human Rights in History* (Cambridge, MA: Harvard University Press, 2010); Mark Lewis, *The Birth of the New Justice: The Internationalization of Crime and Punishment, 1919–1950* (Oxford: Oxford University Press, 2014); Mark Mazower, *No Enchanted Palace: The End of Empire and the Ideological Origins of the United Nations* (Princeton: Princeton University Press, 2009); Samantha Power, *"A Problem from Hell": America and the Age of Genocide* (New York: Basic Books, 2002); Philippe Sands, *East West Street: On the Origins of "Genocide" and "Crimes Against Humanity"* (New York: Knopf, 2016); Douglas Irvin-Erickson, *Raphael Lemkin and the Concept of Genocide* (Philadelphia: University of Pennsylvania Press, 2017); and Mary Ann Glendon, *A World Made New: Eleanor Roosevelt and the Universal Declaration of Human Rights* (New York: Random House, 2001).

The past several years have seen a surge in interest in the Soviet Union's role in the development of international law. On Aron Trainin's contribution to the dialogue about aggressive war see Kirsten Sellars, *"Crimes against Peace" and International Law* (Cambridge: Cambridge University Press, 2015). On Trainin's life and work see Michelle Jean Penn, "The Extermination of Peaceful Soviet Citizens: Aron Trainin and International Law" (PhD diss., University of Colorado at Boulder, 2017). On the Soviet role in deliberations about genocide and human rights see Anton Weiss-Wendt, *The Soviet Union and the Gutting of the UN Genocide Convention* (Madison: University of Wisconsin Press, 2017), as well as Jennifer Amos, "Embracing and Contesting: The Soviet Union and the Universal Declaration of Human Rights, 1948-1958," in *Human Rights in the Twentieth Century,* ed. Stefan-Ludwig Hoffmann (New York: Cambridge University Press, 2011), 147–165. On the politics of the United Nations see Ilya V. Gaiduk, *Divided Together: The United States and the Soviet Union in the United Nations, 1945-1965* (Washington, DC: Woodrow Wilson Center Press, 2012).

On the history of Russian and Soviet law see Peter H. Solomon Jr., *Soviet Criminal Justice under Stalin* (Cambridge: Cambridge University Press, 1996); Tarja Langstrom, *Transformation in Russia and International Law* (Leiden: Martinus Nijhoff, 2003); Lauri Mälksoo, *Russian Approaches to International Law* (Oxford: Oxford University Press, 2015); and James Heinzen, *The Art of the Bribe: Corruption under Stalin,*

1943-1953 (New Haven: Yale University Press, 2016). Those who read Russian will want to look at Aleksandr Zviagintsev's work on the Soviet legal system, particularly A. G. Zviagintsev, *Prigovorennye vremenem: Rossiiskie i sovetskie prokurory XX vek, 1937–1953* [Sentenced by Time: Russian and Soviet Prosecutors of the 20th Century, 1937-1953] (Moscow: ROSSPEN, 2001), and Aleksandr Zviagintsev and Iurii Orlov, *Prokurory dvukh epokh: Andrei Vyshinskii i Roman Rudenko* [Prosecutors of Two Eras: Andrei Vyshinsky and Roman Rudenko] (Moscow: Olma Press, 2001).

On the origins of the Soviet show trial see Elizabeth Wood, *Performing Justice: Agitation Trials in Early Soviet Russia* (Ithaca: Cornell University Press, 2005). On Andrei Vyshinsky's pivotal role at the nexus of law and diplomacy see Arkady Vaksberg, *Stalin's Prosecutor: The Life of Andrei Vyshinsky*, trans. Jan Butler (New York: Grove, 1990). Also see Donald Raysfield, *Stalin and His Hangmen: The Tyrant and Those Who Killed for Him* (New York: Random House, 2005), and O. E. Kutafin, ed., *Inkvizitor: Stalinskii prokuror Vyshinskii* [Inquisitor: Stalin's Prosecutor Vyshinsky] (Moscow: Respublika, 1992). The classic account of the Stalinist show trials remains Robert Conquest, *The Great Terror* (New York: Oxford University Press, 1990). For a new and compelling account, see Lynne Viola, *Stalinist Perpetrators on Trial: Scenes from the Great Terror in Soviet Ukraine* (New York: Oxford University Press, 2017).

There is a growing literature on the Soviet experience of the Second World War. See for example Richard Overy, *Russia's War: A History of the Soviet War Effort, 1941-1945* (New York: Penguin, 1997); Catherine Merridale, *Ivan's War: Life and Death in the Red Army, 1938-1945* (New York: Picador, 2005); Amir Weiner, *Making Sense of War: The Second World War and the Fate of the Bolshevik Revolution* (Princeton: Princeton University Press, 2002); Karel C. Berkhoff, *Motherland in Danger: Soviet Propaganda during World War II* (Cambridge, MA: Harvard University Press, 2012); and Jochen Hellbeck, ed., *Stalingrad: The City That Defeated the Third Reich*, trans. Christopher Tauchen (New York: PublicAffairs, 2015). For a gripping account of the Battle of Berlin, see Antony Beevor, *The Fall of Berlin 1945* (New York: Viking, 2002). On the Molotov-Ribbentrop Pact and Stalin's state of mind on the eve of the war see Stephen Kotkin, *Stalin: Waiting For Hitler, 1929-1941* (New York: Penguin, 2017).

On the Holocaust in the Soviet Union see David Shneer, *Through Soviet Jewish Eyes: Photography, War, and the Holocaust* (New Brunswick: Rutgers University Press, 2012), and the essays in *The Holocaust in the East: Local Perpetrators and Soviet Responses*, ed. Michael David-Fox, Peter Holquist, and Alexander M. Martin (Pittsburgh: University of Pittsburgh Press, 2014). Also see the excellent document collection edited by Joshua Rubenstein and Ilya Altman, *The Unknown Black Book: The Holocaust in German-Occupied Soviet Territories* (Bloomington: Indiana University Press, 2007). On the Soviet Union as a perpetrator of atrocities in Eastern Europe see Timothy Snyder, *Bloodlands: Europe Between Stalin and Hitler* (New York: Basic Books, 2012), and Anne Applebaum, *Iron Curtain: The Crushing of Eastern Europe* (New York: Doubleday, 2012).

There is a vast literature exploring the origins and development of the Cold War. On wartime politics and the early Cold War see S. M. Plokhy, *Yalta: The Price of Peace* (New York: Viking, 2010), and Geoffrey Roberts, *Stalin's Wars: From World War to Cold War, 1939–1953* (New Haven: Yale University Press, 2007). On the Soviet Military Administration in Germany and the politics of postwar reparations, see Norman M. Naimark, *The Russians in Germany: A History of the Soviet Zone of Occupation, 1945–1949* (Cambridge, MA: Harvard University Press, 1997), and Filip Slaveski, *The Soviet Occupation of Germany: Hunger, Mass Violence, and the Struggle for Peace, 1945–1947* (Cambridge: Cambridge University Press, 2013). On the Cold War and the movement for human rights, see Mary Dudziak, *Cold War Civil Rights: Race and the Image of American Democracy* (Princeton: Princeton University Press, 1994); Benjamin Nathans, "Soviet Rights-Talk in the Post-Stalin Era," in *Human Rights in the Twentieth Century*, ed. Stefan-Ludwig Hoffmann (New York: Cambridge University Press, 2011), 166–190; Tony Judt, *Postwar: A History of Europe Since 1945* (New York: Penguin, 2005); and Carole K. Fink, *Cold War: An International History* (Boulder: Westview Press, 2017).

INDEX

pretrial preparation and negotiations and, 123, 124

prosecution case and, 139, 212, 466n48

Bourke-White, Margaret, 320

Brauchitsch, Bernd von, 249–50

Brauchitsch, Walther von, 126, 161, 284, 358–59, 365

Brown, D. W., 37, 38

Brownshirts. *See* SA

Buben, Ivan, 175–77

Bubrik, Samuil, 462n55

Buchenwald concentration camp, 156, 208–9, 217–18, 355–56, 362

Budnik, David, 228

Bukharin, Nikolai, 26–27, 164

Burdenko, Nikolai, 25–26, 34, 86

Burdenko Report, 34, 86, 185, 225–26, 241, 247, 250, 293–94, 295, 308–10, 320–21, 326, 328, 333, 436n72

Burson, Harold, 174–75

Buschenhagen, Erich, 196, 213, 220–21, 224–25

Byrnes, James F., 42–43, 46, 63–64, 71, 72, 200, 242, 290, 353, 396

Cappelen, Hans, 209–10, 211

Cassin, René
IMT judgment and, 391
international law debates and, 34–35, 36
in post-IMT period, 393–94, 399–400, 401–2, 405, 406–7, 409

Central Studio of Documentary Films, 179

Chamberlain, Neville, 100, 174

Cheremnykh, Mikhail, 373*f*

Chicago Tribune on Stalin's health, 99–100

Chuikov, Vasily, 489n7

Churchill, Winston, 23, 24–25, 53, 72, 234–35, 245–46, 252, 254–55, 290, 393
Efimov caricatures of, 164
Katyn Forest massacre and, 29
Moscow Declaration and, 32
Tehran Conference and, 32–33
Yalta Conference and, 40–41

Clay, Lucius D., 64–65, 205, 290–91, 388–89, 442n86

collective guilt, 347–67. *See also* Gestapo; Leadership Corps of the Nazi Party; Reich Cabinet; SA (Sturmabteilung aka Brownshirts); SD (Sicherheitsdienst)
IMT judgment and, 376, 379–80, 383–84
in international law, 62
prosecution case and, 204

Committee of Chief Prosecutors (IMT)
defense case and, 281, 308–9
Indictment and, 80, 81, 91, 98
pretrial preparation and negotiations and, 74–75
prosecution case and, 169, 174, 179, 184

common law system, 60–61

complicity, 36

conspiracy
defense case and, 284–85, 286, 296, 316, 339, 341
IMT judgment and, 370, 371–72, 376, 377, 382, 385–87
Indictment and, 62, 80–81, 87, 91, 100
in international law, 36, 38, 39
pretrial preparation and negotiations and, 46, 62, 80–81, 116, 128
prosecution case and, 139, 141–42, 147, 151, 153, 154–55, 185, 195, 197–98, 199–200, 201, 213, 217, 219, 220

Cory, Thomas J., 412

Stalin, Joseph, 18–19, 24–25, 26–27,
28–29, 79–80, 83–84, 86,
89–90, 91, 92, 94, 99–100,
101, 104–5, 265–66, 272,
396–97, 398
death of, 413
and Efimov, 164
Extraordinary State Commission for
Ascertaining and Investigating
German- Fascist Crimes in the
USSR and, 25
German-Soviet Non-Aggression
Pact and, 265
Great Terror, 21, 32–33, 89, 430n6
health of, 99–100
IMT judgment and, 377–78
Krasnodar Trial (1943) and, 29
Moscow Declaration and, 32
Nikitchenko appointed by, 368–69
Potsdam Conference and, 70, 204–5
and press corps reports, 173–74
and press corps selections, 108–9
press coverage of IMT and, 11
pretrial preparation and negotiations
and, 4, 8–9, 47, 55, 56–57,
71, 72, 75
prosecution case and, 143–44,
158, 171, 195–96, 202, 220,
227, 242
repatriation of Soviet citizens
and, 188–89
Rudenko appointed by, 77,
78–79, 217
Tehran Conference and, 32–33
Trotskyists and, 431–32n18
Vishnevsky and, 191–92
Vyshinsky and, 21–22
Vyshinsky Commission and, 213–14
Yalta Conference and, 40–41
Zorya selected for prosecution team
by, 221
Starikov, K. F., 398–99
State Department (U.S.), 37, 55–56, 82

Steengracht, Gustav Adolf von, 263
Steinbauer, Gustav, 337
Stettinius, Edward, Jr., 39–40, 42,
44, 46–47
Stimson, Henry L., 38, 39–40, 42, 46
Stokes, Richard L., 303
Storey, Robert, 87, 185–86, 192–93
Streicher, Julius
defense case for, 263, 284–85, 322
IMT judgment and, 378, 387
Indictment and, 448n83
pretrial preparation and negotiations
and, 120, 121–22, 123, 127
prosecution case and, 139, 466n38
Strogovich, Mikhail, 501n4
Stupnikova, Tatiana
defense case and, 267, 276, 284–85,
304–5, 315, 326, 329
organizational guilt cases and, 347,
350–51
Sukharev, Pavel, 486–87n59
superior orders, defense of, 31–32,
33, 36, 64, 194, 351, 385–86,
391, 410,
Sutzkever, Abraham, 228–30, 229f,
232–33, 235, 236, 237–38,
240, 415–16
Sutzkever, Freydke, 228–29, 229f
Svilova, Elizaveta, 462n55
Svoboda, Ludvik, 282–83
Szmaglewska, Seweryna, 238, 239

Tarkovsky, Stanislav, 228, 235
TASS, 108–9, 125, 126–27, 149–50,
172
correspondents for, 450n2
on reparations, 51–52
Secret Department, 171–73,
175–77
Taylor, Telford
defense case and, 258, 275, 289,
292, 322–24, 327–28, 329, 335
IMT judgment and, 380–81